DATE DUE

EVANGELICALS

AND SCIENCE IN

HISTORICAL

PERSPECTIVE

Recent titles in

RELIGION IN AMERICA SERIES
Harry S. Stout, General Editor

Mormons and the Bible
The Place of the Latter-day Saints in American Religion
Philip L. Barlow

Episcopal Women
Gender, Spirituality, and Commitment in an American Mainline Denomination
Edited by Catherine Prelinger

Old Ship of Zion
The Afro-Baptist Ritual in the African Diaspora
Walter F. Pitts

Keepers of the Covenant
Frontier Missions and the Decline of Congregationalism, 1774–1818
James R. Rohrer

Saints in Exile
The Holiness-Pentecostal Experience in African American Religion and Culture
Cheryl J. Sanders

Democratic Religion
Freedom, Authority, and Church Discipline in the Baptist South, 1785–1900
Gregory A. Wills

The Soul of Development
Biblical Christianity and Economic Transformation in Guatemala
Amy L. Sherman

The Viper on the Hearth
Mormons, Myths, and the Construction of Heresy
Terryl L. Givens

Sacred Companies
Organizational Aspects of Religion and Religious Aspects of Organizations
Edited by N. J. Demerath III, Peter Dobkin Hall, Terry Schmitt, and Rhys H. Williams

Mary Lyon and the Mount Holyoke Missionaries
Amanda Porterfield

Being There
Culture and Formation in Two Theological Schools
Jackson W. Carrol, Barbara G. Wheeler, Daniel O. Aleshire, Penny Long Marler

The Character of God
Recovering the Lost Literary Power of American Protestantism
Thomas E. Jenkins

The Revival of 1857–58
Interpreting an American Religious Awakening
Kathryn Teresa Long

American Madonna
Images of the Divine Woman in Literary Culture
John Gatta

Our Lady of the Exile
Diasporic Religion at a Cuban Catholic Shrine in Miami
Thomas A. Tweed

Taking Heaven by Storm
Methodism and the Popularization of American Christianity, 1770–1820
John H. Wigger

Encounters with God
An Approach to the Theology of Jonathan Edwards
Michael J. McClymond

Evangelicals and Science in Historical Perspective
Edited by David N. Livingstone, D. G. Hart, and Mark A. Noll

EVANGELICALS

AND SCIENCE IN

HISTORICAL

PERSPECTIVE

Edited by

David N. Livingstone

D. G. Hart

Mark A. Noll

New York ● Oxford

Oxford University Press

1999

Oxford University Press

Oxford   New York
Athens   Auckland   Bangkok   Bogotá   Buenos Aires   Calcutta
Cape Town   Chennai   Dar es Salaam   Delhi   Florence   Hong Kong   Istanbul
Karachi   Kuala Lumpur   Madrid   Melbourne   Mexico City   Mumbai
Nairobi   Paris   São Paulo   Singapore   Taipei   Tokyo   Toronto   Warsaw

and associated companies in
Berlin   Ibadan

Copyright © 1999 by David N. Livingstone, D. G. Hart, and Mark A. Noll

Published by Oxford University Press, Inc.
198 Madison Avenue, New York, New York 10016

Oxford is a registered trademark of Oxford University Press

Library of Congress Cataloging-in-Publication Data
Evangelicals and science in historical perspective / edited by
David N. Livingstone, D. G. Hart, Mark A. Noll.
p.   cm.—(Religion in America series)
Includes bibliographical references.
ISBN 0-19-511557-0
1. Religion and science—History.   2. Evangelicalism—History.
I. Livingstone, David N., 1953– .   II. Hart, D. G. (Darryl G.)
III. Noll, Mark A., 1946– .   IV. Series: Religion in America
series (Oxford University Press)
BL245.E93   1998
261.5'5—dc21   97-24739

1 3 5 7 9 8 6 4 2
Printed in the United States of America
on acid-free paper

Contents

EVANGELICALS
AND SCIENCE IN
HISTORICAL
PERSPECTIVE

Introduction

Placing Evangelical Encounters with Science

Until relatively recently, and under the influence of a number of late Victorian works of historical apologetic, the connections between science and religion were routinely cast in the pugilistic language of warfare, struggle, and conflict. Such aggressive metaphors have been common currency at least since the mid-nineteenth century writings of John William Draper and Andrew Dickson White,[1] and the supposed fracas between Samuel Wilberforce and Thomas Henry Huxley at the 1860 Oxford meeting of the British Association for the Advancement of Science—a symbolic altercation which, like that of Galileo, occupies a strategic place in the cartography of the conflict interpretation.[2] The inadequacies of this portrayal of *systemic* strife, however, have now been fully exposed,[3] and stimulating work on the social origins of the conflict thesis produced.[4] Even for the Darwinian epoch, revisionists have pointed to some of the ways in which many of the theologically orthodox accommodated to evolutionary, if not more narrowly Darwinian, science.[5]

Given the prevalence, until recently, of this confrontational historiography, it is scarcely surprising that studies of the encounters between evangelicalism and science are, with few exceptions, conspicuous by their absence. To be sure we have a series of biographical studies of key scientific figures who were also theologically conservative Protestants—Asa Gray, Benjamin Silliman, Hugh Miller, Michael Faraday, David Brewster, to name but a few;[6] social, intellectual, and legal accounts of the modern creationist movement;[7] and some surveys of the reaction of Protestants to science in general and Darwinian evolution in particular.[8] But serious investigation into more systematic association between evangelicalism and science has implicitly assumed either that the techniques of an anthropologist schooled in the rituals of a primitive society would be required, or that the investigation was necessarily contributing to an exposé of the antiscientific and antirationalist maneuvers of an embattled culture group that, despite demographic strength, was intellectually moribund. The triumphalist machinations of those wedded to what has been referred to—rather sloppily—as the Enlightenment project, however, have increasingly been exposed to serious critique from postfoundationalist epistemologists, revisionist historians of science, and sociologists of scientific knowledge.[9] The cumulative consequence of these moves has been to open up a new range of historiographical questions, questions that lay aside presuppositions about the assumed cognitive superiority of scientific knowledge, or the triumph of western scientific rationality over other thought forms, or the victory of scientists over theologians in the struggle for cultural authority.[10]

The essays drawn together here are presented in this spirit, and are therefore suggestive rather than exhaustive, illustrative rather than comprehensive. They seek to place a sequence of key moments in evangelical engagements with a variety of scientific claims. Doubtless there are major gaps in need of further attention, and it is as well to acknowledge some of them that we see.

At the same time, however, limitations that we recognize should not compromise the substantial contributions of this book. Thus, it situates distinct evangelical encounters with science into broader landscapes of scientific history and fuller accounts of British and North American religious life. It shows, as in John Hedley Brook's overview, that before the twentieth century supposedly "evangelical" approaches to science often simply illustrated intellectual orthodoxies of the day. It demonstrates, as in the chapters of David Bebbington, David Livingstone, and Ronald Numbers, that evangelicalism could encompass a wide range of engagements with science, depending upon time, place, and intellectual environment. It indicates, as in the chapters by Mark Noll, Jonathan Topham, Allen Guelzo, Michael Gauvreau and Nancy Christie, and D. G. Hart, that some of the most far-reaching implications of science for evangelicals have concerned not the physical world but the social uses to which evangelicals and their contemporaries put science. Even in the chapters that show evangelicals engaging in displays of the academically outré, as in James Moore on Darwin's purported deathbed conversion or Larry Eskridge on the search for Noah's Ark, the book reveals anything but simplistic cultural logic beneath such expressions. In sum, this book, while far from the last word on its subject, makes a very substantial start.

Gaps, nonetheless, must be acknowledged. The significant impact of the missionary movement on the development of anthropology, for example, is conspicuous by its absence, as is consideration of evangelicalism's engagement with the modern environmental movement or the role of such formal societies as the Victoria Institute in Britain and the American Scientific Affiliation.[11] Besides, the whole arena of medicine remains beyond our purview as have individual biographical studies of leading scientists with evangelical convictions.

It is worth recording, however, that on some of these topics significant progress is beginning to be made. The question of missionary science, for example, has recently been the subject of a number of essays in a volume reassessing the significance of science in the Pacific world during Darwin's century.[12] Here Neil Gunson, for instance, has shown that evangelical missionaries, through their cooperation with scientific expeditions, were often at the forefront of scientific advance making significant contributions to natural history, geography, and ethnography. Their findings, moreover, were published not only in religious periodicals, but also in the journals of learned societies. In the same volume, Janet Browne uncovers the significance—for Darwin's project—of the missionary assurance that "savage races" could be improved, while Sara Sohmer's discussion of the Melanesian mission highlights its significance for the development of comparative approaches to the study of language and myth—a key contribution illustrating a perhaps unexpected "intellectual flexibility" among the missionary minded. Again John Stenhouse, in reassessing the connections between Darwinism and New Zealand politics, pinpoints some of the ways in which missionaries and Maoris stood together against the settlers' repressive deployment of Social Darwinian rhetoric. These essays cumulatively highlight the potential for further investigation of missionary encounters with a variety of scientific disciplines.

So far as evangelicalism and environmentalism is concerned, there are, for example, a variety of critiques of the famous or infamous thesis promulgated by Lynn White, Jr., who urged that Christianity bore a huge burden of responsibility for our environmental degradation due to a theology supposedly hostile toward the natural order.[13] Some of these reassessments have uncovered hitherto hidden conservationist principles embedded in the Christian traditions of the West[14] or an environmental ethic that remains theologically robust yet affirming of the natural order.[15] The effect of these reappraisals has been to point to the need for the drafting of a new map of the connections between ecology and theology.

Having acknowledged both the lacunae in our survey and the episodic nature of our enterprise, we must also note that just as temporal comprehensiveness has not been our aim, neither has spatial inclusiveness. The diverse ways in which evangelical cultures in different continental, national, and regional settings encountered the scientific enterprise receive no systematic scrutiny, though some efforts have been made to take the particulars of different situations into account.[16]

For all that, we have still been able to cover much of the chronology of evangelical history since the Reformation. Contributions thus range from the early days of the Scientific Revolution in the seventeenth century to the creationist movements of the twentieth century. Accordingly, the essays presented here are intended to open different episodes in the history of a rich and complex encounter between evangelical religion and scientific endeavor, two domains typically regarded as having little to do with one another.

In an enterprise such as this, then, there are numerous dangers and pitfalls. Besides those to which we have already adverted, there are problems of definition, both of what counts as evangelical and—every bit as important—what passes as science. Essentialist definitions that seek to transcend the particularities of history and geography have been eschewed in the recognition that what evangelicalism and science were considered to be were—in all likelihood— different from time to time and from place to place. In general we have preferred to work with looser coalitions of themes according some priority to actors' perceptions of the theological tradition in which they were domiciled.

Still, an effort to define "evangelicalism" in ways that preserve both genuine historical connections and consistently recurring convictions must be made. For our purposes, then, we mean by "evangelical" those Protestant groups that were especially affected by the eighteenth-century revivals (associated with the names of John and Charles Wesley, George Whitefield, Jonathan Edwards, John Newton, Daniel Rowland, and similar figures) or who trace their descent from that moment. The fact that the eighteenth-century evangelical surge in Britain, Ireland, and North America was intimately connected with similar developments on the continent should suggest how flexible historical definitions must remain.[17] A similar flexibility is required when attempting to isolate convictions and characteristics of evangelical movements. Nonetheless, the fourfold definition that David Bebbington uses in his history of British evangelicalism has won an unusual measure of acceptance. In this definition evangelicals are marked by "conversionism, the belief that lives need to be changed; activisim, the expression of the gospel in effort; biblicism, a particular regard for the Bible; and what may be called crucicentrism, a stress on the sacrifice of Christ on the cross."[18] Thus armed with both historical and structural coordinates, observers of evangelicalism know with some reliability what they are looking for. Yet however helpful such definitions are, they should not be considered the last word.

It should be noted, however, that quandaries of definition are not limited to the question of how to define evangelicalism. There are also difficulties to be found in defining the space between the terms in our title, evangelicals and science. In his introductory overview John Brooke addresses precisely this issue by illustrating the diverse range of ways in which those with evangelical sympathies may take an interest in science, and teasing out the wide variety of forms evangelical theology's interactions with scientific endeavor may take. All of this tends toward a pluralizing of encounters, a humility about specifying unilinear correlations, and a sensitivity toward the possibility of definitional circularity. Yet none of this means that it is impossible to uncover connections between evangelical conviction and scientific enterprises. Brooke illustrates these links conceptually and biographically through his portrayal of an "archetypal evangelical scientist" and the career of the Scottish polymath Hugh Miller, even while remaining alert to the temporal and spatial contingencies that modulate doctrinal and scientific determinisms. Ever with an eye to the unexpected and the ironic, Brooke concludes with some sage comments on the reverse of the question, namely, the dynamics of de-conversion which bring to light hidden dimensions of "the evangelical encounter with science."

After Brooke's methodological reflections, and in the interests of providing historical depth, we begin our first substantive section on "Orientations" by revisiting the so-called Puritan thesis according to which science owed a special debt to the principles and practices of English Puritanism. In his investigation of the role of English Puritans in the development of science, John Morgan reminds us that the label "Puritan" is not transparent; it is problematic. It is mistaken to regard Puritans or "Puritanism" as a fixed entity. Instead Morgan takes the entirely right-headed turn toward endeavoring to figure out how Puritans themselves saw their own context. Morgan also makes much of recent scholarship arguing that the forces shaping English science had historically deeper roots than is frequently thought, and that the English universities in the pre-1640 period were nowhere as moribund as is conventionally believed. Of course, we do not mean to imply that Puritan encounters with science can be considered evangelical in precisely the same way in which that label later came to designate a certain tradition, or family, within Protestantism.[19] To do so would be historically anachronistic. But since the self-conscious evangelical movement of the eighteenth century did look back to its Puritan antecedents, and given the resonances between these theological traditions, an investigation of how that branch of English nonconformity interacted with the new science during the crucial moment known as the Scientific Revolution turns out to anticipate some of the associations that resurfaced in different guises later in evangelical history.

In our second orientating contribution, Ted Davis takes up the argument of Michael Beresford Foster, which stressed the key role of voluntarist theology in the genesis of modern science. Davis abjures the absolutist-sounding character of this causal claim; but at the same time he does want to retrieve something of Foster's concerns by arguing that although it is wrong to say that voluntarism *produced* science, this does not mean that it had no role to play. Indeed by examining the key cases of Galileo, Descartes, and Boyle, he shows substantial infiltration of voluntarism into their metaphysical outlook. The significance of Davis's contribution thus lies in his subverting of simple, unilinear connections between scientific practice and theological conviction.

We then move into the eighteenth century as Mark Noll, in his consideration of American evangelicals and science taken in the long view, persistently finds that changes in the philosophical temperature and the scientific fashion among American evangelicals turn out to be rooted in social realities. The need to find legitimate moral and political authority in sources other than cultural heritage, societal hierarchy, or received tradition, for example, encouraged evangelicals during the Revolutionary period to turn away from Edwardsian idealism toward Scottish common-sense realism. This particular intellectual trajectory is seen as symptomatic of a tradition deploying scientific knowledge as a resource for responding to the pressing political concerns of a wider social agenda.

In a parallel chapter for Britain, David Bebbington shows that, while there certainly was some suspicion of scientific endeavor within the evangelical movement, particularly in its earlier phases, the overall pattern was one of accommodation, with science being mobilized as the "handmaid of evangelical theology." In fact, maintaining the connection between God's word and God's world, to use a conventional trope, implicated evangelicals in a number of more or less imaginative strategies, such as their elaboration of a variety of harmonizing schemes to square the biblical creation narratives with geology's portrayal of a deep past, their remarkable willingness to countenance the existence of other inhabited worlds, and their accommodationist attitude toward a variety of evolutionary proposals. All these confirm the long-standing evangelical concern to keep science and faith in conceptual equilibrium.

In recent years much insightful work on the nineteenth century has high-lighted the crucial role played by natural theology in providing a context for scientific research. Natural theology could meet a variety of needs. It could regulate scientific theorizing by disposing practitioners toward agreeable solu-tions to problems; it could help obviate the seeming conflict between believing piety and the infidelity of mechanical theories by projecting images of a divine mechanic or architect; it could facilitate the presentation of potentially seditious science in religious vocabulary thereby shielding scientists from suspicions of heterodoxy; and it could provide answers to specific problems—such as pos-tulating creationist explanations for patterns of geographical distribution.[20] The deceptive simplicity of natural theology as a coherent framework for understand-ing the context and content of science is exposed in Jon Topham's exposition of the case of Thomas Chalmers. Topham uses Chalmers to illustrate not only the changing vesture of natural theology, but the acknowledged limits of ratio-nality by spokesmen for natural theology. The significant contrast between Scot-tish Presbyterian and English Anglican renditions of the natural theology tradi-tion also reminds us of the importance of contextual factors in the debates.

Having scrutinized these theological engagements, we turn to a suite of spe-cific encounters ranging from nineteenth-century Scriptural Geology to the re-cent fundamentalist expeditions in search of Noah's Ark. Throughout these two centuries evangelical engagements with science have been anything but mono-lithic. Rather they have been both varying and contested. Consider, for ex-ample, Rodney Stiling's examination of Scriptural Geology in America during the same period. What is clear here is that, in the pre-Darwinian era, it was only a small group of conservative Christians who opted for reading geology through the spectacles of a literalistic biblical hermeneutic. And it turns out that some of the fiercest criticism of this project was forthcoming from other evan-gelical geologists who had found ways of accommodating biblical hermeneutics to what they understood were the deliverances of science.

The importance of location also features in David Livingstone's examination of the responses to evolution by evangelicals in three different cities. In Edin-burgh, Belfast, and Princeton—all key Calvinist spaces in the late Victorian era—the clerical-intellectual elites responded differently to the new biology de-spite remarkably similar theological commitments. Why? Because in these different places, different local circumstances prevailed, which in turn condi-tioned both the responses of the Calvinist intellectual leadership to evolution and the sorts of things they could say about it, given the prevailing conditions.

By now it will be evident that this volume displays a range of historical styles, from historiographical reflection to narrative. And nowhere is the latter more evident than in James Moore's scrutiny of the legend of Darwin's deathbed conversion. Here the story told by Lady Hope is placed in the context of Vic-torian deathbed scenes and its diagnostic tropes. But Moore goes further, using the storytelling strategy as a means of reflecting both on how evangelicals deal with narrative,—biblical and extrabiblical—and on how they have been help-lessly, not to say hopelessly, attracted to Lady Hope's tale. It was, indeed, the triumph of "Hope" over experience! In a similar narrative vein, Larry Eskridge recounts the quests for Noah's Ark that have littered both Mount Ararat and fundamentalist history throughout this century. The stories themselves are the stuff of motion picture. But here again, as in Moore's story, there is more; for we find exposed something that takes us to the heart of the fundamentalist psyche—the passion to hammer down history, to touch the transcendental, to earth the supernatural in the mundane. Whether in human nature or in nature itself there remains a persistent longing for evidence of the divine at work.

As has already been indicated, much recent historical writing has dismantled the warfare model of the history of relations between Christianity and science. The idea of persistent struggle or conflict has been shown to be as much the creation of late-nineteenth-century historical commentators as anything else. And yet, for all that, there certainly have been conflicts. The latter-day emergence of creation science is one such arena, and Ronald Numbers directs our attention to the genesis of this modern movement. His investigation, moreover, links with the same sorts of issue about labels and terms that Morgan addressed for a earlier period. In Numbers's telling, the meaning of the term "creationist" has itself evolved over time; it is, like Puritanism, Darwinism, even evangelicalism, a contested term, a negotiated entity, with contingent historical circumstances determining who wins out in the battle to control definitions and to manufacture meaning.

These various engagements with natural science, of course, do not exhaust the range of arenas in which evangelicals have encountered the scientific *mentalité*. In the realms of moral philosophy, sociology, and biblical criticism evangelicals have sustained ambiguous relations with a variety of positivistic currents. Allen Guelzo thus inaugurates the final section of the book on these wider domains by elucidating a fleeting, though extraordinarily important, moment in the relations between evangelicalism and science in the post-Enlightenment period through his interrogation of the rise and decline of moral philosophy in the United States. Seen from today's perspective the moral philosophy enterprise can too easily be dismissed as an illicit marriage between moral discourse and the methods of natural philosophy. Thereby the moral philosophers sought to milk metaphysical meaning out of mundane science, transcendental truths out of the mere material. Here Protestant intellectuals sought some rapprochement with Enlightenment values, though running the threat of a panmechanization that even engulfed human nature and social polity. A profound irony surfaces here, moreover; for while some evangelicals were demonizing the naturalizing tendencies of science in one mode, the moral philosophers were valorizing it in another. The constitutional strictures of the new republic forced advocates of moral philosophy to seek for ways of preserving a Christian public order without any explicit appeal to orthodox Christianity. The only route they could find was to say that the scientific study of the human constitution inevitably would display the very universal moral sense adumbrated in Christian theism.

The concentration on the theoretical engagement between scientific thought and evangelical theology can too easily obscure practical interactions. In Britain we now know something of the scientific significance of Michael Faraday's Sandemanian outlook and William Buckland's evangelical religion. But as yet we know all too little about how their evangelicalism affected, if at all, the empirical side of Benjamin Silliman's geology, James Dwight Dana's mineralogy, Arnold Guyot's glacial geomorphology, Joseph Henry's physics, Matthew Fontaine Maury's oceanography, to take just a few American examples. Through the work of Michael Gauvreau and Nancy Christie we see just how important practical engagement was in the arena of sociology. For it turns out that Canadian sociology in the decades around 1900 emerged out of a Christian tradition of social survey energized by social conscience. Here the theoretical works of Marx, Durkheim, and Spencer were largely irrelevant to the initial growth of the social sciences where practical involvement and the search for the resolution of pressing urban and rural social problems were the real catalysts.

In a different arena again D. G. Hart highlights another battlefield—that over the nature of the biblical documents. The struggle by evangelical Christians committed to an inerrant view of the Bible to find a place in the modern academy and the varying ways in which they have engaged "scientific" biblical scholarship are thus the objects of his scrutiny. These in turn become the vehicles by which Hart provides commentary on the uneasy relationship evangelical communities have sustained with the secular world of the university in the twentieth century.

Our last chapter offers a reward for readers who persevere to the end. The dialogue that George Marsden overheard on Mt. Olympus among Socrates, Thomas Jefferson, and William Jennings Bryan is filled with whimsey of a deadly serious sort. What these three worthies have to say about science *in se* as well as about science for its social and political purposes amounts to a final rationale for the book as a whole. By recording encounters of evangelicals and science, the volume demonstrates again what has been shown so often before, that study of the physical universe matters in western society because, for at least 500 years, science has always concerned much more than science.

Evangelicals and Science in Historical Perspective is to be regarded more as a beginning than an ending. It begins the task of uncovering the historical connections between the cultures of evangelical religion and scientific endeavor. If it succeeds in its aims it will convince readers that a full history of the connections between various sciences and various branches of evangelicalism, as well as other forms of religion, is a real desideratum. The essays drawn together here are designed to illustrate something of the rich material that is available for just such a synthetic study and to hint at how complex, though enriching, that story will eventually turn out to be.

NOTES

1. John William Draper, *History of the Conflict between Religion and Science* (London: Henry S. King, 1875); Andrew Dickson White, *A History of the Warfare of Science with Theology in Christendom*, 2 vols. (London: Macmillan, 1896).

2. For revisionist accounts of this episode see J. R. Lucas, "Wilberforce and Huxley: A Legendary Encounter," *Historical Journal*, 22 (1979): 313–30; Sheridan Gilley, "The

Huxley-Wilberforce Debate: A Reconstruction," in Keith Robbins (ed.), *Religion and Humanism* (Oxford: Blackwell, 1981), pp. 325–40; J. Vernon Jensen, "The Wilberforce-Huxley Debate," *British Journal for the History of Science*, 21 (1988): 161–79.

3. See, for example, David C. Lindberg and Ronald L. Numbers, "Beyond War and Peace: A Reappraisal of the Encounter between Christianity and Science," *Church History*, 55 (1986): 338–54; David C. Lindberg and Ronald L. Numbers (eds), *God and Nature: Historical Essays on the Encounter between Christianity and Science* (Berkeley: University of California Press, 1986); John Hedley Brooke, *Science and Religion: Some Historical Perspectives* (Cambridge: Cambridge University Press, 1991); Colin A. Russell, *Cross-Currents: Interactions between Science and Faith* (Leicester: Inter-Varsity Press, 1985).

4. Colin A. Russell, "The Conflict Metaphor and Its Social Origins," *Science and Christian Belief*, 1 (1989): 3–26.

5. James R. Moore, *The Post-Darwinian Controversies: A Study of the Protestant Struggle to Come to Terms with Darwin in Great Britain and America, 1870–1900* (Cambridge: Cambridge University Press, 1979); David N. Livingstone, *Darwin's Forgotten Defenders: The Encounter between Evangelical Theology and Evolutionary Thought* (Grand Rapids: Eerdmans; Edinburgh: Scottish Academic Press, 1987).

6. See Hunter Dupree, *Asa Gray* (Cambridge: Harvard University Press, 1959); Chandos Michael Brown, *Benjamin Silliman: A Life in the Young Republic* (Princeton, N.J.: Princeton University Press, 1989); Michael Shortland (ed.), *Hugh Miller* (Oxford: Oxford University Press, 1966); Geoffrey Cantor, *Michael Faraday: Sandemanian and Scientist* (London: Macmillan, 1991); A. D. Morrison-Low and J. R. R. Christie (eds), *"Martyr of Science": Sir David Brewster, 1781–1868* (Edinburgh: Royal Scottish Museum, 1984).

7. See, for example, Edward J. Larson, *Trial and Error: The American Controversy over Creation and Evolution* (New York, 1985); Ronald L. Numbers, *The Creationists* (New York: Alfred A. Knopf, 1992); George E. Webb, *The Evolution Controversy in America* (Lexington: University of Kentucky Press, 1994).

8. Besides those works listed above, see John Dillenberger, *Protestant Thought and Natural Science* (London: Collins, 1961); Richard Westfall, *Science and Religion in Seventeenth Century England* (New Haven: Yale University Press, 1958); R. Hooykaas, *Religion and the Rise of Modern Science* (Edinburgh: Scottish Academic Press, 1972); B. A. Gerrish, "The Reformation and the Rise of Modern Science," in Jerald C. Brauer (ed), *The Impact of the Church Upon Its Culture* (Chicago: University of Chicago Press, 1968), pp. 231–275; Douglas S. Kemsley, "Religious Influences in the Rise of Modern Science: A Review and Criticism, Particularly of the 'Protestant-Puritan Ethic' Theory," *Annals of Science*, 24 (1968): 199–226; Eugene Klaaren, *Religious Origins of Modern Science* (Grand Rapids: Eerdmans, 1977); Theodore Dwight Bozeman, *Protestants in an Age of Science: The Baconian Ideal and Antebellum American Religious Thought* (Chapel Hill: University of North Carolina Press, 1977); Frederick Gregory, "The Impact of Darwinian Evolution on Protestant Theology in the Nineteenth Century," in David C. Lindberg and Ronald L. Numbers (eds.), *God and Nature: Historical Essays on the Encounter between Christianity and Science* (Berkeley: University of California Press, 1986), pp. 369–90; Jon Roberts, *Darwinism and the Divine in America: Protestant Intellectuals and Organic Evolution, 1859–1900* (Madison: University of Wisconsin Press, 1988). More specialist accounts include Jonathan Wells, *Charles Hodge's Critique of Darwinism: An Historical-Critical Analysis of Concepts Basic to the 19th Century Debate* (Lewiston: The Edwin Mellen Press, 1988).

9. See, for instance, Zygmunt Bauman, *Modernity and Ambivalence* (Ithaca: Cornell University Press, 1991); Michel Foucault, *The Archeology of Knowledge* (New York: Pantheon, 1982); David Harvey, *The Condition of Post-Modernity* (Oxford: Blackwell, 1989); Jean François Lyotard, *The Postmodern Condition: A Report on Knowledge* (Minneapolis:

University of Minnesota Press, 1984); Richard Rorty, *Objectivity, Realism and Truth* (New York: Cambridge University Press, 1991); Steven Shapin, *A Social History of Truth: Civility and Science in Seventeenth-Century England* (Chicago: University of Chicago Press, 1994); and Fredric Jameson, *Postmodernism, or, the Cultural Logic of Late Capitalism* (Durham, N.C.: Duke University Press, 1991).

10. For such arguments, coming from very different points on the theological compass, see as examples David Bloor, *Knowledge and Social Imagery*, 2nd ed. (Chicago: University of Chicago Press, 1991); John Milbank, *Theology and Social Theory: Beyond Secular Reason* (Cambridge, Mass.: Blackwell, 1991); Alisdair MacIntyre, *Three Rival Versions of Moral Inquiry* (Notre Dame, In.: University of Notre Dame Press, 1990); Edward Said, *Orientalism* (New York: Vintage, 1979); and Nicholas Wolterstorff, *Reason Within the Bounds of Religion*, 2nd ed. (Grand Rapids: Eerdmans, 1984).

11. Mark Kalthoff is completing a doctoral thesis on this latter organization at the University of Indiana.

12. The essays referred to here are Neil Gunson, "British Missionaries and Their Contribution to Science in the Pacific Islands"; Janet Browne, "Missionaries and the Human Mind: Charles Darwin and Robert Fitzroy"; Sara Sohmer, "The Melanesian Mission and Victorian Anthropology: A Study in Symbiosis"; and John Stenhouse, "The Darwinian Enlightenment and New Zealand Politics". All appear in Roy MacLeod and Philip F. Rehbock (eds.), *Darwin's Laboratory: Evolutionary Theory and Natural History in the Pacific* (Honolulu: University of Hawaii Press, 1994).

13. Lynn White, Jr., "The Historical Roots of our Ecologic Crisis," *Science*, 155 (1967): 1203–7.

14. See, for example, Robin Attfield, "Christian Attitudes to Nature," *Journal of the History of Ideas*, 44 (1983): 369–86; Robin Attfield, *The Ethics of Environmental Concern* (New York: Columbia University Press, 1983); David N. Livingstone, "The Historical Roots of Our Ecological Crisis: A Reassessment," *Fides et Historia*, 26 (1994): 38–55.

15. For various theological approaches to this problem see: W. F. Welbourn, "Man's Dominion," *Theology*, 78 (1975): 561–68; Rowland Moss, *The Earth in Our Hands* (Leicester: Inter-Varsity Press, 1982); Stephen V. Monsma (ed.), *Responsible Technology: A Christian Perspective* (Grand Rapids: Eerdmans, 1986); Ron Elsdon, *Bent World: Science, the Bible, and the Environment* (Leicester: Inter-Varsity Press, 1981); J. A. Walter, *The Human Home: The Myth of the Sacred Environment* (Tring, Herts: Lion Publishing, 1982); John Black, *The Dominion of Man* (Edinburgh: Edinburgh University Press, 1970); H. Paul Santmire, *The Travail of Nature: The Ambiguous Ecological Promise of Christian Theology* (Philadelphia, 1985). A good introduction to other contributions toward a theology of environment, particularly in the periodical literature, is provided in chapter 4, "The Greening of Religion," in Roderick Frazier Nash, *The Rights of Nature: A History of Environmental Ethics* (Madison: University of Wisconsin Press, 1989).

16. Recent comparative evaluations of evangelicalism in different national settings include Mark A. Noll, David W. Bebbington, and George A. Rawlyk (eds.), *Evangelicalism: Comparative Protestantism in North America, the British Isles, and Beyond* (Oxford: Oxford University Press, 1994); David Hempton, *Religion and Political Culture in Britain and Ireland: From the Glorious Revolution to the Decline of Empire* (Cambridge: Cambridge University Press, 1996).

17. For those connections, see especially W. R. Ward, *The Protestant Evangelical Awakening* (Cambridge: Cambridge University Press, 1992).

18. D. W. Bebbington, *Evangelicalism in Modern Britain: A History from the 1730s to the 1980s* (London: Unwin Hyman, 1989), pp. 2–3.

19. Outstanding histories of evangelicalism now abound for different national arenas;

see, for example, Bebbington, *Evangelicalism in Modern Britain*; George M. Marsden, *Understanding Fundamentalism and Evangelicalism* (Grand Rapids: Eerdmans, 1991); David Hempton and Myrtle Hill, *Evangelical Protestantism in Ulster Society, 1740–1890* (London: Routledge, 1992); George A. Rawlyk (ed.), *Aspects of the Canadian Evangelical Experience* (Montreal and Kingston: McGill-Queen's University Press, forthcoming); and for a more general picture, Keith Robbins (ed.), *Protestant Evangelicalism: Britain, Ireland, Germany and America c. 1750–c.1950* (Oxford: Basil Blackwell, 1990).

20. See the fine overview in Brooke, "Natural Theology," chapter 6, *Science and Religion*, pp. 192–225. See also some of the essays in Robert M. Young, *Darwin's Metaphor: Nature's Place in Victorian Culture* (Cambridge: Cambridge University Press, 1985).

PART I

OVERVIEW

1

The History of
Science and Religion

Some Evangelical Dimensions

JOHN HEDLEY BROOKE

Introduction: Taking an Interest in Science

In the beginning, as students of American evangelicalism often remind us, was Jonathan Edwards. In many respects it is difficult to imagine a more auspicious beginning for the relations between an evangelical theology and science. For Edwards, the beauties of nature are communications of God's excellence.[1] Moreover, scientific knowledge provides a theoretical rationale for affirming that beauty is not merely in the eye of the beholder: Edwards wrote that "light, or our organ of seeing, is so contrived that an harmonious motion is excited in the animal spirits and propagated to the brain."[2] That use of the word *harmony* was sanctioned by reference to Newton, whose division of the spectrum had been modeled on divisions of the musical scale.[3] As Edwards put it, the "mixture of all sorts of rays, which we call white, is a proportionate mixture that is harmonious (as Sir Isaac Newton has shewn) to each particular simple color and contains in it some harmony or other that is delightful."[4]

Those who have been enchanted by Edwards's spider papers will know that there were other sorts of delight in nature: in their flying, even the most despicable of God's creatures could take "their sort of pleasure."[5] In their exuberance one glimpsed "the exuberant goodness of the Creator."[6] Edwards helps us to see how an evangelical might take more than a passing interest in science. But he also helps us to identify two preliminary problems:

1) What does it mean when we say that someone *takes an interest* in science?
2) What does it mean when we say that someone takes an interest in *science*?

1) A moment's reflection shows that taking an interest in science may mean many different things. It may mean no more than reading about science as part of one's self-education. It may mean reading about science with a view to

examining its implications for one's faith. On the positive side this may lead to the appropriation of knowledge in the proclamation of one's faith—as when Edwards drew on Newton's *Optics* to give objective content to concepts of harmony; or as when he drew on Henry Pemberton's *View of Sir Isaac Newton's Philosophy* to demonstrate divine wisdom: " '[T]is wisely ordered that when [comets] are nearest the sun, where they are amongst the planets, and where their orbits come nearest together, they move swiftest and stay but a little while; which renders 'em less liable to be disturbed in their motions."[7] Unless things had been as they are, they would have been decidedly worse.

There may, however, be a negative aspect to this sort of interest in science, if the purpose is not to appropriate the latest news but to reject it. We all have our colorful examples of this sort of interest: when the Scottish evangelical Hugh Miller read *Vestiges of the Natural History of Creation* (1844), he declared it to be "one of the most insidious pieces of practical atheism that has appeared in Britain during the present century."[8] That "fellow-traveller" with the evangelicals, Adam Sedgwick, was even more vitriolic: confronted with such a "foul" mish-mash of materialism, phrenology, and transmutation, Sedgwick was driven to quoting Shakespeare: "[G]ive me an ounce of civet, good apothecary, to sweeten my imagination."[9] It is obvious that evangelical interest in science has often had such negative features, when appraising science that might be deemed unsound.

With this in mind, there is a stronger sense of taking an interest in science: this would be offering patronage to wholesome scientific projects, to trusted individuals who could be relied upon to promote acceptable science, and to educational institutions that promised the teaching of science in ways that would help students to resist the secular baggage that the sciences have increasingly carried since the nineteenth century. One early nineteenth-century beneficiary of evangelical patronage was the Oxford geologist William Buckland. Because he was working so hard to show that geology was confirming a biblical flood, he won the patronage of such evangelical luminaries as Shute Barrington, bishop of Durham, and John Bird Sumner, an eventual archbishop of Canterbury. There is a letter from Barrington to Robert Banks, second earl of Liverpool, in which he spoke of the "great public importance" of keeping Buckland at Oxford. Geology was "capable of abuse and mischief" but Buckland had "applied himself to clearing it from all its most dangerous doubts and difficulties." It had been made "a very useful auxiliary to the cause of revealed Religion."[10]

This particular dimension of evangelical interest in science needs to be studied carefully not only because patronage can be fickle but also because science moves on. When Buckland published his *Bridgewater Treatise*, his retreat, like that of the floodwaters, left him exposed. Some evangelicals would now be among his enemies, agreeing with Dean Cockburn of York that the Bible must needs be defended against the British Association for the Advancement of Science. And as recent scholarship has shown, not even Buckland himself could keep control of the meanings read into his treatise. A scheme of progressive creation could so easily be read as support for the progressive transformation of species, even if that was the last thing Buckland had wanted.[11]

Taking an interest in science might mean more: one might sense a calling to write about it in some systematic way. In the beginning there was also John Wesley. And we know that in 1763 Wesley published what he called a *Compendium of Natural Philosophy* which was at the same time *A Survey of the Wisdom of God in the Creation*. The conception, and especially the execution, of a systematic text demanded not only time but a strong teacher's commitment to the value of at least some forms of science. A systematic text on natural philosophy had featured in Jonathan Edwards's plans though it was never completed.[12]

It may seem prosaic to insist on these various distinctions but there is good reason. One could be a reader of science, one could think about the relations between science and faith, one could be a patron of safe science, one could be an author and a teacher of science—without actually doing any. One of the reasons that Jonathan Edwards is such an appealing figure is that we know he did some. He did not merely write about flying spiders but set himself the "scientific" task of explaining how they fly. This allowed the editor of volume 6 of his collected works, Wallace Anderson, to argue that Edwards's interest was not so much the archetypal interest of the amateur in natural history but the rather deeper interest of one who, versed in mechanics, drew on the principles of buoyancy to explain how the lightness of the spider's web enabled it to build bridges between bushes and to go ballooning in fair weather.[13]

As soon as we begin to consider evangelicals as practitioners of science, the problems begin to multiply. If we take the strongest sense of having an interest in science to mean having a career in science, then the evaluation of an evangelical contribution may become problematic for other reasons. While it is possible to identify evangelical scientists of the highest caliber, we must be alive to the fact that during a scientific career the perceived competence of a scientific researcher may change. As Martin Rudwick has shown, it is impossible to trace the course of a scientific controversy in detail without examining these perceived competences as they were attributed at the time.[14] In one of the controversies I know best, that concerning the substitution of chlorine for hydrogen in organic compounds, the most reactionary participant, Berzelius, fell down the gradient of attributed competence as a consequence of the controversy.[15] Evangelicals who made a career out of science could suffer in the same way. The Scotsman David Brewster made major empirical contributions to the study of optics, but his antipathy to the emerging wave theory was undoubtedly damaging—certainly as perceived from Cambridge.[16] It is perhaps an obvious point, but we should not delude ourselves into thinking that the appraisal of a career in science is a straightforward matter. And the difficulty is surely compounded by multiplicities of meaning associated with the word "science" itself.

2) To say of someone that they "took an interest in science" may be richly ambiguous because so much can hinge on the particular freight the word "science" is intended to carry. One obvious problem is that meanings have changed with time. Both Jonathan Edwards and John Wesley were writing before the word "scientist" had even been coined. With the increasing differentiation of ever more specialized sciences, it became possible in the nineteenth century to be an expert in one science and an amateur in another. As an illustration of the

problem, one might point to the Cambridge scientist George Stokes, who as Lucasian Professor of Mathematics was an acknowledged authority on the physical sciences. But how would one evaluate his pronouncements on the life sciences? Was his evangelicalism reflected in his grave suspicion of evolutionary theory? He worried that advocates of organic evolution sometimes spoke as if evolution "must" be true—the sure sign of what he described as an "*animus* in the direction of of endeavouring to dispense with a Creator."[17] Here we see a distinguished physicist, promoting *his* science but rejecting the science of others. The point is not whether he was correct to do so but rather the fact that if we speak of evangelical attitudes toward "science" we are already oversimplifying. The point surely applies for the whole of the nineteenth century. Most religious commentators, whether evangelical or not, preferred the science of Cuvier to that of Lamarck during the first half of the century. Yet it would be churlish to deny Lamarck's system the name of science when it is generally agreed that he defined the science of biology in its modern sense[18] and when, later in the nineteenth century, his mechanisms for evolution were preferred to those of Darwin by religious thinkers who would have been the very ones, earlier in the century, to denounce him.[19]

There is a second problem associated with the general use of the word "science." Historians who have written on evangelicalism and science have usually found it necessary to distinguish between "good science" and "bad science," or between pure science and its corruptions. In his book *The Age of Atonement*, Boyd Hilton writes there were ways in which "Christianity promoted rather than impeded scientific investigation, though of course it often distorted scientific interpretation."[20] And speaking later of James McCosh he simply states that McCosh "used a distorted version of Darwin."[21] The same has often been said of Henry Drummond because of the central place he gave to altruism in the evolutionary process. It is difficult for historians to avoid these kinds of judgments. The need to make them was the base on which James Moore erected his taxonomy for positions taken during the post-Darwinian controversies.[22] Again it is not a straightforward matter: Darwin's own retreat on the scope of natural selection within evolutionary dynamics[23] might allow one to say that Darwin himself "used a distorted version of Darwin"! But the underlying point remains. Evangelicals who might be placed on parade as exemplars of an interest in "science" might turn out on closer inspection to be enamoured of a distorted or even idiosyncratic "science." How one determines criteria for what constitutes development and what constitutes distortion might be well worth discussing. But a category of idiosyncratic science is hardly an empty one. An extreme example might be the "science" of Dudley Joseph Whitney, the moving spirit behind the Religion and Science Association, one of the ephemeral creationist organizations recently discussed by Ronald Numbers.[24] The suggestion of Whitney that caught my eye concerned the shortage of space on Noah's Ark: "[I]f we insist upon fixity of species we make the Ark more crowded than a sardine can."[25] Whitney's solution was to propose descent with modification from the relatively few passengers on the ark. By any definition this surely was idiosyncratic. From the standpoint of an evolutionist such rapid diversification was more incredible than the slow gradual evolution over millions of years that Darwin had proposed. And from the standpoint of a fellow creationist such as Byron Nelson, Whitney had "given up half of the battle" to the evolutionists.[26]

I have been suggesting in this introduction that to assess the relationship between evangelical culture and the culture of science is an intriguing but complicated project. "Taking an interest in science" can mean and has meant many different things. One reason that it is intriguing is that we may wish to ask whether an evangelical interest in science has been distinctive in some way—compared, for example, with the interest shown by other religious traditions. It is to this question that I now turn.

The Relevance of Evangelicalism to the Portrayal of Science

In broaching this question I am conscious of at least four historiographical problems that ought perhaps to be aired. The first is simple. Just because an evangelical happens to take an interest in science, it may not mean that that interest has been fired by faith. The problem is how to tell if and when it has.

A second problem concerns our methodology. If we examine only those evangelicals who, as a matter of fact, did take an interest in science, are we not in danger of distorting our description of evangelical values? Too strong a claim for the relevance of those values to science would seem to be compromised by the existence of so many who have been utterly indifferent, or even hostile to scientific enquiry. I should express my debt to John Morgan for this point since he has made the same methodological objection with reference to the alleged correlation between puritan values and science in seventeenth-century England.[27] A commitment to revelation and the primacy of soteriological concerns was liable to displace other priorities. One of his exemplars, Richard Greenham, declared: "[T]here are many things to be learned, which we cannot attaine unto by naturall reason onely, without spirituall revelation."[28]

There is a third and associated problem. In general discussions of relations between science and religion, a standard move has been to distinguish between moderate and extreme representatives of a particular tradition. The attraction of the move is that one may then say that there was, for example, a correlation between moderate puritanism and science in mid-seventeenth-century England[29]; or between moderate Anglicanism and science in the post-Restoration period[30]; or between the Cambridge "broad church network" and science in the first half of the nineteenth century.[31] There is a case for such discrimination. My worry is that we risk making these correlations circular by taking as one of the criteria for moderatism or latitudinarianism the very interest in science that is the matter in question.[32]

The fourth of my worries arises from the fact that what may appear to be a distinctively evangelical view can be found in other and often antithetical theologies. Jonathan Edwards again affords a useful example.

Spiders fly because they seem to enjoy the experience; but in one of the spider letters, Edwards asserts that "the chief end of this faculty is not their recreation but their destruction."[33] The argument is simple: spiders enjoy flying in a warm westerly breeze, not in the cold, wet airstreams from the Atlantic. The consequence is that along with airborne insects they eventually meet their doom when they fall into the ocean. A skeptic would not find it difficult to caricature the argument. In his goodness it would seem that God had given the spiders a faculty, the end of which was their end! They go smiling all the way to their funeral. To be fair, the argument is more subtle than this. There has to be destruction to maintain the balance of nature—a balance that itself reveals the mathematical skill of the Creator.[34] And this is not all. The most engaging point is still to come: the destruction of the spiders is all part of a divinely ordained mechanism for removing what Edwards calls "the corruption and nau-seousnes of the air."[35] Flying insects are collections of this noxious air, and since spiders eat insects they are, in his own words, "collections of these collections." In short, nature is a system in which there is a wonderful contrivance for the remedy of corruption—for the annual disposal of toxic waste. As one commentator has observed, "Edwards' thoughts were much more given to reflection upon the power and wisdom of God in contriving the whole system of nature, than to searching out the special benefit brought by particular things in it."[36]

Now we have reached the problem, for exactly the same has been said of the English Unitarian, Joseph Priestley.[37] Priestley, like Edwards, was concerned with replenishing the air. In fact he did rather more serious science in investigating the manner in which plants render the air, in his terms, less phlogisticated. He did not understand the details of photosynthesis, nor did he even accept the word "oxygen." But in the memorable words of Sir John Pringle, who presented him with the Royal Society's Copley Medal, he did show that "no vegetable grows in vain."[38] Evidence of divine contrivance was visible in the system as a whole, in the mechanisms of refurbishment. The parallel with Edwards is striking. Might we not say of Edwards that he had shown that no spider flies in vain? In structure their respective natural theologies were remarkably alike. And yet in almost every other respect, it would be difficult to imagine two more disparate figures. The Calvinism Edwards had come to embrace was the very theology against which Priestley rebelled.[39] Whereas Edwards saw in the material world symbols of a pervasive spiritual reality,[40] Priestley famously collapsed a matter/spirit duality.[41] Whereas Edwards responded warmly to the platonism of Henry More,[42] Priestley saw in Plato's philosophy that which had corrupted Christianity.

The problem that I want to underline is simply this. We may look for the relevance of evangelical theology to particular constructions of nature. And we may think we have found it, as in Edwards's natural theology. But it may turn out not to be distinctive at all. An emphasis on nature as a whole, as an economic system, was, in the case of Priestley, integral to an utterly different theological and political vision. In looking for a distinctively evangelical appraisal of "science" we may unwittingly glide over the doctrinal, social, and political issues that may have separated evangelicals from their opponents. I cannot imagine either Edwards or John Wesley asserting, as Priestley did, that "the English hierarchy (if there be anything unsound in its constitution) has equal reason to tremble at an air pump, or an electrical machine."[43]

With these problems in mind can we still identify ways in which evangelical beliefs might have been relevant to the portrayal of "science"? I think we can and in several respects. Here I shall follow the functional analysis that I have employed elsewhere.[44]

An evangelical emphasis on the faithfulness of God could certainly find expression in one of the presuppositions of natural science—namely the uniformity and regularity of nature. One did not have to be an evangelical to make the point. For the Cambridge philosopher William Whewell it was obvious that a law presupposed an agent[45] and the same had been true for Newton.[46] But a sense of the dependence of nature on a faithful God was certainly expressed by evangelicals with an interest in the sciences. It is particularly clear in the Scottish evangelical Thomas Chalmers[47], and it had been just as clear in Jonathan Edwards. Corollary 15 in his paper on atomism amounts to the proposition that what we call the "laws of nature" are "the stated methods of God's acting with respect to bodies, and the stated conditions of the alteration of the manner of his acting."[48]

Evangelical belief could also provide sanction for scientific activity in that the book of God's works invited some, if not as much, attention as the book of His words. The claim that the two books could not ultimately disagree has been described by James Moore as the "Baconian compromise."[49] But until well into the nineteenth century, it was a common resource. There was no reason that evangelicals should not have marveled at the wisdom, economy, and beauty of nature as Edwards clearly had. The sufficiency of natural theology was quite another matter.

The motivation to address specific scientific issues could also come from evangelical convictions. One might wish to defend a biblical perspective on some point of natural philosophy; or one might, for example, wish to privilege one form of science over another if it happened to fit one's apologia. There may have been other reasons that Edwards was drawn to a discussion of matter theory, but one reason at least was for the access it gave to statements about divine power: "The infinite power of God," he wrote, "is necessary to keep the parts of atoms together."[50]

Religious beliefs have also played a selective role in the context of choosing between competing theories. The role of religious predisposition may sometimes have been unconscious, but it has surely been real enough. Jack Haas has recently written of John Wesley that "he was willing to accept new scientific ideas except where they threatened Christian faith."[51] What this could mean in practice is nicely illustrated by Wesley's ready acceptance of the "Great Chain of Being," his adoption of a preformationist position in embryology, and his rejection of Buffon's theory of the earth as "wild and whimsical."[52]

An evangelical concern for the correct exegesis of Scripture could also be relevant to concerns associated with the sciences. Within evangelical movements one can of course find sophisticated concepts of biblical "accommodation," which do not require that the Bible has to be authoritative on technical scientific matters. Among the reformers Calvin himself had affirmed that if one wished to learn about astronomy it was not to the Bible one should turn.[53] This had not, however, stopped Calvin from casting aspersions on the idea of a moving earth.[54] Attempts to deduce a "science" of nature from Scripture have been common in conservative evangelical circles, and it is for that reason that it may be appropriate to speak of the constitutive role of religious belief in such cases. An obvious example would be accounts of the earth's history in which the biblical flood is made constitutive of geological theory.[55] A more subtle case might be represented by the view that the Bible gives one the outlines of a science, with the details still to be filled in. The in-filling then takes on a religious dimension precisely because the object is to vindicate the authenticity of the outline. For a specific example one might point to the Scottish evangelical Hugh Miller, who saw a perfect concordance between the order of creation in *Genesis* and that disclosed in the rocks.[56] The task of the evangelical geologist was to supply and properly interpret the geological details.

Many an excursion into natural theology has been sanctioned by the exegesis of Rom. 1: 20. Put simply, the point is that scientific research can be conceived, and has been, as an aid to the correct interpretation of Scripture. In such cases there can be a hermeneutic of reciprocity in that biblical motifs may well appear in the science that is supposed to corroborate a particular exegesis. The kind of reciprocity I have in mind is exemplified by Thomas Chalmers. In 2 Cor. 4: 18 Chalmers read that "the things which are seen are temporal; but the things which are not seen are eternal." In his view this required that the visible world be considered transitory, and he was therefore untroubled by any scientific evidence that seemed to make it so.[57] The impress of a Scottish voluntarist theology has in fact been seen in the subsequent development of thermodynamics. The principle of energy conservation was a reminder that only God could create and destroy that which drove the universe, while the principle of energy dissipation was a potent reminder that the present form of the visible world was indeed transitory. William Thomson was a friend of Chalmers and attended his services. In a preliminary draft of his "dynamical theory of heat" Thomson wrote of a "tendency in the material world . . . for motion to become diffused."[58] There was a "reverse of concentration . . . gradually going on." In his own mind there was resonance with Psalm 102: "[O]f old hast thou laid the foundation of the earth: and the heavens are the work of thy hands. They shall perish, but thou shalt endure: yea, all of them shall wax old like a garment."[59]

The Archetypal Evangelical Scientist

If an evangelical faith could leave an imprint on particular forms of science, the question arises as to whether we might not go further and construct a model of the archetypal evangelical scientist. It is certainly tempting to do so. Provisionally at least we might suggest the following characteristics.

One would expect to find that she or he holds a biblically informed philosophy of nature. This would not have to mean that the Bible would be cited in technical scientific papers. But it might mean appeals to Scripture on metaphysical issues on the margins of science. When Chalmers tried to take the sting out of a plurality of worlds, he had recourse to the parable of the lost sheep. Did it really matter if other worlds were inhabited? Did it even matter if the inhabitants had not fallen from grace? After all, it was consonant with Christ's teaching that even if ours was the one world that had gone astray, it would still be brought to safety.[60] His compatriot David Brewster was even more succinct on the same subject. Other worlds were surely sanctioned by Christ's remark: "[O]ther sheep I have which are not of this fold." Or if that was not convincing enough: "In my Father's house are many mansions."[61]

Our archetypal scientist would also see the world as a theatre of redemption. Chalmers's God, for example, was one of justice and righteousness not the soft touch of more liberal theologies.[62] Though the Atonement might be explicated in terms of debt and ransom, what mattered to Hugh Miller was not how it worked but the fact that it was a doctrine perfectly adapted to the human condition.[63] We might expect our evangelical scientist to believe that sin demands punishment and that this temporal sequence might even be inscribed in nature itself.[64] Might we also expect a degree of ambivalence toward the control of those natural forces that, on a conservative reading, had often been interpreted as agents of punishment?

An evangelical scientist would be likely to favor inductivist accounts of scientific methodology. Humility before God's word, Francis Bacon had said, demanded humility before His works. And that meant divesting the mind of arrogant hypotheses. Appeal to the sanctity of Baconian induction became a standard move in polemics against Darwin.[65] The use of well-attested hypotheses in the organization of data would not have to be outlawed, but an aversion to *speculative* hypotheses had been a recurring characteristic. A rhetorical appeal to the discipline of induction would surface whenever there was a whiff of danger. Another of the Scottish evangelicals, John Fleming, makes a striking case study because, like his friend Charles Lyell, he believed that appeals to global catastrophes went beyond the limits of inductive science. Although it is possible to exaggerate the similarity, he was a kind of actualist before Lyell. But it was this same insistence on an inductive method that armed him against the subversive cycles of James Hutton. Fleming declared Hutton's speculations suspect precisely because they *were* speculations, conducted without examination of the rocks.[66] There was something of the same spirit in Brewster's critique of Whewell. In his *Bridgewater Treatise* Whewell had seen evidence of design in the provision of an ether perfectly adapted to the transmission of light waves. Which was all very well, said Brewster, if one happened to believe in the wave theory. But he for one did not; and it was surely dangerous to suspend one's natural theology from theoretical constructs that might prove ephemeral and misconceived.[67]

A sensitivity to the uses but also to the limitations of natural theology would surely be another feature of our evangelical scientist. The "qualified endorsement of an empirically based natural theology" that is to be found in John Wesley[68] is certainly to be found among other evangelicals. It is possible that among practicing scientists the qualifications have been less visible than among clerical commentators. The pressures to show that one's science is not to be viewed with suspicion can provoke exaggerated claims for its religious utility. Yet the overall insufficiency of natural theology would surely be conceded. Chalmers devoted an entire chapter of his *Bridgewater Treatise* to its limitations. The appearance of design in nature might shed powerful light on the existence of God; it could even generate "a considerable degree of probability, both for his moral and natural attributes."[69] But in the context of evangelism, the most it could do was persuade unbelievers to reconsider their position. It might raise questions in their minds, but it could not provide the answers that really mattered. It said nothing of a covenant between God and His people, nothing of a plan of salvation. It simply could not answer the question "what shall I do to be saved?"[70] Whilst they might contribute to preevangelism, arguments for design were less propitious than an appeal to the human conscience. Qualifications could arise from another source. Because evangelical natural theology was rarely, if ever, an independent rational theology, because it was informed by the biblical image of a fallen nature, it could distance itself from facile claims that this is the best of all possible worlds. For Thomas Gisborne, writing in 1818, it was obvious from the chaos of rock formations that we live in a ruined world, one that testifies to divine punishment. As Boyd Hilton shrewdly observed, this was not an abandonment of natural theology, but it was to turn it on its head.[71]

An evangelical scientist would surely resist attempts to exclude God's sovereignty over nature. John Wesley had taken the view that a deity with the power to create such a universe as this most assuredly had the power to intervene if there were good cause. Jonathan Edwards had said much the same. In one of his papers on natural philosophy, he noted "the great wisdom" necessary to "dispose every atom at first, as that they should go for the best throughout all eternity; and in the adjusting by an exact computation, and a nice allowance to be made for the miracles which should be needful."[72] It might be argued that this "nice allowance" for miracles became a problem for evangelical scientists who, during the nineteenth century, were in danger of being swept along on the tide of scientific naturalism.[73] But there is no doubt that the tide was resisted. Neither Chalmers nor Hugh Miller among the Scottish evangelicals wished to reduce his theology of nature to statements about laws of nature. To have done so would have given hostage to deism.[74] There was more to nature than nature's laws. There is a striking example of this antireductionism in George Stokes, who saw both the divine and human will as directive and interventionist. The human will, he suggested, lay outside the energy transactions of the body.[75]

An insistence on harmony between true science and true religion would of course be another characteristic. One might even be tempted to say that among evangelical writers on science, if not among evangelical scientists themselves, there has been a greater interest in the harmony of science and religion than in science for its own sake. At least two resources have made the task of harmonization deceptively easy. The biblical category of "science falsely so called" has not exactly been an empty one! The kind of science one may not like can always be syphoned off leaving "true science" and "true religion" in happy union. The second resource was the provisional character of scientific knowledge, which could always be exploited to argue that a seeming dissonance would at some future date be resolved. There is an engaging letter from John Bird Sumner to Leonard Horner in which this tactic is nicely displayed. The year was 1861 and Horner had recently addressed the Geological Society of London on the antiquity of man. Darwin had been delighted. "You are coming out in a new light as a Biblical critic!" he had jested.[76] One might expect Sumner to have been less amused. But his letter to Horner was both studied and courteous:

> You are, I believe, aware that I have always considered the first verse of Genesis as indicating, rather than denying, a *preadamite world*. And if one may venture to speculate on such unknown ground, it would seem more reasonable to believe that any former system of things should contain creations having the qualities of man than the contrary. Therefore it would be no surprise to me, if further enquiry should confirm what is at present a new and unexpected discovery, and certainly meanwhile, I shall adhere to Paley's rule, and not suffer what I do know, to be distracted by what I do not know.[77]

Because of the deeply personal investment in holding "true" science and "true" faith together, evangelical scholars would develop their own historiography of science. David Brewster, for example, could not tolerate the disconcerting view that Newton had only turned to religion when mentally disturbed or in his dotage. Not for him was Voltaire's jibe that he had actually turned to religion to console the rest of us by showing that he was, after all, fallible and mortal. Brewster rewrote Newton's life to ensure that such constructions were vetoed. And on a smaller scale, Chalmers also rescued Newton from Voltaire, praising his rejection of merely plausible arguments that lacked empirical foundation.[78] The Scottish evangelicals who were active in promoting the sciences certainly shared the vision of Jonathan Edwards that "all the arts and sciences, the more they are perfected, the more they issue in divinity, coincide with it, and appear to be as parts of it."[79]

Some Limitations of the Archetype

We could carry on investing our archetype with other qualities. One of these would certainly be a refusal to concede that scientific knowledge can of itself be sufficient to meet the deepest human needs. But I want to change tack at this point because, as a tool of historical analysis, the use of an archetype also has limitations. It may be instructive to reflect on a few reasons that this is so.

As with all archetypal constructs, we get no real leverage on historical change. If we take Thomas Chalmers as typifying evangelical natural theology, we are left with the problem identified by Jonathan Topham—that Chalmers's views changed during his life, from an almost complete rejection of natural theology, following his conversion and repudiation of moderatism in 1809, to his later, qualified espousal.[80] There could be changes of heart on scientific issues themselves. During the 1830s David Brewster appeared sympathetic to the nebular hypothesis of Laplace.[81] But by the mid 1840s he was distinctly less enamored.[82] Hugh Miller, from having been a champion of progressive creation, began to speak more of "degeneration" within geological epochs.[83] The appeal to some archetypal view of the relations between science and religion can leave us stranded without an explanation. When it comes to larger shifts over longer periods of time, the problem is magnified. The contrast, for example, that Ronald Numbers has drawn between the old-earth creationism of the 1920s and the young-earth creationism of recent times poses a serious challenge for the historian. In his conclusion, Numbers has suggested a correlation that might partly account for the appeal of flood geology. Most of its exponents in America, he notes, came from churches awaiting Christ's imminent return.[84] But as he and others have shown, the rejection of the traditional schemes for the harmonization of Genesis with an earth of great antiquity has been part of a complex historical process in which the "evangelical right" has associated all manner of licentiousness with the bogey of "secular humanism," of which the name of Darwin has been the most potent symbol.[85]

A second problem with use of an archetype is simply the looseness of fit: evangelicals sharing many religious beliefs might nevertheless be on opposite sides of a scientific controversy. In a much earlier beginning was Martin Luther. And the problem of looseness of fit is vividly displayed in the response of two Lutherans to the Copernican innovation. In the young Rheticus there was an evangelistic zeal to promote the new astronomy as a physical and not merely mathematical system. In Melanchthon there was resistance, partly on biblical grounds, to precisely that interpretation.[86] And there is no shortage of later examples. We noted above that the Oxford geologist William Buckland enjoyed the patronage of senior evangelical churchmen. But the most censorious *critic* of his flood geology was the evangelical naturalist John Fleming. It was a travesty of Scripture, so Fleming objected, to suggest that the biblical flood would have left the geological traces to which Buckland referred. It had been a miraculous intervention: the waters had risen and fallen in an almost ghostlike manner and Genesis did not record cataclysmic consequences for the earth's surface.[87] In the light of our preceding problem it is perhaps worth noting that Fleming himself had changed his mind on this very point.[88]

Boyd Hilton has made the general obervation that evangelical communities have often been the locus for division on key issues related to the sciences.[89] An example to which Jim Moore drew attention would be the reception accorded to the liberal evangelical Henry Drummond when he presented his fusion of Evolution and Christianity at a Northfield conference in 1893. "Many fell upon me and rent me" was his woeful report.[90]

Drummond's misfortune introduces a further problem with the use of archetypes. It has been nicely exposed by David Livingstone in his contrast between the reception of Darwinism in Belfast and in Princeton. In both places there were Calvinists who opposed Darwin's theory, but the resistance in Belfast was to prove the more enduring. The reason, he suggests, has to do with local circumstances. There was nothing at Princeton to compare with the Belfast Address of John Tyndall. When Tyndall gave his presidential address at the meeting of the British Association in 1874, he gave a more completely naturalistic account of Darwinism than Darwin himself and pledged to wrest from theology the entire domain of cosmological theory. This, coupled with a rebuke meted out by the association to the Presbyterian theologian Robert Watts, so soured feelings within the Presbyterian camp that Darwinism would henceforward be associated with an intolerant materialism. Watts had prepared a paper for the meeting in which he had urged conciliation between Christianity and science. The rebuke had consisted in a refusal to give it a place in the program. Livingstone's point is that in exploring the historical relations between evangelicalism and science it is not enough to focus on doctrinal issues. Local geography must be considered. His contrast is surely telling: "While MacNaughtan, Porter, and Martin were, in Belfast, using traditional Calvinism to refute both the science and metaphysics of evolution, at Princeton McCosh and Macloskie who had emigrated from Ulster were doing just the opposite. And while Watts was campaigning against evolution as subversive of the Westminster Confession of Faith, Warfield was evolutionising human origins and casting Calvin as the intellectual precursor of Darwin."[91]

A similar contrast might be drawn between Scottish and English evangelicals in their attitudes toward geology. It was certainly drawn by Hugh Miller, who took a dim view of the topography of England. He complained of a great deficiency in the size of its mountains. But he also complained of a deficiency of spirit among its Christians—at least among the evangelicals associated with the publication of the *Record*. While his newspaper, the *Witness*, was doing its best to promote a wholesome understanding of geology, the English evangelicals seemed to be falling headlong into his category of the antigeologists. Miller's contrast was undoubtedly self-centered and overdrawn. There were English evangelicals, such as the Congregationalist John Pye Smith, who were far from obscurantist in their appraisal of geology.[92] Nevertheless, Miller's diagnosis in his *First Impressions of England and Its People* underlines the importance of cultural contrast, both national and local.

A fourth problem with the use of archetypes is largely a corollary of those we have just been considering. Attitudes toward particular scientific hypotheses are unlikely to be derivable (either by the actor or the historian) by a kind of Cartesian deduction from a preexisting theology. When I first studied the plurality of worlds debate between Brewster and Whewell, I had expected to find that the evangelical, Brewster, would be the one to oppose the idea of extraterrestrial life. After all, there could be embarrassing questions about the spiritual state of extraterrestrials. Because Whewell was generally described as a liberal Anglican, I expected the doctrine to hold no terrors for him. But what I actually discovered was that Brewster was the great protector of other worlds, while the master of Trinity was all for dissolving them, leaving him, as one cynic observed, occupying the most prestigious lodge in the universe.[93] How ideas are associated and manipulated by one's opponents would seem to be a crucial factor. It is certainly not surprising that Brewster should have retaliated against Whewell's position. He had earlier been offended by the absence of his name from Whewell's *History of the Inductive Sciences*, indeed the absence, as far as he could see, of the names of all Scotsmen.[94] The well-known case of Charles Lyell, who was not an evangelical, provides an illustration of the basic point. Until he read the work of Lamarck, Lyell had not departed significantly from the progressionist interpretation of the fossil record associated with his teacher Buckland and other clerical geologists. But having once glimpsed that a directionalist account would lend itself to reinterpretation in evolutionary terms, he soon changed his tune.[95] The volte face of Brewster over the nebular hypothesis appears to have followed a similar pattern. Once he saw what damage the hypothesis could do when linked to organic evolution, as it was by the anonymous author of *Vestiges*, he drew back. So did Hugh Miller. It was after 1844 that his account of progressive creation became increasingly darkened with a natural tendency to degeneration. The idea was to scotch the natural trends toward complexity and perfectibility so beloved of the transformists.

Hugh Miller: A Brief Case Study of an Evangelical Scientist

I should like to devote a little more space to Miller because in his enthusiasm for geology there are evangelical dimensions in length, breadth, and depth. In length because, however old the earth, its development could be squared with Genesis as long as the "days" of the creation narrative were elongated, or as long as they referred to successive days on which the inspired author had received visions of how the earth had appeared in each of its six epochs.[96] In breadth because Miller drew arguments from geology to combat every threat to an evangelical faith. By the middle of the nineteenth century it was quite a list: he argued against religious moderates, Puseyites, Mosaic geologists, secularists, skeptics, atheists, and scientific naturalists. There are evangelical dimensions in depth not merely because he dug out fossil fish that supported his case for "degeneration" but also because once his faith had become real to him it suffused his entire perception of nature. Fossils became divine artifacts of great beauty.

As editor of the *Witness*, the organ of the Free Church of Scotland, Miller relished every opportunity to show that Free Church science was best. Writing of the Disruption in 1843, when Chalmers had led the long line of dissidents, Miller reported that "On the one side we saw *Moderate* science personified in Dr. Anderson of Newburgh—a dabbler in geology, who found a fish in the Old Red Sandstone, and described it as a beetle.—we saw science, not *moderate*, on the other side, represented by Sir David Brewster."[97] Scientific credentials and ecclesiastical credibility could be woven into one and the same argument.

It will be clear from the complications I have just identified that it would be a mistake to present Miller as an archetypal figure. But his exploitation of geology to refute rival creeds was both imaginative and resourceful. Geology, properly understood, could hammer the atheist because it afforded proof of new creations. Species appeared in the fossil record that had not been there before. Geology could crush the skeptic because it provided a vicarious "experience of creations." David Hume had argued that in the absence of such experience nothing could be known about the cause of the universe. Hume had also objected that claims to infer the infinite qualities of God from the finitude of nature were doomed because they violated a cardinal principle of reasoning—that causes should always be proportioned to their effects. But Miller turned the tables.

To witness the new forms of life that appeared as one passed from each great epoch to the next was to enjoy that experience in creations that Hume had deemed impossible. More ingeniously still, Miller pointed out that to base one's conception of creative power on the evidence of the earliest epoch would, on Hume's principles, lead to a false result. This was because each subsequent epoch revealed a greater complexity of form—at least before degeneration set in. To follow Hume one would have had to surmise that the Creative force was limited to fishes—only to discover that reptiles were within its power. And likewise in the progression from reptiles to mammals, and from mammals to men. Humean skepticism was misplaced. Comparisons between worlds were after all possible.[98]

The dimension of depth, to which I referred, is visible in Miller as an aesthete. This is an interesting dimension because evangelicals have often been suspicious of the arts—not least because of their association with Catholic or High Church worship. Chalmers noted that men with the most lively of aesthetic sensibilities had shown themselves utterly blind in the understanding of God's word.[99] Miller, however, found in the fossil record a proof of the most fundamental of biblical doctrines—that humanity had been made in the image of God. By describing fossil forms in terms of human architecture, he created a rhetoric that pointed up the resemblance between the human and the divine minds. They shared the same aesthetic sensibilities. As Miller himself put it, "there is scarce an architectural ornament of the Gothic or Grecian styles which may not be found existing as fossils in the rocks."[100] His argument was subtle because it was not that man consciously imitates nature, but that his structures and those of nature betray the same architectonic principles.

Thus the interior arches of ammonites resembled the "groined ribs of a Gothic roof." Even corrugated iron had its precursor in ammonite grooves. The ornately carved columns of Sigillaria were more exquisite than those of Canterbury cathedral. A fossil such as Murchisonia bigranulosa demonstrated the superiority of nature's art over human art. And to cap his argument Miller appealed to one of the most successful designs emerging from the Lancashire calico-printing industry. The pattern known as "Lane's net" had sold more pieces than any other and had led to many imitations. But the most striking imitation of all was to be found in "Smithia Pengellyi"—a coral of the Old Red Sandstone. The "beautifully arranged lines," Miller wrote, "which so smit the dames of England" had been stamped amid the rocks ages before.[101] The fact that no dames had been around then to appreciate them only confirmed that the patterns in the rocks evinced the tastes of the divine designer.

An aesthetic experience of nature can of course serve a surrogate form of piety. But in the wake of his conversion (if that is the right word to describe his resolution of doubt) Miller had fused the material and the aesthetic in ways that conformed to a more conservative piety. In a remarkable letter to Roderick Murchison, Miller reported that he was making a set of casts for Louis Agassiz. These were from specimens of *asterolepis*—the fossil fish that Miller had used to argue against the transformists. What makes his description remarkable is that the material and the aesthetic are fused in his mind in such a way that they generate a religious symbol: "From a curious combination of plates, an angel robed and winged seems to stand in the centre, and the effect is at once so singular, and, to at least the geological eye, beautiful; so much so that I propose getting a pair of them framed."[102]

Coming full circle, Hugh Miller seems to exemplify the point that Jonathan Edwards has so often been used to illustrate. Following conversion, the natural world can take on a refreshing new aspect. One may become aware of a kind of beauty to which one had been blind before. In his "Personal Narrative," Edwards had explained how his conversion had brought a new sense of the presence of God in nature: "God's excellency, his wisdom, his purity and love, seemed to appear in everything; in the grass, flowers, trees; in the water and all nature; which used greatly to fix my mind."[103]

It would be pleasing to stop with that symphony of praise; but there is a coda on which, I believe, we should fix our minds. There are hidden dimensions to the evangelical encounter with science. They have to do not with conversion but with de-conversion.

Some Hidden Dimensions:
De-conversion and Science

There is one form of reaction against evangelical teaching that cannot be described as de-conversion. On exposure to doctrines of election, to accounts of the Atonement in terms of penal substitution, to threats of eternal damnation for the theologically unsound, many have recoiled against it. The relevance of a reaction against evangelicalism to a scientific culture is something we should not exclude from our picture. It is some years now since Jim Moore first suggested that Darwin's theory of evolution was, in some measure, the expression in science of a moral revolt against Christian doctrines that Darwin described as damnable.[104] Darwin's strong words, that he could not see how anyone could wish Christianity to be true, carried emotional weight because so many members of his own family had been heterodox or worse. We cannot forget that Darwin was cooped up for five years with a ship's captain, Robert Fitzroy, whose evangelical, Tory convictions proved to be too claustrophobic. On some issues Darwin and Fitzroy were not divided. They both appreciated the civilizing effects of Christian missionaries in Tahiti.[105] But on others, such as slavery, there were explosive differences.[106]

It would be a different kind of reaction against an evangelical faith if one had first savored it for oneself. Historians of nineteenth-century Britain have often noted how many of the great writers of the Victorian period were troubled souls who, sometimes with pain, sometimes with relief, had come to reject the verities of an evangelical childhood. The names to conjure with include George Eliot, Thomas Carlyle, John Ruskin and, in a rather special category perhaps, John Henry Newman.[107] In what they saw as their emancipation, much was shed; but much was also retained. In Thomas Carlyle, for example, the evangelical habit of searching biblical history for types that prefigured Christ left an indelible mark. He had been accustomed to conceiving human lives in biblical terms and continued to find complex and surprising meanings in the strangest events.[108] In John Ruskin a moral commitment to the accuracy of description survived his de-conversion, and may, with some poignancy, have contributed to it.

Because the loss of faith could follow many paths, I should like to suggest that there is a rich vein here for future enquiry. For evangelical writers on "science and religion" it may be more comfortable to remain with those scientists who preserved their faith intact. But a historian of science has to recognize that new forms of science have sometimes been the last straw in the erosion of belief. And the loss of an evangelical faith could be particularly traumatic because nothing less than one's personal identity was at stake. When correcting the popular image of evangelical puritanism as a dour and restrictive force on human life, George Landow made the perceptive remark that, in fact, "it provided an emotional, imaginative form of belief that endowed its adherents with a sense of their own identities."[109] In forging new identities, the culture of science could be involved in a variety of ways.

It is this variety which needs further exploration. One thinks of T. H. Huxley evangelizing on behalf of scientific naturalism during the 1860s.[110] His mission shows the survival of evangelical forms in the rhetorical defence of science.[111] As Adrian Desmond has recently put it, science, for Huxley, became the path of righteousness.[112] Earlier in Huxley's life there had been an "evangelical anger" in his response to the Catholic festivities on the island of Madeira.[113]

He had indeed been reared by evangelical parents and the imprint survived his disillusionment: "Huxley never lost the intense moral impulses and the urge to proselytize that Evangelicalism inculcated."[114] It is difficult not to see a surrogate form of evangelicalism in his later creed. In his own way Huxley became a "tub-thumper . . . preaching old-time hell-fire."[115] He would complain of an "idolatrous age," of a society "which listens to the voice of the living God thundering from the Sinai of science, and straightaway forgets all that it has heard, to grovel in its own superstitions; to worship the golden calf of tradition; to pray and fast where it should work and obey; and, as of old, to sacrifice its children to its theological Baal."[116] Huxley's sermonizing before working men raises the question "when is an antireligion not a religion?" One can overdo the homologies. A priest hunter may not always be a priest. But when Huxley spoke in Edinburgh in January 1862, the new and the old forms of redemption were clearly locked in a culture clash. The *Witness*, which in Hugh Miller's day had prided itself in promoting scientific education, could not countenance Huxley's performance. And it grieved at the audience's applause when "their kindred to the brute creation was most strongly asserted."[117]

It may not be strictly correct to speak of a de-conversion in Huxley's case. In the spiritual odyssey of John Ruskin it is. In one of his own accounts he could pinpoint the exact moment:

I was still in the bonds of my old Evangelical faith; and, in 1858, it was with me, Protestantism or nothing: the crisis of the whole turn of my thoughts being one Sunday morning, at Turin, when, from before Veronese's Queen of Sheba, and under quite overwhelmed sense of his God-given power, I went away to a Waldensian chapel, where a little squeaking idiot was preaching to an audience of seventeen old women and three louts, that they were the only children of God in Turin; and that all the people in the world out of sight of Monte Viso, would be damned. I came out of the chapel, in sum of twenty years of thought, a conclusively *un*-converted man.[118]

I should like to close with Ruskin because those 20 years of thought had included thinking about science. The springs of his evangelical faith had been in childhood. His mother had made him read the Bible from cover to cover, assiduously and repeatedly. From the age of nine he had been required to take extensive notes.[119] In his intellectual formation a love of the observational sciences as well as Romantic poetry contributed to his identity as an artist. His interest in geology, for example, was strong enough to gain him membership of the London Geological Society. His intellectual biography is one in which, initially at least, there was a harmonious union of his artistic, scientific, and religious interests. Operating with the concept of God's two books he saw himself as supplying the spiritual dimension lacking in neutral descriptions of nature. Ruskin had special respect for Turner and commented that he was a geologist as much as a painter. Above all, Ruskin's evangelicalism generated a high seriousness, a moral commitment to the accuracy of description.[120]

The poignancy, to which I referred earlier, consists in the fact that this very commitment to accuracy eventually militated against the faith that had spawned it. The more he learned of biblical criticism, the more he read the latest geology, the greater did his hidden doubts become. His private frustration was confessed to Henry Acland in a letter that has often been quoted: "You speak of the flimsiness of your own faith. Mine, which was never strong, is being beaten into mere gold leaf, and flutters in weak rags from the letter of its old forms; but the only letters it can hold by at all are the old Evangelical formulae. If only the geologists would let me alone, I could do very well, but those dreadful hammers! I hear the clink of them at the end of every cadence of the Bible verse. . . ."[121]

It is confessions like these which suggest that there are hidden dimensions to the evangelical encounter with science. What commentators find so striking is the contrast between public and private utterance. From Ruskin's publications in the 1850s, notably volume 4 of *Modern Painters*, one would never guess that the private doubts existed. In the chapters "Dry Land" and "Mountain Glory" there is a confident natural theology in which geological and biblical images are united. The mountains have been sculpted to facilitate human habitation, for without them "the air could not be purified, nor the flowing of the rivers sustained." They also have a higher purpose: to "fill the thirst of the human heart for the beauty of God's working." Evangelical motifs can still be discerned. The noble architecture of mountains is, *as far as possible*, to delight and sanctify the heart of man; that is, "as far as is consistent with the fulfilment of the sentence of condemnation on the whole earth."[122] The question is how much torment did a confident natural theology conceal? Even when a rapprochement with disturbing science was achieved, as by the evangelical biologist Philip Gosse, there could still be other kinds of torment. When he published his *Omphalos* in 1857 Gosse thought he had saved a biblical chronology. The earth, he argued, would have the appearance of age, however recently it had been created—just as a tree created yesterday, if it was real tree, would have to have rings. But when his ingenious concept of "pro-chronism" met with a cool reception, he was so deeply affected, according to his son, it was as if he had become angry with God Himself.[123]

By hidden dimensions, I do not merely mean the private as contrasted with the public. There is the question of what values and habits of mind survive deconversion. It is striking that in his letter to Acland, Ruskin should have picked out the "old Evangelical formulae" as those alone from which his fragile faith was suspended. But these too were to crumble if his account of what happened in Turin in 1858 is to be believed. They had proved vulnerable to art as well as to science. When he reflected on the beauty of a Veronese painting, on brilliant music, on gold, pearls, and crystal, in short on what he called the "gorgeousness of life," he had been bound to ask: "Can it be possible that all this power and beauty is adverse to the honour of the Maker of it?" Had God made these things only that they might lead his creatures away from Him?[124] His evangelical mother clearly believed so. In a state of alarm she sent him long remedial instructions and five pounds to donate to the Waldensian chapel.[125]

What did survive, even then, was Ruskin's belief that the question of right belief is one of high seriousness. The specific doctrines of an evangelical theology might be lost, but the importance evangelical preachers gave to doctrine could be ineradicable. Later in life Ruskin saw the sciences going their specialized ways in a manner that left him cold. He never warmed to Darwin's theory despite being Darwin's friend. He felt it was still necessary to put back a spirituality that half-witted scientists were excluding. And he could still be a moral critic of scientific practices. Thus he railed against the diffusion of microscopy because it was associated in his mind with all that was abhorrent in anatomy and vivisection.[126] When he eventually resigned from Oxford in March 1885, he gave as one of his reasons that he could not lecture next to a room in which there was a shrieking cat. There is more to an evangelical encounter with the culture of science than meets the eye.

NOTES

1. Jonathan Edwards, "Beauty of the World," in *The Works of Jonathan Edwards, Vol. 6, Scientific and Philosophical Writings*, edited by Wallace E. Anderson (New Haven: Yale University Press, 1980), pp. 305–6.

2. *Ibid.*, p. 306.

3. Penelope Gouk, "The Harmonic Roots of Newtonian Science," in *Let Newton Be!* edited by John Fauvel, Raymond Flood, Michael Shortland, and Robin Wilson (Oxford: Oxford University Press, 1988), pp. 101–25.

4. Jonathan Edwards, *Works, Vol. 6*, p. 306.

5. *Ibid.*, p. 157.

6. *Ibid.*, p. 158.

7. *Ibid.*, p. 309.

8. Hugh Miller, "The Physical Science Chair," *The Witness*, 17 September 1845.

9. Charles C. Gillispie, *Genesis and Geology* (New York: Harper, 1959), p. 165.

10. Cited by Boyd Hilton, *The Age of Atonement* (Oxford: Clarendon Press, 1988), p. 235.

11. Jonathan Topham, "Beyond the 'Common context': The Readership of the *Bridgewater Treatises*"; unpublished conference paper.

12. Editor's introduction to Jonathan Edwards, *Works, Vol. 6*, pp. 37–52.

13. *Ibid.*, p. 40.

14. Martin J. S. Rudwick, *The Great Devonian Controversy* (Chicago: University of Chicago Press, 1985), pp. 418–26.

15. John Hedley Brooke, "Berzelius, the Dualistic Hypothesis and the Rise of Organic Chemistry," in *Enlightenment Science in the Romantic Era: The Chemistry of Berzelius and its Cultural Setting*, edited by Tore Frangsmyr and Evan Melhado (Cambridge: Cambridge University Press, 1992), pp. 180–221.

16. Jack Morrell and Arnold Thackray, *Gentlemen of Science* (Oxford: Clarendon Press, 1981), pp. 466–72.

17. Cited by David B. Wilson, "A Physicist's Alternative to Materialism: The Religious Thought of George Gabriel Stokes," *Victorian Studies*, 28 (1984), 69–96.

18. Ludmilla Jordanova, *Lamarck* (Oxford: Past Masters series, 1984); Richard W. Burckhardt, *The Spirit of System: Lamarck and Evolutionary Biology* (Cambridge Mass: Harvard University Press, 1977); Pietro Corsi, *The Age of Lamarck* (Berkeley: University of California Press, 1988).

19. Peter J. Bowler, *The Eclipse of Darwinism* (Baltimore: Johns Hopkins University Press, 1983), especially ch. 6.

20. Boyd Hilton, *Age of Atonement*, p. 51.

21. *Ibid.*, p. 364.

22. James R. Moore, *The Post-Darwinian Controversies* (Cambridge: Cambridge University Press, 1979), part 3.

23. Charles Darwin, *The Descent of Man* (London: Murray, 1906), pp. 91–92; first published 1871.

24. Ronald L. Numbers, *The Creationists* (New York: Knopf, 1992).

25. Cited in *ibid.*, p. 109.

26. *Ibid.*, pp. 108–9.

27. John Morgan, "Puritanism and Science: A Reinterpretation," *The Historical Journal*, 22 (1979), 535–60.

28. John Morgan, *Godly Learning: Puritan Attitudes Towards Reason, Learning and Education, 1560–1640* (Cambridge: Cambridge University Press, 1986), p. 51.

29. Robert K.Merton, "Science, Technology and Society in Seventeenth-Century England," *Osiris*, 4 (1938), 360–632.

30. Barbara J. Shapiro, "Latitudinarianism and Science in Seventeenth-Century England," in *The Intellectual Revolution of the Seventeenth Century*, edited by Charles Webster (London, 1974), pp. 286–316; Shapiro, *Probability and Certainty in Seventeenth-Century England* (Princeton: Princeton University Press, 1983).

31. Susan F. Cannon, *Science in Culture: The Early Victorian Period* (New York: Dawson, 1978); Morrell and Thackray *Gentlemen of Science*, pp. 225–29.

32. I have explored these and related problems of categorization in two essays on Wil-

liam Whewell. See John Hedley Brooke, "Joseph Priestley and William Whewell, Apologists and Historians of Science: A Tale of Two Stereotypes," in *Science, Medicine and Dissent: Joseph Priestley*, edited by Robert Anderson and Christopher Lawrence (London: Wellcome Foundation and Science Museum, 1987), pp. 11–27; and "Indications of a Creator: Whewell as Apologist and Priest," in *William Whewell: A Composite Portrait*, edited by Menachem Fisch and Simon Schaffer (Oxford: Clarendon Press, 1991), pp. 149–73.

33. Jonathan Edwards, *Works, Vol. 6*, p. 167.

34. *Ibid.*, pp. 161 and 169.

35. *Ibid.*, p. 168.

36. Wallace E. Anderson, editor's introduction to *ibid.*, p. 49.

37. Simon Schaffer, "Priestley and the Politics of Spirit," in *Science, Medicine and Dissent*, pp. 39–53.

38. Cited by F. W. Gibbs, *Joseph Priestley* (London: Nelson, 1965), p. 81.

39. John Hedley Brooke, " 'A Sower Went Forth': Joseph Priestley and the Ministry of reform," in *Motion Toward Perfection: The Achievement of Joseph Priestley*, edited by A. Truman Schwartz and John G. McEvoy (Boston: Skinner House, 1990), pp. 21–56.

40. Jonathan Edwards, *Works, Vol. 6*, p. 305.

41. Joseph Priestley, *Disquisitions Relating to Matter and Spirit* (London, 1777).

42. Jonathan Edwards, *Works, Vol. 6*, pp. 57–63.

43. Cited by Schaffer, "Priestly and the Politics of Spirit," p. 40.

44. John Hedley Brooke, *Science and Religion: Some Historical Perspectives* (Cambridge: Cambridge University Press, 1991), ch. 1.

45. William Whewell, *Astronomy and General Physics Considered with Reference to Natural Theology* (London: Pickering, 1833); Brooke, "Indications", p. 151.

46. See the four letters of Isaac Newton to Richard Bentley in *Newton's Philosophy of Nature*, edited by H. S. Thayer (New York: Hafner, 1953), pp. 46–65.

47. Thomas Chalmers, *On the Power, Wisdom and Goodness of God as Manifested in the Adaptation of External Nature to the Moral and Intellectual Constitution of Man*, 2 vols., (London: Pickering, 1833), Vol. 2, p. 137. For the best contextual analysis of the *Bridgewater Treatises*, see Jonathan Topham, *"An Infinite Variety of Arguments": The* Bridgewater Treatises *and British Natural Theology in the 1830s*, Lancaster University Ph.D. dissertation, 1993.

48. Jonathan Edwards, *Works, Vol. 6*, p. 216.

49. James R. Moore, "Geologists and Interpreters of Genesis in the Nineteenth Century," in *God and Nature: Historical Essays on the Encounter between Christianity and Science*, edited by David C. Lindberg and Ronald L. Numbers (Berkeley: University of California Press, 1986), pp. 322–50.

50. Jonathan Edwards, *Works, Vol. 6*, p. 214.

51. John W. Haas, Jr., "Eighteenth-Century Evangelical Responses to Science: John Wesley's Enduring Legacy," *Science and Christian Belief*, 6 (1994), 83–100, p. 83.

52. *Ibid.*, pp. 86 and 95.

53. Edward Rosen, "Calvin's Attitude toward Copernicus," *Journal of the History of Ideas*, 21 (1960), 431–41, especially pp. 440–41.

54. Robert White, "Calvin and Copernicus: The Problem Reconsidered," *Calvin Theological Journal*, 15 (1980), 233–43.

55. That geology could corroborate a universal flood was still being argued by the Oxford geologist William Buckland in his *Reliquiae Diluvianae* of 1823. The critique of this view in Charles Lyell's *Principles of Geology*, 3 vols. (London, 1830–33), and Buckland's own retraction in his *Bridgewater Treatise* are often seen as symbolic of the end of this long tradition. It endures of course in the literature of so-called scientific creationism, of which many examples are given by Numbers (see *The Creationists*).

56. Hugh Miller, *The Testimony of the Rocks* (Edinburgh: Nimmo, 1869); first published 1857. See also Gillispie, *Genesis and Geology*, pp. 170–81.

57. Crosbie Smith, "From Design to Dissolution: Thomas Chalmers' Debt to John Robison," *British Journal for the History of Science*, 12 (1979), 59–70; Boyd Hilton, m*Age of Atonement*, pp. 361–62.

58. Crosbie Smith and M. Norton Wise, *Energy and Empire: A Biographical Study of Lord Kelvin* (Cambridge: Cambridge University Press, 1989), p. 330.

59. *Ibid.*, pp. 317 and 330–31.

60. Nor was Chalmers perturbed by the alternative prospect that other worlds might have fallen. For anything the infidel can tell, "many a visit has been made to each of them. . . . For anything he can tell, the redemption proclaimed to us is not one solitary instance, or not the whole of that redemption which is by the son of God." Thomas Chalmers, *Astronomical Discourses* (Glasgow, 1817), 7th edition (Edinburgh, 1817), pp. 78–79, 81, 119, and 180–81.

61. David Brewster, *More Worlds Than One* (London, 1854), pp. 12–14.

62. Boyd Hilton, *Age of Atonement*, p. 291.

63. Peter Bayne, *The Life and Letters of Hugh Miller*, 2 vols. (London: Strahan and Co., 1871), Vol. 1, pp. 403–10.

64. Boyd Hilton, *Age of Atonement*, p. 25.

65. Moore, *Post-Darwinian Controversies*, pp. 194–205. For a typical example, cited by David Bebbington in his contribution to this volume, see Thomas R. Birks, *Supernatural Revelation: or First Principles of Moral Theology* (London: Macmillan, 1879), p. vi. That inferences should be drawn cautiously from facts was so much part of a public perception of what was best in scientific methodology that it was affirmed by Prime Minister Gladstone in a letter to Leonard Horner: "I heartily . . . wish well to all who are engaged in the careful collection of facts, and in concluding with caution from them, and feel that if any fault or error arise, it will come not from the observance of these rules, but from failing to observe them." Letter of W. E. Gladstone to Leonard Horner, 26 March 1861, in *Memoir of Leonard Horner*, edited by Katharine M. Lyell, 2 vols. (London: Women's Printing Society, 1890), Vol. 2, p. 303. I thank Malcolm Fielding for this reference.

66. Leroy E. Page, "Diluvialism and its critics," in *Towards a History of Geology*, edited by Cecil J. Schneer (Cambridge, Mass.: MIT Press, 1969), 259–71.

67. David Brewster, "Review of Whewell's *Bridgewater Treatise*," *Edinburgh Review*, 58 (1834), 422–57, p. 429.

68. Haas, "Eighteenth-Century Evangelical Responses to Science," p. 85.

69. Chalmers, *On the Power, Wisdom and Goodness of God*, Vol. 2, p. 285.

70. *Ibid.*, p. 286.

71. Boyd Hilton, *Age of Atonement*, p. 22

72. Jonathan Edwards, *Works*, Vol. 6, p. 49.

73. Frank M. Turner, *Between Science and Religion* (New Haven: Yale University Press, 1974), pp. 1–37; John Hedley Brooke, "Natural Law in the Natural Sciences: The Origins of Modern Atheism?" *Science and Christian Belief*, 4 (1992), 83–103.

74. Smith, "From Design to Dissolution."

75. Boyd Hilton, *Age of Atonement*, p. 368; Wilson, "A Physicist's Alternative to Materialism".

76. Letter of Charles Darwin to Leonard Horner, 20 March 1861, in *Memoir of Leonard Horner*, Vol. 2, pp. 300–301.

77. Letter of J. B. Sumner to Leonard Horner, 1 April 1861, in *ibid.*, p. 303. For historical orientation on the subject of preadamites, see David Livingstone, "The Pre-

adamite Theory and the Marriage of Science and Religion," *Transactions of the American Philosophical Society*, 82 (1992), 1–81.

78. David Cairns, "Thomas Chalmers's Astronomical Discourses: A Study in Natural Theology," *Scottish Journal of Theology*, 9 (1956), 410–21; reproduced in *Science and Religious Belief*, edited by Colin A. Russell (London: University of London Press in association with Open University Press, 1973), pp. 195–204, especially p. 199.

79. Jonathan Edwards, *Works, Vol.* 6, p. 50.

80. Topham, *"An Infinite Variety of Arguments,"* pp. 70–71; see also Topham's contribution to this volume.

81. Ronald L. Numbers, *Creation by Natural Law: Laplace's Nebular Hypothesis in American Thought* (Seattle: University of Washington Press, 1977), pp. 24 and 34.

82. To my knowledge this point was first made by Paul Baxter, "Natural Law Versus Divine Miracle: The Scottish Evangelical Response to *Vestiges of the Natural History of Creation,*" paper presented to the British Society for the History of Science conference on "New Perspectives on the History of Geology," Cambridge, April 1977.

83. In a note that Miller wrote for the third edition of *The Old Red Sandstone* (1846), he retracted a proposition that had been stated in the two preceding editions, namely that "there is a gradual increase of size observable in the progress of ichthyolitic life, from the minute fish of the Silurian System up to the enormous Holoptychius of the Coal Measures." Following the publication of *Vestiges* he would now stress the evidence that destroyed a simple directional pattern. A ganoid found by Robert Dick proved that "there were giants among the dwarfs." Hugh Miller, *The Old Red Sandstone* (London: Everyman edition, 1906), pp. 16–17.

84. Numbers, *The Creationists*, p. 338.

85. Richard V. Pierard, "The New Religious Right in American Politics," in *Evangelicalism and Modern America*, edited by George Marsden (Grand Rapids, Michigan: Eerdmans, 1984), pp. 161–74; Eileen Barker, "Let There Be Light: Scientific Creationism in the Twentieth Century," in *Darwinism and Divinity*, edited by John R. Durant (Oxford: Blackwell, 1985), pp. 181–204; James R. Moore, "Interpreting the New Creationism," *Michigan Quarterly Review*, 22 (1983), 321–34.

86. Robert S. Westman, "The Melanchthon Circle, Rheticus and the Wittenberg Interpretation of the Copernican Theory," *Isis*, 66 (1975), 165–93; Westman, "The Copernicans and the Churches," in Lindberg and Numbers, eds., *God and Nature*, pp. 76–113.

87. Page, "Diluvialism and Its Critics" Gillispie, *Genesis and Geology*, pp. 123–24.

88. Page, *ibid.*

89. Boyd Hilton, *Age of Atonement* pp. 23 and 370.

90. James R. Moore, "Evangelicals and Evolution," *Scottish Journal of Theology*, 38 (1985), 383–417.

91. David N. Livingstone, "Darwinism and Calvinism: The Belfast-Princeton Connection," *Isis*, 83 (1992), 408–28, p. 427.

92. John Pye Smith, *On the Relation between the Holy Scriptures and Some Parts of Geological Science* (London: Jackson and Walford, 1839).

93. John Hedley Brooke, "Natural Theology and the Plurality of Worlds: Observations on the Brewster-Whewell Debate," *Annals of Science*, 34 (1977), 221–86.

94. *Ibid.*, pp. 243–44.

95. Michael J. Bartholomew, "Lyell and Evolution: An Account of Lyell's Response to the Prospect of an Evolutionary Ancestry for Man," *British Journal for the History of Science*, 6 (1973), 261–303.

96. Miller, *Testimony of the Rocks*, pp. 144–74.

97. Hugh Miller, "The Disruption," *The Witness*, 20 May 1943.

98. Miller, *Testimony of the Rocks*, pp. 184–87.

99. Cairns in Russell, "Thomas Chalmers's Astronomical Discourses," p. 203.

100. Miller, *Testimony of the Rocks*, p. 216.

101. *Ibid.*, p. 220.

102. Bayne, *Life and Letters of Hugh Miller*, Vol. 2, p. 420. My discussion of Miller here is based on a previous essay: John Hedley Brooke, "Like Minds: The God of Hugh Miller," in *Hugh Miller and the Controversies of Victorian Science*, edited by Michael Shortland (Oxford: Oxford University Press, 1996), pp. 171–186.

103. Jonathan Edwards, *Works*, *Vol. 6*, p. 7.

104. James R. Moore, "1859 and All That: Remaking the Story of Evolution-and-Religion," in *Charles Darwin, 1809–1882: A Centennial Commemorative*, edited by R. G. Chapman and C. T. Duval (Wellington, New Zealand, 1982), pp. 167–94.

105. Adrian Desmond and James Moore, *Darwin* (London: Michael Joseph, 1991), pp. 172–76.

106. *Ibid.*, p. 120.

107. George P. Landow, *Victorian Types, Victorian Shadows* (London: Routledge and Kegan Paul, 1980), p. 169.

108. *Ibid.*

109. Landow, *Victorian Types, Victorian Shadows*, pp. 18–19.

110. Frank M. Turner, "The Victorian Conflict between Science and Religion: A Professional Dimension," *Isis*, 69 (1978), 356–76.

111. Colin A. Russell, "The Conflict Metaphor and Its Social Origins," *Science and Christian Belief*, 1 (1989), 3–26.

112. Adrian Desmond, *Huxley: The Devil's Disciple* (London: Michael Joseph, 1994), p. 209.

113. *Ibid.*, p. 55.

114. T. W. Heyck, *The Transformation of Intellectual Life in Victorian England* (London: Croom Helm, 1982), p. 98. Heyck notes that even in renouncing an evangelical Christianity, Huxley would appeal to Luther's plea: "God help me, I can do no other."

115. Desmond, *Huxley*, p. 209.

116. Cited by Desmond, *ibid.*, p. 209

117. Cited by Desmond, *ibid.*, p. 300.

118. *The Works of John Ruskin*, edited by E. T. Cook and Alexander Wedderburn, 39 vols. (London: Library edition, 1903–12), Vol. 29, p. 89. This account, from *Fors Clavigera* of April 1877, is cited with instructive comment by Tim Hilton, *John Ruskin: The Early Years, 1819–1859* (New Haven: Yale University Press, 1985), p. 254.

119. Landow, *Victorian Types, Victorian Shadows*, p. 21.

120. For this point I am indebted to Robert Hewison, "Ruskin and Science," the Ruskin Lecture, Lancaster University, 1994. It is also a pleasure to thank my colleague Professor Michael Wheeler for stimulating conversation on Ruskin, whose archive is shortly to be housed at Lancaster University.

121. Ruskin, *Works* Vol. 36, p. 115; Tim Hilton, *John Ruskin*, p. 167.

122. The quotations here are from *Modern Painters*, Vol. 4, ch. 7.

123. Edmund Gosse, *Father and Son* (London: Heinemann, 1907), ch. 5.

124. Tim Hilton, *John Ruskin*, p. 256.

125. *Ibid.*

126. On the popularization of microscopy in the second half of the nineteenth century, see Graeme Gooday, " 'Nature' in the Laboratory: Domestication and Discipline with the Microscope in Victorian Life Science," *The British Journal for the History of Science*, 24 (1991), 307–41.

PART II

ORIENTATIONS

2

The Puritan Thesis Revisited

JOHN MORGAN

I

Historical explanations of the development and increasing acceptance of "science" in early modern Europe have generally sought to locate these processes within broader social movements. Given the profusion of religious contention, the widely held contemporary view that monopolistic religion was crucial to the stability of the state and to individual morality, and the evident cultural truth that in studying nature one was examining God's handiwork, historians have most commonly attempted to link science to particular strains of early modern Christianity. By far the most prominent and longest-lived of these attempts has been the "puritan thesis." This chapter seeks first to analyze the historiography of this interpretation and secondly to offer certain new suggestions concerning puritans and their views of nature in light of recent more directly political and religious historical reinterpretation of the era.

Though in a sense a historical argument is a progress toward the understanding of terms, it may be helpful, particularly in a largely historiographical paper, to clarify usage at the beginning.[1] The term "puritan" was used primarily as a libel—of somewhat changing meaning—from the 1560s until the religious fragmentation of the early 1640s, when it became far less useful.[2] After much modern debate, puritans are now seen as representing a broad spectrum of ideas; central, however, were a supra-or sublapsarian theory of double predestination, an emphasis on the further reformation of doctrine and ceremony, greater stress on sermons than on sacraments, an insistence on a "reformation of manners," and closer analysis of the question of the visibility of the true church. While on many social and economic issues puritans were indistinguishable from their neighbors, the godly nonetheless saw themselves as people who, by virtue of their regeneration and subsequent inner turmoil, belonged to a distinct community, possessed of special responsibilities.

Historians have also recently become much more sensitive to difficulties in defining "science" for the seventeenth century when that term was not itself used.[3] Where in the past they have sometimes discounted or ignored investigations of nature, either traditional or novel, valued in early modern times but later cast aside, social and cultural historians now wish to comprehend more the processes and various meanings of early modern investigations and debates. What revisionists are finding, not surprisingly, is an enormous complexity of "subcultures"; this has called into doubt notions of a coherence or "essence" in science at this time.[4] Seventeenth-century natural philosophy was indeed an arena of continual contestation and negotiation. It still included forms of knowledge such as astrology and alchemy that would later be extruded from the canon of science. The nature and place of rationalism and experimentalism, of mathematics and mechanical philosophy were all openly debated, even by Fellows of the Royal Society.[5] Natural philosophy still incorporated the work of artisans and virtuosi.[6] It also encompassed a traditionally close relationship between the cultural constructs of creation and God. Recently, even the notion of a scientific revolution has been challenged and is currently being reinterpreted as a conscious break with, but not total repudiation of, previous views of nature.[7] Many contemporary scientists saw the development and application of new knowledge to improve the conditions of existence as an integral part of natural philosophy, but they were also clearly aware of the possibility and desirability of an intellectual achievement distinguishable from its applied results.[8]

Science is now seen as a socially constructed artifact that must be understood, in part, by comprehension of the multiplicity of processes which go into its making, from the origin of questions through discovery and theorizing to institutionalization. Much of the story of later seventeenth-century science was the shaping and controlling of method and thus to some degree, of "truth."[9] Investigative processes, legitimated areas, types of communication, and standards of confirmation or falsification were all in comparatively fluid stages of negotiation. Religious and scientific categories—often imposed later or contemporaneously by opponents—therefore are best seen as spectra of not necessarily wholly consistent ideas that promised an enormous variety of cross-influences. Lines of cultural development in the seventeenth century perhaps resembled a great railway yard, with a huge number of tracks, operating distinctly but sometimes converging and running together for a time, or crossing and diverging, throwing off spurs which might end abruptly, disappear into the hinterland of marginalized ideas, or finally rejoin what perhaps only later becomes evident is the main track. This chapter, then, seeks both to anatomize and contextualize puritan ideas in order to assess which were catalytic to science, which regressive, and what the balance of influences was likely to be. Given the complexity of these matters, it should be stressed that this is intended as an exercise in probabilities.

II

The "puritan thesis" is most closely identified with the sociologist R. K. Merton, who sought to explain why particular aspects of natural philosophy were undertaken and also why the "new philosophy" was established as the norm by the later seventeenth century.[10] That is to say, from the start, the puritan thesis has been concerned with both the doing and the legitimation of natural philosophy. For Merton the answer lay in the growing interest in and approval of science by "puritanism," by which he meant the dominant value system of broadly English "Protestant" religion generally,[11] or as Abraham has explained, a "climate of opinion."[12] Merton was primarily interested in the continuously negotiated "sentiments" that lay behind cultural expressions and historical agencies such as puritanism and that were to him the real motive forces.[13] Following Weber, Merton emphasized that this "Puritan ethic, as an ideal-typical expression of the value-attitudes basic to ascetic Protestantism generally" was an "important element" in increasing the "cultivation of science."[14] While puritanism did not in any exclusive sense *cause* science or "directly influence the method of science," it was a key factor in making "science commendable rather than, as in the mediaeval period, reprehensible or at best acceptable on sufferance."[15] The mechanisms that he identified as the agencies of this cultural shift were, primarily, an increasing emphasis on the faculty of reason, a belief in progress, and the growth of a utilitarian outlook.[16]

At times, however, Merton's use of "puritan" clearly did refer to a particular strain of seventeenth-century English religious thought. Puritanism, he argued, as a *"religious movement"* certainly "adapted" to science but itself "initially involved deep-seated sentiments which inspired its followers to a profound and consistent interest in the pursuit of science."[17] Because reason "enables man more fully to glorify God by aiding him to appreciate His works," puritans, to a greater degree than their contemporaries, had a "tendency to laud the faculty of reason," and were even willing to have reason "test" all religious beliefs save the most basic.[18] Even though some theologians regarded some scientific work as "possibly subversive," a growing emphasis on progress, combined with a belief that natural philosophy was "instrumental . . . in establishing practical proofs of the scientist's state of grace," led "inevitably" to a great interest in science and to the "elimination of religious restriction on scientific work."[19] Puritan attitudes inexorably made the "pursuit of science" a "self-evident value." The desire to act for the "good of the many," for example, caused puritans to appreciate natural philosophy's utilitarianism and its empiricism. The principles of "puritanism" and Baconianism—both crucial to the *institutionalization* of science—proved similar and mutually reinforcing.[20] The test of this view for Merton was an analysis of the early Royal Society; the "originative spirits," he contended, were "markedly influenced by Puritan conceptions."[21] Nonetheless, the "consequences" of puritans' support for science "did not coincide with their expectations." Indeed, awareness of these consequences would have caused puritans to repudiate their support of reason.[22] The "most significant influence of Puritanism upon science" was therefore *"largely unintended* by the

Puritan leaders."[23] Inadvertence was thus a central aspect of Merton's puritan thesis.

Other historians also attempted to connect puritanism with a favorable attitude toward new forms of natural philosophy. Dorothy Stimson similarly argued that puritanism provided a cultural basis for the acceptance specifically of a "Baconian" approach to nature and that a disproportionate percentage of the original members of the Royal Society were puritans.[24] For R. F. Jones, scientific reform was antiauthoritarian, public spirited, and utilitarian, emphasizing the "concrete" and evincing a "distrust of language and hatred of words."[25] The puritan ascendancy brought advocacy of "practical" and "materialistic" reforms, as well as the infiltration of Oxford colleges and London science circles (and thus later the Royal Society) by puritans "interested in the new science."[26] Puritans were able to adopt Baconian approaches to nature specifically because of Bacon's "sharp distinction between religion and science."[27] Perry Miller similarly argued that puritans saw the comprehension of nature as a form of faith, since nature was a "positive declaration of the will of God, a necessary and indispensable complement to Biblical revelation."[28] In the 1960s Christopher Hill resurrected the puritan thesis, referring to the "Puritan antecedents" of "so many of the [Restoration] scientists" of the Royal Society.[29] Hill also sought to locate early modern science not only in the work of the educated elite but also among artisans and tradesmen.[30] Emphasis was also placed on the belief in the social, economic, and moral value of labor. Puritanism linked to Baconianism revealed the "roots of Protestantism's contribution to science."[31] Hill followed Merton both in arguing for a connection rather than a causal relation and in emphasizing that puritanism "*unwittingly* helped to create an atmosphere favourable to science."[32]

Since Merton, however, Charles Webster has offered the most developed form of the puritan thesis. Webster abundantly demonstrated the breadth of scientific activity in the 1640s and 1650s, as well as the variety of social classes involved and the great differences of political, economic, and intellectual interests. He also sought to determine and to locate historically the "cultural conditions essential" to this growth of science. He found his answer in early and mid-seventeenth century millenarian and eschatological views that decreed that unlocking the secrets of nature was a necessary prelude to Christ's rule on earth.[33] The agency of this millennial vision was a puritan opposition party that developed from c.1626.[34] After 1640 a blend of Foxean history and this millenarianism produced a "utopian mentality" that, desirous of overthrowing its "immediate intellectual inheritance," seized upon a reading of Bacon "fully commensurate with puritanism" as a way of confirming and fulfilling God's providence and of rapidly ameliorating the conditions of existence.[35] Here the "puritan" Samuel Hartlib and his labyrinthine connections stand as the most important puritan-Baconian engine for the new natural philosophy and also for broader social reform in the 1640s and 1650s. Hartlib himself contributed a specific puritan ideal of intellectual organization to the Royal Society.[36] Gone was Merton's stress on unintended effects; for Webster the struggle for empirical knowledge of nature became a self-conscious, highly organized, and purposeful aspect of puritans' religious-based intellectual efforts. Nor was this a localized aberration: the *"entire* puritan movement was conspicuous in its cultivation of the sciences."[37] Radicals were credited with much more influence concerning the various directions of scientific enterprise.[38] Even the Royal Society was seen as the end product of a long process of growth and recruitment from the "Puritan Revolution."[39] Although Webster has more recently conceded that within each "sectarian group" there was an "influential party which was anti-science," he has remained adamant that, despite differences of approach and some fragmentation, there was broad agreement among puritans on the principle of "complete harmony" between natural and revealed truth.[40]

To sum up, central to all versions of the puritan thesis is the depiction of a similarity of epistemology and methodology, as well as of social purposes, between puritanism and certain forms of seventeenth-century natural philosophy, particularly Baconianism. Both have been portrayed as possessing an antiauthoritarian view, a critical approach to scholastic learning, a favorable disposition toward the great powers of human reason, a desire to reform the universities toward the new philosophy, a progressive outlook, a utilitarian spirit, and a belief in the centrality of law in creation. Puritan reforms in the universities advantaged natural philosophy; puritans were also disproportionately involved in the formation of the various groups of the 1640s and 1650s that were the Royal Society's forerunners. Nor has the puritan thesis disappeared. Margaret Jacob, following Hill's and Webster's broad definition of "puritan," has recently again emphasized the formation of a Baconian-inspired, Erastian, millenarian, national alliance between "scientific learning" and "Protestant culture."[41]

Over the years, critics have systematically attacked the puritan thesis on methodological, terminological, and evidential grounds.[42] In the process, most of the supposed similarities and connections between puritanism and science have dissolved. Puritan experientialism and the empiricism of natural philosophy, for example, are now understood to be quite different structures of experience.[43] Puritans and Francis Bacon, so often linked, had substantially different approaches to knowledge and to its distribution and use.[44] Such traits as asceticism, dedication to a vocational life, a search for general improvement, the virtues of manual labor, emphasis on things rather than on words, and millenarianism—variously labeled as "puritan" or "Baconian"—have recently been shown to be conventional in the seventeenth century.[45] At the same time, the Merton-Webster approach greatly underestimated the dynamic strength of post-Reformation *Protestant* scholasticism and of continuing attempts, in which puritans were heavily engaged, for example through Ramism, to refine and improve logic and rhetoric rather than to reduce their importance.[46] The concept of an organized puritan party in the 1620s and 1630s has also been shown to have little grounding.[47]

Allegations of inexact or historically confused religious terminology have also featured in the criticism. Those aspects of Merton's thesis dealing with puritans as a specific thread of English seventeenth-century religion have often been seen as miscontextualized. Merton's view, for example, that "Anglicans, Calvinists, Presbyterians, Independents, Anabaptists, Quakers, and Millenarians . . . subscribed to a substantially identical nucleus of religious and ethical convictions"[48] disregarded enormous theological, ecclesiological, and political differences, as well as developments within factions. In failing to integrate the continuing importance and popularity of episcopal, Book-of-Common-Prayer Protestantism and the rise of "anti-Calvinism" into his view of religion, Merton miscomprehended the "religious ethos" on which he wished to focus. As well, Merton's ideas that puritans were particularly interested in the "good of the many" or that they exhibited an especial "hostility toward the existing class structure"[49] have not been substantiated by later research. That there was the "deepest interpenetration between science and religion within the English scientific movement"[50] seems to have been true along almost all the spectrum of seventeenth-century natural philosophers. There is little evidence that *contemporaries* widely identified science disproportionately as a puritan activity or interest. One of the chief problems here has been the proponents' reliance on a selection of evidence that privileged the puritan thesis.[51] Webster notes his reliance on puritan scientists who have left evidence in the form of autobiographical description that "unambiguously suggests" [*sic*] the "motivation" that they "*derived* from religious sources," a rather distant and tenuous link.[52] Similarly, that sectaries interested in natural philosophy had once been "puritans" (where true) does not establish that puritanism was the origin of, or continuing motivation behind, this interest.[53] One could engage in natural philosophy and still oppose specific *religious* claims for it that went beyond the convention that nature revealed the existence and power of God.

In light of research on the place of natural philosophy in the universities before 1640,[54] the view that Restoration science was the "end-product of a long process of growth and development which had taken place during the decades of the Puritan Revolution" is perhaps misleadingly truncated.[55] Recent work on the period 1640–60 has discounted also the idea that the puritan authorities or Visitors seriously pushed curriculum revision other than on more overtly religious questions, and has established that most of the intruded Heads were theologians. While a few were scientists, so were some of those removed from headships and lectureships because of religious unreliability. The circle around Wilkins at Wadham College is now explained more as a collection of dedicated natural philosophers of various religious and philosophical views seeking respite from outside pressures than as a puritan circle.[56] Webster has undoubtedly established that Hartlib was of enormous importance in facilitating the exchange of ideas and in helping to hold together a critical mass in London for the reform of natural philosophy.[58] But Hartlib's "Baconian" ideas may well have had an intellectual pedigree traceable more directly to the Calvinism of central Europe and to the dominance of Ramism there.[59] Early enthusiasm in the House of Commons and later in the Council of State for Hartlib's reforms languished; sums of money voted to Hartlib and to others, while sometimes generous, did not reflect consistent support.[60] Nor should this limited level of assistance to natural philosophy from puritans in authority be surprising in light of much evidence that pre-1640 puritan school and college statutes and practices (as at Emmanuel, Sidney Sussex, and Harvard) are identifiable primarily by greater

insistence on purified religion and not by any connection with natural philosophy.[57] That there was an active investigation of nature during the 1640s and
1650s is not in dispute, but it is not easily directly affiliated primarily with puritan
inspiration, direction, control, or approval.[61] As well, in light of the factional
quarreling and international wars of the 1640s and 1650s, it is difficult to see the
eirenic approach of John Dury (linked to Hartlib) as representing a specifically
puritan policy.

Head counting of Royal Society Fellows by religious affiliation has also
proved inconclusive; given a greater understanding of religious positions and a
remodeling of categories, Stimson's and Merton's figures on puritans in the early
Royal Society are now seen as inflated.[62] A statistical approach also has some
difficulty gauging the pressures that natural philosophers or their supporters may
well have felt to justify their scientific activities in the religious conventions, or
to the political masters, of the moment. The Royal Society's early active members are now best seen as exhibiting such a collection of "diverse philosophical
commitments" that "no one metaphysical, methodological, or ideological view
could be truly representative."[63]

III

Broad criticism of the puritan thesis did not challenge the belief of most historians in a relationship between organized religion and the growth of science.
Instead, alternative theses arose. As part of his own critique Kemsley detected
what he termed an "Anglican" via media, dating from the early days of the
English Reformation, which differed from other Christian streams of thought
in a way "closely similar" to that in which the new philosophy of the Royal
Society differed from other scientific streams, old and new.[64] Shapiro argued
that a particular strain within English religious thought, known to contemporaries as latitudinarianism, was most closely connected to, and conducive of, the
growth of English science in the 1650s and thereafter.[65] This view developed
very quickly and indeed was not wholly rejected by proponents of the puritan
thesis.[66]

The term "latitudinarian" probably originated at Cambridge in the 1650s as
a slur to describe anti-Calvinists who preferred an episcopal church. Especially
after 1660, amid a scramble to be reintegrated into restored structures of authority, latitudinarianism was equated with time-serving, or a willingness to
subordinate individual beliefs to the public order requirements of the civil government of the day.[67] Latitudinarians supposedly emphasized the capabilities of
human reason, attacked scholasticism, preferred a plain prose style, accepted
notions of human fallibility and the nature of probability, displayed a lack of
interest in fine points of theological dogma, and stressed instead morality and
an epistemology that supported both rationalized religion and natural theology.[68]
That leading organizers and defenders of natural philosophy such as Wilkins,
Glanvill, Sprat, and "S. P." could be labeled latitudinarian seemed further to
establish the compatibility of latitudinarian religious views with the beliefs and
methods of the new philosophy.[69] The relationship even seemed symbiotic. Nat-

ural philosophy, in rooting firm knowledge of God's creation in experience rather than in illumination or even in Scripture, could offer a "*via media* between scepticism and dogmatism" and thus help, in turn, to heal the religious wounds of the seventeenth century.[70] The debt of latitudinarianism to humanism, particularly concerning the compatibility of religion and learning, has also been established.[71] Merton's "puritan" characteristics on this reading devolved from humanism and were far more likely to be found in latitudinarian forms of Anglicanism. The interpenetration of religious and secular interests and the balance between latitudinarianism and the new science offered fertile soil for intellectual developments in late seventeenth-century England and beyond.[72]

This proposed connection also quickly ran into difficulty, however, since natural philosophy did not remain the captive of latitudinarian interests, even if they had served as the early catalyst. Latitudinarianism itself has also been reappraised. Recent studies have discerned that latitudinarians were engaged in an effort, not much different from that of other Anglican clerics after 1660, to recycle old views of certainty and to use moralism and rationality as slogans against puritan soteriology (particularly notions of limited atonement and reprobation) and in favor of Arminian ideas such as free will and cooperation in grace.[73] Natural philosophy was of interest (as with Glanvill) primarily because it could lend support to the old Hookerian notion of the rehabilitation of reason in religion.[74] The much-vaunted latitudinarian "moderation" precluded neither an emphasis on obeisance to authority above public expression of liberty of conscience nor persecution of those who would not be comprehended within a Church of England whose leaders were willing to offer only minor changes over *adiaphora*.[75] Even the latitudinarian epistemology and methodology employed by natural philosophers were in fact common to "all the major factions of the English Reformed Church." Similarly, notions of probabilism, so important in seventeenth-century English natural philosophy, were traced beyond the latitudinarians to the "anti-dogmatism and sceptical epistemology" of the early English Reformers.[76] Thus we are faced with much the same conclusion as had been reached about puritans: some latitudinarians performed or supported natural philosophy, but the supposed causes (such as "rationality" or "moderation") of their engagement in these activities cannot be demonstrated to have been specific to latitudinarians. As well, many latitudinarians showed no interest at all in experimental philosophy; any link was thus not a necessary aspect of the set of values called "latitudinarianism."[77]

In an attempt to rescue the latitudinarian thesis from these intellectualist shortcomings, James and Margaret Jacob emphasized "social processes, and particularly the social dynamics of the two English revolutions of mid-and late-century."[78] Latitudinarian Anglicanism, emerging out of puritanism through the dialectics of the English Revolution, managed in the early Restoration to develop a "position in which science and moderation were held to function as agents of social control, material acquisition and empire." This was made manifest in Thomas Sprat's *History of the Royal Society* (1667), which represented, under the aegis of the Royal Society, "an aggressive, acquisitive, mercantilist ideology justified in the name of both restoration and reformation."[79] The Royal

Society served as a counterrevolutionary agency, attempting to be the "key to the successful operation of the monarchy."[80] Even the mechanical philosophy was constructed as it was for ideological reasons to defeat both radicalism and republicanism.[81] This view has the great advantage of situating science firmly in the political, social, and economic turmoil of the Restoration. As yet, however, it is a more appealing argument concerning what mainstream science *became* in its general thrust in the Restoration rather than concerning its origins or specific activities. There is no clear or convincing explanation of how or why puritan-ism—or certain particular strains of it—metamorphosed into a form of "Angli-canism" nor of what "liberal" means when applied to these beliefs.[82] The notion of an easy metamorphosis also does not seem to square with latitudinarian hos-tility toward Dissenters in the Restoration.

IV

The continued emphasis on associating identifiable groups with particular views of nature and thus with the potential or actual growth and legitimation of science reflects in part a degree of continuing isolation of the history of science. Recent political and religious historical studies have forcefully contested the nature and structure of differences in seventeenth-century England. Since the 1970s a num-ber of historians, once called "revisionists," have offered withering criticism of what they take to be teleological approaches (Whig or Marxist) based on know-ing the results or future (in this case the 1640s or post-1660 period) and then depicting the previous era as (in many cases *only as*) the causes of those results. Revisionists deny the existence of deep, ideological differences and therefore rule out the conceptual possibility within this society of long-term causation concerning the civil wars. "Doctrinal puritanism" of the 1610s and 1620s— much as the original term "puritanism" of the 1560s and thereafter—was a libel, a propagandistic-purposed invention of enemies rather than an accurate descrip-tion of any real divide within the broadly unified and unitary worldview of the Church of England and of English culture generally. James I especially is pictured as following a policy of inclusion and balance of all but extremist views. There is a lack of evidence that people in England in the 1620s and 1630s desired, foresaw, or planned civil war or revolution. Contingent—and largely unfore-seen—events, and not a disintegration of fundamental structures, brought En-gland to crisis in 1638–41 and to war in 1642. Without this functional failure no reform thrust in England would have been capable of fracturing the body politic and the body cultural. This view sought to destroy finally the idea of a puritan revolution since puritans, on this reading, had become a conventional part of the mainstream of a stable and consensus church and worldview, and had all but disappeared as an identifiable force.[83]

These arguments clearly play heavily also upon explanations of long-term association of particular cultural thrusts with the new philosophy, yet they have seldom been integrated. By looking at myriad small pieces of evidence rather than at large, unwieldy, and contentious categories and relationships, and through their insistence on a closer narrative of the pre-1642 period, the revisionists delivered a serious setback to *any* grand theory that depends on the assertion of fundamental social, political, economic, or ideological differences among a set of people called puritans. It becomes prima facie less likely that such an assimilated thrust would produce a clearly differentiated view of the purposes and value of the study of nature. This view, while currently dominant, has, however, not gone unchallenged. Postrevisionists have very recently begun to reemphasize pluralism and conflict, even as part of the intellectual framework of early seventeenth-century England.[84] The debate, with direct relevance to the puritan thesis, now turns on questions of ideology, consensus and conflict, and stability; puritans are once again seen to be agents of recognizably different thought and action.[85]

V

In light of these new arguments it is necessary to reexamine certain aspects of the puritans themselves. Given contemporary religious, political, linguistic, and social conventions, what *could* puritans have meant by their texts and what did they hope their readers and auditors would do in response to their utterances? In early modern England (as in many societies) there was a variety of prescriptive views, that is, different conventions, as well as a variety of meanings for each convention.[86] Revisionists have commonly emphasized harmony over conflict as the dominant convention of the early seventeenth century. The two should not, however, be seen as mutually exclusive or as diametrically opposed. Harmony and consensus *encompassed* conflict as a necessary dialectical mechanism, a way, that is, of constantly modifying the status quo, whether at the level of marital relations, village confrontations, or metapolitics. Indeed, the language of "contrarieties" and "exaggerated dichotomies" was pervasive in early modern England. While inversion techniques were used ritually to reimpose coercively the appearance of public religious, political, social and neighborly unity, the purpose of such conflict was not principally to destroy but to emphasize the need for *readjustment* so that the different parties could achieve greater satisfaction.[87]

At the same time, conflict *as a mode of existence* (as distinct from the ulterior purpose of the conflict) also had its followers. At the core of what made puritans reformers was not an eagerness for assimilation into a single set of values. Rather, the clearly dominant convention for the godly—concerning double predestination, the visibility or invisibility of the church, preaching, communion, and antipopery—was the notion of division.[88] Indeed, the urge to divide things (thus providing a site for conflict) has been called the best defining inward trait of puritans.[89] Contention was not just of the moment; it was providential. Agreement on some, many, even most questions could not eradicate the expectation that some form of conflict was the norm of true Christian existence (and even proof of election) since on earth the godly would always be at a disadvantage. Part of the notion of contention for puritans was a self-fashioning as perpetually the underdog, struggling to hold to a godly course against the sometimes overwhelming force of the reprobates. Puritans neither saw themselves nor within their *mentalité ever* could see themselves as the mainstream in England. Virtue lay not in the pursuit of the mean but rather in obeying the will of a binary-minded God who had divided humanity into reprobate, languishing in the covenant of works, and regenerate, blessed in the covenant of grace.[90] The most important image of the history of the church for the godly was that crafted by Foxe: the endurance of the faithful through godly warfare against a succession of oppressors.[91] God also chose particular peoples and imposed collective responsibilities upon them. While "Israel" as a national paradigm became conventional, it was puritans who emphasized, beyond the norm, that territories once won for godliness could be lost completely, and might have to be physically abandoned, if the nation did not continue to follow godly policies such as the spiritual, as well as physical, battle against Rome.[92]

In the early seventeenth century changing circumstances heightened the puritans' sense of being an embattled minority and therefore transformed the intellectual context in which they must be historically located. In 1595–96 at Cambridge Peter Baro (Lady Margaret Professor of Divinity) and William Barrett (a fellow of Caius) variously criticized English Calvinist theology. In defense Cambridge Calvinists and Archbishop Whitgift produced the Lambeth Articles, a strong reassertion of Calvinist predestinarianism.[93] Both Elizabeth and James I, however, rejected the Articles as an authoritative statement of the faith of the Church of England. Under James, thereafter, the upper echelons of the Church of England became increasingly "latitudinarian." Although he was a Calvinist, James apparently desired a via media in England (and abroad) based on a "wide range of Protestant opinion" including anti-Calvinists.[94] Quiet disagreement was to be permitted on secondary doctrines on which certainty could not be established. James seldom applied a binary paradigm to religious questions; indeed, he even seemed willing to prevaricate, at least for political advantage, over whether the Pope was Antichrist.[95] He saw himself as the Janus-faced arbiter: "I am," as he put it, "for the medium in everything. . . ."[96]

A more intellectual challenge to orthodox English Calvinism arose in the 1590s from Richard Hooker. Hooker saw God's fundamental act as the establishment of laws to govern his creation. He denied the strict English Calvinist claim that God acted from will alone; God's will was based on reasons and in reason.[97] Hooker also minimized the effects of the Fall on nature and humans, positing an injured but still fundamentally cooperative and capable human reason.[98] Against puritan views that scripture was self-authenticating, Hooker insisted that it was reason that, through the institution of the Church, had to establish both scripture's divine origin and the literal construction of the text, as well as devise modern rules for the Church.[99] Since there were seldom "reasons demonstrative," or certainty, in controversy, Hooker accepted the legitimacy of different interpretations; it was no coincidence that he was critical of puritan scripturalism and of Ramism. He veered away from a binary view, criticizing double predestination and instead emphasizing the sacraments partly as a way to incorporate all into a comprehensive church. Not surprisingly, he was more respectful of the historical role of the Church of Rome.[100] Hooker thus offered, by the end of the sixteenth century, a mixture of rationalism, probabilism, and *avant la lettre* latitudinarianism.

Hooker's views were roundly attacked by the godly.[101] In response, puritans increasingly offered "exaggerated dichotomies."[102] The starting point was the twin effects of the Fall: the immediate, though not absolute, crash of Adam and Eve, and the continued further degradation of each human being thereafter. Human history was not a Hookerian narrative of a gradual climb back from the depths, of humans rehoning their natural abilities and connecting closely with God on a rational plane. While humans could still discern some portion of natural law through reason—a necessary ability for civil society—that this knowledge had been attained by pre-and non-Christian societies was an indication of its disconnection from the process of salvation. The Fall had in no sense been "fortunate." Carnal reason was seen in the main as clouded, vain, and presumptuous, and by itself more likely to lead humans away from God.[103] Similarly to Hooker, puritans posited two conditions of reason. Here, however, one was not presented as a divinely assisted *extension* of the other; rather they were seen as contraries. Natural reason was the respondent in the covenant of works; the elect, welcomed into the covenant of grace, alone had their reason regenerated. The doctrine of perseverance, stressed in the Lambeth Articles, allowed regenerate reason some reliability. While puritans did not doubt the abilities of the human intellect with regard to earthly tasks, they took especial pains to distance such knowledge from any soteriological value. Indeed, "knowledge" itself also took on peculiar meanings. Puritans saw the highest forms of knowledge—of God and, more specifically, of assurance of their own salvation—as a sui generis blend of private struggle and public involvement in the godly community, aided by expert mediation. The "truth" might arrive in a piercing moment during a sermon or more privately at home but it was singular, often unwitnessed (though frequently recorded in a diary), and by definition unrepeatable. As well, the election of others was not fully demonstrable, though observed tendencies might be assessed by the unimpeachable gathered godly judges of "truth."[104]

It was the structures of Ramism that both provided safe use of reason and at the same time confirmed aspects of the puritans' binary approach. Ramism claimed to provide, through "technologia," an infallible way of dividing the arts, whose principles conformed to the eternal laws of nature, and of assigning the proper tasks to each art, thus helping to provide knowledge for *use*.[105] Propositions that followed Ramus's three laws would be axiomatic and therefore commonly would not need proofs. This reinforced the desire of stricter English Calvinists for some form of certain a priori knowledge. Induction, as an English Ramist explained, was important only at the earlier stage of gathering "many specialls [into] a generall or universall conclusion."[106] A Ramist argument, perfectly organized from the most general statement to the least general, therefore paralleled and supported the puritan sermon arrangement of doctrines, uses, and applications. Since certainty rather than probability was the hallmark of Ramism, the system allowed the minister to feel intellectually *assured* that he was delivering to his congregation the true meaning of the Word.[107] In English adaptations, Ramus's system became a dichotomized offering of alternatives, employing the conventional heuristic of inversion, of knowing what was right by being presented with what was wrong. Its common diagrammatic form provided a wonderful spatial representation of the binary *mentalité*. Contrarieties, too, reflected the mind of God.[108]

VI

Nature, God's other book, served as a macrocosmic convention that in turn legitimated certain of the human-made paradigms of the microcosm. The complexity and yet constancy of nature led to the commonplace that God, in designing the natural world, had installed hierarchy and order, that is, the patterns of harmony. There was a widespread belief that he had also bound himself to his rules. When he chose to exercise his will he was now content, by and large, to act through secondary causes, though most commentators, insistent upon God's voluntarism and omnipotence, argued both that matter contained no self-willed purpose and that God could suspend or circumvent the operation of natural law and act directly through special providences. Natural philosophy could therefore be utilitarian not only in supplying information for carnal existence but also in providing knowledge about the intentions and practices of the Creator.[109]

As Calvin had explained, in order "to call us to the knowledge of him, [God] setteth before our eyes the workmanship of heaven and earth. . . ."[110] As well, Calvin's acceptance of the theory of accommodation probably removed wide potential for puritan objections to new astronomical ideas on the basis of apparent contradiction of scripture.[111] Not surprisingly, puritans also participated in this convention. Edward Dering insisted that the heavens revealed God's "greatnesse," the earth his "providence," and the "unchaungeable course" of nature the "constant wisedome & goodnesse" of such a Creator. A later puritan preacher similarly argued that the great variety and yet unity of nature "works for the glory of God" and proved "the manifold wisdome and goodness of God in creation." There was "nothing superfluous and nothing without function." John Preston, master of Emmanuel College, Cambridge, was one of many who used the clock analogy to argue the existence of design, hence also of a Creator.[112] That Preston's sermon was delivered before Charles I, no puritan or scientist, should, however, serve as a reminder of the ubiquity, that is, the conventionality, of this view. Empirical knowledge of nature, as with arts such as logic and rhetoric, was thus as practically useful to puritans as to many of their contemporaries. If natural philosophy could instil in people a desire to attempt to obey God's laws for humans, as the universe obeyed its own divine system of laws, then the covenant of works would be a slightly less unruly realm, and the elect in each age might suffer fewer hardships.

Puritans also frequently praised and pursued empirical knowledge. The knowledge of the craftsman or traveler was considered to be superior to and more "assured" than that of the book reader. John Downame spoke of "the skill and knowledge of civill and mechanicall Arts and Sciences . . . which are in themselves good, as being the common gifts of Gods spirit, and his profitable talents, which being well used, do much redound to the glorie of God, the author of them, and to the good of the Church and Common-wealth. . . ." More specifically, Thomas Granger advised practical experience, rather than simply a knowledge of Galen or Hippocrates, in investigating medical questions.[113] Some puritans went beyond commentary and even engaged in natural philosophy. William Fulke approached the question of meteors from a rational perspective; Henry Gellibrand addressed the problem of magnetism. Henry Briggs was the first Gresham professor of geometry and later Savilian professor of astronomy.[114]

The interest of some puritans in natural philosophy may well also have been encouraged by certain apparent similarities of view in Francis Bacon. Bacon was interested in developing a system of knowledge that would lead to a "certitude of physics" and then to the "forms."[115] While Bacon criticized Ramus's idea of a single method and denounced his emphasis on dichotomy and on words rather than things, he did accept two of the three Ramist "laws" and praised Ramus for cutting down much of the old scholastic brush.[116] Bacon's belief that his new method would in time produce axioms echoed Ramism. Bacon also argued that his own approach to natural philosophy would enhance the religious proclivities of the individual scientist. At the same time, his admission that the study of nature could not lead to "any light for the revealing of the nature or will of God" paralleled Calvinist emphasis on a distinction between Word and world.[117] Bacon's four Idols also recounted the incapacities of the human mind and the fallibilities of human knowledge. So Thomas Granger, a puritan preacher, in addressing his Ramist logic manual to Bacon, praised him both for rooting his logical system in the reflection of the mind of God and for emphasizing experiential knowledge over arguments from authority and from tradition.[118]

Yet nature was not God. And so more often than they expressed support for natural philosophy, and certainly in more vehement language, puritans voiced their concern that the successes of science would lead to vanity and presumption, and subordinate the Word to the discoveries and proofs of human reason.[119] Calvin himself had warned that God's works had to be studied through the prism of Scripture.[120] The evidences of a greater structure could be understood only by testing them syllogistically against the Word. As Thomas Shepard put it, "the major [premise] is the word, the minor [premise] experience."[121] As well, the puritan view of election was not easily made compatible with any idea that knowledge of God's universe (and therefore of God himself) was equally available to all, regardless of their spiritual condition. John Preston's conventional comment that nature offered "such letters as *every one* may understand and reade"[122] in effect denied a correlation between the study of nature and regeneration. Even Bacon's comments on the value of natural philosophy to religion were likely to raise questions concerning the *nature* of that religion, especially as Bacon was himself at times highly critical of puritans.[123] And if nature itself had decayed since the Fall, then what one could now learn might well not tell much about God's original intentions.[124] Another problem was that many natural philosophers increasingly challenged traditional notions of certainty. The grow-ing sense of "probabilism" exhibited by John Wilkins's recommendation of constraint in both religion and science where victory could not be had and by Robert Hooke's argument that one should not fix axioms dogmatically was epistemologically and methodologically divergent from, if not actually contrary to, the thrust of Ramist logic and that strain of English Calvinism summed up by the Lambeth Articles and continued through the Irish Articles of 1615 and the Westminster Confession of 1646/48. These had offered axiomatic knowl-edge as well as certainty of faith and also certainty of assurance, at which anti-Calvinists had baulked. Puritans thus do not seem to have been epistemologically situated to deal (as well as the non-Calvinist strain within the Church of En-gland) with the probabilism which became so prominent in seventeenth-century English natural philosophy.

The anti-Copernican views of John Cotton, one of the most important pur-itan ministers of his generation, similarly reveal not only astronomical conser-vatism but also an unwillingness to invest the agency of nature with specific religious meaning.[125] Hornberger suggested that Cotton was "clearly interested . . . in physical causes and in natural phenomena."[126] The work on which this comment was based, however, as its contemporary editor explained, was con-cerned with the theme of loss of "national" covenant.[127] Cotton offered con-ventional comment on the power and glory of God and advised the utility of natural philosophy for both health (through the discovery of new medicines) and wealth (through improved agriculture). When Cotton argued that "to study the nature and course, and use of all Gods works, is a duty imposed by God upon all sorts of men," his most likely meaning, since this construction was also used in discussing the distribution of election, was that some people of every "sort" (social rank) should be involved, that is, that knowledge of nature was useful throughout the social hierarchy.[128] William Perkins had termed this duty "general" calling: the obligation of all humans to honour God and to know his works.[129] Yet Cotton elsewhere specifically downgraded the value of natural knowledge precisely because it was only "unsafe and obscure" compared to the "more evident and *certain*" knowledge in scripture. He explained that while Christ "doth not mislike the study of nature" or reject "conjectures" concerning the weather, even if predictions were always reliable "and the reasons were evident," it was not the sort of knowledge that was important enough "as that a man should busie himselfe with the observation of it" since it was knowledge useful only for the day.[130] There may also have been a specific objection to weather prediction, beyond a point, as divination. But in general, for puritans such as Cotton the particular interpretation of the structure and rules of the universe does not seem to have held intrinsic interest.[131]

The intricacies of puritan views concerning the study of nature lead into the troubling question of astrology, still a very deep aspect of late sixteenth-and seventeenth-century English culture. Most disturbing to clerics, because it rep-resented in some ways potentially a rival belief system, was "judicial" astrology: the idea that the positions of the planets affected each human life in particular ways. In vesting authority in the heavenly bodies (which might thus be seen as animistic) rather than in the will of God, astrology seemed to challenge the value of prayer and thus to subvert religion. Published in hundreds of almanacs, astrology increasingly came to depend, in the search to produce more probable prediction, on the new widely available astronomy and on mathematics.[132] Not only many leading mathematicians but also astronomers were directly involved with, or respectful of, astrology.[133] Yet while astrology depended on firm rules as the basis of reliable prediction, theologically puritans stressed a covenant made by and with a highly voluntaristic ruler of the universe. Although some Independents and leaders of the Army in the 1640s and 1650s expressed interest in astrology and protected certain astrologers,[134] puritans were commonly seen by contemporaries as the fiercest opponents of prediction based on an analysis of nature.[135]

The logician Peter Ramus had also written texts on arithmetic and geometry,[136] and had stressed not only direct observation but also the value of mathematics in astronomy and mechanics as well as in more practical daily affairs such as trade.[137] Given his stature, this may well have influenced some English puritans toward a degree of acceptance of both empirical and mathematical science. Yet the inchoate signs and symbols of mathematics, seen as un-Christian forms of ceremony, may also on occasion have raised Protestant suspicions of diabolical association.[138] That mathematics teachers advertised in almanacs likely compounded the association. It was the mixing of the realms that perturbed the godly.[139] John Downame, for example, questioned the application of a form of speculation not based in the Word to an illegitimate purpose (probing God's providence):

> What benefit have they by their exquisite skill in Arithmetike, whereby they are able to number numbers numberlesse, if they want [lack] skill to number their daies, that they may applie their hearts to true wisdome? What though like good Geometricians they could measure all the parts of the earth and take the height, and demonstrate the bignes of all the starres of heaven; if they have no measure in their passions, appetites, and earthly desires? What though like cunning Astronomers and Astrologians, they knew the number of the starres, with all their motions, the constellations, aspects and influences of these celestiall bodies, and could neerely gesse at future contingents, and things to come; if their hearts and affections remaine fastned to the earth . . . ?[140]

From a perception of godly religion under attack, Downame sought to issue a forceful reminder of the limitations placed by God on carnal reason and the *inutility*, in religious terms, of explanations based upon secondary causes:

> What will it helpe skilfull Philosophers, though they were able to unbowell the secrets of nature, to know the causes and yeeld the reason of all things, which curiositie her selfe, could inquire, if they be ignorant of the great Creator, and of themselves, neither knowing the corruption of their nature, nor the meanes how to be freed from it?[141]

Knowledge of God's physical creation was not to be compared to the understanding of the godly path available from Scripture and to self-comprehension gained through repentance motivated by faith. Without the latter, the former had no religious value since the reprobates did not participate in true religion. And yet possessed of the latter, a Christian had no *soteriological* need of knowledge of the particulars of the creation, though such knowledge might well of course prove useful on earth. Puritans' comments on the superiority of empirical to mathematical knowledge were by no means out of keeping with developments in English science,[142] but they were not intended to promote experimentalism as the Royal Society would later fashion it. They were rather a reflection of the puritan view that regeneration and life in the covenant of grace constituted an experiential process rather than a piece of theoretical knowledge. They were also a form of recognition by puritans of the conventionality of the "empirical" attitude present in a milieu in which the great majority of adults engaged in farming or commerce.

VII

Establishing the puritan thesis requires two proofs: disproportionate involvement of puritans in studying nature (and evidence that they were involved because of their religious views) and especial efforts to spread approval of a new cultural role for natural philosophy. The vast evidence available about the broader puritan *mentalité*—from sermons, tracts, letters, diaries and official papers—makes it difficult to discern a strongly positive connection between this worldview and natural philosophy. Nor has it proved possible to establish that more than a few scientists actually became such because of their specifically puritan (as distinguished from generalized Christian or Protestant) religious ideas. Although puritan involvement now clearly seems outweighed by an "Anglican-humanist" background, there continues to be a methodological as much as evidential problem. The cultural variety so evident in early modern England (as outlined above) is starting to be emphasized against the older stress on "cultural coherence," that is, that a set of ideas X was more likely to produce a set of activities Y.[143] It is enormously difficult to trace the clear and distinct pedigree of ideas, as was suggested above concerning the intricate relationship of Baconianism and Ramism. While natural philosophers themselves are increasingly being seen as minds composed of a great variety of cultural threads, not all of them apparently seen as coherent even by contemporaries—Newton is the most obvious example— almost monolithic cultural forces such as puritanism (or Anglicanism, to say nothing of Roman Catholicism) are still called upon to serve as agents of motivation. Puritans constituted a broad spectrum of religious opinion. They were neither a party nor a denomination; there was never a single "puritan" church. Yet they have sometimes been portrayed as possessing a cohesive cultural view which in turn motivated certain activities. Unfortunately for the general argument, these purported views and activities cannot be found in most examples of that spectrum of *religious* opinion. There is a clear need for acceptance of cultural eclecticism—the notion that the particular amalgam of (sometimes inconsistent and even contradictory) views that constitutes the individual may have enormously divergent and indirect origins and ramifications. The importance of laws in seventeenth-century scientific conceptualizing, for example, may, if religious influence is sought, be traced to Richard Hooker's *Laws of Ecclesiastical Polity*, yet it may also be traced further back to humanism and even perhaps to Thomist philosophy. Similarly, "voluntarism"—so obvious in the ideas of Boyle—was a theological commonplace of the Reformation, and before that of medieval nominalists.

The study of nature, beyond acknowledging the power and authority of God and beyond also immediately utilitarian aspects, was for many puritans perhaps a form of adiaphora. Since neither cosmological theory nor questions of vacuums had evident soteriological value or spoke to the identification and preservation of the saints, puritan religiosity was not directly concerned with them. But even adiaphora were not located in an unbounded realm of indifference. They could (and in other cases clearly had) become contentious if they were imbued with too much importance. While nature was certainly also God's text, it was at once more fundamental and less fulfilling. It spoke to everyone, nourished all humans indiscriminately as physical creatures, and echoed God's original offer to humanity. But it does not seem to have been fitted into the *ordo salutis* by puritans. There seems to be little or no evidence that puritans broadly took the intensive intellectual (as opposed to ubiquitous daily-utilitarian) study of nature to be a particular covenantal duty of the elect. Indeed, in many ways, the natural was equated with the realm of the covenant of works. The text of the Word, on the other hand, while it had a moral and judicial message for all, alone served a salvific purpose for the elect.

There may also have been a difficult decision for puritans in the 1650s and 1660s. The realm of religious existence had to be kept separate from, and superior to, natural knowledge, since God's will could not be constructed as confined to his particular deeds. At an operational level knowledge of nature had to be rid of any connection to soteriological conditions that might lead reason to poach on the grounds of revelation and encourage a doctrine of works rather than faith. On this basis puritans would have been able to use the work of other Protestant and even Romanist scientists as they also sometimes admired Jesuit *methods* of education. But this may well have been, from the start, a chimera. An age that did not distinguish welfare, gender relations, crime and punishment, politics, and war from its relationship with God was unlikely to be able to study God's creation without finding particular supernatural meaning. Perhaps the greater difficulty for puritans in this was that traditionally they had *not* separated from the Church of England; rather, they had turned to gathering the godly as a way of publicly announcing their distinction from the ungodly and their culture. Each ritual, each form of socialization, each belief had then to be tested against whether it would aid the permanently beleaguered cause of godliness. In some ways, it may be that the radicals who had separated from the Church did not feel that they had to distinguish themselves so greatly on other matters.[144] This may have been, in part, the reason behind the puritans' insistence that natural philosophy not make grandiose claims for its religious utility. That is, as in matters of ecclesiology, they were not far enough apart, and did not feel themselves to be adequately secure, to ignore or to cooperate with views with which they disagreed. Their social, ecclesiastical, and political standing, as well

as their Ramism, kept them on edge. Natural philosophy was therefore historically likely to be a contested site for them. As well, separation of religion and
natural philosophy was not what occurred in the Restoration. Rather, an Anglican tradition seized hold of the agencies of authority and propaganda in the
Royal Society and, among other things, denounced the historical effects of "puritanism." It would be useful to have more work on whether Dissenters, in
continuing puritan strategies, worked out new methods of resistance to, or accommodation with, the dominant religious-political-scientific nexus of the Restoration. There is, however, the vastly difficult question of self-(re-)fashioning
in the political-religious turmoil of the Restoration. As political and external
religious conditions changed, so, too, did the rhetoric of science (and perhaps
the science itself). Separation at the level of the "actual science" may have
permitted puritans/Dissenters to participate in natural philosophy even while
they were excluded from the dominant construction of its cultural, political,
and religious meaning.

Work on the early legitimation of natural philosophy in England has concentrated on scientific groups in the 1640s and 1650s and on the Royal Society
in the Restoration. It is not at all clear, however, that attempts at legitimation
that included or heavily emphasized religious value *appealed* to audiences on the
same bases, that is, that the response to natural philosophy was predicated on
the same grounds as the way in which it was represented. As far as attempted
legitimation is concerned—and here I understand that term to refer to an elite
cultural process (distinct from wider "acceptance")—the historical role would
not seem to lie with puritans, who gave it comparatively little official effort in
the 1640s and 1650s. Legitimation, as understood above, was a process which
largely began—partly because of public criticism—in the early Restoration, in
the hands of the Royal Society or of (at first) independent writers such as Joseph
Glanvill who supported the Royal Society.

Here Thomas Sprat's *History of the Royal Society* may provide further suggestive evidence for the nonpuritan track to definition and acceptance of natural
philosophy. While Sprat's *History* did not accurately reflect the great variety of
scientific views and methods among the Fellows of the Royal Society,[145] his
great effort to illustrate the long tradition and continuing popularity of a broadly
based seventeenth-century "Anglicanism" and to connect its post-Reformation
religious and intellectual sympathy with natural philosophy (and thus of course
with the Royal Society) is of great importance to the question of legitimation.[146]
Indeed, in linking the experimental method with conventional virtues such as
affability and friendship,[147] he apparently strove to distance new science from
the well-known puritan experientialism and its criticisms of traditional neigh-
borliness and also from the application of binary divisions that had produced
"Twenty Years Melancholy." Conversely, he praised the Wadham group and
the Royal Society for abandoning any attempt at uniformity of religious opinion.[148] That Sprat downplayed puritanism says nothing about its historical contribution to the development of science. But in terms of our second question—
legitimation—his not wholly unreasonable attempt to tie the Royal Society to
the *longue durée* of seventeenth-century Anglican religion says much about con-

temporary elite attempts to define and direct natural philosophy and to tie it to a specific historical interpretation. Given that the early Restoration was a period of repression of other religious views and expressions, and that many former supporters of, or at least collaborators with, the Commonwealth and Protectorate were scrambling to distance themselves from their own past and to construct historical memories of the correctness of what they had done, the Anglican-latitudinarian dominance of early Restoration natural philosophy and its legitimation is hardly surprising.

The two tasks of doing and legitimating science consist of different activities, quite possibly engaged in for very different social, cultural, and political purposes and should not be conflated. For many natural philosophers it is simply impossible to establish any motivation or intention linking their specific religious beliefs and their science. It is substantially different with legitimation, a social process that could be accomplished only through conventions. It is virtually inconceivable that an attempt to legitimate science (or almost anything else) could have been made in seventeenth-century England without the promise of religious advantage. In this the "Anglicans" of the Restoration had the enormous privilege not only of political authority but also of being able, before a population weary of armies, religious extremists, war, and high taxes, to reconstruct post-Reformation English history and to insert into the narrative a particular type of science represented to the spiritual, political, and material advantage of restored state and church.[149] While certain of the effects of engaging in natural philosophy and of legitimation may well have been inadvertent—it is difficult to see how they could not have been, on *anyone's* part, given the enormous novelty of ideas and practices involved—legitimation may well have been a much more carefully and thoughtfully constructed process.

As well, the centrifugal—at times even anarchistic—tendencies of radical Protestantism moved in the opposite direction from Anglican legitimation (and so *construction*) of the new science. The Royal Society natural philosophers strove, in part, to establish consistent experimental standards and arrange socially and politically (as well as intellectually) acceptable forums, which quickly appropriated and reconfigured one of the most important conventions, the assigning of *public* truth value. Radical Protestantism, on the other hand, already by the late sixteenth century, was moving either toward "gathered" believers, who voluntarily associated themselves with beliefs for which they offered (if at all) proof that had to be incontrovertible only to themselves or toward individual illumination answerable to no one. Concerning nature, this culminated in the view that God was immanent in matter and could be grasped through individual sensuous experience. To the "left" and to the "right" of puritans, then, there were both science and legitimation. But within puritanism as a religious phenomenon, while there was some participation, there seems, on the whole, to have been wariness—as of any interest or authority not obviously leading to godliness—and, mostly, an indifference. On this reading, the most significant contribution to legitimation made by puritans may well have been individual decisions not to wage intellectual war on the involved study of nature, provided always that it did not directly challenge their theology.

NOTES

I should like to thank the Office of Research Services and the Dean of Arts of Ryerson Polytechnic University for a special research leave period during which this chapter was researched and drafted. My thanks go also to David Lindberg and to the readers for comments on an earlier version, and Adrian Foti and Clare Dale for their computer skills. Unless stated otherwise, the place of publication of all works cited is London. Spelling, punctuation, and capitalization follow the original in all quotations and titles of books. Certain aspects of the author's English usage and spelling have been changed to conform to house style.

1. But see also the cautionary note provided in J. H. Brooke, *Science and Religion: Some Historical Perspectives* (Cambridge: Cambridge University Press, 1991), pp. 6–10.

2. Concerning definitions of "puritan" and "puritanism," P. Lake, *Moderate Puritans and the Elizabethan Church* (Cambridge: Cambridge University Press, 1982) and P. Collinson, *The Religion of Protestants: The Church in English Society 1559–1625* (Oxford: Clarendon Press, 1982) have been especially influential recently. I have explained at some length my preference for the more nominalist "puritan" over the more essentialist "puritanism" in J. Morgan, *Godly Learning: Puritan Attitudes towards Reason, Learning and Education, 1560–1640* (Cambridge: Cambridge University Press, 1986), ch. 1. I revert to using "puritanism" on occasion here primarily because the term has been so widely used in the literature with which I am concerned.

3. It would be inordinately difficult to eliminate the term "science" from modern discourse about the early modern period. While I hope that this chapter reflects an awareness of the substantial differences, "science" is used here interchangeably with, and as shorthand for, "natural philosophy," and all that that term entailed in the sixteenth and seventeenth centuries.

4. S. Shapin, *The Scientific Revolution* (Chicago: University of Chicago Press, 1996), pp. 168–72; J. Schuster, "The Scientific Revolution," *Companion to the History of Modern Science*, ed. R. C. Olby et al. (London: Routledge, 1990), esp. pp. 223, 230–32, 239.

5. E. McMullin, "Conceptions of science in the Scientific Revolution," pp. 27–86 in *Reappraisals of the Scientific Revolution*; ed. David Lindberg and Robert Westman, (Cambridge: Cambridge University Press, 1990); Brooke, *Science and Religion*, p. 26; T. Hoppen, cited in P. B. Wood, "Methodology and Apologetics: Thomas Sprat's *History of the Royal Society*," *The British Journal for the History of Science*, 13, 1980, p. 5; M. B. Hall, *Promoting Experimental Learning: Experiment and the Royal Society 1660–1727* (Cambridge: Cambridge University Press, 1991), *passim*, e.g., pp. 10–11, 154–63; M. Hunter, *Establishing the New Science. The Experience of the Royal Society* (Woodbridge: Boydell Press, 1989); S. Shapin, *Scientific Revolution*, e.g., pp. 90–93, 130, 172; T. Kuhn, "Mathematical versus Experimental Traditions in the Development of Physical Science," in Kuhn, ed., *The Essential Tension: Selected Studies in Scientific Tradition and Change* (Chicago: University of Chicago Press, 1977), pp. 31–65; Schuster, "Scientific Revolution," esp. pp. 223–27; M. Jacob, *The Cultural Meaning of the Scientific Revolution* (Philadelphia: Temple University Press, 1988), pp. 34–35.

6. On the contribution to "science" of non-university-trained people, especially in the 1640s and 1650s, see C. Webster, *The Great Instauration: Science, Medicine and Reform 1626–1660*, (Duckworth, 1975) [hereafter, *GI*]; M. Hunter, *Science and Society in Restoration England* (Cambridge: Cambridge University Press, 1981), esp. pp. 89–91.

7. For cogent approaches to these problems see R. S. Westman and D. C. Lindberg, "Introduction," *Reappraisals of the Scientific Revolution*, pp. xx–xxi; Lindberg, "Concep-

tions of the Scientific Revolution from Bacon to Butterfield: A Preliminary Sketch" in *Ibid.*, pp. 1–26; I. B. Cohen, *Revolution in Science* (Cambridge, Mass.: Belknap Press, 1985), esp. ch. 5; Shapin, *Scientific Revolution*, esp. "Introduction"; Schuster, "Scientific Revolution," esp. pp. 217–24; J. H. Brooke, "Science and Religion" in *Ibid.*, esp. pp. 763–66.

8. Thomas Sprat, the most important early propagandist of English science, stressed this point from Bacon: Sprat, *The History of the Royal Society of London [1667]*, ed. J. Cope and H. Jones (St. Louis: Washington University Press, 1958), p. 245.

9. See the comment by Schuster, "Scientific Revolution," p. 222. The most thorough recent attempt at examining the phenomenon of truth making is S. Shapin, *A Social History of Truth: Civility and Science in Seventeenth-Century England* (Chicago: University of Chicago Press, 1994), though see also the reviews by M. C. Jacob, *Albion*, 27, 1995, pp. 300–302 and by M. Feingold, *Isis*, 87, 1996, pp. 131–39 and subsequent correspondence in *Isis*.

10. R. K. Merton, *Science, Technology and Society in Seventeenth-Century England* (New York: H. Fertig, 1970, orig. 1938) [hereafter *STS*]. The "puritan thesis," it should be noted, was only part of Merton's broader explanation of the development of early modern science; too often the two have been conflated.

11. Merton, *STS*, pp. 78, 82. Merton defended his terminological usage by arguing that all Protestant groups (with the curious exception of the Lutherans) "subscribed to a substantially identical nucleus of religious and ethical convictions." He acknowledged that this was not the common usage of the term but excused himself on the grounds that his interest was "social" rather than "ecclesiastic": Merton, *STS*, 1970, pp. 57–58. On Merton's concept of "institutionalization," see Gary Abraham, "Misunderstanding the Merton Thesis: A Boundary Dispute between History and Sociology," *Isis*, 74, 1983, esp. pp. 374–376; also P. Rattansi, "Puritanism and Science: The 'Merton Thesis' after Fifty Years," in J. Clark, C. Modgil, and S. Modgil, eds., *Robert K. Merton: Consensus and Controversy* (New York: Folmer Press 1990), p. 353.

12. Abraham, "Misunderstanding," p. 373; see also I. B. Cohen, "The Impact of the Merton Thesis," in Cohen, ed., *Puritanism and the Rise of Modern Science* (New Brunswick, N.J.: Rutgers University Press, 1990) p. 63.

13. Shapin, "Understanding the Merton Thesis," *Isis*, 79, 1988, esp. pp. 598, 601; but see also Shapin, *Scientific Revolution*, p. 195; Shapin, "Science and the Public," *Companion*, p. 999. Also J. Ben-David, "Puritanism and Modern Science," in Cohen, ed., *Puritanism*, p. 248.

14. R. K. Merton, "Puritanism, Pietism, and Science," in Merton, ed., *Social Theory and Social Structure* (Glencoe, Ill.; Free Press 1957), p. 574. On Merton in the Weberian tradition, see Rattansi, "Puritanism and Science," esp. pp. 351–52; I. B. Cohen, "Some Documentary Reflections on . . . the 'Merton Thesis' " in J. Clark, C. Modgil, and S. Modgil, eds., *Robert K. Merton: Consensus and Controversy*, pp. 314, 342 note 21. On the caution in Merton's thesis, see Shapin, "Understanding the Merton Thesis," esp. pp. 594–96. See also Merton, "The Sorokin-Merton Correspondence . . . 1933–34" in *Sorokin and Civilization . . .* , ed. J. B. Ford et al. (New Brunswick, N.J.: Transaction Publishers, 1996), pp. 21–28. I am grateful to Doug Webb for this last reference.

15. Merton, *STS*, p. 94. Cohen, "Impact of Merton Thesis," p. 11.

16. Merton, *STS*, e.g., pp. 63, 66, 72, 81, 104, 233–34.

17. Merton, *STS*, p. 82, emphasis added.

18. Merton, *STS*, pp. 66, 67–68, 85, 110; Merton, "Puritanism and the Rise of Modern Science," p. 580.

19. Merton, *STS*, pp. 99–100, 115.

20. *Ibid.*, pp. 87–90, 92–93. On Merton's view of the confluence of a "puritan ethos"

and the "spirit of science," see Ben-David, "Puritanism and Modern Science" in Cohen, ed., *Puritanism*, esp. p. 249.

21. Merton, *STS*, p. 112ff., quotation at p. 114.

22. *Ibid.*, pp. 79, 68.

23. *Ibid.*, p. 58 note 6, emphasis added; reiterated at p. 100.

24. D. Stimson, "Puritanism and the New Philosophy in 17th Century England," *Bulletin of the Institute of the History of Medicine*, 3, 1935, pp. 321–24.

25. R. F. Jones, *Ancients and Moderns: A Study of the Rise of the Scientific Movement in Seventeenth-Century England* (New York: Washington University Press, 1982, orig. 1936), pp. 91, 115.

26. *Ibid.*, pp. 91, 109, 117, ch. 5 *passim*.

27. *Ibid.*, pp. 92, 115–17.

28. P. Miller, *The New England Mind: The Seventeenth Century* (Cambridge, Mass., 1954, orig. 1939), esp. pp. 207–15, quotation at p. 211; also ch. 8.

29. C. Hill, "The Intellectual Origins of the Royal Society—London or Oxford," *Notes and Records of the Royal Society*, 23, 1968, p. 151.

30. C. Hill, *Intellectual Origins of the English Revolution* (1972, orig. London: Panther Books, 1965), esp. chs. 2 and 3; Hill, *The World Turned Upside Down* (Temple Smith, 1972).

31. Hill, *Intellectual Origins*, pp. 169, 124 note 4.

32. *Ibid.*, pp. 25, 26, emphasis added.

33. Webster, *GI*, ch. 1 and pp. 491, 506–7.

34. *Ibid.*, p. xiv.

35. *Ibid.*, pp. 3–44; see also pp. 497, 511, 520. On the redesigning of Bacon by 'puritans', generally supporting Webster's views, see J. Martin, "Natural Philosophy and Its Public Concerns," in *Science, Culture and Popular Belief in Renaissance Europe*, ed. S. Pumfrey et al. (Manchester: Manchester University Press, 1991), p. 114. M. Jacob, *Cultural Meaning*, p. 34, also stresses Bacon's millenarianism. See also K. Firth, *The Apocalyptic Tradition in Reformation Britain, 1530–1645* (Oxford: Oxford University Press, 1979), esp. pp. 204–07.

36. Webster, *GI*, *passim*, e.g. at pp. 511–12; Webster, "Benjamin Worsley: Engineering for Universal Reform from the Invisible College to the Navigation Act," pp. 213–35 in M. Greengrass et al., ed., *Samuel Hartlib and Universal Reformation: Studies in Intellectual Communication* (Cambridge: Cambridge University Press, 1994). See also G. H. Turnbull, "Samuel Hartlib's Influence on the Early History of the Royal Society," *Notes and Records of the Royal Society of London*, 10, 1952–57, pp. 101–30; H. Floris Cohen, *The Scientific Revolution: A Historiographical Inquiry* (Chicago: University of Chicago Press, 1994).

37. *Ibid.*, pp. 505–6, 510; quotation at p. 503, emphasis added.

38. *Ibid.*, e.g. pp. 498–99, 502–3, 511–12. Also Webster, "Puritanism, Separatism, and Science," in D. Lindberg and R. Numbers, eds., *God and Nature: Historical Essays on the Encounter between Christianity and Science* (Berkeley: University of California Press, 1986), pp. 208, 210–11, 213, where religious differences, as for example between radicals and university puritans, were said to have produced differences of approach and interest between, respectively, "Biblicist metaphysical" (and more utilitarian) and more "mechanical."

39. *Ibid.*, pp. 485–86, 488–91.

40. Webster, "Puritanism," pp. 199–205.

41. M. Jacob, *Cultural Meaning*, pp. 32–34. Also *Ibid.*, p. 74, on the "linkage between science and the Puritan reformers," and *Ibid.*, pp. 74–76, 81, 83, for "reforming Puritan

savants," "experimentalism of the Puritan savants," "Puritan scientists," "Puritan scientific vision," "Puritan philosophers grafted their reforming science. . . ."

42. Among the works directly critical of the "puritan thesis" are: T. K. Rabb, "Puritanism and the Rise of Experimental Science in England," *Journal of World History*, 7, 1962, pp. 46–67; A. R. Hall, "Merton Revisited or Science and Society in Seventeenth-century England," *History of Science*, 2, 1963, pp. 1–16; L. Solt, "Puritanism, capitalism, democracy, and the new science," *American Historical Review*, 73, 1967, pp. 18–29; B. Shapiro, "Latitudinarianism and Science in Seventeenth-Century England," reprinted as pp. 286–316 in *The Intellectual Revolution of the Seventeenth Century* (ed. C. Webster: Routledge and Kegan Paul, 1974); L. Mulligan, "Civil War Politics, Religion and the Royal Society," pp. 317–346 in *Ibid.*; H. F. Kearney, "Puritanism, capitalism and the Scientific Revolution," pp. 218–42 in *Ibid.*; L. Mulligan, "Puritans and English Science: A Critique of Webster," *Isis*, 71, 1980, pp. 456, 469; R. L. Greaves, "Puritanism and Science: the Anatomy of a Controversy," *Journal of the History of Ideas*, 30, 1969, pp. 345–68; D. Kemsley, "Religious Influences in the Rise of Modern Science," *Annals of Science*, 24, 1968, pp. 199–226; J. Morgan, "Puritanism and Science: A Reinterpretation," *The Historical Journal*, 22, 1979, pp. 535–60; Hunter, *Science and Society*, esp. pp. 113–16.

43. E.g., in Greaves, "Puritanism and science," pp. 353–55; Shapin, *Scientific Revolution*, pp. 80–85, 129–30.

44. J. Martin, *Francis Bacon, the State, and the Reform of Natural Philosophy* (Cambridge, 1992), esp. pp. 45–71. Abraham, "Misunderstanding," p. 382, comments that it has not yet been demonstrated that there was an appreciable number of "Puritan Baconians" or even how to identify them. A similar criticism appears in Q. Skinner's review of Webster, *GI*, in *The Times Literary Supplement*, 2 July 1976.

45. Mulligan, "Puritans and English Science," p. 469; Shapin, *Scientific Revolution*, pp. 68–72, 149–50; James R. Jacob, *The Scientific Revolution: Aspirations and Achievements, 1500–1700* (Atlantic Highlands, N.J.: Humanities Press, 1998), *passim.*

46. Merton, *STS*, p. 71. In *Great Instauration* "Ramism" and "Ramus" have one listing each in the index. On puritan use of logic, see Miller, *New England Mind*; W. J. Ong, *Ramus, Method and the Decay of Dialogue* (Cambridge, Mass.: Harvard University Press, 1958); W. Howell, *Logic and Rhetoric in England 1500–1700* (Princeton: Princeton University Press, 1956); K. L. Sprunger, "Technometria: a prologue to puritan theology," *Journal of the History of Ideas*, 29, 1968, pp. 115–22; Morgan, *Godly Learning*, esp. pp. 106–12.

47. Especially by the work of C. Russell, *Parliaments and English Politics 1621–1629* (Oxford: Oxford University Press, 1979); *idem, The Causes of the English Civil War* (Oxford: Clarendon Press, 1990). These works did not address the history of science.

48. Merton, *STS*, p. 57.

49. *Ibid.*, p. 81.

50. Webster, "Puritanism, Separatism, and Science," p. 200.

51. Merton conceded that what he was arguing had "been accentuated through a biassed selection" but excused himself by arguing that "this sort of bias is common to all positive enquiries." Merton, *STS*, p. 80. This teleological approach is replicated in C. Hill, *Intellectual Origins*, p. vii.

52. *Ibid.*, p. 203, emphasis added. The reliability of autobiographies on such matters as religious motivation is also questionable.

53. Webster (*Ibid.*, p. 200) has attempted to defend himself against criticisms of emphasis on puritans in *GI* by offering the *reductio* that it would be "unrealistic to expect the worldview of the Puritans to be *totally different* from that of other English Protestants" (emphasis added). As far as I know no one has suggested this position within this debate. Similarly, his comment that "*no amount* of antiscientific feeling emanating from Puritan

sources logically entails that all members of that group should come to the same conclu-sions" (*Ibid.*, p. 202, emphasis added) is of course true but each instance of such feeling does, I think, further imperil any puritan thesis.

54. For the view critical of the pre-1640 universities (concerning science): Merton, *STS*, p. 116; Hill, *Intellectual Origins*, esp. appendix, pp. 301–14. For the contrary position see, for example, M. H. Curtis, *Oxford and Cambridge in Transition 1558–1642* . . . (Oxford: Clarendon Press, 1959); B. Shapiro, "The Universities and Science," *Journal of British Studies*, 10, 1971, pp. 47–82; R. G. Frank, "Science, Medicine and the Universities," *History of Science*, 11, 1973, pp. 194–216 and 239–269; N. Tyacke, "Science and Religion at Oxford," in D. Pennington, ed., *Puritans and Revolutionaries* (Oxford: Clarendon Press, 1978), pp. 73–93; H. Kearney, *Scholars and Gentlemen: Universities and Society in Pre-Industrial Britain, 1500–1700* (Ithaca, N.Y., 1970); J. Gascoigne, "A Reappraisal of the Role of the Universities," in D. Lindberg, ed., *Reappraisals of the Scientific Revolution*, pp. 207–60; M. Feingold, *The Mathematicians' Apprenticeship: Science, Universities and Society in England, 1560–1640* (Cambridge: Cambridge University Press, 1984). Feingold, pp. 5–6, even criticizes Frank, "Science, Medicine and the Universities" for arguing that students' exposure to science came only at the M.A. level.

55. Webster, *GI*, p. 486. While critical at times, Webster takes rather a middling position (*GI*, pp. 115–29) on the question of pre-1640 universities.

56. Shapiro, "Latitudinarianism," pp. 21–29; Shapiro, "Universities," pp. 57–61. In "Latitudinarianism" Shapiro argues that "there is not a single unambiguous and fully committed puritan in the entire scientific leadership" of the Oxford circle: (p. 25). See also Hunter, *Science and Society*; J. R. Jacob, "Restoration, Reformation and the Origins of the Royal Society." *History of Science*, 13, 1975, pp. 155–76.

57. Morgan, *Godly Learning*, chs. 9–13.

58. Hartlib's "fundamental importance" was recently emphasized by Greengrass *et al.*, "Introduction," p. 18 in Greengrass et al., ed., *Samuel Hartlib*.

59. Howard Hotson, "Philosophical Pedagogy in Reformed Central Europe between Ramus and Comenius: A Survey of the Continental Background of the 'Three Foreigners,' " in Greengrass *et al.*, ed., *Samuel Hartlib, passim,* esp. p. 32ff.

60. See, e.g., Webster, *GI*, pp. 73–74; Webster, "Benjamin Worsley," esp. pp. 229–31; Hill, *Intellectual Origins*, p. 101; Jones, *Ancients*, p. 118; K. Dunn on the impoverished end of Gabriel Plattes: "Milton among the monopolists . . . ," in Greengrass et al., ed., *Samuel Hartlib*, pp. 178–79, 183 note 17.

61. Jones, *Ancients*, esp. ch. 5, seems to have fallen into the trap of thinking that things which occurred in the 1640s and 1650s were at least prima facie to be considered "puritan." Similarly, the rhetorical value of the term *"Puritan Revolution"* is retained by Webster, though by few other historians. Webster, writing of the pre-1640 period, argues that the "significance of the religious dimension can be inferred from the fact that the opposition party was firmly identified as 'Puritan' by its monarchist and Laudian opponents. . . ." Webster, "Puritanism, Separatism, and Science," p. 195. Labeling political, religious, or other opponents clearly tells us more about the rhetorical terms that the labeler thinks will advantage his own cause than about the object of the political rhetoric. One of the now well-recognized political ploys of the anti-Calvinists in the Church of England in the 1620s and 1630s was to label *anyone* who was not with them, a "puritan." On this see, e.g., Russell, *Causes of the English Civil War*, p. 85; A. Hughes, *The Causes of the English Civil War* (Houndmills, Basingstoke: Macmillan 1991), pp. 90–91; Thomas Cogswell, "England and the Spanish Match," in R. Cust and A. Hughes, eds., *Conflict in Early Stuart England* (London: Longman 1989), p. 129; P. Lake, 'Anti-Popery: The Structure of a Prejudice," in *Ibid.*, pp. 86–87.

62. Merton, *STS*, p. 112ff.; D. Stimson, "Puritanism and the New Philosophy," p. 321ff. Mulligan, "Civil War Politics," provided the most significant challenge; see also Kemsley, "Religious Influences," *passim*; Brooke, *Science and Religion*, pp. 114–15; Shapiro, "Latitudinarianism"; Mulligan, "Puritans and English Science"; J. R. Jacob, "Restoration, Reformation and the Origins of the Royal Society," *History of Science*, 13, 1975, pp. 155–76; Hunter, *Science and Society*, pp. 115–17.

63. Wood, "Methodology and Apologetics," 1980, p. 5.

64. Kemsley, "Religious Influences," p. 226. This general view has been criticized in D. MacCulloch, "The Myth of the English Reformation," *Journal of British Studies*, 30, 1991, pp. 1–19, and in N. Tyacke, "Anglican Attitudes: Some Recent Writings on English Religious History . . . ," *Journal of British Studies*, 35, 1996, pp. 139–67. "Anglican" is also a difficult term since it was not much used before the 1640s to mean a particular theological or ecclesiological strain within the Church of England.

65. Shapiro, "Latitudinarianism"; Shapiro, *John Wilkins 1614–1678: An Intellectual Biography* (Berkeley, 1969); Shapiro, "Early Modern Intellectual Life: Humanism, Religion and Science in Seventeenth Century England," *History of Science*, 29, 1991, pp. 45–71.

66. Hill, *Intellectual Origins*, p. 103; Webster, *GI*, p. 497.

67. Spurr, " 'Latitudinarianism' and the Restoration Church," *The Historical Journal*, 31, 1988, pp. 63–68; J. I. Cope, " 'The Cupri-Cosmits': Glanvill on Latitudinarian Anti-Enthusiasm," *Huntington Library Quarterly*, 17, 1953–1954, esp. p. 271, quoting from Glanvill's "Bensalem" MS.; S. P., *A Brief Account of the New Sect of Latitude-Men* (1662); J. M. Levine, "Latitudinarians, Neoplatonists, and the Ancient Wisdom" in Richard Kroll et al., eds., *Philosophy, Science, and Religion in England 1640–1700* (Cambridge, 1992), p. 85.

68. Shapiro, "Latitudinarianism," pp. 29, 35ff.; Shapiro, "Early Modern Intellectual Life," esp. pp. 58–60; L. Mulligan, "Anglicanism, Latitudinarianism and Science in Seventeenth Century England," *Annals of Science*, 30, 1973, p. 214. J. R. Jacob and M. C. Jacob, "The Anglican Origins of Modern Science: The Metaphysical Foundations of the Whig Constitution," *Isis*, 71, 1980, pp. 25–67; J. Spurr, *The Restoration Church of England, 1646–1689* (New Haven and London, 1991). For a very useful analysis of latitudinarian intellectual attitudes, see I. Rivers, *Reason, Grace, and Sentiment: A Study of the Language of Religion and Ethics in England, 1600–1780*, vol. 1 (Cambridge: Cambridge University Press, 1991), esp. ch. 2.

69. On Wilkins, see esp. Shapiro, *John Wilkins*; on Glanvill, esp. J. I. Cope, *Joseph Glanvill: Anglican Apologist* (St. Louis, 1956); S. P., *A Brief Account*, esp. pp. 14–24. S. P. may have been Simon Patrick.

70. Shapiro, "Latitudinarianism," p. 35; M. C. Jacob, *The Newtonians and the English Revolution* (1976), pp. 34–35; Rivers, *Reason, Grace, and Sentiment*, ch. 2.

71. Shapiro, "Early Modern Intellectual Life," esp. pp. 47–54, 57–58 Rivers, *Reason, Grace, and Sentiment*, esp. pp. 35–37, 87; Jacob, *Scientific Revolution*, p. 130.

72. Shapiro, "Early Modern Intellectual Life," pp. 60–62. On the interconnection of humanism and science, see J. V. Field and F. A. J. L. James, eds., *Renaissance and Revolution: Humanists, Scholars, Craftsmen and Natural Philosophers in Early Modern Europe* (Cambridge, 1993) and A. Grafton, *Defenders of the Text: The Traditions of Scholarship in an Age of Science, 1450–1800* (Cambridge, Mass., 1991).

73. Spurr, "Latitudinarianism," pp. 81–82; Levine, "Latitudinarians," pp. 89–90; Jacob, *Scientific Revolution*, pp. 108–09. See also the important article by N. Tyacke, "Arminianism and the Theology of the Restoration Church," in S. Groenveld and M. Winkle, eds., *The Exchange of Ideas: Religion, Scholarship and Art in Anglo-Dutch Relations in the Seventeenth Century* (Zutphen: Walburg Institut, 1994), pp. 68–83.

74. Spurr, "Latitudinarianism," esp. pp. 65–72, 81–82; Cope, *Glanvill*, esp. pp. 43–52.

75. John Marshall, "The Ecclesiology of the Latitude-Men 1660–1689: Stillingfleet, Tillotson and 'Hobbism,' " *Journal of Ecclesiastical History*, 36, 1985, esp. pp. 411, 416–17, 421–22; Richard Ashcraft, "Latitudinarianism and Toleration: Historical Myth versus Political History," in R. Kroll, ed., *Philosophy, Science, and Religion*, pp. 152–54; Spurr, *Restoration Church, passim*.

76. John Henry, "The Scientific Revolution in England," in R. Porter and M. Teich, eds., *The Scientific Revolution in National Context* (Cambridge: Cambridge University, Press, 1992), pp. 190–91, 201; Shapiro, "Early Modern Intellectual Life," esp. pp. 58–59; Shapiro, *Probability and Certainty in Seventeenth-Century England* (Princeton: Princeton University, Press, 1983); H. G. van Leeuwen, *The Problem of Certainty in English Thought, 1630–1690* (The Hague: Martinus Nijhoff, 1970, orig. 1963); I. Hacking, "Probability and Determinism, 1650–1900," *Companion*, esp. pp. 693–94.

77. Mulligan, "Anglicanism," p. 216. Mulligan accused Shapiro of defending the connection by focusing the definition of "latitudinarianism" so narrowly that the "conscious reconciliation of science and religion" was the "ultimate defining characteristic of latitudinarianism." *Ibid.* See also J. R. Jacob's and M. C. Jacob's review of Shapiro, *Wilkins*: "Scientists and Society: the Saints Preserved," *Journal of European Studies*, 1, 1971, pp. 87–90; M. Hunter, "The Debate over Science," J. R. Jones, ed., *The Restored Monarchy 1660–1688* (London: Macmillan 1979), pp. 185–87 and sources cited there.

78. J. R. Jacob and M. C. Jacob, "The Saints Embalmed, Scientists, Latitudinarians, and Society: A Review Essay," *Albion*, 24, 1992, pp. 439–40.

79. Jacob, "Restoration," pp. 169, 171. J. R. Jacob, *Robert Boyle and the English Revolution* (New York: Burt Franklin, 1977), p. 155, termed Sprat's *History* a "latitudinarian manifesto," though the point is specifically denied by M. Hunter, "Latitudinarianism and the 'Ideology' of the Early Royal Society: Thomas Sprat's *History of the Royal Society* (1667) reconsidered," in Kroll, ed., *Philosophy, Science, and Religion*, pp. 210–11.

80. J. R. Jacob, "Restoration Ideologies and the Royal Society," *History of Science*, 18, 1980, p. 28; J. R. Jacob, " 'By an Orphean Charm': Science and the Two Cultures in Seventeenth-Century England," in *Politics and Culture in Early Modern Europe*, ed. P. Mack and M. C. Jacob (Cambridge, 1987), p. 248.

81. Jacob and Jacob, "Anglican Origins," pp. 254, 258 and *passim*; also Jacob, "Scientists and Society," p. 89; Jacob, *Robert Boyle*, p. 155.

82. E.g., Jacob and Jacob, "Anglican Origins," p. 258; M. Jacob, *Cultural Meaning*, pp. 85, 109. For criticisms of the Jacobs' general interpretation, see Hunter, *Science and Society*, p. 29; Hunter, "Latitudinarianism," p. 212. For other criticisms, implicit and explicit, see Wood, "Methodology," *passim*; Henry, "Scientific Revolution," esp. pp. 200–01; Spurr, "Latitudinarianism," *passim*; Shapin, *Scientific Revolution*, p. 205. James Jacob has recently slightly modified his earlier views. In his *Scientific Revolution* he argues that "it was not Puritanism and capitalism that provided the ideological underpinnings of English science. . . . It was, rather, a reaction that set in among scientific thinkers to what they took to be the excesses of Puritan enthusiasm and Hobbist materialism" (pp. 130–31) and that the moral theology of people such as Wilkins and Boyle "emerged during the midcentury upheaval in reaction to the Puritanism, radical sectarianism, and Hobbism that were thought to jeopardize true religion, social order, and private property" (p. 130; see also pp. 105–106).

83. The term "revisionist" is less in use now; as revision of the former picture grows rapidly, the category becomes meaningless. Among the important contributions are N. Tyacke, *Anti-Calvinists: The Rise of English Arminianism, c.1590–1640* (Oxford: Clarendon

Press, 1987); Collinson, *Religion of Protestants*; P. Lake, "Calvinism and the English Church 1570–1635," *Past and Present*, No.114, 1987, pp. 32–76; C. Russell, *Causes of the English Civil War*, esp. ch. 4; J. Davies, *The Caroline Captivity of the Church* (Oxford: Clarendon Press 1992); K. Fincham, "Introduction," in K. Fincham, ed., *The Early Stuart Church, 1603–1642* (Houndmills, Basingstoke: Macmillan 1993); K. Fincham and P. Lake, "The Ecclesiastical Policies of James I and Charles I" in *Ibid.*, pp. 23–49; P. White, "The Rise of Arminianism Reconsidered," *Past and Present*, No.101, 1981, pp. 34–54; *White, Predestination, Policy and Polemic* (Cambridge: Cambridge University Press, 1992); G. W. Bernard, "The Church of England c.1529–1642," *History*, 75, 1990, pp. 183–206; K. Sharpe, *Politics and Ideas in Early Stuart England* (London: Pinter 1989); *Sharpe, The Personal Rule of Charles I* (New Haven: Yale University Press 1992), esp. ch. 6; C. Hill, "Archbishop Laud's place in English History," in C. Hill, *A Nation of Change and Novelty* (London Routledge 1990), pp. 56–81; J. P. Sommerville, *Politics and Ideology in England 1603–1640* (London: Longman 1986).

84. See, for example, R. Cust and A. Hughes, "Introduction" in Cust and Hughes, eds., *Conflict in Early Stuart England*, pp. 1–46; Hughes, *The Causes of the English Civil War*; John Fielding, "Arminianism in the Localities," in Fincham, ed., *Early Stuart Church*, pp. 93–114.

85. For summaries of the debate, see Glen Burgess, "Revisionism, Politics and Political Ideas in Early Stuart England," *The Historical Journal*, 34, 1991, pp. 465–78; Thomas Cogswell, "Coping with Revisionism in Early Stuart History," *Journal of Modern History*, 62, 1990, pp. 538–51; John Kenyon, "Revisionism and Post-Revisionism in Early Stuart History," *Journal of Modern History*, 64, 1992, pp. 686–99.

86. Q. Skinner, "Motives, Intentions and the Interpretation of Texts," *New Literary History*, 3, 1972, pp. 393–408; K. Sharpe, "A Commonwealth of Meanings: Languages, Analogues, Ideas and Politics," pp. 3–71 in K. Sharpe, *Politics and Ideas in Early Stuart England*.

87. Cust and Hughes, "Introduction," *Conflict in Early Stuart England*, p. 17. S. Clark, "Inversion, Misrule and the Meaning of Witchcraft," *Past and Present*, No.87, 1980, pp. 98–110; M. Ingram, "Ridings, Rough Music, and the 'Reform of Popular Culture' in Early Modern England," *Past and Present*, No.105, 1984, pp. 79–113; P. Collinson, *The Birthpangs of Protestant England* (Houndmills, Basingstoke: Macmillan 1988), pp. 107–8.

88. William Perkins saw the church not as an all-inclusive institution but rather as the "body of the predestined": Quoted in D. Wallace, *Puritans and Predestination: Grace in English Theology* (Chapel Hill, N.C., University of North Carolina Press, 1982), p. 60.

89. M. McGiffert, "Grace and Works: The Rise and Division of Covenant Divinity in Elizabethan Puritanism," *Harvard Theological Review*, 75, 1982, p. 465. Patrick Collinson argues that "a Puritanism which was no longer in contention, no longer setting itself against the stream, would cease to be in any very meaningful sense Puritanism." P. Collinson, *The Puritan Character: Polemics and Polarities in Early Seventeenth-Century English Culture* (Los Angeles William Andrews Clark Library, University of California, Los Angeles, 1989), p. 12, also pp. 25, 32; Collinson, *Religion of Protestants*, p. 199 and ch. 6, *passim*; Collinson, *From Iconoclasm to Iconophobia: The Cultural Impact of the Second English Reformation* (Reading University of Reading, 1986), p. 6.

90. On the covenant, see Morgan, *Godly Learning*, esp. pp. 26–30 and sources cited there. Covenant theology was not exclusive to puritan divines. See Neil Lettinga, "Covenant Theology Turned Upside Down: Henry Hammond and Caroline Anglican Moralism: 1643–1660," *Sixteenth Century Journal*, 24, 1993, pp. 653–69.

91. See McGiffert, "Grace and Works," p. 465; Collinson, *Birthpangs*, esp. ch. 5.

92. See esp. M. McGiffert, "God's Controversy with Jacobean England," *American Historical Review*, 88, 1983, pp. 1151–52; modified in *Ibid.*, 89, 1984, pp. 1217–18; T. D. Bozeman, "Federal Theology and the 'National Covenant' ", *Church History*, 61, 1992, pp. 394–407. On English Protestant views of Rome, see A. Milton, *Catholic and Reformed: The Roman and Protestant Churches in English Protestant Thought 1600–1640* (Cambridge: Cambridge University Press, 1995).

93. H. C. Porter, *Reformation and Reaction in Tudor Cambridge* (Cambridge, 1958), pp. 281–82, 336–39; 344–45; 376; 381–84; Lake, *Moderate Puritans*, ch. 9.

94. Fincham and Lake, "Ecclesiastical Policies," *passim*.

95. Milton, *Catholic and Reformed*, pp. 108, 121–22, 222; Fincham and Lake, "Ecclesiastical Policies," p. 28

96. Quoted in Sharpe, "Commonwealth of Meanings," p. 14.

97. R. Hooker, *Of the Laws of Ecclesiastical Polity* (Cambridge, Mass.: Harvard University Press, 1977), I.2.4; I.2.5; I.3.3. Arguing that God acted for "reasons" in establishing double predestination raised the possibility of judgment on the basis of foresight, theologically anathema to orthodox English Calvinists. See P. Lake, *Anglicans and Puritans? Presbyterian and English Conformist Thought from Whitgift to Hooker* (London: Allen and Unwin 1988), ch.4; on Hooker's views of reason, see esp. Gunnar Hillerdal, *Reason and Revelation in Richard Hooker* (Lund: C. W. K. Gleerup, 1962). On the similarity between Hooker and the episcopal "anti-Calvinists," see K. Fincham, *Prelate as Pastor: the Episcopate of James I* (Oxford: Clarendon Press, 1990), p. 232; Fincham, "Episcopal Government, 1603–1640," in Fincham, ed., *Early Stuart Church*, pp. 75–78. On the medieval background of many of the issues of law, necessity, and voluntarism see Francis Oakley, *Omnipotence, Covenant, and Order: An Excursion in the History of Ideas from Abelard to Leibniz* (Ithaca: Cornell University Press, 1984).

98. Hooker, *Laws*, I.8.10; I.8.11; I.3.1; I.3.3; I.3.4; I.7.7.

99. *Ibid.*, I.13.3; I.14.1,2; II.4.2; II.5.5; II.7.4,9; II.8.5,6; III.8.6,11,13,14. J. Booty, "Hooker and Anglicanism" in W. Speed Hill, ed., *Studies in Richard Hooker . . .* (Cleveland: Press at Case Western Reserve University, 1972), esp. pp. 217–18; Lake, *Anglicans and Puritans?*, p. 152; R. Almasy, "The Purpose of Richard Hooker's Polemic," *Journal of the History of Ideas*, 39, 1978, esp. pp. 263–66; Debora Shuger, *Habits of Thought in the English Renaissance*, (Berkeley: University of California Press, 1990), pp. 28–29, 31–38; Hillerdal, *Reason*, pp. 42–49.

100. Hooker, *Laws*, I.6.4; III.1.9–10; IV.7.6; IV.14.6.

101. Early responses included the *Christian Letter* (1599, possibly by Andrew Willet) and the anonymous *Abridgment . . . Booke . . . Ministers . . . Lincoln* (1605).

102. See, for example, W. Perkins, *A christian and plaine treatise and order of predestination* (trans. F. Cacot and T. Tuke) (1606), "Introduction."

103. Morgan, *Godly Learning*, ch. 3. On concepts of "right reason," P. M. Rattansi, "Some Evaluations of Reason in Sixteenth-and Seventeenth-Century Natural Philosophy," in M. Teich and R. Young, eds., *Changing Perspectives in the History of Science* (London: Heinemann Education 1973), pp. 148–166; C. Hill, " 'Reason' and 'Reasonableness' " in C. Hill, *Change and Continuity in Seventeenth-Century England* (1974), pp. 103–26; L. Mulligan, " 'Reason,' 'right reason,' and 'revelations' in mid-seventeenth-century England," in B. Vickers, ed., *Occult and Scientific Mentalities in the Renaissance* (Cambridge: Cambridge University Press, 1984), pp. 375–401. On ideas in such important figures as Paracelsus, Bruno, and Bacon that the Fall had provided a "fortunate" opportunity for the development of human potential, see Jacob, *Scientific Revolution*, pp. 32, 57, 104–105.

104. The gathering of "truth-assessors" was itself conventional, as in dunking suspected witches, organizing rough music, or calling juries.

105. Howell, *Logic*, esp. p. 151ff; Morgan, *Godly Learning*, pp. 106–07.

106. Thomas Granger, *Syntagma Logicum Or, The Divine Logike* (1620), pp. 276–77.

107. Morgan, *Godly Learning*, p. 107; Howell, *Logic and Rhetoric*, p. 151ff. S. Egerton, *The Practice of Christianitie* (1618), pp. 288–90; also p. 292.

108. See, for example, Granger, *Syntagma Logicum*, Book III, chs. 17 and 18 on "disjunctive syllogisms."

109. Thomas Sprat even suggested that natural philosophers might know God more thoroughly than other humans could. T. Sprat, *History of the Royal Society*, e.g., pp. 82, 111, 132, 349–50, 351, 352.

110. J. Calvin, *A Commentarie . . . upon . . . Genesis* (1578 transl.), p. 18, quoted in J. Briggs, *Francis Bacon and the Rhetoric of Nature* (Cambridge, Mass.,: Harvard University Press, 1989), p. 46.

111. The Genevan Bible (1560), for example, offered no marginal comment on the astronomical questions contained in Joshua 10.12–13 and Psalm 93.1.

112. E. Dering, *XXVII Lectures* (1576), sigs. E.vii–E.vii verso; Granger, *Syntagma Logicum*, Address to Bacon; J. Preston, *Sermons Preached Before His Majestie . . .* (1634), p. 68; Morgan, "Puritanism and Science," p. 555.

113. See, for example, R. Rogers, *Seven Treatises*, pp. 279, 281; A. Dent, *A Pastime for Parents . . .* (1606), unpaginated; S. Bird, *The Lectures of Samuel Bird of Ipswidge . . .* (1598), sigs. A2 verso–A3. J. Downame, *The Second Part of the Christian Warfare; or the Contempt of the World . . .* (1611), p. 101. T. Granger, *The Application of Scripture. . . .* (1616), p. 5ff.

114. W. Fulke, *A goodly gallerye with a most pleasant prospect, into the garden of naturall contemplation . . .* (1563); H. Gellibrand, *An Institution Trigonometricall . . .* (1635); P. Kocher, *Science and Religion in Elizabethan England* (New York: Octagan Books, 1969, orig. 1953), p. 165. On Gellibrand's relationship with Hartlib, see S. Pumfrey, " 'These 2 Hundred Years Not the Like Published as Gellibrand Has Done de Magnete': The Hartlib Circle and Magnetic Philosophy" in Greengrass *et al.*, eds., *Samuel Hartlib*, pp. 247–67. On Briggs's "puritanism," see Hill, *Intellectual Origins*, p. 57, but also I. Adamson, "The Foundation and Early History of Gresham College London, 1596–1704," unpublished 1974 University of Cambridge Ph.D. thesis, p. 133. For other examples, see Webster, *GI, passim;* also Martin, *Francis Bacon*, p. 55; Dunn, "Milton," pp. 178–79.

115. Shapiro, *Probability and Certainty*, p. 24.

116. P. Rossi, *Francis Bacon: From Magic to Science* (transl. 1968 London: Routledge and Kegan Paul, orig. 1957), pp. 66, 174, 68, 148, 151, 159, 195–98. Bacon called Ramus "a hide-out of ignorance, a pestilent bookworm, a begetter of handy manuals". *Ibid.*, p. 195.

117. Francis Bacon, *Works* (ed. Spedding, Ellis, and Heath)(Boston: Braun and Tagard 1857–74), III, pp. 267–68 ("Advancement of Learning"), and III, p. 488 ("Valerius Terminus").

118. Granger, *Syntagma Logicum*, "Address to Bacon." On another connection of Ramism and science, see Hill's comment on Timothy Bright in *Intellectual origins*, p. 133.

119. E.g., W. Pemble, *Salomons Recantation And Repentance . . .* (1628), pp. 9–10, 21–22, 34; S. Hieron, *A Helpe Unto Devotion in Sermons* (1624), p. 751. Morgan, "Puritanism and Science," *passim*.

120. Calvin, *Commentarie . . . upon . . . Genesis*, p. 20, cited in Briggs, *Francis Bacon*, p. 47.

121. Quoted in T. Webster, "Writing to Redundancy: Approaches to Spiritual Journals and Early Modern Spirituality," *The Historical Journal*, 39, 1996, p. 50, from Shepard, *Parable of the ten virgins*.

122. Quoted in Miller, *New England Mind*, p. 209; emphasis added.

123. Bacon, *Works*, IV, pp. 87–88 ("New Organon"), III, pp. 267–68 ("Advancement of Learning"); Martin, *Francis Bacon*, pp. 38–44, 62–63.

124. For an example of the decay argument, see Thomas Granger, *A Familiar Exposition or Commentarie on Ecclesiastes* (1621), p. 21. Kocher, *Science and Religion*, p. 87, suggests that it was "not one of the ruling ideas of the Elizabethan period." However, the forcefulness of George Hakewill's argument *against* the notion (*An Apologie of the Power and Providence of God* [1627]) perhaps suggests the strength of the idea.

125. On the popularity among divines of pre-Copernican astronomy, see Kocher, *Science and Religion*, p. 154. Brooke, "Science and Religion," *Companion*, p. 769, notes opposition to Copernicanism because it seemed to *raise* the status of humans.

126. T. Hornberger, "Puritanism and Science: The Relationship Revealed in the Writings of John Cotton," *New England Quarterly*, 10, 1937, p. 510.

127. John Cotton, *A Briefe Exposition . . . Ecclesiastes* (1654). The work, published posthumously, contained an introduction by Anthony Tuckney, later master of Emmanuel College and then of St. John's College, and also Regius Professor of Divinity at Cambridge.

128. *Ibid.*, pp. 23–24.

129. William Perkins, *A Treatise of the Vocations, or Callings of Men* (Cambridge, 1603). See, similarly, Downame, *Second Part of the Christian Warfare*, p. 102.

130. John Cotton, *Gods Mercie Mixed with His Justice* (1641), pp. 112–113, 134, 115.

131. On this point see also Miller, *New England Mind*, pp. 216–17, 219, 224.

132. Thomas Digges's *A Perfit Description of the Caelestiall Orbes*, published together with *Prognostication everlastinge* in 1576, contained not only the first diagram in an English publication of the Copernican heavens—a system that Digges enthusiastically supported—but also the first published suggestion of the infinity of the heavens. F. R. Johnson, *Astronomical Thought in Renaissance England: A Study of the English Scientific Writings from 1500 to 1645* (Baltimore: Johns Hopkins University Press, 1937), esp. pp. 391–94, 404.

133. B. Capp: *Astrology and the Popular Press: English Almanacs 1500–1800* (London: Faber, 1979), pp. 188–92; P. Wright, "Astrology and Science in Seventeenth-Century England," *Social Studies of Science*, 5, 1975, esp. p. 404ff.

134. K. Thomas, *Religion and the Decline of Magic* (London: Weiderfeld and Nicolson, 1971), pp. 437, 438, 440–47, argues that support for astrology at this time reflected heightened millenarian interest and the temporarily greater power available to lower social classes rather than the traditional *mentalité* of puritans.

135. Capp, *Astrology*, pp. 143–44; Thomas, *Religion*, esp. ch.12.

136. Ramus's mathematical works appeared in English before 1640 as *The art of arithmetike* (transl. W. Kempe, 1592); *The elements of geometrie* (transl. T. Hood, 1590); *The way to Geometry* (transl. and enlarged by W. Bedwell, 1636). On mathematics in England, see E. G. R. Taylor, *The Mathematical Practitioners of Tudor and Stuart England* (Cambridge: Cambridge University Press, 1954); Feingold, *Mathematicians' Apprenticeship*; Gascoigne, "Reappraisal of the Role of the Universities," pp. 103–104.

137. *Dictionary of Scientific Biography*, "Ramus, Peter"; Gascoigne, "Reappraisal of the role of universities," p. 223; Schuster, "Scientific Revolution," pp. 233–34. Bedwell, translator of *The way to geometry*, also produced almanacs and popular science manuals: Hill, *Intellectual Origins*, p. 64.

138. Thomas, *Religion and the Decline of Magic*, pp. 430–31. Bishop Hooper (executed 1555) regarded geometry and arithmetic as "necessary for every man" yet referred to astrology as "this damnable art mathematical." Quoted in Kocher, *Science and Religion*, p. 153.

139. H. Gellibrand's *Institutional Trigonometricall* may have been acceptable because it made no religious claims for mathematics.

140. Downname, *Second Part of the Christian Warfare*, pp. 95–96.

141. *Ibid.*, p. 95.

142. See, for example, Dent, *Pastime for Parents*, sigs. Cvi verso, Cvii, on the superiority of travel to the knowledge offered by the "mathematicall geographers." E. G. R. Taylor argued that geography entered a mathematical phase after 1583, especially through the link with astronomy. Taylor, *The Mathematical Practitioners*, p. 68.

143. On this point, see also the comments by L. Daston, *Minerva*, 32, 1994, pp. 113–14.

144. C. Marsh, " 'A Gracelesse, and Audacious Companie'?: The Family of Love in the Parish of Balsham, 1550–1630," pp. 191–208 in *Voluntary Religion*, ed. P. Collinson et al., *Studies in Church History*, 24, (Oxford: Published for the Ecclesiastical Historical Society by B. Blackwell 1986).

145. Wood, "Methodology," *passim*, e.g., pp. 8, 12.

146. Sprat, *History*, pp. 370–73. As early as 1585 Richard Bostock compared the Copernican and Paracelsan revolutions with the Protestant Reformation: Hill, *Intellectual Origins*, pp. 25–26. On the continued popularity of the (non-Laudian) Church of England, see J. Morrill, "The Church in England 1642–1649," now reprinted in J. Morrill, *The Nature of the English Revolution* (London: Longman 1993), pp. 148–75; Lettinga, "Covenant Theology"; Spurr, *The Restoration Church of England*, esp. ch. 1; Ronald Hutton, *The British Republic 1649–1660* (1990).

147. Wood, "Methodology," p. 15.

148. Sprat, *History*, pp. 58, 56, 47, 53.

149. I hope to demonstrate this in a forthcoming essay on Sprat.

3

Christianity and
Early Modern Science

The Foster Thesis Reconsidered

EDWARD B. DAVIS

> What I'm really interested in is whether God could have made the
> world in a different way; that is, whether the necessity of logical
> simplicity leaves any freedom at all.
>
> —Albert Einstein

Introduction: On Interpreting Christianity and
Early Modern Science

Did Christianity "cause" modern science? The question would have shocked
Voltaire, provoked a heated denial from Andrew Dickson White, and knocked
George Sarton entirely off his chair. According to the Enlightenment tradition
in which each of these men lived and moved and had their being, the very
possibility that theology could have had *any* formative influence on an enterprise
as "rational" and fruitful as the natural sciences was almost unthinkable: at best,
theology had sometimes provided (the wrong) motivation for some people to
pursue the life of science; at worst, theology had often played the role of the
obscurantist, standing in the way of scientific progress like Bellarmino en-
trenched before Galileo. On this view, the normative relation between Christianity and science in all periods has been one of cultural and intellectual conflict
rather than cooperation or conversation.

Fortunately such a view is no longer in vogue. Although reports of the
demise of the "warfare" school of writing the history of religion and science
may yet be premature,[1] it seems safe to say that it has had a near-death experience, at least among professional historians of science. Much recent historiography has underscored the shallowness, futility, and wrongheadedness of treating controversies involving religion and science simply as skirmishes in an
ongoing, inevitable conflict between contradictory ways of viewing the world.[2]

75

We have been urged to probe beneath the surface of apparent conflicts in search of the underlying reasons why people with different beliefs have come to disagree so deeply about matters involving science, and to accept the realities of a historically complex situation that resists *any* overly simple analysis—whether it is couched in the terms of conflict or its polar opposite, harmony, for both have been guilty of distorting the truth through an excess of emotion. At the same time, we must seek to make significant statements about the historical situation, not to bury our efforts with trivial conclusions. As Floris Cohen has recently said, "To find the proper balance between detachment and involvement seems almost beyond reach when this particular subject [religion and science] comes up for discussion—partisanship and irrelevance being the Scylla and the Charybdis on which more than one historiographical ship has been wrecked."[3]

The decline of the warfare thesis has left a large hole in the conceptual apparatus of historians, causing David C. Lindberg and Ronald L. Numbers to lament that "we will never find a satisfactory alternative of equal simplicity"[4] to replace it. And John Hedley Brooke, the author of a recent comprehensive study, concludes that "[s]erious scholarship in the history of science has revealed so extraordinarily rich and complex a relationship between science and religion in the past that general theses are difficult to sustain. The real lesson turns out to be the complexity."[5] This is not a problem unique to questions about religion and science; various questions about all sorts of historical events are difficult to answer simply, without sacrificing too much of the truth. Historians have a different sense of causality than scientists, and with good reason: human actions are complex, resulting from diverse motives and reflecting diverse beliefs and perceptions, a situation that is made only more complex for major events by the involvement of more people. Thus we are led to this paradoxical conclusion: the larger the historical target, the harder it is to hit; or, as Brooke has said with understatement, "general theses are difficult to sustain."

It is in this light that we ought to evaluate the question with which this essay begins: whether Christianity "caused" modern science. If a new sensitivity and subtlety have freed us from bondage to the warfare thesis, thereby creating the space in which questions about the religious roots of modern science may be asked without inviting scorn, they have also made it much more difficult—I am tempted to say impossible—to phrase *any* historical question about religion and science quite so baldly. If we insist on simple answers to simple questions, we will end up with what A. Rupert Hall has called a "one-legged interpretation,"[6] in which just one of several factors (say, Christianity) relevant to understanding a phenomenon (say, the rise of modern science) is identified as the sole "cause" of that phenomenon. More than anything else, this is why attempts to show that Christianity in one form or another (usually Roman Catholic or Reformed) "caused" modern science have failed to convince most historians, including me: what was once seen as an absurd question is now seen as hopelessly naive.

More modest claims about Christianity and science, however, can be much easier to support convincingly. John Brooke has identified several "levels on which statements about nature and statements about God have coexisted," yielding a number of ways in which religious beliefs have influenced science: as presuppositions underwriting science, as sanctions and motives for doing science, as principles for regulating scientific methodology and for selecting acceptable theories, and as theological explanations for events that are otherwise inexplicable.[7] My own typology, not much different from his, looks like this (the more fundamental questions are higher up in the table):

Can science be done? (Is a science of nature possible?)	The possibility question
Why should science be done?	The morality/motivation/justification question
How should science be done?	The methodology/epistemology question
What sorts of theories are acceptable?	The regulative question

Although these questions are not posed in explicitly religious terms, the answers various people have given will reflect their religious or metaphysical beliefs, as well as their beliefs about the nature of science as a form of knowledge. Furthermore, each general question could in principle be transformed into a specific historical question about connections between religious beliefs and beliefs about the nature of science in a particular period. For example, we might ask, why did (a specific group of) early modern scientists believe that it was possible to construct a science of nature? This is not the same thing as asking whether Christianity caused modern science, but it is a related question to which a definite answer might be obtained.

One of the most famous inquiries of this sort was taken up more than 50 years ago by the great American sociologist Robert Merton (b. 1910), whose work on the influence of puritanism on the *social activity* of science in England has led to a veritable mountain of research, most of it ultimately inconclusive but still of great interest to students of the seventeenth century, as the chapter by John Morgan has detailed for us. Although Merton was interested in several questions, it is what he said about the motivation-justification question (Why did particular English scientists decide that science was worth doing?) that has drawn the lion's share of attention, a fact that has surprised Merton himself, since his book was actually much broader in scope. "Had educated and articulate Puritans of the seventeenth century been social scientists," Merton reflected in 1970, "they would have found this focus of interest passing strange," for they assumed almost without question that science could only support theology.[8] Yet what we have grown accustomed to call the "Merton thesis" did not at first seem very persuasive. By Merton's own admission, many scholars saw it as "an improbable, not to say, absurd relation between religion and science." This was because John William Draper and Andrew Dickson White had convinced a generation of scholars that conflict between religion and science was a "logical and historical necessity," so that "a state of war between the two was constrained to be continuous and inevitable."[9]

Merton was not the only one to challenge that assumption in the mid-1930s. Unbeknownst to Merton, at the very time when he was engaged in his research on the influence of the puritan *"ethos"* on the *reception* of science, the late British philosopher Michael Beresford Foster (1903–59) was writing about the influence of Christian *theology*, especially the voluntarist variety, on the *content* of early modern natural philosophy.[10] Where Merton pursued an "externalist" inquiry, Foster followed an "internalist" line by asking the methodology question.[11] It, too, has inspired much research, though a mere foothill next to Merton's mountain.

Foster made his long, convoluted, often confusing argument in a series of three articles published in the journal *Mind* in the mid-1930s, early in his career as a tutor at Christ College, Oxford.[12] He focused on the doctrine of creation as the vehicle through which theology impinged on natural philosophy, a particularly promising approach because most natural philosophers of the early modern period believed without question that the world and the human mind had been created by the omnipotent God of the Judeo-Christian tradition. The classic triangle of relations between God, nature, and the human mind determined the way in which they viewed scientific knowledge (Fig. 3.1): both the manner in which and the degree to which the universe could be understood depended on how God had acted in creating it and how God continued to act in sustaining it. Over the centuries Christian thinkers, though reaching a consensus on the reality and goodness of the creation, have differed widely on the precise nature of the created order. Nevertheless, it is possible to say in general that the history of the Christian doctrine of creation often involves a dialogue between an emphasis on God's unconstrained will, which utterly transcends the bounds of human comprehension, and an emphasis on God's orderly intellect, which serves as the model for the human mind. This dialogue rose to prominence in the late middle ages, when theologians developed the distinction between God's absolute power (*potentia absoluta*) and God's ordained power (*potentia ordinata*). In the words of William Courtenay, this meant "that according to absolute power God, inasmuch as he is omnipotent, has the *ability* to do many things that he does not *will* to do, has never done, nor ever will do." Medieval theologians used this distinction to affirm divine freedom in creation and to underscore the contingent, covenantal character of all created things.[13] Early modern Christian thinkers worked within the linguistic boundaries of a similar dialectic. Typically they would acknowledge that God has both will and reason, but then stress one more than the other. Those emphasizing the divine will are often called "voluntarists," and those emphasizing the divine reason are often called "rationalists."[14]

Ernan McMullin has noted the existence of an equivalent dynamic in the history of science since antiquity. Science has always been marked by what he described as "a tension between two views concerning the nature of science, which we call the *conceptualist* and the *empiricist* views." Where "the conceptualist supposes that a direct access to the essence or structure of natural objects is available," the empiricist "believes that evidence for a scientific statement cannot be found in the concepts utilized in the statement, but only in the singular

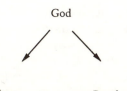

God

Nature ←——————→ People
(Created order)   (Created minds)

FIGURE 3.1. God, Nature, and the Human Mind

observations on which the statement rests." Conceptualist science "will be certain and definitive"; empiricist science "will be tentative, approximate, progressive." McMullin offers the following historical analysis in terms of these categories: although "severely challenged" by the "quasi-positivism" of the later nominalists, "the dominant medieval theory of science was conceptualist." The science of the early seventeenth century "was still strongly conceptualist," but it "became more and more empiricist in tone" as the century progressed—a trend that was reversed in the eighteenth century, at least in the science of mechanics.[15]

Though it came long before McMullin's analysis, Foster's work can be understood as an attempt to establish a direct link between the theological and scientific forms of this dialectic. "The method of natural science," he argued, "depends upon the presuppositions which are held about nature, and the presuppositions about nature [depend] in turn upon the doctrine of God." Foster identified two basic attitudes toward God that differ substantially in their implications for scientific methodology. Rationalist theology "is the doctrine that the activity of God is an activity of reason." Since "God is nothing but reason, there is . . . nothing mysterious or inscrutable in his nature." Such a theology, Foster said, "involves both a rationalist philosophy of nature and a rationalist theory of knowledge of nature." As a product of divine reason, the world must embody the ideas of that reason; and our own reason, "in disclosing to us God's ideas, will at the same time reveal to us the essential nature of the created world." A voluntarist theology, on the other hand, "attributes to God an activity of will not wholly determined by reason." Thus the products of God's creative activity are not necessary, but contingent. Since our minds cannot have demonstrative a priori knowledge of a contingent reality, the created world can be known only empirically.[16]

For Foster, the connection between Christian theology and the presuppositions of modern science was itself logically necessary, not historically contingent.[17] It seems fair to say that his articles go beyond historical revisionism to the point of engaging in apologetics:[18] by showing the fundamental significance of Christian theology for modern science, he hoped to use the prestige of the latter to benefit the former. This approach has provoked an important critique by the German theologian Rolf Gruner, who does not share the high view of science held by Foster, as well as by many opponents of Christianity. Gruner takes issue with all those who see Christianity as the source of modern science, hoping to put a stop to the apologetic uses of revisionism. It would be more promising, he says, for theologians in the future "to further the prestige of their religion by maintaining that it demands man's respect for his so-called environment rather than its manipulation and control."[19] This is a point well worth making—science and technology are no longer viewed uncritically as unmixed blessings in many circles[20]—but it fails to touch the substance of Foster's argument, and it can only preach to, not argue with, those who do not share Gruner's negative opinion of modern science. Gruner does raise several other objections to the Christianity-and-science thesis, including some that might be called historical in the very broadest sense,[21] but most of his objections are theological, and none of them confronts the actual historical situation in the seventeenth century, when what we now recognize as modern science came slowly into existence. Ultimately Gruner realizes that the revisionist case "is really the case of Bacon refurbished for the twentieth century,"[22] in that revisionists are simply repeating Bacon's attempt to show that the new science was closely tied to Christian assumptions. But this is to concede the very historical point I want to make: the revisionist case remains attractive to many precisely because it does ring true for certain aspects of seventeenth-century natural philosophy.[23]

Perhaps the most serious objection to Foster's work, however, is that his articles are profoundly unhistorical, dwelling in an abstract space somewhere above the plain of real thinkers constructing real natural philosophies. Although he argued vigorously what a consistently pursued theology of creation *ought* to have entailed for early modern natural philosophy, he did very little to show what had actually been the case. Yet he focused our attention on two of the right questions—how in fact did early modern thinkers construe the relation between God and the creation? and, what did they think this meant for human efforts to understand the created order? Picking up on Foster's essential insights, a growing number of scholars have begun to fashion a more genuinely historical form of revisionism. These would include John H. Brooke, Reijer Hooykaas, Eugene Klaaren, J. E. McGuire, Francis Oakley, and Margaret J. Osler[24]—individuals who do not share a common ideology (so far as I know), and therefore cannot be accused as a group of engaging in thinly veiled apologetics. Taken together, their work goes a long way toward bridging the gap between Foster's abstract assumptions and the complex historical reality of early modern science.

It is from my own work, however, that I will offer some representative examples of how different theologies of creation were used to undergird different conceptions of scientific knowledge by early modern natural philosophers. Elsewhere I have given a lengthy account of the substantive role of voluntarist theological assumptions in the scientific thought of Isaac Newton (1642–1727), which readers are encouraged to study as a supplement to this essay.[25] Here I will consider, of necessity much more briefly, three other major natural philosophers of the seventeenth century: Galileo Galilei (1564–1642), René Descartes (1596–1650), and Robert Boyle (1627–91).[26] These case studies, which should be viewed as vignettes taken from much longer essays written several years ago,[27] will be used to test the Foster thesis by sketching the answers to three main questions: How was God's relationship to the human mind understood? How was God's relationship to nature understood? What overall view of the nature of scientific knowledge was proclaimed? Although I will not always quote authors directly, I have been careful to rely on their explicit statements about God, and to avoid arguing (as Foster sometimes did) by implication and inference. As we will see, Foster was correct to suggest that theological assumptions were closely associated with conceptions of scientific knowledge. However, Foster's belief that Christian theology had actually *caused* the rise of modern science turns out to be as much an oversimplification of the actual situation as the belief that warfare between religion and science is inevitable.

Three Case Studies, Briefly Considered

Apart from his famous letter to Christina de Medici, written in response to a specific threat to freedom of thought, Galileo Galilei never wrote extensively or systematically about any theological subject—at least not for publication.[28] Nevertheless, he made enough explicit theological statements for us to assemble a picture of his theology of creation that is consistent with everything else we know about him. In confronting the qualitative Aristotelian philosophy of nature that dominated the universities of his age, Galileo was forced to justify his alternative view that physics was essentially mathematics applied to matter, and the justification he provided was couched in the language and concepts of theology. Galileo's ideal of a mathematical, a priori science of nature was grounded explicitly on a rationalistic, highly Platonic, understanding of God's relation to created objects and to created minds.

This is not to deny that Galileo performed many experiments, which certainly helped him formulate propositions about nature. I mean simply that his *ideal* of scientific knowledge was that of mathematical demonstration, which he believed to be the only way to achieve certainty. In this respect, his conception of scientific knowledge was still largely Aristotelian—certainty rather than probability was the ultimate goal of science.[29] It is now clear that he was heavily influenced in this by the Jesuits of the Collegio Romano, whose view of science as demonstrative knowledge Galileo maintained, though he molded it to fit his mathematical and experimental methods.[30] For Galileo, science was true and necessary knowledge of nature, just as mathematics was true and necessary demonstration. Thus mathematics was truly the proper language of science. He sought not to persuade opponents by probable arguments but to prove his conclusion "by necessary demonstrations from their primary and unquestionable foundations."[31] Natural truths, he said, "must follow necessarily, in such a way that it would be impossible for them to take place in any other manner," for "just as there is no middle ground between truth and falsity in physical things, so in rigorous proofs one must either establish his point beyond any doubt or else beg the question inexcusably."[32] It was the failure of other natural philosophers to do just this that Galileo was wont to criticize most. Thus he said of William Gilbert's work on magnetism, that his reasons "lack that force which must un-questionably be present in those adduced as necessary and eternal scientific con-clusions."[33]

Galileo realized that a truly demonstrative science would be possible only if God, as Author of the great book of the universe, guaranteed that nature dis-played the same necessity as the mathematical language in which it was written, and further guaranteed that the human mind was capable of reading that lan-guage. He claimed nothing less. As "the obedient executrix of God's com-mands," nature was "inexorable and immutable," never transgressing "the laws imposed upon her."[34] Since he took "matter to be inalterable—that is, always the same," it was evident that for any "eternal and necessary property, purely mathematical demonstrations can be produced."[35] Now Galileo was not a pure Platonist: unlike Plato, he thought we could attain true knowledge of material bodies. But he confessed that he was not "far from being of the same opinion" with Plato, who "admired the human understanding and believed it to partake of divinity simply because it understood the nature of numbers."[36] Within the range of mathematical demonstration, Galileo claimed, human "knowledge equals the Divine in objective certainty, for here it succeeds in understanding necessity, beyond which there can be no greater sureness."[37]

Galileo did place limits upon our ability to plumb the depths of nature, but these arose from our status as creatures with finite minds rather than from an exercise of divine freedom. Thus we could not know infinitely many truths, he admitted, for we are not God. We could know discursively by reason some of the truths that God knows instantly by intuition, and here our knowledge was equal to God's.[38] But our limited capacity to comprehend the subtle mathematics of infinity, which God had sometimes used in making the world, meant there were some things about nature we would never fully understand. In an inter-esting letter to Gallanzone Gallanzoni, secretary to Cardinal François de Joyeuse (1559–1615), Galileo identified three classes of proportions—the perfect, be-tween proximate numbers; the less perfect, between "more remote prime num-bers"; and the imperfect, between incommensurables, such as ratios of square roots to one another. If it were up to us to arrange the motions of the celestial bodies, Galileo said, "we should have to rely on proportions of the first type, which are the most rational." But God, "not bothering about symmetries that man can understand," had used imperfect proportions, which were not only "irrational, but totally inaccessible to our intelligence." Likewise, Galileo con-tinued, if a famous architect were to distribute the fixed stars throughout the vault of heaven, he would employ regular geometric figures and familiar ratios. But God, "by apparently scattering them at random, impresses us as having arranged them without heeding any rules or any demands of symmetry and elegance."[39] Nor could we determine whether the world was finite or infinite in size, Galileo told the philosopher Fortunio Liceti (1577–1657) late in his life. Galileo leaned toward an infinite world simply because "I feel that my incapacity to comprehend might more properly be referred to incomprehensible infinity, rather than to finiteness, in which no principle of incomprehensibility is re-quired." Ultimately, he confessed, this was one of those questions that was "happily inexplicable to human reason, and similar perchance to predestination, free will, and others in which only Holy Writ and divine revelation can give an answer to our reverent remarks."[40]

For all of Galileo's willingness to surrender infinity to God's unlimited mind, God's will had almost no place in Galilean natural philosophy, not even in thought experiments, the traditional vehicle for the consideration of supernatural possibilities. For example, Galileo twice suggested the experiment of dropping a body into a tunnel through the center of the earth, precisely the sort of situation in which many medieval natural philosophers would have invoked God's absolute power to do such a thing. Neither time did Galileo suggest an agent.[41] Equally he refused to accept without sarcasm supernatural possibilities proposed by others.[42] The principal role for God's power in Galileo's natural philosophy was implicit rather than explicit: to ensure that God's geometrical thoughts would be completely realized in the objects of his making, so that even the accidental complexities of real bodies would be subject to the exacting scrutiny of geometry.[43] Although nature was not simple, it was nevertheless almost wholly explicable in mathematical terms. As Thomas McTighe has put it, there was for Galileo "no intractable surd in the things of nature which defies rationalization."[44] And since the world was mathematical to the core, our failure completely to know God's works was attributed much more to the defect of a finite human understanding than to the exercise of divine freedom. Thus Galileo's theology of creation, like his conception of science, was essentially rationalistic.

The same could be said of René Descartes, who ironically used a most extreme form of voluntarism as a tool to help establish the rationalistic natural philosophy that grew out of his vigorous attempt to answer skepticism. In emphasizing God's utter transcendence, Descartes denied that any limits could be placed on God's power to create a boundless universe[45] or eternal truths incomprehensibly different from those that the human mind perceived as necessary: he refused to deny that God could make mountains without valleys, or make the sum of one and two not to equal three.[46] In this he went even further than almost every medieval nominalist.[47] However, Descartes' God could not change his mind once he had chosen which truths to create, because he was perfect and his will and intellect were one. Thus if we could somehow gain knowledge of these truths, that knowledge would be permanent and necessary, not contingent. We could indeed get such knowledge, Descartes believed, for God had given us certain innate truths. Here Descartes retreated from the radical voluntarism he expressed elsewhere. A perfect God could not deceive us by implanting in our souls seeds of error rather than seeds of truth. Thus the human mind became the touchstone for created reality: what it could not comprehend, God obviously had not chosen to create.[48]

Thus Descartes used the voluntarist notion of a free creator as a reductio ad absurdum, in a way that closely paralleled the process of methodic doubt for which he is so well known. The evil genius who haunted Descartes' sleep of reason was exactly like the radically free God who could create arbitrary and continually changing truths. Either one would undermine the possibility of absolute certainty, which Descartes could not allow. Both the evil genius and the nightmare God had to be dismissed by an act of faith in the veracity of a more reasonable God who could not change his mind or deceive his human creations.

At the same time, God's freedom to employ his absolute power was not altogether denied. Initially to determine which laws to make true and which mechanisms to place in nature remained the privilege of the divine will, not the human mind; and the results of that determination were shared only partially. The general fabric of the world followed from the first principles of Cartesian physics (the laws of motion, and the equivalence of matter and extension), which were fully revealed to us by the light of reason and could not be otherwise, so that there could only be one *kind* of world.[49] But within this world, God could have placed an infinity of particular things, unfettered by the necessity to choose one or another to instantiate.[50] And the general principles by which Descartes sought to explain these contingent things were "so vast and so fertile," "so simple and so general," that a particular phenomenon could be explained in any number of ways.[51] God could have chosen to employ any one of an infinite number of possible mechanisms to produce a given phenomenon. Which one he had actually chosen could be found only from experimentation.[52] The human mind could not separate reality from possibility, actuality from contingency, without an appeal to experience. (See Fig. 3.2 for an illustration of the structure of his scientific epistemology.)

Descartes therefore saw the impossibility of creating a purely a priori physics all the way down to the last detail. In a letter to the Minim friar Marin Mersenne (1588–1648) that is strikingly similar to Galileo's letter to Gallenzoni, Descartes told of how he had sought to find "the cause of the position of each fixed star." Though they seemed "very irregularly distributed in various places in the heavens," Descartes believed there was "a natural order among them which is regular and determinate." To discover this would be "the key and foundation of the highest and most perfect science of material things which men can ever attain. For if we possessed it we could discover *a priori* all the different forms and essences of terrestrial bodies, whereas without it we have to content ourselves with guessing them *a posteriori* from their effects." But such a discovery would depend on having an exhaustive knowledge of particular facts about the stars, which Descartes despaired of gaining. "The science I describe," he had to admit, "is beyond the reach of the human mind; and yet I am so foolish that I cannot help dreaming of it though I know this will only make me waste my time . . ."[53]

But Descartes' dream of an a priori science was never really given up. In spite of an unmistakable element of voluntarism in his theology of nature, Descartes' *ideal* of science remained (like Galileo's) essentially rationalistic. Though God was free to produce the particulars of nature in a variety of ways, the fundamental laws of nature necessarily conformed absolutely to the innate truths implanted in our souls, or else God would be deceiving us. Grounded on such a theology of creation, Cartesian natural philosophy was largely rationalistic; experience was required to augment pure reason precisely and only where the vestiges of divine will remained.

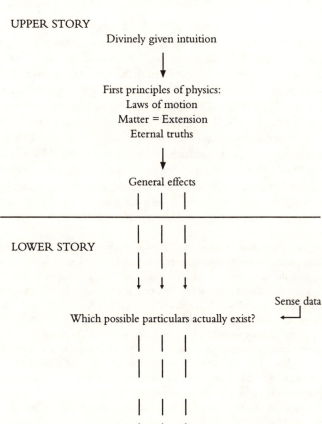

FIGURE 3.2. The Relation between Created Minds and Created Objects

Robert Boyle agreed with Descartes in identifying the basic laws of mathematics and logic as eternal truths that functioned as the foundation of all knowledge, including theology as well as science. He also affirmed that God, as "the author of our reason, cannot be supposed to oblige us to believe contradictions," and that God's veracity and boundless knowledge prevented him from deceiving us.[54] But where Descartes also embraced the proposition that all things perceived clearly and distinctly are true—including the fundamental laws of nature, which could therefore be known from pure reason—Boyle placed the foil of divine freedom abruptly in the path of a rationalistic science. We "mistake and flatter human nature too much," he said, "when we think our faculties of understanding so unlimited, . . . as many philosophers seem to suppose." Boyle emphasized that we were created, "as it pleased the almighty and most free author of our nature to make us." Our mental abilities were "proportionable to God's designs in creating us, and therefore may probably be supposed not to be capable of reaching to all kinds . . . of truths, many of which may be unnecessary for us to know here . . ."[55] As "purblind mortals," we could be only "incompetent judges" of God's power, which could "justly be supposed to reach farther than our limited intellects can comprehend; or for that reason, without a saucy rashness, can presume to bound."[56] "For if we believe God to be the author of things," he continued a bit later, "it is rational to conceive that he may have made them commensurate, rather to his own designs in them, than to the notions we men may best be able to frame of them." In an unpublished manuscript from the 1680s that stresses the significance of the act of divine creation for the ; limits of human reason, Boyle went even further than this, suggesting that the laws of reason themselves might have been otherwise. "It may be a useful supposition," he said to an unknown amanuensis around 1680,

> to Imagine such a state of things as was that which preceeded the beginning of the Creation for since then there was noe being besides God himselfe who is Eternall and Beings of what kind soever that had a beginning must derive there natures & all their faculties from his Arbitrary will; & consequently man himselfe & all intellectuall as well as all Corporeall Creatures, were but just shuch [such] as he thought fitt to make them. And as he freely establisht the affections of schemetisms & the Laws of Motion by which the universe was framed, & doth act; so he freely constituted the Reason of Man & other created intellects, & gave them those Ideas and Measures of truth by which they are guided in all their Ratiotinations. And the very Axtioms or most acknowledg'd truths being but Relations resulting [crossed out: that] from the nature of the mind & the things 'tis conversant about, God might have so ordered things that propositions very differing from these might have been true. [Here there is a blank space in the middle of a line.] As he might have contriv'd the palate, that honey had tasted bitter to men, & gall sweet.[57]

As he said elsewhere, the world was made before human beings, who had not been consulted in its construction! The author of nature "made things in such a manner as he was pleased to think fit," leaving people "to speculate as well as they could upon those corporeal, as well as other things."[58]

Boyle's concept of a scientific law was wholly consistent with this voluntarist attitude toward God's creative activity. The laws of nature, no less than the rest of the creation, were imposed upon matter by the free choice of a sovereign God. Natural laws, as Boyle put it, "did not necessarily spring from the nature of matter, but depended on the will of the divine author of things. . . ." [59] Boyle did not believe that matter is wholly passive *mechanically* (entirely without powers of its own), as some scholars have thought,[60] but he absolutely believed that matter is wholly passive *ontologically*. He put this very clearly in an unpublished manuscript from the late 1680s:

> The Primordial system of the universe, or the great & Original fabrick of the world; was as to us arbitrarily establisht by God. Not that he created things without accompanying, & as it were regulating, his omnipotence, by his boundless wis-

dome; & consequently did nothing without weighing reasons: but because those reasons are a priori [crossed out: unsearchable] undiscoverable by us: such as are the number of the fixt stars, the colocation as well as number of the planetary globes, the lines & period of their motion, . . . the bigness, shapes, & differing longevity of Living creatures; & many other particulars: of which the onely Reason we can assign, is that it pleasd God at the beginning of things, to give the world & also its parts the disposition. (This may also be applied to the states of bodys & the rules of motion.)[61]

Thus we find Boyle saying of other worlds, that they "may be framed and managed in a manner quite differing from what is observed in that part of the universe, that is known to us." The kind of matter, the laws of motion, and the living creatures might be highly unlike those in our own world.[62] Similarly, in the new heaven and earth that God will some day substitute for this one, "the primordial frames of things, and the laws of motion, and consequently, the nature of things corporeal, may be very differing from those that obtain in the present worlds."[63] As he said elsewhere, only "God knows particularly, both why and how the universal matter was first contrived into this admirable universe, rather than a world of any other of the numberless constructions he could have given it. . . ."[64]

Surely this was a voluntarist's world. Because the creator had worked and continued to work in accordance with his free will and not out of necessity, the order of nature was contingent and could not be known a priori. Boyle said as much when he described physical laws as "collected or emergent" truths "gathered from the settled phaenomena of nature," not "axioms metaphysical, or universal, that hold in all cases without reservation."[65] Boyle's theology of creation was markedly more voluntaristic than that of Galileo or Descartes, precisely because he had much less confidence in fallen human minds, and placed much more emphasis on God's freedom and absolute power. The key word here is "emphasis." Certainly Galileo and Descartes *believed* in divine freedom and power—what seventeenth-century Christian did not? But did they *emphasize* them to the extent that Boyle did? I think not. Where Galileo and Descartes reluctantly conceded that some things lay beyond the power of finite minds to know, Boyle practically gloried in our status as "purblind mortals," and constantly reminded his readers that it would be "saucy rashness" for them to "presume to bound" God's freedom to make the world as he saw fit.

Conclusions

What can now be said about the relation between theology of creation and philosophy of nature in the seventeenth century? At the very least, we have seen that theological presuppositions were closely allied with conceptions of scientific knowledge, and in just the way that Foster suggested. Galileo's lack of emphasis on divine freedom was mirrored in his a priori attitude toward scientific knowledge. Descartes' belief that God cannot deceive us led him to claim that the first principles of physics can be discovered by pure reason. For

Boyle, however, an emphasis on divine will went hand in hand with a commitment to the primacy of phenomena.[66]

But were these parallel emphases any more than just parallel emphases, as interesting as it may be to discover them? No single answer is likely to satisfy everyone. If one believes (as I do) that thoughtful people like those studied here tend to strive for consistency among various parts of their minds, then these parallel emphases are in and of themselves evidence that a genuine conversation between science and theology has taken place, leading toward a unified vision of reality. As Alexandre Koyré once observed, "The God of a philosopher and his world are correlated."[67] Others might call for more words of the conversation, as it were, spelling out precisely when a given thinker came to believe precisely what about God or the world for a specific reason. For them, a definitive answer would require detailed biographical studies of a sort that have not yet really been done for any of the three figures here.[68] Still others might claim that theological language is never able to do any more than to give ultimate expression to beliefs one has already formed on more purely philosophical or scientific grounds. Adherents of the conflict model of theology and science, for example, would find it hard to admit even the possibility that theology has helped shape the modern conception of scientific knowledge: for them, theology can only retard genuine science, not inform it. The statements quoted in this chapter are not likely to convince them that a genuine dialogue has taken place; nor can I imagine what sort of account *would* be convincing, given their particular bias.

There remains yet another group: those who are convinced, as Foster was, that Christian theology actually *caused* modern science, insofar as it led early modern thinkers to break with Greek notions of science in direct response to biblical teaching about the contingency of created nature. I reject such a claim— not because I doubt that theology influenced science in this way, but because I do not accept the narrow definition of modern science that is implicit in the claim.[69] During what is often called the "scientific revolution,"[70] several fundamental changes took place, each the result of a variety of factors. To give just one example, the change in world picture from geocentrism to heliocentrism certainly shows the influence of Neoplatonism on men like Copernicus, Kepler, and Galileo; but voluntarist theology contributed little or nothing to this central feature of the scientific revolution.

What voluntarism *did* affect was an important debate *within* the scientific revolution that was already under way—the debate about what sort of knowledge the new science ought to take for a foundation: necessary truths demonstrable from pure reason, or contingent truths emergent from phenomena. If many natural philosophers of the early modern period were convinced that the Aristotelian worldview had to be replaced, they were not all equally eager to abandon the Aristotelian notion that science consists of (or at least contains) necessary truths. Many of those who took this step were, like Boyle and Newton, committed to a high view of divine freedom that was undoubtedly related to their understanding of the Bible—and this is an important historical claim that suggests a strong consonance between modern science and a particular form of Christian theology.

But we must not be too quick to conclude that theological voluntarism was either necessary or sufficient to bring about an empirical science of nature. The very fact that Descartes used radical voluntarism to uphold his program of pure reason gives the lie to such a *simple* claim about voluntarist theology. Nor is there any obvious connection between theology of creation and the religious split caused by the Reformation, although the particular group of people explored in this chapter might suggest that. For every Protestant voluntarist like Boyle, there was a Catholic voluntarist like Pierre Gassendi; for every Catholic rationalist like Galileo, there was a Protestant rationalist like Gottfried Leibniz. Furthermore, theological factors were not the *only* ones of importance to this issue. When Renaissance humanists rediscovered the ancient skeptics, they gave European thinkers a foil to rationalism so powerful that Descartes made it the prime target of his program to reconstruct knowledge. His countryman Pierre Gassendi, however, made a mitigated pyrrhonian skepticism the epistemological basis for his version of the mechanical philosophy, which was itself deeply influential on both Boyle[71] and Newton. To bring the argument round full circle, we note that Reformation debates about the sources of religious authority were in turn a principal factor in creating a skeptical climate in the first place.[72] The full historical picture is complex: science, philosophy, and theology are inextricably intertwined. To single out one factor as the sole cause is to misrepresent the actual situation. Voluntarist theology neither "caused" modern science nor acted as the single cause of a particular kind of science. It was rather one factor, albeit a very important one, in giving modern science its strong empirical bent.

NOTES

This chapter is an expanded version of an earlier essay, "Rationalism, Voluntarism, and Seventeenth-Century Science," in *Facets of Faith and Science*, ed. Jitse M. van der Meer (Lanham, Maryland: University Press of America, 1996), vol. 3, pp. 135–54. Much of the material has been taken with suitable revisions from my doctoral dissertation, "Creation, Contingency, and Early Modern Science: The Impact of Voluntaristic Theology on Seventeenth-Century Natural Philosophy," Indiana University (1984), written with generous support from the Charlotte W. Newcombe Foundation. Earlier versions of this chapter were presented at the August 1985 meeting of the American Scientific Affiliation at St. Catherine's College, Oxford, where the commentator was the late Reijer Hooykaas; the October 1985 meeting of the History of Science Society at Indiana University; and in a session honoring Robert K. Merton at the December 1988 meeting of the American Historical Association in Cincinnati.

1. Though conflict metaphors and assumptions are no longer operative for many historians and social scientists, they remain common with journalists, much of the American public, and more than a few academics. Within the community of natural scientists,

for example, warfare language is still routine. Whether this is owing to historical naïveté, biographical circumstances, or deliberate ideological choice varies with the individual scientist.

2. The work to do this most forcefully is James R. Moore, *The Post-Darwinian Controversies: A Study of the Protestant Struggle to Come to Terms with Darwin in Great Britain and America, 1870–1900* (Cambridge: Cambridge University Press, 1979), the first part of which is an extended essay on the damage done to historiography by the use of military metaphors. An early challenge was raised by Colin A. Russell, "Some Approaches to the History of Science," in *The "Conflict Thesis" and Cosmology* (Milton Keynes: Open University Press, 1974), ed. C. A. Russell, R. Hooykaas, and D. C. Goodman, pp. 5–50. For a recent funeral service, see David C. Lindberg and Ronald L. Numbers, "Beyond War and Peace: A Reappraisal of the Encounter between Christianity and Science," *Perspectives on Science and Christian Faith* 39 (1987), 140–9; and the introduction to *God & Nature: Historical Essays on the Encounter between Christianity and Science*, ed. Lindberg and Numbers (Berkeley: University of California Press), pp. 1–18.

3. H. Floris Cohen, *The Scientific Revolution: A Historiographical Inquiry* (Chicago: University of Chicago Press, 1994), p. 308.

4. Lindberg and Numbers, "Beyond War and Peace," p. 148.

5. J. H. Brooke, *Science and Religion: Some Historical Perspectives* (Cambridge: Cambridge University Press, 1991), p. 5.

6. The term is found in A. R. Hall, "The Rise and Fall of Science," *Nature* (1994) 372: 51–52, on p. 51.

7. Brooke, *Science and Religion*, pp. 18–33, quoting p. 18.

8. See the preface to Robert K. Merton, *Science, Technology, and Society in Seventeenth-Century England*, 2nd ed. (New York: Harper & Row, 1970), pp. xv–xvi.

9. *Ibid.*, p. xvi.

10. Merton told me that Foster's work was unknown to him until he read a draft of an earlier version of this essay in 1988.

11. Some might follow Cohen, *The Scientific Revolution*, and call both of these approaches "externalist," in that they seek the causes of certain aspects of the scientific enterprise "outside" of science itself, namely in religion or theology. I prefer to see Merton's work as "externalist" because it invokes social causes, and Foster's work as "internalist" because it invokes intellectual causes. This is admittedly an old-fashioned distinction, and I use it with some hesitation, but I believe it helps us properly to understand the differences in these two approaches. Merton himself regarded his approach as "externalist," and thought (as I do) that he had not touched upon the "internal" history of science itself. See Merton *Science, Technology, and Society*, p. 75.

12. See M. B. Foster, "The Christian Doctrine of Creation and the Rise of Modern Natural Science," *Mind* (1934) 43: 446–68, and "Christian Theology and Modern Science of Nature," *Mind* (1935) 44: 439–66 and (1936) 45: 1–27. For a biography of Foster, see Cameron Wybrow, "Introduction: The Life and Work of Michael Beresford Foster," in *Creation, Nature, and Political Order in the Philosophy of Michael Foster (1903–1959): The Classic 'Mind' Articles and Others, with Modern Critical Essays*, ed. C. Wybrow (Lewiston, N.Y.:Edwin Mellen Press, 1992), pp. 3–44, a thoroughly researched essay that goes well beyond the limited information available in the obituaries in the *London Times*, 16 October 1959, p. 15, and the *Manchester Guardian*, 16 October 1959, p. 19; and the memorial sermon by V. A. Demant in *The Christian Scholar* (1959) 43: 3–7. Wybrow includes a splendid overview of the whole range of Foster's thought. The same volume contains a critical analysis of the internal logic of Foster's argument; see I. Weeks and S. Jacobs, "Theological and Philosophical Presuppositions of Ancient and Modern Science: A Crit-

ical Analysis of Foster's Account," on pp. 255–68. For more extensive comments on Wybrow's collection of essays, see my review in *Isis* (1994) 85: 127–29.

13. On the origins and uses of this distinction, see William J. Courtenay, "Nominalism and Late Medieval Religion," in *The Pursuit of Holiness in Late Medieval and Renaissance Religion*, ed. C. Trinkaus and H. Oberman (Leiden: E. J. Brill, 1974), pp. 26–59, esp. pp. 37–43; quoting p. 37, his italics. Technically, *potentia absoluta* (God's power considered absolutely) and *potentia ordinata* (God's power as ordained through his will for the creation) are not identical with will and reason per se, but they reflect the same dialogue between freedom and order.

14. These terms are used by Foster, and in much of the secondary literature cited in this essay.

15. Ernan McMullin, "Empiricism and the Scientific Revolution," in *Art, Science, and History in the Renaissance*, ed. C. S. Singleton (Baltimore: Johns Hopkins University Press, 1967), pp. 331–69, quoting pp. 332–34.

16. Quotations taken from Foster, "Christian Doctrine of Creation," p. 465; and Foster, "Christian Theology," pp. 1, 10, and 5n, respectively.

17. His essays are replete with statements that would support this, although it is rarely stated directly. An exception is found on p. 11 of the 1936 article. If it should happen that certain aspects of Cartesian philosophy are "compatible with a theology which has been found to be unorthodox, and therefore unchristian," Foster says, "the whole contention that there is a necessary implication between Christian theology and modern natural science would be imperilled."

18. I am using this term descriptively, not pejoratively: we are here to evaluate Foster, not to attack him. Foster's advocacy of the strong claim that Christianity caused modern science is not hard to understand, given that he was writing at a time when secular scholarship was dominated by the confict model of religion and science. We ought not to dismiss his insights with a pejorative label simply because he overstated his case.

19. Rolf Gruner, "Science, Nature, and Christianity." *Journal of Theological Studies* (1975) 26: 55–81, p. 56.

20. As Matt Cartmill, *A View to a Death in the Morning: Hunting and Nature through History* (Cambridge: Harvard University Press, 1993) observes (p. 215), "The Baconian tradition no longer has any literary champions. There is a growing consensus—outside the scientific research community, at any rate—that limits must be placed on human power over nature."

21. For example, his point that modern science did not appear for more than fifteen hundred years after the origin of Christianity, which seems to counter the claim that Christianity was so favorable to it.

22. Gruner, "Science, Nature, and Christianity," p. 65.

23. Whether one ought to take the historical argument further, by heaping praise on Christianity for its role in helping to shape modern science, is another question entirely. No doubt some people would be impressed with such an argument. But others might be just as tempted to use alternative historical arguments to blame Christianity for such things as anti-Semitism, the torture and execution of witches, or (as Gruner fears) environmental exploitation.

24. Representative works include J. H. Brooke, *Newton and the Mechanistic Universe* (Milton Keynes: Open University Press, 1974); R. Hooykaas, "Science and Theology in the Middle Ages," *Free University Quarterly* (1954) 3: 77–163; Hooykaas, *Religion and the Rise of Modern Science* (Grand Rapids: Eerdmans, 1972); Eugene Klaaren, *Religious Origins of Modern Science* (Grand Rapids: Eerdmans, 1977); J. E. McGuire, "Force, Active Principles, and Newton's Invisible Realm," *Ambix* (1968) 15: 154–208; McGuire, "Boyle's

Conception of Nature," *Journal of the History of Ideas* (1972) 33: 523–42; Francis Oakley, "Christian Theology and the Newtonian Science: The Rise of the Concept of the Laws of Nature," *Church History* (1961) 30: 433–57; Oakley, *Omnipotence, Covenant, and Order: An Excursion in the History of Ideas from Abelard to Leibniz* (Ithaca: Cornell University Press, 1984); M. J. Osler, "Descartes and Charleton on Nature and God," *Journal of the History of Ideas* (1979) 40: 445–56; Osler, "Eternal Truths and the Laws of Nature: The Theological Foundations of Descartes' Philosophy of Nature," *Journal of the History of Ideas* (1985) 46: 349–62; Osler, "The Intellectual Sources of Robert Boyle's Philosophy of Nature: Gassendi's Voluntarism and Boyle's Physico-theological Project," in *Philosophy, Science, and Religion in England, 1640–1700*, ed. R. Kroll, R. Ashcraft, and P. Zagorin (Cambridge: Cambridge University Press, 1992), pp. 178–98; Osler, *Divine Will and the Mechanical Philosophy: Gassendi and Descartes on Contingency and Necessity in the Created World* (Cambridge: Cambridge University Press, 1994). It is impossible to cite more than just a few of the numerous books and articles related to the Foster thesis. I have chosen a group of scholars whose works have been, in my judgment, among the most influential on others. It is worth noting that at least two members of this group did not know of Foster's work until their own work was quite advanced. In commenting on an earlier version of this chapter at another conference, the late Reijer Hooykaas said as much, adding that he learned about Foster from the late British cyberneticist Donald M. MacKay. (*Religion and the Rise of Modern Science* is dedicated to MacKay's mother.) Francis Oakley first saw Foster's articles in 1959–60, after his ideas were "essentially in place and complete." See the afterword to the reprint of his article in Wybrow, *Creation, Nature, and Political Order*, pp. 209–11.

25. E. B. Davis, "Newton's Rejection of the 'Newtonian world view': The Role of Divine Will in Newton's Natural Philosophy," *Science & Christian Belief* (1991) 3: 103–17.

26. I am convinced that the best test of the Foster thesis is to apply it to some of those who were regarded by their contemporaries as the leading natural philosophers of the age. It is not "whiggish" or unhistorical to say this: it is one thing to select a group of individuals based solely upon our perception *today* that their ideas led to where we are *now*; but it is another thing entirely to select thinkers who were seen *at the time* to be the thinkers whose ideas were of the greatest significance *for that time*. Each of the three people chosen here was viewed in that way; the fact that we also tend to see them as having led to where we are now does nothing to alter their importance in the context of the scientific revolution, or to diminish their suitability as subjects of this study.

27. It is assumed that this essay is aimed at a broad scholarly audience, who are likely to have less interest in the details and more in the overall argument and conclusions. For more comprehensive treatments, readers are invited to consult E. B. Davis, "Creation, Contingency, and Early Modern Science," chaps. 2 and 4; and "God, Man, and Nature: The Problem of Creation in Cartesian Thought," *Scottish Journal of Theology* (1991) 44: 325–48.

28. He did write two early essays on divine creation that were never published. See Winifred L. Wisan, "Galileo and God's Creation," *Isis* (1986) 77: 473–86.

29. For accounts of Galileo's rationalism with which I wholeheartedly agree, see McMullin, "Empiricism and the Scientific Revolution," and "The Conception of Science in Galileo's Work," in *New Perspectives on Galileo*, ed. R. E. Butts and J. C. Pitt (Dordrecht: Reidel, 1978), pp. 209–57; and A. C. Crombie, "Galileo's Conception of Scientific Truth," in *Literature and Science: Proceedings of the Sixth Triennial Congress of the International Federation for Modern Languages and Literature* (Oxford: Basil Blackwell, 1954), pp. 132–38, and "The Sources of Galileo's Early Natural Philosophy," in *Reason, Exper-*

iment, and Mysticism in the Scientific Revolution, ed. M. L. Righini Bonelli and W. R. Shea, (New York: Science History Publications, 1975), pp. 157–75, a study of Galileo's early writings that stresses the degree to which he accepted the Aristotelian notion of scientific knowledge as certain knowledge.

30. William A. Wallace "Galileo's Concept of Science: Recent Manuscript Evidence," in *The Galileo Affair: A Meeting of Faith and Science, Proceedings of the Cracow Conference, 24 to 27 May 1984*, ed. G. V. Coyne, M. Heller, and J. Życiński (Vatican City: Specola Vaticana, 1985), pp. 15–35, quoting p. 33. On the magnitude of Galileo's debt to the Jesuits, see Wallace, *Galileo and His Sources: The Heritage of the Collegio Romano in Galileo's Science* (Princeton: Princeton University Press, 1984).

31. Galileo Galilei, *Discourses on Two New Sciences*, trans. Stillman Drake (Madison: University of Wisconsin Press, 1974), p. 15.

32. Taken (respectively) from Galileo Galilei, *Dialogue Concerning the Two Chief World Systems—Ptolemaic & Copernican*, trans. Stillman Drake (Berkeley: University of California Press, 1953), p. 424; and Galileo Galilei, *The Assayer*, trans. Stillman Drake, in *The Controversy on the Comets of 1618*, ed. S. Drake and C. D. O'Malley (Philadelphia: University of Pennsylvania Press, 1960), p. 252. Cf. *Dialogue*, pp. 157ff.

33. *Dialogue*, p. 406.

34. Galileo Galilei, *Letter to the Grand Duchess Christina*, trans. Stillman Drake, in *Discoveries and Opinions of Galileo*, ed. S. Drake (Garden City: Doubleday, 1957), pp. 175–216, quoting p. 182. Cf. the similar passage from his *Letters on Sunspots* on p. 136 in the same volume; and his letter to Elia Diodati, quoted by T. P. McTighe, "Galileo's Platonism: A Reconsideration," in *Galileo: Man of Science*, ed. E. McMullin (New York: Basic Books, 1967), pp. 365–87, quoting p. 375.

35. *Two New Sciences*, p. 13.

36. *Dialogue*, pp. 11f.

37. *Dialogue*, pp. 103f.

38. *Ibid.*

39. The letter is quoted at length in Maurice Clavelin, *The Natural Philosophy of Galileo: Essay on the Origins and Formation of Classical Mechanics*, trans. A. J. Pomerans (Cambridge, Mass.: MIT Press, 1974), pp. 447ff.

40. Quoted by Alexandre Koyré, *From the Closed World to the Infinite Universe* (Baltimore: Johns Hopkins University Press, 1957), p. 98. As Koyré notes just before this, Galileo flatly denied the infinite size of the world in the *Dialogue*, but this may have been done simply to get the book approved.

41. *Dialogue*, pp. 22 and 236.

42. For more on this aspect of his writing, see E. B. Davis, "Creation, Contingency, and Early Modern Science," pp. 54–58. His refusal to take seriously the possibility that God's absolute power might undermine our ability to know the truth about nature is well documented in Wisan, "Galileo and God's Creation."

43. This is how I understand passages such as pp. 203–8 in the *Dialogue;* and pp. 12–13 in *Two New Sciences*.

44. McTighe, "Galileo's Platonism," p. 369.

45. See, among other places, a remark in the *Excerpta ex Cartesio: MS de Leibniz*, in *Oeuvres de Descartes*, ed. C. Adam and P. Tannery, 12 vols (Paris: Leopold Cerf, 1897–1913), vol. 11, p. 656.

46. Descartes discussed the eternal truths several times in his correspondence, and in a few other places. The examples chosen here are found at the end of his letter of 29 July 1648 to the Jansenist theologian and philosopher Antoine Arnauld (1612–94); see *Oeuvres de Descartes*, vol. 5, p. 223.

47. An exception was Peter Damian, who argued that God's absolute power could alter even the laws of logic. See Osler, *Divine Will and the Mechanical Philosophy*, p. 19.

48. For a more extended discussion of these points, see E. B. Davis, "God, Man, and Nature," pp. 328–35. M. J. Osler does not agree that Descartes's position on the eternal truths constitutes voluntarism; see *Divine Will and the Mechanical Philosophy*, esp. pp. 146–52. For a clear discussion of the difficulties involved in classifying someone like Descartes, see Jan W. Wojcik, *Robert Boyle and the Limits of Reason* (Cambridge: Cambridge University Press, 1997), pp. 190–99.

49. It is clear that Descartes thought that these principles were evident from metaphysical considerations. The identity of matter and extension followed from his inability to conceive them clearly as separate things; and the laws of motion followed from the immutability of God. See the second part of the *Principles of Philosophy*, in *Oeuvres de Descartes*, vol. 8A, pp. 40–79.

50. This is a central point of the famous passage on scientific method in the sixth part of the *Discourse on Method*; see *Oeuvres de Descartes*, vol. 6, pp. 63–65.

51. *Principles of Philosophy* 3. 4, in *Oeuvres de Descartes*, vol. 8A, pp. 81ff; and the sixth part of the *Discourse on Method*, in *Oeuvres de Descartes*, vol. 6, pp. 64.

52. *Principles of Philosophy* 3. 46, in *Oeuvres de Descartes*, vol. 8A, pp. 100ff.

53. Quoting from the translation by Anthony Kenny, *Descartes: Philosophical Letters* (Oxford: Oxford University Press, 1970), pp. 23ff. Had Descartes somehow managed to gain the exhaustive knowledge of particulars he lacked, it would only have shown him once again the necessity of having empirical knowledge for answering certain questions.

54. See *The Christian Virtuoso*, in *The Works of the Honourable Robert Boyle*, ed. Thomas Birch, 6 vols. (London: Millar, 1772), vol. 6, pp. 709–12, and vol. 5, p. 529; hereafter cited as *Works*. At the same time, he acknowledged that certain revealed truths (such as predestination and free will) might appear contradictory to the human mind. But God, he thought, is able to reconcile these "unsociable" truths, even if we cannot. See *A Discourse of Things above Reason*, in *Works*, vol. 4, pp. 408–9. For a fuller discussion of this point, see Jan W. Wojcik, *Robert Boyle and the Limits of Reason*, pp. 100–108.

55. *A Discourse of Things above Reason*, in *Works*, vol. 4, p. 410. Boyle's position on these sorts of truths is fully explicated in Jan W. Wojcik, "The Theological Context of Boyle's *Things Above Reason*," in *Robert Boyle Reconsidered*, ed. Michael Hunter (Cambridge: Cambridge University Press, 1994), pp. 139–55.

56. From *The Christian Virtuoso*, in *Works*, vol. 6, pp. 676ff.

57. Royal Society, Boyle Papers, vol. 36, fol. 46v, quoted with permission of the president and Fellows of the Royal Society. Apparently from Boyle's unfinished treatise on "The Excellency of Christianity," this is one of several snippets from various works that were copied out in a single place for future reference.

58. *The Christian Virtuoso*, in *Works*, vol. 6, p. 694.

59. *The Christian Virtuoso*, in *Works*, vol. 5, p. 521.

60. See, e.g., McGuire, "Boyle's Conception of Nature," and Gary B. Deason, "Reformation Theology and the Mechanistic Conception of Nature," in *God and Nature*, ed. Lindberg and Numbers, pp. 167–91. For a useful corrective, see Timothy Shanahan, "God and Nature in the Thought of Robert Boyle," *Journal of the History of Philosophy* (1988) 26: 547–69.

61. Royal Society, Miscellaneous MS 185, fol. 29, quoted with permission of the President and Fellows of the Royal Society. The manuscript, in the hand of Boyle's amanuensis Thomas Smith, is from an intended appendix for *A Disquisition about the Final Causes of Natural Things*, in *Works*, vol. 5, pp. 392–444.

62. *Of the High Veneration Man's Intellect Owes to God*, in *Works*, vol. 5, p. 139.

63. *The Christian Virtuoso*, in *Works*, vol. 6, pp. 788ff. The importance of statements about other worlds, including the new one God has not yet made, for studies of the limits of scientific knowledge in the seventeenth century must not be overlooked.

64. *High Veneration*, in *Works*, vol. 5, pp. 149ff.

65. *Things above Reason*, in *Works*, vol. 4, pp. 462ff.

66. As I have shown in "Newton's Rejection of the 'Newtonian World View,' " divine will was also primary for Isaac Newton, who held similar views about the laws of nature and our inability to discover them from pure reason. An emphasis on the dominion of an ever-active, omnipresent, and free creator lay at the heart of Newton's natural philosophy.

67. Koyré, *From the Closed World to the Infinite Universe*, p. 100.

68. Existing biographical studies explore both scientific and theological beliefs, but do not focus on the questions asked in this essay. Although I have made some attempt to construct such accounts in "Newton's Rejection of the 'Newtonian World View' " and "God, Man, and Nature," mostly I have been concerned simply to recover what each of these thinkers actually said about God, nature, and the human mind. Placing their statements more fully within the context of intellectual biography remains to be done.

69. To say nothing about the inadequate notion of Greek science that is often part of the same claim.

70. I recognize that quite a few scholars would reject this term entirely, though its use remains widespread, and I think it still has validity (though I lack the space here to defend this). For a good sense of the state of the debate, see Cohen, *The Scientific Revolution*.

71. On this particular point, see Osler, "The Intellectual Sources of Robert Boyle's Philosophy of Nature." What Osler overlooks in her study is the degree to which the Bible was a source of Boyle's voluntarism.

72. On Descartes, Gassendi, the revival of scepticism, and the role of the Reformation, see Richard Popkin, *A History of Scepticism, from Erasmus to Spinoza*, rev. ed. (Berkeley: University of California Press, 1979).

PART III

THEOLOGICAL ENGAGEMENTS

4

Science, Theology, and Society

From Cotton Mather to
William Jennings Bryan

MARK A. NOLL

The evangelical engagement with science in America during the eighteenth and nineteenth centuries was a complicated matter. Complications arose from the fact that "science," variously conceived, played a major role in many evangelical enterprises—promotion of natural theology and moral philosophy; appropriations of democratic ideology, republican political theory, and economic liberalism; and practices of biblical interpretation and theological construction. In addition, one form or another of science regularly featured large in evangelical struggles for the control of public discourse. The subject is also complicated because "science" and "evangelical" have both softer and harder meanings. On the one hand, the meanings of "science" become ever fuzzier the further one moves away from the empirical toward the cosmological.[1] The meaning of "evangelical" poses a different problem. In the American context, "evangelical" comes into sharpest focus when applied to religious and cultural practices. Evangelicals, that is, stress the new birth, evangelism, and holy living; they tend toward populism, pietism, and biblicism; they have been deeply marked by revival. When it comes to specific intellectual or theological content, however, especially of the sort that can be set alongside the clearer aspects of "science," evangelicalism too becomes increasingly fuzzy. Evangelicals usually embrace Christian orthodoxy in some form, but, beyond that general commitment, variety rules. It is thus, for example, no difficulty to recognize as evangelicals both the philosophical idealist Jonathan Edwards and the philosophical realist John Witherspoon, both the Calvinist Charles Hodge and the anti-Calvinist Charles Finney; both the Americanizing Lutheran Samuel Schmucker and the Methodizing African American Richard Allen; both the holiness preacher Phoebe Palmer and the advocate of Southern conservatism Robert L. Dabney; both B. B. Warfield, who was classically educated, and Billy Sunday, who was educated on a baseball diamond.[2] A considerable problem does exist, however, in finding for such a range of figures the kind of theological specificity that bears on

99

scientific questions—for example, attitudes toward the material world, toward natural theology, toward hermeneutics, toward, in short, the whole domain of practices and beliefs where science has been important for the history of religion in America.

The historical problem becomes even more difficult if the historian, as in my case, is an evangelical with opinions. Because I believe that Christian faith, properly understood, should promote a certain set of attitudes toward study of the material world, my historical account is biased from the start. Specifically, I hold that Christian beliefs concerning God, the creation, human nature, the Incarnation, and the Atonement demand for science a resolute combination of realism and skepticism—realism about the possibility that humans can truly know certain features of the material world as it really is, skepticism because purported knowledge about the material world always serves social, political, and psychological ends having little to do with the way the material world really is. With such beliefs, it is painful to write about evangelical engagement with science in America because I find controversy over the aims and purposes of science regularly crowding out patient attention to the natural world; I see struggles over social, political, and psychological hegemony masquerading as debates about the character of the natural world; and I discover evangelical intellectual paralysis manifesting itself as resentment of science in the broader culture alongside wholesale incorporation of supposedly scientific procedures in apologetics, natural theology, and biblical interpretation.[3]

Complicated and painful as this subject may be, it is still possible to hazard a general historical thesis about the evangelical engagement with science during the Protestant period of American history, that is, from the age of the puritans through the 1920s. The thesis is that the evangelical engagement with science belongs more to the domain of social history than to intellectual history. To be sure, certain evangelicals at certain times have worked diligently on *intrinsic* connections between science and theology, but that work has regularly been subordinated to *extrinsic* connections between science and society.[4]

The tendency in America to talk about science while thinking about something else is by no means limited to evangelicals. In fact, one of the reasons that broader cultural matters have so thoroughly dominated the evangelical engagement with science in America is that broader cultural appropriations have loomed so large for American science in general. It is little wonder, for example, that at the start of the twentieth century scientific questions became for evangelicals even more thoroughly political than before, since that was the era when post-Protestant denizens of America's new universities were making their most extravagant claims for the extrinsic social and metaphysical achievements of science. In Bruce Kuklick's fine summary, "Dewey, Royce, Charles Peirce, and others . . . urged that loyalty to science would enable human beings to achieve existential integration most adequately. Mankind would make its greatest advance when the scientific method was applied to questions of ethics. Control would grow ever more rich and complex. The quality of human experience would change for the better and, consequently, human selves also."[5] For evangelicals to respond in kind to the cosmological claims put forth by leaders of the new university under the name of science was, however, simply to refurbish a long tradition. A science put to use in shaping or promoting large-scale interpretations of the world, rather than for focusing study on the material world, was a science as old as American evangelicalism itself.[6]

Originally, this chapter was to have been titled, "Science and Theology from Edwards to Warfield," but the title as it now stands—"Science, Theology, and Society: from Cotton Mather to William Jennings Bryan"—reflects more accurately the main traditions of American evangelical science. The contributions of theologians like Edwards and Warfield, though developed in settings rife with extrinsic political interest, featured a concern for intrinsic theological-scientific investigation setting them apart from the concerns of popularizers like Mather and Bryan. To a very large degree, the history of evangelical engagement with science in America simply is a history of extrinsic social or metaphysical concern.

Or, at the very least, the growing literature on science and evangelicalism in American experience suggests that it is, since this literature highlights the prominence of extrinsic concern for matters linking science and society much more than intrinsic concerns of science, or of science and theology.[7] Thus, the questions that scholars have canvassed most, and with most illumination, are issues such as the role of science in shaping antebellum worldviews, which has received splendid treatment in recent decades,[8] the images of science incorporated into theological practice,[9] and the history of biblical interpretation in response to scientific investigation.[10] Similarly, concerns extrinsic to the actual doing of science have dominated a fledgling literature that seeks to compare the intellectual or cultural history of evangelicals in various regions of the North Atlantic world.[11] Intrinsic concerns do play a larger role in writings about reactions to Darwin[12] and on the perils of natural theology.[13] But literature on Darwin and natural theology deals more with how evangelicals reacted to large-scale cosmological implications of various scientific results than to the results and procedures of the science itself.[14]

By contrast, the literature on what might be considered more intrinsically scientific questions is much thinner. For example, I am not aware of any effort to show what might have been evangelical in the practice of mainline science during the nineteenth century by evangelicals or those linked with evangelicalism—such as James Dwight Dana, Joseph Henry, J. W. Dawson, John Wesley Powell, Asa Gray, G. F. Wright, or William Berryman Scott.[15] In like manner, I am not aware of work on what may have been the actual experiments attempted, or stimulated by, the long line of American theologians who have written on cosmological aspects of science. Nor has there been serious consideration of how denominational or theological traditions affected the actual practice of science.[16]

If extant historiography reflects a real situation, Cotton Mather rather than Jonathan Edwards is the figure with which to begin an account of the American evangelical engagement with science. Mather may be said to have established the main evangelical tradition with the publication in 1721 of *The Christian Philosopher*, a formidable volume of physico-theological erudition. As recently detailed in Winton Solberg's fine edition of this work, Mather's attention to scientific detail was intense.[17] Yet the volume aimed not simply, and not even primarily, at the practice of science, narrowly conceived, but at the meaning of science in very grand terms.

In the words of Thomas Bradbury, who introduced the book to its English audience, "every Observation" that Mather made on the natural world was "improv'd to the Ends of Devotion and Practice." As an example, when he wrote about the nature of snow, Mather cited metereological observations from several learned Europeans before ending with the citation of another European concerning the need for all humans to have their sins made white as snow. Mather began the book with the intention to "demonstrate," as he put it, "that *Philosophy* is no *Enemy*, but a mighty and wondrous *Incentive* to *Religion*."[18] Mather's achievement in this book was intellectually impressive, but it was not a narrowly scientific achievement. As the best history of early American philosophy concludes, Mather was taking the measure of science for purposes not directly related to understanding the physical world itself: "Mather accepted the new science and sought to incorporate it into his own theologically oriented world view. He did so because his own world view sanctioned science and assured him of its consistency with theology, and because the new science was so obviously useful to him. But he also accepted it because by doing so he was able to vindicate the claim of the clergy to intellectual leadership in the colony."[19]

William Jennings Bryan is likewise a fitting endpoint for this chapter because his scientific interests were almost exclusively external. At the Scopes trial in 1925, Bryan may have embarrassed himself on scientific and theological details, but such matters had never been the focus of his interest in evolution. For Bryan, it was necessary to oppose evolution, not because it imperiled traditional interpretations of Genesis 1, or because it sabotaged empirical investigations, but because evolution was a threat to a treasured social ideal. As Bryan put it in 1925, evolution is "an insult to reason and shocks the heart. That doctrine is as deadly as leprosy; . . . it would, if generally adopted, destroy all sense of responsibility and menace the morals of the world."[20]

The conclusion that social uses of science, as illustrated by Mather and Bryan, have always taken precedence for American evangelicals over more intrinsic attention to science as such or theology as such cannot be demonstrated in a short essay, but it can be suggested by attention to several episodes in the eighteenth, nineteenth, and early twentieth centuries. These episodes are of different kinds, but they illustrate the common evangelical tendency to move instinctively away from science, narrowly conceived as an experimental exercise focused on the natural world, toward science broadly conceived as an ideological principle bearing primarily on the public sphere.

The Transition from Jonathan Edwards to John Witherspoon

The first episode is the intellectual transition among American evangelicals symbolized by the replacement of Jonathan Edwards by John Witherspoon as president of Princeton College, but also as guiding intellectual force. Edwards served only briefly at Princeton before his death in 1758, but before arriving in New Jersey he had largely completed a grand theological project that could have set the practice of science, as well as ethics and theology, on a new course. Like Cotton Mather, Edwards was much concerned that the new science of his day—both Newtonian physical science and affectional moral philosophy associated with Shaftesbury, Hutcheson, and Locke—was undercutting traditional Christian faith. Mather had held out for moral philosophy of an older puritan sort that, as had been described most influentially by William Ames, denied the ability of the non-elect to act with true virtue.[21] But Mather's attitude toward natural science was quite different in *The Christian Philosopher*, for Mather thought it was a relatively straightforward matter to show how the natural science of Boyle and Newton could be made to support traditional Christianity. In contrast to Mather, who worked on the major intellectual problems of his day ad hoc, Edwards sought a comprehensive intellectual solution. He found it in Calvinistic theological idealism.[22] Edwards thought he had discovered in God-centered philosophical idealism a way to incorporate both modern natural science and the new moral philosophy, while at the same time defanging their threat to the faith. His view of reality as dependent every moment on the thinking of God meant that an affectional ethics such as that presented by the leading lights of the new moral philosophy and a mechanistic science as presented by Newton could become Christian pursuits. Edwards's own youthful exploration in natural philosophy (such as his investigations of the spider's web) as well as his lifelong engagement with moral philosophy showed the potential of his grand theocentric vision actually to bear fruit in specific research. To be sure, Edwards's interests were always intensely metaphyiscal and theological. But at the same time, he construed those interests in such a way as to promote relatively open-ended (or intrinsic) explorations of the physical world.

The catch was Edwards's stiff Augustinianism. In both moral philosophy and, by implication at least, in natural science, real truth would be found only by those who constantly remembered that true knowledge of nature, as well as true virtue, depended on God's moment-by-moment re-creation of the world. Edwards's idealism was the linchpin of his entire system—it held scientific materialism and ethical egocentricism at bay, while at the same time actually encouraging research. At least in principle, one could not find out the truth about the physical world (and thereby about the God who made it new every moment) unless one did actual experiments in the physical world. What soon made this intellectual system problematic, however, was its Calvinism. Edwards's road to genuine knowledge—in science and ethics both—was open only to the elect. But at least for the elect—and especially because natural and moral philosophy were linked so securely in that era—this was an intellectual system that encouraged actual research into both the character of ethical structures and the character of the physical world.

John Witherspoon arrived in Princeton in 1768, only a decade after Edwards's death. Immediately upon his arrival Witherspoon jettisoned Edwards's system. Witherspoon's first biographer linked the Edwardsean system to Bishop Berkeley, probably because Edwards, as promoter of revivals, was too sacrosanct to criticize. But under whatever name, the fate of any form of theocentric idealism was doomed: "The Berklean system of Metaphysics was in repute in the college when he entered on his office. The tutors were zealous believers in it, and waited on the President, with some expectation of either confounding him, or making him a proselyte. They had mistaken their man. He first reasoned against the System, and then ridiculed it, till he drove it out of the college."[23] In its place, Witherspoon put a variant of the common-sense realism that he had learned in his native Scotland. As the biographer of one of Witherspoon's first students put it:

> Dr. Witherspoon arrived from Scotland, and bringing with him . . . the recently broached principles of [Thomas] Reid, [James] Oswald, and [James] Beattie, furnished him [the student] with a clue by which he was conducted out of the dark labyrinth into which he had been betrayed by bishop Berkeley. . . . From the cloudy speculations of immaterialism, he was now brought back to the clear light of common sense. Nature was again reinstated in her rights, and the external world, which had been banished for a while, returned and resumed its place in creation.[24]

As was the case for Edwards's intellectual system, Witherspoon's too had a major stake in science. In the Scottish pattern—which several other American savants were promoting at the time of Witherspoon's arrival—deliberations in all areas of life were supposed to be conducted inductively, on a Baconian model. So whether in moral philosophy, natural science, politics, or any other sphere of thought, truth could be had by systematically arranging sense impressions—whether of the mental world, the physical world, or the political world.

The key point for our purposes is why Americans generally, including American evangelicals, so rapidly abandoned Edwards's idealism for Witherspoon's realism, for in fact Witherspoon's kind of mental science spread like wildfire from the 1770s among all American thinkers. Just as rapidly did a theistic form of this mental science, with a special concern for apologetical natural theology, spread among American evangelicals.

The reason, when considered as a question in the history of science, was entirely extrinsic; it had nothing to do with the relative ability of idealism or realism actually to promote understanding of the physical world. The reason was that theistic mental science on the Scottish model met so precisely the social, political, and cultural needs of evangelicals at the time of the American Revolution.

In the revolutionary period it was not research in science or theology that led American evangelicals to a full-scale embrace of philosophical realism, an ideology of Baconianism, a doxological view of science as showing the glory of God's handiwork, and a dedicated commitment to natural theology as an apologetical device. It was rather that Witherspoon's version of the Scottish Enlightenment offered Americans exactly what they seemed to require to master the tumults of the revolutionary age. In the midst of what Nathan Hatch has called "a cultural ferment over the meaning of freedom,"[25] the intuitive, sensationalist ethics provided by the Scots offered an intellectually respectable way to establish public virtue in a society that was busily repudiating the props upon which virtue had traditionally rested—tradition itself, divine revelation, history, social hierarchy, inherited government, and the authority of religious denominations. As Norman Fiering has put it, the "moral philosophy" of the eighteenth-century Scottish Enlightenment "was uniquely suited to the needs of an era still strongly committed to traditional religious values and yet searching for alternative modes of justification for those values."[26] For Protestants who wanted to preserve traditional forms of Christianity without having to appeal to hereditary religious authorities, no less than for patriots who wanted to justify their break from Great Britain by appealing to "self-evident truths" and founding fathers who wished to establish an orderly and prosperous republic based upon what James Madison and Alexander Hamilton both styled the "science of politics," the common-sense reasoning of Scotland's theistic mental science was the answer.

In Revolutionary America, citizens of the new nation were desperate for intellectual authorities that could replace deference, tradition, the weight of history, and preemptory hierarchy as intellectually compelling supports for the break with Britain, for the reestablishment of social order, and for the defense of Christianity. In these circumstances, only two authorities escaped the stigma of tyranny with which the traditional intellectual authorities of Europe were marked. These untainted authorities were science and the Bible.

At the dawn of Protestantism, reformers had joined the Bible to history in order to assault the authority of Roman Catholic tradition.[27] Now in America, Protestant descendants of the Reformers linked science to the Bible as a way of escaping the evil influences of history. Science, in the form of common-sense Baconianism, and the Bible, now liberated as a book to be read by all, were both untouched by associations with tyranny. In a world of self-evident political principles, ideological equality, and a determination not to repeat the errors of decadent Europe, science and the Bible were the only authorities with broad social suasion that remained uncontaminated. The potential of Edwards's metaphysics for promoting actual study of the physical world was just as irrelevant as the potential of doxological Baconianism for the same purpose. In the evangelical appropriation of Witherspoon's theistic mental science, the need for mental constructs to maintain public order and to defend the Christian faith meant everything. Research into the character of the physical world meant almost nothing.

The Bible Only and the Failure of Hutchinsonian Science

The second episode concerns a nonevent, the failure of American evangelicals to promote the anti-Newtonian science of John Hutchinson. Hutchinson's science might seem to have been a natural for American evangelicals because it was an explanation of nature taken straight from the Bible and because it enjoyed considerable intellectual cachet in Britain during the founding years of the United States when evangelical commitment to "the Bible alone" was never stronger.[28] In other intellectual spheres, such as the literal application of the Bible to current events or the apocalyptic future, Bible-onlyism flourished in early

America. The application of apocalyptic texts to American events during the Revolution, the War of 1812, and the Civil War[29]—as well as the huge popularity of William Miller's literal apocalypticism in the 1830s[30]—showed that evangelicals in the new American republic could, for some purposes, follow "the Bible only" with no reserve. Why not in science?

John Hutchinson (1674–1737) developed his views of the material world in direct opposition to what he held to be materialistic implications of Newton's gravitational mechanics.[31] If in the Newtonian world objects could attract each other at a distance with no need for an intervening medium, Hutchinson concluded that Newton was setting up the material world as self-existent and hence in no need of God. From a painstakingly detailed study of the linguistic roots, without vowel points, of Old Testament Hebrew, Hutchinson thought he had discovered an alternative Bible-based science. The key was the identity of the roots for "glory" and "weight," which led Hutchinson to see God actively maintaining the attraction of physical objects to each other through an invisible ether. Moreover, by analogous reasoning from the New Testament's full development of the Trinity, it was evident that a threefold reality of fire, air, and light offered a better explanation for the constituency of the material world than did modern atomism.

Hutchinson's ideas seem bizarre now, but they did not look that way to everyone in his age. A series of distinguished professors at Oxford and of highly placed bishops in the Church of England adopted Hutchinsonian science, along with Hutchinson's principles for the use of Hebrew. As late as the 1820s, Samuel Taylor Coleridge spoke with respect about certain aspects of the Hutchinsonian system that had survived for a full century as a Bible-based alternative to Newtonianism.

Why did not America's evangelical Bible-only Christians adopt Hutchinsonianism? Probably the main reason was that they were so thoroughly committed to Newtonian-Baconian ideals, and that some evangelicals, at least by the 1830s, had begun to contribute their own research and interpretations to the transatlantic community defined by the normal science of the era.

As it happens, however, at least a few American evangelicals did seem to have been attracted to the Hutchinsonian system. Archibald Alexander, first professor at Princeton Theological Seminary, paused during his inaugural sermon of 1812—which was devoted to a defense of the Bible—to comment on Hutchinsonianism. It was clear that Alexander's own loyalty to Scripture had found something attractive in Hutchinson, even if it was not enough:

> [T]here have been some who believed, that the scriptures not only furnish a rule to guide us in our religion, but a complete system of *philosophy*; that the true theory of the universe is revealed in the first chapters of Genesis; and that there is an intimate connexion betwixt the natural and spiritual world. The one containing a sort of emblematical representation of the other; so that even the high mystery of the Trinity is supposed to be exhibited by the material fluid, which pervades the universe, in its different conditions, of fire, light, and air. *John Hutchinson*, Esq. of *England*, took the lead in propagating this system, and has been followed by some men of great name and great worth. *Jones, Horne, Parkhurst, Spearman*, and

Bates, would be no discredit to any cause. But, although we acknowledge that there is something in this theory which is calculated to prepossess the pious mind in its favour; yet is too deeply enveloped in clouds and darkness to admit of its becoming generally prevalent. And if what these learned men suppose, had been the object of revelation, no doubt, some more certain clue would have been given to assist us to ascertain the mind of the Spirit, than the obscure, though learned, criticisms of *Hutchinson*.[32]

Alexander's comments are cryptic. But a speculative case can be made that the major objection from American evangelicals to Hutchinsonianism was social rather than scientific. A clue supporting this line of reasoning is the fact that the major American Hutchinsonians of the eighteenth and nineteenth centuries were high-church Anglicans and Episcopalians, of whom the most ardent had been the American Samuel Johnson, first president of Columbia and with Jonathan Edwards the most sophisticated American philosopher of his era.[33] Hutchinsonianism also survived into the nineteenth century in the circle of high-church Episcopalians clustered around John Henry Hobart of New York.[34]

If these churchmen—who lingered at the fleshpots of tyrannical Britain, or Egypt, as Britain was so often styled by colonials during the first half-century of the new nation's existence—could put Hutchinsonianism to use, it was unlikely that any American evangelical, committed to civil as well as theological liberty, would have anything to do with it. Although a few British evangelicals seem to have adopted Hutchinsonianism,[35] its science was too much of a piece with what J. C. D. Clark has described as "the divine appointment of kings, . . . in alliance with a priesthood similarly sanctioned; the complete dependence of man on God, the impossibility of self-sufficiency for man in the civil sphere, and the necessity of dependence and social subordination," to ever have a chance with American evangelicals at the very time when they were defining themselves in opposition to royalism, traditional ecclesiastical authority, and British gentile dependence.[36]

If Tory elitism was not enough to warn American evangelicals away from Hutchinsonianism, then the expertise it required in Hebrew was. Such expert knowledge might be respected for limited purposes in the early United States, but not if it kept the full meaning of the Bible from the minds of ordinary people.

Hutchinsonian Bible-only science, it might be argued, was fatally compromised among American evangelicals by its Toryism more than by the character of its science. That sort of judgment may possibly also explain why, later in the century, the views published by Philip Henry Gosse in Britain in 1857—to the effect that the marks of old age in the earth were deliberately planted by God as a kind of mental test of faith for his latter-day children—did not catch on. In the United States, a variation of this view, with reference to Gosse by name, was propounded with considerable vigor by Robert Lewis Dabney, the most persistent, and also most bitter, southern theological opponent of the North's conduct in the Civil War. In several major essays throughout his career, Dabney set out a Bible-only position on science—for example, from 1861: "If . . . the Bible, properly understood, affirms what geology denies, the difference is irreconcilable; . . . it can only be composed by the overthrow of the authority of one or the other of the parties."[37] In the same essay, as well as later in 1871 and 1873, Dabney floated Gosse's proposal, that, as he put it in 1871, "Grant me any creative intervention of a God, in any form whatsoever, and at any time whatsoever, then it is inevitable that any individual thing, produced by that intervention, must have presented, from its origin, every trait of naturalness [including the appearance of development]."[38]

I may be mistaken in thinking that Dabney's Gosseism did not spread among American evangelicals, but if it did not, the reason may have had more to do with Dabney's suspect role as defender of the South's Lost Cause than because the scientific vision he proposed was intrinsically offensive to American evangelical thinking.

Whatever the case with Gosse and Dabney, Hutchinsonian Bible-only science could never work among American evangelicals in the early nineteenth century because of its Tory, elitist, and prelatical overtones. It would, of course, be different when at the start of the twentieth century a Bible-only science that was democratic, populist, voluntarist, and that required no special expertise in Hebrew appeared on the scene precisely when tensions were growing between evangelical believers in Scripture and the practitioners of mainstream science.[39]

The Weakness of Empiricism in an Era of Transition

The relation of evangelicals to science, as indeed the perception of science itself, underwent a great shift between the Civil War and World War I. In antebellum America, evangelicals had been among the most ardent promoters of mainstream science (as doxological, Baconian, and realist), but developments in geology and biology, as well as in the organization of university learning, created a new situation after the Civil War.[40] As American intellectuals gradually moved from static to organic views of the natural world, evangelicals broke step. They were troubled by possible atheism lurking in ateleological evolution, by agnostic conclusions promoted by popularizers of the new science, by the heartache in abandoning traditional interpretations of Scripture, and by efforts of scientific professionals to replace religious professionals as society's key arbiters of truth. It was an era in which the tone was set by sallies like those of Andrew Dickson White, who claimed that Cornell University, over which he presided, would "afford an asylum for Science [note capitalization]—where truth shall be sought for truth's sake, where it shall not be the main purpose of the Faculty to stretch or cut sciences exactly to fit 'Revealed Religion.' "[41]

In this environment, evangelicals vacillated. For roughly half a century before 1920, evangelical views of science were in flux. Some clung resolutely to the old ways and so naturally came both to oppose the new patterns of science and to resent the rising power of those who evangelized on behalf of social ideals thought to arise from the new science. Other evangelicals made the effort to adjust larger patterns of metaphysics and biblical interpretation to the new scientific mainstream.[42] In this changing situation, a few evangelical theologians also gave fresh attention to the potential of empirical research. Such ones edged closer to advocating scientific investigation as a means of finding out about nature, rather than as a means for making apologetical, cosmological, or political capital.

This last option found clearest expression at Princeton Theological Seminary. While Princeton theologians were occupied in the effort to shore up standards of biblical inspiration, they were also contending for a much more frankly empirical approach to the natural world. Charles Hodge, who asked to have Darwin's *Voyage of the Beagle* reread to him in the last weeks of his life,[43] initiated this push toward empiricism with his attitude toward the historic "two books." As early as 1863, Hodge offered a forthright defense of the rights of empirical science in response to criticism of his *Biblical Repertory and Princeton Review*. When the editor of a religious newspaper attacked an article in the *Review* for giving up the Bible too easily when new scientific results contradicted traditional biblical interpretations, Hodge leapt to the challenge. Even as he reaffirmed a full doctrine of biblical infallibility, he also affirmed in sharpest terms the need for unfettered empirical practice in the investigation of nature:

> The proposition that the Bible must be interpreted by science is all but self-evident. Nature is as truly a revelation of God as the Bible; and we only interpret the Word of God by the Word of God when we interpret the Bible by science. . . . There is a two-fold evil on this subject against which it would be well for Christians to guard. There are some good men who are much too ready to adopt the opinions and theories of scientific men, and to adopt forced and unnatural interpretations of the Bible, to bring it to accord with those opinions. There are others, who not only refuse to admit the opinions of men, but science itself, to have any voice in the interpretation of Scripture. Both of these errors should be avoided. Let Christians calmly wait until facts are indubitably established, so established that they command universal consent among competent men, and then they will find that the Bible accords with those facts. In the meantime, men must be allowed to ascertain and authenticate scientific facts in their own way, just as Galileo determined the true theory of the heavens. All opposition to this course must be not only ineffectual, but injurious to religion.[44]

Hodge would later become better known for attacking the underlying philosophical basis of Darwin's evolution. But even in the last stage of his career, when he made his fullest assaults on what he regarded as Darwin's ateleological philosophical atheism, Hodge continued to argue that Christians needed to give the fullest possible scope to the independent empirical inquiries of the scientists.[45]

B. B. Warfield, who became Hodge's successor as Princeton's major theologian, maintained this same position to the end of his lifelong interest in science. To Warfield, who read with close attention much of the best general literature on science for over 40 years, the question of science and religion came down, not to metaphysics, but to facts. In 1895, he wrote that, "The really pressing question with regard to the doctrine of evolution is not . . . whether the old faith can live with this new doctrine. . . . We may be sure that the old faith will be able not merely to live with, but to assimilate to itself all facts. . . . The only living question with regard to the doctrine of evolution still is whether it is true." By "true" Warfield did not have in mind a question of scriptural exegesis but a question of empirical science: whether "(1) we may deduce from the terms of the theory all the known facts, and thus, as it were, prove its truth; and (2) deduce also new facts, not hitherto known, by which it becomes predictive and the instrument of the discovery of new facts, which are sought for and observed only on the expectation roused by the theory."[46]

With their relative naiveté about the possibility of a bare approach to questions of fact, Hodge and Warfield bore the marks of the nineteenth-century Baconian realism in which they had both been reared. Since they could not benefit from the kind of analysis that has been illustrated so ably in recent years by, for example, Adrian Desmond and James Moore or by Steven Shapin, they were not as aware as they would have been that empirical experience can provide only a certain level of verification or falsification for only a certain level of middle-range hypotheses, or that it is necessary to pay closer attention to encompassing worldviews in order to ascertain the deeper social axioms that function like necessary hypotheses for the doing of science.[47] But such adjustments having been made, we still see in Hodge and Warfield a theological commitment to the virtues of empirical investigation that opened the possibility of a new direction for American evangelicals.

Creation Science as a Successful Use of the Bible Only

With only a few exceptions, American evangelicals did not pursue the possibility that Hodge and Warfield opened up. In the modern research university doxological Baconianism became as irrelevant as Hutchinsonianism had been in the early cosmos of democratic doxological Baconianism. In the history of evangelicalism, however, the elitist pronouncements of the new university scientific spokesmen sounded like a new form of Hutchinsonianism. The democratic, populist, voluntary features of American evangelicalism that made Hutchinsonianism irrelevant in the early nineteenth century were the very features that created evangelical disquiet with the modern research university. In contrast to the earlier neglect of Hutchinsonianism, creation science and flood geology arose in a lived world that fit with the ideological shape of American evangelicalism. Modern university science seemed, that is, to oppose both the Bible and the populist biblicism of the nineteenth-century evangelical heritage.

The rise of creation science as a democratic Bible-onlyism, however, did not take place immediately with the rise of the new university. It was, rather, not until the perceived crisis of civilization—which George Marsden has documented convincingly as arising from the events of the First World War[48]—that evangelical opposition to evolution as a threat to civilization, and evangelical support for creation science as a defense of civilization, came to dominate evangelical attitudes toward science. It was, for instance, only after William Jennings Bryan resigned as Woodrow Wilson's secretary of state over Wilson's handling of early tension with Germany that Bryan transformed his earlier disquiet with evolution into a full-scale political crusade. From roughly the time of the war, antievolution became more and more important in American evangelicalism, but also less and less directly concerned about science narrowly conceived.

Until the perceived crisis of civilization associated with World War I, it was by no means certain that the evangelical engagement with science would take this antievolutionary path and so continue to feature extrinsic over intrinsic aspects of science. In *The Fundamentals*, for example, which were published from 1910 to 1915, at least two evangelical voices could be heard with respect to science. On the one side were those who, while not necessarily sharing the same views on evolution, nonetheless were trying to sort out differences between intrinsic and extrinsic aspects of the problem. Thus, James Orr, once he had made what seemed to him necessary emendations to Darwin's ideas, felt free to say that " 'Evolution' . . . is coming to be recognized as but a new name for 'creation,' only that the creative power now works from *within*, instead of, as in the old conception, in an *external*, plastic fashion. It is, however, creation none the less."[49] Similarly G. F. Wright felt confident enough in factuality (although still of the nineteenth-century sort) to say that "The worst foes of Christianity are not physicists but metaphysicians. . . . Christianity, being a religion of fact and history, is a free-born son in the family of the inductive sciences, and is not specially hampered by the paradoxes inevitably connected with all attempts to give expression to ultimate conceptions of truth."[50] For Orr and Wright, in other words, the meaning of science depended upon the proper prosecution of science.

A second voice in *The Fundamentals* was, by contrast, nearly overwhelmed by the extrinsic meanings thought to reside in broad discussions of evolution. To J. J. Reeve, evolution was a "world-view"; it was "wonderfully fascinating and almost compelling"; and ex hypothese it spoke for a universe in which "there can be no miracle or anything of what is known as the supernatural."[51] Henry H. Beach was similarly certain about the large-scale implications of modern evolution: "Darwinists have been digging at the foundations of society and souls. . . . Natural selection is a scheme for the survival of the passionate and the violent, the destruction of the weak and defenseless."[52] If in *The Fundamentals* Orr and Wright still were trying to make space for an intrinsic attention to experimental results, Reeve and Beach were arguing that the modern climate made it necessary to concentrate preeminently on the evil social uses to which science was being put.

Opinions in the *Princeton Theological Review* likewise illustrate this shift from an evangelical world in which intrinsic competed against extrinsic implications of science to one in which the extrinsic prevailed over all. In 1901 an author could treat the question of whether the human body descended from animal ancestors as an open question to be adjudicated by research: "The difference between his [the human's] physical structure, with his erect posture, his greater weight of brain, etc., and that of the other primates is indeed striking, but does not exclude the hypothesis of common origin. In many of his mental characteristics again man shows a kinship with the brutes." And the reason the author could countenance such a question as a proper subject for research was because of the distinction he had drawn between science as empirical research and science as metaphysical statement. "Darwinism," he concluded, "has made men think. . . . The outcome of forty years of scientific investigation and apologetic discussion is, however, the growing conviction both among scientists and theologians that evolution as a scientific theory and theology have very little to do with each other, and that evolution neither increases materially the theologian's difficulties, nor helps him to solve them."[53]

Within 20 years, and after the death of B. B. Warfield in 1921, the tone of the *Princeton Theological Review* changed to stressing the totalizing extrinsic character of scientific work. Thus, in a series of articles in the early 1920s, the Princeton assessment of various scientific experiments came to focus on broader, extrinsic concerns. In 1922, it was contended that the "world-view" of evolution "because of its monism, is both at first so attractive and afterwards so compelling that, if yielded to, it must at last revolutionize civilization."[54] In 1924 an author raised the issue of speciation to ultimate heights:

> The other adequate explanation of this similarity [of features in different species] is found in the assumption of a creation of each species by a personal God. On independent grounds the theist reaches the conclusion that a personal God exists. If this conclusion is correct, and if God is the actual ground for the existence of the universe and of matter and if even on an evolutionary hypothesis the only adequate explanation of the existence of the first living cell is to suppose that God created it, there is no presumption against the possibility of his having created each species. If he *did* create each species, then the similarity between the species would be adequately accounted for by the fact that the different species were created on a similar plan by the same Great Architect.[55]

In 1925, a biblical doctrine of "a completed Creation" was posed against what the author calls "this essentially pagan or atheistic theory" of evolution.[56]

These accounts in the *Princeton Theological Review* from the mid-1920s show several things—that the empirical option that Hodge and Warfield tried to open up had failed, that the effort to differentiate intrinsic from extrinsic scientific concerns (which could still be glimpsed in *The Fundamentals*) had become passé, and that evangelicalism was ready for the Scopes trial. As was the case in the first half of the nineteenth century, so also now in the third decade of the twentieth: much more was at stake for American evangelicals in the cosmological meaning of science, much less in the actual doing of science.

Conclusion

Since evangelicalism became so strong in America through its full exploitation (and absorption) of traits in the early republic, it is little wonder that the attitudes toward science of the early republic would continue to exert such force even after the intellectual and cultural situations of the early republic had changed. In a world where most other traditional supports of Christianity no longer prevailed—including the sanction of state churches, the patronage of elites, and the weight of historic patterns of deference—it is not surprising that American evangelicals would lean as hard as they did on science, as one of the few supports left with which to recommend the Christian faith. Such a social setting helps explain why American evangelicals always took extrinsic issues of science more to heart than their peers in other regions of the North Atlantic. As Michael Gauvreau, for example, has shown, evangelical intellectuals in nineteenth-century Canada prosecuted natural theology and explained the harmonies of mental and physical science with as much vigor as their peers in the United States. But the Canadians never regarded their efforts with quite the deadly seriousness found in the United States and, as therefore could be expected, experienced a good deal less trauma in the early years of the twentieth century in adjusting to new intrinsic and extrinsic patterns of science.[57]

In a similar way, formulations of natural theology by Archibald Alexander and Thomas Chalmers, which were both published in 1836, revealed that implications for scientific questions were different in evangelical Scotland as compared to the evangelical United States. For Alexander,

> In receiving . . . the most mysterious doctrines of revelation, the ultimate appeal is to reason: not to determine whether she could have discovered these truths; not to declare whether considered in themselves they appear probable; but to decide whether it is not more reasonable to believe what God speaks, than to confide in our own crude and feeble conceptions. . . . There is no just cause for apprehending that we shall be misled by the proper exercise of reason on any subject which may be proposed for our consideration. . . . But what if the plain sense of Scripture be absolutely repugnant to the first principles of reason? Let that be demonstrated and the effect will be rather to overthrow the Scriptures, than to favour such a method of forming a theory from them. But no such thing can be demonstrated.[58]

Alexander, in other words, raised the stakes very high for the extrinsic implications of the era's scientific reasoning.

For his part, Chalmers did not back away from defending the value of natural theology, which he described as reasoning from God's "adaptation of External Nature to the Mental Constitution of Man." But Chalmers at the start of a long exercise in natural theology still wanted readers to understand limitations that Alexander was loath to admit. Wrote the Scot: "It is well to evince, not the success only, but the shortcomings of Natural Theology; and thus to make palpable at the same time both her helplessness and her usefulness—helpless if trusted to as a guide or an informer on the way to heaven; but most useful if, under a sense of her felt deficiency, we seek for a place of enlargement and are led onward to the higher manifestations of Christianity."[59] Once again, it is no surprise that later transitions in Scotland brought about by shifts in the character of science were less traumatic than those taking place in the United States.

Evangelicalism in America has been proprietary, scholastic, and pious—in each instance, often honorably so. It has been proprietary in its persistent concern for public order; it has been scholastic in promoting natural theology and its own forms of Bible-only religion; it has been pious in stressing the religion of the heart. For each trait, particularly American circumstances have exaggerated those aspects in the evangelical engagement with science that stressed extrinsic meanings at the expense of intrinsic practices. The result by 1925 was a divided situation. From the angle of deeply held views on the extrinsic meanings of science, the evangelical engagement had been persistent, profound, sometimes savvy, and regularly alert to the political implications of intellectual discourse. From the angle of science as an intrinsic exercise, it was not clear what evangelical engagement meant. Although a worthy list of evangelicals had been noteworthy practitioners of intrinsic science, the face of evangelicalism as a movement was turned so consistently to extrinsic matters that the bearing of evangelical faith on the intrinsic practices of science remained a mystery, undefined by practitioners and undisturbed by later historians of their work.

NOTES

1. For helpful studies on the larger, fuzzier meanings of science in American history, see Charles E. Rosenberg, *No Other Gods: On Science and American Social Thought* (Baltimore: Johns Hopkins University Press, 1976); Cynthia Eagle Russett, *Darwin in America: The Intellectual Response* (San Francisco: W. H. Freeman, 1976); and Nathan Reingold, ed., *The Sciences in the American Context: New Perspectives* (Washington, D.C.: Smithsonian Institution Press, 1979).

2. In addition to the immense body of literature that now exists on evangelical traditions in America, some of the most useful writing for gaining perspective on American developments is the growing literature on evangelicalism in other national settings—for example, David W. Bebbington, *Evangelicalism in Modern Britain: A History from the 1730s to the 1980s* (London: Unwin Hyman, 1989); David Hempton and Myrtle Hill, *Evangelical Protestantism in Ulster Society, 1740–1890* (London: Routledge, 1992); Mark Ellingsen, *The Evangelical Movement* (Minneapolis: Fortress, 1988), with excellent treatment of Continental movements; George A. Rawlyk, *The Canada Fire: Radical Evangelicalism in British North America, 1775–1812* (Montreal and Kingston: McGill-Queen's University Press, 1994); John G. Stackhouse, Jr., *Canadian Evangelicalism in the Twentieth Century* (Toronto: University of Toronto Press, 1993); Mark Hutchinson and Edmund Campion, *Re-Visioning Australian Colonial Christianity, 1788–1900* (New South Wales: Centre for the Study of Australian Christianity, 1994); and Stuart Piggin, *Evangelical Christianity in Australia: Spirit, Word, and World* (Melbourne: Oxford University Press, 1996). Questions of definition are canvassed in the introduction to *Evangelicalism: Comparative Studies of Popular Protestantism in North America, the British Isles, and Beyond, 1700–1900*, ed. Mark A. Noll, David W. Bebbington, and George A. Rawlyk (New York: Oxford University Press, 1994).

3. These prejudices are expanded upon in *The Scandal of the Evangelical Mind* (Grand Rapids: Eerdmans, 1994). This chapter also draws on material published in *Princeton and the Republic, 1768–1822* (Princeton: Princeton University Press, 1989); "The Rise and Long Life of the Protestant Enlightenment in America," in *Knowledge and Belief in America*, ed. Michael Lacey (New York: Cambridge University Press, 1995); and Charles Hodge, *What Is Darwinism? And Other Writings on Science and Religion* (Grand Rapids: Baker, 1994), which I edited with David N. Livingstone.

4. I do not view "intrinsic" science as objective, neutral, and free of social influences, for all science is done by humans, within human social settings, and for human purposes. Nevertheless, it does seem self-evident that "intrinsic" questions such as "what am I seeing through this microscope now?" are influenced by ideology and social setting in different, less obvious, ways than "extrinsic" questions such as "what do someone else's conclusions about variations in a pigeon population suggest about the presence or absence of design in the universe?"

5. Bruce Kuklick, *Churchmen and Philosophers from Jonathan Edwards to John Dewey* (New Haven: Yale University Press, 1985), 202.

6. In this American situation I am talking about something different than what Steven Shapin describes in *A Social History of Truth: Civility and Science in Seventeenth-Century England* (Chicago: University of Chicago Press, 1994), where broad, underlying, all-but-invisible cultural assumptions are described as shaping, or determining, the credibility of scientific conclusions. Rather, I am describing a situation where political, ideological, cosmological, and metaphysical matters have been self-consciously at work in relation to the practice and place of science in American society.

7. The indispensable secondary accounts for beginning any discussion of evangelicals and science are essays in the last half of *God and Nature: Historical Essays on the Encounter Between Christianity and Science*, ed. David C. Lindberg and Ronald L. Numbers (Berkeley: University of California Press, 1986); and the oeuvre of John C. Greene, including *American Science in the Age of Jefferson* (Ames: Iowa State University Press, 1984); *Science, Ideology, and World View* (Berkeley: University of California Press, 1981); and *Darwin and the Modern World View* (Baton Rouge: Louisiana State University Press, 1961).

8. D. H. Meyer, *The Instructed Conscience: The Shaping of the American National Ethic* (Philadelphia: University of Pennsylvania Press, 1972); Henry F. May, *The Enlightenment in America* (New York: Oxford University Press, 1976); Theodore Dwight Bozeman, *Protestants in an Age of Science: The Baconian Ideal and Antebellum American Religious Thought* (Chapel Hill: University of North Carolina Press, 1977); Drew Gilpin Faust, *A Sacred Circle: The Dilemma of the Intellectual in the Old South, 1840–1860* (Philadelphia: University of Pennsylvania Press, 1977); E. Brooks Holifield, *The Gentlemen Theologians: American Theology in Southern Culture, 1795–1860* (Durham: Duke University Press, 1978); Herbert Hovenkamp, *Science and Religion in America, 1800–1860* (Philadelphia: University of Pennsylvania Press, 1978); James Oscar Farmer, Jr., *The Metaphysical Confederacy: James Henley Thornwell and the Synthesis of Southern Values* (Macon, Ga.: Mercer University Press, 1986); and Walter H. Conser, Jr., *God and the Natural World: Religion and Science in Antebellum America* (Columbia: University of South Carolina Press, 1993).

9. Besides the works in note 5, see also Kuklick, *Churchmen and Philosophers;* George M. Marsden, *The Evangelical Mind and the New School Presbyterian Experience* (New Haven: Yale University Press, 1970); Marsden, *Fundamentalism and American Culture, 1870–1925* (New York: Oxford University Press, 1980); John Dillenberger, *Protestant Thought and Natural Science* (Nashville: Abingdon, 1960); and Grant Wacker, *Augustus H. Strong and the Dilemma of Historical Consciousness* (Macon, Ga.: Mercer University Press, 1985.

10. Besides the works in note 5, see the very full contribution by Davis A. Young, *The Biblical Flood: A Case Study of the Church's Response to Extrabiblical Evidence* (Grand Rapids: Eerdmans, 1995).

11. George Marsden, "Fundamentalism as an American Phenomenon: A Comparison with English Evangelicalism," *Church History* 46 (1977): 215–32; Richard Carwardine, *Trans-Atlantic Revivalism: Popular Evangelicalism in Britain and America, 1790–1865* (Westport: Greenwood, 1978); David N. Livingstone, "Darwinism and Calvinism: The Belfast-Princeton Connection," *Isis* 83 (1992): 408–28; David W. Bebbington, "Evangelicalism in Its Settings: The British and American Movements since 1940," in *Evangelicalism;* Michael Gauvreau, "The Empire of Evangelicalism: Varieties of Common Sense in Scotland, Canada, and the United States," in *ibid.;* Barry Mack, "Of Canadian Presbyterians and Guardian Angels," in *Amazing Grace: Evangelicalism in Australia, Britain, Canada, and the United States*, ed. George A. Rawlyk and Mark A. Noll (Grand Rapids: Baker, and Montreal: McGill-Queen's University Press, 1994); David W. Bebbington, "Evangelicalism in Modern Britain and America: A Comparison," in *ibid.;* and Mark A. Noll,

"Revival, Enlightenment, Civic Humanism, and the Evolution of Calvinism in Scotland and America, 1735–1843," in *ibid.*

12. See especially James R. Moore, *The Post-Darwinian Controversies* (New York: Cambridge University Press, 1979); Jon H. Roberts, *Darwinism and the Divine in America: Protestant Intellectuals and Organic Evolution, 1859–1900* (Madison: University of Wisconsin Press, 1988); and David N. Livingstone, *Darwin's Forgotten Defenders: The Encounter Between Evangelical Theology and Evolutionary Thought* (Grand Rapids: Eerdmans, 1987).

13. Stephen Toulmin, "The Historicization of Natural Science: Its Implications for Theology," in *Paradigms in Theology*, ed. Hans Küng and David Tracy (New York: Crossroad, 1989); John Hedley Brooke, *Science and Religion: Some Historical Perspectives* (New York: Cambridge University Press, 1991), 192–225; John C. Vanderstelt, *Philosophy and Scripture: A Study in Old Princeton and Westminster Theology* (Marlton, N.J.: Mack, 1978); and James Turner, *Without God, Without Creed: The Origins of Unbelief in America* (Baltimore: Johns Hopkins University Press, 1985).

14. The most exactingly researched history of science for evangelicals concerns such broader extrinsic matters almost exclusively—viz., Edward B. Davis, "A Whale of a Tale: Fundamentalist Fish Stories," *Perspectives on Science and Christian Faith* 43 (Dec. 1991): 224–37; and James R. Moore, *The Darwin Legend* (Grand Rapids: Baker, 1994).

15. Ronald Numbers, *The Creationists: The Evolution of Scientific Creationism* (New York: Knopf, 1992), includes descriptions of scientific practice, but for a contingent of evangelicals who have operated in opposition to the mainstream. Description of scientific practice by evangelicals, but only for the twentieth century, is found in the historical articles noting the 50th anniversary of the American Scientific Affiliation, *Perspectives on Science and Christian Faith* 44 (Mar. 1992): 1–24.

16. A partial exception to that generalization is attention to how southern settings affected the dismissal of Alexander Winchell from Vanderbilt in 1878 (for holding to the existence of "preadamites," human beings before Adam) and the debate over James Woodrow's views on evolution in the 1870s and 1880s. See David N. Livingstone, *The Preadamite Theory and the Marriage of Science and Religion*, Transactions of the American Philosophical Society, Vol. 82, P. 3 (Philadelphia: American Philosophical Society, 1992), 40–52; and George H. Daniels, "Science and Religion," *Encyclopedia of Religion in the South*, ed. Samuel S. Hill (Macon, Ga.: Mercer University Press, 1984), 672–77.

17. Cotton Mather, *The Christian Philosopher*, ed. Winton U. Solberg (Urbana: University of Illinois Press, 1984); see also Solberg, "Science and Religion in Early America: Cotton Mather's *Christian Philosopher*," *Church History* 56 (1987): 73–92.

18. Cotton Mather, *The Christian Philosopher: A Collection of the Best Discoveries in Nature, with Religious Improvement* (London: E. Mathews, 1721), iv, 60–61, 1.

19. Elizabeth Flower and Murray G. Murphey, *A History of Philosophy in America*, 2 vols. (New York: Capricorn, 1977), 1:79–80.

20. William Jennings Bryan, *The Last Message of William Jennings Bryan* (New York: Fleming H. Revell, 1925), 51. On Bryan's social opposition to evolution, see Lawrence Levine, *Defender of the Faith, William Jennings Bryan: The Last Crusade, 1915–1925* (New York: Oxford University Press, 1965), 261–70; and Garry Wills, *Under God: Religion and American Politics* (New York: Simon and Schuster, 1990), 97–106.

21. See Noll, *Princeton and the Republic*, 46.

22. The critical documents, with learned commentary, are in *The Works of Jonathan Edwards: Scientific and Philosophical Writings*, ed. Wallace E. Anderson (New Haven: Yale University Press, 1980). Extraordinarily helpful is also Norman Fiering, *Jonathan Edwards's Moral Thought and Its British Context* (Chapel Hill: University of North Carolina Press, 1981).

23. Ashbel Green, *The Life of the Revd. John Witherspoon*, ed. Henry Lyttleton Savage (Princeton: Princeton University Press, 1973), 132.

24. Frederick Beasley, "An Account of the Life and Writings of the Rev. Samuel Stanhope Smith," *Analectic Magazine* 1 (June 1820): 449–50.

25. Nathan O. Hatch, *The Democratization of American Christianity* (New Haven: Yale University Press, 1989), 6.

26. Norman Fiering, *Moral Philosophy at Seventeenth-Century Harvard: A Discipline in Transition* (Chapel Hill: University of North Carolina Press, 1981), 300.

27. A. G. Dickens and John M. Tonkin, *The Reformation in Historical Thought* (Cambridge, Mass.: Harvard University Press, 1985), 7–57.

28. See Hatch, *The Democratization of American Christianity;* and Hatch, "*Sola Scriptura* and *Novus Ordo Seclorum*," in *The Bible in American Culture*, ed. Nathan O. Hatch and Mark A. Noll (New York: Oxford University Press, 1982).

29. Ruth Bloch, *Visionary Republic: Millennial Themes in American Thought, 1756–1800* (New York: Cambridge University Press, 1985); William Gribbin, *The Churches Militant: The War of 1812 and American Religion* (New Haven: Yale University Press, 1973); and on the literal application of the Bible at the time of the Civil War, Mark A. Noll, "The Image of the United States as a Biblical Nation, 1776–1865," in *The Bible in America*, 40–41, 48–50.

30. Eric Anderson, "The Millerite Use of Prophecy," in *The Disappointed: Millerism and Millenarianism in the Nineteenth Century*, ed. Ronald L. Numbers and Jonathan M. Butler (Bloomington: University of Indiana Press, 1987).

31. I have found helpful on this subject, David S. Katz, "The Hutchinsonians and Hebraic Fundamentalism in Eighteenth-Century England," in *Sceptics, Millenarians and Jews*, ed. David S. Katz and Jonathan I. Israel (Leiden: E. J. Brill, 1990); Albert J. Kuhn, "Glory or Gravity: Hutchinson vs. Newton," *Journal of the History of Ideas* 22 (1961): 303–22; and Brooke, *Science and Religion*, 190.

32. *The Sermon, Delivered at the Inauguration of the Rev. Archibald Alexander, D. D., as Professor of Didactic and Polemic Theology, in the Theological Seminary of the Presbyterian Church, in the United States of America . . .* (New York: J. Seymour, 1812), 77.

33. On Johnson's Hutchinsonianism, see Flower and Murphy, *Philosophy in America*, 1: 85–86; and Joseph Ellis, *The New England Mind in Transition: Samuel Johnson of Connecticut, 1696–1772* (New Haven: Yale University Press, 1973), 228–32.

34. Robert Bruce Mullin, *Episcopal Vision/American Reality: High Church Theology and Social Thought in Evangelical America* (New Haven: Yale University Press, 1986), 19, 67n., 189.

35. Bebbington, *Evangelicalism in Britain*, 57; Margaret C. Jacob, *The Radical Enlightenment: Pantheists, Freemasons and Republicans* (London: George Allen & Unwin, 1981), 96, citing Bernard Semmel, *The Methodist Revolution* (New York: Basic Books, 1973), 20.

36. J. C. D. Clark, *English Society, 1688–1832* (New York: Cambridge University Press, 1985), 218, with illuminating comments on Hutchinson extending to p. 219.

37. R. L. Dabney, "Geology and the Bible" (orig. July 1861), in *Discussions by Robert L. Dabney, Vol. III: Philosophical*, ed. C. R. Vaughan (Richmond, Va.: Whittet & Shepperson, 1892), 95.

38. Dabney, "A Caution Against Anti-Christian Science" (orig. Oct. 1871), in *ibid.*, 131; see "The Caution Against Anti-Christian Science Criticised by Dr. Woodrow" (orig. Oct. 1873), in *ibid.*, 169–70, with specific mention of Gosse on 170.

39. I owe my first awareness of Hutchinsonianism, the social-political milieu in which it flourished, and its parallels to later creationism to a brief reference in James R. Moore, "Interpreting the New Creationism," *Michigan Quarterly Review* 22 (1983): 324. David

Katz views Hutchinsonianism as anticipating both fundamentalist creationism and nineteenth-century historical criticism of Scripture; Katz, "Hutchinsonians and Hebraic Fundamentalism," 254–55.

40. Especially helpful on the contexts of these transitions are Alexandra Oleson and John Voss, eds., *The Organization of Knowledge in Modern America, 1860–1920* (Baltimore: Johns Hopkins University Press, 1979); Burton J. Bledstein, *The Culture of Professionalism: The Middle Class and the Development of Higher Education in America* (New York: Norton, 1976); and George M. Marsden, *The Soul of the American University: From Protestant Establishment to Established Nonbelief* (New York: Oxford University Press, 1994).

41. Quoted in Henry Warner Bowden, *Church History in the Age of Science: Historiographical Patterns in the United States, 1876–1918* (Chapel Hill: University of North Carolina Press, 1971), 7.

42. See especially Livingstone, *Darwin's Forgotten Defenders*.

43. William Berryman Scott, *Some Memories of a Palaeontologist* (Princeton: Princeton University Press, 1939), 75, which reports the title as *Voyage of a Naturalist*.

44. Charles Hodge, letter to the *New York Observer*, March 26, 1863, 98–99; with discussion in *What Is Darwinism?* ed. Noll and Livingstone, 51–56. For fuller context, see Bradley John Gundlach, "The Evolution Question at Princeton, 1845–1929" (Ph.D. diss., University of Rochester, 1995).

45. For attacks on ateleology, see Charles Hodge, *What Is Darwinism?* (New York: Scribner, Armstrong, and Co., 1874); and Hodge, *Systematic Theology*, 3 vols. (New York: Charles Scribner's Sons, 1872–73), 1: 550–74, 2: 3–41. For a repetition of his convictions on the rights of an independent science, see *Systematic Theology*, 1: 59, 170–71, and 573–74 (reprinted and annotated in *What Is Darwinism?* ed. Noll and Livingstone, 56–59).

46. Benjamin B. Warfield, "The Present Status of the Doctrine of Evolution," *The Presbyterian Messenger* 3:10 (Dec. 5, 1895), 7–8.

47. That is, Shapin is convincing in arguing that it took a particular social environment, in which it seemed both rational and commendable to trust the word of a gentleman, in order for empirical science of the sort promoted by Robert Boyle to advance. Desmond and Moore are likewise convincing in suggesting that, because of the social construction of ameliorative ideals of Design in the 1830s and 1840s, only "revolutionaries" were able to look for, or perhaps even see, evidence pointing to the distribution of "species" along a continuum without rigid boundaries. Shapin, *A Social History of Truth;* Adrian Desmond and James Moore, *Darwin: The Life of A Tormented Evolutionist* (New York: Warner, 1991).

48. Marsden, *Fundamentalism and American Culture*.

49. James Orr, "Science and Christian Faith," *The Fundamentals*, 4 vols. (Grand Rapids: Baker, 1972; orig. 1917), 1:346. Excellent on the context for Orr's scientific thinking is Glen G. Scorgie, *A Call for Continuity: The Theological Contribution of James Orr* (Macon, Ga.: Mercer University Press, 1988).

50. George Frederick Wright, "The Passing of Evolution," *Fundamentals*, 4: 87. Excellent on Wright is Ronald L. Numbers, "George Frederick Wright: From Christian Darwinism to Fundamentalist," *Isis* 79 (1988): 624–45.

51. J. J. Reeve, "My Personal Experience with the Higher Criticism," *Fundamentals*, 1:349–50.

52. Henry H. Beach, "Decadence of Darwinism," *Fundamentals*, 4: 60, 67.

53. William Hallock Johnson, "Evolution and Theology Today," *Princeton Theological Review* 1 (1903): 417, 422. For the broader context in which these changes took place, see Gundlach, "The Evolution Question at Princeton."

54. William Brenton Greene, Jr., "Yet Another Criticism of the Theory of Evolution," *Princeton Theological Review* 20 (Oct. 1922): 537.

55. Floyd E. Hamilton, "The Evolutionary Hypothesis in the Light of Modern Science," *Princeton Theological Review* 22 (1924): 422.

56. George McCready Price, "Modern Botany and the Theory of Organic Evolution," *Princeton Theological Review* 23 (1925), 65.

57. Michael Gauvreau, *The Evangelical Century: College and Creed in English Canada from the Great Revival to the Great Depression* (Montreal and Kingston: McGill-Queen's University Press, 1991).

58. Archibald Alexander, *Evidences of the Authenticity, Inspiration, and Canonical Authority of the Holy Scriptures* (Philadelphia: Presbyterian Board, 1836), 10, 15.

59. Thomas Chalmers, *On Natural Theology* (New York: Robert Carter, 1844; orig. Edinburgh, 1836 [preface dated Dec. 1835]), xiv.

5

Science and Evangelical Theology in Britain from Wesley to Orr

DAVID W. BEBBINGTON

Evangelicals, in Britain as elsewhere, have often been seen as wary of science. The movement springing from the Evangelical Revival, it has been supposed, generated a species of religion alien to painstaking research. The hothouse atmosphere of evangelicalism, marked by intense feeling and sudden conversions, seemed unlikely to nurture the calm, reflective temper of scientific investigation. Historians have pointed out that it was not evangelicals but liberal Anglicans of the Broad Church school, often seconded by Unitarians, who were at the heart of British science.[1] Evangelicals, by contrast, appeared the defenders of a literal interpretation of the Bible that made them suspicious of advances in the understanding of nature. It has been suggested, furthermore, that their antiscientific stance was theologically grounded. They so exalted biblical revelation as to cast aspersions on other sources of religious knowledge. Hence evangelicals, it has recently been argued, were marked by a "rejection of the natural theology" that bound together science and religion during the eighteenth century.[2] The idea that the Creator could be known through his works, on this view, was dismissed as a vain human fancy. "For an evangelical minister," Adrian Desmond has written, "revelation overshadowed natural theology; it made any attempt to prove God's actions from nature not only redundant but actually pernicious."[3] The belief has become widespread that evangelicals were hostile to natural theology because of their fundamental religious convictions. Their characteristic devotion to the Bible ranged them among the opponents of scientific progress.

Suspicions of Science

It must be conceded at the outset that there is an element of truth in this picture. Since evangelicals were constantly aware of the illumination they derived from Scripture, they tended to minimize the role of other sources of light. Thus in the later eighteenth century Thomas Haweis, a leading Anglican evangelical and associate of the countess of Huntingdon, contrasted the glowworm ray of human reason with the glory of the Sun of righteousness.[4] Haweis's contemporary, the influential clergyman John Newton, drew out the stern implication for the examination of creation. "The study of the works of God," he wrote, "independent of his word, though dignified with the name of *philosophy*, is not better than an elaborate trifling and waste of time."[5] It is hardly surprising that John Foster, a later Baptist essayist who was personally much better disposed toward scientific endeavour, complained that among serious persons there was an irreligious neglect of the works of the Almighty, which they tended to deprecate in relation to his word.[6] Likewise it was noted that in Scotland many Christians raised an outcry against any coverage in the pulpit of topics relating to the work of God in nature because they were thought to be remote from the doctrines of grace.[7] The evangelicals' preoccupation with issues of salvation goes a long way towards explaining their reservations about giving a larger place to natural philosophy, but another reason was doubt about its epistemological status. The Bible, according to a correspondent of the evangelical Anglican *Christian Observer* in 1839, "ought not to be bended and conformed to philosophy, but more plastic science should rather be assimilated to . . . Scripture."[8] Science was plastic because the investigators of the natural world were constantly changing their minds. Why should their results be treated with wholehearted deference? Certainly there seemed no good reason for preferring scientific findings to the assured teachings of the Bible. Accordingly there was a thread of skepticism running through evangelical attitudes to the accomplishments of researchers. Science seemed shifting sands; the Bible was a solid rock.

Hence evangelicals were sometimes lukewarm toward natural theology. For John Newton, to attempt to reason toward God from the phenomena of nature was in itself fruitless. "The works of creation," he wrote, "may be compared to a fair character in cipher, of which the Bible is the key; without this key they cannot be understood."[9] The evidence for this conclusion was plain to anyone acquainted with the classics: the ancients were not persuaded by arguments drawn from the natural world to believe in the true God. Their authors dwelt on the harmony and design of the universe, pointed out J. B. Sumner, later the first evangelical archbishop of Canterbury, but to no avail. That left us "undisputable proof that the God of NATURAL THEOLOGY will never be any thing more than the dumb idol of philosophy: neglected by the philosopher himself, and unknown to the multitude; acknowledged in the closet, and forgotten in the world."[10] Even if, on occasion, the arguments of the philosophers carried conviction to the intellect, that was not far enough. "The works of creation," commented Daniel Wilson, later bishop of Calcutta, "wonderful as they are, are incapable of changing the heart."[11] Even Thomas Chalmers, the leading early nineteenth-century evangelical in the Church of Scotland who wrote extensively on natural theology, held that the discipline had only limited powers. It shed light on the being of God and the human predicament, but had nothing to say about the way of salvation. "Natural theology," he declared, "might announce the problem, but cannot resolve it."[12] He was aware that some distrusted the whole enterprise as an apparent attempt to supplant the gospel by another system of belief.[13] That suspicion Chalmers deplored; but his own stance is a clear sign that even among its exponents evangelicals imposed strict limits on what natural theology was supposed to achieve.

The exaltation of Scripture and the downgrading of natural theology could issue in a marginalization of science. Although the evangelist George Whitefield might allude to astronomy in his preaching, he injected little learning into his gospel sermons and was accused by a Cambridge don of decrying human reasoning altogether.[14] John Newton was willing to admit that Christians, as opposed to unbelievers, might trace God's wisdom in his works, but only "if their inquiries are kept within due bounds, and in a proper subservience to things of greater importances." In any case, he added, "they are comparatively few who have leisure, capacity, or opportunity for these inquiries."[15] Likewise Thomas Robinson, vicar of St. Mary's, Leicester, believed that though the investigation of God's wisdom in his works was legitimate, "we shall find much matter for devout admiration, rather than for curious research and critical explanation."[16] In 1780 John Venn, subsequently the spiritual mentor of the Clapham Sect, warned his Cambridge friend Francis Wollaston not to let a passion for chemistry eclipse his work as a minister of Christ. "What comparison," he exclaimed, "can there be between saving a soul and analysing a salt!"[17] It is hardly strange that a religious movement should make religion its priority, but it has to be acknowledged that it also gave rise to bad science. The school of "Scriptural Geology," beginning in 1826 with a book of that title by the evangelical clergyman George Bugg, tried to eliminate the apparent threat to the early chapters of Genesis from practicing geologists. The British Association for the Advancement of Science, which gathered together many real practitioners in the 1830s, was denounced by another evangelical, Frederick Nolan, for aiming at "the ascendancy of philosophy on the ruins of religion."[18] J. Mellor Brown, another of Bugg's school, was typical in denying that any particular expertise was needed for entering on scientific questions. The natural world could be sufficiently understood a priori by the devout reasoner from the pages of the Bible.[19] Such an opinion, though having a long lineage, was tottering toward extinction. The Scriptural Geologists illustrate that evangelicals were capable of closing their eyes to empirical science altogether.

Sympathy for Science

The evidence reviewed so far shows why the idea has sprung up that evangelicalism was inimical to science. Allegiance to the Bible could lead the movement's adherents to disparage natural theology and to neglect or distort scientific endeavour itself. Yet that is a very partial sampling of their attitudes. Many of these instances—such as the views of Thomas Haweis and John Newton—come from the early days of the revival when it was small and embattled, struggling to make an impression on the mass of unbelief around it by summoning hearers to conversion. The pressing need was for preachers of the gospel, not for academics in any field. Thus the curriculum of the dissenting theological colleges associated with evangelicalism concentrated on giving men basic Bible knowledge, not on turning them into scholars.[20] The movement's apologists were inclined to set out their central doctrines rather than to pursue related matters. Thus in his *Essays on the Most Important Subjects in Religion* (1794), Thomas Scott, well known as a commentator on the Bible, deals with topics such as the inspiration of the Scriptures and the deity of Christ, justification and regeneration, never touching on questions of natural theology.[21] As time passed, however, there was a tendency for intellectual curiosity, which had never been dead, to branch out in fresh directions. Evangelical authors became more numerous; evangelical periodicals multiplied; and topics were treated for the first time from an evangelical angle. In the first half of the nineteenth century ideas that had previously existed only in germ within the movement began to be elaborated more fully. Sympathy for science was voiced more often. Although there were sometimes worries about its implications, the prevailing attitude was one of confidence that God's works were in harmony with God's word. "Nature and Revelation," wrote the leading Congregational theologian John Pye Smith in 1839, "are both beams of light from the same Sun of eternal truth; and there cannot be discordance between them."[22] Evangelical theology revealed an alignment with the scientific enterprise.

Consequently the leaders of evangelical thought were on the same side as the broader Anglicans who endorsed and practiced the science of the day. William Buckland, professor of geology at Oxford, received the backing of the evangelicals J. B. Sumner and G. S. Faber.[23] William Whewell and Adam Sedgwick, the leading Cambridge authorities on science, were quoted deferentially by J. H. Pratt, the evangelical archdeacon of Calcutta, in his *Scripture and Science Not at Variance* (1856).[24] W. D. Conybeare, with the editor's approval, defended what has been called "the liberal Anglican position" on geology in the pages of *The Christian Observer*, the magazine of the moderate evangelicals in the Church of England.[25] Although it gave space to the fulminations of George Bugg against infidel tendencies in geology, *The Christian Observer*, unlike the more conservative evangelical journal *The Christian Guardian*, came down consistently against Bugg and the other Scriptural Geologists.[26] So did Pye Smith, the most respected dissenting theologian of the period.[27] Around Thomas Chalmers in Scotland there was a circle of distinguished men who blended evangelical theology with scientific practice: Sir David Brewster, a specialist in optics and eventually principal of the University of Edinburgh; John Fleming, professor of natural history at King's College, Aberdeen; and, among amateurs, Hugh Miller, the stonemason turned littérateur who pursued and popularized geological investigation.[28] Cambridge produced a crop of eminent scientific evangelicals including Isaac Milner, Francis Wollaston, and William Parish, successive occupants of the Jacksonian chair of natural and experimental philosophy.[29] The university's graduates, many evangelicals among them, sometimes imbibed a taste for experiment. John Venn, despite his warning to Wollaston about the siren appeal of chemistry, filled his notebooks with diagrams on optics, astronomy, hydrostatics, and mechanics.[30] Likewise John Ryland, principal of Bristol Baptist College, was said to delight in natural history, being "much assisted by the structure of his eyes which were a kind of natural microscope."[31] The passion for fossils of Philip Gosse, a member of the Brethren, has become enshrined in English literature.[32] Scientific pursuits could be little more than a hobby; but equally they could form the basis of a career. To uphold evangelical theology was certainly no bar to scientific interests.

An Enlightenment Approach

It was not merely that the two—evangelicalism and science—were compatible; rather, there was a tight bond between them. Both as they were pursued in the late eighteenth and early nineteenth centuries bore the marks of the Enlightenment. Few would doubt that the Newtonian framework of British science was associated with the Age of Reason: the enlightened ideal of free enquiry leading to greater understanding through empirical investigation was itself modeled on scientific method. Increasingly it has also been recognized that evangelical thought shared the same values, with reason occupying the supreme place.[33] When, in 1801 and again in 1813, the Eclectic Society of leading evangelicals met to consider the province of reason in religion, they decided that it fulfilled a central role. "I do not oppose reason and revelation," declared Thomas Scott. "Reason is the eye, revelation the sun."[34] Hence there was no intrinsic a antithesis between vital region and learning. Cornelius Winter, a younger associate of George Whitefield, for instance, began his ministry without a classical education, yet valued erudition, gained skill in Greek and Hebrew, read and corresponded in Latin, and became proficient in French.[35] John Wesley was constantly urging his preachers to read and to promote reading among the early Methodists.[36] The Scriptures themselves seemed to sanction the pursuit of natural philosophy in particular. "Though they give us no system of astronomy," wrote the Baptist divine Andrew Fuller, "yet they urge us to study the works of God, and teach us to adore him upon every discovery."[37] Wesley, who took a serious interest in scientific matters, issued a two-volume *Survey of the Wisdom of God in the Creation* (1763).[38] His central preoccupation, in typical Enlightenment fashion, was with the usefulness of new discoveries. In another work, *The Desideratum: or Electricity Made Plain and Useful* (1760), he set out the therapeutic value of electrical current. It was, he remarked with his accustomed precision, a "general and rarely failing remedy, in nervous cases of every kind (old palsies excepted)."[39] Science, as an essential component of the Enlightenment worldview, came naturally to most evangelicals.

The most striking exceptions in the evangelical community confirm this analysis. By the 1820s the Romantic reaction against Enlightenment thought was making headway in society at large. Mediated through Coleridge and others, intellectual dispositions that had previously been more powerful in Germany began to penetrate the British evangelical world. The values of the previous century—reason, utility, free inquiry—were eagerly discarded by a small number of individuals who began to dwell on dramatic religious themes such as the second advent and the revival of glossolalia. At their head was Edward Irving, minister of the Church of Scotland congregation in Hatton Gardens, London.[40]

Scientific investigation soon fell under suspicion in this group. "Again," asked Irving in a lecture of 1828, "are you students and inquirers into any region of nature? then, be assured, that the understanding will blind the reason: the understanding which judgeth by the sense of the nature of things, will blind the reason, which judgeth by the conscience. And of all blinds and eclipses, this is the most helpless which bath darkened all our scientific men to the light of God. . . ."[41] Irving exploited the Coleridgean distinction between "understanding," mere sense perception, and "reason," with the peculiar meaning of moral intuition, in order to mount his blanket denunciation. Similarly his associate Henry Drummond condemned the habit of looking into secondary causes, as did scientists, instead of contemplating the first Cause of all things. This approach to the world, he claimed, was to live by sight rather than by faith.[42] Some years later William Tarbet, a minister of the Catholic Apostolic Church created by Irving and Drummond, expounded some of the consequences. "It is by faith, then, and not by science that we can understand *how* God made the world. He has revealed it to us. And *He* ought to know."[43] Astronomy and geology must bow before the letter of the Scriptures. Similar attitudes appeared in the diatribe against natural theology issued by the Tractarian William Irons in 1836.[44] Tractarians shared with the knot of radical evangelicals around Irving a reverence for authority and an exaltation of faith that were profoundly hostile to free inquiry.[45] Here, in the church groupings most swayed by Romanticism, there were deep-seated antiscientific convictions. They were not present, however, among the mass of evangelicals who remained faithful to the legacy of the Enlightenment.

That is evident in the widespread respect, almost amounting to adulation, for the memory of Sir Isaac Newton. Wesley led the way with a striking eulogy. "The immortal man," he wrote in his *Concise Ecclesiastical History* (1781), "to whose immense genius and indefatigable industry philosophy owed its greatest improvements, and who carried the lamp of knowledge into paths of knowledge that had been unexplored before, was Sir Isaac Newton, whose name was revered, and his genius admired, even by his warmest adversaries."[46] Later Methodists, including the polymath Adam Clarke and the theologian Richard Watson, treated Newton with deference.[47] So did the evangelical Anglicans Joseph Milner, J. B. Sumner, and, later on, T. R. Birks, who referred to the "immortal writer of the Principia."[48] The Baptist Andrew Fuller yoked Newton's name with those of Bacon and Boyle as admirable examples of the combination of philosophy and Christianity.[49] In Scotland Thomas Chalmers contrasted Newton's sound reasoning with the "unfounded imaginations of Des Cartes" and devoted the second of his *Astronomical Discourses* (1817) to praise of the scientist.[50] Sir David Brewster wrote two separate lives of Newton, in 1831 and again in 1855.[51] Newton's Arianism, of which Chalmers and Brewster were both aware, did little in their eyes to detract from his greatness. Even the Scriptural Geologist George Bugg claimed to be a Newtonian.[52] It might be supposed that the rival Hutchinsonian scheme of natural philosophy drawn from the Hebrew text of the Bible would appeal to evangelicals.[53] Certainly William Romaine, the earliest evangelical Anglican to occupy a London pulpit, used his single series of lectures

as Gresham Professor of Astronomy to assail Newtonian philosophy on Hutchinsonian lines.[54] As late as 1828 an evangelical Oxford graduate, claiming that
Newton's followers rather than the great man himself had made most of the
mistakes, professed himself a Hutchinsonian.[55] But Thomas Haweis was more
representative in being initially attracted by the devotional spirit of the Hutchinsonians but then alienated by their High Church sacramentarianism.[56] Wesley
was fascinated by their strangely cabalistic scheme but found it untenable.[57] So
it was Newtonianism that claimed the allegiance of nearly all the branches of
the evangelical community.

The shaping hand of the Enlightenment is equally evident in evangelical
statements of scientific method. Chalmers was an uncompromising champion of
simple induction. "Nothing," he wrote, "can be more safe or more infallible
than the procedure of inductive philosophy as applied to the phenomena of
external nature. . . . It is at liberty to classify appearances, but then in the work
of classifying, it must be directed only by observation."[58] Similarly Wesley,
whose *Survey of the Wisdom of God* included a history of empiricism, was so
wedded to experience as the grand source of knowledge that he wished to banish
hypotheses from experimentation altogether.[59] Others were more sophisticated.
Brewster, under the influence of the Scottish common-sense philosophy of Thomas Reid and Dugald Stewart, believed that imaginative hypotheses were essential.[60] Pye Smith recognized that deduction had a place as well as induction.
"In Physical Science," he explained, "the evidence of truth is obtained by drawing inferences from observations of facts made known by our senses; and confirmed in many cases, and those the most important, by the application of Mathematics. . . ."[61] His fellow Congregationalist Henry Rogers perceived the need
for both induction and deduction in scientific activity but, like Pye Smith, gave
induction the priority.[62] In the same way as scientists, evangelicals habitually
appealed to observation and experience. Describing their faith as "experimental
Christianity,"[63] they saw no difference between procedures in religion and science. "We are applying," declared Chalmers, "the very same principles to a
system of theism, that we would do to a system of geology." In order to understand the ways of God in either salvation or creation there was but one
requirement. "Give us the facts," demanded Chalmers.[64] The result of the application of empirical technique in either field was an assured grasp of reality.
Although their formulations differed, evangelicals accepted the standard method
of the Enlightenment as the high road to knowledge.

Natural Theology

Because theology and science shared the same modus operandi, the two disciplines could be closely integrated with each other. Their intersection was chiefly
in the field of natural theology, which therefore calls for more detailed examination. This department of divinity was succinctly defined by Thomas Gisborne,
an evangelical Anglican specialist in the subject, as "that knowledge concerning
the Deity and our relations to Him, which by observation and natural reasoning
man is capable of attaining."[65] It encompassed more than the semiscientific prov-

ince of what could be observed in creation of the Creator. It included as well the dimension of a priori reasoning for the existence of God. Although the Methodist Adam Clarke set out the five classic arguments presented by Aquinas and found them "powerfully convincing," he was unusual among evangelicals in giving them substantial weight.[66] The Newtonianism of the evangelicals normally predisposed them in favor of concentrating on the evidence of the Almighty in the natural world. They were aware of standing in a long tradition. *The Methodist Magazine*, for example, quoted Cicero's argument for a Creator at length in successive issues between February and June 1804.[67] Richard Watson and many others listed later authorities, almost always including John Ray's *The Wisdom of God Manifested in the Works of Creation* (1691) and William Derham's *Physico-Theology* (1713).[68] *The Methodist Magazine* went out of its way to note Derham's evidence for a benevolent Deity from the fact that eyelashes grow only to a suitable length and so never need cutting.[69] There was a chorus of approval for the latest statement of the overall case in William Paley's *Natural Theology* (1802).[70] The theological tradition least enthusiastic about this strand of Christian apologetic, it has recently been pointed out, was High Churchmanship, where the Hutchinsonian leaven was still at work. William Van Mildert, in his Boyle Lectures for 1802–5, was extremely reserved about the light shed by nature on the Creator.[71] Evangelicals, by contrast, were usually eager to avail themselves of the armory of natural theology.

What did they hope to achieve? John Brooke has drawn attention to the variety of purposes that natural theology was meant to serve.[72] Within the heterogeneous evangelical movement, virtually every suggested aim was pursued by at least a few. The small number of scientists, such as John Fleming, who after his time at King's College, Aberdeen, became first professor of natural science at New College, Edinburgh, found physico-theology a useful vehicle for the promotion of science and a source of regulative principles for the discipline.[73] Archdeacon Pratt wrote his *Scripture and Science Not at Variance* to provide reassurance for fellow believers and to indicate the most tenable apologetic positions. Pye Smith, in putting down the Scriptural Geologists, was similarly showing a legitimate way of reconciling science and religion but was also taking the opportunity to celebrate the powers of reason against misdirected enthusiasm. There was sometimes an element of social conservatism about the enterprise: in 1803 a contributor to *The Christian Observer*, probably William Wilberforce, by alluding to the recent open atheism in France that natural theology could counteract, was implicitly suggesting a remedy for the revolutionary chaos of the previous decade.[74] A less epic form of social control was in the mind of Pye Smith when he remarked on the leisure enjoyed by young people in the evening. "The cultivation of Natural History and the Sciences," he observed, "will be a dignified means of excluding those modes of abusing time which are the sin and disgrace of many young persons. . . ."[75] Not only did natural theology provide common ground for church and chapel, as John Brooke has suggested, but it also mediated, within the evangelical movement, between Arminians and Calvinists.[76] Arguments for God's existence drawn from nature were also valued as the stock-in-trade of the missionary. For preevangelism among the heathen, Gisborne pointed out, it was essential to gain access to their minds through natural theology.[77] By far its most important function, however, was the defense of Christianity against skepticism at home. "In these days," wrote Adam Clarke, "when blasphemy stalks abroad unmolested, and the Bible is treated with malicious and satanic indignity—every Christian, who has it in his power, and especially every Christian minister, should acquaint himself with these arguments!"[78] Thus equipped, the disciple could give a reason for the hope within him that might awaken the careless unbeliever. Natural theology was intrinsic to the missionary strategy of evangelicalism.

The kernel of physico-theology was the argument for the existence of God from design in external nature. It rested, as Chalmers explained, on an analogy between human and divine craftsmanship. Just as a house, the result of contrivance, indicated a contriver, so the world, adapted to the welfare of its inhabitants, implied an architect.[79] The appropriate inference was the reality of a Being infinite in power, wisdom, and goodness. References to the "final cause" of the created order illustrate the rooting of this mode of thinking in the scholastic tradition,[80] but evangelicals commonly presented this teleological argument in distinctively Newtonian guise. Adam Clarke discussed elliptic orbits, Pye Smith traced the causes of motion, and both J. B. Sumner and Richard Watson stressed the simplicity of gravitation as evidence for divine wisdom.[81] The idea of adaptation—what Chalmers called contrivance—was pivotal to the argument. When plants were so formed as to be nourished by moisture and animals so constituted as to be nourished by plants, the whole structure of nature seemed to manifest design. The adaptations were the effects, the Designer the cause. The eighteenth century, however, had witnessed a powerful challenge to this mode of thinking from David Hume. Subsequent writers usually located the problem in his analysis of causation. Any cause, Hume held, was only contingently related to its alleged effect. If he was right, the design argument fell to the ground. The rebuttal of Hume, implicitly or explicitly, was therefore a standard element in the evangelical case. The contention of Thomas Reid and Dugald Stewart that the concept of causation was part of the data of human experience was repeated by apologists in England as well as in their native Scotland.[82] Evangelicals adopted the same groundwork of reasoning as their British contemporaries.

Yet evangelicals typically pressed the argument further than the other thinkers of their day.[83] Although they agreed with the thrust of William Paley's classic statement of the case, they found aspects of it unsatisfactory. The reviewer in *The Christian Observer*, probably Wilberforce, criticized Paley on the one hand for denying the inherent sinfulness of human nature and on the other for a shallow treatment of the problem of the existence of venomous and predatory animals. This dysfunctional aspect of creation could not be explained away, in the manner of Paley, as being outbalanced by the evidence of benevolence. Rather, along with the other signs of natural and moral evil, it was an indication that the world was in a state of degradation resulting from the fall of humanity. Natural theology taught the holiness of God, the sinfulness of human beings, and even the need for redemption.[84] Likewise the Methodist Richard Watson, though following Paley about animal suffering, argued that "we see natural evils, and punitive acts of the divine administration, not because God is not good, but because he is just as well as good."[85] The geological strata illustrating past convulsions of the world, according to *The Methodist Magazine* for 1825, together with volcanoes, earthquakes, thunderstorms, tempests, and hurricanes, showed that human beings could not be innocent.[86] The irregularity and confusion of the earth, Thomas Gisborne similarly believed, revealed the holiness of the Almighty in punishing sin.[87] This type of theodicy was systematically stated by Chalmers. The miseries of life, he contended, could be explained only as a consequence of the displeasure of a righteous God. Since so much physical evil was the result of moral evil, the world would be happy if it were not depraved. Its present state taught that "while God loves the happiness of His children, He loves their virtue more."[88] Partly because of Chalmers's influence, and partly because it possessed the clear merit of grappling with the twin problems of suffering and evil, this version of natural theology spread. Inevitably it shaped the thinking of Chalmers's fellow Free Churchman William Cunningham, but hints of a similar approach can also be detected in the Anglican William Whewell.[89] The evangelical modification of natural theology extended beyond the boundaries of the movement to become the prevailing attitude in the early Victorian years.

Challenges from Science

The tradition of reasoning from natural phenomena toward the Christian God, enriched by this evangelical input, was nevertheless encountering fresh difficulties. One was the problem of the immensity of space. During the eighteenth century astronomers had discovered an ever-expanding array of stars. The increasing likelihood that other worlds were populated posed a question for faith. To believe that God created a plurality of inhabited worlds, according to the deist Thomas Paine, was incompatible with Christian belief. The idea that the obscure earth was the scene of the death of the Son of God seemed ridiculous in the light of the extent of the universe.[90] Andrew Fuller, the Baptist theologian, was the first to respond to this assault on the central evangelical doctrine of the Atonement. There was no reason, Fuller contended, why one small part of creation should not be chosen as the theater of God's most glorious works, though the theologian treated life on other planets as no more than hypothetical.[91] Chalmers, who elaborated some of Fuller's points in his *Astronomical Discourses*, was less tentative. "Worlds roll in these distant regions," he declared; "and worlds must be the mansions of life and of intelligence."[92] Chalmers popularized among evangelicals the idea of intelligent extraterrestrial life. The Baptist essayist John Foster, an evangelical Anglican contributor to *The Christian Observer*, and the Scottish Secessionist Thomas Dick all endorsed the opinion.[93] Sir David Brewster did battle for it in a celebrated exchange with Whewell.[94] Although, in deference to the view of Wesley, the Methodist *London Quarterly Review* was staunchly sceptical about Brewster's position, nearly three-quarters of non-Unitarian Protestant opinion took his side.[95] It seems remarkable that evangelicals should hold a speculative notion that potentially endangered the Atonement, but, as one of them put it, "the wisdom and goodness of God would be compromised by a material creation, stupendous and astounding as that which astronomy discloses, and yet wholly discontinuous from moral life."[96] If the galaxies lacked intelligent beings, the purposiveness of the universe would be undermined. The strength of the belief by evangelicals in the plurality of inhabited worlds is a further sign of their commitment to the argument from design.

A second problem concerned not space, but time. In the early nineteenth century the rising science of geology raised insistent questions about the interpretation of the Bible. Fossils from the rocks revealed extinct creatures that had roamed the earth in a remote and unimagined past. The fact that some had evidently been carnivorous challenged the belief, endorsed in the New Testament, that death entered the world through the fall of humanity. The biblical text was consequently reinterpreted as teaching that Adam's sin was responsible only for the introduction of the death of human beings.[97] Many evangelicals were capable of taking, the absence of evidence for Noah's flood equally in their stride. John Fleming, himself a practicing scientist, accepted as early as 1826 that, since the waters rose and fell gradually, it was unsurprising that there were no geological signs of catastrophe, and informed opinion followed his teed in seeing no disharmony between the biblical text and scientific discovery.[98] More intractable was the reconciliation of fresh evidence with the opening of Genesis. How could the vast aeons of geological time be matched with the information that creation occupied a mere six days? One answer, retaining a literal interpretation of the six days, was to hypothesize an interval, perhaps of enormous duration, between the creation "in the beginning" recorded in the Bible's first verse and the ordering of the present state of the world described from the second verse onward. Chalmers adopted this viewpoint in his preevangelical period and propagated it steadily afterwards.[99] The theory became precarious, however, when Charles Lyell demonstrated that rocks laid down before the human era contained fossils of species still living, so undermining the idea of a break between the early tracts of the planet's history and the phase following the six days' work.[100] Despite ingenious attempts to shore up the tottering interpretation, many evangelicals followed Hugh Miller in turning to the scheme earlier proposed by the French natural philosophers Buffon and Cuvier according to which the "days" were to be understood figuratively as protracted epochs.[101] Although there was considerable difficulty in fitting the sequence of the strata into the order of the days in Genesis, this speculation gained ground during the later nineteenth century and was still being advanced by James Orr in the twentieth.[102] The two schemes of harmonization proved popular because they appeared to uphold the integrity of science as well as scripture. Unlike on the one hand the liberal Anglican Baden Powell, who resorted to treating Genesis as myth, and on the other the Scriptural Geologists, who closed their eyes to fresh discoveries, many evangelicals ardently wished to believe in both. Their allegiance to the Bible is predictable; what is striking is the degree of their commitment to science.

A third, and ultimately the greatest, challenge to the synthesis of theology and science came from the idea of the transformation of species. If plants and animals could adapt themselves, the evidence for contrivance in the natural world vanished. The new doctrine, in the form of the evolutionary thought of the French naturalist Lamarck, became rooted by the 1830s in the radical circles of London medicine.[103] The discovery of the law of the conservation of energy in the following decade encouraged expectations that similar natural continuities awaited discovery elsewhere. The rising tide of a broadly Romantic temper, expressed in a vogue for German *Natürphilosophie*, undergirded the drift of opinion.[104] The trends culminated in the appearance in 1859 of Charles Darwin's *Origin of Species*. There were evangelicals who showed sympathy for this movement of thought. Pye Smith, for example, maintaining the high probability of Laplace's nebular hypothesis, drew the inference that God originally created a small number of simple bodies, which, operating according to laws, produced "all the forms and changes of organic and inorganic natures."[105] The publication in 1844 of Robert Chambers's *Vestiges of the Natural History of Creation*, however, provoked a dismayed reaction. The book exploited Laplace to maintain the transformation of species as a universal law and so appeared to imply that everything in creation was ultimately material. Brewster, who, like Pye Smith, had previously endorsed the nebular hypothesis, now repudiated it; a chair of natural science was established at New College, Edinburgh, to counter erroneous theories; and Hugh Miller denounced *Vestiges in his Foot-prints of the Creator* (1847).[106] Evangelicals tended to become more wary of development in the natural world, stressing instead the immediacy of divine intervention. That was to leave many of them more vulnerable to the coming Darwinian revolution. Yet the door was left open, at least by the far-sighted Miller, to a means of reconciling evolution with natural theology. "God," he wrote, "might as certainly have *originated* the species by a law of development, as he *maintains* it by a law of development;—the existence of a First Great Cause is as perfectly compatible with the one scheme as with the other. . . ."[107] It was along these lines that other evangelicals were to come to terms with Darwin.

Those who anathematized Darwin and all his works were at first outspoken. A botanist who reviewed *The Origin of Species* in *The Christian Observer* condemned the book as biased, negligent of Scripture, unsupported by facts, and designed "to cast God out of His own creation."[108] The Nonconformist readers of *The Eclectic Review* were told that Darwin's thesis, while suffering from an absence of evidence, implicitly denied immortality and showed an "absolute incompatibility" with any faith in revelation.[109] But as the new theory gained general approval in the scientific community, opinion mellowed. By the early 1870s much less outright resistance remained among evangelical theologians. The most strident opponent was T. R. Birks, vicar of Holy Trinity Church, Cambridge, and from 1872 Knightbridge professor of moral philosophy in the university there. Birks, like many contemporaries, closely associated the scientific understanding of evolution with Herbert Spencer's "social Darwinism," and attacked both for teaching that humanity was ultimately no different from the material world.[110] Against Darwin in particular he argued that the experience of the ages showed that like produced like. Only by overthrowing "the inductive principles of Bacon and Newton" could a false science maintain the transformation of species.[111] Evolution, he asserted, proposed a universe that was "nothing but a Proteus without reason or intelligence."[112] The theory, in Birks's mind, was simply an upstart rival to the Christian doctrine of creation.[113] The Wesleyan theologian W. B. Pope, though conceding (unlike Birks) that others might assume that the Creator used the method of evolution, argued strongly against that supposition. "No theory of evolution or development," he wrote, "that seems to trace a regular succession of forms through which organic existence has passed, in obedience to a plastic law originally impressed upon matter, can be made consistent with Scripture."[114] Still, in the early 1880s at the Baptist college founded by C. H. Spurgeon, the tutor in philosophy maintained a "protest against being considered a blood relation of the ape or the oyster."[115] There were circles where Darwinian evolution appeared unscientific, antiscriptural, and nonsensical.

Accommodation with Evolution

Yet during the last third of the nineteenth century it was more common to try to reach an accommodation with the new approach to science. Here natural theology came into its own, providing the intellectual framework within which the absorption of the Darwinian style of thinking could take place. Those who had been trained before the appearance of *The Origin of Species* did not abandon their belief in design but enlarged it to take account of the fresh evidence. Thus Robert Rainy, when delivering in 1874 his inaugural address as principal of New College, Edinburgh, contended that the conditions of the argument for the existence of God had not been altered by evolution. Each "stream of processes" revealed by the scientist had distinct value for the natural theologian.[116] Rainy's colleague John Duns, the professor of natural science at New College, still asserted "the doctrine of final causes" even though he believed there must be a "frank acceptance of the law of development from lower to higher." The argument from design, he contended, must go beyond special adaptations of particular organisms in the manner of Paley to correspondences of whole systems such as the bones in the skulls of carnivores.[117] The younger Free Churchman James Orr similarly held that when evolution was granted, the argument from design stood, but with its sphere extended.[118] There was disagreement about whether natural selection had to be rejected in the name of design. John Laidlaw, like Duns, believed that it did;[119] James Iverach, like Orr, thought that it did not. "Supposing natural selection true," wrote Iverach, "what is it but another way of indicating design."[120] So long as there were a directing power, purpose could be discerned in the process. Nor was this position restricted to Presbyterians with their Reformed heritage. The Wesleyan W. H. Dallinger, accepting "the Darwinian law of evolution," saw it as only a method of universal design.[121] The General Baptist John Clifford declared that evolution, if proved to be true, would not lessen the force of the witness to design of the physical nature of man.[122] Far from dying out in the 1860s and 1870s, natural theology discovered a new role. It became a means by which evangelicals adjusted their faith to post-Darwinian science.

For those who wished to reach an accommodation with developmental thinking there were three potential sticking points. One such point was before surrendering the idea of creation as something separate from evolution. Sir George Stokes, the Lucasian professor of mathematics at Cambridge and the leading evangelical Anglican scientific thinker of the late nineteenth century, wanted to continue to distinguish exertions of creative power from the continuity of the evolutionary process.[123] Others, however, encouraged by the willingness of biblical scholars to treat Genesis metaphorically, agreed with Orr that the terms "evolution" and "special creation" could in some sense be synthesized. Certainly there was no contradiction between them.[124] A second sticking point was at the transition from the inorganic to the organic. Duns denounced the Lamarckian idea of latent vitality in matter because he was sure it would lead to materialism.[125] The danger of a materialistic philosophy was already patent in the thought of Spencer and in the exotic monism of the German Ernst Haeckel, whose system, as Orr pointed out, spelled the death of God, freedom, and immortality.[126] Against them it was possible to recruit the authority of the militant agnostic scientist T. H. Huxley, who could see no link between the living and the not living.[127] Yet even on this issue there were those such as Rainy who claimed that if life were shown to derive from matter, the foundations of natural theology would remain undisturbed.[128] For a large number, among whom Orr was the most prominent, the greatest sticking point was the connection of humanity with the rest of the evolutionary series. Orr perceived in the assimilation of human beings to the animal world a threat to their rationality, moral freedom, and religious capacity, and beyond that to the recognition of their sinfulness and ultimately to the need for atonement.[129] Yet many others—including Rainy, Dallinger, and Clifford—saw no problem in accepting the physical continuity of the human race with the animal kingdom because a spiritual discontinuity could still be postulated.[130] At each point there were some who were willing to take the radical course. There was great diversity in the evangelical responses to the Darwinian revolution, but perhaps what is most remarkable is the degree of novelty so many were willing to adopt.[131]

While their attitude to science was being transformed, the evangelicals' natural theology, though remaining in place, was inevitably modified. Since evolution entailed an immense extension of the reign of law, there was a move toward a broader style of teleological reasoning. The emphasis in the design argument shifted from special adaptation to cosmic order. "Teleology," wrote W. H. Dallinger, "does not now depend for its existence on Paleyan 'instances'; but all the universe, its whole progress in time and space, is one majestic evidence of teleology."[132] The older form of the case had argued *from* design, from the premise of adaptation to an intelligent Creator. The theistic conclusion, however, was no longer necessary when natural selection constituted an alternative and perhaps more plausible interpretation of the evidence for adaptation. Hence the revised form of the case had to argue *for* design, from the premise of order to the existence of a plan.[133] It was no longer an argument in favor of theism but merely an argument for the compatibility of the evidence with theism. It made no presence to have demonstrated the being of God. In his Gifford Lectures for 1893 at Edinburgh, Sir George Stokes delivered an elaborate account of design in the human eye. Although he himself attributed its intricate structure to a directing power, he admitted that it was possible to explain the eye in terms of natural selection. The evidence, he conceded, in no sense compelled a verdict in favor of divine superintendence.[134] Christians could now merely choose to believe what they could not prove. Since design had become a far less powerful weapon, they were thrown onto the defensive. The evidence of natural phenomena now had to be interpreted sympathetically if it was to match theological claims. Before Darwin, science had been an asset. After him, and throughout the twentieth century, there was a constant struggle to avoid its becoming a liability.

Nor could evangelical theology itself escape the encounter with scientific evolution unaffected. Anglicans of the High and Broad Church schools already gave priority to the doctrine of the incarnation, and from *Lux Mundi* (1889) onward High Churchmen normally stressed the immanence of God. The two themes became the hallmarks of Anglican thought down to World War II.[135] Both were deployed to incorporate an evolutionary perspective into theology. Orr was unusual in the evangelical community in emphasising incarnationalism,[136] but it was immanence that he, like many others, related directly to evolution. "Assume God," he wrote, ". . . to be immanent in the evolutionary process. . . . The real impelling force of evolution is now from *within*. . . ."[137] The most celebrated figure to take this course was the evangelist Henry Drummond, the author of the immensely popular *Natural Law in the Spiritual World* (1883), whose chief debt was to Herbert Spencer.[138] By 1894 he saw no need to reconcile Christianity and evolution because, as he ingenuously put it, "the two are one."[139] Another very liberal thinker, the Congregationalist W. F. Adeney, was delighted that religion had turned to immanentism. "The great Gardener," he wrote, "is always moving about among His plants, fostering and feeding them." Perhaps, he added, Origen had been right that the eternal God was eternally creating.[140] Although the celebration of immanence as the true meaning of evolution is found in theologians less given to speculation such as the Free Church of Scotland's James Iverach and A. B. Bruce,[141] there is no doubt that this theme pointed in a liberal direction. Vernon Storr, who was to be the inspiration of the liberal evangelical movement in the interwar Church of England, restated natural theology in 1906 in terms of immanence.[142] The same idea was to be the burden of *Evolution and the Christian Concept of God* (1936) by Charles Raven, Regius Professor of Divinity at Cambridge and another leading liberal evangelical.[143] Because immanence was not a traditional theme among evangelicals, and because it was harder to relate the doctrine to their central preoccupation with the atonement than to other Anglicans' emphasis on the incarnation, its unaccustomed prominence changed the balance of their thinking. For good or ill, evolution had the effect of broadening the evangelical mind.

The conclusion must be that on the whole evangelicalism in Britain was not hostile to science. Although there were some reservations about the value of natural philosophy, especially in the eighteenth century, the movement's adherents were not generally the foes of learning, research, and the intellect; and, even if they ranked these matters below conversion, revelation, and the spirit, they normally regarded scientific investigation in particular as bound up with the knowledge of God through natural theology. The worldview of the Enlightenment, fully shared by most of them, encouraged reverence for Newtonianism, induction, and the argument for God from design in nature. They created a distinctive version of physico-theology that, like the Atonement itself, took account of the pain and suffering of the world. Their presentation of the design argument, particularly as expounded by Chalmers, was the substance of the revitalization of Natural theology around the 1830s.[144] Endorsement by evangelicals gave the British tradition of argument from design a new lease on life in a period when their assumptions tinctured the whole intellectual atmosphere. The style of reasoning proved flexible, accommodating the problems of space and time on the borders of science and religion, and, even when challenged by developmental thinking, enabled many evangelicals to come to terms with Darwinism. If their theology altered in the process, finding a larger place for immanence, so did their attitude toward natural phenomena. The world examined by scientists, though compatible with theistic belief, no longer appeared to demonstrate the divine. Science itself turned into a potential threat, and evangelicals in the twentieth century were often to be wary of it. Before then, however, the progress of discovery was usually hailed as an ally. In the era between Wesley and Orr science was a handmaid of evangelical theology.

NOTES

1. Walter F. Cannon, "Scientists and Broad Churchmen: An Early Victorian Intellectual Network," *Journal of British Studies*, 4, 1964, pp. 65–88. Jack Morrell and Arnold Thackray, *Gentlemen of Science: Early Years of the British Association for the Advancement of Science* (Oxford: Clarendon Press, 1981), pp. 224–45.

2. John Gascoigne, *Cambridge in the Age of the Enlightenment: Science, Religion and Politics from the Restoration to the French Revolution* (Cambridge: Cambridge University Press, 1989), p. 262. Similarly, the invaluable recent biography of Michael Faraday comments that natural theology was attacked by evangelicals alongside Tractarians and Scriptural Geologists. Geoffrey Cantor, *Michael Faraday: Sandemanian and Scientist* (London: Macmillan, 1991), p. 137.

3. Adrian Desmond, *The Politics of Evolution: Morphology, Medicine and Reform in Radical London* (Chicago: University of Chicago Press, 1989), p. 64.

4. [Thomas Haweis], *Essays on the Evidence, Characteristic Doctrines, and Influence of Christianity* (Bath: S. Hazard, 1790), pp. iv, v. quoted by Arthur Skevington Wood, *Thomas Haweis, 1734–1820* (London: Society for Promoting Christian Knowledge, 1957), p. 176.

5. John Newton, "A Plan of a Compendious Christian Library," in *The Works of the Rev. John Newton*, 6 vols. (London: for the author's nephew, 1808), 1, p. 215. Cf. Doreen Rosman, *Evangelicals and Culture* (London: Croom Helm, 1984), p. 228.

6. John Foster, "Astronomy and Christian Revelation," *Critical Essays Contributed to The Eclectic Review*, ed. J. E. Ryland, 2 vols. (London: George Bell and Sons, 1879–85), 2, p. 367.

7. Thomas Dick, *The Christian Philosopher*, 2 vols. (Glasgow: William Collins, 1846), 1, p. 26.

8. F. S. to editor, *The Christian Observer*, March 1839, p. 154.

9. Newton, "A Plan," p. 215.

10. John B. Sumner, *A Treatise on the Records of the Creation*, 2 vols., 5th ed. (London: T. Hatchard, 1833), 1, p. x.

11. John H. Pratt, ed., *The Thought of the Evangelical Leaders: Notes of the Discussions of The Eclectic Society, London, During the Years 1798–1814* (Edinburgh: Banner of Truth Trust, 1978), p. 496.

12. Thomas Chalmers, *Institutes of Theology*, 2 vols. (Edinburgh: Sutherland and Knox, 1849), 2, p. 135.

13. *Ibid.*, p. 133.

14. William Jay, *Memoirs of the Life and Character of the Late Rev. Cornelius Winter*, 2nd ed. (London: for William Baynes, 1812), p. 31. Gascoigne, *Cambridge*, p. 261.

15. Newton, "A Plan," p. 215.

16. Thomas Robinson, *The Christian System Unfolded in a Course of Practical Essays on the Principal Doctrines and Duties of Christianity*, 3 vols. (London: for the author, 1805), 1, p. 41.

17. John Venn to F. J. H. Wollaston, 15 June 1789, quoted by Michael Hennell, *John Venn and the Clapham Sect* (London: Lutterworth Press, 1958), p. 52.

18. Frederick Nolan, *The Analogy of Revelation and Science* (Oxford, 1833), p. viii. On "scriptural geology," see Milton Millhauser, *Just Before Darwin: Robert Chambers and Vestiges* (Middletown, Conn.: Wesleyan University Press, 1959), pp. 46–57.

19. James Mellor Brown, *Reflections on Geology: Suggested by the Perusal of Dr. Buckland's Bridgewater Treatise* (London: James Nisbet, 1838), p. 52.

20. Geoffrey F. Nuttall, *The Significance of Trevecca College, 1768–91* (London: Epworth Press, 1969).

21. Thomas Scott, *Essays on the Most Important Subjects in Religion* (London: D. Jaques, 1794).

22. John Pye Smith, *On the Relation between the Holy Scriptures and Some Parts of Geological Science* (London: Jackson and Walford, 1839), p. 168.

23. Nicolaas A. Rupke, *The Great Chain of History: William Buckland and the English School of Geology (1814–1849)* (Oxford: Clarendon Press, 1983), p. 14.

24. John H. Pratt, *Scripture and Science Not at Variance*, 3rd ed. (London: Thomas Hatchard, 1859), pp. 25, 108, 87. Both Whewell and Sedgwick had evangelical leanings, but neither was an adherent of the evangelical party. Cf. John H. Brooke, "Indications of a Creator: Whewell as Apologist and Priest," in Menachem Fisch and Simon Schaffer, eds., *William Whewell: A Composite Portrait* (Oxford: Clarendon Press, 1991), pp. 161–162. The remaining distance between Sedgwick and evangelicalism is indicated in *The Christian Observer*, June 1834, p. 371n.

25. *The Christian Observer*, May 1834, pp. 306–9. Cf. Morrell and Thackray, *Gentlemen of Science*, p. 236.

26. *The Christian Observer*, October 1829, pp. 647–48; April 1834, p. 207n; June 1834, pp. 369–85; July 1834, p. 395n; August 1834, p. 482n. Cf. Boyd Hilton, *The Age of Atonement* (Oxford: Clarendon Press, 1988), p. 23.

27. Pye Smith, *On the Relation*, pp. 172–97.

28. Paul Baxter, "Science and Belief in Scotland, 1805–1868: The Scottish Evangelicals," unpublished Edinburgh Ph.D. dissertation, 1985.

29. Rosman, *Evangelicals and Culture*, p. 205.

30. Hennell, *Venn*, p. 42.

31. Robert Hall, *Sermon Occasioned by the Death of the Rev. John Ryland, D. D.* (London, 1825), p. 43, quoted by Herbert MacLachlan, *English Education under the Test Acts: Being the History of the Nonconformist Academies, 1662–1820* (Manchester: Manchester University Press, 1931), p. 97.

32. Edmund Gosse, *Father and Son* (London: William Heinemann, 1907), chap. 5.

33. Roger Anstey, *The Atlantic Slave Trade and British Abolition, 1760–1810* (London: Macmillan, 1975), chaps. 7 and 8. Bernard Semmel, *The Methodist Revolution* (London: Heinemann, 1974). Frederick Dreyer, "Faith and Experience in the Thought of John Wesley," *The American Historical Review*, 88 (1983), pp. 12–30. David W. Bebbington, *Evangelicalism in Modern Britain: A History from the 1730s to the 1980s* (London: Unwin Hyman, 1989), chap. 2. David W. Bebbington, "Revival and Enlightenment in Eighteenth-Century England," in Edith L. Blumhofer and Randall Balmer, eds., *Modern Christian Revivals* (Urbana: University of Illinois Press, 1993), pp. 17–41.

34. Pratt, ed., *Thought of the Evangelical Leaders*, pp. 230–32, 523–24, spec. p. 231.

35. Jay, *Winter*, p. 249.

36. Horace F. Mathews, *Methodism and the Education of the People, 1791–1851* (London: Epworth Press, 1949).

37. Andrew Fuller, "The Gospel Its Own Witness," in Andrew G. Fuller, ed., *The Complete Works of the Rev. Andrew Fuller*, 5 vols. (London: Holdsworth and Ball, 1831), I, p. 121.

38. John Wesley, *A Survey of the Wisdom of God in the Creation*, 2 vols. (Bristol: William Pine, 1763). Cf. John W. Haas, Jr., "Eighteenth Century Evangelical Responses to Science: John Wesley's Enduring Legacy," *Science and Christian Belief*, 6 (1994), pp. 83–102.

39. John Wesley, "The Desideratum: or Electricity Made Plain and Useful," *The Works of the Rev. John Wesley, M. A.*, 32 vols. (Bristol: William Pine, 1773), 24, p. 287.

40. Bebbington, *Evangelicalism*, chap. 3.

41. Edward Irving, "Lectures on the Parable of the Sower," *Sermons, Lectures and Occasional Discourses*, 3 vols. (London: R. B. Seeley and W. Burnside, 1828), 2, p. 709.

42. [Henry Drummond], *Dialogues on Prophecy* (London: James Nisbet, 1827), p. 346.

43. [William Tarbet], *Astronomy and Geology as Taught in the Holy Scriptures* (Liverpool, 1855), p. 17, quoted by Michael J. Crowe, *The Extraterrestrial Life Debate, 1750–1900: The Idea of a Plurality of Worlds from Kant to Lowell* (Cambridge: Cambridge University Press, 1986), p. 338.

44. William J. Irons, *On the Whole Doctrine of Final Causes* (London, 1836). Cf. Pietro Corsi, *Science and Religion: Baden Powell and the Anglican Debate, 1800–1860* (Cambridge: Cambridge University Press, 1988), pp. 179–80.

45. Rupke, *Great Chain of History*, chap. 20.

46. John Wesley, *A Concise Ecclesiastical History from the Birth of Christ to the Beginning of the Present Century* (London: Paramore, 1781), 3, p. 332, quoted by John C. English, "John Wesley and Isaac Newton's 'System of the World,' " *Proceedings of the Wesley Historical Society*, 48 (1991), p. 73.

47. Adam Clarke, "Some Observations on the Being and Providence of a God," *Discourses on Various Subjects Relative to the Being and Attributes of God and His Works in Creation, Providence and Grace*, 3 vols. (London: J. and T. Clarke, 1828–30), 2, pp. 385–86. Richard Watson, *Theological Institutes*, 1, p. 407.

48. Joseph Milner, "A Selection of Tracts and Essays, Theological and Historical," in Isaac Milner, ed., *The Works of Joseph Milner*, 8 vols. (London: for T. Cadell and W.

Davies, 1810), 8, p. 285. Sumner, *Treatise*, 1, p. 325. Thomas R. Birks, *The Bible and Modern Thought* (London: Religious Tract Society, 1862), p. 310.

49. Fuller, "Gospel Its Own Witness," p. 117.

50. Chalmers, *Evidence and Authority*, p. 189. Thomas Chalmers, *A Series of Discourses on the Christian Revelation Viewed in Connection with the Modern Astronomy*, 4th ed. (Glasgow: for John Smith and Son, 1817), pp. 56–93.

51. Sir David Brewster, *The Life of Sir Isaac Newton* (London: John Murray, 1831); *Memoirs of the Life, Writings and Discoveries of Sir Isaac Newton* (Edinburgh: T. Constable and Co., 1855).

52. *The Christian Observer*, June 1828, p. 367.

53. The best exposition is G. N. Cantor, "Revelation and the Cyclical Cosmos of John Hutchinson," in L. J. Jordanova and Roy S. Porter, eds., *Images of the Earth: Essays in the History of the Environmental Sciences* (Chalfont St. Giles, Bucks: British Society for the History of Science, 1979), pp. 3–22.

54. William B. Cadogan, "The Life of the Rev. William Romaine, M.A.," in *Works of the Late Reverend William Romaine, A.M.*, 8 vols. (London: for T. Chapman, 1796), 7, p. 34.

55. *The Christian Observer*, October 1828, pp. 631–32.

56. Wood, *Haweis*, pp. 46–47.

57. English, "John Wesley and Isaac Newton's 'System,' " pp. 84–85.

58. Chalmers, *Evidence and Authority*, p. 191.

59. John Wesley, "Primitive Physic," *Works*, 25, p. 8.

60. Baxter, "Science and Belief," p. 117.

61. Pye Smith, *On the Relation*, p. 21.

62. Alan P. F. Sell, "Henry Rogers and the Eclipse of Faith," *Dissenting Thought and the Life of the Churches: Studies in an English Tradition* (San Francisco: Mellen Research University Press, 1990), pp. 492–93.

63. E.g., Edward William, *An Essay on the Equity of Divine Government and the Sovereignty of Divine Grace*, 3rd ed. (London: for Francis Westley, 1825), p. xlviii.

64. Chalmers, *Evidence and Authority*, p. 204.

65. Thomas Gisborne, *The Testimony of Natural Theology to Christianity* (London: for T. Cadell and W. Davies, 1818), p. 1.

66. Clarke, *Discourses*, 1, p. 6; 2, pp. 375–79.

67. *The Methodist Magazine*, February 1804, pp. 78–81; March 1804, pp. 127–28; April 1804, pp. 168–71; May 1804, pp. 217–20; June 1804, pp. 265–68.

68. Watson, *Theological Institutes*, 1, p. 445n. Pye Smith, *On the Relation*, p. 27. James McCosh, *The Method of the Divine Government Physical and Moral*, 11th ed. (London: Macmillan and Co., 1878), p. 3.

69. *The Methodist Magazine*, April 1804, p. 167n.

70. Sumner, *Treatise*, 1, p. 30n. Watson, *Theological Institutes*, 2, pp. 8–10, 51–55, 122–27. William Cunningham, *Theological Lectures on Subjects Connected with Natural Theology, Evidences of Christianity, the Canon and Inspiration of Scripture* (London: James Nisbet and Co., 1878), p. 107.

71. Elizabeth A. Varley, *The Last of the Prince Bishops: William Van Mildert and the High Church Movement of the Early Nineteenth Century* (Cambridge: Cambridge University Press, 1992), pp. 39–45.

72. John H. Brooke, "The Natural Theology of the Geologists: Some Theological Strata," in Jordanova and Porter, eds., *Theories of the Earth*, esp. p. 40. Brooke, "Indications of a Creator," esp. pp. 149–51.

73. John Fleming, *The Institutes of Natural Science* (Edinburgh: for the author, [1846]).

74. *The Christian Observer*, March 1803, p. 162. Wilberforce is known to have held the estimate of Paley contained in this review: Rosman, *Evangelicals and Culture*, p. 44.

75. Pye Smith, *On the Relation*, p. 327.

76. E.g., the Methodist Richard Watson cited writers from the Reformed tradition such as Thomas Gisborne: *Theological Institutes*, 2, pp. 134–43.

77. Gisborne, *Testimony of Natural Theology*, p. 2.

78. Clarke, *Discourses*, 1, pp. 129–30.

79. Chalmers, *Institutes*, 1, p. 91.

80. Sumner, *Treatise*, 1, p. 29. Watson, *Theological Institutes*, 2, p. 109. Fleming, *Institutes*, p. 6.

81. Pye Smith, *On the Relation*, pp. 25–26. Clarke, *Discourses*, 2, pp. 384–87. Sumner, *Treatise*, 2, p. 8. Watson, *Theological Institutes*, 2, p. 111.

82. E.g., Sumner, *Treatise*, 1, pp. 300–316. Watson, *Theological Institutes*, 1, pp. 418–24.

83. Rosman, *Evangelicals and Culture*, pp. 44–47. Hilton, *Age of Atonement*, pp. 21–22. Daniel F. Rice, "Natural Theology and Scottish Philosophy in the Thought of Thomas Chalmers," *The Scottish Journal of Theology*, 24 (1971), pp. 36–37.

84. *The Christian Observer*, June 1803, pp. 371–73, esp. p. 373.

85. Watson, *Theological Institutes*, 2, p. 133.

86. *The Methodist Magazine*, April 1826, pp. 240–44.

87. Gisborne, *Testimony of Natural Theology*, esp. pp. 29, 69.

88. Chalmers, *Theological Institutes*, 1, p. 110.

89. Cunningham, *Theological Lectures*, p. 120. Brooke, "Indications of a Creator," p. 154.

90. Thomas Paine, "The Age of Reason: Part First," in Bruce Kuklick, ed., *Thomas Paine: Political Writings* (Cambridge: Cambridge University Press, 1989), p. 243.

91. Fuller, "Gospel Its Own Witness," pp. 119, 118.

92. Chalmers, *Modern Astronomy*, p. 41.

93. Foster, "Astronomy and Christian Revelation," esp. pp. 359–60. *The Christian Observer*, July 1834, pp. 1834, pp. 388–95. Dick, *Christian Philosopher*, 1, p. 100.

94. John H. Brooke, "Natural Theology and the Plurality of Worlds: Observations on the Brewster-Whewell Debate," *Annuals of Science*, 34 (1977), pp. 222–84.

95. Crowe, *Extraterrestrial Life Debate*, pp. 338, 352.

96. *The Christian Observer*, July 1834, p. 390.

97. Pye Smith, *On the Relation*, pp. 294–98. Pratt, *Scripture and Science*, pp. 41–43.

98. Pye Smith, p. 113n (quoting Fleming). Pratt, *Scripture and Science*, pp. 45–46.

99. Baxter, "Science and Belief in Scotland," pp. 71–72.

100. Pratt, *Scripture and Science*, pp. 63–65.

101. Hugh Miller, *The Two Records: Mosaic and Geological* (n.p., 1854), pp. 17–33. Cf. Hugh Miller, *The Testimony of the Rocks* (Edinburgh, 1857).

102. James Orr, "Science and Christian Faith," in *The Fundamentals*, 12 vols. (Chicago: Testimony Publishing Co., [1910–15]), 4, p. 101.

103. Desmond, *Politics of Evolution*.

104. Hilton, *Age of Atonement*, pp. 309–11.

105. Pye Smith, *On the Relation*, pp. 281–82.

106. Paul Baxter, "Deism and Development: Disruptive Forces in Scottish Natural Theology," in Stewart J. Brown and Michael Fry, eds., *Scotland in the Age of Disruption* (Edinburgh: Edinburgh University Press, 1993), pp. 106–8.

107. Hugh Miller, *Foot-prints of the Creator* (London, 1847), p. 13.

108. *The Christian Observer*, August 1860, pp. 561, 562–63, 565, 570.

109. *The Eclectic Review,* March 1860, pp. 234, 230.

110. Thomas R. Birks, *Modern Physical Fatalism and the Doctrine of Evolution* (London: Macmillan and Co., 1876).

111. Thomas R. Birks, *Supernatural Revelation: or First Principles of Moral Theology* (London: Macmillan and Co., 1879), p. vi.

112. *Ibid.,* p. 136.

113. Thomas R. Birks, *The Scripture Doctrine of Creation* (London: Society for Promoting Christian Knowledge, 1872), chap. 11.

114. William B. Pope, *A Compendium of Christian Theology,* 2nd ed., 3 vols. (London: for the author at the Wesleyan Methodist Book Room, 1880), I, p. 398. David Livingstone has stressed Pope's concession whereas John Kent treats his views as the epitome of conservatism on the issue. David N. Livingstone, *Darwin's Forgotten Defenders: The Encounter between Evangelical Theology and Evolutionary Thought* (Grand Rapids, Michigan: William B. Eerdmans, 1987), pp. 135–36; John Kent, *From Darwin to Blatchford: The Role of Darwinism in Christian Apologetic, 1875–1910* (London: Dr. Williams's Trust, 1966), pp. 11–14.

115. *Annual Paper Concerning the Lord's Work in Connection with the Pastors' College, Newington, London, 1881–82* (London: Alabaster, Passmore, and Sons, 1882), p. 17. Some other persistent opponents of evolution are noted by Livingstone, *Darwin's Forgotten Defenders,* pp. 131–32, and by James R. Moore, *The Post-Darwinian Controversies: A Study of the Protestant Struggle to Come to Terms with Darwin in Great Britain and America, 1870–1900* (Cambridge: Cambridge University Press, 1979), chap. 9.

116. Robert Rainy, *Evolution and Theology: Inaugural Address* (Edinburgh: Maclaren and Macniven, 1874), pp. 9, 14.

117. John Duns, *Science and Christian Thought* (London: Religious Tract Society, [1866]), pp. 22, 122, 59–60.

118. James Orr, *The Christian View of God and the World as Centring in the Incarnation,* 2nd ed. (Edinburgh: Andrew Elliot, 1893), p. 119.

119. John Duns, *On the Theory of Natural Selection and the Theory of Design,* Part II, paper for Victoria Institute, [1887], author's copy, New College, Edinburgh, p. 1. John Laidlaw, *The Bible Doctrine of Man* (Edinburgh: T. & T. Clark, 1879), p. 39.

120. Orr, *Christian View,* p. 120. James Iverach, *Christianity and Evolution,* 3rd ed. (London: Hodder and Stoughton, 1900), p. 79.

121. William H. Dallinger, *The Creator and What We May Know of the Method of Creation* (London: T. Woolmer, 1887), pp. 66, 61.

122. John Clifford, "Charles Darwin or Evolution and Christianity," *Typical Christian Leaders* (London: Horace Marshall and Son, 1898), p. 233.

123. Sir George G. Stokes, *Natural Theology: The Gifford Lectures Delivered before the University of Edinburgh in 1893* (London: Adam and Charles Black, 1893), p. 150.

124. James Orr, *God's Image in Man and Its Defacement in the Light of Modern Denials* (London: Hodder and Stoughton, 1905), p. 87. For exegetical developments, see Richard A. Riesen, *Criticism and Faith in Late Victorian Scotland: A. B. Davidson, William Robertson Smith and George Adam Smith* (Lanham, Maryland: University Press of America, 1985), pp. 383–88.

125. Duns, *Science and Christian Thought,* chap. 5.

126. Orr, *God's Image,* p. 5. On Haeckel, see Paul Weindling, "Ernst Haeckel, Darwinismus and the Secularisation of Nature," in James R. Moore, ed., *History, Humanity and Evolution: Essays for John C. Greene* (Cambridge: Cambridge University Press, 1989), pp. 311–27.

127. Dallinger, *The Creator,* p. 32.

128. Rainy, *Evolution and Theology*, p. 9.

129. Orr, *God's Image*, pp. 146–50, 10. James Orr, *Sin as a Problem of To-day* (London: Hodder and Stoughton, 1910). Cf. Glen G. Scorgie, *A Call for Continuity: The Theological Contribution of James Orr* (Macon, Georgia: Mercer University Press, 1988), chap. 6.

130. Rainy, *Evolution and Theology*, p. 15. Dallinger, *The Creator*, pp. 79–81. Clifford, "Charles Darwin," p. 234.

131. Moore, *Post-Darwinian Controversies*, part 3. Livingstone, *Darwin's Forgotten Defenders*, chap. 4.

132. Dallinger, *The Creator*, p. 74.

133. This analysis is indebted to L. E. Hicks, *A Critique of Design-Arguments* (New York: Charles Scribner's Sons, 1883), esp. p. 27.

134. Stokes, *Natural Theology*, pp. 62–108, 138–39, esp. p. 139. On Stokes's "directionism," see David B. Wilson, "A Physicist's Alternative to Materialism: The Religious Thought of George Gabriel Stokes," *Victorian Studies*, 28 (1984), pp. 69–96. Cf. Peter J. Bowler, *The Eclipse of Darwinism: Anti-Darwinian Evolution Theories in the Decades around 1900* (Baltimore: Johns Hopkins University Press, 1983), p. 45.

135. Arthur Michael Ramsey, *From Gore to Temple: The Development of Anglican Theology between "Lux Mundi" and the Second World War, 1889–1939* (London: Longmans, 1960).

136. Scorgie, *Call for Continuity*, pp. 50–51.

137. Orr, *God's Image*, p. 96.

138. James R. Moore, "Evangelicals and Evolution: Henry Drummond, Herbert Spencer and the Naturalisation of the Spiritual World," *The Scottish Journal of Theology*, 38 (1985), pp. 395–99.

139. Henry Drummond, *The Lowell Lectures on the Ascent of Man* (London: Hodder and Stoughton, 1894), p. 438.

140. W. F. Adeney, *A Century's Progress in Religious Life and Thought* (London: James Clarke and Co., 1901), pp. 102–3.

141. Iverach, *Christianity and Evolution*, p. 206. Alexander B. Bruce, *The Providential Order of the World* (London: Hodder and Stoughton, 1897), p. 57.

142. Vernon F. Storr, *Development and Divine Purpose* (London: Methuen and Co., 1906), esp. pp. 132–34.

143. Charles E. Raven, *Evolution and the Christian Concept of God* (London: Oxford University Press, 1936).

144. John Gascoigne, "From Bentley to the Victorians: The Rise and Fall of British Newtonian Natural Theology," *Science in Context*, 2 (1988), pp. 240–41. Gascoigne, however, does not recognize the evangelical dimension of the revitalization (p. 249).

6

Science, Natural Theology, and Evangelicalism in Early Nineteenth-Century Scotland

Thomas Chalmers and the Evidence Controversy

JONATHAN R. TOPHAM

It has often been noted that evangelical attitudes were of enormous importance in shaping British culture in the early nineteenth century, having considerable impact on everything from politics and business to literature and art.[1] Yet surprisingly little has been written concerning the relevance of evangelicalism to science in that period. The fact that there were exceedingly few evangelicals among the gentlemanly elite of science (a phenomenon itself clearly deserving of attention) by no means excuses this omission. One of the most important aspects of the creation of modern, specialist science in Britain in the course of the nineteenth century was that it involved the development of a community that claimed a unique right to pronounce authoritatively about nature.[2] To ignore the wider public from whom such authority was won, or at least that large proportion who were to varying degrees touched by evangelical religion, is thus to ignore a central component in the development of modern science. It is not enough for historians of early nineteenth-century science merely to refer, in passing, to evangelical opponents of the scientific elite, such as the Scriptural Geologists of the 1820s and 1830s.[3] We need also to begin to chart out the views of nature held by evangelicals more generally in that period, and to examine the extent to which such views were also shared by some who were not evangelicals. Clearly such a task is both vast and daunting, and this chapter makes no pretence to address it in anything other than a limited way. My objective here is to identify the historiographical issues that are raised by such an undertaking, before turning to a case study that illustrates some of those issues.

One reason why evangelical attitudes toward nature have received so little attention has been the tendency to assume that evangelicals could not have been greatly involved in the project of natural theology, on the grounds that its rational approach would be alien to those who cleaved to a religion of the heart. Such a view rests, first, on a stereotyped view of evangelicals as being necessarily and uniformly antagonistic to the Enlightenment emphasis on reason. However, this supposition has received considerable criticism over recent years, and it has been persuasively argued that, on the contrary, the theology of many British evangelicals—particularly those within the established churches—rested to a large extent on Enlightenment assumptions. It is argued that evangelicals often laid considerable emphasis on the value in religious belief of reason, as opposed both to mystery and emotion, and of experience, as opposed both to ecclesiastical authority and "speculative" theology.[4] The supposition that evangelicals were uninterested in natural theology rests secondly on a stereotyped conception of nineteenth-century natural theology, in which the confident rationalism of William Paley's *Natural Theology* (1802) is seen as representative of most subsequent expositions of the subject.[5] However, it has now been repeatedly demonstrated that, far from being uniformly Paleyan, natural theology in the early nineteenth century was extremely diverse.[6] In particular, it is clear that there were a number of evangelical scientists who warmly embraced distinctively evangelical forms of natural theology, most notably the Scottish Presbyterians Thomas Chalmers and David Brewster.[7]

As yet, however, such studies of evangelical natural theology are few, and little has been done to map out more generally the sometimes widely diverging views of evangelicals in both established and dissenting congregations. One notable exception is Boyd Hilton's recent book *The Age of Atonement*, in which he argues that, rather than rejecting the program of natural theology, those whom he designates "moderate evangelicals" merely sought to redefine its scope and nature to meet their particular concerns. The fundamental shift was, he argues, from "*evidences* to *paradoxes*, that is, from examples of benign contrivance in the natural world to demonstrations of how superficial misery may work inner improvement."[8] Where Paley's optimistic natural theology rested on a conviction that nature attested to the existence of a benevolent creator, Hilton's "moderate evangelicals," imbued with a lapsarian and postrevolutionary pessimism, argued that nature evinced a righteous judge, stern in disciplining his wayward creatures.

Groundbreaking as it is, Hilton's account clearly has limitations. One of the least satisfactory features of his analysis is his division of evangelicals into "moderates" and "extremists"—the former encompassing "the respectable Clapham Sect and its followers," and the latter encompassing "the pentecostal, premillenarian, adventist, and revivalist elements."[9] Like most dichotomies, this categorization begins to break down as soon as it is examined in any detail, and one is forced instead to recognize the complexities of the divergences within evangelicalism. In part Hilton's simplification merely reflects the limits that he deliberately sets to his study. As he makes clear, he is concerned primarily with "the mind of the middle and upper classes," and his main emphasis is on "the established clergy, Anglicans and Scottish Presbyterians."[10] As a result, he generally excludes from consideration the dissenting clergy, most evangelical laity, and others outside the middle and upperclasses who were to some degree influenced by evangelicalism. Clearly, then, a more general survey of the attitudes of evangelicals to nature and science is still needed.

I have argued elsewhere that there existed within evangelicalism a debate about natural theology that ran across denominational lines.[11] However, rather than seeking merely to codify the different factions, it is helpful to examine the debate itself, and to see the divergent positions as part of an ongoing dialectic. The task is complicated by the evangelicals' fervent interest in conversion,[12] which makes the question of strategy particularly critical. In a religious culture dominated by the Pauline ideal of being "all things to all men" for the sake of the gospel (1 Cor. 9:22), the arguments endorsed by evangelicals had a pragmatic orientation and depended heavily on the context in which they were being deployed. This often makes the exact beliefs lying behind the statements of evangelicals difficult to determine, and it is only by examining the context in which such statements are made that the underlying issues begin to emerge. For example, many evangelicals who considered natural theology to be either positively harmful or of limited value in the context of religious apologetics could still enthuse about works of natural theology in a devotional context. Evangelicals might disagree on the question of whether the sinful human mind could grasp anything of God's nature in isolation from revelation, while at the same time agreeing entirely about the *devotional* value of works intended to evince the power, goodness, and wisdom of God from the created order.

The variety of strategic functions that works of natural theology might fulfil highlights a further issue that has been largely neglected in scholarship concerning evangelicalism and science. The historical literature relating to the attitudes of religious believers toward science in early nineteenth-century Britain has generally focused on beliefs about natural theology, frequently with the corollary, noted above, that since natural theology could not have appealed to evangelicals, they could have had little positive to say on the subject of science. While, as we have seen, the supposition of a general antipathy among evangelicals toward natural theology is based on inadequate views of both evangelical religion and natural theology, a more fundamental concern must relate to the assumption that the interest of religious people in science and nature in this period was structured primarily by a discourse of natural theology. For, as the foregoing discussion implies, many evangelicals rejected natural theology as a legitimate theological enterprise, but nonetheless welcomed discourse about nature that related the natural world to the divine dispensation—that is, what is more properly called a theology of nature.

Although this distinction between natural theology and theology of nature was elucidated by John Brooke more than twenty years ago,[13] it is still frequently ignored by historians, and evidently requires further emphasis. Strictly speaking, a "natural" theology is one based on the exercise of "natural" reason alone, without reference to revelation. By contrast, "theology of nature" denotes a body of theological beliefs about the meaning of the natural world and God's relationship to it that might equally be based on natural reason, on revelation, or on any combination of the two. It may be objected that the latter is not a term that had currency in the early nineteenth century, and it is certainly the case that commentators in the period did not always make such a distinction, let alone in as many words. Indeed, as we shall see, they sometimes deliberately sought to blur the issue, in order to avoid making explicit claims about what may be known by natural reason alone.[14] Yet the distinction surfaced frequently in most of the evangelical debates about natural theology and was evidently one about which evangelicals in particular were intensely concerned.[15] In the light of this, the tendency of historians to infer from references to design a commitment on the part of the author to the project of natural theology clearly has to be countered before evangelical attitudes toward nature can be properly understood. It is only by giving due consideration to the exact nature of the claims being made, and their strategic importance with respect to the particular audience being addressed, that the parameters of the debate can be identified.

My object in this chapter is to illustrate these general historiographical points by the example of one of the most prominent evangelical advocates for science in early nineteenth-century Britain, the Scottish theologian and churchman Thomas Chalmers. Chalmers has long been invoked as the outstanding exponent of a distinctively evangelical natural theology in the period, and with good cause, since few evangelicals have ever written so much or so systematically on the subject. Moreover, his analysis was of the first importance in the later formulation of evangelical views on natural theology, especially in Scotland, where his reputation and influence were immense. Yet in his earliest theological publication, an article entitled "Christianity" published in 1813 in the *Edinburgh Encyclopedia* (1808–30), Chalmers gave a strikingly less positive account of natural theology. In his mature work, Chalmers argued that natural theology (particularly the argument from the felt supremacy of conscience) should play an important, if circumscribed, role in the evangelistic enterprise. However, in his earliest publication on the subject, he repudiated natural theology as speculative and unscientific, arguing that it was completely useless to convert the infidel and that, insofar as it encouraged skeptics to bring the truths of revelation to the bar of their own speculations, it was a positive hindrance to the evangelist. Not, however, that Chalmers believed scientific reason to be inapplicable to the subject of religion. Indeed, it was on avowedly Baconian grounds that Chalmers repudiated natural theology. In its place, he advocated as a corrective to skepticism the scientific study of the historical evidence of Christianity, conducted according to Baconian principles.

Chalmers's changing views on natural theology highlight a number of important themes. Firstly, his early position nicely demonstrates that the tendency of historians of science to equate rational religion with natural theology is by no means reliable. Chalmers's account of Christianity was based explicitly on scientific reasoning, and yet his repudiation of natural theology was remarkable for its force. Secondly, Chalmers's science of revelation, presented as it was in company with an attack on natural theology as unscientific speculation, illustrates that the combination of religious belief with an interest in science, or in the scientific method, did not necessarily involve a commitment to the project of natural theology.[16] Finally, his remarkable change of view illustrates that the debate about natural theology within evangelicalism was not static. As David Bebbington has shown in his contribution to this volume, views on this subject changed as evangelical religion itself changed. However, there has, as yet, been very little work devoted to analyzing the diversity of evangelical positions as part of an ongoing and changing debate. Chalmers's change of view provides an opportunity to begin to sketch out this debate.

In what follows, I begin by briefly outlining the continuing debate about natural theology within the Church of Scotland during the early nineteenth century, particularly in regard to the conflict between the two main church parties—the Evangelicals and the Moderates[17]—and more especially as illustrated by the Leslie affair of 1805. I then describe the early development of Chalmers's views against this background, before examining the argument of Chalmers's article on Christianity in some detail. Next I consider the reactions to Chalmers's article of the two parties in the Scottish church, and of the Evangelical party in the English Church, noting that the Evangelical debate in the two countries was distinctly different. Finally, I make some preliminary observations on the development of Chalmers's mature view of natural theology, briefly illustrating how that view developed out of the concerns of the Evangelical party during the controversy surrounding his article.

Natural Theology and the Leslie Affair

Born in 1780, the son of a strict and devout Calvinist father, Thomas Chalmers came of age in a Church of Scotland marked by increasing evangelical activity and organization.[18] In addition to homegrown revivalism, contact between the Scottish Evangelicals and the Evangelical party in the Church of England (particularly with the "Clapham Sect") provided inspiration and practical assistance in the organization of evangelistic enterprises. Moreover, with a new party machinery, the Scottish Evangelicals also began, around the turn of the century, to mount a serious challenge to the 50-year-old domination of the General Assembly by a rationalist and anti-Calvinist Moderate party.

The changing balance of power was signaled particularly clearly by the celebrated Leslie affair of 1805, when the Evangelicals inflicted on the Moderates their first defeat in the General Assembly for 50 years. In a contested election for the chair of mathematics at Edinburgh University, the Moderates had attempted to secure the post for one of their own party, by impugning the religious orthodoxy of the successful candidate, John Leslie.[19] In evidence, they cited Leslie's *Experimental Enquiry into the Nature and Propagation of Heat* (1804), in which he had endorsed David Hume's doctrine of causation. Critically, Hume's denial of any necessary connection between cause and effect undermined the logical basis of the argument from design. The question at issue was whether Leslie had thus put himself outside the terms of the Westminster Confession of Faith, to which all university professors in Scotland were formally obliged to subscribe.

The Westminster Confession left the status of natural theology somewhat open to dispute, asserting that "Although the light of nature, and the works of creation and providence, do so far manifest the goodness, wisdom, and power of God, as to leave men inexcusable; yet they are not sufficient to give that knowledge of God, and of his will, which is necessary unto salvation: therefore it pleased the Lord, at sundry times, and in divers manners, to reveal himself, and to declare that his will unto his Church."[20] The Moderates argued that natural theology—particularly the argument from design—was fundamental to the entire enterprise of Christian theology. Once accept Hume's doctrine of causation, they claimed, and the entire Christian superstructure would tumble to the ground. By contrast, leading Evangelicals rapidly came to the fore, both in the General Assembly and in the pamphlet war spawned by the controversy, in defence of the proposition that natural theology was not the only foundation on which Christian faith might be established. William Laurence Brown, principal of Marischal College, Aberdeen, told the General Assembly that if Leslie thought the argument a posteriori to be inconclusive, he might still ground his belief in God on the argument a priori, the argument from the universal consent of mankind, or the argument from conscience. If that were the case, Brown asked, was Leslie to be "accounted an atheist, because he is persuaded of this great truth on fewer grounds than those on which we maintain it?"[21] The young Andrew Mitchell Thomson, later leader of the Evangelical party, went further. Leslie could, he asserted, "discard all the ordinary foundations of natural religion, and assert, at the same time, his claim to the character of a sound theist."[22]

Ian Clark has argued persuasively that one outcome of the Leslie affair was that "the frontier between Natural Religion and Revelation" in the Kirk shifted, so that a more circumscribed view of the role of natural theology came to supplant the Enlightenment view propounded by the Moderates.[23] In developing this new approach to the subject, he suggests, the Evangelicals of the early nineteenth century were in some sense indebted to David Hume's critique of Enlightenment natural theology in upholding their belief that Christianity was more properly based on "[b]iblical revelation and the conscious subjective experience of God's activity in the world at large and in the souls of individuals" than on "the 'proofs' and 'evidences' of 18th century Moderatism."[24] In responding to Hume, Clark observes, the Moderates had adopted "the famous principles of the 'Scottish Philosophy'—*common sense, the natural convictions of mankind, intuitive belief* etc." He considers, however, that it was their Evangelical opponents who constructed from those principles "an autonomous theology in which things natural and revealed were no longer kept apart or superimposed in unstable layers."[25]

This view of the distinctive character of Scottish natural theology in the early nineteenth century is elaborated in greater detail by Harry Phillips, in a study of the development of demonstrative theism in nineteenth-century Scotland.[26] Pointing out that the Enlightenment tradition of natural theology was never so prevalent in Scotland as in England, Phillips argues that at the same time as Hume's critique caused problems for the English tradition of natural theology, it presented an opportunity in Scotland for the development of a distinctive natural theology based on human nature. The whole thrust of Hume's critique was to establish that all our knowledge, with the sole exception of mathematics, consists of essentially nonrational beliefs. Reason itself, he famously wrote, "is and ought to be the slave of the passions." According to Phillips, this view was more in keeping with the theology of Scottish Confessionalism than were the rational proofs of English natural theology, and he argues that the emergence in nineteenth-century Scotland of a tradition of natural theology based on human nature had its roots in Hume's analysis. Moreover, Phillips, like Clark, identifies Chalmers as one of the central figures in the development of this Scottish tradition of natural theology.

There is certainly evidence to support the suggestion that the revitalized Scottish Evangelical party that earned its spurs in the Leslie affair developed distinctive and markedly more circumscribed views of natural theology than were to be found among members of the Evangelical party in the Church of England. Only three years before the Leslie controversy, a reviewer (almost certainly Wilberforce[27]) writing in the Anglican Evangelical party journal, the *Christian Observer*, warmly welcomed Paley's *Natural Theology*, not only for its value in confirming faith but also for its value in confronting skepticism and unbelief. In a lengthy review, the journal endorsed Paley's exposition of the argument, maintaining that contrivance afforded "satisfactory proof of the *existence, agency, and wisdom* of a supreme designer." Only at the very end did the reviewer seriously diverge from Paley in what he considered to be an inadequate discussion of the world as a state of probation, and of the natural evidence for the moral attributes of God. On these subjects he considered Paley's remarks to be "highly prejudicial to the cause of true religion."[28] This public position was echoed in private comments: Hannah More, for instance, considered Paley's a "very able work," and well designed to achieve a "grand purpose," though nonetheless "deficient in some essential parts."[29] Moreover, the Claphamites actively sought to address what they considered Paley's failings in regard to the natural evidence of the moral attributes of God. In 1818, Thomas Gisborne, a leading member of the group and one of its chief apologists,[30] published his *Testimony of Natural Theology to Christianity* as an explicit extension of Paley's *Natural Theology*. Gisborne applauded Paley's work, but argued that it encompassed "a part only of its legitimate subject." In addition to demonstrating the existence and natural attributes of God, he argued, natural theology afforded "specific and appropriate and most valuable aid" in demonstrating God's holiness, human fallenness, the consequent penal obligations and hope of mercy, and "other fundamental truths lying at the root of the gracious plan of salvation through a Redeemer."[31]

Yet, while a case can be made for a great circumspection toward natural theology on behalf of the Scottish Evangelicals, especially in contrast to the Evangelical party in the English Church, it is important to appreciate the strategic function of the positions they took during the Leslie affair. Even those historians most interested by the metaphysical substance of the controversy have acknowledged that the Evangelicals and their Whig intellectual allies attacked the Moderate view of natural theology chiefly because it presented them with an unwonted opportunity of challenging the Moderate-Tory hegemony.[32] Consequently, as Paul Baxter suggests, the differences between them were "perhaps exaggerated in the heat of party strife."[33] This is confirmed by the example of William Brown, who in 1805 argued that Leslie need not believe in the design argument in order to be a Christian. A decade later, by contrast, Brown presented one of the most extensive endorsements of the argument from design hitherto published in Scotland in his *Essay on the Existence of a Supreme Creator* (1816).[34] Moreover, this was consistent with his stance in 1805, since on that occasion he had clearly assumed the truth of the argument from design, at the same time as denying that it was a necessary foundation for Christian belief.

Furthermore, it is significant that, as Stewart Brown has indicated, the first decade of the nineteenth century saw the emergence to positions of influence in the Evangelical party of a group of young clergymen, Andrew Thomson among them, who "endeavoured to combine Popular party Calvinism with Enlightenment concepts of the harmony of nature and the progress of society."[35] Duncan Rice argues that this group, who were "often learned, and often even fashionable," allied themselves with the high Enlightenment Scottish common-sense philosophers.[36] More generally, the leaders of the new Scottish Evangelical party, like their Claphamite peers, were concerned to demonstrate the rationality and respectability of Evangelical religion. Indeed, as we have seen, the Leslie affair had the effect of reversing the allegiances of half a century, in that it was now the Evangelicals, rather than the Moderates, who found themselves defending the intellectual freedom of university professors from Confessional demands.

Clearly, then, one must be wary of assuming that the Evangelicals in the Kirk were generally or uniformly antipathetic either to natural theology or to reasoned religion. Indeed, Paul Baxter, who attempted to assess the extent to which views about natural theology expressed by Evangelicals during the Leslie affair were typical of the period as a whole by carrying out a survey of the views expressed in the Scottish evangelical periodicals, concluded that there was "no consensus in the Evangelical party about the status and utility of the design argument" during the early decades of the century.[37] Yet, by analyzing the divergences that Baxter identifies in the context of a particular debate, it is possible to demonstrate some of the issues that were at stake for the Scottish Evangelicals in the ongoing debate about natural theology. In the following two sections, I will use the controversy surrounding Chalmers's article "Christianity" to illuminate the interest of the rejuvenated Scottish Evangelical party in formulating a rational religion that would attract the cultured middle classes, while maintaining a scriptural and soteriological emphasis distinct from the largely ethical emphasis of the Moderates.

Thomas Chalmers and the Science of Theology

Though he later came to personify the evangelical revival of early nineteenth-century Scotland, Thomas Chalmers for many years showed nothing but distaste for Evangelicalism. Indeed, some contemporaries considered him to have been a member of the Moderate party,[38] although his alienation from the patronage network of the leader of that party, George Hill, makes such an alignment untenable.[39] However, in his clerical practice and in his abhorrence of "enthusiasm," Chalmers had much in common with the Moderatism of the period. Licensed as a preacher at the exceptionally young age of 19, as "a lad o' pregnant pairts,"[40] he quickly demonstrated that (like many Moderates) he viewed the clerical profession as a suitable base from which to pursue his mathematical and scientific interests, and, in particular, his ambition of being a university professor. Moreover, Chalmers's recent biographer, Stewart Brown, speaks of his religious ideas encompassing "a loosely-defined natural theology, combined with a distaste for the rigid scholastic Calvinism of his father, and indeed for all forms of religious enthusiasm," and of his being in this regard "essentially a Moderate."[41] However, Chalmers's early theological views—particularly respecting natural theology—are not so straightforward as this might suggest, and it is important before considering his position in the *Edinburgh Encyclopedia* article briefly to review what is known about the earlier development of his theology. The subject is needful of more detailed study, but within the confines of this chapter I shall rely chiefly on the account given in William Hanna's extensive memoir of his father-in-law, and on Chalmers's own published statements.[42]

According to Hanna, Chalmers's third session at St. Andrews University, that of 1793–4, was his "intellectual birth-time": it was then, at the age of thirteen, that he began to display his remarkable aptitude for mathematics, and also to take an interest in political and metaphysical subjects. Through his mathematical lecturer, James Brown, Chalmers came into contact with a set of aspiring men of science (among them John Leslie) who had acquired the reputation of being ultra Whigs. Whether it was through their influence and through Chalmers's reading of William Godwin's *Enquiry Concerning Political Justice* (1793), as Hanna suggests,[43] or through his encounter with the Moderates who then held ascendancy in St. Andrews, Chalmers clearly made a conscious break at this time from his paternal Calvinism. He later recalled of his time at St. Andrews that the university was "overrun with Moderatism, under the chilling influences of which we inhaled not a distaste only but a positive contempt for all that is properly and peculiarly gospel, insomuch that our confidence was nearly as entire in the sufficiency of natural theology as in the sufficiency of natural science."[44] Yet, like that of many Moderates, Chalmers's confidence in natural theology did not involve an approach to deism: he was apparently deeply attached to the Christian scriptures and to Christian morality, if not to the doctrine of the atonement. One of his peers later recalled that, during his first session in the Divinity Hall (1795–6), Chalmers's theology comprised "sublime ideas of the Divine Omnipresence, Omnipotence, Omniscience, and Goodness, and the grandeur, extent, and variety of His works, combined with some lively conceptions of the character, the teaching, and the example of the Author of Christianity."[45]

Toward the end of his first session in the Divinity Hall, Chalmers read the Calvinist Jonathan Edwards's necessitarian *Freedom of the Will* (1754), and, profoundly impressed by its account of the necessary sequence of causes in the natural world, reportedly "rose to the sublime conception of the Godhead, as that eternal, all-pervading energy by which this vast and firmly knit succession was originated and sustained."[46] His own later recollections are instructive:

> I remember, when a student of divinity, and long ere I could relish evangelical sentiment, I spent nearly a twelvemonth in a sort of mental elysium, and the one

idea which ministered to my soul all its rapture was the magnificence of the God-head, and the universal subordination of all things to the one great purpose for which He evolved and was supporting creation. I should like to be so inspired over again, but with such a view of the Deity as coalesced and was in harmony with the doctrine of the New Testament.[47]

As he pursued his studies in divinity through four further sessions, Chalmers presumably made some efforts to acquire a theological education as befitting an aspiring clergyman, but while he was to be found in the 1796–7 session debating the question "Is a Divine Revelation necessary?" on the affirmative side, there is little to indicate the exact tenor of his religious beliefs. Yet, although he was licensed to preach in 1799, Hanna argues that Chalmers had by then had the confident bubble of his natural theology pricked by the pin of Baron D'Holbach's *Système de la nature* (1770).[48] He probably read the book in 1798, and he apparently found his religious views entirely undermined by D'Holbach's materialism, his doubts not being fully assuaged until he came under the teaching of the common-sense school in Edinburgh two or three years later.

Having been licensed to preach, Chalmers began a long wait for ecclesiastical patronage but showed no great desire to fulfil his clerical vocation. He continued, instead, his mathematical and metaphysical studies at Edinburgh University, hoping to support himself by taking pupils and clearly hoping that he might ultimately obtain a university chair. It was here that Chalmers imbibed the Scottish common-sense philosophy from its source, and, according to Hanna, that he found his way out of his D'Holbach-induced "state of philosophical scepticism." In retrospect, Chalmers considered that he was "most indebted for [his] deliverance" to James Beattie's *Essay on Truth* (1770) and to the lectures at Edinburgh by the professor of natural philosophy, John Robison. He was particularly impressed, he recalled, by their grand argument that the agreement between the natural world and the intuitive belief in the uniformity of nature represented evidence of divine design.[49] Yet even as this natural theology provided Chalmers with his escape route from skepticism, he apparently began to move away from the Moderate reliance on natural theology. This may have been, as Phillips suggests, a "conscious reaction" to the views of the Moderate party leader, George Hill, who had taught Chalmers in St. Andrews.[50] Such an interpretation has much to recommend it, not only in view of Chalmers's alienation both from Hill's Toryism and from his patronage network, but also in view of Chalmers's increasing contact with the Whigs among the Edinburgh intelligentsia. In addition, however, the enduring influence of Chalmers's Calvinist upbringing should not be discounted, and it seems likely that the development of his views also owes much to this.

Whatever the cause, Chalmers was shortly to be found expounding a rational defense of the Christian religion well suited to the middle-class intelligentsia among whom he moved, but clearly distinct from the theology of the Moderates. In September 1802, for instance, Chalmers, while talking of "the difficulties which students met with in searching after divine truth," reportedly "considered the historical evidence of Christianity the most satisfactory," attaching "little value" to the evidence derived from the reasonableness of its doctrines.[51] As we shall see, this statement closely mirrors Chalmers's position 10 years later in his *Edinburgh Encyclopedia* article, when he refused to make the truth of the Christian revelation dependent on its consistency with preconceived notions of the divine character. Chalmers was more explicit in a lecture probably delivered to students at St. Andrews a year or two later, in which he recommended that they study the evidences of Christianity, arguing:

> The truth of Christianity is neither more nor less than the truth of certain facts that have been handed down to us by the testimony of reporters. Let the historical evidences on which it rests be made to pass in review and become the subject of sober inductive examination . . . let the enemies of our faith . . . bring along with them the spirit of cool and candid reflection, an anxiety after truth, and a ready submission to evidence. How little do they think, as they strut along in the pride of the infidel philosophy, how little of the spirit and temper of true philosophy is in them—of that humble cautious spirit which Bacon taught, and on which Newton rests the immortality of his genius[52]

Here, again, are indications of the position later elaborated in Chalmers's article on "Christianity," with its emphasis on the scientific study of the historical evidence of Christianity, conducted according to Baconian principles. Moreover, some of those who heard Chalmers's earliest sermons later claimed to recognize in the article "Christianity" views delivered from the pulpit 10 years before.[53]

It is interesting to place Chalmers's theological position at this time against the background of the Leslie affair. Such a comparison has particular keenness since Chalmers actually contributed to the pamphlet war spawned by the controversy. However, while Moderates and Evangelicals were disputing the relevance of natural theology to Christian orthodoxy, Chalmers merely felt it necessary to publish a pamphlet on the "mathematical pretensions of the Scottish clergy."[54] This anonymous work answered the charge made in an earlier pamphlet by the Edinburgh professor of natural philosophy, John Playfair, that there existed "a certain degree of inconsistency" between mathematical studies and "the studies to which clergymen are naturally led by their profession."[55] While Playfair's attack was aimed at the Moderate/Tory candidate Thomas M'Knight, Chalmers, himself both a clergyman and a candidate for the disputed chair, understandably responded by presenting the old Moderate consensus that scientific learning and the clerical office were not incompatible, famously stating: "A minister has five days in the week for his own free and independent exertions."[56] However, it is significant that, while Chalmers argued that the two activities were consistent, he did not consider that there was any fruitful interplay between them and made no attempt to play the Moderate trump card of natural theology.

From all the foregoing, it is clear that, as a young clergyman, Chalmers was at the very least unsympathetic to the Moderate system of theology, with its foundational natural theology. According to Hanna, it was Joseph Butler's *Analogy of Religion* (1736), with its famous argument that the difficulties attending revealed religion were no greater than those attending natural religion, which convinced him that "there was nothing either in the contents or credentials of Christianity to weaken the force, much less to warrant the setting aside, of its own proper and peculiar proofs."[57] Chalmers was clearly impressed with Butler's fundamental methodological principle that the truth of Christianity should be judged according to the historical facts and that preconceived assumptions about what was to be expected of a revelation should not be allowed to overbear such solid evidence. This position had much in common with Chalmers's later espousal of Baconianism in theology, and it is not insignificant that Chalmers came to view Butler as the "Bacon of Theology."

Yet, while Chalmers is reputed to have said that "it was Butler's Analogy that made him a Christian,"[58] it is clear that the development of his Baconian science of revelation was also rooted in his experiences during his two years as a student in Edinburgh. It was the Scottish common-sense philosophers who, as the historian Henry Hallam put it, led the way in turning the "blind veneration" of Bacon into a "rational worship,"[59] and Chalmers had attended with particular effect the Baconian lectures of John Robison, professor of natural philosophy.[60] Hanna claims of Chalmers's attendance at Robison's lectures that he would not have so readily hailed Butler, or done him "such full homage," as the "Bacon of Theology," had he "not been at this period so thoroughly imbued with the true spirit of the inductive philosophy."[61] Indeed, it is significant that when Chalmers later systematized his application of Baconianism to Christianity in his *Edinburgh Encyclopedia* article, he cited as a precedent and pretext the successful application in recent years of the principles of Baconian induction to moral and intellectual subjects by the philosophers of the Scottish common-sense school.[62] Such a view provides support for the contention of Ian Clark and Harry Phillips that the distinctive view of natural theology developed by Scottish Evangelicals in the early nineteenth century owed much to the analysis of the common-sense philosophers. Indeed, Chalmers's debt to the common-sense philosopy in developing his Baconian science of theology (a debt that Theodor Bozeman shows to have been shared by American Presbyterians[63]) serves to reemphasize the extent of his appropriation, even in his denial of the apologetic value of natural theology, of the Enlightenment tradition in Scotland. Moreover, Chalmers's invocation in his article of the common-sense philosophy allowed him to maintain the bearing of the Leslie affair in demonstrating that the Evangelical party were the true supporters of Scotland's illustrious philosophers.[64]

Chalmers's considerable debt to Butler has long been recognized, and Boyd Hilton has convincingly argued that it was Chalmers, more than anyone else, "who adapted Butler's ethics and theology to nineteenth-century evangelicalism."[65] However, it is not commonly recognized that Chalmers's attachment to Butler dates from his early pre-Evangelical period or that he was beginning to use Butler's attributed "Baconianism" to establish the independence of the Christian revelation from natural theology at this time. A more detailed study of the early development of Chalmers's theology is evidently desirable, but would require primary research beyond the scope of this chapter. Yet it is already clear that the theological views that Chalmers expounded as a young Evangelical author developed before ever he became an Evangelical. Such continuity between Chalmers's pre-Evangelical and Evangelical views sheds interesting light on the remodeling of the Scottish Evangelical party in the early nineteenth century, with its increased reliance on the insights of the Scottish Enlightenment.

Between 1809 and 1811, Chalmers experienced a series of personal and family crises that precipitated an evangelical conversion. A significant part of the process, as Stewart Brown has shown, was his growing contact, through his connections among the Whig intelligentsia of Edinburgh, with the young Evangelical intellectuals of the Church of Scotland.[66] According to Brown, Chalmers appreciated the young Evangelicals "for many of the same reasons he respected the young Whigs," namely, because they demonstrated "high ideals" instead of the vested interests of the Moderate-Tory placemen, and "offered opportunities to young men of talent" rather than engaging in nepotism. Moreover, Brown suggests that with the failure of his academic aspirations, Chalmers found involvement in the Evangelical party attractive as a means of increasing his influence in the Church.[67] Yet Chalmers had a long-standing aversion to what he perceived to be the "enthusiasm" of Evangelical religion, and it is clear that his experience of the Enlightenment-inspired form of evangelicalism current among the young intellectuals also had a considerable impact on him. It is of no small significance, for instance, that his reading of William Wilberforce's *Practical View of the Prevailing Religious System of Professed Christians* (1797) left him feeling, as he later recalled, "on the eve of a great revolution in all [his] opinions about Christianity."[68] More than any other book of the period, Wilberforce's work presented evangelical piety in a way that the educated middle and upper classes found attractive: far from being enthusiasm, evangelicalism in Wilberforce's hands was a rational and practical religion ideally suited to the cultured man of influence. Chalmers's subsequent career, and his acclaim among the Claphamites, marks him out as one of the best exemplars of Wilberforce's ideal, and there seems little doubt that his conversion was to a large extent prompted by the new sense of vocation that the evangelicalism of Wilberforce and the young Scottish Evangelicals presented to him.

Among Chalmers's Edinburgh associates had been the Whig natural philosopher David Brewster, who was not only an Evangelical but also the brother of a leading Evangelical clergyman, and a close friend of the Evangelical leader Andrew Thomson. Brewster had been appointed editor of the *Edinburgh Encyclopedia*, a project devised by a group of young Evangelical clergymen and Whig intellectuals as a platform from which to criticise the Tory-Moderate hegemony, and early in 1808 he commissioned Chalmers to contribute scientific articles to the publication. In the autumn of that year, after the death of his sister, Chalmers asked Brewster if he might also undertake the article on Christianity. "In selecting the Christian Evidences, he was," as his son-in-law points out, "neither influenced by any novelty in the subject, nor any change in his convictions regarding it."[69] But he expressed extreme anxiety to do the subject justice and told Brewster he would spend three or four months in St. Andrews in order to consult the appropriate books. Chalmers's Evangelical backers were pleased to have him carry out the commission. The article had been committed to Thomson, but, on hearing of Chalmers's strong desire to undertake it, Thomson agreed to withdraw.[70] Brewster had high hopes of Chalmers, telling him that, while the public had "an aversion to theological subjects however ably they are treated," he expected that in Chalmers's hands "Christianity" would "become alluring to many who would otherwise be alarmed at such a subject."[71]

Chalmers wrote the article intermittently over the three-year interval during which his evangelical conversion took place, and it provided him with an ideal opportunity to elaborate a rational defense of his newfound evangelical faith. Yet what is perhaps most striking is the similarity of his approach in this article to that which he first adopted in Edinburgh some 10 years before. The chief object of his account was to establish the truth of Christianity on Baconian principles. According to Chalmers, the divine origin of the Christian revelation could be established scientifically on the basis of its historical evidences—the miracles and prophecies attending it, and the credibility of its first witnesses, as reported by human testimony. Such a Baconian induction, he asserted, was as sound as any in the physical sciences. This claim was consciously designed to answer religion's cultured despisers. Far from being a subject in which prejudice prevailed, consideration of the claims of Christianity required that the enquirer "should train his mind to all the hardihood of abstract and unfeeling intelligence." Noting that many contemporary philosophers were inclined to despise theology as a subject unfit for "liberal enquiry," Chalmers argued that such a feeling was "an offence against the principles of just speculation." "We are not preaching against it," he continued, "we reason against it. We contend that it is a transgression against the rules of the inductive philosophy."[72]

Chalmers's science of theology was based strictly on historical evidence. This comprised chiefly the "external evidence" of the truth of the Christian revelation (the miracles and prophecies attending it), but also included one branch of the "internal evidence," namely the "marks of truth" in the New Testament considered as a human composition, and the evidence provided by the text as to the character of its authors. These inferences were sound, he argued, since they were based on observations of human nature, of which people have much empirical experience.[73] By contrast, he considered the remaining branch of what was usually considered to be the "internal evidence" of the truth of the Christian revelation, namely the reasonableness of its message, to be unscientific and consequently unreliable. This was so, he claimed, because we have "no experience whatever" of the "invisible God," and his government must consequently be a subject "inaccessible to our faculties."[74] Thus, to judge the truth of Christianity on the reasonableness of its doctrines, or any supposed agreement between the nature of the Christian religion and the character of the supreme being, was, according to Chalmers, to rely on a priori speculation, and was consequently strictly anti-Baconian and unscientific. Contrasting the historical evidences, based on human testimony, with these internal evidences, based on what he considered to be unempirical speculation about the divine character, he deemed the former to be like the sure ground of Newton's physics, and the latter to be "like the ether and whirlpools, and unfounded imaginings of Des Cartes."[75]

Chalmers's language makes it difficult to determine the extent to which he intended his argument to undermine natural theology as a legitimate form of theological discourse. Indeed, some historical commentators have sought to play down the extent of Chalmers's antagonism toward natural theology in this work by pointing out that its subject, the evidence of Christianity, was one in which natural theology could be said properly to have no part.[76] However, this was precisely the point at issue, since, as Chalmers explicitly acknowledged, many contemporaries, especially the Moderates, considered natural theology to be the logical foundation of Christian belief, on which the claims of revelation must be established. There was, he noted, "a numerous class of very sincere and well disposed Christians" who "antecedent to the study of the Christian revelation altogether, repose a very strong confidence in the light of natural religion, and think that, upon the mere strength of its evidence, they can often pronounce with a considerable degree of assurance on the character of the divine administration." But for Chalmers "this attempt to reconcile the doctrines of Christianity with the light of natural religion [was] superfluous. Give them historical evidence for the truth of Christianity," he continued, "and all that natural religion may have taught them will fly like so many visionary phantoms before the light of its overbearing authority."[77]

This and similar statements seem to imply that Chalmers had not totally abandoned the a posteriori arguments of natural theology—merely that he considered them to be superseded by the historical evidence of Christianity. Such a view is supported by other evidence. First, there is the apparent continuity across this time period of Chalmers's belief in the "uniformity" argument of the common-sense school referred to above. Second, and apparently conclusively, there is a statement in his famous review of Georges Cuvier's *Essay on the Theory of the Earth*, published in the *Edinburgh Christian Instructor* for April 1814, which appears to concede a natural argument for the existence and power, if not for the other attributes, of God. Reviewing the evidence given by Cuvier that the oldest geological strata contained no animal remains, Chalmers contended that this afforded "an argument for the exercise of a creative power, more convincing, perhaps, than any that can be drawn from the slender resources of natural theism."[78] However, while this statement clearly concedes some minimal validity to natural theology, it also clearly demonstrates Chalmers's low estimate of natural theology. Moreover, he evidently considered that little beyond the mere existence of a deity could be known without recourse to revelation.

At the very least, Chalmers's position in the *Evidence* entailed the proposition that natural theology was not a logically necessary, nor even a desirable, foundation for Christianity—the very question that had formed the subject of heated debate in the Leslie affair. Chalmers was thus firing a broadside at the rationalist system of Moderate theology—a point that, as we shall see, Moderates were not slow to perceive. Moreover, he argued that natural theology encouraged a speculative mentality that militated against Christian belief. "Viewed purely as an intellectual subject," he claimed, the mind of an atheist was "in a better state of preparation for the proofs of Christianity than the mind of a Deist," since the former was "a blank surface, on which evidence may make a fair impression," while the latter was "occupied with pre-conceptions."[79] Thus, according to Chalmers, natural theology was not only unnecessary in engendering Christian belief, it was positively detrimental.

The point was given more explicit treatment in sermons of the period. In 1812, for instance, Chalmers announced to his congregation in sonorous tones: "I throw aside the speculations of our theistical philosophers and bring God before you in the living characters of revelation." Pointing out that "the leading peculiarity of the Christian faith was that all true disciples approached God through the mediation of Christ, he continued:

> It is not the God of natural religion whom they recognize[:] that tremendous metaphysical being whom to know is but to tremble. Not the God of the Schools. Not that God which the Fancy of philosophers has formed, and propped upon the feeble imagination of a priori and a posteriori arguments. It is God such as he has chosen to reveal himself[.] It is the God of the New Testament.[80]

Chalmers continued by observing that Jesus alone had entered "within that veil that necessarily hangs betwixt every corporeal being and the God who is a spirit and is invisible." "What conception then can I [hope] to form of God," he enquired, "that secret principle, which no eyes can see, which no ear can hear, no sense can recognize?" Unfortunately, the end of the sermon is not extant, but it is clear that Chalmers was even more forceful in his repudiation of natural theology in sermons than in his article. There is also a distinct hint here of autobiography—a verbal echo of that youthful year in a "mental elysium," when Chalmers knew well "that tremendous metaphysical being whom to know is but to tremble." Only when D'Holbach had destroyed this confident but speculative natural theology did Chalmers consider that he had been able to find his way to a proper understanding of scriptural truth.

That Chalmers at this time considered natural theology utterly irrelevant to the Christian apologist is also forcefully demonstrated by his own later recollections. When, in the 1830s, Chalmers came to rewrite his article for publication in an edition of his complete works, he reflected in regard to the change in his views respecting the miraculous evidence of Christianity: "There is a previous natural religion on whose aid we call for the determination of this matter. It is an authority that we at one time should have utterly disregarded and contemned; but now we hold it in higher reverence, since, reflecting on the supremacy of conscience within us, we deem this to be the token of an ascendent principle of morality and truth in the universe about us."[81] This confirms that Chalmers's repudiation of natural theology was for all practical purposes, comprehensive, even including the arguments for divine existence that, as we have seen, he allowed to have some limited logical validity. This is an interpretation of Chalmers's view that, as we shall see, many of his contemporaries shared.

As I argued in the introduction, Chalmers's position here undermines a number of common historical assumptions. Rarely has a theological author adopted a form of scientific reasoning more explicitly and wholeheartedly than Chalmers did in this article; yet the whole weight of his argument was to deny the utility and scientificity of natural theology, and to establish in its place a science of

Scripture. Moreover, the argument against natural theology was marshaled in the context of a new Scottish Evangelical party that was determined to demonstrate its rationality and to establish its claims to cultural supremacy over an effete Moderate party.

Chalmers's position bears a striking resemblance to that espoused by the young Anglican theologian and natural philosopher Baden Powell, in his *Rational Religion Examined* (1826). Baden Powell, though later renowned for his theological liberalism, was at that time still a High Churchman. In view of the similarity of their views, it is instructive briefly to compare the contexts in which they were writing, since it nicely confirms what we have already seen of Chalmers's concerns. Like Chalmers, Baden Powell was attempting to counter what he considered to be a sterile and flawed rationalism with what he presented as a truly rational religion. Where Chalmers's chief target was the theologically rationalist Moderate party, Baden Powell's was Unitarianism, the intellectual revival of which in England had prompted a widespread reaction among members of the High Church party.[82] As with Chalmers's attack on Moderatism, Baden Powell's strategy was to seek to demonstrate both the rationality of High Church doctrine and the irrationality of Unitarianism by establishing methodological guidelines for the interpretation of the Christian scriptures modeled on scientific methodology. He did not assign a central role in his "rational religion" to natural theology, arguing (as Pietro Corsi puts it) that "matters involving the nature of the deity and the scheme of his dispensation to man, by far exceeded the powers of human understanding."[83] In particular, like Chalmers, he argued that the content of the scriptures was above the reach of human reason, and he sought to indict Unitarians for disregarding the "facts" of revelation in favor of their own general theories.[84]

While there are certainly differences between the positions espoused by Chalmers and Baden Powell, especially in regard to their use of scientific methodology, it is interesting to reflect on their similarities. Corsi has shown that Baden Powell considered the existence of God and the truth of revelation to be "noncontentious issues." He argues that not only were all the major religious denominations in Britain agreed on these points but by the 1820s the deism and atheism prevalent among working-class radicals was "politically defeated."[85] Baden Powell's main purpose was, by developing a science of revealed theology, to convince professing Christians of another, avowedly rational, denomination, of the truth of High Church doctrine. The parallel with Chalmers on this point is instructive. For, while Chalmers may indeed have been concerned about the deism of working-class radicals, his main concern in the article on Christianity (as the expensive form in which it was first published confirms) was to convince professing Christians of the cultured middle classes of the truth of Evangelical doctrine, by demonstrating the rationality of the Evangelical approach to the Christian scriptures and the irrationality of the Moderate approach. His repudiation of natural theology and his emphasis on the science of revealed theology thus reflect the nature of his intended audience—chiefly the theologically rationalist Moderate party, against which the Evangelical party defined itself. This view of Chalmers's position is borne out by the reactions to his article of members of the Evangelical and Moderate parties in Scotland, and it is to these reactions that we now turn.

"The Theological War . . . in the North": The Evidence Controversy

Chalmers's article on Christianity enjoyed considerable celebrity in his native land, and before he could even ask, the proprietors of the *Encyclopedia* were themselves suggesting that he should publish it separately.[86] *The Evidence and Authority of the Christian Revelation* appeared in a large first edition of 1,500 copies in 1814 and made rapid progress, with seven editions in circulation within ten years. In addition, the Glasgow Religious Tract Society approached him with a request for permission to publish extracts from the work as an eight-page tract, which went on sale in 1815 at 2s. 8d. per hundred.[87] Yet, for all its popularity, or perhaps because of it, the work prompted what one commentator considered a veritable "theological war" in Scotland.[88]

Evangelical reviewers and readers were particularly taken with Chalmers's book for its proof of the rationality of evangelicalism. One of the most striking reactions was that of Chalmers's sister, who, in applauding the rational character of the book, saw an immediate (if ironic) parallel in that regard with William Paley's *Natural Theology*.[89] The evangelical journals echoed this sentiment. According to the reviewer in the *Christian Herald*, the general dissatisfaction of evangelicals with existing books on the evidences of Christianity had been used to prove that their faith was "unreasonable," and that they were "enemies to reason." That Chalmers's book had been so extensively circulated, the reviewer continued, proved the contrary.[90] The Evangelical party journal, the *Edinburgh Christian Instructor*, also considered the great importance of Chalmers's book to be its display of rationality. Not, the reviewer wrote, that we should "imagine that the most convincing proofs will bring conviction to those who have an interest in not being convinced," but such reasoning could protect the young from "plausible sophisms." Moreover, the reviewer argued, it was, in view of the infidel's representation of Christians as "weak and credulous people," of the utmost importance "for Christians to have the victory on the ground of argument and reason, *and to make it manifest to the world that it is so.*" In this regard, Chalmers's work, the most celebrated of all the "small works" published in defense of Christianity in recent years, excelled. "A piece of more conclusive reasoning, united with all the graces of eloquence," the reviewer stated, "we do not recall to have met with."[91]

Yet even before the article was ready, Chalmers was encountering criticism of his argument. As he rehearsed his views in sermons, several friends remonstrated with his rejection of that branch of the internal evidence relating to the reasonableness of the message. In February 1812, for example, his friend the Moderate clergyman Samuel Charters wrote to him: "Your sermon minded me of a book that once made some noise *Christianity not grounded on argument* to which D^r. Doddridge made a good reply. It is right to avow your own sentiments but is it right to announce hostility against Clarke Butler and Locke's reasonableness of Christianity—men who assuredly believed, and whose writings have aided the belief of many."[92] Chalmers's science of revelation—his "philology"—might be excellent for the learned and the leisured, Charters conceded, but for the unlearned, the internal evidence was the great prop of religion.

To another critical friend, the Baptist theologian and physician Charles Stuart, Chalmers conceded that he had "not yet arrived at a right settlement of opinion" regarding the value of the internal evidence. Moreover, when his article appeared in book form, Chalmers appended a brief explanatory advertisement, in which he drew back somewhat from his earlier position. He was, he wrote, "far from asserting the study of the historical evidence to be the only channel to a faith in the truth of Christianity." There undoubtedly were, he continued, "thousands and thousands of Christians, who bear the undeniable marks of the truth having come home to their understanding 'in demonstration of the Spirit and of power' " (I Cor. 2: 4). They had "an evidence within themselves which the world knoweth not, even the promised manifestations of the Saviour." Yet, while this was " 'a sign to them that believe,' " he observed, the Bible also spoke of " 'a sign to them which believe not' " (I Cor. 14: 22), and this was the value of the historical evidence of Christianity.[93]

Chalmers's disclaimer was enough to satisfy the *Christian Herald* that he had not intended to undermine the internal evidence, but the reviewer still regretted that Chalmers had not made more of the appeal of the message of revelation to the human condition. This was, the reviewer insisted, the real internal evidence—not the attempt to judge revelation by the light of a priori speculation, which Chalmers was right to condemn. The reviewer in the *Edinburgh Christian Instructor* was also respectfully critical of Chalmers's position on the internal evidence, while largely upholding his view of natural theology. On the latter subject, the reviewer considered that Chalmers held to "the impossibility of our knowing any thing about the counsels and operations of a Being who is infinite and eternal," independent of revelation. "We go so far along with him here," the reviewer declared, "as to be firmly persuaded, that had it not been owing to revelation, or to tradition, which is the same, mankind would either have had no ideas of God, or of his will at all, or false ones." He concluded that Chalmers was consequently right to say that such antecedent conceptions of God were improper grounds on which to judge of the truth of any professed revelation.[94] Yet just as one might be capable of apprehending the truth of a scientific theory that could be discovered only by a mind of greater powers, so the reviewer considered that one might be capable of apprehending the truth of a divine revelation, the content of which one could not have discovered oneself. Moreover, according to the *Christian Instructor* this was the path to truth of most who truly believed. Those who read the Christian scriptures found in them an accurate account of the human condition and a convincing statement of its remedy.

The reactions of these reviewers indicate that while the Scottish Evangelicals generally approved Chalmers's scientific defense of the reasonableness of Christian belief, as recommending Christianity to people of refined taste and intellectual habits, they considered the appeal of the message of revelation to the human condition, the evidential value of which Chalmers had eschewed, to be of more universal application. In all this discussion, however, criticism of Chalmers's views on natural theology was singularly absent, and one might reasonably conclude that his views on this question were unobjectionable to most of his Evangelical readers in the Kirk. Such a conclusion is clearly suggestive, in view of Ian Clark's analysis of the Leslie affair, as implying a tendency within the Evangelical party to place little or no reliance on natural theology. However, it is interesting to consider the issues that were at stake for the Evangelical party in this discussion. Firstly, in applauding Chalmers's book, the reviewers emphasized the apologetic importance of demonstrating the rationality of evangelical religion. Not that such rational arguments would ever convince a mind alienated from God, but they were important in removing the opprobrium of "enthusiasm" or credulity from evangelical religion, and in protecting the young from plausible sophisms. In this regard, however, most evangelical commentators in Scotland seem to have found Chalmers's science of revealed theology quite as serviceable, and more acceptable, than the science of natural theology. Secondly, however, the reviewers were concerned to maintain the apologetic bearing of evangelical preaching—namely, the exposition of the inherent appeal of the gospel message to the wayward sinner—and it was in this regard that Chalmers's work failed to meet their requirements.

The contrast in this regard with the reaction of the Evangelical party in the Anglican church is very striking. The Evangelicals of Wilberforce's circle had found in the publications of the newly converted Chalmers a man much to their own taste and purpose, a fact that is abundantly clear from the review of his *Evidence* that appeared in their party journal, the *Christian Observer*. Yet while the reviewer applauded in warm terms Chalmers's application of Baconian principles to the historical evidences, he argued that Chalmers should have extended the same approach both to the internal evidences of Christianity and to natural theology. Conceived as an argument a posteriori, natural theology constituted, the reviewer suggested, an acceptable Baconian induction. Moreover, he continued, a knowledge of the Creator was an essential foundation of any appeal that might be made to persuade the infidel to examine the evidence of the Christian revelation.[95] The contrast here between the Claphamites' positive assessment of the natural powers of the human mind and the much more circumscribed view propounded by the Scottish Evangelical journals tends to reinforce the assessment of Clark and Phillips concerning the distinctive theological development in the two nations.

This contrast is made more striking by the fact that the *Christian Observer*'s criticism of Chalmers's position paralleled very closely that made by Chalmers's principal Moderate critic, Duncan Mearns. In April 1818, Mearns, who was professor of divinity at King's College, Aberdeen, and a leading minister in the Moderate party, challenged Chalmers's theological orthodoxy in the church courts, on the grounds that his *Evidence* was inconsistent with Kirk doctrine. Although Mearns's attempt was defeated before the case could even reach the General Assembly,[96] his vitriolic attack, made on Chalmers in the Aberdeen

Synod, was expanded and published later in the year with the title *Principles of Christian Evidence Illustrated by an Examination of Arguments Subversive of Natural Theology and the Internal Evidence of Christianity, Advanced by Dr. T. Chalmers in his "Evidence and Authority of the Christian Revelation."*

In his preface, Mearns sought to undermine Chalmers's central objective: that of presenting evangelicalism as a rational religion. Chalmers, he claimed, was one of a class of theologians who were so anxious to counter "the erroneous reasoning and insidious devices of those, who with singular absurdity appropriate to themselves the title of 'rational Christians,' " that they "have unwarily employed expressions and arguments which give countenance to errors of an opposite nature;—and have thus laid religion open to the attacks of infidels, whose representations of Christianity, as having no foundation in reason, but in some inexplicable principle which *they* style faith, correspond very nearly with the sentiments held by religious enthusiasts in all ages."[97] Mearns proceeded to argue that, in his attempt to thwart theological rationalism, Chalmers had "avowedly subverted" the conclusions of "natural theology and the internal evidence of Christianity." Such a position was extreme, he noted, even by evangelical standards. Citing the statement of the Anglican Evangelical John Bird Sumner that "[t]he chief use of natural religion, is to shew the high probability of that being true which revelation declares,"[98] he argued that it had "been common, even for those who place no high degree of confidence in the light of nature, to display the chief arguments which reason draws from observation of natural phenomena in favour of the existence, attributes, and moral government of God, as coinciding with and corroborating the declarations of revelation regarding these fundamental doctrines."[99]

The crux of Mearns's attack was his argument that natural theology and the internal evidence of Christianity were fundamental to Christian belief and that by denying their validity, Chalmers was indirectly subverting his own argument from historical evidence. Pointing out that the argument from historical evidence had been, at the hands of Hume, the object of "the most formidable assault which Christianity has of late encountered," Mearns argued that the only way in which Hume's argument against miracles could be neutralized was by appealing to prior knowledge of God, and to the antecedent probability of his performing miracles in particular circumstances.[100] More generally, he claimed, antecedent knowledge of God was necessary for miracles to be of use in engendering belief in the Christian revelation, and miracles on their own could never convince an atheist.

According to Mearns, Chalmers's views undermined the whole Christian superstructure in a second and more fundamental way. Discussing Chalmers's account of the inductive philosophy, Mearns charged him with having fallen into what he considered to be the Humean fallacy of making sense experience the only source of human knowledge, to the exclusion of those instinctive beliefs about causation and the uniformity of nature that were central to the analysis of the common-sense school. This followed, he claimed, from Chalmers's statement that "we have no experience of God," since such a statement could only be made if one admitted sense experience alone and denied the legitimacy of

reasoning from causes to effects.[101] What Chalmers had failed to notice, according to Mearns, was that in adopting "this common sceptical maxim," he had
undermined the historical evidence of Christianity as much as natural theology
or the internal evidence. He argued that "we have, philosophically speaking, no
experience of any Efficient Cause, either in miraculous or natural phenomena;—
that knowledge of the moral qualities of our fellow men cannot be derived from
mere experience;—that it is not experience which teaches us the intellectual
existence of others;—and that therefore we cannot learn from experience solely,
that any credit is due to testimony."[102]

It is particularly striking that Mearns's attack on Chalmers parallels very
closely the Moderate party's attack on Leslie, some 13 years previously. As we
have seen, Mearns represented Chalmers as being (like Leslie) an adherent to
Hume's doctrine of causation, and he even went so far as to refer, suggestively,
to "the principles of Hume and of Dr. C." [103] That Mearns was being disin-
genuous in making such a connection, and in his reading of Chalmers's work
more generally, is indubitable—he was, after all, one of the more partisan members of the Moderate party, and his target was a rising star of the increasingly
powerful Evangelical party—yet it is nonetheless interesting to observe the
ground on which he had chosen to impugn Chalmers's orthodoxy.[104] Mearns
evidently still considered the Evangelical position on natural theology to be
vulnerable to attack, even after the Moderate defeat on this issue 13 years previously, and his attack clearly signals the continuing danger for the Evangelicals
of being cast as an antirational, anti-intellectual party of "religious enthusiasts."

Such a critique was certainly bad publicity for those Evangelicals, Chalmers
included, determinedly fashioning an Evangelical religion that could claim to be
rational. Chalmers himself, though urged to do so, declined to answer the
charges put to him,[105] but the annoyance is visible in the review of Mearns's
book that appeared in the *Edinburgh Christian Instructor*, written by the same
reviewer who had previously praised Chalmers's *Evidence*. The reviewer was
strongly critical of the tone of Mearns's attack and of his party spirit, but he was
now also more critical of Chalmers himself, reflecting that his piety and rhetoric
had "outshone his logic."[106] The main object of the review, however, was to
show that Mearns had misconstrued Chalmers's meaning, and to defend Chalmers from the charge of denying "the conclusions of natural theology." In
further echoes of the Leslie affair, the reviewer started by pointing out that, even
had Chalmers rejected the *evidence* of natural theology more decidedly than he
had done, there could be no doubt that he accepted its *conclusions*, albeit on
different grounds. However, the reviewer claimed, Chalmers's strongest statement respecting natural religion—that it was totally insufficient "to pronounce
on the works of any revelation"—was by no means inconsistent with the proposition that "natural religion teaches a great deal."[107] Mearns had missed the
central point, he continued, namely that Chalmers's argument was addressed to
deists, in whose hands natural theology was a weapon against revelation, rather
than to those writers on natural theology like Samuel Clarke and William Paley,
who "merely laboured to extract the same conclusions from nature which are
taught by revelation."[108]

There was a certain sleight of hand here between a demonstrative natural theology and a theology of nature based on revelation but corroborated by the observation of nature—a point that one of Mearns's supporters, writing under the name "Venusinus," was quick to point out in a pamphlet pouring scorn on the pretensions to rationality of the Evangelical party. "The idea of drawing the conclusions of Natural Theology from Scripture, not from the light of Nature," he scoffed, "is a very happy one."[109] Yet this running together of natural and revealed theology was precisely the intention of the *Christian Instructor's* reviewer. He thought it no coincidence that all the works of natural theology had been written by men who had read and believed revelation "before they ever thought of looking after proofs from any other source." Moreover, he argued, while it was undoubtedly true that "the invisible things of God may be clearly seen by the things which he has made" (Rom. 1: 20), in their present condition, humankind were "so destitute either of the inclination or ability to see these displays, that in fact they go for almost nothing without some further instruction." The reviewer challenged Mearns to identify a single person who without revelation had obtained "just ideas of the being and character of God." Natural theology was far from being the foundation of religion: "We who enjoy revelation can now read the book of nature—we are delighted to find a great number of the same truths taught in both these books; and we think it a sound conclusion that, by their agreement, the argument for the truth of revelation is not a little strengthened. But the process by which we come at this conclusion, we consider as the very reverse of that which Dr. Mearns has stated."[110] Indeed, the reviewer concluded, Mearns was unintentionally giving countenance to Unitarianism by giving the impression "that revelation is a very secondary matter, that natural religion and natural reason are far above it," and that the former is to be judged by the latter.[111]

While the *Evidence* controversy was a somewhat quieter shadow of the Leslie affair, the views of the Scottish Evangelicals on this occasion seem to confirm Ian Clark's view of that earlier encounter—that it marks a significant change of emphasis in the Kirk, from natural to revealed theology. Indeed, Clark's suggestion that the theology of the Evangelical party was in some sense indebted to David Hume's critique of Enlightenment natural theology is given somewhat ironic expression by Mearns's portrayal of Chalmers as adopting Hume's doctrine of causation. Within the context of the *Evidence* controversy, the suggested contrast between the Scottish and English Evangelicals on the question of natural theology seems to hold good. At the same time, however, their reactions confirm that the Scottish Evangelical party, no less than the English, was profoundly interested in making its theology bear rational scrutiny, and in this regard the Scottish Evangelicals found Chalmers's science of revealed theology extremely attractive. Moreover, as with Chalmers himself, an interest in the rationality of religion did not necessarily require the elaboration of a demonstrative natural theology. Chalmers's peers in the Scottish Evangelical party were aware from the start that capital could be made out of any explicit rejection of natural theology, in undermining their claims to rationality, and the point was forcibly brought home to them by Mearns's book. Yet while the Evangelical reviewers were undoubtedly embarrassed by such criticism, they were not to be shamed into giving natural theology theological primacy, choosing instead to collapse it into revealed theology, as a corroborative theology of nature.

Chalmers's great failing, as far as the Scottish Evangelical party was concerned, was not that he denied the usefulness of demonstrative natural theology but that he had underplayed the appeal of the gospel message to the human condition—a central strand in evangelical apologetic. In this sense his approach was too academic, and not sufficiently rooted in pastoral concerns. In crafting an evangelicalism that could bear scrutiny by the cultured man of influence, Chalmers had, his peers considered, weakened its appeal to the great unwashed.

Chalmers and the Natural Theology of Conscience

If Chalmers was out of step with many of his Evangelical peers in the Church of Scotland in his rejection of the internal evidence of Christianity, he was not so for long. It is the argument of this final section that Chalmers responded to their criticisms of his *Evidence* by developing a theology that not only effectively reinstated the internal evidence of Christianity but also provided evangelicals with a natural theology that, while not pretending to be the logical foundation of Christianity, could be made the "basis of Christianization." Chalmers's mature position, famously enunciated in his *Bridgewater Treatise* of 1833, involved an account of the pilgrim's progress from atheism to Christian belief that was radically different from the view given in the *Evidence*. His ideal skeptic was still the Baconian atheist, but Chalmers now considered that natural theology could serve a real purpose in placing a moral obligation on the skeptic to examine the evidences of Christianity. The natural theology on which he laid most emphasis was that based on the felt supremacy of the human conscience, which, he considered, constituted the strongest presumptive evidence for the existence of a moral governor. Only a righteous Creator, he argued, would wish to make "the obviously superior faculty in man, so distinct and authoritative a voice on the side of righteousness."[112] This simple argument was, he considered, "of more force than all other arguments put together, for originating and upholding the natural theism which there is in the world." It was, he considered, "of wider diffusion" and "far more practical influence than the theology of academic demonstration."[113]

One notable feature of this argument was that it maintained Chalmers's earlier commitment to the Baconian method. Far from requiring great knowledge of the divine administration previous to examining the claims of revelation, it required merely a limited induction drawn from the observation of human nature. In this regard, Chalmers continued to draw explicitly on the insights of the common-sense school, most particularly on its Baconian science of human nature. Yet, in his emphasis on the appeal made by the New Testament to the human condition, Chalmers's natural theology of conscience also has particular resonances with the criticisms leveled at his *Evidence* by the Scottish evangelicals. This dual debt to the common-sense philosophy and to the Calvinist tradition of Scottish evangelicalism has been identified by a number of authors.[114] However, none of these authors has sought to trace the development of Chalmers's views within the context of the ongoing debate about natural theology in the Evangelical party. While it is clearly beyond the scope of this essay to give a full account of the development of Chalmers's views on natural theology, it is nevertheless instructive briefly to examine the evidence that his change of view dates from the time of the *Evidence* controversy.

While Chalmers did not fully expound his natural theology of conscience in print until 20 years after the publication of his article on Christianity, there are indications from a number of published and unpublished sources that he began to formulate this analysis very soon after his article on Christianity was published. It is evident that Chalmers took very seriously the remonstrations of his friends and made a particular study of the subject of the internal evidences in the midst of the controversy.[115] He even apparently toyed with the idea of publishing an appendix to deal with this question in the second edition of the *Evidence*,[116] but no such appendix was ever published.

The impact of the criticism of his *Evidence* is visible in his *Discourses on the Christian Revelation Viewed in Connexion with the Modern astronomy* (1817), a work based on the immensely popular series of sermons that he delivered from a Glasgow pulpit in 1815 and 1816. Although this work has often been treated as a work of natural theology,[117] that characterization is a misreading of Chalmers's enunciation of a theology of nature based on revelation. Indeed, the shape of his argument in the *Discourses* was structured by precisely the same Baconian principles as appear in the *Evidence*. The unambiguous object of the book was to defend the Christian revelation from objections that had been brought against it on the grounds of the vastness of the universe.[118] In the final discourse, however, "On the slender influence of mere taste and sentiment in matters of religion," Chalmers addressed his readers with a direct appeal to believe the gospel. He pointed out that the sense of wonder engendered by contemplation of the astonishing phenomena of astronomy had no power to impel them to true religion. Even if such contemplation could lead an atheist to a belief in "the design and authority of a great presiding Intelligence," it could never by itself lead him to obedience to the divine will, or humble him "to acquiesce in the doctrine of that revelation which comes to his door with such a host of evidence, as even his own philosophy cannot bid away."[119] It was "only by insisting on the moral claim of God to a right of government over His creatures" that the preacher could carry his hearers to "loyal submission to the will of God. Let him keep by this single argument," Chalmers insisted, "and then . . . he may bring convincingly home upon his hearers all the varieties of Christian doctrine."[120] In his insistence that the preacher's appeal to the human conscience was essential to impel the atheist to consider the historical evidences, and in his insistence that this argument was infinitely more powerful than any argument from external nature, we see a clear indication of Chalmers's developing views.

Further developments can be seen in other sermons about this time. On 14 May 1817, when Chalmers made his much-feted debut as a preacher in London, he chose to preach the annual sermon of the London Missionary Society on the subject of Christian evidence, but this time he emphasized the power of the internal evidence of Christianity in engendering belief (especially the resonance of the gospel message with the human condition), almost at the expense of the external evidence (to such an extent, ironically, that one of the Claphamites, the vicar of Harrow, John William Cunningham, was a little disquieted).[121] A sermon on the "reasonableness of faith," also preached about this time from his Glasgow pulpit, shows that Chalmers was now prepared to meet disciples of "the school of Natural Religion" on their own terms. He was still dismissing the "rash and unphilosophical audacity" of their presumption that the human mind was competent "to know God by the exercise of its own faculties." Yet he was now happy to start from their assertion of "the judicial government of God over moral and accountable creatures," to proceed by showing them the abundant evidence that people had violated that government, to demonstrate that "the Gospel of the New Testament" offered the only remedy, and by such means to "shut them up unto the faith" (Gal. 3: 23).[122]

It is probable that the systematic development of this view had much to do with Chalmers's role from 1823 as professor of moral philosophy at St. Andrews University, and, more importantly, from 1828 as professor of divinity at Edinburgh University, when the construction of a comprehensive system of evangelical theology became a particular priority.[123] Indeed, manuscript notes of his divinity lectures indicate that he was already rehearsing the themes of his *Bridgewater Treatise* with his students as early as 1828. He emphasized the value of natural theology for the preacher in terms that recall the words of his erstwhile critics: "Natural Theology is the Church calling Bill to the Peasantry," he stated. "The internal evidences are the grand thing that leads on the Peasant to religion."[124] When the Quaker philanthropist Joseph John Gurney met Chalmers in 1830, they discussed the evidences of Christianity and very quickly came to the subject of the human conscience. Chalmers explained that, while he thought the historical evidences "abundantly sufficient to satisfy the scrutinizing researches of the learned," the internal evidence—the comparison of the message of the Bible with the records of one's own experience—lay "within the grasp of *every* sincere inquirer." "I love this evidence," he continued. "It is what I call the *portable* evidence of Christianity."[125]

The later development of Chalmers's views on natural theology, and their role in the ongoing debate within evangelicalism, is a subject on which much more deserves to be written. However, it is clear from the foregoing that the development of Chalmers's natural theology of conscience occurred within a peculiarly Scottish tradition. In this chapter I have argued that the English tradition of demonstrative natural theology, exemplified by Paley, was much less attractive to the Evangelical party in the Church of Scotland than to the Claphamites. Indeed, we have seen that the young Chalmers denied demonstrative natural theology any place whatever in his "rational religion," initially without incurring the censure of his fellow Evangelicals. The chief impetus for the later development of Chalmers's natural theology, however, came from within the Evangelical party. For, in seeming to deny that a sense of judgement issuing from the natural human conscience testified to the inherent truth of the message of the Christian revelation (that is, by denying the internal evidence of Christianity), Chalmers found himself profoundly at odds with his Evangelical peers. It was in response to their criticism that Chalmers came to construct his distinctive natural theology, based on the doctrine that the human conscience gave grounds for supposing there to be a moral governor whose laws all had violated. In developing this view, Chalmers evidently also drew on the Scottish common-sense tradition of the scientific analysis of human nature. Moreover, even though Chalmers's reliance on the English apologist Joseph Butler in his account of the human conscience should warn us against any simplistic national dichotomy, it is nonetheless the case, as Boyd Hilton has shown, that it was he who did most to make Butler relevant to the English as well as the Scottish Evangelicals of the mid-nineteenth century.[126]

It has been the purpose of this chapter to show that the historical interconnections between natural theology, science, and "rational" religion are not so predictable as is commonly supposed. Chalmers "rational religion," with its science of revealed theology, and its repudiation of natural theology on scientific grounds, clearly demonstrates that the situation could be much more complex. That this is so should warn against any simplistic assumption that evangelicals have historically been ill disposed toward or uninterested in science, but it should also serve to suggest that the connections historically made by evangelicals between their religion and science were much more sophisticated than has often been assumed.

NOTES

The Chalmers papers are quoted with the kind permission of the Librarian of New College, Edinburgh. I would like to acknowledge the helpful comments and suggestions of Bill Astore, David Bebbington, John Brooke, Geoffrey Cantor, Patricia Fara, Marina Frasca-Spada, David Livingstone, Jim Secord, and Roberta Topham. I would also like to thank the library staff of New College, Edinburgh for their cheerful and unwearying assistance.

1. See, for example, R. D. Altick, *The English common reader: a social history of the mass reading public, 1800–1900*, Chicago: University of Chicago Press, 1957, p. 99; D. W. Bebbington, *Evangelicalism in modern Britain: a history from the 1730s to the 1980s*, London: Unwin Hyman, 1989, p. ix; and Boyd Hilton, *The age of atonement: the influence of evangelicalism on social and economic thought, 1785–1865*, Oxford: Clarendon Press, 1988, pp. 7, 26–35. See also Ernest Marshall Howse, *Saints in politics: the "Clapham Sect" and the growth of freedom*, London: George Allen & Unwin, 1953, and Doreen M. Rosman, *Evangelicals and culture*, London: Croom Helm, and 1984.

2. On the origin of modern science in the nineteenth century see Andrew Cunningham and Perry Williams, "De-centring the 'big picture': *The Origins of Modern Science* and the modern origins of science," *British Journal for the History of Science* 26 (1993): 407–32. On the question of authority see, for instance, Richard Yeo, "Science and intellectual authority in mid-nineteenth-century Britain: Robert Chambers and *Vestiges of the Natural History of Creation*," *Victorian Studies* 28 (1984): 5–31.

3. Of course, Scriptural Geology itself represents an important untold history. There is some discussion of the scriptural geologists in John David Yule, "The impact of science

on British religious thought in the second quarter of the nineteenth century," Unpublished Ph.D. thesis, University of Cambridge, 1976. See also Charles Coulson Gillispie, *Genesis and geology: a study in the relations of scientific thought, natural theology, and social opinion in Great Britain, 1790–1850*, New York: Harper & Row, 1959.

4. See, for example, Bebbington, *Evangelicalism in modern Britain*, pp. 50–60, and Hilton, *Age of atonement*, pp. 20–26.

5. The most explicit statement of this position is to be found in Robert Young's famous thesis that in early nineteenth-century Britain there was "a relatively homogeneous and satisfactory natural theology, best reflected in William Paley's classic *Natural Theology* (1802) and innumerable works reflecting the same point of view," and that this formed the basis for a "common intellectual context." Robert M. Young, *Darwin's metaphor: nature's place in Victorian culture*, Cambridge: Cambridge University Press, 1985, pp. 127–28. However, similar views still permeate the literature. Adrian Desmond even coins the word "Paleyism" to describe what he takes to be the common view of natural theology. See Adrian Desmond, *The politics of evolution: morphology, medicine and reform in radical London*, Chicago: University of Chicago Press, 1989, p. 260.

6. See, for instance, John Hedley Brooke, "Natural theology and the plurality of worlds: observations on the Brewster-Whewell debate," *Annals of Science* 34 (1977): 221–86; Brooke, "The natural theology of the geologists: some theological strata," in L. J. Jordanova and Roy S. Porter, eds., *Images of the earth: essays in the history of the environmental sciences*, Chalfont St. Giles: British Society for the History of Science, 1979; Brooke, *Science and religion: some historical perspectives*, Cambridge: Cambridge University Press, 1991; and Jonathan R. Topham, " 'An infinite variety of arguments': the *Bridgewater Treatises* and British natural theology in the 1830s," Unpublished Ph.D. thesis, University of Lancaster, 1993.

7. On Brewster see Brooke, "Plurality," and Paul Baxter, "Brewster, evangelism and the disruption of the Church of Scotland," in A. D. Morrison-Low and J. R. R. Christie, eds., *"Martyr of science": Sir David Brewster 1781–1868*, Edinburgh: Royal Scottish Museum, 1984. On Chalmers see Hilton, *Age of atonement*; Daniel F. Rice, "Natural theology and the Scottish philosophy in the thought of Thomas Chalmers," *Scottish Journal of Theology* 24 (1971): 23–46; and Crosbie Smith, "From design to dissolution: Thomas Chalmers' debt to John Robison," *British Journal for the History of Science* 12 (1979): 59–70. Paul Baxter has made one of the most systematic surveys, setting Chalmers, Brewster, John Fleming, and Hugh Miller in context within the Evangelical party of the Church of Scotland, and, later, within the Free Church of Scotland. See Paul Baxter, "Science and belief in Scotland, 1805–1868: the Scottish Evangelicals," Unpublished Ph.D. thesis, University of Edinburgh, 1985; and Baxter, "Deism and development: disruptive forces in Scottish natural theology," in Stewart J. Brown and Michael Fry, eds., *Scotland in the age of the Disruption*, Edinburgh: Edinburgh University Press, 1993, pp. 98–112. See also William Joseph Astore, "Observing God: Thomas Dick (1774–1857), evangelicalism and popular science in Victorian Britain and antebellum America," Unpublished DPhil thesis, University of Oxford, 1995.

8. Hilton, *Age of atonement*, pp. 21–22.

9. *Ibid.*, p. 10.

10. *Ibid.*, pp. 1, 7.

11. Jonathan R. Topham, "Science and popular education in the 1830s: the role of the *Bridgewater Treatises*," *British Journal for the History of Science* 25 (1992): 397–430.

12. See, for instance, Bebbington, *Evangelicalism in modern Britain*, pp. 2–10.

13. John H. Brooke, "Natural theology from Boyle to Paley," in John H. Brooke, R. Hooykaas, and Clive Lawless, *New interactions between theology and natural science*, Milton Keynes: Open University Press, 1974, pp. 8–9.

14. I have argued in my doctoral thesis that several of the authors of the *Bridgewater Treatises*, notably William Whewell, used the language of design in such a way as to leave rather ambiguous the status of their claims for what could be known by reason alone. See Topham, " 'An infinite variety of arguments,' " chapter 4. See also John Hedley Brooke, "Indications of a creator: Whewell as apologist and priest," in Menachem Fisch and Simon Schaffer, eds., *William Whewell: a composite portrait*, Oxford: Clarendon Press, 1991.

15. See, for instance, [Anon.], "Gisborne's Natural Theology," *Congregational Magazine* 1 (1818): 426.

16. This point has been made extremely well by John Brooke, but still clearly requires reiteration. See Brooke, *Science and religion*, pp. 19–33.

17. I have followed the common practice of using the capitalized form "Evangelical" when referring to the religious parties in the established churches of England and Scotland, and of using "evangelical" when also referring to nonconformists.

18. Stewart J. Brown, *Thomas Chalmers and the godly commonwealth in Scotland*, Oxford: Oxford University Press, 1982, pp. 3, 43–49.

19. The standard account is Ian D. L. Clark, "The Leslie controversy, 1805," *Records of the Scottish Church History Society* 14 (1960–2): 179–97. However, see also J. B. Morrell, "Professors Robison and Playfair, and the *Theophobia Gallica*: natural philosophy, religion and politics in Edinburgh, 1789–1815," *Notes and Records of the Royal Society* 26 (1971): 43–63; Morrell, "The Leslie affair: careers, kirk and politics in Edinburgh in 1805," *Scottish Historical Review* 54 (1975): 63–82; and John G. Burke, "Kirk and causality in Edinburgh, 1805," *Isis* 61 (1970): 340–54.

20. *Westminster confession of faith*, rpt., Glasgow: Free Presbyterian Publications, 1976, p. 1.

21. Clark, "The Leslie controversy," p. 192.

22. *Ibid.*, p. 193.

23. *Ibid.*, p. 194.

24. *Ibid.*, p. 196. On the Evangelical "debt" to Hume, see also Morrell, "Robison and Playfair," pp. 54–55.

25. Clark, "The Leslie controversy," pp. 195–96.

26. Harry P. Phillips, Jr., "The development of demonstrative theism in the Scottish thought of the nineteenth century," Unpublished Ph.D. thesis, University of Edinburgh, 1950.

27. Compare Wilberforce's views as given in the letter from William Wilberforce to Ralph Creyke, 8 January 1803, in Robert Isaac and Samuel Wilberforce, eds., *The correspondence of William Wilberforce*, 2 vols., London: John Murray, 1840, 1: 250–52. This attribution is also suggested in Hilton, *Age of atonement*, p. 178.

28. [William Wilberforce?], "Review of Paley's Natural Theology," *Christian Observer* 2 (1803): 162–66, 240–44, 369–74, pp. 373, 165.

29. William Roberts, *Memoir of the life and correspondence of Mrs. Hannah More*, 2nd ed., 4 vols., London: R. B. Seeley and W. Burrside, 1834, 3: 191.

30. See John H. Overton, *The English church in the nineteenth century (1800–1830)*, London: Longmans, Green, 1894, pp. 74–6.

31. Thomas Gisborne, *The testimony of natural theology to Christianity*, London: T. Cadell and W. Davies, 2nd ed., 1818, pp. 5, 7–8.

32. Clark, "The Leslie controversy," Burke, "Kirk and causality." The political aspects of the affair are particularly emphasized in Morrell, "The Leslie affair."

33. Baxter, "Science and belief," p. 73.

34. See Phillips, "The development of demonstrative theism," p. 74. It should, how-

ever, be noted that Brown was born in Utrecht, and became minister of the English church there, before fleeing to Scotland after the French invasion of Holland. Nevertheless, his work on natural theology was prompted by an essay prize founded by an Aberdeen merchant, John Burnett, who left money to be awarded for a treatise on "The Evidence that there is a Being all powerful, wise, and good, by whom every thing exists; and particularly to obviate Difficulties regarding the Wisdom and the Goodness of the Deity; and this, in the first place, from Considerations independent of written Revelation; and in the second place, from the Revelation of the Lord Jesus." William Laurence Brown, *Essay on the existence of a supreme creator, possessed of infinite power, wisdom, and goodness; containing also the refutation, from reason and revelation, of the objections urged against his wisdom and goodness; and deducing, from the whole subject, the most important practical inferences*, Aberdeen: A. Brown, 1816, pp. xxix–xxx. Moreover, Brown's treatise gave more scope and consideration to natural theology than did the entry for the Burnett Prize by the Anglican Evangelical, John Bird Sumner (see n. 98, below).

35. Brown, *Thomas Chalmers*, p. 48.

36. C. Duncan Rice, *The Scots abolitionists 1833–1861*, Baton Rouge: Louisiana state University Press, 1981, p. 25. On Chalmers's debt to the Scottish common-sense tradition, see Rice, "Natural theology."

37. Baxter, "Science and belief," pp. 108, 41. See also Phillips, "The development of demonstrative theism," p. 90.

38. See, for instance, [John Wilson], "Review.—Dr Chalmers's Discourses," *Blackwood's Edinburgh Magazine* 1 (1817): 73–5, p. 74.

39. See Brown, *Thomas Chalmers*, pp. 16–29.

40. William Hanna, ed., *Memoirs of Thomas Chalmers, D.D. LL.D.*, 2 vols., Edinburgh: Thomas Constable, 1854, 1: 19.

41. *Ibid.*, 1: 43, 49.

42. An account of Chalmers's early religious views is given in Rice, "Natural theology," but it merely repeats and amplifies that given in Hanna, *Memoirs of Thomas Chalmers*.

43. While Godwin made his philosophical necessitarianism support a Pyrrhonian skepticism, it was certainly possible, as Hanna argues, to make it serve a quasi-deistical piety; however, its exact effect on Chalmers remains undetermined. See Hanna, *Memoirs of Thomas Chalmers*, 1: 11–13, 28. There is a largely derivative discussion of Chalmers's political radicalism at this period in William Matthews Kirkland, "The impact of the French revolution on Scottish religious life and thought with special reference to Thomas Chalmers, Robert Haldane and Neil Douglas," Unpublished Ph.D. thesis, University of Edinburgh, 1951, chapter 3.

44. Robert Coutts, *Sermons by the late Rev. Thomas Coutts, Brechin, with a preface by Thomas Chalmers, and a memoir by the Rev. Thomas Guthrie*, Edinburgh: John Johnstone, 1847, p. vii.

45. Hanna, *Memoirs of Thomas Chalmers*, 1: 12.

46. *Ibid.*, 1: 13.

47. Letter from Thomas to Grace Chalmers, 26 February 1821, quoted in ibid., 1: 13.

48. *Ibid.*, 1: 29, 19.

49. *Ibid.*, 1: 27–28.

50. Phillips, "The development of demonstrative theism," p. 101.

51. Hanna, *Memoirs of Thomas Chalmers*, 1: 105.

52. *Ibid.*, 1: 106.

53. *Ibid.*, 1: 105. The early sermons published in [William Hanna], ed., *Sermons by*

the late Thomas Chalmers, D.D. LL.D., illustrative of different stages in his ministry, 1798–1847, Edinburgh: Thomas constable, 1849, do not shed any light on this question, and a study of the surviving manuscripts of Chalmers's early sermons at New College, Edinburgh, is particularly desirable in this regard.

54. [Thomas Chalmers], *Observations on a passage in Mr Playfair's Letter to the Lord Provost of Edinburgh relative to the mathematical pretensions of the Scottish clergy*, Cupar, Fife: R. Tullis, 1805.

55. Quoted in *ibid., p. 4*.

56. *Ibid.*, p. 11.

57. Hanna, *Memoirs of Thomas Chalmers*, 1: 107.

58. *Ibid.*

59. Henry Hallam, *Introduction to the literature of Europe in the fifteenth, sixteenth and seventeenth centuries*, 4 vols., London: John Murray, 1838–9, 3: 227. On Baconianism in the Scottish common-sense school see Richard Yeo, "An idol of the market-place: Baconianism in nineteenth century Britain," *History of Science* 23 (1985): 251–98, pp. 259–67.

60. Hanna, *Memoirs of Thomas Chalmers*, pp. 26–28. See also Smith, "From design to dissolution."

61. *Ibid.*, 1: 27.

62. Thomas Chalmers, *The evidence and authority of the Christian revelation*, Edinburgh: William Blockwood, 1814, pp. 194–95, 213–14.

63. Theodor Dwight Bozeman, *Protestants in an age of science: the Baconian ideal and antebellum American religious thought*, Chapel Hill: University of North Carolina Press, 1977.

64. Rice, "Natural theology."

65. Hilton, *Age of atonement*, p. 183.

66. Brown, *Thomas Chalmers*, pp. 50–51.

67. *Ibid.*, p. 52.

68. Letter from Thomas to Alexander Chalmers, 14 February 1820, quoted in Hanna, *Memoirs of Thomas Chalmers*, 1: 138.

69. *Ibid.* 1: 105.

70. *Ibid.* 1: 104–5. Some accounts suggest that Thomson actively recruited Chalmers to carry out the article (see Brown, *Thomas Chalmers* p. 51, and Margaret Maria Gordon, *The home life of Sir David Brewster*, 2nd ed., Edinburgh: Edmonston and Douglas, 1870, p. 79). However, Hanna's account appears to be based on correspondence that is not now extant.

71. David Brewster to Thomas Chalmers, 3 September 1810, Chalmers Papers, New College, Edinburgh (hereinafter cited as CHA), 4.1.15.

72. Chalmers, *Evidence and authority*, pp. 196–97.

73. *Ibid.*, pp. 186–88.

74. *Ibid.*, p. 5. See also pp. 188–89.

75. *Ibid.*, pp. 188–89.

76. Baxter, "Science and belief," pp. 73–75. By contrast, Harry Phillips argues that Chalmers's "earlier published views specifically repudiated any interest in any rational or moral considerations apart from those contained in revelation itself." Phillips, "The development of demonstrative theism," p. 98.

77. Chalmers, *Evidence and authority* pp. 220–21.

78. Thomas Chalmers, "Remarks on Cuvier's Theory of the Earth," *Edinburgh Christian Instructor* 8 (1814): 261–74, p. 270.

79. Chalmers, *Evidence and authority* pp. 225–26.

80. Sermon on Heb. 6: 17–20, [10 August 1812?], CHA 6.15.128.

81. Thomas Chalmers, *On the miraculous and internal evidences of the Christian revelation, and the authority of its records*, 2 vols., Glasgow: William Collins, [1836], 1: 385.

82. Pietro Corsi, *Science and religion: Baden Powell and the Anglican debate, 1800–1860*, Cambridge: Cambridge University Press, 1988, pp. 61–63.

83. *Ibid.*, p. 65.

84. *Ibid.*, p. 67.

85. *Ibid.*, p. 64.

86. Hanna,*Memoirs of Thomas Chalmers* 1: 278.

87. Letter from William M'Gavin to Thomas Chalmers, 29 March 1815, CHA 4.4.37. The tract appeared as Thomas Chalmers, *Extracts from Evidences of Christianity*, [Glasgow]: Glasgow Religious Tract Society, 1815.

88. "Venusinus," *Remarks on the Edinburgh Christian Instructor's review of Dr. Mearns' "Principles of Christian evidence;" with a proposal for publishing and circulating, under the sanction of the General Assembly of the Kirk of Scotland, an improved edition of that review; humbly submitted to the consideration of Dr. Chalmers' friends*, London: R. Hunter, 1819, p. 2.

89. She told him: "it is the kind of reading I am particularly fond of[.] [W]e have been ingaged lately reading Paley's natural theology with which we are highly delighted." Letter from Jane Morton to Thomas Chalmers, 3 December 1814, CHA 4.3.43.

90. [Anon.], "Review of Chalmers on Christianity," *Christian Herald* 2 (1815): 99–105, p. 100.

91. [Anon.], "Review of Chalmers' Evidences of Christianity," *Edinburgh Christian Instructor* 14 (1817): 19–41, pp. 24, 25.

92. Letter from Samuel Charters to Thomas Chalmers, 29 February 1812, CHA 4.2.3. The sermon to which this letter relates has not been identified; however, see the sermon from August 1812 quoted earlier in the chapter. Charters refers to [Henry Dodwell], *Christianity not founded on argument; and the true principles of Gospel-evidence assigned: in a letter to a young gentleman at Oxford*, London: M. Cooper, 1741; and Philip Doddridge, *An answer to a late pamphlet, intitled, Christianity not founded on argument, &c.: in three letters to the author*, 3 pts., London: M. Fenner and J. Hodges, 1743.

93. Chalmers, *Evidence and authority*, p. vi.

94. [Anon.], "Review of Chalmers' Evidences," pp. 33, 34.

95. [Anon.], "Review of Chalmers's Evidence and Authority of Revelation," *Christian Observer* 14 (1815): 236–48.

96. Brown, *Thomas Chalmers* p. 114.

97. Duncan Mearns, *Principles of Christian evidence illustrated*, Edinburgh, 1818, pp. xii–xiii.

98. John Bird Sumner, *A treatise on the records of the creation, and on the moral attributes of the creator; with particular reference to the consistency of the principle of population with the wisdom and goodness of the Deity*, 2 vols, London: J. Hatchord, 1816, pp. x–xi.

99. Mearns, *Principles of Christian evidence* pp. 26–27.

100. *Ibid.*, pp. 32–33.

101. *Ibid.*, pp. 102–3; cf. pp. 48–51.

102. *Ibid.*, p. 103.

103. *Ibid.*, pp. 70n.

104. Brown implies that Mearns only used Chalmers's *Evidence* as a pretext for his attack, in the midst of the controversy sparked by Chalmers's public appeal for an end to anti-Catholic prejudice. See Brown *Thomas Chalmers*, p. 114.

105. *Ibid.*

106. [Anon], "Review of Mearns's 'Principles of Christian Evidence,' " *Edinburgh Christian Instructor* 17 (1819): 180–204, p. 182.

107. *Ibid.*, pp. 181, 182.

108. *Ibid.*, p. 182.

109. "Venusinus," *Remarks*, p. 14.

110. [Anon.], "Review of Mearns's 'Principles' " pp. 198, 197, 199.

111. *Ibid.*, p. 204.

112. Thomas Chalmers, *On the power, goodness and wisdom of God as manifested in the adaptation of external nature to the moral and intellectual constitution of man*, 2 vols., London: William Pickering, 1833, 1: 72.

113. *Ibid.*, 1: 77.

114. Rice, "Natural Theology," and Phillips, "The development of demonstrative theism."

115. In particular, friends supplied him with suitable reading matter for his studies; see, for instance, Hanna, *Memoirs of Thomas Chalmers* 1: 279, and the letter from Charles Stuart to Thomas Chalmers, 29 April 1813, CHA 4.2.41.

116. There is a manuscript in CHA 6.4.5, partially in shorthand, which has been catalogued as a draft appendix to Chalmers's *Evidence*. While nothing in the longhand portion of the manuscript identifies it definitively with this work, the introduction is suggestive: "Since the appearance of the first edition of this little work, I have had much interesting conversation with Christian friends upon its subject, and some of whom have expressed in my hearing their doubtfulness as to the soundness and tendency of the whole argument. My own impression is that the difference betwixt us does not lie in any of our opinions about the truth as it is in Jesus, but in our mode of putting that truth. I am sure however from the respectability of the people to whom I allude and from the eminent stations which some of them habit in the religious community that they represent a large portion of sentiment among the Christians of this country. To them I address these few additional pages."

117. See, for example, Baxter, "Science and belief," pp. 76f.

118. That this is not a work of natural theology is persuasively argued in David Cairns, "Thomas Chalmers' *Astronomical discourses*: a study in natural theology?" *Scottish Journal of Theology* 9 (1956): 410–21.

119. Thomas Chalmers, *Discourses on the Christian revelation viewed in connection with the modern astronomy*, Edinburgh: Thomas Constable and Co., 1859, pp. 171–72, 173–74.

120. *Ibid.*, p. 178.

121. For an account of this remarkable occasion, see Hanna, *Memoirs of Thomas Chalmers*, 1: 422–23. The text of the sermon is in CHA 6.17.50. See also the letter from John William Cunningham to Thomas Chalmers, 18 January 1818, CHA 4.7.32.

122. Thomas Chalmers, *Sermons preached at St. John's Church, Glasgow*, Glasgow: Chalmers and Collins, 1823, pp. 246–52.

123. On the importance of Chalmers's appointment as an academic theologian for the development of his views, see Baxter, "Science and belief," p. 69. See also Phillips, "The development of demonstrative theism," p. 102.

124. "Notes from Dr. Chalmers' lectures on theology," n. d. (watermark 1827), Edinburgh University Library, Special collections, Dc.7.81–82; quoted in Baxter, "Science and belief," p. 90.

125. Joseph John Gurney, *Chalmeriana; or, colloquies with Dr. Chalmers*, London: R. Bentley, 1853, pp. 3–4, 6–7.

126. Hilton, *Age of atonement* p. 183.

PART IV

SPECIFIC
ENCOUNTERS

7

Scriptural Geology
In America

RODNEY L. STILING

According to historian Milton Millhauser, the nineteenth-century line of thinking known as Scriptural Geology probably takes its name from a two-volume
work by that name published in 1826 and 1827 by English clergyman George
Bugg (1769?–1851). More a school of thought than an organized movement,
Scriptural Geologists sought to protect and preserve the Bible from the perceived
encroachments of a threatening science, but more to the point, to throw back
any hermeneutical compromises that ill-advised interpreters of Genesis might
inappropriately grant to promoters of geology. Never dominant, Scriptural Geology nonetheless became quite visible for a time in Great Britain, and to a
somewhat lesser extent in the United States, where, in the middle of the century,
America produced a handful of intriguing authors of this school.[1]

Very little of the biblical text refers specifically to nature or natural phenomena, but in those few places where Scripture makes reference to nature, Christians committed to the time-honored notion that the one God is the author of
both a general revelation in nature and a special revelation in Scripture would
insist that these "two books" in some real sense actually agree. As the science
of geology developed in the late eighteenth and early nineteenth centuries, it
became increasingly difficult for the geological interpretation of the history of
the earth to conform to the traditional interpretation of the biblical history of
the earth as outlined in the Creation and Flood accounts of Genesis. There were
two main areas of tension: the age and composition of the earth, and the effect
and extent of the Genesis Flood. By 1800, fewer and fewer geologists, even
those deeply sympathetic to these biblical concerns, could affirm that the earth
was merely several thousands of years old. Increasingly, estimates drawn from
observations of the earth suggested ages vastly greater than that. Further, geologists placed less and less confidence in the idea that the existence of the stratified
deposits and their fossil contents could be attributed to the singular action of

the Flood of Noah's time. Although the traditional understanding of the biblical narrative had served for some centuries as a very useful framework for geology, ethnology, and even biogeography, by the late eighteenth century, the accumulation of new information from nature eventually demanded a reexamination of that traditional understanding.

Scriptural Geology in Great Britain

At the risk of oversimplifying a complex problem, in the late eighteenth and early nineteenth century the options before science-minded Christian thinkers committed both to the study of nature and to the divine character of Scripture were three: 1) that human scientific observation should have the dominant or determining role in the study of nature and the Bible should assume a responding or submissive role (or no role); 2) that the Bible should have the dominant or determining role in the study of nature and human scientific observation should assume a submissive role; 3) that the Bible and human scientific observations of nature have equally important and valid roles—either may be adjusted so as to bring the two into agreement, but agreement must be achieved. As the need to seek a new biblical understanding of geological phenomena grew, the third option became the path most traveled. However, as historian James R. Moore has pointed out, the so-called Baconian Compromise required of option three that most of the adjustment be made on the part of interpreters of the Bible rather than by the interpreters of earth history.[2]

An important example of this kind of adjustment appeared in 1815, when the Scottish kirkman Thomas Chalmers (1780–1847) published a small book entitled *Evidence and Authority of the Christian Revelation* in which he argued that the language of Genesis chapter one implied that a time interval or "gap" existed between its first two verses. This proposed interval provided an indefinite chronological space into which, according to Chalmers, vast stretches of geological time could be inserted and then after which the customarily received six-day creation would have taken place. In this interpretation, the traditional creation narrative was understood to describe a *re*-creation of the earth—a restoration that followed ages and ages of activity and devastation on earth that lay recorded in the earth but not on the pages of the sacred text. Chalmers's ingenious interpretation provided for a neat and almost complete reconciliation of geology and Genesis by placing most of geological history beyond biblical comment. The scheme rather rapidly became a standard one in Great Britain, being adopted by prominent clergy, respected popular writers, and influential geologists such as William Daniel Conybeare (1787–1857) and William Buckland (1784–1856).[3]

In this context, the appearance of a Scriptural Geology in Great Britain may be best described as a response rather than an initiative. Scriptural Geologists insisted on a literal six-day creation and a short (less than 10,000-year) chronology of earth history. In addition, adherents to this line of thinking suggested that all geological formations were generated either by the action of the primeval waters of Genesis 1, or by the action of natural (perhaps accelerated) geological processes during the 1,700 years between the creation and the Genesis Flood, or by the actions of water and cataclysm during and shortly after the Flood, or by any combination of the three. Therefore, seeing the new "gap theory" interpretation of Genesis as a threat to faith and orthodoxy, concerned authors of the Scriptural Geology school began to publish in the 1820s a string of strongly worded books in Great Britain—notably Granville Penn's (1761–1844) *Comparative Estimate of the Mineral and Mosaic Geologies* (1822) and George Bugg's *Scriptural Geology*—all protesting any approach to geology that would sacrifice the traditional understanding of Genesis. In the 1830s, another wave of such books gathered in response to the publication of Lyell's *Principles of Geology* (1830–1833) and to William Buckland's shift away from identifying the Genesis Flood with the diluvial formations in his Bridgewater Treatise of 1836. Prominent in this round were George Fairholme's *General View of the Geology of Scripture* (1833) and *The Mosaic Deluge* (1837). These argued for the reestablishment of geology on its previous scriptural foundations.[4]

New Geology in America

Meanwhile, in the United States, the idea of a modified interpretation of Genesis was finding additional adherents. Geological study in mid-nineteenth-century America rested firmly in the hands of orthodox Christian leaders who were committed to the preserving of geology as a servant of the faith and to the reconciliation of geology and Genesis. Leading geologists such as Yale's Benjamin Silliman (1779–1864), for example—no theological liberal—on the one hand defended the Bible against the likes of the infamous philosophical materialist and chemist Thomas Cooper (1759–1839), and on the other hand reinterpreted the Bible by adopting a "day-age" reconciliation scheme for Genesis and geology of the sort more popular in Europe. Cooper attacked the Bible as "detestable" and "unauthenticated" and attacked Silliman's geology as so unconventional that there were not even "half a dozen Geologists in Europe who would venture to coincide with your views." Undaunted, Silliman published his *Outlines of the Course of Geological Lectures, Given at Yale College* (1829), "Consistency of Geology with Sacred History" (1833), "Relation of Geology to Early Scripture History" (1839), and dozens of other editorials, letters, and articles in which he argued for the compatibility of science and Scripture.[5]

Silliman's student, colleague, and friend Edward Hitchcock (1793–1864), while preaching against "infidel" interpretations of geology and warning that "the very stones cry out" against unbelievers, developed the idea of the "Christian Geologist," whose task it was "to reconcile the facts . . . with the Mosaic account." From the beginning to the end of his fruitful career, Hitchcock believed in the harmony of Genesis and geology: "If both records are from God," he wrote, "there can be no real contradiction between them." Hitchcock wrote dozens of essays, lectures, articles, and books, among which are titles such as "Connection of Geology with Theology" (1820s), "The Connection Between Geology and Natural Religion" (1835), "The Connection Between Geology and the Mosaic History of Creation" (1835), and *The Religion of Geology* (1851). Hitchcock's system of reconciling Genesis and geology involved the use of Chalmers's system for inter-preting Genesis 1 and the successive employment of four different models of the Genesis Flood. He did whatever was necessary to maintain the compatibility of the Mosaic account with the accumulation of geological observations. Capturing the deepest convictions of the Christian Geologists in a slogan, Hitchcock once wrote: "We sincerely protest against any such efforts to divorce science from re-ligion. What 'God hath joined together, let no man put asunder.' "[6]

Silliman and Hitchcock both affirmed the "new views" that the earth was geologically ancient and both opposed the idea that the Flood could account for the formation of the extensive consolidated fossil-bearing strata. Hitchcock wrote that geology revealed the "arcana" of "the vast and varied plans of Je-hovah," which were buried in "deep and illimitable" time. Silliman once re-ferred to the idea of creation in "six days of twenty-four hours" as "puerile and vulgar." Hitchcock considered the idea that the fossil-bearing strata had been formed by the Flood as "not possible" and "entirely absurd." He felt it "painful" that the fossils "were still referred to as evidences of that convulsion" because it could give the impression to "infidel geologists" that theologians were be-coming desperate in their defense of Moses. More important, Hitchcock and Silliman believed that Christian geologists like themselves should be enlisted, indeed consulted, by theologians involved in the interpretation of Genesis. Fur-ther, they were convinced that without input from geologists who were "dis-posed to reverence the scriptures" as they were, "no *mere* divine, no *mere* critic in language" could possibly get Genesis right.[7]

This conviction that "mere theologians" (Hitchcock's word) were inadequate for the task led to a confrontation between Silliman and Hitchcock with former Yale friend Moses Stuart (1780–1852), an Andover Seminary Hebrew scholar. Despite Hitchcock's matrimonial rhetoric about the union of science and Scrip-ture, Stuart resented the encroachment of the Christian geologists into the theo-logians' study. He argued that the question of the meaning of Genesis "is one of *philology*" not geology: "The sacred writers," Stuart observed, "were not com-missioned to teach geology." While Stuart explicitly claimed to believe that "God will not contradict in one book, what he has taught in another," he contended that at present, the language of Genesis chapter one could be understood in no other terms than those of six twenty-four days and a short age of the earth.[8]

Although he rejected any reinterpretation of Genesis to accommodate geo-logical theory, Moses Stuart should not be regarded as a Scriptural Geologist, because he made no attempt to modify geology. He offered no reinterpretation of geology to fit the old traditional understanding of Genesis; he was merely defending the separate turf of philology and hermeneutics. But his objections to the reconcilers foreshadowed the modest wave of Scriptural Geology that broke over American geology in mid-century.

The Stirring of Scriptural Geology

American writers who might qualify as Scriptural Geologists were not that nu-merous[9] to begin with, but three in particular fit the profile. Interestingly, all were situated in New York City, all wrote in objection to the reconciling trend, and all wrote before the advent of Darwinism. (If there was anything that Scriptural Geology was *not* about, it was not about combating evolution.)

The publication of Edward Hitchcock's *Religion of Geology and Its Connected Sciences* in the spring of 1851 seemed to mark the occasion for the appearance of Scriptural Geology in the United States. A classic science-Scripture reconciliation, Hitchcock's book triggered a reaction later that same year entitled *The Epoch of Creation: The Scripture Doctrine Contrasted with the Geology Theory.* The author, Eleazar Lord (1788–1871), was a successful and respected New York City insurance and railroad executive who retired about 1835 when not yet fifty to devote himself nearly exclusively to writing and religious activities. A frequently published author, Lord had earlier anonymously declared that the ideas of an old earth and a geologically insignificant Genesis Flood were "wholly at war with the Bible" and "puerile." Lord attacked "theoretical" geology with its views of an old earth and a limited or insignificant Flood, and called readers back to the basic beliefs held by previous generations: a young earth, the rapid deposition of the fossil-bearing sedimentary strata at the time of the Flood (or in the brief 1,700-year interval between the creation and the Flood), and the imminent return of Christ.[10]

Eleazar Lord complained especially about Hitchcock's insistence that to accept miracles as a possible factor in earth history was to preclude scientific investigation: "if it was miraculous," Hitchcock had written of the geologic past, "we must give up the idea of philosophizing about it." Lord disagreed. He felt strongly that nature could testify even to the supernatural. The *"facts of geology,"* he argued, reveal neither when nor how rapidly the fossils were buried. Conclusions on those matters were founded upon interpretations, and the interpretations rested upon assumptions. Assume a possibly miraculous Genesis Flood, for example, instead of one strictly governed by natural law, and the "facts of geology" would support a different interpretation, that is, that the fossiliferous strata *were* a product of the Flood. Lord's solution to the puzzle of the fossil record was straightforward: he assigned the surface drift phenomena, the coal beds, and all of the sedimentary strata to the period associated with the Flood:

> The whole mass of sedimentary matter was dissolved, intermixed with the existing plants and animals, and held in solution in the waters of the deluge; and under the influence of mechanical, chemical, galvanic, electric, and perhaps other forces, precipitated, distributed into beds of diverse mineral composition, consolidated, and subsequently elevated above sea level.

Lord was critical of virtually every aspect of Hitchcock's conciliatory volume and even managed to attack Hitchcock himself: the book effectively illustrated, Lord marveled, that "the mind of a geologist, devout and conversant with the Scriptures though he be, may be mystified and bewildered by physical studies, theories, and associations."[11]

Most prominent among Eleazar Lord's publishing outlets stood the *Theological and Literary Journal*, a New York quarterly dedicated to promoting a conservative millenarian theology. The journal was founded in 1848 and then edited by none other than Eleazar's like-minded younger brother David Nevins Lord (1792–1880), a prosperous New York dry goods merchant. David Lord proved to be the dominant force at the *Journal*, contributing nearly a score of articles himself during its 13-volume career. Beginning in 1852, he offered his own responses to Hitchcock's *Religion of Geology*, criticizing Hitchcock's interpretation of the creation and the Flood. David Lord's criticisms were most heavily leveled at what he considered two root problems: first, the naturalistic assumptions of geology, and second, the whole reconciliation enterprise, the very idea of accommodating Scripture with science. The success of Hitchcock's efforts rested on these very assumptions: that geological processes operate in accord with natural law, and that nature and the Bible constituted the works of a single divine author, and thus were necessarily reconcilable. To David Lord, all of naturalistic geology was founded upon "postulates that are gratuitously assumed" which contradict even "the laws themselves of matter." The whole enterprise, he suggested, "manifestly needs a reconstruction." He summed up Hitchcock's reconciling effort as "altogether mistaken" and a "fantastic dream, without a shadow of evidence to sustain it, unphilosophical in every respect." Unsatisfied with mere assault on a fellow Christian, Lord also battered Hitchcock's work as a "direct and fatal contradiction to the teachings of revelation," as "natural and powerful auxiliaries of scepticism and infidelity," and in short, "a great evil."[12]

David Lord felt that reconciliation schemes fostered apostasy. "Let any one converse with the sceptical," Lord complained in a review in 1854, "and learn what the considerations were which led them to renounce their faith in the inspiration and authority of the sacred volume; and he will find that these doctrines of Dr. Smith, Dr. Hitchcock, Hugh Miller, and their colaborers in the propagation of the system, were among the causes of their disbelief, and are among the reasons by which they justify it."[13]

In 1855, David Lord compiled his views into a volume with the telling title of *Geognosy, or the Facts and Principles of Geology Against Theories*. Technically, "geognosy" is the practice of studying or describing the composition and arrangement of the materials in the earth without speculating how they came to be so composed or arranged. By "facts" Lord meant the observable geological phenomena. The "principles" included the belief in the Bible as a guide to geological problem solving. The "theories," of course, included the assumed effectiveness of geological causes now in action and the resulting erroneous theories of an old earth and a gradual creation. Ironically David Lord's version of geological history required him to do substantial speculating of his own. The "materials of the earth," he surmised, "must have been drawn from the interior of the globe. . . . [T]hey were thrown up from the depths of the earth, and arranged in their present form *within the period* that is implied in the Mosaic history of the world from the creations to the remodification of its surface at the deluge." This scheme would eliminate the need of "assigning to the earth any earlier date than that which is ascribed to it by the history in Genesis." The only proof required, he argued, was to show that the idea was "compatible with the laws of nature, and therefore possible and probable; as [sic; and?] that being shown, the consistency of the facts of geology with the Scriptures is established." So much for geognosy.[14]

Though undeniably articulate, Eleazar and David Lord both developed a reputation for energetic expositions of simplistic notions. The *Biblical Repertory and Princeton Review* criticized Eleazar Lord's *Epoch of Creation* for doing "more harm than good" with its shallow view of science and its uncharitable attack on Edward Hitchcock. A writer in the *Presbyterian Quarterly Review* considered Eleazar Lord to be full of "the most blind and misguided zeal." A particularly pointed review in the *New Englander* accurately described Eleazar Lord's volume as belonging "geologically speaking, to an earlier period" and as having an air of "overbearing authority" and "dogmatic intolerance" about it. It would "confirm the prejudices of the ignorant, and give a temporary relief to the half-informed," the reviewer concluded.[15]

Brother David Lord also garnered his own critics. A reviewer in the *Protestant Episcopal Quarterly Review* in 1856 criticized David Lord's *Geognosy*, especially his insistence that the earth was only 6,000 years old and his linkage of the fossil-bearing strata with this brief earth history and the Flood. "Respectable geologists can now no more believe this," the reviewer scoffed, "than astronomers can credit the sun's traveling daily around the earth." In 1850, the *American Church Review*, an independent Episcopal journal, characterized David Lord as full of "dogged obstinacy" and "bitter vituperation." A decade later writers in the *Southern Presbyterian Review* still complained of Lord's unrelenting arrogance, reminding him that "humility becomes all who would approach God in the study either of His Works or His Word." An editor in that journal branded the brothers Lord simply as "antigeologists."[16]

Despite their brusque manner, the Lords did receive some support, mainly from yet another New Yorker, Dr. Martyn Paine (1794–1877), who significantly extended their views. Born into an influential Vermont family, Martyn Paine was educated at Harvard, where he also received his medical degree. His father, Elijah, served in the U.S. Senate and then for decades as a U. S. district court judge in Vermont. His brother Charles served as governor of Vermont. But Martyn moved to New York City in 1822 and resided there until his death 55 years later. He was a member of the founding faculty of medicine in 1841 of the new Medical College of the University of the City of New York, and continued there teaching and authoring textbooks as a professor of therapeutics and materia medica for 25 years. A reviewer of one of Paine's medical textbooks once characterized Martyn Paine as a "genius" with "independence of mind" who also happened to be—in an understatement—a "firm opposer of modern geology."[17]

In a lengthy exposition in the *Protestant Episcopal Quarterly Review* in 1856 and in his later *Physiology of the Soul and Instinct* (1872), Paine endorsed the exhortations of the Lord brothers, praising their "spirit of forbearance and courtesy." Paine portrayed himself as a kind of colaborer with them in their work of "recalling the faith of the Christian world to the Mosaic narrative of Creation and of the General Deluge." Paine considered criticism of authors like David Lord to be indicative of the sorry state of geology: the acceptance of a nonliteral interpretation of the creation account seemed to reveal a dangerous concession made to "theoretical geology."[18]

Theoretical geology, a technical term (intended pejoratively) employed by both the Lords and Martyn Paine, was built, according to them, on the underlying assumptions that the sediments of the fossiliferous strata were deposited under relatively tranquil conditions and at a gradual and uniform rate. These constituted mere assumptions, they argued, because no human observer witnessed the actual deposition of the strata. Any inferences built upon these assumptions were thus tagged "theoretical" geology: especially damaging had been the suggestions that the earth was ancient and that the effects and extent of the Flood had been limited. The Bible, by contrast, offered inspired infallibility rather than mere assumption and explicit description in the place of invalid inference. The Creator Himself served as the witness, making possible the perfectly trustworthy alternative to the untrustworthy "theoretical geology": Dr. Paine called it "theological geology." Paine deeply feared the theological and cultural implications of modern geology. "Theoretical geology," Paine warned those enamored with reconciliation schemes, "must surrender its ground or abandon Revelation." Christians could not have both modern geology and the Bible. One had to go. Like the Lord brothers, Paine was certain that compromises with theoretical geology had "opened the door for a wide-spread infidelity."[19]

Like others of the school of Scriptural Geology, Paine argued for a literal understanding of the creation account, a young earth, and a Flood narrative to be taken in its "obvious sense." The stratified fossil-bearing rocks could not be accounted for in the fashion of theoretical geology—by extending the geological age of the earth—so Paine attributed these formations to the Flood. "This catastrophe will explain all the geological 'enigmas,' " he wrote, even though "theoretical geology repudiates the event." To explain all enigmas, the Flood therefore must have been nothing short of a worldwide affair, and he criticized attempts to interpret it otherwise as "sarcastic" toward the biblical text.[20]

Paine rested his view of the all-effectual universal Flood on three supports: the Old Testament account of the Flood in Genesis, the New Testament references to the Flood by Jesus and the apostles, and the coal formations. These formed what Paine called a "united testimony" for universal effectiveness of the Flood. The first two supports found their basis deep in his religious commitments to the inspiration of the Bible and to its literal interpretation. But most of Paine's speculative energies were devoted to the idea that "the *coal-formations* are the offspring of the general deluge." If these formations deep in the earth proved to be products of the Flood, he thought, then the plausibility that the other consolidated strata were also products of the Flood would be dramatically enhanced.[21]

All geologists agreed that the coal formations were composed of heavily concentrated once-living plant matter that had been buried and pressed into strata. But Paine traced this phenomenon to the Flood. He argued that one "necessary result of our flood would have been an uprooting of all the forests of the globe." These floating forests were then washed up onto the North American continent, he speculated, by cataclysmic oceanic surges from the southeast and then buried in the sediments that precipitated from the waters as the Flood calmed. By analogous processes all the sedimentary layers were formed, but the coal formations, he felt, bore a special witness to the effect. In this way, the Flood could be enlisted to explain the entire set of fossil-bearing sediments.[22]

The Eclipse of American Scriptural Geology

By the time the American Civil War had come to a close, the *Theological and Literary Journal* had ceased publication, Paine was retiring from medical education, and the three New York–based promoters of Scriptural Geology ranged in age from 71 to 77 years. They had been sincere, dedicated, conspicuous, and annoyingly logical, yet their program had not developed into a serious option for geology-minded evangelical Americans. In the end, the "party of reconciliation" or the "*Christian* Geologists" proved to enjoy the largest following. The reasons for this were several. From its earliest years, geology in America was essentially a Christian pursuit. Although the expression "evangelical" may be a bit anachronistic for the period, the fact remains that the leaders and most influential people in the young discipline were without doubt what one would consider evangelical today. Virtually all of them contended vigorously for the accommodation of science and Scripture and specifically for the reconciliation of Genesis and geology—all, they believed, for the sake of the integrity both of the Scripture and the Christian faith.

Yale's Benjamin Silliman became the foremost geological educator of the first half of the nineteenth century, training many future geologists and orienting a host of students heading into other professions to the basics and benefits of geological study. Silliman took every occasion to outline the compatibility between geological study and the Bible, arguing that not only do the two not conflict but they strengthen and validate one another. As editor of the foremost scientific (and geological) journal in America of the era, *The American Journal of Science*, Silliman extended his influence well beyond the classroom. Most important, however, Silliman's personal piety was widely known and trusted. Persevering in difficult personal circumstances, from suffering financial want to grieving over children lost to illness, Silliman maintained a sincerity and faith that completely precluded any attempt at attributing his views to creeping infidelity or liberalism.

Silliman's friend Edward Hitchcock became perhaps the most influential reconciler of nineteenth-century America. As a dedicated young Congregationalist clergyman, Hitchcock became interested in geology on an amateur basis first. Deciding to leave his pastorate, he studied with Silliman at Yale and then took a post at Amherst College as a professor of natural sciences. Maturing into a geological master, Hitchcock eventually rose to the presidency of Amherst College, became the first to conduct a government-funded statewide geological survey (Massachusetts, 1830s), became the author of the first comprehensive American geology textbook for college-level study, and was elected the first president of the Association of American Geologists and Naturalists (later to become the American Association for the Advancement of Science). Hitchcock's dedication to Christian mission, to Christian character and growth, and to theological accuracy was deep and sincere. He, too, engaged in battles for the soul of geology, combating "infidels" on the left and exclusive philological professionals on the right. He, too, mourned the deaths of children and struggled with difficult personal hardships. Because character and leadership were unquestioned, his views on the compatibility of Scripture and science were widely respected and emulated.

More important, perhaps, was the legacy of these two influential leaders. Silliman's student and son-in-law, James Dwight Dana (1813–1895), a deeply religious man, became one of the leading geologists in the entire century, with influence deep into the present century. Dana also became a professor at Yale, and later succeeded Silliman as editor of *The American Journal of Science*. He contended vigorously for the compatibility of Genesis and geology and for the right of evangelical scientists to have a part or input into the interpretation of the Bible. Dana became especially well known and respected for his views on geological origins, which featured the "day-age" reconciliation schema. Dana's version of this scheme was reminiscent of his father-in-law's view and was also derived in part from the ideas of physical geographer Arnold Guyot (1807–1884), a friend of Dana's.[23]

Later in the century, in the era of Darwin, other evangelical "great men of geology," such as the prolific and influential Canadian geologist-educator John William Dawson (1820–1899) and Congregationalist geologist and editor George Frederick Wright (1838–1921), became widely known and frequently quoted authorities for the reconciliation of Genesis and geology. Their character and commitment beyond question, these men supported the creative day-age interpretations of Genesis and embraced a local Flood idea. Dawson's reputation in and out of religious circles was profound, and he became the only person ever to serve simultaneously as president both of the British Association for the Advancement of Science and the American Association for the Advancement of Science. Wright's geological expertise and writing brought him respect both from circles sympathetic to Darwinism and from the editors of the *International Standard Bible Encyclopedia* and of the World War I–era series *The Fundamentals*.[24]

These thinkers, all dedicated to maintaining a compatibility between Genesis and geology, exerted a wide and profound influence on American evangelicalism. The acceptance of nonliteral creative days of Genesis chapter one and a regional or nonuniversal Genesis Flood were central to the framework for compatibility. In other hands, perhaps such views might have seemed reckless, irresponsible, or anti-Christian. But in the hands of highly respected professionals whose expertise, integrity, and piety rendered them even of "good reputation with those outside the church," they became the bedrock of orthodoxy for nineteenth-century American evangelicalism. In addition, the reconcilers, or "Christian" Geologists—Silliman, Hitchcock, Dana, Wright, and others—were actually practicing geologists. While the Scriptural Geologists were skilled writers and editors who sometimes exhibited scholarly skill and penetrating insight, their practical experiences were drawn from the railroad and insurance businesses and from academic medicine. They were not, it turns out, geologists at all. Thus, while it may be proper to speak of Scriptural *Geology*, it is not really accurate to speak of Scriptural *Geologists*. The views of the reconcilers, the "new views" that Hitchcock and Silliman had euphemistically spoken of in the 1820s, became dominant in countless American Bible dictionaries, encyclopedias, handbooks, commentaries, and apologetics works in the latter half of the nineteenth century and in the early part of the twentieth. The views of the deliberate and dedicated "Christian" Geologists thus simply overwhelmed and drowned out those of the uncompromising and at times seemingly unfriendly "Scriptural" Geologists.[25]

The Echo of Scriptural Geology

Scriptural Geology, did, however, reappear in the late nineteenth century and early twentieth century, and it is still with us today by a different name and with a reformulated mission. In 1864 Seventh-day Adventist prophet Ellen Gould White (1827–1915) published an account of a vision experience in which she claimed to have been shown the Genesis Flood. She saw the violence and worldwide extent of the catastrophe, she beheld the doomed plants and animals being crushed into layers of rock and fossil as they were buried by the sediments of the Flood, and she witnessed the formation of the coal beds as whole forests were swept away by raging floodwaters and buried under layers of sediment. The published account of White's vision was embraced by the self-taught Adventist geological writer George McGready Price (1870–1963), who melded this extrabiblical revelation with scriptural accounts and his personal geological observations into what he called "Flood Geology." Twentieth-century flood geology proved to be essentially the same as nineteenth-century Scriptural Geology: both advocated a literal six-day creation, a short age of the earth, and the idea that all of the fossil-bearing strata were formed during and shortly after the Flood, or during the time between the creation and the end of the Flood. Price's views, best elucidated in his influential 1923 book *The New Geology*, found their way into established evangelical publishing outlets such as the *Princeton Theological Review* and the Fleming H. Revell publishing firm in New York. Eventually the views of flood geology caught the interest of theologian John Whitcomb (b. 1924) and hydrologist Henry Morris (b. 1918), whose 1961 publishing success *The Genesis Flood* has promoted the idea before evangelical readers ever since.[26]

Interestingly, American flood geology seems to have had no genetic relationship with the earlier Scriptural Geology. The phenotypic resemblance, so to speak, is there, but an examination of the genotype turns up no connection. White's and Price's accounts of the creation, age of the earth, and the Flood bear a very strong resemblance to the views of the Lords and especially to those of Martyn Paine. Perhaps there is another smoking gun of plagiarism in this subject as Ronald L. Numbers and others have found in other topics in White's writing. Such a case may be plausible, but the evidence remains soft, circumstantial, and inconclusive. But despite their strong resemblances, flood geology and Scriptural Geology differ in one important regard: they serve different functions. The heyday—if that expression pertains in this case—of Scriptural Geology came before the publication of Darwin's *Origin of Species*. Thus, its objective was simply to contend for the reputation and integrity of the biblical text as judged from the point of view of a literal, nonfigurative interpretative framework. To alter or broaden the interpretation of the text merely in the face of the claims of geological science was to threaten, it was feared, the security of the Bible and the Christian faith. In short, Scriptural Geology was a defense of a hermeneutical preference.[27]

Flood geology, on the other hand, became a weapon against a specific new threat to the faith as a whole: evolutionary theory. The main function of flood geology was not to engage the theory of evolution directly—that is, to debate the merits of the various proposed evolutionary mechanisms and processes—but rather to attack a foundational assumption: whether there had been enough time for evolution to have occurred. Recall that well before the publication of the *Origin of Species*, most American evangelical writers, at least as measured by reference works and study publications, had accepted the notion that the earth was indefinitely old. More importantly, this understanding was worked out in the absence of any influence of Darwinian evolution. Thus when the *Origin of Species* was published, it was not the question of the age of the earth that American evangelicals balked at, but the philosophical materialism and the anti-supernaturalistic tendencies of the theory. Charles Hodge summarized in a famous phrase about Darwinism that "it is atheism," a charge from which Darwin himself did not shrink. Nevertheless, the program of flood geology did not even need to address these larger philosophical and theological issues if it could achieve its main objective: to demonstrate that the earth is young. If the age of the earth could be measured in mere thousands of years, then the theory of evolution, which by definition requires millions and billions of years, would fall down without further consideration or debate. In a sense, it was the advent of Darwinian evolution that revived the fortunes of the old nineteenth-century Scriptural Geology, by giving it a new practical purpose, a new name, and a new set of advocates.[28]

Finally, American Scriptural Geology of the last century proved to be less about geology than about Scripture, and less about the content of Scripture than about its interpretation. In the end, Scriptural Geology and its more modern version, flood geology, were and are really symbols of a different question: how is the Bible to be interpreted, and how is information from outside the Bible to be considered and incorporated—if at all—in the interpretation of Scripture? In short, Scriptural Geology was not about geology; it was all about hermeneutics. Thus, while the story of Scriptural Geology and its successor flood geology will doubtless in time be increasingly regarded as marginal episodes in American evangelical history, the larger questions they symbolized will and perhaps should always remain near the center of American evangelical dialogue.[29]

NOTES

1. Milton Millhauser, "The Scriptural Geologists," *Osiris*, 1954, 11:65–86.
2. James R. Moore, "Geologists and the Interpreters of Genesis in the Nineteenth

Century," in *God and Nature: Historical Essays on the Encounter Between Christianity and Science*, ed. David C. Lindberg and Ronald L. Numbers (Berkeley: University of California Press, 1986), pp. 322–50, on pp. 322–25.

3. Thomas Chalmers, *Evidence and Authority of the Christian Revelation* (Edinburgh, 1815). Originally published as an *Encyclopaedia Britannica* article in 1814. W. D. Conybeare and William Phillips, *Outlines of the Geology of England and Wales, with Introductory Compendium of the General Principles of that Science and Comparative Views of the Structure of Foreign Countries* (London: W. Phillips, 1822); William Buckland, *Reliquiae Diluvianae; or observations on the Organic Remains Contained in Caves, Fissures, and Diluvial Gravel and on Other Geological Phenomena Attesting to the Action of an Universal Deluge* (London: John Murray, 1823 [New York: Arno Press, 1978]); William Buckland, *Geology and Mineralogy Considered with Reference to Natural Theology*, American Edition (Philadelphia: Carey, Lea, and Blanchard, 1837).

4. Millhauser, "Scriptural Geologists," pp. 70–75; Buckland, *Geology and Mineralogy* [his Bridgewater Treatise].

5. [Thomas Cooper], *Fabrication of the Pentateuch Proved, by the Anachronisms contained in those Books* (Granville, N.J.: George H. Evans, 1829, 1840); Thomas Cooper, *On the Connection between Geology and the Pentateuch: In a Letter to Professor Silliman, from Thomas Cooper, M.D. to Which Is Added the Defence of Dr. Cooper Before the Trustees of the South Carolina College* (Columbia, S.C.: Printed at the Times and Gazette Office, Jan. 1833); Cooper to Silliman, 17 December 1833, in Nathan Reingold, ed., *The Papers of Joseph Henry* (Washington: Smithsonian Institution Press, 1975), vol. 2, pp. 134–137; Benjamin Silliman, *Outline of the Course of Geological Lectures, Given in Yale College* (New Haven: Hezekiah Howe, 1829); Benjamin Silliman, "Supplement by the Editor—Consistency of Geology with Sacred History," in Robert Bakewell, *An Introduction to Geology* (New Haven: Hezekiah Howe, 1833). Benjamin Silliman, "Relation of Geology to the Early Scripture History," in Robert Bakewell, *An Introduction to Geology*, third American edition (New Haven: Hezekiah Howe, 1839).

6. Edward Hitchcock, *Utility of Natural History; A Discourse Delivered Before the Berkshire Medical Institution* (Pittsfield: Phinehas Allen, 1823), p. 24; Hitchcock, "The Connection Between Geology and The Mosaic History of Creation," *American Biblical Repository*, 1835, 5:439–51; Hitchcock, *The Religion of Geology* (Boston: Phillips, Sampson, and Company, 1854), pp. 4–5, 14; [Edward Hitchcock], "Notice and Review of the 'Reliquiae Diluvianae,'" *American Journal of Science*, 1824, 8:155. The reference was to Granville Penn's *Comparative Estimate of the Mineral and Mosaical Cosmologies* (London, 1822).

7. Edward Hitchcock, *The Highest Use of Learning: An Address Delivered at His Inauguration to the Presidency of Amherst College* (Amherst, Mass.: J. S. & C. Adams, 1845), p. 33; Edward Hitchcock, *The Utility of Natural History* (Pittsfield, Mass.: Phinehas Allen, 1823), pp. 20–24; Silliman to Hitchcock, 18 August 1820, Edward Hitchcock Papers.

8. Hitchcock to Silliman, 1 December 1822, Edward Hitchcock Papers; Silliman to Hitchcock, 5 May 1823, Edward Hitchcock Papers; Moses Stuart, "Critical Examination of Some Passages in Gen. I; with Remarks on Difficulties That Attend Some of the Present Modes of Geological Reasoning," *American Biblical Repository*, 1836, 7: 46–105, on pp. 49–52.

9. Possible candidates might include James Mease, *A Geological Account of the United States; Comprehending a Short Description of Their Animal, Vegetable, and Mineral Productions, Antiquities and Curiosities* (Philadelphia: Birch and Small, 1807); Howard Malcom, *A Dictionary of Important Names, Objects, and Terms Found in the Holy Scriptures* (Boston: Lincoln and Edmands, 1830); J. L. Comstock, *Outlines of Geology: Intended as a Popular*

Treatise of the Most Interesting Parts of the Science (Hartford: D. F. Robinson and Co., 1834).

10. Eleazar Lord, *The Epoch of Creation: The Scripture Doctrine Contrasted with the Geology Theory* (New York: Charles Scribner, 1851); [Eleazar Lord], "Epoch of Creation," *Literary and Theological Review*, 1837, 4: 526–38, on p. 538; A Layman [Eleazar Lord], *Geological Cosmology; or an Examination of the Geological Theory of the Origin and Antiquity of the Earth (and of the Causes and Object of the Changes It Has Undergone)* (New York: Robert Carter, 1843), p. 155.

11. Eleazar Lord, *Epoch of Creation*, pp. 165–67, 177–80, 230–40.

12. David Nevins Lord, "Genesis and the Geological Theory of the Age of the Earth," *The Theological and Literary Journal*, 1852, 4:529–614, on p. 613; D. N. Lord, "The Theory on Which Geologists Found Their Deduction of the Great Age of the World," *The Theological and Literary Journal*, 1853, 5:1–74 and 177–233, on pp. 72 and 232; D. N. Lord, "Review of *The Religion of Geology and Its Connected Sciences*," *The Theological and Literary Journal*, 1853, 5:353–403, on pp. 355, 385, and 402.

13. D. N. Lord, "Review of *The Two Records; the Mosaic and the Geological*. A Lecture Delivered before the Young Men's Christian Association in Exeter Hall, London by Hugh Miller, (Boston: Gould and Lincoln, 1854)," *Theological and Literary Journal*, 1855, 7:119–144, on p. 140.

14. David N. Lord, *Geognosy, or the Facts and Principles of Geology Against Theories* (New York: Franklin Knight, 1855), pp. 316–17. Two years earlier he had argued that "strata may have been formed within the period of eighteen hundred to two thousand years from the creation." D. N. Lord, "The Theory on Which Geologists Found Their Deduction of the Great Age of the World," *The Theological and Literary Journal*, 1853, 5:1–74 and 177–233, on p. 228.

15. "Review of Eleazar Lord's *Epoch of Creation*," *Biblical Repertory and Princeton Review*, 1851, 23: 696–98, on p. 697; "Is the Science of Geology True?" *Presbyterian Quarterly Review*, 1853, 1:83–106, on p. 87; "Lord's Epochs of Creation," *New Englander*, 1851, 9: 510–31, on pp. 510 and 531.

16. Review of Tayler Lewis's *Six Days of Creation* (1855) and Hugh Miller's *The Two Records: The Mosaic and Geological* (1954), *Protestant Episcopal Quarterly Review*, 1856, 3: 35–62, on p. 38; "Notice of *Theological and Literary Journal*," [American] *Church Review*, 1850, 3:462; J. R. Blake, "David N. Lord's Geological Writings," *Southern Presbyterian Review*, 1860, 13:537–78; James Woodrow, "Geology and Its Assailants," *Southern Presbyterian Review*, 1861, 14:549–74.

17. "Notice of Martyn Paine's *Institutes of Medicine* (New York: 1862)," *Methodist Quarterly Review*, 1863, 45:352–353.

18. A reviewer in the *Knickerbocker* once expressed appreciation for Eleazar Lord's *Epoch of Creation*, while explicitly disagreeing with Lord's views, encouraging him to press ahead and to disregard negative reviews. Nashville's *Southern Baptist Review and Eclectic* was actually enthusiastic about David Lord's *Geognosy*, urging "every Baptist minister to procure at once, and study thoroughly this work," adding that "every Christian should aid in its circulation." "Notice of Eleazar Lord's *Epoch of Creation*," *Knickerbocker*, 1851, 38:546–47; "Review of David Lord's *Geognosy*," *Southern Baptist Review and Eclectic*, 1855, 1:755–57.

19. Martyn Paine, "A Review of Theoretical Geology," *Protestant Episcopal Quarterly Review*, 1856, 3:161–281, on p. 163 and 171; Martyn Paine, *Physiology of the Soul and Instinct, as Distinguished from Materialism* (New York: Harper and Brothers, 1872), pp. 358–59.

20. Martyn Paine, *Physiology of the Soul and Instinct*, pp. ix, 358–64; Paine, "A Review of Theoretical Geology," p. 225.

21. Paine, "Review of Theoretical Geology," pp. 225, 234–35, 263.

22. Paine, "Review of Theoretical Geology," p. 248; Paine, *Physiology of the Soul and Instinct*, 664–707.

23. James D. Dana, *The Genesis of the Heavens and the Earth and All the Host of Them* (Hartford: The Student Publishing Company, 1890); Arnold Guyot, *The Biblical Cosmology in Light of Modern Science* (New York: Charles Scribner's Sons, 1884). See also Ronald L. Numbers, *Creation by Natural Law: LaPlace's Nebular Hypothesis in American Thought* (Seattle: University of Washington Press, 1977), pp. 91–95.

24. For example, J. W. Dawson, *Archaic: or Studies of the Cosmology and Natural History of the Hebrew Scriptures* (Montreal: B. Dawson and Son, 1860); J. W. Dawson, *Nature and the Bible* (New York: Robert Carter and Brothers, 1875); G. Frederick Wright, *Scientific Aspects of Christian Evidences* (New York: D. Appleton and Company, 1898); G. Frederick Wright, *Scientific Confirmations of Old Testament History* (Oberlin, Ohio: Bibliotheca Sacra Co., 1906); *The Fundamentals: A Testimony to the Truth* (Chicago: Testimony Publishing Company, 1910–1915), vols. 1–12; Ronald L. Numbers, "George Frederick Wright: From Christian Darwinist to Fundamentalist," *Isis*, 1988, 79:624–45; James Orr, gen. ed., *The International Standard Bible Encyclopedia* (Chicago: Howard-Severance Company, 1915).

25. For example, *Cyclopedia of Biblical Literature*, ed. William Lindsay Alexander, originally edited by John Kitto (Edinburgh: Adam and Charles Black, 1862); Milton Spenser Terry, *Biblical Hermeneutics: A Treatise on the Interpretation of the Old and New Testaments*, vol. 2 of the *Library of Biblical and Theological Literature*, ed. George R. Crooks and John F. Hurst (New York: Phillips and Hunt, 1883); *A Dictionary of the Bible: Comprising Its Antiquities, Biography, Geography, and Natural History*, ed. William Smith (London: John Murray, Walton and Maherly, 1863). Smith's *Dictionary* appeared in America as *Dr. William Smith's Dictionary of the Bible; Comprising Its Antiquities, Biography, Geography, and Natural History*, ed. H. B. Hackett and Ezra Abbot (New York: Hurd and Houghton, 1868) and also took on other forms: Samuel W. Barnum, *A Comprehensive Dictionary of the Bible, Mainly Abridged from Dr. Wm. Smith's Dictionary of the Bible* (New York: D. Appleton and Co., 1868), *Holman's Bible Teacher's Textbook and Student's Scripture History: A Treasury of Religious Knowledge* (Philadelphia: A. J. Holman and Co., 1877), and it even appeared as volume 5 of *The Bible Lover's Illustrated Library* (Chicago: Sears, Roebuck and Co., 1920); John M'Clintock and James Strong, *Cyclopaedia of Biblical, Theological, and Ecclesiastical Literature* (New York: Harper and Brothers, 1867–1881), 10 volumes, plus 2 volume *Supplement*, 1885–1887; Philip Schaff, *A Dictionary of the Bible: Including Biography, Natural History, Geography, Topography, Archaeology, and Literature*, fourth edition (Philadelphia: The American Sunday-School Union, 1887). Earlier editions were published in 1880, 1881, and 1885. Plus many, many others.

26. Ellen G. White, *Spiritual Gifts: Important Facts of Faith in Connection with the History of Holy Men of Old* (Battle Creek, Mich.: Seventh-day Adventist Publishing Association, 1864), vol. 3, pp. 64–79; George McGready Price, *The New Geology* (Mountain View, Calif.: Pacific Press, 1923); Price, *Q. E. D.; or New Light on the Doctrine of Creation* (New York: Fleming H. Revell Company, 1917); Price, "The Fossils as Age-Markers in Geology," *Princeton Theological Review*, 1922, 20:585–615; John C. Whitcomb, Jr., and Henry M. Morris, *The Genesis Flood: The Biblical Record and Its Scientific Implications* (Philadelphia: Presbyterian and Reformed Publishing Co., 1961). See also Ronald L. Numbers, "The Creationists," in *God and Nature: Historical Essays on the Encounter between Christianity and Science*, ed. David C. Lindberg and Ronald L. Numbers (Berkeley: University of California Press, 1986), pp. 391–423; Henry M. Morris, *A History of Modern Creationism* (San Diego: Master Books, 1984), pp. 118–19; and Numbers, *The Creationists* (New York: Alfred A. Knopf, 1992), the authoritative treatment of this movement.

27. The intervention of the Civil War, the Darwinian hypothesis, and acceptance of the Ice Age theory in the United States all undoubtedly could have contributed to the lack of a link between Scriptural geology and flood geology. Accordingly, the names of the Lord brothers or Martyn Paine do not appear in Byron Nelson's *The Deluge Story in Stone: A History of the Flood Theory of Geology* (Minneapolis: Augsburg Publishing House, 1931), Whitcomb and Morris's *Genesis Flood* (1961), or Henry Morris's *History of Modern Creationism* (1984).

28. See, for example, Henry M. Morris, *Scientific Creationism* (San Diego, Calif.: Creation-Life Publishers, 1974), p. 252; Whitcomb and Morris, *Genesis Flood*, p. 118; John D. Morris, "Does Scripture Require a Global Flood?" ("Back to Genesis" No. 32 for August 1991), *Acts and Facts*, 1991, 20:d.

29. Davis Young's *The Biblical Flood: A Case Study of the Church's Response to Extra-biblical Evidence* (Grand Rapids, Mich.: William B. Eerdmanns Publishing Co., 1995) is specifically devoted to an analysis of this very question of the role of extrabiblical information in hermeneutics.

8

Situating Evangelical
Responses to Evolution

DAVID N. LIVINGSTONE

On Situating Science and Religion

In recent years there has been a remarkable "spatial turn" among students of society and culture. The genealogy of this twist of events is both multifaceted and complex. But among philosophers, social theorists, and historians of science there has been a renewed emphasis on the significance of the local, the specific, the situated. Some philosophers thus argue that what passes as a good reason for believing a claim is different from time to time, and from place to place. Rationality, it turns out, is in large measure situation specific such that what counts as rational is contingent on the context within which people are located. "Good grounds" for holding a certain belief is evidently different for a twelfth-century milkmaid, a Renaissance alchemist, and a twentieth-century astrophysicist. Among social theorists there has also been a recovery of spatiality. The importance of the diverse locales within which social life is played out has assumed considerable significance with such writers as Clifford Geertz, Erving Goffman, Anthony Giddens, Michel Foucault, and Edward Said.[1]

Survey, however, is not my intention here. Rather it is to call attention to an increasing acknowledgment of the spatial in cultural life—an awareness that is being increasingly recognized among historians of science.[2] Thus, attention has been called to the role of experimental space in the production of scientific knowledge, the significance of the uneven distribution of scientific information, the diffusion tracks along which scientific ideas and their associated instrumental gadgetry migrate, the management of laboratory space, the power relations exhibited in the transmission of scientific lore from specialist space to public place, the political geography and social topography of scientific subcultures, and the institutionalization and policing of the sites in which the reproduction of scientific cultures is effected. The cumulative effect of these investigations is to draw attention to the local, regional, and national features of science—an enterprise hitherto regarded as prototypically universal.

The implications of these recent moves for my present task are of considerable dimensions. My suspicion is that the project of reconstructing the historical relations between science and religion might similarly benefit from a localizing strategy that seeks to situate "responses" or "encounters" in their respective sociospatial settings. To pursue such a program, I suggest, will inevitably mean abandoning grand narratives that trade in abstract and idealist "isms." It will not do to speak of "the" encounter between evangelicalism and evolutionism or Calvinism and Darwinism. Instead I think we will be better advised to seek to uncover how *particular* religious communities, in *particular* space-time settings, developed *particular* tactics for coping with *particular* evolutionary theses. Here I want to make a preliminary stab at elucidating the responses of certain conservative Christians to evolutionary claims in a number of different locales during the second half of the nineteenth century. If my argument is in the neighborhood of a correct analysis, the specifics of these situations turn out to be of crucial importance.

Calvinists Encounter Evolution

During 1874, in three different cities, Presbyterians with remarkably similar theological commitments issued their judgments on the theories of evolution that were gaining ascendancy in the English-speaking intellectual world. In Edinburgh, Belfast, and Princeton, differing assessments of the new biology were to be heard; in these different situations varying rhetorical stances were adopted; for in these religious spaces different circumstances prevailed.

1874: Three statements

RAINY IN EDINBURGH   In October of 1874 Robert Rainy, the new principal of New College, Edinburgh—the theological college of the Free Church—delivered his inaugural address. His subject was "Evolution and Theology" and, according to his biographer Simpson, it "attracted considerable attention." "The religious mind of the day," according to Simpson "was disturbed about Darwinism and apprehensive lest it should affect the foundations of faith; and that a man of Dr. Rainy's known piety and orthodoxy should, from the Principal's chair of the New College, frankly accept the legitimacy of the application of evolution even to man's descent and find it a point on which the theologian 'may be perfectly at ease' reassured many minds."[3] Indeed, Rainy did make it clear that while some found evolution objectionable, he himself did not feel justified "in imputing an irreligious position to the Evolutionist." Accordingly, he insisted that even if "the evolution of all animal life in the world shall be shown to be due to the gradual action of permanent forces and properties of matter"—a claim he himself actually doubted—that would have no bearing on "the argument of the Theist [or on] the mind of a reverent spectator of nature."[4] Methodologically, Rainy was prepared to allow considerable autonomy to the scientific enterprise, believing that it was "often in its right in keeping to its own path" irrespective of interpretations of Scripture. Indeed he had already applied the principles of inductive philosophy to the question of miracles.[5] But this certainly did not mean that Christians were never justified in "contesting the ground." To the contrary, evolution could be mobilized for infidel purposes; these simply had to be challenged. As illustration, he referred to the atomic theory of Democritus—an example that, as we shall see, had a particular poignancy in the winter of 1874. And yet, for all that, Rainy was remarkably sanguine about evolutionary speculation, even to the extent of welcoming evolutionary interrogations of human development. Not that he ruled out divine intervention in human origins; he certainly insisted on "direct Divine interposition."[6] But by decorporealizing the *imago dei*, he found it possible to liberate Christian anthropology from detailed questions over similarities in the human and anthropoid skeletons. Thereby the door was opened to an evolutionary account of the human physical form.

PORTER IN BELFAST   That same winter in Belfast, J. L. Porter, professor of biblical criticism in the General Assembly's College (and later president of Queen's College), delivered the opening address to the Presbyterian faculty and students.[7] Here he ominously spoke of the "evil tendencies of recent scientific theories"—and that of evolution in particular—which threatened to "quench every virtuous thought." The need for theological colleges was thus more urgent than ever so that "heavenly light is preserved and cherished." What was more, he declared that he was "prepared to show that not a single scientific fact has ever been established" from which the pernicious dogmas of Huxley and Tyndall could be "logically deduced."[8] Within a few weeks, on the last day of November, Porter would pursue this same theme in an address on "Science and Revelation: Their Distinctive Provinces" which inaugurated a series of winter lectures on "Science and Religion" in Rosemary Street Church in downtown Belfast. The need for a clear-cut boundary line—in terms of both content and methodology—between the provinces of science and theology was of the utmost importance to Porter, and while he was happy to insist that "no theological dogma can annul a fact of science" the question of "crude theories and wild speculations"—in which evolutionists were all too prone to engage—was a different matter. As for Darwin's own interventions, *The Origin of Species* was described as having made empirically "one of the most important contributions to modern science"; in logic, by contrast, it was "an utter failure." The facts, in other words, were welcome; the theory, alien. The problem was that the latter was utterly unsupported by the former. In sum, the book was "not scientific." Darwin was not to be substituted for Paley.[9] In the key Calvinist spaces of Belfast and Edinburgh, different attitudes toward evolution theory were already being promulgated.

HODGE IN PRINCETON   Earlier in May of that same year, Charles Hodge, arguably the most influential theologian at Princeton Theological Seminary during the first century of its existence, had published his last book, *What Is Dar-*

winism? It contained Hodge's considered treatment of the Darwinian theory and can appropriately be regarded as an extended exercise in definition. Thereby Hodge believed its nature could be ascertained and the lineaments of an appropriate Christian response plotted. Because he was certain that Darwin's use of the word "natural" was "antithetical to supernatural," Hodge insisted that "in using the expression Natural Selection, Mr. Darwin intends to exclude design, or final causes." Here the very essence of the theory lay exposed. That "this natural selection is without design, being conducted by unintelligent physical causes," Hodge explained, was "by far the most important and only distinctive element of his theory." In a nutshell, the denial of design was the very "life and soul of his system" and the single feature that brought "it into conflict not only with Christianity, but with the fundamental principles of natural religion."[10] By this definitional move, Hodge could set the terms of the debate and adjudicate on who was or was not a Darwinian. It plainly meant that those like Asa Gray who considered themselves Christian Darwinians were either mistaken or just plain mixed-up; that label had no meaning. Thus for all his efforts to "teleologize" Darwinism, Gray simply was "not a Darwinian."[11] That he was a Christian *evolutionist* Hodge had no doubt; but that was a different matter. For to Hodge, Darwinism simply was "atheism."

Three situations

These key pronouncements were not elaborated in a vacuum. Rather they were broadcast in differing ideological contexts. My suggestion is that in these diverse arenas different issues were facing Presbyterian communities and that these were crucially significant in conditioning the rhetorical stances that were adopted by a variety of religious commentators on evolutionary theory. Besides this, different voices were being sounded in different ways, and their modes of expression, whether bellicose or irenic, did much to set the tone of the local science-religion "encounter." I suggest that such prevailing circumstances—and no doubt there are many more—had an important influence on the style of language that was available to theologically conservative spokesmen pronouncing on evolution, which in turn determined not only what could be *said*, but what could be *heard*, about evolution in these three different localities.

EDINBURGH   In Edinburgh Robert Rainy attempted to "retain the evangelical heritage of the F[ree] C[hurch] while keeping pace with rapid contemporary developments"—a strategy that increasingly made him a controversial figure. To much of the secular press he became known as "Dr Misty as well as Dr Rainy," even though he was named by Gladstone as the greatest living Scotsman. Later in his career as an ecclesiastical statesman and architect of the union of the Free Church and the United Presbyterian Church[12] he found it necessary to "offer unlimited hospitality to biblical criticism." And if in the case of William Robertson Smith he judged it politic to sacrifice that particular critic, he later protected Marcus Dods, A. B. Bruce, and George Adam Smith in a sequence of heresy trials—judgments that secured the later censure of those retaining the classical Calvinism of the Free Church.[13] Certainly Rainy's forté was ecclesiastical polity rather than intellectual engagement. But what *is* significant is that because, as Drummond and Bulloch put it, he "was circumspect and heedful of public reactions," his endorsement of an evolutionary reading of human descent at New College in 1874 is indicative of a general lack of anxiety about evolution among Scottish Calvinists.[14]

The earlier furor surrounding Huxley's iconoclastic assault on the biblical account of creation to Edinburgh's working class at the Queen Street Hall in 1862, which had *The Witness* venting its spleen, had evidently been long forgotten.[15] Besides, already by 1866, the Free Church editor of the *Daily Review*, David Guthrie, although antievolutionary himself, made it clear that Darwinism was not incompatible with faith.[16] Moreover, during the 1870s in Edinburgh, the Darwinian issue had paled in significance beside two other intellectual currents assaulting the orthodox Scottish mind. To be sure it was, as Simpson writes, a "period when a somewhat scornful materialism was asserting itself—it was the time of Tyndall's famous British Association speech about 'the promise and potency of matter,' " but, in Simpson's judgment these issues did not "greatly affect Scottish thought."[17] Of much greater moment was the matter of biblical criticism and the influence of German idealist philosophy.[18] As for the former, matters came to a head in 1876 when the protracted heresy trial concerning William Robertson Smith began, litigation that would, in due course, result in his dismissal from the Old Testament chair at the Free Church College in Aberdeen. What had sparked off the matter was Smith's contribution to the ninth edition of the *Encyclopaedia Britannica*—the "canonical expression," according to Alasdair MacIntyre, of the Enlightenment thrust of contemporary Edinburgh high culture.[19] Smith's entries on "Angel" and "Bible" revealed his espousal of the Graf-Wellhausen theory of the Pentateuchal documents.[20] And this, together with the ninth edition's progressivist ethos, threatened to subvert the traditional authority of Scripture by promising to provide an architectonic overview of knowledge.

In an environment where biblical criticism and idealist philosophy were considered much more threatening than science[21]—after all, the prestigious Lord Kelvin of the University of Glasgow (later president of the Royal Society) was an Episcopalian of low church sympathies who regularly worshiped in a Free Church congregation—the need for a rational defense of Christianity was felt by those like Lord Gifford who endowed the celebrated series of lectures on natural theology that bears his name. In many ways this was an attempt to out-rationalize the rationalists; thereby the Gifford lecturers deployed the very tools of those whom they sought to outmaneuver.[22] If intellectual energies *were* to be deployed by conservative Christians in the combating of the new infidels, these were the arenas in which engagement was seen to be required. By contrast, science—at least in its most Baconian form—had long been domesticated to the needs of Scottish Calvinism as harmonizing strategies had been forged to meet challenges from a variety of sources.[23]

BELFAST   Though no less enthusiastic about the scientific enterprise, the situation over the Darwinian intervention was radically different in Belfast. On Wednesday, 19 August 1874, the *Northern Whig* enthusiastically announced the coming of the "Parliament of Science"—the British Association—to Belfast. Ironically, the meeting was being welcomed to the city as a temporary respite from "spinning and weaving, and Orange riots, and ecclesiastical squabbles." Nevertheless "some hot discussions" were predicted "in the biological section," between advocates of human evolution and those "intellectual people—not to speak of religious people at all—who believe there is a gulf between man and gorilla."[24] The Belfast meeting was to be what Moore and Desmond call "an X Club jamboree" with its priestly coterie of Huxley, Hooker, Lubbock, and of course Tyndall himself, all speechifying.[25] If indeed an assault was to be mounted by the new scientific priesthood on the old clerical guardians of revelation and respectability, Scripture and social status, then what better venue could there be for a call to arms than the BA's meeting in Calvinist Belfast? Tyndall's pugnacious performance did not fall short of expectations. In an Ulster Hall garnished with accompanying orchestra, he delivered—with nothing short of evangelical fervor—a missionary call to "wrest from theology the entire domain of cosmological theory." His conclusion was that all "religious theories, schemes and systems which embrace notions of cosmogony . . . must . . . submit to the control of science, and relinquish all thought of controlling it".[26] The gauntlet had been thrown down.

Events moved quickly. On Sunday, 23 August, Tyndall's address was the subject of a truculent attack by Rev. Professor Robert Watts at Fisherwick Church in downtown Belfast.[27] Watts, the Assembly's College Professor of Systematic Theology—and an erstwhile student of Princeton Seminary in the United States—had good reason for spitting blood. He had already submitted to the organizers of the Biology Section of the Belfast British Association meeting a paper congenially entitled "An Irenicum: Or, a Plea for Peace and Cooperation between Science and Theology."[28] They flatly rejected it.[29] It must have seemed to Watts that the scientific fraternity was not interested in peace. The spurned lecture, which Watts—not prepared to waste good words already committed to paper—delivered at noon the following Monday in Elmwood Presbyterian Church, revealed just how enthusiastic he could be about science.[30] But the BA's rebuff *had* stung and chagrin over his expulsion from the program put him in a bad mood. Yet this was nothing to the anger that Tyndall's address aroused in him. So when on the Sunday following the infamous address he turned his big guns on Tyndall in a sermon preached to an overflowing evening congregation at Fisherwick Place Church in the center of Belfast, the irenic tone of the rejected paper was gone. Tyndall's mention of Epicurus was especially galling; that name had "become a synonym for sensualist," and Watts balked at the moral implications of adopting Epicurean values. To him Epicureanism was a system that had "wrought the ruin of the communities and individuals who have acted out its principles in the past; and if the people of Belfast substitute it for the holy religion of the Son of God, and practise its degrading dogmas, the moral destiny of the metropolis of Ulster may easily be forecast."[31]

Watts, of course, was not a lone voice imprecating Tyndall-style science. On the very same Sunday that he was arraigning atomism before the downtown congregation of Fisherwick Place, the same message was buzzing through the ears of other congregations.[32] That evening none other than W. Robertson Smith found himself preaching from Killen's North Belfast pulpit. And while he did not speak out there and then on Tyndall's speech, he had certainly caught the prevailing mood, for he was moved within the week to write to the press challenging Tyndall's assertions about early religious history, castigating his "pragmatic sketch of the history of atomism," and complaining that he was "at least a century behind the present state of scholarship" concerning the Christian Middle Ages.[33] Small wonder that Tyndall reflected: "Every pulpit in Belfast thundered of me."[34] It was the BA event that set the agenda for Porter's opening speech at the Assembly's College that winter, and for the Belfast response to evolution for a generation.

PRINCETON   In Princeton, things were different yet again. Of crucial importance, I think, was the fact that Hodge's powerful voice was not the only one to be heard. The judgments of James McCosh, president of the College of New Jersey since 1868, were also audible. In fact, as Gundlach has convincingly shown, there was little real difference of substance between Hodge and McCosh on the Darwinian question.[35] Both were determined to resist any removal of design from the natural order; teleology, not transmutation, was the key theological issue for both. But there *was* a difference in rhetorical style such as to secure McCosh's reputation as the foremost Protestant reconciler of theology and Darwinism in the New World. Thus at the 1873 New York meeting of the Evangelical Alliance, McCosh told his hearers that, instead of denouncing the theory of evolution, "Religious philosophers might be more profitably employed in showing . . . the religious aspects of the doctrine of development; and some would be grateful to any who would help them to keep their new faith in science."[36] In later years he could produce such works as *The Religious Aspect of Evolution*—a title, I suspect, that Hodge would never have adopted.

McCosh, as I have implied, was every bit as unnerved by the naturalism of the Darwinian vision as Charles Hodge, and thus devoted considerable intellectual energy to the task of producing an evolutionary teleology. But by lapsing into a Lamarckian-style evolutionism that conceived of organic progress along predetermined paths, he was able to couch his response in terms of a sympathetic rereading of the evolutionary story and thereby to do what he could to avert what one of his students, Rev. George Macloskie, called a potentially "disastrous war between science and faith."[37] It further enabled him, when reminiscing on 20 years as Princeton's president, to confess that much of his time had been devoted to "defending Evolution, but, in so doing, [I] have given the proper account of it as the method of God's procedure, and find that when so understood it is in no way inconsistent with Scripture."[38]

It was back in Belfast, however, that McCosh had learned how to use words wisely—and on a rather different issue. During the momentous events of 1859 he found it possible to query the Ulster revival's "physiological accidents."

But—and this is crucial—by casting his diagnosis in the language of defense he could insist that the "deep mental feeling" that induced somatic convulsions was itself "a work of God."[39] Thereby he came to be seen as the key theological apologist for revival. Precisely the same was true of his evolutionary stance. Remote from the Tyndall episode, McCosh was free to maneuver his theology around science.[40] Like his Belfast colleagues, McCosh too had drunk deeply at the waters of Scottish common-sense philosophy. But whereas Tyndall's naturalism predisposed them to marshall its inductive principles in opposition to evolution, McCosh could mobilize William Hamilton's neo-Kantian reformulations of the Scottish philosophy to construct a rather more idealist response. By renegotiating natural theology in a less Paleyan way, that is by loosening the ties between design and perfect adaptation, he found resources to accommodate biological transformism.[41] So, whether speaking of divine visitation or Darwinian vision, rhetorical nuance counted for much, cognitive content for little. For it was style of communication rather than substance of argument that secured history's judgment on McCosh as the defender of religious revival *and* evolutionary theory. By keeping the rhetorical space of Princeton open to the possibility of evolution theory—whatever his reservations about Darwinian naturalism—he did much to determine that the theory would at least be tolerated at American Presbyterianism's intellectual heartland.

Three stories

Given the different sets of circumstances prevailing in Edinburgh, Belfast, and Princeton, it is now understandable why the subsequent histories of conservative Christian responses to evolution were different in these Calvinist cities. In a nutshell, the theory of evolution was absorbed in Edinburgh, repudiated in Belfast, and tolerated in Princeton. This, I hope, can be illustrated by a brief survey of the judgments issued by a number of key individuals in these different places.

EDINBURGH—ADOPTION   Henry Calderwood was a lifelong member of the United Presbyterian Church.[42] During the latter part of the nineteenth century, this Presbyterian body—which in 1900 joined with the Free Church to form the United Free Church—had increasingly adopted aspects of liberal theology that frequently issued in a relatively radical political outlook. According to S. D. Gill, "while other Presbyterian Churches in Scotland were being rocked by the issue of higher criticism the UPC remained comparatively unaffected."[43] Calderwood himself remained substantially evangelical in his outlook, supporting the evangelistic activities of Moody and Sankey in Edinburgh, and retaining the modified Calvinism (which, according to some, demonstrated Arminian infiltration[44]) embodied in the United Presbyterians' Declaratory Act of 1879 with which he was closely associated.[45] At the same time, his staunch defense of Scottish common-sense philosophy enabled him to maintain philosophical continuity with the tradition of Scottish realism. This stance had involved him in a critique of his teacher William Hamilton's idealist inclinations. As Pringle-

Pattison put it: "Calderwood may be said to have been the first to reassert . . . the traditional doctrine of Scottish philosophy against the agnostic elements of Kantianism which Hamilton had woven into his theory."[46] This early work,[47] which appeared in 1854, established his philosophical reputation and, after serving as a United Presbyterian minister in Glasgow from 1861 until 1868, he was appointed to the chair of moral philosophy in Edinburgh in 1868. Significantly, one of the first letters of congratulation was received from James McCosh at Princeton, who wrote enthusiastically of his appointment but also spoke of "a dark thread running through the white of my feeling. . . . I looked to you as my successor, and had laid plans to secure it. You would have had the support of the College and of my old pupils in the Presbyterian Church. As it is, I am now fairly at sea."[48] Clearly McCosh had hoped that Calderwood would follow in his own footsteps and cross the Irish Sea to assume the professorship of logic and metaphysics at the Queen's University of Belfast.

In the case of Calderwood (and indeed McCosh) the commonly held view that common-sense philosophy was typically deployed against evolutionary theory certainly does not seem to hold good. In 1877 Calderwood took up the issue of ethical evolution in *The Contemporary Review*. Here he left to one side all questions of evolution as a strictly biological theory, and turned to its use as an account of moral development. For this is what Calderwood found objectionable—the attempt to read human values through the spectacles of natural selection and heredity. And so, using the example of human altruism, he argued for evolution's inability to account for self-denial without compromising the very principles of selection and competition intrinsic to the theory.[49] Yet despite these scruples, he was far from denying evolution and, like Rainy in the Free Church, certainly did not oppose it as a bona fide scientific theory. In 1881, for example, he observed:

> [B]iological science must be credited with the new departure which has given fresh stimulus to thought, and has succeeded in gaining wide support to a theory of Evolution. To Mr. Darwin, as a naturalist, belongs the indisputable honour of having done service so great as to make its exact amount difficult of calculation, involving, as it does, vast increase of our knowledge of the relations and interdependence of various orders of animate existence. "Origin of species" may not be the phrase which exactly describes the sphere of elucidation, over the extent of which all students of Nature now acknowledge indebtedness to Mr. Darwin; but "development of species" does express an undoubted scientific conclusion, which has found a permanent place in biological science.[50]

That same year Calderwood delivered the Morse lectures at Union Theological Seminary in New York on the subject "The Relation of Science and Religion." Here he insisted that even if "the theory of the Development of Species by Natural Selection . . . were accepted in the form in which it is at present propounded, not only would the rational basis for belief in the Divine existence and government not be affected by it, but the demand on a Sovereign Intelligence would be intensified." Again, he assured his hearers that Darwin's theory "is no more at variance with religious thought, than with ordinary notions of preceding times" and that "the fewer the primordial forms to which the multiplicity of existing species can be traced, the greater is the marvel which science presents, and the more convincing becomes the intellectual necessity by which we travel back to a Supernatural intelligence as the source of all."[51] And again:

> The scientific conception of the history of animal life is, that there has been a historical progression in the appearance of animals, in so far as lower orders took precedence of higher, while the higher have shown large power of adaptation to the circumstances in which they have been placed. In accordance with the whole principles regulating the relations of religion and science, religious men, scientific and non-scientific, will readily acquiesce in this modification of general belief, as largely favored by evidence which geology supplies, and supported by testimony drawn from the actually existing order of things; and they will do so with clear recognition that this view involves no conflict with scriptural statement, and in so far from containing in it any thing antagonistic to the fundamental conception of the supernatural origin of existence, that it harmonizes with it, even intensifying the demand upon a transcendent cause for the rational explanation of the admitted order of things.[52]

Not surprisingly, when Calderwood participated in the 1884 third General Council of the Alliance of Reformed Churches in Belfast, he steadfastly supported George Matheson's presentation on "The Religious Bearings of the Doctrine of Evolution" and urged that Darwin's theory afforded an even grander conception of the designer than had hitherto been glimpsed.[53] Such a perspective was not exactly shared by his Belfast colleagues present at the meeting.

Subsequently Calderwood delivered his mature reflections on the whole subject, first in a short article for the *Proceedings of the Royal Society of Edinburgh*,[54] and then at much greater length in *Evolution and Man's Place in Nature*. In two editions of this work—the second a more or less complete reworking—which came out in 1893 and 1896, respectively, he sought to exempt rational life from the reign of evolutionary law by arguing that "Animal Intelligence shows no effective preparation for Rational Intelligence."[55] Yet this did not prevent him from declaring that "Evolution stands before us as an impressive reality in the history of Nature,"[56] for he was convinced that the evidence for "descent with modifications" was "so abundant and varied, as to leave no longer any uncertainty around the conclusion that a steady advance in organic form and function has been achieved in our world's history."[57]

To be sure, none of this can be construed as unqualified endorsement for the Darwinian scheme. Throughout, Calderwood was insistent on the need for creative activity in the *origin* of life and for constant providential superintendence. But his rhetorical style was radically different from that of the Belfast Calvinists who, as we shall presently see, maintained an attitude of "no compromise" with the new biology. Thus in a number of brief but sympathetic sketches of Darwin's early life for the readers of the *United Presbyterian Magazine* in 1888 (of which he was editor), Calderwood used Darwin's school experiences as the vehicle for raising some troubling educational questions. "How many really gifted minds, concealed in the order of mediocrity," he pondered, "are left just as they are received? How far is there a risk that we provide education of the ordinary type, without suceeding in doing other things which might also be accomplished. This school life of Charles Darwin suggests many things deserving of being pondered."[58]

I have been dwelling for some time on the work of Henry Calderwood since my focus at this point is on Edinburgh. But it would be remiss to ignore altogether the contributions of other Scots such as James Iverach and James Orr. By the time Iverach was appointed to a chair at the Free Church of Scotland's college in Aberdeen in 1887, he had already begun his assessment of Darwinism in *The Ethics of Evolution Examined* (1886); subsequently, in 1894, he would also publish *Evolution and Christianity*. His defense of Robertson Smith certainly condemned him in the eyes of more conservative elements in the Free Church. But his renowned intellectual stature and his strategic position in the Free Church, and its successor the United Free Church, meant that his acknowledgment of Darwin's theory of evolution by natural selection as a good working hypothesis—within limits—further contributed to obviating Scottish conflict between faith and science. As he put it, the conflict was "not between 'evolution' and what our friends call 'special creation.' It is between evolution under the guidance of intelligence and purpose, and evolution as a fortuitous result."[59]

Like Calderwood, James Orr's ecclesiastical home was the United Presbyterian Church. His major assessments of evolution appeared in print after he moved from Edinburgh to assume the chair of apologetics and systematic theology at the new United Free Church College in Glasgow in 1900.[60] Nevertheless, in the same year that he was appointed to the professorship of church history at the Divinity Hall in Edinburgh he told the hearers of his Kerr Lectures in 1891 that "On the general hypothesis of evolution, as applied to the organic world, I have nothing to say, except that, within certain limits, it seems to me extremely probable, and supported by a large body of evidence."[61] Subsequently Orr confirmed this stance when he made it clear that there was no reason to dispute the "genetic derivation of one order or species from another,"[62] although, like Calderwood, he wanted to preserve a teleological metaphysics and an act of special creation in the origin of the human species.[63] Even in his contribution at the end of his life to the *Fundamentals*, published between 1910 and 1915, he tellingly quipped that " 'Evolution', in short, is coming to be recognised as but a new name for 'creation,' only that the creative power now works from *within*, instead of, as in the old conception, in an *external*, plastic fashion."[64]

Also of considerable importance at this late Victorian moment was Robert Flint, who moved from the chair of moral philosophy in St. Andrews to assume the professorship of divinity in Edinburgh University in 1876. He had grown up in the Free Church but as a student became disenchanted with what he took to be its intellectual narrowness and was ordained to the Church of Scotland. To be sure, his rationalistic defense of traditional theism, reminiscent of the eighteenth century, might well be out of spirit with aspects of Scotland's evangelical traditions, but his capacity to deliver a natural theology of evolution would have done much to confirm the stance taken by such men as Calderwood and Orr. For Flint, with his passionate concern to establish the rationality and objectivity of belief in God, was convinced that neither evolution in general nor Darwinism in particular had weakened the design argument; the "law of heredity," the "tendency to definite variation," the "law of over-production," the "law of sexual selection," and even the "law, or so-called law, of natural selection" could all be seen as the expression of divine purpose. All in all, he was convinced, as he put it in his first series of Baird lectures in 1876, that "the researches and speculations of the Darwinians have left unshaken the design argument. I might have gone further if time had permitted, and proved that they had greatly enriched the argument."[65]

Two other figures also bear mentioning as contributing significantly to the Edinburgh ethos on Presbyterianism and science—George Matheson and Henry Drummond. In Matheson's case, Spencer's "Unknowable" was ultimately nothing less than Almighty God, and so he could happily tell the Presbyterians gathered for the 1884 congress in Belfast that if we "agree to call [Spencer's] Force an inscrutable or unsearchable Will, we shall have already established a scientific basis, not only for the belief in a guiding Providence, but for the possibility of an efficacious prayer."[66] Undeterred by local opposition, Matheson elaborated these themes in extenso the following year. In *Can the Old Faith Live with the New?* he not only welcomed an evolutionary account of human origins but insisted that evolution also shed light on such Christian concerns as the workings of providence, the operations of the Spirit, and human immortality.[67] The selfsame concern to place Christian theology on a solid scientific footing was the driving force behind Henry Drummond's life and work. A professor of natural science at the Free Church College in Glasgow who gave weekend classes to the Edinburgh divinity students, and a close friend of D. L. Moody, Drummond set forth his "Spencerization" of evangelicalism in *Natural Law in the Spiritual World* and *The Ascent of Man*.[68] It amounted to an attempt to find a law of continuity connecting the material and spiritual worlds, and was widely interpreted as an underwriting of faith by the latest science. In the long run its opiating strategy contributed significantly to what Jim Moore calls the naturalization of the supernatural.

By retrieving these pro-evolutionary sentiments among Edinburgh Calvinists I do not mean to give the impression that absolutely no opposition was expressed toward the new biology. Consider, for example, the stance advocated by John Duns, the successor of John Fleming as the New College professor of natural science since 1864.[69] Even while Rainy, the principal of New College, was flirting with evolutionary theses, Duns maintained a firm attitude of opposition. He had already pronounced on *The Origin of Species* just after its publication.[70] By 1877 he still found the speculative "hypothesis of organic evolution" distinctly harmful to theology, and those who were finding "scope for the principle in Scripture, or in history, [had] generally very indistinct notions as to its full scientific import."[71] And later in his investigation of the connection between natural selection and the theory of design he repudiated the efforts of those such as Asa Gray who insisted on the possibility of an evolutionary teleology.[72] For all that, however, I think it is clear that Duns is the exception that proves the rule.

BELFAST—REPUDIATION   In Belfast, the Tyndall event brought terror to the hearts of solid Presbyterians for more than a generation. But there was still a sense that Tyndall's act of aggression was ultimately to be welcomed, for it displayed to the world the machinations of the materialist school. It was precisely because he had spoken so plainly that the editor of *The Witness* (the weekly Presbyterian newspaper) could observe that "We now know exactly the state of matters, and what is to be expected from Professor Tyndall and his school, and we shall be able to take our measures accordingly."[73] And measures the Presbyterian Church did take. Plans were hastily laid for a course of evening lectures to be given at Rosemary Street Church during the winter months on the relationship between science and Christianity. In time these addresses would be drawn together into a book, distributed on both sides of the Atlantic, under the title *Science and Revelation: A Series of Lectures in Reply to the Theories of Tyndall, Huxley, Darwin, Spencer, Etc.*

During that 1874–75 winter of discontent, eight Presbyterian theologians and one scientist joined together to stem, from the Rosemary Street pulpit, any materialist tide that Tyndall's rhetoric might trigger. Just as the villagers of medieval Europe and colonial New England annually beat the bounds—marked out the village boundaries—so the Presbyterian hierarchy needed to reestablish its theological borders. Indeed, it is precisely for this reason, I would contend, that the winter lecture series at Rosemary Street Church included ministerial addresses—by A. C. Murphy on proofs of the Bible as divine revelation, by John McNaughtan on the reality of sin, by John Moran on the life of Christ, and by William Magill on the divine origin of Scripture—which made no specific reference to Tyndall, Darwin, Spencer, or any version of evolutionary theory. That they were included in the series attests to the perceived need to reaffirm systematically the cardinal doctrines of the faith so as to ensure that Presbyterian theological territory remained intact.

Just over a year earlier the Catholic serial *The Irish Ecclesiastical Record* had presented an evaluation of Darwinism in which its correspondent castigated the "Moloch of natural selection" for its "ruthless extermination of . . . unsuccessful competitors," for its lack of evidence for transitional forms, for its failure to account for gaps in the fossil record, and for its distasteful moral implications.[74] As for the latest clash in Belfast, the Catholic archbishops and bishops of Ireland issued a pastoral letter in November 1874 in which they repudiated the "blasphemy upon this Catholic nation" that had recently been uttered by the "professors of Materialism . . . under the name of Science." This certainly was no new warfare, they reflected; but the Catholic hierarchy perceived that this most recent incarnation of materialism unveiled more clearly than ever before "the moral and social doctrines that lurked in the gloomy recesses of [science's] speculative theories." Quite simply it meant that moral responsibility had been erased, that virtue and vice had become but "expressions of the same mechanical force," and that sin and holiness likewise vanished chimeralike into oblivion. Everything in human life from "sensual love" to religious sentiment were "all equally results of the play between organism and environment through countless ages of the past." Such was the brutalizing materialism that now confronted the Irish people.[75]

The congruence between these evaluations and those of the Presbyterian commentators we have scrutinized is certainly marked. So why then should

Watts, in a subsequent reprint of his pamphlet "Atomism: Dr. Tyndall's Atomic Theory of the Universe Examined and Refuted," incorporate in an appendix "strictures on the recent Manifesto of the Roman Catholic Hierarchy of Ireland in reference to the sphere of Science"? That he wished to distance himself from their proposals is clear: it was "painful," he noted, "to observe the position taken by the Roman Catholic hierarchy of Ireland in their answer to Professors Tyndall and Huxley." So just what was the problem? Simply this—Watts felt that the Catholic willingness to compartmentalise science and religion would lead to "the secularisation of the physical sciences." Because Cardinal Cullen and his coreligionists seemed only too willing to follow Newman in restricting the physicist to the bare empirical, Watts insisted that since "the Word of God enjoins it upon men as a duty to infer the invisible things of the Creator from the things that are made," the Roman Catholic hierarchy of Ireland had, by their declaration, "taken up an attitude of antagonism to that Word, prohibiting scientists, as such, from rising above the law to the infinitely wise, Almighty Lawgiver."[76]

The sectarian traditions in Irish religion doubtless had a key role to play in these particular machinations. The furor surrounding the Tyndall event merely became yet another occasion for Ulster Nonconformity to uncover its sense of siege. In his confrontation with evolutionary theory Watts wanted to cultivate and tend to his own tradition's theological space, and not engage in extramural affiliations. And by seeking to cast secularization and Catholicism as subversive allies against the inductive truths of science and the revealed truths of Scripture, he found it possible to conflate as a single object of opprobrium the old enemy—popery—and the new enemy—evolution. To Watts these were indeed the enemies of God. Writing to A. A. Hodge in 1881 he observed: "Communism is, at present rampant in Ireland. The landlords are greatly to blame for their tyranny, but the present movement of the Land League, headed by Parnell, is essentially communistic. He and his coconspirators are now on trial, but with six Roman Catholics on the jury there is not much likelihood of a conviction."[77] And later in 1890, poised between Gladstone's two Home Rule Bills, he wrote again to Warfield, castigating both the Free Church and the United Presbyterians in Scotland and adding: "Both these churches are so bent on Disestablishment that they are quite willing to sustain Mr. Gladstone's Irish policy & deliver their Protestant brethren into the hands of the Church of Rome, to be ruled by her through a band of unmitigated villains."[78]

For their part, the Catholic hierarchy did not miss the opportunity of firing its own broadsides at Protestantism. For the bishops and archbishops felt it would "not be amiss, in connection with the Irish National system of education, to call attention to the fact that the Materialists of to-day are able to boast that the doctrines which have brought most odium upon their school have been openly taught by a high Protestant dignitary." It only confirmed them in their uncompromising stance on the Catholic educational system. Had it not been for their own vigilance, an unbelieving tide would have swept through the entire curriculum. Such circumstances justified "to the full the determination of Catholic Ireland not to allow her young men to frequent Universities and Colleges where

Science is made the vehicle of Materialism." Accordingly, the bishops and arch-bishops rebuked "the indifference of those who may be tempted to grow slack in the struggle for a Catholic system of education."[79] Tyndall's speech, it seems, succeeded not only in fostering the opposition of both Protestants and Catholics in Ireland to his own science, but in furthering their antagonism to each other.

As for Watts, he maintained his antagonistic attitude to evolution for the rest of his life. At that 1884 pan-Presbyterian meeting in Belfast, even while Matheson and Calderwood were endorsing an evolutionary viewpoint, the redoubtable Watts told the company that evolution was a "mere hypothesis" with "not one single particle of evidence" to support it. The need for embarking on any doctrinal reconstruction—including the exegesis of Genesis—did not exactly commend itself to him. Indeed, he had long been campaigning—both in Belfast and Scotland—against Spencer's system because to him it was explicitly designed "to overthrow the Scripture doctrine of special creations," as he had realized in *An Examination of Herbert Spencer's Biological Hypothesis*—his winter address of 1875. Again in 1887 he wrote: "[d]espite the efforts of evolutionists, the laws which protect and perpetuate specific distinctions remain unrepealed, and Science joins its testimony to that of Revelation in condemnation of the degrading hypothesis that man is the offspring of a brute."[80] Here we witness a much narrower biblicist rejection of evolution than was evident in either Edinburgh or Princeton.

Not surprisingly Watts utterly repudiated the efforts of Henry Drummond to evolutionize theology and to import Spencer's evolutionary laws into the supernatural realm. To him Drummond's project was just a mess—theologically *and* scientifically. To be sure, his aim of removing "the alleged antagonism" between science and religion was a worthy objective. But the Drummond strategy ultimately was "not an Irenicum between science and religion or between the laws of the empires of matter and of spirit" at all. Rather it only displayed the expansionist character of natural law. Watts found the whole project so bizarre that, as he worked up to his conclusion, he felt "inclined to apologise for attempting a formal refutation of a theory which, if it means anything intelligible, involves the denial of all that the Scriptures teach, and all that Christian experience reveals."[81]

By now, not surprisingly, Watts had grown entirely disillusioned with the Edinburgh New College network; but he continued to cultivate links with Princeton. This is clearly apparent in extant correspondence from Watts to Warfield, though there is just the slightest whiff of suspicion that Watts was beginning to have concerns on the evolution front there too. Writing in 1889 to Warfield he began: "It would seem as if Princeton is going to absorb Belfast. Here I am asked to introduce to you, I think, the fifth student, within the past few weeks. Well, over this I do not grieve but rather rejoice. I am glad that our young men are setting their faces towards your venerable and orthodox institution instead of turning their backs upon orthodoxy and seeking counsel at the feet of men who are trampling the verities of Revelation under foot."[82] In introducing yet another student to the Princeton campus he wrote to Warfield in 1893: "I am greatly pleased to find that our young men have turned their eyes to Princeton instead of Edinburgh, and I owe you my warmest thanks for the great kindness you have shown them."[83] Indeed he had already reminded Warfield that he had been writing a series of articles on the changing attitudes toward inspiration in the Free Church, reporting at the same time on the current heresy hunting of A. B. Bruce and Marcus Dods. Predictably, Watts took a dim view of these teachers. "How has the fine gold of the disruption become dim!" he sighed. "The men of '43 would have made short work of these cases."[84] And later that same year, having sent Warfield two days earlier a copy of his new book *The New Apologetic, or the Down-Grade in Criticism, Theology, and Science*,[85] he concluded yet another letter with the comment: "I dread the influence of the Scotch Theological Halls, as you may learn from my book."[86]

Still, in a reply to Warfield in 1894 thanking him for sending a copy of William Brenton Greene's inaugural lecture, Watts felt constrained to comment:

> I admired Dr. Greene's Inaugural, but I am sorry that he passed such high eulogium upon Mr. Herbert Spencer. My revered father, Professor Wallace, author of an immortal work, entitled 'Representative Responsibility,' had, for Spencer, supreme contempt as a professed philosopher. Immediately after the meeting of the British Association in Belfast, in 1874, I reviewed Spencer's Biological Hypothesis, & proved that he was neither a philosopher, nor a scientist. Someone sent him a paper containing only one half of my review, &, assuming that what the paper gave was the whole of my address, he took occasion in an issue of his book, then passing through the Press, to charge me with misrepresentation. I called his attention to the mistake of his correspondent, but he had not the courtesy to withdraw the charge. Dr. McCosh's successor in the Queen's College here, trots out Spencer to our young men in their undergraduate course, and one of my duties, in my class work, is to pump out of them Mill & Spencer.[87]

Clearly even after 20 years the recollection of the Tyndall event remained unsullied and Watts neither would, nor could, release his grip on that bitter memory.

PRINCETON—TOLERATION   In 1916, reflecting on his undergraduate days at Princeton, B. B. Warfield recalled the coming of James McCosh to take up the presidency of the College of New Jersey. Yet in one sense Warfield made it clear that McCosh's coming had no influence on him . . . and that was on the question of Darwin's theory of evolution. For Warfield already was, by his own admission, "a Darwinian of the purest water" before McCosh's presence graced the Princeton campus. To be sure, Warfield would later depart from what he took to be McCosh's Darwinian "orthodoxy," but he would remain open to the possibility of evolutionary transformism through a range of mechanisms besides Darwinian natural selection.[88] We should recall that in 1916, when Warfield penned these recollections, Darwinism was in eclipse in the scientific world. In the interim, evolutionary theses flourished—neo-Lamarckism, orthogenesis, the mutation theory of Hugo de Vries and so on—though without assuming the gradualism or the central significance of natural selection that Darwin's disciples had promulgated.[89]

Long before Warfield ever expressed himself in print on the evolution question, however, he had evidently thought seriously about the issue. This I believe
stemmed from the long-standing interest both he and his father, William, had
in shorthorn cattle breeding. Indeed in 1873, prior to entering Princeton Seminary as a student for the ministry, he had been livestock editor for the *Farmer's
Home Journal* of Lexington, Kentucky. He maintained this interest for the remainder of his life and carefully kept a scrapbook of clippings—mostly those of
his father—on what he called "Short Horn Culture."[90] It is not surprising
therefore to find the following words in the preface to William Warfield's *The
Theory and Practice of Cattle-Breeding*:

> I wish to take this opportunity to acknowledge the assistance my sons have given
> me in preparing all my work for the press. Without their aid much—even most—
> of it could never have been done. . . . Great credit is also due to my elder son,
> Prof. Benjamin B. Warfield, D. D., now of Princeton, N.J., whose energy and
> vigor of thought and pen gave me such essential aid in the earlier years of my
> connection with the press; nor has the pursuit of the more weighty things of
> theology destroyed his capacity for taking an occasional part in the active discussion
> of cattle matters. The papers which have appeared over my signature have thus to
> quite a large degree been of family origin.[91]

This affirmation is, I think, particularly significant because in the course of his
discussion of such key issues as variation, heredity, atavism, and reversion to
type, William Warfield quoted liberally from Darwin's *Animals and Plants under
Domestication*.[92] Moreover, he directly endorsed the theory of evolution by natural selection when he wrote:

> Nature's method seems to be a wide and general system of selection, in which the
> strong and vigorous are the winners and the weaker are crushed out. Among wild
> cattle the more lusty bulls have their choice of the cows in a way that under
> natural selection insures the best results to the race. . . . If the conditions of life
> should suddenly change the result on such wild cattle would be to deteriorate or
> to improve the average according as the change was for their advantage or dis-
> advantage. It is quite apparent that no question of breeding intrudes itself here.
> Nature's selection, while always in favor of the maintenance of the animals in the
> best manner, yet is impartial, and under ordinary circumstances would maintain
> an average.[93]

Like Darwin himself, B. B. Warfield encountered natural selection through an
intense study of breeding.[94] And this, I believe, is why he could, early in his
career, describe himself as a pure Darwinian—he met the theory empirically, as
it were, not theologically or philosophically.

While Warfield's espousal of Darwinism evidently predated the coming of
McCosh to Princeton in 1868, some of his earliest published statements on
evolutionary theory date from 1888—significantly just the year after he returned
from Western Theological Seminary near Pittsburgh to take up the chair of
didactic and polemic theology at Princeton. By this stage Warfield's reservations
about Darwinism as a comprehensive system had begun to manifest themselves.
In his Lectures on Anthropology, begun that same year, he took up the subject

"Evolution or Development" and made it clear that in his view Darwinism did not enjoy anything like the scientific status of the Newtonian system, for there were just too many unresolved geological, zoological, and paleontological anomalies—anomalies he did not hesitate to itemize. And yet he was prepared to leave the truth or falsity of the Darwinian theory an "open question." In sum: "The whole upshot of the matter is that there is no *necessary* antagonism of [Christianity] to evolution, *provided that* we do not hold to too extreme a form of evolution." If the constant supervision of divine providence and the "occasional supernatural interference" of God were retained, then, he concluded, "we may hold to the modified theory of evolution & and be [Christ]ians in the ordinary orthodox sense. I say we may do this. Whether we ought to accept it, even in this modified sense is another matter, & I leave it purposely an open question."[95] If Warfield's sense of equivocation is evident here, so too is the openness of his stance on the whole issue, and his willingness to test the theory by its empirical adequacy.

During the 1880s, of course, other issues had been occupying Warfield and other conservative Presbyterian theologians—matters that, I suspect, rather cast the Darwinian threat in the shade. Of primary importance was the whole issue of biblical criticism that dramatically manifested itself in the years 1881–1883 when the *Presbyterian Review* published an exchange of essays on the subject in the wake of the Robertson Smith affair in Scotland. Along with A. A. Hodge and Francis L. Patton, Warfield provided a conservative critique of the position advanced by Charles A. Briggs, Henry Preserved Smith, and Samuel I. Curtiss. Having said this, as Noll has pointed out, in the early 1880s the two sides personified in Briggs and Hodge enjoyed "a reasonably satisfactory relationship" and it was not until the following decade that the conservatives, increasingly worried about the critics' radicalism, took action that would lead to heresy charges against Briggs and his eventual suspension from the ministry. Because, as Noll puts it, "ecclesiastical control seemed fully on the side of the conservatives," they retained a cultural hegemony in the last decade of the century that their Scottish counterparts did not enjoy.[96]

By the early years of the new century, Warfield's theological tentativeness over the evolution question progressively declined as he came to adopt a decidedly more partisan stance. The depth of evolutionary penetration into his thinking as the first decade of the twentieth century wore on is particularly evident on two issues of burning concern, namely, the origin and the unity of the human species. In 1906, a review of James Orr's *God's Image in Man* afforded him the opportunity to spell out in more detail his own thinking on the subject. In this work, Orr had argued for the entirely supernatural origin of the first human, on the grounds that the complex physical organization of the brain—necessary he believed for *human* consciousness—made it impossible to postulate a special origin for the mind and not for the body. To Warfield, however, Orr's objection could effectively be undermined by the idea of evolution by mutation. Thereby Warfield proposed a kind of emergent evolutionary solution to the problem. As he put it: "If under the directing hand of God a human body is formed at a leap by propagation from brutish parents, it would be quite consonant with the fitness of things that it should be provided by His creative energy with a truly human soul."[97]

Warfield's self-perception as perpetuating orthodox Calvinism, even in this concession to the possibility of a human evolutionary history and a theologically permissible explanatory "naturalism," is nowhere more dramatically displayed that in his 1915 exposition of "Calvin's Doctrine of the Creation" for the *Princeton Theological Review*. Here he made much of Calvin's insistence that the term "creation" should be strictly reserved for the initial creative act. For the subsequent "creations" were—technically speaking—*not* creations ex nihilo, but were, rather, modifications of the primeval "indigested mass" by "means of the interaction of its intrinsic forces." The human soul was the only exception, for Calvin held to the Creationist (as opposed to the Traducianist) theory that every human soul throughout the history of propagation was an *immediate* creation out of nothing. To Warfield, then, Calvin's doctrine opened the door to a controlled "naturalistic" explanation of natural history—including the human physical form—in terms of the operation of secondary causes. These, to be sure, were directed by the guiding hand of divine providence; but this conviction did not prevent him from asserting that Calvin's doctrine of creation actually turned out to be "a very pure evolutionary scheme." In addition, Warfield's architectonic defense of biblical inerrancy did not prevent him from departing from a literalistic interpretation of the early Genesis narratives. Thus while acknowledging that Calvin himself had understood the days of creation as six literal days, he still believed that Moses, "writing to meet the needs of men at large, accommodated himself to their grade of intellectual preparation, and confine[d] himself to what meets their eyes." Now in the twentieth century Warfield suggested that in order to perpetuate the spirit of Calvin's hermeneutic genius "it was requisite that these six days should be lengthened out into six periods—six ages of the growth of the world. Had that been done Calvin would have been a precursor of the modern evolutionary theorists. As it is, he only forms a point of departure for them to this extent—that he teaches, as they teach, the modification of the original world-stuff into the varied forms which constitute the ordered world, by the instrumentality of second causes—or as a modern would put it, of its intrinsic forces."[98] Recalling that Warfield penned these words in 1915, around the time he reminisced on his student days with McCosh and observed that he later abandoned the Scotsman's Darwinian orthodoxy, certainly helps us to see that departing from classical Darwinism evidently did not mean abandoning evolutionary transformism.

Warfield, of course, was not alone in the evolutionary sentiments expressed at Princeton. Among figures like A. A. Hodge, Francis L. Patton, and Casper Wistar Hodge, not to mention James McCosh and George Macloskie, similarly cautious attitudes may be discerned.[99] Of these the most considered treatments were forthcoming from the two arrivals from Belfast—McCosh and Macloskie. It seems as though their removal from Belfast to the New World facilitated a rhetorical liberation that allowed them to express their reservations about *Dar-*

winism in a muted way, and to find *evolution* theologically congenial. I have already commented on McCosh's essentially neo-Lamarckian proclivities; a few comments on Macloskie will suffice to complete my survey.

George Macloskie, a minister of the Presbyterian Church in Ireland, followed his teacher McCosh to Princeton University in 1875 to take up the position of professor of biology. From the time he arrived there Macloskie vigorously promoted science among orthodox Presbyterians and consistently urged the value of a chastened Darwinian perspective, notwithstanding his friendship with Robert Watts.[100] Achieving this, however, required Macloskie to jettison the Scottish philosophy's inductive strictures on the scientific imagination. To him speculation was not only inevitable; it was a necessity.[101] Hypothesizing, even of the Darwinian variety, was thus to be welcomed[102] and, when given a suitably Calvinist gloss, it might even be acceptable as an account of human origins:

> Evolution, if proven as to man, will be held by the biblicist to be a part, the naturalistic part, of the total work of his making, the other part being his endowment miraculously with a spiritual nature, so that he was created in the image of God. . . . As a member of the animal kingdom, man was created by God, probably in the same naturalistic fashion as the beasts that perish; but, unlike them, he has endowments that point to a higher, namely a supernaturalistic, order of creation.[103]

Not surprisingly, he applauded A. A. Hodge's words that "we have no sympathy with those who maintain that scientific theories of evolution are necessarily atheistic." More, he insisted that attempts to make evolution a heresy—he seems to have had the James Woodrow case in mind[104]—were disastrous for religion and science alike, and he applauded both McCosh and Asa Gray for their "great service" in demonstrating that evolution "is not dangerous."[105]

Managing Theological Space

In the latter decades of the nineteenth century, the intellectual leadership of the Presbyterian citadels of Edinburgh, Belfast, and Princeton was involved in the production and reproduction of theological space. In all three, the fields of discourse these figures had done so much to manage set limits on the assertable—on what could be *said* about evolution, and on what could be *heard*. In Edinburgh the concerns with biblical criticism, idealist philosophy, confessional modification in the wake of ecclesiastical reunions, and the pro-evolution sentiments of key leaders all made rapprochement with evolutionary theory intellectually congenial. In Belfast, the infamous BA meeting made it exceptionally difficult to be sympathetic to those who might argue that evolution could be construed in terms other than that of Tyndall's supposed philosophical naturalism. Besides, even if this possibility had been grasped, it would have been exceedingly difficult to *express* it in the doctrinal locality they had labored so diligently to reproduce. In Princeton the cautious words of Warfield and the strenuous efforts of McCosh to produce an evolutionary teleology, together with the conservative success in domestic Presbyterian debates over biblical criticism, permitted evolution, if not Darwinism, to be tolerated. It did not need to be absorbed or proscribed.

Local circumstances, I contend, are thus crucial to understanding how Calvinists in these different places chose to negotiate their way around the issues that science seemed to be placing in one way or another on their agendas. By extension: to understand "the encounter between science and religion," I submit, will require us to take with greater seriousness the situatedness of both scientific and religious discourses.

NOTES

I am greatly indebted to Rev. William O. Harris, archivist at the Speer Library, Princeton Theologial Seminary, and to Mr. Bradley Gundlach for much assistance with archival queries when I visited the Speer Library. Their generosity and help are deeply appreciated. Mark Noll made a number of helpful observations on an earlier draft of this chapter, which I also very gratefully acknowledge.

1. See, for instance, Clifford Geertz, *Local Knowledge: Further Essays in Interpretive Anthropology* (New York: Basic Books, 1983); Erving Goffman, *The Presentation of Self in Everyday Life* (London: Allen Lane, 1969); Anthony Giddens, *The Constitution of Society: Outline of the Theory of Structuration* (Oxford: Polity Press, 1984); Michel Foucault, "Of Other Spaces," *Diacritics*, 16 (1986): 22–27; Edward W. Said, "Narrative, Geography and Interpretation," *New Left Review*, 180 (1990): 81–97; Said, "Travelling Theory," in *The World, the Text and the Critic* (London: Vintage, 1991).

2. I have surveyed some of these matters in "The Spaces of Knowledge: Contributions Towards a Historical Geography of Science," *Society and Space*, 13 (1995): 5–34.

3. Patrick Carnegie Simpson, *The Life of Principal Rainy*, 2 vols., (London: Hodder and Stoughton, 1909), Vol. 1, p. 285. A. C. Cheyne agrees, commenting that the pro-evolution sentiment of Rainy and Robert Flint "is a measure of the rapid intellectual transformation that had taken place in Scotland in less than half a century." A. C. Cheyne, *The Transforming of the Kirk. Victorian Scotland's Religious Revolution* (Edinburgh: St. Andrews Press, 1983), pp. 77–78.

4. Robert Rainy, *Evolution and Theology: Inaugural Address* (Edinburgh: Maclaren & Macniven, 1874), pp. 6, 9.

5. Robert Rainy, "On the Place and Ends of Miracles," in *Christianity and Recent Speculations. Six Lectures by Ministers of the Free Church*, with a preface by Robert S. Candlish (Edinburgh: John Maclaren, 1866), pp. 33–65.

6. Rainy, *Evolution and Theology*, p. 18.

7. I have discussed the Belfast Calvinist response to Darwin in "Darwinism and Calvinism: The Belfast-Princeton Connection," *Isis*, 83 (1992): 408–28; and "Darwin in Belfast: the Evolution Debate," in John Wilson Foster (ed.), *Nature in Ireland: A Scientific and Cultural History* (Dublin: Lilliput Press, 1997), pp. 387–408.

8. J. L. Porter, *Theological Colleges: Their Place and Influence in the Church and in the World; With Special Reference to the Evil Tendencies of Recent Scientific Theories. Being the Opening Lecture of Assembly's College, Belfast, Session 1874–75* (Belfast: William Mullan, 1875), p. 8.

9. J. L. Porter, *Science and Revelation: Their Distinctive Provinces. With a Review of the Theories of Tyndall, Huxley, Darwin, and Herbert Spencer* (Belfast: William Mullan, 1874), pp. 3–4, 5, 20, 22.

10. Charles Hodge, *What Is Darwinism?* (New York: Scribner's, 1874), pp. 41, 48, 108, 52.

11. *Ibid.*, pp. 174.

12. The Free Church of Scotland was formed in 1843 by the evangelical party which withdrew from the Established Church of Scotland. In large measure this Disruption, when over 450 ministers seceded to form the new body, was over the assertion of the church's spiritual independence from civil powers. The United Presbyterian Church originated in 1847 and brought together elements from two earlier secessions from the Church of Scotland. The United Presbyterians were missionary orientated and revisionist with respect to the Westminster Confession of Faith through their deployment of Declaratory Acts, which allowed signatories liberty with respect to certain doctrinal points. The consequence was to moderate Calvinism in the direction of Wesleyanism. The Union of the Free Church and the United Presbyterian Church was finally brought about in 1900 when the United Free Church came into being. A number of Free Church ministers remained outside this union adhering more uncompromisingly to Westminster Calvinism; this group and its successors constitute the Free Church of Scotland. See the relevant entries in Nigel M. de S. Cameron (ed.), *Dictionary of Scottish Church History and Theology* (Edinburgh: T & T Clark, 1993).

13. K. R. Ross, "Rainy, Robert," in Cameron, *Dictionary of Scottish Church History.* For such reasons he remained suspect-as did James Orr-to figures like John Macleod of the Free Church, who interpreted Scottish Theology to American Calvinists in his lectures at Westminster Theological Seminary. See John Mcleod, *Scottish Theology in Relation to Church History Since the Reformation* (Edinburgh: Free Church of Scotland, 1943).

14. Andrew L. Drummond and James Bulloch, *The Church in Victorian Scotland 1843–1874* (Edinburgh: St. Andrews Press, 1975), p. 234. It should be noted, however, that in his 1927 lectures on the Calvin Foundation at the Free University of Amsterdam, Donald Maclean, professor of church history at the Free Church College in Edinburgh, did note that "In the scientific world the theory of Darwin profoundly affected theological thinking with resultant doctrinal accommodations that lessened the authority of the Word of God as a rule of faith and conduct." Maclean reported that Darwinism "has been severely challenged by the science of the twentieth century. All its outstanding principles have been the subject of the most adverse criticism. It has no explanation of the "sudden apparition of species," or of "terminal forms," or of the great "gaps" in series of living forms, or of "inversions" in the geological records. It has no concrete proof whatever of genetic continuity, which is fundamental to the theory." Donald Maclean, *Aspects of Scottish Church History* (Edinburgh: T. & T. Clark, 1927), pp. 105, 149. Nevertheless, Maclean's assessment did dwell at considerably greater length on the issue of biblical criticism.

15. See Adrian Desmond, *Huxley: The Devil's Disciple* (London: Michael Joseph, 1994), pp. 300–301. Free Church responses appeared in "The Philosophical Institution and Professor Huxley," *The Witness* (14 January 1862), and "Professor Huxley's Theory of the Origin and Kindred of Man," *The Witness* (18 January 1862).

16. David Guthrie, *Christianity and Natural Science: A Lecture Delivered Before the Young Men's Association of the Free Tolbooth Church* (Edinburgh, 1866). I have derived this information from an undergraduate dissertation prepared by James Scowen, "A Study in the Historical Geography of Ideas: Darwinism in Edinburgh 1859–75," Department of Geography, University of Edinburgh, 1996. I am grateful to Professor Charles Withers for calling it to my attention.

17. Patrick Carnegie Simpson, *The Life of Principal Rainy*, 2 vols., (London: Hodder and Stoughton, 1909), Vol. 1, p. 406.

18. See Andrew L. Drummond and James Bulloch, *The Church in Late Victorian Scotland 1874–1900* (Edinburgh: St. Andrews Press, 1978), chapter 5, "The Mind of the Church."

19. Alasdair MacIntyre, *Three Rival Versions of Moral Enquiry: Encyclopaedia, Genealogy, Tradition* (London: Duckworth, 1990), p. 18.

20. See the discussions in Simpson, *Rainy*, pp. 306–403; A. C. Cheyne, *The Transforming of the Kirk. Victorian Scotland's Religious Revolution* (Edinburgh: St. Andrews Press, 1983), pp. 44–52; Richard Allen Riesen, *Criticism and Faith in Late Victorian Scotland: A. B. Davidson, William Robertson Smith and George Adam Smith* (Lanham, Md.: University Press of America, 1985), pp. 94–251.

21. On earlier evangelical enthusiasm for science in Scotland see Paul Baxter, "Science and Belief in Scotland, 1805–1868: The Scottish Evangelicals," Ph.D. dissertation, University of Edinburgh, 1985. The shifting role of natural theology among pre-Darwinian Scottish evangelicals is the subject of Paul Baxter, "Deism and Development: Disruptive Forces in Scottish Natural Theology," in Stewart J. Brown and Michael Fry (eds.), *Scotland in the Age of the Disruption* (Edinburgh: Edinburgh University Press, 1993), pp. 98–112.

22. In his Gifford lectures delivered in the late 1930s, Karl Barth argued that the entire enterprise of natural theology was based upon a radical theological error. See Karl Barth, *The Knowledge of God and the Service of God* (London, 1938).

23. See, for example, Thomas Smith, "The Bible Not Inconsistent with Science," in *Christianity and Recent Speculations*, pp. 1–32.

24. *The Witness*, 19 August 1874.

25. Adrian Desmond and James Moore, *Darwin.* (London: Michael Joseph, 1991), p. 611.

26. John Tyndall, *Address Delivered Before the British Association Assembled at Belfast, with Addition.* (London: Longmans, Green, and Co., 1874). See the discussion in Ruth Barton, "John Tyndall, Pantheist. A Rereading of the Belfast Address." *Osiris*, 2nd series, 3 (1987): 111–34.

27. On Watts more generally, see Robert E. L. Rodgers, "The Life and Principal Writings of Robert Watts, D.D., LL.D. An Historico/Theological Examination of the Life and Principal Writings of Robert Watts with Particular Reference to the Doctrine of the Verbal Inspiration of Holy Scripture," Th.D. thesis, Faculté Libre de Théologie Réformée, Aix-en-Provence, 1984. Also see Alan Sell, "An Englishman, An Irishman and A Scotsman . . ." *Scottish Journal of Theology* 38 (1985): 41–83. Here Sell discusses Watts, William Burt Pope, and Andrew Martin Fairbairn.

28. Robert Watts, "An Irenicum: Or, a Plea for Peace and Co-operation between Science and Theology," in *The Reign of Causality: A Vindication of the Scientific Principle of Telic Causal Efficiency.* (Edinburgh: T. & T. Clark, 1888).

29. *The Witness*, 9 October 1874.

30. *Northern Whig*, 25 August 1874, 8. Also *The Witness*, 9 October 1874.

31. Robert Watts, "Atomism-An Examination of Professor Tyndall's Opening Address before the British Association, 1874," in *The Reign of Causality*.

32. Rev. John MacNaughtan at Rosemary Street Presbyterian Church, Rev. George Shaw at Fitzroy, and Rev. T. Y. Killen at Duncairn all took up the cudgels.

33. Robertson Smith, "Letter," *Northern Whig* (27 August 1874).

34. Cited in Barton, "Tyndall."

35. Bradley John Gundlach, "The Evolution Question at Princeton, 1845–1929", Ph.D. dissertation, University of Rochester, New York, 1995.

36. James McCosh, "Religious Aspects of the Doctrine of Development," in S. Irenaeus Prime (ed.), *History, Orations, and Other Documents of the Sixth General Conference of the Evangelical Alliance* (New York: Harper, 1874), pp. 264–71.

37. William Milligan Sloane, *The Life of James McCosh: A Record Chiefly Autobiographical* (Edinburgh: T. & T. Clark, 1896).

38. Sloane, *Life of McCosh*, p. 234. The standard biography of McCosh is J. David Hoeveler, *James McCosh and the Scottish Intellectual Tradition* (Princeton: Princeton University Press, 1981).

39. James McCosh, *The Ulster Revival and Its Physiological Accidents. A Paper Read Before the Evangelical Alliance, September 22, 1859* (Belfast: C. Aitchison, 1859).

40. This certainly does not mean that Princetonians were unaware of the Tyndall episode. *The Presbyterian Quarterly and Princeton Review*, for example, carried "An Open Letter to Professor Tyndall" from Rev. John Laing of Dundas, Ontario, in 1875, Vol. 4, pp. 229–53.

41. I discuss this in *Darwin's Forgotten Defenders*, pp. 107–108.

42. Biographical details are drawn from W. L. Calderwood and David Woodside, *The Life of Henry Calderwood* (London: Hodder and Stoughton, 1900).

43. S. D. Gill, "United Presbyterian Church," in Cameron (ed.), *Dictionary of Scottish Church History*.

44. See John Mcleod, *Scottish Theology in Relation to Church History Since the Reformation* (Edinburgh: Free Church of Scotland, 1943), p. 307.

45. For all that, Calderwood, according to his biographer, "regarded with equanimity the new views promulgated by the late W. Robertson Smith and others in this country regarding the authorship of certain books of the Old Testament, and had a firm conviction that these did not touch the real question of inspiration or the abiding influence of the Word of God." Calderwood and Woodside, *Life of Henry Calderwood*, p. 275. His concerns were much more focused on issues of moral philosophy and the creeping influence of German idealism.

46. A. Seth Pringle-Pattison, "The Philosophical Works," in Calderwood and Woodside, *Life of Henry Calderwood*, p. 423.

47. Henry Calderwood, *Philosophy of the Infinite* (London: Macmillan, 1854). Calderwood was also the author of the popular student text, *Handbook of Moral Philosophy* (London: Macmillan, 1888). By 1902 it had gone through 14 editions.

48. Cited in Calderwood and Woodside, *Life of Calderwood*, p. 159.

49. Henry Calderwood, "Ethical Aspects of the Theory of Development," *Contemporary Review*, 31 (December 1877): 123–32.

50. Henry Calderwood, "Evolution, Physical and Dialectic," *Contemporary Review*, 40 (December 1881), pp. 865–76, on pp. 867–68.

51. Henry Calderwood, *The Relations of Science and Religion* (New York: Wilbur B. Ketcham, 1881), pp. 21, 134–35.

52. Calderwood, *Relations of Science and Religion*, pp. 153–54.

53. George D. Mathews (ed.), *Alliance of the Reformed Churches Holding the Presbyterian System. Minutes and Proceedings of the Third General Council, Belfast 1884* (Belfast: Assembly's Offices, 1884), pp. 250–51.

54. Henry Calderwood, "On Evolution and Man's Place in Nature," *Proceedings of the Royal Society of Edinburgh* 17 (1890): 71–79.

55. Henry Calderwood, *Evolution and Man's Place in Nature* (London: Macmillan, 1893), p. 337. This aspect of the book drew praise from A. R. Wallace himself, who reviewed the book in *Nature*. See Calderwood and Woodside, *Life of Henry Calderwood*, p. 190.

56. Calderwood, *Evolution and Man's Place in Nature* (1893), p. 340.

57. Henry Calderwood, *Evolution and Man's Place in Nature* (2nd edition, London: Macmillan, 1896), p. 33.

58. Henry Calderwood, "Charles Darwin: His Boyhood," *United Presbyterian Magazine* (1888): 15–18, on p. 18. Other pieces by Calderwood in this series included "Charles

Darwin: His Youth," pp. 58–60; "Darwin Under Weigh as a Naturalist," pp. 113–116; and "Charles Darwin: His Theory as to Coral Reefs," pp. 254–57.

59. James Iverach, *Evolution and Christianity* (London: Hodder & Stoughton, 1894), p. 104.

60. See Alan P. F. Sell, *Defending and Declaring the Faith. Some Scottish Examples 1860–1920* (Exeter: Paternoster Press, 1987), pp. 137–171.

61. James Orr, *The Christian View of God and the World* (Edinburgh: Elliott, 1893), p. 99.

62. James Orr, *God's Image in Man and Its Defacement in the Light of Modern Denials* (London: Hodder & Stoughton, 1905), p. 88.

63. I discuss Orr's thinking on this matter in *Darwin's Forgotten Defenders. The Encounter between Evangelical Theology and Evolutionary Thought* (Grand Rapids and Edinburgh: Eerdmans and Scottish Academic Press, 1987), pp. 140–44.

64. James Orr, "Science and Christian Faith," in *The Fundamentals*, (Chicago: Testimony Publishing Co., 1910–1915), Vol. 4, p. 103.

65. Robert Flint, *Theism* (Edinburgh: Blackwood & Sons, 3rd ed., 1880), pp. 201–206, 208.

66. George Matheson, "The Religious Bearings of the Doctrine of Evolution," in *Alliance of the Reformed Churches Holding the Presbyterian System: Minutes and Proceedings of the Third General Council, Belfast 1884* (Belfast: Assembly's Offices, 1884), p. 86. See also Matheson's "Modern Science and the Religious Instinct," *Presbyterian Review* 5 (1884): 608–21.

67. George Matheson, *Can the Old Faith Live with the New? or, The Problem of Evolution and Revelation* (Edinburgh: William Blackwood & Sons, 1885).

68. The best analysis of Drummond's efforts is James R. Moore, "Evangelicals and Evolution: Henry Drummond, Herbert Spencer, and the Naturalisation of the Spiritual World," *Scottish Journal of Theology*, 38 (1985): 383–417.

69. Technically, Duns occupied the position as lecturer from 1864 to 1869 due to some doubts expressed by the General Assembly of 1864 about the propriety of retaining natural science in the theological curriculum. A bequest provided for the endowment of a professorial chair in 1869 and Duns occupied that position until his death during the General Assembly of 1903.

70. John Duns, Review of *The Origin of Species*, *North British Review* 32 (1860): 455–86.

71. John Duns, *Creation According to the Book of Genesis and the Confession of Faith. Speculative Natural Science and Theology. Two Lectures* (Edinburgh: Maclaren & Macnivan, 1877), p. 36.

72. John Duns, "On the Theory of Natural Selection and the Theory of Design," *Transactions of the Victoria Institute*, 1892. Duns also maintained this viewpoint in *Christianity and Science* (Edinburgh: William P. Kennedy, 1860), and *Science and Christian Thought* (London: Religious Tract Society, n.d.).

73. "The British Association," *The Witness*, 28 August 1874. It should not be assumed that there were no less strident voices. Rev. George Macloskie, in a letter to the *Northern Whig* on 26 August, for example, insisted that there was no desire in Belfast "to stifle free scientific inquiry." *Northern Whig*, 27 August 1874, p. 8.

74. J. G. C., "Darwinism," *Irish Ecclesiastical Record* 9 (1873): 337–61.

75. "Pastoral Address of the Archbishops and Bishops of Ireland." *Irish Ecclesiastical Record* 11 (November 1874).

76. Robert Watts, *Atomism: Dr. Tyndall's Atomic Theory of the Universe Examined and Refuted. To Which Are Added, Humanitarianism Accepts, Provisionally, Tyndall's Impersonal Atomic Deity; and a Letter to the Presbytery of Belfast; Containing a Note from the Rev. Dr.*

Hodge, and a Critique on Tyndall's Recent Manchester Recantation, Together with Strictures on the Late Manifesto of the Roman Catholic Hierarchy of Ireland in Reference to the Sphere of Science (Belfast: Mullan, 1875), pp. 34, 38, 39. The addition of Hodge's endorsement evidently meant a great deal to Watts. He regarded Hodge as "the author of the greatest work on systematic theology which has ever issued from the pen of man." And later in a letter to A. A. Hodge in 1881 thanking him for sending a copy of the biography of his father, Watts wrote: "Precious indeed it is to me and mine. We feel towards it as if it were the history of one of our own kith and kin." Letter, Robert Watts to A. A. Hodge, 1 January 1881, Archives, Speer Library, Princeton Theological Seminary. Earlier in 1879 he had supplied A. A. Hodge with copies of letters from Charles Hodge to Principal Cunningham. Letter, Robert Watts to A. A. Hodge, 2 December 1879, Archives, Speer Library, Princeton Theological Seminary.

77. Letter, Robert Watts to A. A. Hodge, 1 January 1881, Archives, Speer Library, Princeton Theological Seminary.

78. Letter, Robert Watts to B. B. Warfield, 18 June 1890, Warfield Papers, Archives, Speer Library, Princeton Theological Seminary.

79. "Pastoral Address," On earlier controversies between Catholics and Protestants over higher education in Ireland see T. W. Moody, "The Irish University Question in the Nineteenth Century," *History*, 43 (1958): 90–109.

80. Watts, "Evolution and Natural History," in *The Reign of Causality*, pp. 316–17. This review had originally appeared in the April 1887 issue of the *British and Foreign Evangelical Review*.

81. Robert Watts, "Natural Law in the Spiritual World," *British and Foreign Evangelical Review* (1885), reprinted in *The Reign of Causality*. See also Robert Watts, *Professor Drummond's "Ascent of Man," and Principal Fairbairn's "Place of Christ in Modern Theology," Examined in the Light of Science and Revelation* (Edinburgh: R. W. Hunter, n.d., circa 1894).

82. Letter, Robert Watts to B. B. Warfield, 23 September 1889, Warfield Papers, Archives, Speer Library, Princeton Theological Seminary.

83. Letter, Robert Watts to B. B. Warfield, 5 October 1893, Warfield Papers, Archives, Speer Library, Princeton Theological Seminary.

84. Letter, Robert Watts to B. B. Warfield, 18 June 1890, Warfield Papers, Archives, Speer Library, Princeton Theological Seminary.

85. In a postcard to Warfield dated 11 February 1891, he reported to Warfield that "Spurgeon's 'Sword and Trowel', 'Expository Times', 'United Pres. Mag.' & 'The Theological Monthly' have all given most flattering reviews of my 'New Apologetic &c.' "

86. Letter, Robert Watts to B. B. Warfield, 13 October 1890, Warfield Papers, Archives, Speer Library, Princeton Theological Seminary. These same sentiments were also expressed in a letter of 31 May, the following year. Of course, he dreaded no less the inroads biblical criticism was making in the United States too and chose to provide a detailed critique of Briggs's Biblical Theology in his opening address to the Assembly's College in November 1891. See letter, Robert Watts to B. B. Warfield, 22 July 1891, Warfield Papers, Speer Library, Princeton Theological Seminary.

87. Letter, Robert Watts to B. B. Warfield, 20 February 1894, Warfield Papers, Archives, Speer Library, Princeton Theological Seminary.

88. B. B. Warfield, "Personal Reflections of Princeton Undergraduate Life: IV—The Coming of Dr. McCosh," *The Princeton Alumni Weekly*, 16, No. 28 (19 April 1916): 650–53, on p. 652.

89. See the discussion in Peter J. Bowler, *The Eclipse of Darwinism: Anti-Darwinian Evolution Theories in the Decades around 1900* (Baltimore: Johns Hopkins University Press, 1983).

90. This scrapbook is extant in the Speer Library, Princeton Theological Seminary. Most of the clippings are from the *National Livestock Journal*. The Speer Library also retains a number of books on shorthorn cattle from B. B. Warfield's personal library.

91. William Warfield, *The Theory and Practice of Cattle-Breeding* (Chicago: J. H. Sanders Publishing Company, 1889).

92. From the Darwin volumes in Warfield's personal library, it is clear that the second volume of this work was the first of Darwin's books to be purchased by B. B. Warfield. It is dated May 1st 1868. *The Origin of Species* and *The Descent of Man* are both dated 1871. In 1872, while in London, B. B. Warfield purchased *The Expression of the Emotions*.

93. W. Warfield, *Cattle-Breeding*, pp. 85–86. William Warfield also enthusiastically commended a volume by J. H. Sanders, *Horse-Breeding: Being the General Principles of Heredity Applied to the Business of Breeding Horses . . .* (Chicago: J. H. Sanders, 1885), in which Darwin's evolutionary thinking was promulgated. Warfield particularly endorsed the long first chapter, which dealt with these general principles.

94. See James Secord, "Nature's Fancy: Charles Darwin and the Breeding of Pigeons," *Isis*, 72 (1981): 163–186.

95. B. B. Warfield, "Lectures on Anthropology" (December 1888), Speer Library, Princeton University.

96. Mark A. Noll, *Between Faith and Criticism: Evangelicals, Scholarship, and the Bible in America* (New York: Harper and Row, 1987), pp. 28, 29. See also the introduction in Mark A. Noll, *The Princeton Theology: Scripture, Science, and Theological Method from Archibald Alexander to Benjamin Warfield* (Grand Rapids: Baker, 1983).

97. B. B. Warfield, Review of *God's Image in Man*, by James Orr, *Princeton Theological Review*, 4 (1906): 555–58

98. B. B. Warfield, "Calvin's Doctrine of the Creation," *Princeton Theological Review*, 13 (1915): 190–255.

99. See my discussion in *Darwin's Forgotten Defenders: The Encounter between Evangelical Theology and Evolutionary Thought* (Grand Rapids: Eerdmans; Edinburgh: Scottish Academic Press, 1987).

100. When Watts visited Princeton in 1880, he wrote to his wife: "After writing you at Professor Green's on Monday, Dr. M'Closkie who you remember lost his dredge in Belfast Lough when our little boys were out with him in a boat, called according to promise and took me over all the buildings of Dr M'Cosh's College." Letter, Robert Watts, West Philadelphia, to his wife, 17 September 1880, in "Family Letters of Revd. Robert Watts, D. D., LL. D.," compiled by his wife (typescript). I am grateful to Dr. R. E. L. Rodgers for making this typescript available to me.

101. George Macloskie, "Scientific Speculation," *Presbyterian Review*, 1887, 8: 617–25.

102. See George Macloskie, "Concessions to Science," *Presbyterian Review*, 1889, 10: 220–28; Macloskie, "Theistic Evolution," *Presbyterian and Reformed Review*, 1898, 9: 1–22; Macloskie, "The Outlook of Science and Faith," *Princeton Theological Review*, 1903, 1: 597–615; Macloskie, "Mosaism and Darwinism," *Princeton Theological Review*, 1904, 2: 425–51. I discuss the contents of these articles in *Darwin's Forgotten Defenders*, pp. 92–96.

103. George Macloskie, "The Origin of Species and of Man," *Bibliotheca Sacra*, 1903, 60: 261–75, on p. 273.

104. Macloskie's papers at the Princeton University Library contain *The Examination of the Rev. James Woodrow D. D. by the Charleston Presbytery* (Charleston, S. C.: Lucas & Richardson, 1890). Carton 2, Macloskie Papers, CO498, Princeton University Library.

105. Mss. Notebook by George Macloskie, "Drift of Modern Science," Carton 1, Macloskie Papers, CO498, Princeton University Library.

9

Telling Tales

Evangelicals and the Darwin Legend

JAMES MOORE

The anecdote is the literary form that uniquely *lets history happen* by virtue of the way it introduces an opening into the teleological, and therefore timeless, narration of beginning, middle, and end. The anecdote produces the effect of the real, the occurrence of contingency, by establishing an event as an event within and yet without the framing context of historical successivity. . . . The opening of history that is effected by the anecdote, the hole and rim—using psychoanalytic language, the orifice—traced out by the anecdote within the totalizing whole of history, is something that is characteristically and ahistorically plugged up by a teleological narration that, though larger than the anecdote itself, is still constitutively inspired by the seductive opening of anecdotal form—thereby once again opening up the possibility, but, again, *only* the possibility, that this new narration, now complete within itself, and thereby rendered formally small—capable, therefore, of being anecdotalized—will itself be opened up by a further anecdotal operation, thereby calling forth some yet larger circumcising circumscription, and so, so on and so forth.

Joel Fineman

And he spake also a parable unto them; No man putteth a piece of a new garment upon an old; if otherwise, then both the new maketh a rent, and the piece that was taken out of the new agreeth not with the old.

Luke 5:36 (King James Version)

It is open season on edifying anecdotes. The last decade has seen an orgy of historical debunking as evangelical academics and their allies scrambled to scotch the folk fables of neocreationism. Tom McIver regaled the readers of *The Skeptical Inquirer* by exploding the so-called NASA-IBM discovery of "Joshua's missing day." Ted Davis got hooked on "fundamentalist fish stories" and slapped an international whale ban on modern Jonahs. Dan Wonderly, too, went over-board, trawling for Bible-science "myths" about marine fossils; and some be-lievers, still at sea, even pour cold water on sightings of Noah's Ark.[1]

Such concern with creationist tall tales marks a rising self-consciousness among evangelicals and a growing need to hold themselves accountable to schol-arly norms.[2] The tall tales, the edifying anecdotes, are an embarrassment. They offend, they taunt, they *tell*. They rend the fine fabric of evangelical history and expose a checkered past. Debunkers rush in to make repairs. They tie up loose ends, patch and stitch—even stitch up culprits—making the past smooth and serviceable again. Fact confronts fiction, reason corrects error, believers are ad-monished. Critical history thus bears witness to the one who proclaimed himself "the truth," as well as "the way" and "the life."

Whatever one may think of this procedure, it does not square readily with evangelical attitudes toward other edifying anecdotes. Modern, documented Joshua, Jonah, and Genesis stories may be exposed in the clear, cold light of reason, but ancient accounts, for which little or no independent corroboration exists, are taken as statements of fact—the original stories of Joshua and Jonah, for instance, or the miracle reports of the apostolic church. Here historicity is defended in the same way that the Calvinist divine B. B. Warfield once dis-missed postapostolic miracle claims: not by means of evidence—"there is," he allowed, "a much greater abundance and precision of evidence, such as it is, for miracles in the fourth and the succeeding centuries, than for the preceding ones"—but on the basis of scriptural authority.[3] In history as elsewhere, evan-gelicals remain rationalists manqués.

Lest I be misunderstood, my aim is not to cast doubt on sacred texts nor to devalue critical historical methods. So far I merely wish to suggest that evan-gelicals as a whole suffer from an epistemic split. They straddle the hermeneutic great divide of the seventeenth and eighteenth centuries.

In part they remain premodern, supposing that Bible stories depict real events, and these stories, of themselves, interpret history. The Fall and the Flood, the Crucifixion and the Resurrection, the first Pentecost and the Final Judgment—all equally are said to take place in space and time, and demonstrate divine purpose. To doubt this would impugn the truth and perspicuity of God's written Word. Yet, for all their literalism, many evangelicals are also modern interpret-ers. They adopt precisely the opposite attitude toward certain extrabiblical sto-ries: for *not* to doubt what these depict as history would, it is believed, implicitly dishonor God's Word incarnate, who proclaimed himself "the truth." Missing days in jammed computers, sailors surviving in whales, "fossil" limestone pre-cipitating from a mineral-laden Flood—such events are to be exposed as gra-tuitous fictions through minute empirical research.

For evangelicals, then, a self-consistent hermeneutic would appear to be un-attainable without toppling into either credulity or secularity. The belief that some stories are true because they appear in the Bible, while certain others, which do not, can or should be refuted, is intellectually precarious.[4]

But again, I do not intend to play the skeptic. Having pointed up the di-lemma that flows from privileging Bible stories, I want instead to question a further, more general belief on which *both* modern and premodern evangelical understanding depend: the notion that the meaning of certain stories—biblical or not—derives primarily from their historicity. This belief runs deep and is ironically one source of critical attitudes that evangelicals routinely (though selectively) deplore.

The reduction of a text's meaning to that of its " 'true' historical occasion or setting" led last century to what Hans Frei calls "the eclipse of biblical narrative." Bit by bit the Bible was shredded. Books, chapters, and even verses were ripped apart as provenance and authorship came under fire. Scholars restitched the fragments, creating polychrome Pentateuchs and anodyne lives of Jesus, but at a cost. Holy Scripture became a coded palimpsest, understandable by the few. Its rich old stories, full of memorable characters with credible destinies in real-life settings, were impoverished, not merely as literature, but for didactic and devotional purposes as well.[5]

Today evangelical scholars tackle such "destructive criticism" on its own terms, defending the Bible with ever more erudite arguments. At the same time, they applaud their own home-grown critics for debunking extrabiblical myths. The unity in these attitudes is, I believe, as striking and salutary as their irony. For by insisting on *either* hand that historicity and meaning stand or fall together, the wider significance of narratives is lost. Whether they be Bible stories or edifying anecdotes, narratives are passed on as wholes, telling while being told, succoring or scandalizing the "evangelical mind." Their first meaning is to be sought in what they mean to those who repeat them, not in what scholars declare they should mean in the light of historical research.[6]

Thus I myself believe that Bible stories have a pithiness, a poignancy, even a grandeur that no criticism can dispel. So also to a lesser extent do creationist folk fables. Individual texts may be deconstructed, analysed, pulled to bits, but each has an inner integrity and a rich legacy of recensions. The stories of Cain and Abel, Abraham and Issac, Jacob and Esau, Moses and Aaron, David and Goliath, Joseph and Mary, Jesus and Nicodemus, Paul and Timothy, and many others are passed on with mother's milk. In their constant retelling they remain ever memorable, ever instructive. So also, for better or worse, do the creationist anecdotes. Some may seem silly, others sinister, but all speak a tell-tale language that opens up the past. In their forging and flourishing we may even glimpse that "primal, almost universal motive" to find eternal truth in time.[7]

"The entrance of thy words giveth light"

Now let me come clean. For twenty years I myself was a closet debunker. Quietly, some say quixotically, I chipped away at that most notorious of creationist anecdotes, the story of Charles Darwin and Lady Hope. How I got wrapped up in it would itself make a good story, so a word about this first.

Tall tales can be intractable, with anonymous subjects, apocryphal settings, or indefinite origins. The Darwin–Lady Hope anecdote has none of these. Its subjects were eminent Victorians—a Fellow of the Royal Society, the dowager of a fleet-admiral in the Royal Navy—and its provenance is given precisely. In

short, it is a debunker's dream. Nor is the story merely amusing, like others—
a funny fib, outlandish but innocent. Quite the contrary, it spawned the ghast-
liest piece of gossip about any modern scientist: the legend that Darwin on his
deathbed renounced evolution and professed the Christian faith. Many have
dismissed this as a feeble slander; the Darwin family tried to crush it by sheer
authority. But the legend lives on.

For such reasons I was drawn to the Darwin–Lady Hope story. I chased up
clues like schoolboys collect stamps, and the sleuthing became obsessive. My
findings are published in *The Darwin Legend*, so I need not detail them here.
Briefly, I conclude that the deathbed tale, like other legends, is a "grotesque
gloss on real historical events"; an "actual meeting between Darwin and Lady
Hope" probably lay at its root. What concerns me now is the likely impact of
a book that claims to expose the deathbed business "once and for all." My
colleague Jim Secord calls it *The Darwin Legend* "an exemplar of targeted debunking," but I wonder whether it will hit the mark.[8] Can a century's chit-
chat be undone in 200 pages? Does truth triumph through footnotes?

Here, frankly, I *am* skeptical. My faith in debunking has waned. Outside the
evangelical academy, sanctified storytelling is rife. In pulpit and pew the "faculty
of deglutition" (as phrenologists would say) is overdeveloped. Ask any group of
ordinary Bible-believing Protestants what they know about Darwin, and the
odds are someone will pipe up expectantly, "Didn't he die a Christian?" No
matter that many have doubted and a few denied it, the deathbed legend is
deeply imbedded in the folk consciousness of modern evangelicalism.[9] Rooting
it out will be hard.

Mass communication is partly to blame. Since it was first published 80 years
ago, the Darwin–Lady Hope story has been recycled constantly in religious
magazines, books, and tracts. Its radio exposure seems scant, but telepreachers
like Jimmy Swaggart have exploited it, and hi-tech hucksters promise more—a
dying Darwin, born-again on interactive CD-ROM; do-it-yourself Darwin
conversions in virtual reality. Even so, all God's gadgetry will not convince
people who lack a reason to believe. A motive is needed, a mind-set that makes
a Darwin repentance not just desirable but deeply plausible. Evangelicals, I think,
possess that uniquely. They know from Bible stories that God saves lost souls.
His power is real to them because they believe the stories are true. The Darwin–
Lady Hope story gives further proof of God's grace and is read in the same way.
It moves the heart even as it cuts to the heart of evangelicalism. It exposes a
hermeneutic raw nerve.

To understand this operation we must get past debunking and bring the
whole story into focus.

The original, 521-word anecdote appeared in August 1915 in America's oldest and largest Baptist magazine, the Boston-based *Watchman-Examiner*. Its spon-
sor was the distinguished editor himself, Curtis Lee Laws, who in an issue five
years later would plead the cause of those he christened "fundamentalists." Laws
noted that the story had been told only days before, during a Christian workers'
conference held at the Northfield, Massachusetts, girls' school founded by D. L.
Moody. It had even been repeated from the conference platform by the main

speaker, Professor A. T. Robertson, a noted New Testament scholar and eminent Southern Baptist. The source of the "remarkable story," said Laws, was a "consecrated English woman" attending the conference. She had written it out at his request under her nom de plume "Lady Hope."

And who was this noble guest? In Britain her name had been as worthy as the company she kept at Northfield. Elizabeth Cotton, the firstborn of an army general, had come to prominence as a temperance campaigner in the 1870s. For years she rolled the wagon around the country, opening coffee houses and cultivating the great and good. Lord Shaftesbury sang her praises, Moody employed her during his British missions, and in 1877 another soldier of the Cross, Admiral Sir James Hope, commander-in-chief in China during the second Opium War, took her as his wife. The lady carried on bountifully, with noblesse oblige. She read the Bible from door to door and wrote treacly tracts and novels. After the admiral's death, in 1893, she married an elderly millionaire and acquired a London address to match. But still she traded off her second-hand title, calling herself Lady Hope.

Her largesse now grew lavish, her lifestyle grand. She swapped the temperance wagon for a motor car and raced back and forth to Keswick conventions at unholy speeds. Creditors finally caught up with her. Months after her second husband died, she had squandered not only his £1500 jointure, but the £1000 annuity left her by the admiral. None of her devout West End friends—not even the late head of Scotland Yard—could keep the courts at bay. Her bankruptcy in 1911 was splashed all over, headlined "A Widow's Affairs." Discharged a year later, she retreated to New York City, ostensibly "to overcome the grief of her husband's death." Less plausibly, after the *Watchman-Examiner* story came out, she claimed that her flight was "to avoid the persecution of the Darwins."[10]

Not that Americans minded. Most knew nothing of Lady Hope; those who did forgave. What counted was her story, which spread like wildfire. Editors reprinted it, preachers repeated it, fundamentalists swallowed it. Few indeed could refuse. The story had integrity—the "ring of truth"—like Scripture. "The entrance of thy words giveth light; it giveth understanding unto the simple." Here is Darwin, aged and bedridden, cradling an open Bible, his head haloed by an autumn sunset. Lady Hope attends him, basking in the "brightness and animation" of his face, nodding as he speaks of " 'the grandeur of this Book.' " The imagery is familiar, irresistible, overwhelming. "Write the vision, and make it plain upon tables, that he may run that readeth it." This is a deathbed scene— Darwin has been converted!

Such stories vouched for themselves and evangelicals were inured to them. The deathbed gave rise to the archetypal anecdote, pathetic and plausible at once.[11] Thousands of "dying sayings" and "dying hours," "last days" and "last words," had been compiled. *Death-bed Scenes* was the grandest, a British blockbuster published in 1832 in four, 400-page tomes. In New York a 500-page collection with the same title ran to a sixth edition in 1869. These books edified; others admonished: *The Closing Scene; or, Christianity and Infidelity Contrasted in the Last Hours of Remarkable Persons*, stood by genteel bedsides, while *The Dying Pillow*, a penny pamphlet comparing "the last days of infidels and Christians," was aimed at the homeless poor. Victorians wallowed in such works but the genre did not die out. In the past century at least a dozen more deathbed collections have circulated in Britain and the United States.[12]

Lady Hope tapped this huge voyeurs' market. Had Darwin not been her subject, her story would still have sold. Shrewdly crafted, it reported neither a death scene nor a repentance, but it aped such tales to perfection by playing up the drama and playing down the date—six months before Darwin died. "To bring about a death-bed conversion was the highest accolade an Evangelical could win," and the noble lady passed a brilliant counterfeit.[13] Bankrupt abroad, she sought spiritual credit in the States, and she got it, pressed down, full and overflowing.

Nor was this her first effort at self-aggrandizement. In Britain she had honed her anecdotal skills in dozens of books and tracts. Her embroidery was exquisite, coloring her own good deeds, appealing to pious sentiment. The Darwin anecdote was only her latest life-and-death "true story."

Here is Lady Hope at work. She climbs a narrow dingy staircase and enters a humble room. From his bed a dying miner reaches out and, seizing her hand, kisses it. "I was wanting to see you once more," he sighs. "I have been very ill—yes—but it is *all right*. Jesus is with me. I cannot think much—no—but *He thinks for me*. Jesus is very kind. Oh! He is kind." The man remembers his unchurched neighbors. "Speak to them, speak to them," he pleads, "and have all the meetings you can." The lady prays by the bedside, then bids him farewell, knowing they will be reunited "at the Throne of Glory above!" Later she describes the scene in a letter to Christian friends.[14]

Again, picture the same noble lady waiting at a rural railway station "late on a summer afternoon." A young gentleman on the platform addresses her.

"You have been hurried in trying to be here in time."

She does not recognize him at first but responds politely, "Yes, I have been very busy for several hours amongst the people, visiting from house to house."

He nods, "You are always busy, are you not?"

"Oh!" she answers, "my life is so full of interest! It is such a joy to be able to take to the people the message of Christ's love and mercy."

"You believe in him?" he asks.

"Believe in him! Do you not believe in Him? He is all in all to me."

The man shakes his head and mutters softly, "I am not sure of anything. I have no beliefs at all now, for I do not know what is true and what is not true. Life is an entire mystery, and a very sad one, I think."

The train comes and they part. The lady now remembers the young man as a local doctor, "so earnest and thoughtful," and resolves to get him "on the right side." "It would be a grand thing if he could learn to believe," she says. But they never meet again. Three hours later, alone in his room, the doctor scribbles a message and slits his throat. The lady, stricken by the news, recounts "this tragic little history" to illustrate the "misery that can take possession of a mind that has not the rest of saving faith."[15]

Now, once more, picture the noble lady visiting an elderly "professor." He is propped up in bed, wearing a rich purple gown. As she sits beside him he gestures with one hand toward the sunset scene beyond his window, while in the other he holds an open Bible.

> "What are you reading now?" she asks.
>
> "Hebrews!" he replies, "—still Hebrews. The Royal Book, I call it. Isn't it grand?"
>
> The lady mentions the Book of Genesis, for the "professor" is a famous scientist who wrote about "the history of the Creation."
>
> At this he seems "greatly distressed," his fingers twitch "nervously," and with a "look of agony" he sighs, "I was a young man with unformed ideas. I threw out queries, suggestions, wondering all the time over everything; and to my astonishment the ideas took like wildfire. People made a religion of them."
>
> Then he pauses, and after remarking on "the holiness of God" and the "grandeur" of the Bible, he suddenly says, "I have a summer house in the garden. . . . I want you very much to speak there. . . . To-morrow afternoon I should like the servants on the place, some tenants and a few of the neighbors to gather."
>
> "What shall I speak about?" the lady asks.
>
> "CHRIST JESUS!" he says, smiling brightly, ". . . and his salvation. Is not that the best theme? And I want you to sing some hymns with them. . . . If you take the meeting at three o'clock this window will be open, and you will know that I am joining in with the singing."

Her vignette finished, the lady longs to give her readers a indubitable record: "How I [wish] that I could have made a picture of the fine old man and his beautiful surroundings on that memorable day!"[16]

As if further proof were needed—a photograph—that she told the truth. For who could doubt it? Lady Hope described her visit to Darwin in the same well-worn idiom used in her accounts of the dying miner and the depressed doctor. The bedside scene, the outstretched hand, the anguished utterance, the agony of doubt, the approach of death, the hope of salvation, the missionary zeal—all were authenticating marks, tried and true, a thousand-fold familiar from death-bed tales. Such stories bore a redeeming message, like the Bible's; they pointed to the one who proclaimed himself "the truth" as well as "the way" and "the life." Little wonder, then, that evangelicals read Lady Hope's story as "true."

"He that is spiritual judgeth all things"

It is high time for historical criticism. Time to scrutinize sources, tease out discrepancies, and say what really happened that autumn afternoon. Time to reveal the man of history behind the icon of faith—the *historische* Charles behind the *geschichtliche* Darwin.

But no. Such is mere debunking, at which evangelical scholars already excel. I might show how Lady Hope turned into Lady Pope; how Darwin became a knight and she his nurse; or how Northfields proliferated. I might trace the shifting time frame, from Darwin's "last illness" to his "last days" to his "last hours," when on his "deathbed" he uttered to Lady Hope "almost [his] last words."[17] I might point up and parcel out blame for all these howlers, then offer the "true" version of events, and yet still not get one step closer to understanding what Lady Hope's story has meant to evangelicals. So I leave the "Darwin of history" to debunkers and move on.

Commentary is somewhat telling. Lady Hope's story is never placed in context—anecdotes have none—but always given a spiritual gloss. Editors milk it for meaning, extracting lessons for all. Young men are admonished about their "unformed ideas," modernists rebuked for making evolution into a religion, and unbelievers warned that a theory is worse than worthless "when the solemn realities of eternity stare a man in the face." Any argument detectable here is roughly a fortiori: the enormity of Darwin's transgressions points to a still greater salvation. As "Darwin . . . was mercifully delivered from his doubts and fears," so also "the Holy Spirit is still working, and brands from the burning are daily becoming trophies of grace." In Darwin "Satan tried to make a monkey out of man," so "aren't you glad that God has made it possible that you can be His son?"[18]

But logic chopping yields little from such remarks. The screed is hard, hiding nothing profound. Concrete men, dealers in the practical and superficial, have glossed the story, and their glibness tells less about God, Darwin, or Lady Hope than themselves.

Oswald J. Smith was the editor par excellence. Born in 1889 to a Canadian telegraph operator, he was converted by R. A. Torrey and received a Bible college and seminary education. He became a Presbyterian preacher, then a roving evangelist, and founded the famous People's Church in Toronto, where he served for sixty years. During his ministry he wrote hundreds of hymns and gospel tracts. Many of the latter were based on sermons, such as "Why I Am Against Evolution," published in 1946. This gave the Darwin–Lady Hope story verbatim, a "remarkable picture," Smith called it, exposing "the very soul of tragedy." He had culled the story with bits of commentary from versions published in the 'twenties, and the Peoples Church sold it as a tract until the 1970s.[19] Others in turn recycled the tract, so that today "Darwin's Confession" is the most widely read version of Lady Hope's story.

Yet times have changed, apparently. A sermon published a half-century ago is no longer thought authoritative. Even the People's Church has doubts. The senior minister Paul Smith, son of Oswald, explains that the tract was discontinued because it lacked documentation. "I am reasonably sure that when father first wrote, he could have validated it but unfortunately he did not do so. During those earlier years a great many godly men wrote things and they did not think it was necessary to document their sources. Most of us today would not do that."[20]

Wouldn't they? In pulpit and pew, I repeat, sanctified story-telling is rife. My files are awash with the flotsam of Darwin's deathbed. Popular credulity has sunk to new lows with help from the likes of Jimmy Swaggart. In 1984, a few years before his fall, he lifted the Oswald Smith text from an obscure magazine and retailed it, typos and all, in a syndicated telecast. "Charles Darwin refuted the devilish, hellish *lie* of evolution, and embraced the King of Glory," he exulted, shouting "Hallelujah! . . . Praise the Lord!" An impertinent viewer wrote in and challenged Swaggart to document the story. The archfoe of "devilish, hellish" lies prevailed on his poor wife, Frances, to supply an umpteenth generation photocopy, absurdly entitled "The Untold Story of Charles Darwin." "I am sorry," she confessed, "but this is all the information we have. . . . We ask that you continue to lift up this Ministry in your prayers as we endeavor to carry on God's work."[21]

Alas, it will take more than prayers to lift up historical Elmer Gantryism on this scale from the pit it hath digged for itself and naive viewers. Frances Swaggart wrote not six months before Paul Smith declared such practices to be passé, and still, a decade later, the arrogance of evangelical epistemology is astounding. Even upwardly mobile creationists, keen to debunk the Darwin anecdote, possess a wonderful sixth sense for reaching historical truth a priori.

"He that is spiritual judgeth all things, yet he himself is judged of no man." Belief in direct and unaccountable access to truth is the enthusiast's failing and the evangelical's foible. The Darwin anecdote exposes it like nothing but Bible stories themselves. Lady Hope's account "is not only likely true; it is pretty certainly true," declared William Bell Riley's *Christian Fundamentalist* in 1927. "It is hardly conceivable that Lady Hope, wonderful Christian woman that she was, would ever manufacture a story of this sort. . . . We give this story, having little doubt that it is absolutely accurate and true." Now fast-forward 55 years and mark the verdict issued by Creation-Life Publishers: "It is difficult to imagine a deeply religious Christian . . . fabricating the account and then publishing it. Any check which revealed its falsity would bring great discredit upon the originator."[22] The same argument, trotted out endlessly, is used to vindicate the New Testament witnesses to the Resurrection. Spontaneously, even habitually, evangelicals read and defend Lady Hope's history like they do the Bible's.

Creationist debunkers—lately on the rise—take the opposite tack, arguing with all the presumption of the Bible critics they deplore. Thus, "biographies of Darwin do not mention . . . an incident" like Lady Hope's; "there is not a particle of evidence that his mind changed" and "no evidence of his being bedridden"; the Darwin family said nothing about a conversion at the time, nor can Lady Hope "even be identified," and so on. I need hardly point out that such arguments from silence cut two ways, and may undermine Scripture as readily as an edifying anecdote. Or, indeed, that arguments from authority may do so even quicker. "Several scientists who have made a study of Darwin's life . . . do not accept as factual Lady Hope's account of his deathbed conversion," crowed the ultra lowbrow *Bible-Science Newsletter*, the "scientists" of course being creationists.[23] Scientific authorities, Christian or otherwise, who "do not accept as factual" the early chapters of Genesis would be much easier to cite, never mind those actually qualified to assess such things—historians.

To be fair, at least one U.S. creationist has made a show of suspended judgment. Like William Jennings Bryan, who promised $100 to any professor who could reconcile evolution and the Bible (and once actually paid it), Bolton Davidheiser has "a standing offer of $25" to anyone who can prove Lady Hope's story true. The anecdote has "all the features of a hoax," he admits, but "it would be worth more than $25 to find that . . . Darwin did [m]ake a confession of faith." This is a voice crying in a wilderness of foregone conclusions. Truth, like salvation, is priceless to American evangelicals; it cannot be bought. History may be hard work for some, truth laboriously acquired, but debunkers of Lady Hope, like her defenders, are amazingly saved by grace: their history is made by hunch. The Darwin anecdote is "apocryphal . . . a figment of the imagination . . . completely false." "The events evidently took place only in Lady Hope's mind." "The story is, of course, nonsense—a myth. . . . When I saw it I knew *at once*, even with my limited knowledge, . . . that it could not be true."[24]

"The truth shall make you free"?

Puff this as "common sense realism" or "democratic epistemology," it is still Yankee cock-sureness to the core. All the key documents needed to evaluate Lady Hope's story have sat on open shelves for over half a century. At any time, any ordinary conscientious debunker could have run it to ground. A hardline British Communist proved as much, almost cracking the story in the 1960s. His atheist initiative seems all the more remarkable for decades of evangelical inertia.[25] God-fearing, truth-loving, Bible-believing Americans—fundamentalists first, then neocreationists—have persistently taken short cuts, appealing to authority, negative evidence, or Lady Hope's presumed probity, rather than conduct the necessary research. With one or a few texts before them, defenders and debunkers alike have exhibited the same invincible intuition, the same sixth sense for historicity, that evangelicals learn before an open Bible. "The entrance of thy words giveth light; it giveth understanding unto the simple." Truth rises from the text, self-attesting, to anecdotal minds.[26]

Britain is no historian's Havana, but evangelicals there—like that sixties' Stalinist—have been more critical. It was *The Christian*, the great revivalist weekly founded by R. C. Morgan, that in 1922 published the thunderous rebuke to Lady Hope by Darwin's own daughter Henrietta, commenting: "it is well that the facts should be known." Since then only a clutch of obscure writers have endorsed the Darwin anecdote; evangelical leaders on the whole have kept an open mind.[27] "Unable to pin it down," the chemist and apologist Robert E. D. Clark simply "did not mention it" in his 1948 study, *Darwin, Before and After*. Nor did F. F. Bruce, New Testament scholar extraordinaire, rush to take sides. The "only surprising thing . . . to me" about Darwin's reported admiration for the Book of Hebrews, he wrote in 1976, "would be that it seems inconsistent with another piece of tradition, according to which he is said to have remarked that his minutely scientific studies had taken away his former capacity for aesthetic appreciation."[28]

Such judiciousness is perhaps to be expected in circles where Lady Hope's memory may survive, and it shows a certain deference to the Darwin family that rugged individualists may find repellant. Even so, I suggest that British attitudes to Lady Hope's story may also stem from chastened views of Scripture, and habits of Bible reading formed less democratically than those of most Americans. Narratives of faith take on rich meanings where tradition and authority are upheld; truth and historicity may be detached. Whether or not this is so across the British churches, it surely holds within individual denominations. The silence of Roman Catholics about Lady Hope's story is particularly eloquent. Only one :omment have I found, slating it as "pathetic but mendacious," an instance of the crude, anecdotal methods used by Protestant polemicists.[29]

What then does all this augur for the reception of a book purporting to expose the Darwin deathbed legend "once and for all"? More of the same, I suspect. My colleague Frederick Burkhardt, American man of letters and senior editor on the Darwin correspondence project at Cambridge University Library, credits *The Darwin Legend* as a "paradigm of serious scholarly investigation" but fears that, "fundamentalists being what they are, you will have encouraged a revival" of Lady Hope's story.[30] I think Burkhardt may well be right, though the revival will not be straightforward.

Let me explain. Hermeneutic naivete will remain endemic among evangelicals so long as the Bible is not interpreted as Benjamin Jowett in 1860 famously insisted it should be, "like any other book."[31] Stories will interpret themselves, speaking truth to spiritual minds, so long as the Bible's are read routinely as simple statements of historical fact. But in the case of the Darwin legend, the story has now been greatly enlarged. It is no longer just Lady Hope's, or one of the countless recensions; it is the new narrative about Darwin with which I have framed the original anecdote. And my retelling in its turn may be "anecdotalized" as evangelicals retell it and make telling new tales of their own.[32]

The Darwin Legend all but invites this. In the main text I give a slick teleological account, tidying up history, drawing lessons, making morals. I never presume to say what actually passed between Lady Hope and Darwin, but in good debunking fashion I historicize her anecdote and give its "true" meaning. Then, however, I pack the appendixes with my sources, which can be read in various ways. Compared and cross-examined, these documents may stimulate fresh stories about Darwin, new and telling anecdotes. These in turn will circulate among evangelicals and eventually disrupt my own account. Others will debunk them, my account itself will be debunked, and so on. If *The Darwin Legend* has a "sobering message about the nature of truth" (as Mark Noll says in his kind foreword), it is surely that the truth about Darwin will never finally be told. The book not only reconstitutes its subject; it also joins its subject's literature. The title is self-referential.

Truth "will out," but when? Not so long as people live by legends. The "truth" about the past will only go on being outed. It is itself historical.

NOTES

1. Tom McIver, "Ancient Tales and Space-Age Myths of Creationist Evangelism," *Skeptical Inquirer*, 10 (1986), 258–76; Edward B. Davis, "A Whale of a Tale: Fundamentalist Fish Stories," *Perspectives on Science and Christian Faith*, 43 (1991), 224–37; Daniel E. Wonderly, "Fanciful Bible-Science Stories' Harm: A Call to Action," *Perspectives on Science and Christian Faith*, 44 (1992), 131–33; Howard M. Teeple, *The Noah's Ark Nonsense* (Evanston, Ill.: Religion & Ethics Institute, 1978); Lloyd R. Bailey, *Where is Noah's Ark?* (Nashville, Tenn.: Abingdon, 1978); Larry Eskridge, chap. 11, this book.

2. Mark A. Noll, *Between Faith and Criticism: Evangelicals, Scholarship, and the Bible in America* (San Francisco: Harper & Row, 1986), pp. 163–98.

3. Benjamin B. Warfield, *Counterfeit Miracles* (New York: Scribner's, 1918), p. 10.

4. Cf. the porous "great divide" described in Noll, *Between Faith and Criticism*, chaps. 7–8, esp. pp. 181–82.

5. Hans Frei, *The Eclipse of Biblical Narrative: A Study in Eighteenth and Nineteenth Century Hermeneutics* (New Haven, Conn.: Yale University Press, 1974), pp. 1–16.

6. Mark A. Noll, *The Scandal of the Evangelical Mind* (Grand Rapids, Mich.: Eerdmans, 1994). For evidence of this changing hermeneutic emphasis, see George P. Landow, *Victorian Types, Victorian Shadows: Biblical Typology in Victorian Literature, Art and Thought* (Boston: Routledge & Kegan Paul, 1980), and Martin Warner, ed., *The Bible and Rhetoric: Studies in Biblical Persuasion and Credibility* (London: Routledge, 1990).

7. H. H. Milman, *History of Latin Christianity*, quoted in Baden Powell, "On the Study of the Evidences of Christianity," in Frederick Temple et al., *Essays and Reviews*, 4th ed. (London: Longman, Green, Longman, & Roberts, 1861), p. 111. For the cultural history of a favorite creationist Bible story, see Don Cameron Allen, *The Legend of Noah: Renaissance Rationalism in Art, Science, and Letters* (Urbana: University of Illinois Press, 1949); Jack P. Lewis, *A Study of the Interpretation of Noah and the Flood in Jewish and Christian Literature* (Leiden: E. J. Brill, 1978); Alan Dundes, ed., *The Flood Myth* (Berkeley: University of California Press, 1988); Lloyd R. Bailey, *Noah: The Person and the Story in History and Tradition* (Columbia: University of South Carolina Press, 1989); and Norman Cohn, *Noah's Flood: The Genesis Story in Western Thought* (New Haven, Conn.: Yale University Press, 1996).

8. James Moore, *The Darwin Legend* (Grand Rapids, Mich.: Baker, 1994), pp. 23, 172; J. Secord to the author, Jan. 23, 1995.

9. The public too is generally clued in. After my lecture on the Darwin legend at a 1994 Open University summer school, members of the audience retired to a local park for libations and late-night revelry. They were joined by a passing stranger, himself the worse for wear, who had overheard Darwin mentioned. Composing himself, he solemnly informed the group that the great man died a Christian. Nor does the legend just crop up among the legless. In November 1994, while giving a live interview to BBC Radio Berkshire about his splendid new biography, *Huxley*, my colleague Adrian Desmond was pressed to say whether Darwin repented on his deathbed.

10. [L. Legge to E. W. Denny], June 16 and 30, Aug. 4 and 26, 1906, Denny Family Papers, Hingham, Norfolk; ". . . A Widow's Affairs . . . ," *The Times*, July 10, 1911, p. 3; Moore, *Darwin Legend*, pp. 125, 131.

11. See the deathbed chapters in E. M. Forster, *Marianne Thornton, 1797–1887: A Domestic Biography* (London: Edward Arnold, 1956); A. O. J. Cockshut, *Truth to Life: The Art of Biography in the Nineteenth Century* (London: Collins, 1974); John R. Reed, *Victorian Conventions* (Athens, Ohio: Ohio University Press, 1975); and Ralph Houlbrooke, ed., *Death, Ritual and Bereavement* (London: Routledge, 1989).

12. John Warton, *Death-bed Scenes and Pastoral Conversations*, 5th ed., 4 vols. (London: John Murray, 1826–32); Davis Clark, ed., *Death-bed Scenes; or, Dying with and without Religion: Designed to Illustrate the Truth and Power of Christianity* (New York: Lane & Scott, 1851; 6th ed. 1869); [Erskine Neale], *The Closing Scene; or, Christianity and Infidelity Contrasted in the Last Hours of Remarkable Persons*, 2 vols. (London: Longman, Brown, Green, & Longmans, 1848–49); *The Dying Pillow: The Last Days of Infidels and Christians Contrasted*, 12th ed. rev. (London: William Wileman, [1889]).

13. R. Cecil, "Holy Dying: Evangelical Attitudes to Death," *History Today*, Aug. 1982, p. 31.

14. Lady Hope, *Lines of Light on a Dark Background* (London: James Nisbet, 1879), pp. 153–54.

15. Lady Hope, *Heavenly Blossoms on Earth's Pathway* (London: S. W. Partridge, 1899), pp. 68–71.

16. Lady Hope, "Darwin and Christianity," *Watchman-Examiner*, n.s., 3 (Aug. 19, 1915), 1071.

17. John Ellis Currey, "The Good Word: Darwin's Beliefs Defended," *Evening Telegram* (St. John's, Newfoundland), Aug. 7, 1993, p. 15a ("Lady Pope," "last illness"); Jimmy Swaggart's sermon "That I May Know Him" (preached in Honolulu, Mar. 30, 1984), telecast Sept. 30, 1984 ("Sir Charles"), transcription by courtesy of Craig Pringle; E. K. Victor Pearce, "Darwin, Charles Robert (1809–1882)," in J. D. Douglas, ed., *The New International Dictionary of the Christian Church* (Exeter, Devon: Paternoster Press, 1978), p. 283 ("his nurse's record"); Anon., "Darwin's Last Days," *Christian Fundamentalist* (Minneapolis), 1 (Dec. 1927), 12 ("Northfield, England"); F. S. Dunkin, "Darwin's Deathbed" (letter), *Local Preacher's Magazine* (London), 78 (Jan. 1928), 18–19 ("Northfields, Massachusetts"); C. W. Hale Amos, "Darwin's Last Hours," *Reformation Review* (Amsterdam), 4 (Oct. 1956), pp. 56–57; A. J. Pollock, "Charles Darwin's Deathbed," *Churchman's Magazine* (London), 79 (Mar. 1925), 69; L. T. Townsend, *Collapse of Evolution*, rev. ed. (Louisville, Ky: Pentacostal Publishing Co., [1921]), pp. 122–24 ("almost the last words").

18. [S. Chadwick], "The Editor's Letter: . . . Darwin on Darwinianism," *Joyful News and Methodist Chronicle* (London), Mar. 8, 1928, p. 3; H. Enoch, "Darwin's Recantation," *Evolution or Creation* (London: Evangelical Press, 1966), pp. 165–67; A. J. Pollock, "Charles Darwin's Deathbed," *British Evangelist* (London), 47 (Dec. 1920), 92; Alexander Hardie, *Evolution: Is It Philosophical, Scientific or Scriptural?* (Los Angeles: Times-Mirror Press, 1924), pp. 159–61; Alasdair Johnston, "Like Darwin, I doubt . . ." (letter), *The Scotsman* (Edinburgh), Apr. 15, 1958, p. 6; Pastor Mel, " 'Learn from the Mistakes of Others and You Won't Live Long Enough to Make Them All Yourself,' " *Faith Seed* (?), [1983?].

19. Warren W. Wiersbe, "Oswald J. Smith—The People's Preacher," *Confident Living*, Sept. 1986, pp. 36–39; Oswald J. Smith, *The Story of My Life and the Peoples Church* (London: Marshall, Morgan & Scott, 1962); idem, "Why I Am Against Evolution," *The Challenge of Life* (London: Marshall, Morgan & Scott, [1946]), pp. 104–106, drawing on Pollock, "Charles Darwin's Deathbed," and Anon., "Darwin's Last Days"; Oswald J. Smith, ed., *Darwin's Confession* (Willowdale, Ont.: People's Church, n.d.).

20. P. B. Smith to C. J Pringle, Jan. 7, 1987, by courtesy of Craig Pringle.

21. C. J. Pringle to Jimmy Swaggart Ministries, June 7, 1986; F. Swaggart to C. J. Pringle, July 9, 1986; and telecast transcription, all by courtesy of Craig Pringle. See also McIver, "Ancient Tales and Space-Age Myths."

22. Anon, "Darwin's Last Days"; M[alcolm] Bowden, "A Return to Faith?" *The Rise of the Evolution Fraud: An Exposure of Its Roots* (San Diego: Creation-Life Publishers, 1982), pp. 188–93.

23. Bolton Davidheiser, *Science and the Bible* (Grand Rapids, Mich.: Baker, 1971), p. 89; idem, *Evolution and Christian Faith* (Grand Rapids, Mich.: Baker, 1969), p. 66; R. E. Kofahl to the author, Dec. 1, 1987; Wilbert H. Rusch, Sr., "Darwin's Last Hours Revisited," *Creation Research Society Quarterly*, 21 (June 1984), 37–39; idem, "Darwin's Last Hours," *Creation Research Society Quarterly*, 12 (Sept. 1975), 99–102; David Herbert, "Deathbed Repentance: Fabricated or True?" *Darwin's Religious Views: From Creationist to Evolutionist* (London, Ont.: Hersil, 1990), pp. 85–93; Ian T. Taylor, *In the Minds of Men: Darwin and the New World Order* (Toronto: TFE Publishing, 1984), p. 137; Preston

P. Phillips, in *Creation Research Society Quarterly*, 26 (1989), 150; Anon., "Magazine Articles," *Bible-Science Newsletter*, Dec. 15, 1969, p. 7.

24. Paolo E. Coletta, *William Jennings Bryan: III. Political Puritan, 1915–1925* (Lincoln: University of Nebraska Press, 1969), p. 219; B. Davidheiser to C. Russell, Apr. 25, 1979, by courtesy of Colin Russell; B. Davidheiser to the author, Oct. 9, 1980; Rusch, "Darwin's Last Hours;" P. A. B., "Questions and Answers on Creationism," *Bible-Science Newsletter*, Dec. 1986, p. 16; R. E. Kofahl to the author, Dec. 1, 1987 (emphasis added). Bryan himself does not seem to have doubted Lady Hope's story, only the wisdom of using it: Moore, *Darwin Legend*, pp. 127–28, 130–31.

25. Pat Sloan, "The Myth of Darwin's Conversion," *The Humanist* (London), 75 (Mar. 1960), 70–72; idem, "Demythologizing Darwin," *The Humanist* (London), 80 (Apr. 1965), 106–10.

26. Cf. Noll, *Scandal of the Evangelical Mind*, and Os Guinness, *Fit Bodies, Fat Minds: Why Evangelicals Don't Think and What to Do About It* (Grand Rapids, Mich.: Baker, 1994). In "The Evangelical Heart and Mind," (*Sojourners*, Mar.–Apr. 1995, p. 63), Bob Hulteen comments on the authors' approaches to evangelical readers: "Noll cites facts and figures and Guinness tells anecdotes." One need hardly wonder which book will have the greater impact?

27. Among the endorsers, L. R. Croft, *The Life and Death of Charles Darwin* (Chorley, Lancs.: Elmwood, 1989), is the most presumptuous.

28. Moore, *Darwin Legend*, p. 146; R. E. D. Clark to F. F. Bruce, Nov. 12, 1976, by courtesy of F. F. Bruce; F. F. Bruce to the author, Nov. 9, 1976.

29. D. W. Bebbington, *Evangelicalism in Modern Britain: A History from the 1730s to the 1980s* (London: Unwin Hyman, 1989), pp. 161, 188–91; Anon., "News and Notes," *The Tablet* (London), 145 (May 2, 1925), p. 576.

30. F. Burkhardt to the author, Feb. 18, 1995. Burkhardt is not convinced by the book's case for a meeting between Darwin and Lady Hope.

31. Benjamin Jowett, "On the Interpretation of Scripture," in Temple et al, *Essays and Reviews*, p. 377.

32. Or as the *Catholic Herald*, July 28, 1995, p. 6, explains, with an evolutionary twist: "Legends are extremely sophisticated survival systems, and the one about Darwin's deathbed conversion will soon adapt to its new environment, with or without Lady Hope."

10

Creating Creationism

*Meanings and Uses since
the Age of Agassiz*

RONALD L. NUMBERS

In an elegant essay titled "Deconstructing Darwinism" James R. Moore several years ago noted how strikingly "little effort had been expended by historians of science in tracing the proliferation of Darwin-related vocabulary and interpreting its function in public discourse." To help remedy this deficiency, he carefully examined the metamorphosis of the term "Darwinism" from a synonym for naturalistic evolution generally to a label for evolution by natural selection specifically, illustrating in the process how malleable and politically serviceable such labels can be. Recently Mark A. Noll and David N. Livingstone drew attention to the historical significance of efforts to define terms in the Darwinian debates. Definitions "are designed to demarcate the true from the false, the legitimate from the illegitimate, the relevant from the irrelevant," they wrote. "Accordingly, the control of definitions is of enormous consequence for intellectual debate, since definitions position both ideas and people on particular sides of debates." Like Moore, they, too, focused on Darwinism.[1]

Despite the utility of such exercises, no one has yet looked at the deployment of the terms "creationism" and "creationist" in the late nineteenth and twentieth centuries. Even I, in a 450-page book on the history of modern creationism, failed to address the issue of when these terms first came into use.[2] In this essay I would like to draw on my previous research and some subsequent explorations to address the following queries: When, why, and how were the terms "creationism" and "creationist" first employed? At what point did they come to be associated primarily with the community of evangelical Christians; and, finally, under what circumstances did those militant evangelicals known as fundamentalists capture creationism to represent their own distinctive interpretation of Genesis? Most of my discussion will concentrate on American usages, from the Darwinian debates of the late nineteenth century through the fundamentalist controversy of the early twentieth century and on to the rise of "scientific creationism" in recent decades.

Creation and Evolution in the Nineteenth Century

When Charles Darwin published his essay *On the Origin of Species* in 1859, the term "creationist" commonly designated a person who believed in the special creation of a soul for each human fetus, as opposed to a traducianist, who believed that the souls of children were inherited from their parents. Nevertheless, just one day after his book appeared, Darwin employed the label to refer to opponents of evolution. "What a joke it would be," he wrote to T. H. Huxley, "if I pat you on the back when you attack some immovable creationist!" Since at least the early 1840s Darwin had occasionally referred to "creationists" in his unpublished writings, but the epithet remained relatively uncommon. In 1873 we find the American botanist Asa Gray describing a "special creationist" (which he placed in quotation marks) as one who maintained that species "were supernaturally originated just as they are," and in 1880 he briefly contrasted Darwinism with "direct Creationism." Similarly, in the 1890s the priest-scientist John A. Zahm of Notre Dame occasionally used "creationist" as a synonym for antievolutionist. But the practice of describing antievolutionists as creationists remained relatively infrequent during the nineteenth century— and confined, it seems, largely to persons who no longer believed in special creations. As far as I can tell, such prominent North American anti-Darwinists as Louis Agassiz, Arnold Guyot, and John William Dawson neither called themselves creationists nor referred to their views as creationism. During the 75 years or so after the appearance of the *Origin of Species* opponents of evolution were denoted by such terms as "advocates of creation," "exponents of the theory of the immutability of species" or, increasingly, "anti-evolutionists."[3]

One of the reasons that the label "creationist" languished in obscurity for so long was the immense diversity of opinion among the dissenters from Darwinism. In the *Origin of Species* Darwin took issue with "the ordinary view of creation," but he failed to identify the particular view he had in mind. Almost certainly he was not referring to the biblically inspired Linnaean notion of the simultaneous creation in one locale of single pairs, which then multiplied and migrated to their eventual homes. More likely he had in mind Charles Lyell's alternative suggestion of various "*centres* or *foci* of creation," separated spatially and temporally—or possibly Louis Agassiz's proposal of repeated plenary creations, which stipulated that "species did not originate in single pairs, but were created in large numbers," in the habitats the Creator intended them to populate. Agassiz, whose earlier studies of glaciers had led him to postulate the existence of an ice age, believed that the geological record revealed a series of catastrophes and special creations by which the earth had been repeatedly depopulated and repopulated. For him, species were linked by the mind of the Creator, not by common descent from Eden or Ararat. When the Harvard botanist Asa Gray referred to "the commonly received doctrine" of creation, he explicitly connected it with this unbiblical doctrine of Agassiz's.[4]

It is impossible to determine how many Americans followed Agassiz in seeing creative activity this way. Most conservative Christians never expressed themselves on the matter, though many of them undoubtedly clung to the traditional view that God had created the heaven and the earth in six literal days about six thousand years ago. This reading of Genesis necessitated rejecting the rapidly growing body of geological and paleontological evidence of the earth's great antiquity, but it could be defended on the grounds that scientists had not correctly interpreted their data. At mid-century one American observer estimated that perhaps "one half of the Christian public" still adhered to this position. The remainder, he claimed, had divided largely into two rival camps: those who accommodated the findings of historical geology by interpreting the days of Genesis 1 to represent vast ages in the history of the earth (the so-called day-age theory) and those who did so by separating a creation "in the beginning" from a much later Edenic creation in six 24-hour days (the gap theory).[5]

To compound the confusion about special creation, its most vocal scientific proponents disagreed markedly over the number of supernatural interventions required. As we have seen, Agassiz, a fair-weather Unitarian, called for a virtual infinitude of miracles, while his Swiss-born compatriot Arnold Guyot, an evangelical Presbyterian, demanded only three divine intrusions into the natural order: for the special creation of matter, life, and humans. The Presbyterian geologist John William Dawson, who served as principal of McGill University in Montreal, took an intermediate position. He followed his mentor Charles Lyell in postulating successive creations in various "centres" but stopped short of insisting that "all groups of individual animals, which naturalists may call species, have been separate products of creation."[6]

Although a few advocates of creation, such as the British naturalist Philip Gosse, indulged in speculating about the details of creation—he suggested, for example, that God had created Adam with a navel, thus giving him the appearance of age at the time of his creation—most nonevolutionists resolutely avoided the topic. Louis Agassiz on more than one occasion frustrated colleagues by refusing to provide a single specific description of how a species came into existence. "When a mammal was created, did the oxygen, hydrogen, nitrogen, and carbon of the air, and the lime, soda, phosphorus, potash, water, &c., from the earth, come together and on the instant combine into a completely formed horse, lion, elephant, or other animal?" inquired Agassiz's Harvard colleague Jeffries Wyman, who noted that if this question were "answered in the affirmative, it will be easily seen that the answer is entirely opposed by the observed analogies of nature." The ichthyologist Theodore N. Gill, who likewise complained about the "vague and evasive" responses of nonevolutionists when called upon for scientific explanations, quoted Darwin in demanding answers to such questions as: "Did 'elemental atoms flash into living tissues?' Was there vacant space one moment and an elephant apparent the next? Or did a laborious God mould out of gathered earth a body to then endue with life?" In his opinion, such information was a prerequisite to conceiving of creation in any scientifically useful way.[7]

Creationism and Its Critics

In 1899 Dawson, the last major nineteenth-century scientist to defend special creation, passed away. By this time the scientific community was promoting organic evolution as an established "fact," even as members quarreled among themselves over the exact mechanisms of change. About the only Americans left debating the merits of special creation were conservative, often evangelical, Christians. In the early 1920s the most concerned critics of human evolution launched a movement to eradicate the offending belief from the churches and schools of America. But throughout the so-called fundamentalist controversy, their goal remained the elimination of evolution, not the promotion of a particular doctrine of creation. They dedicated their organizations to "Christian Fundamentals," "Anti-Evolution," and "Anti-False Science," not to creationism.[8]

Evangelicals had still reached no consensus about the correct reading of Genesis 1, although even the most conservative commentators had come to terms with the antiquity of life on earth and a deluge of local or geologically superficial significance. Leaders of the fundamentalist movement tended to promote either the day-age theory, endorsed by William Jennings Bryan and William Bell Riley, or the gap (or ruin-and-restoration) interpretation, taught in the popular Scofield Reference Bible and preached by the evangelist Harry Rimmer. About the only Christians to insist on the recent appearance of life and on a fossil-burying flood were the Seventh-day Adventist disciples of Ellen G. White, who claimed to have witnessed the creation of the world in vision. Shortly after the turn of the century the self-instructed Adventist geologist George McCready Price began advocating a scientific version of White's views that he called "the new catastrophism," "the new geology," or simply "flood geology." According to Price, a correct reading of Genesis 1 ruled out any notion of "creation on the installment plan," that is, creative acts interspersed over millions of years, which he regarded as a "burlesque" of creation. The gap theory required too much verbal "dodging and twisting" to conform to his standards of biblical literalism, and the day-age theory was even more egregious. This "libel on Moses" struck at the very basis of the Sabbath—and the identity of Seventh-day Adventists—by suggesting that the seventh day of creation had not been a literal 24-hour period. The Bible, as Price saw it, allowed for only "*one act of creation*," which, he said, may easily be supposed to have included all of those ancestral types from which our modern varieties of plants and animals have been derived."[9]

Early in his career Price toyed with the idea of starting a magazine called *The Creationist* to popularize his views, but for years he avoided equating his theory of flood geology with creationism generally. As far as I can tell, it was not until 1929 that one of his students, Harold W. Clark, a Berkeley-trained biologist, explicitly packaged Price's new catastrophism as "creationism." In a brief self-published book titled *Back to Creationism* Clark urged readers to quit simply opposing evolution and to adopt the new "science of creationism," by which he clearly meant Price's flood geology.[10]

In the mid-1930s Dudley Joseph Whitney, one of Price's earliest non-Adventist converts to flood geology, observed that fundamentalists were "all mixed up between geological ages, Flood geology and ruin, believing all at once, endorsing all at once." How, he wondered, could evangelical Christians possibly convert the world to creationism if they themselves could not even agree on the meaning of Genesis 1? To bring order to this chaotic state of affairs, he pushed for the establishment of a society to create a united fundamentalist front against evolution, the Religion and Science Association. In a press release Price declared that the association backed flood geology as "by far the best and most reasonable explanation of the facts of the fossils and the rocks," while "condemning and repudiating the only other possible alternatives about the fossils: (a) The Day-Age theory, which is false scientifically and cannot be made to harmonize with the record of Genesis I; and (b) The Pre-Adamic Ruin Theory, which makes nonsense of the scientific facts and is utterly fantastic theologically." This description represented mere wishful thinking on Price's part. The infant association died within two years of birth largely because its leaders could not agree on a common interpretation of the first chapter of Genesis.[11]

Unfortunately for Price and Whitney, they had recruited for the association's presidency a Wheaton College chemist, L. Allen Higley, who, like so many fundamentalists, believed in the truth of the ruin-and-restoration theory as adamantly as they believed in flood geology. In Whitney's opinion, the views Higley espoused had become "a *Fundamentalist* dogma; and when I say dogma in that connection I mean DOGMA and then some. . . . The thing is an *obsession*." Whitney had initially hoped to convert the "Wheaton crowd" to flood geology, believing that "the more Wheaton can be played up in our association, the more influence it will have with the Fundamentalist." When the Wheaton establishment proved immovable, Whitney despaired of the future for flood geology. Nevertheless, in 1937 he began circulating a mimeographed sheet, *The Creationist*, hoping thereby to identify creationism with the Price school.[12]

Such efforts to co-opt the creationist label did not go uncontested for long, in part because evangelical scientists who did not subscribe to flood geology could ill afford to have their constituencies view them as noncreationists. Thus leaders of the American Scientific Affiliation (ASA), organized in 1941, waged a two-pronged campaign in the 1940s and 1950s to discredit flood geology as "pseudo-science" while cloaking their own quasi-evolutionary views in the mantle of creationism. The anthropologist James O. Buswell III, who introduced fellow evengelicals to the evidence for human antiquity and development, decried the common tendency of evolutionists to equate creationists with "hypertraditionalist" fundamentalists like Price. He winced when he heard the paleontologist George Gaylord Simpson declare in 1950 that "creationists are found today only in non-or anti-scientific circles." Buswell argued for a broad understanding of creationism that would allow both rigid hypertraditionalists and progressive scientists like himself, "who constantly allow their interpretations to be open to the acceptance of newly discovered facts," to be called creationists. He boldly, but unsuccessfully, urged evangelicals ranging from progressive creationists to theistic evolutionists to march under the banner of "scientific creationism."[13]

The Wheaton biologist Russell L. Mixter, who gently prodded the ASA to accept more and more evidence of organic evolution, pushed for a similarly inclusive definition of creationism. "Creationists of today are not in agreement concerning what was created according to Genesis," he announced in a controversial mid-century monograph in which he defended the evolution of species within major groups of animals. "In this sense," he noted provocatively, "Creationists can be called evolutionists." Indeed, they could; but as he soon discovered, they might not want to be if they desired to teach at schools like Wheaton. In terms of job security at Christian colleges, it was far better to be an evolutionist who called himself a creationist. Adopting Mixter's nomenclature, Wheaton president V. R. Edman was able to assure a concerned board of trustees in 1957 that "We at Wheaton are avowed and committed creationists."[14]

The ASA progressives received a boost in 1954, when Bernard Ramm, a Baptist philosopher and theologian, brought out an influential treatise called *The Christian View of Science and Scripture*. Convinced that Price's scientifically disreputable views had come to form "the backbone of much of Fundamentalist thought about geology, creation, and the flood," he urged fellow evangelicals to repudiate such "narrow bibliolatry" and adopt what he called "progressive creationism," a position far to the left of fiat creationism but slightly to the right of theistic evolution. It did away with the necessity of believing in a young earth, a universal flood, and the recent appearance of humans, but still required that "from time to time the great creative acts, *de novo*," had taken place.[15]

Such attempts to stretch the meaning of creationism—almost to the point of accepting divinely guided evolution—provoked a backlash among the increasingly outspoken advocates of Price's flood geology. In 1961 John C. Whitcomb, Jr., and Henry M. Morris published *The Genesis Flood*, which sought to establish a recent special creation and flood geology as the only orthodox understanding of Genesis. Two years later a group of 10 like-minded scientists formed the Creation Research Society (CRS) to promote this point of view. To enter the public schools of America, these creationists in the early 1970s peeled off the biblical wrappings of flood geology and repackaged it as "creation science" or "scientific creationism." This relabeling reflected more than euphemistic preference; it signified a major tactical shift among strict six-day creationists. Instead of denying evolution its scientific credentials, as biblical creationists had done for a century, these scientific creationists argued for granting creation and evolution equal scientific standing. And instead of trying to bar evolution from the classroom, as their predecessors had done in the 1920s, they fought to bring creation into the schoolhouse and shunned the epithet "antievolutionist." "Creationism is on the way back," Morris proudly announced in 1974, "this time not primarily as a religious belief, but as an alternative scientific explanation of the world in which we live."[16]

The ASA's drift toward theistic evolution and the CRS's insistence on young-earth creationism left many self-described creationists feeling left out in the cold. As the Canadian antievolutionist John R. Howitt, a gap theorist, put it, while many ASA members were embracing theistic evolution "or some such rubbish, the true fundamentalists are all going over to flood geology. Oh me, oh my!" In the mid-1960s he begged CRS leaders not to make flood geology a test of creationist orthodoxy. "Let it be truly a Creation Research Society," he urged, "seeking for truth, no matter where it ends up,—as flood geology, the gap theory, theistic evolution or what not." By the early 1970s, however, he had abandoned any hope of reconciliation. "The flooders are getting pretty dogmatic these days," he noted with sadness, and not a little irritation. Before long even in Great Britain, where evangelical antievolutionists had long kept the flood geologists at bay, the so-called young earthers captured the Evolution Protest Movement, condemned the gap and day-age theories as unscriptural, and reinvented themselves as the Creation Science Movement.[17]

Although many evangelicals who regarded themselves as creationists, from Billy Graham to Jimmy Swaggart, resisted the allure of scientific creationism, by the last decades of the twentieth century Price's intellectual heirs had virtually co-opted the creationist label for their own interests. Even their severest critics often conceded as much. When in 1984 the National Academy of Sciences issued an official condemnation of "creationism," that august body defined it as comprising beliefs in a young earth and universe, flood geology, and the miraculous origination of all living things. Writing in the early 1980s in defense of the day-age theory and against flood geology, the Calvin College geologist Davis A. Young noted regretfully that, although he still believed in the biblical story of creation, he was opposed to creationism. This ironic turn of events had resulted because "those who advocate the creation of the world in seven literal days only a few thousand years ago have come to be known generally as creationists." When he and two Calvin colleagues, Howard J. Van Till and Clarence Menninga, later collaborated on a book titled *Science Held Hostage* (1988), they assigned equal blame for this terrorist act to "naturalism" and "creationism," which they explicitly identified with the views of the scientific creationists.[18] Latter-day flood geologists may not have liked being lumped together with godless evolutionists as enemies of true science (and religion), but they could only have appreciated the often grudging but increasingly widespread recognition that their once marginal views, inspired by the visions of an obscure Adventist prophetess, now defined the very essence of creationism.

NOTES

This essay is reprinted from Ronald L. Numbers, *Darwinism Comes to America* (Cambridge, MA: Harvard University Press, 1998). I am indebted to Edward J. Larson, Paul A. Nelson, and especially Jon Topham for their helpful criticisms and suggestions.

1. James Moore, "Deconstructing Darwinism: The Politics of Evolution in the 1860s," *Journal of the History of Biology* 24 (1991): 353–408, quotation on p. 359; Mark A.

Noll and David N. Livingstone, "Charles Hodge and the Definition of 'Darwinism,' " in *What Is Darwinism? and Other Writings on Science and Religion*, by Charles Hodge (Grand Rapids, Mich.: Baker Books, 1994), p. 34.

2. Ronald L. Numbers, *The Creationists* (New York: Alfred A. Knopf, 1992).

3. *The Oxford English Dictionary*, 2nd ed., 20 vols. (Oxford: Clarendon Press, 1989), 3: 1135; Charles Darwin to T. H. Huxley, November 25, 1859, *The Correspondence of Charles Darwin*, 9 vols. to date (Cambridge: Cambridge University Press, 1985–), 7: 398; Asa Gray, *Darwiniana: Essays and Reviews Pertaining to Darwinism*, ed. A. Hunter Dupree (Cambridge, Mass.: Harvard University Press, 1963), p. 204, from "The Attitude of Working Naturalists Toward Darwinism," originally published in the *Nation*, October 16, 1873; Gray, *Natural Science and Religion: Two Lectures Delivered to the Theological School of Yale College* (New York: Charles Scribner's Sons, 1880), p. 89; J. A. Zahm, *Evolution and Dogma* (Chicago: D. H. McBride, 1896), pp. 73–75; J. W. Dawson, *The Story of the Earth and Man* (New York: Harper & Brothers, 1873), p. 352; [Alexander Agassiz], "A Natural Theory of Creation," *Nation* 8 (1869): 193–94, quotation on p. 193. E. D. Cope contrasted the "creativist doctrine" with the "derivatist doctrine"; Cope, "A Review of the Modern Doctrine of Evolution," *American Naturalist* 14 (1880): 166–79, quotations on p. 166. Before 1859 Darwin also referred to "creationist" or "creationists" in his unpublished essay of 1842 [Charles Darwin, *The Foundations of the Origin of Species: Two Essays Written in 1842 and 1844*, ed. Francis Darwin (Cambridge: Cambridge University Press, 1909), pp. 31, 49–50; in his unpublished essay of 1844 (ibid., pp. 182, 193), in an 1854 (?) note (*Correspondence*, 5:234), and in two letters to J. D. Hooker in 1856 (ibid., 6:170, 304). I am indebted to Jon Topham for information about the Darwin manuscripts and to Sarah Pfatteicher for searching nineteenth-century dictionaries.

4. Charles Darwin, *On the Origin of Species*, with an introduction by Ernst Mayr (Cambridge, Mass.: Harvard University Press, 1966), p. 437; Tore Frangsmyr, "Linnaeus as a Geologist," in *Linnaeus: The Man and His Work*, ed. Tore Frangsmyr (Berkeley and Los Angeles: University of California Press, 1983), pp. 110–55, especially p. 122; Charles Lyell, *Principles of Geology*, 3 vols. (London: John Murray, 1830–1833), 2: 123–26; Louis Agassiz, *Essay on Classification*, ed. Edward Lurie (Cambridge, Mass.: Harvard University Press, 1962), pp. 173–75; Asa Gray, *Natural Science and Religion*, p. 35. For Darwin's early views on special creation, see his unpublished 1842 and 1844 essays in Darwin, *The Foundations of the Origins of Species*, pp. 22–23, 31, 49–50, 168–71, 182, 191–94, 249–51. Without clarification, he refers to "the common view" of creation in a letter to J. D. Hooker, March 13, 1846 (*Correspondence*, 3: 300); and in a letter to J. D. Dana, November 11, 1859 (ibid., 7: 368). Regarding Agassiz's views, see also Ernst Mayr, "Agassiz, Darwin, and Evolution," *Harvard Library Bulletin* 13 (1959): 165–94; and Mary P. Winsor, "Louis Agassiz and the Species Question," *Studies in History of Biology* 3 (1979): 89–117. For a survey of creationist views before Darwin, see Edwin Tenney Brewster, *Creation: A History of Non-Evolutionary Theories* (Indianapolis: Bobbs-Merrill, 1927), which is the unacknowledged source for much of Frank L. Marsh's chapter "Creationist Theories" in *Studies in Creationism* (Washington: Review and Herald Publishing Association, 1950), pp. 22–40.

5. William B. Hayden, *Science and Revelation; or, The Bearing of Modern Scientific Developments upon the Interpretation of the First Eleven Chapters of Genesis* (Boston: Otis Clapp, 1852), p. 77. On pre-Darwinian views of Genesis, see Chapter 8, "The Mosaic Story of Creation," of Ronald L. Numbers, *Creation by Natural Law: Laplace's Nebular Hypothesis in American Thought* (Seattle: University of Washington Press, 1977), pp. 88–104.

6. Arnold Guyot, *Creation; or, The Biblical Cosmogony in the Light of Modern Science* (New York: Charles Scribner's Sons, 1884), pp. 116–28; J. W. Dawson, *The Story of the*

242 o SPECIFIC ENCOUNTERS

Earth and Man (New York: Harper & Brothers, 1873), pp. 340–41, 352; J. W. Dawson, *The Origin of the World, According to Revelation and Science* (Montreal: Dawson Brothers, 1877), pp. 238, 371. On Protestant antievolutionism in the late nineteenth century, see Jon H. Roberts, *Darwinism and the Divine in America: Protestant Intellectuals and Organic Evolution, 1859–1900* (Madison: University of Wisconsin Press, 1988), pp. 209–31.

7. J[effries] W[yman], Review of *Monograph of the Aye-Aye*, by Richard Owen, *American Journal of Science* 86 (1863): 194–99, quotation on p. 196; Theodore Gill, "The Doctrine of Darwin," *Proceedings of the Biological Society of Washington* 1 (1880–1881): 47–55, quotation on p. 52; Darwin, *On the Origin of Species*, p. 483. T. H. Huxley was making the same points; see Adrian Desmond, *Huxley: From Devil's Disciple to Evolution's High Priest* (Reading, MA: Addison-Wesley, 1997), pp. 225–26, 256. On Agassiz's refusal to describe creation, see Jeffries Wyman to Burt G. Wilder, May [?], 1871, quoted in Burt G. Wilder, "Jeffries Wyman, Anatomist (1814–1874)," in *Leading American Men of Science*, ed. David Starr Jordan (New York: Henry Holt, 1910), pp. 171–209, quotation on p. 194; and Nathaniel Southgate Shaler, *The Autobiography of Nathaniel Southgate Shaler* (Boston: Houghton Mifflin, 1909), p. 128. On Gosse, see Frederic R. Ross, "Philip Gosse's *Omphalos*, Edmund Gosse's *Father and Son*, and Darwin's Theory of Natural Selection," *Isis* 68 (1977): 85–96.

8. Numbers, *The Creationists*, p. 49.

9. George McCready Price, *The Phantom of Organic Evolution* (New York: Fleming H. Revell, 1924), pp. 99–100 (burlesque and one act); Geo. E. McCready Price, *Outlines of Modern Christianity and Modern Science* (Oakland, Calif.: Pacific Press, 1902), pp. 125–27 (libel and dodging); On the views of Price, see Numbers, *The Creationists*, pp. 72–101.

10. W. W. Prescott to G. M. Price, November 6, 1908, and C. C. Lewis to G. M. Price, October 23, 1908, both in the George McCready Price Papers, Adventist Heritage Center, Andrews University; Harold W. Clark, *Back to Creationism* (Angwin, Calif.: Pacific Union College Press, 1929), p. 135.

11. D. J. Whitney to G. M. Price, December 11, 1935, Byron C. Nelson Papers, Institute for Creation Research, El Cajon, Calif. On the Religion and Science Association, see Numbers, *The Creationists*, pp. 102–17, from which this account is extracted.

12. D. J. Whitney, "For the Consideration of the Directors of the Religion and Science Association," August 6, 1935, Nelson Papers (obstacle); D. J. Whitney to G. M. Price, December 11, 1935, Price Papers (dogma); D. J. Whitney to G. M. Price, September 9 and 14, 1934, Price Papers (Wheaton). For extant issues of *The Creationist*, see Ronald L. Numbers, ed., *Early Creationist Journals*, Vol. 9 of *Creationism in Twentieth-Century America: A Ten-Volume Anthology of Documents, 1903–1961* (New York: Garland Publishing, 1995).

13. Interview with J. Laurence Kulp, July 23, 1984 (pseudo-science); James O. Buswell III, "A Creationist Interpretation of Prehistoric Man," in *Evolution and Christian Thought Today*, ed. Russell L. Mixter (Grand Rapids, Mich.: Wm. B. Eerdmans, 1959), pp. 165–89, quotations on pp. 169, 188–89. On evolution in the ASA, see Numbers, *The Creationists*, pp. 159–81; and Mark A. Kalthoff, ed., *Creation and Evolution in the Early American Scientific Affiliation*, Vol. 10 of *Creationism in Twentieth-Century America: A Ten-Volume Anthology of Documents, 1903–1961* (New York: Garland Publishing, 1995).

14. Russell L. Mixter, *Creation and Evolution*, Monograph Two (Wheaton, Ill.: American Scientific Affiliation, 1950), pp. 1–2; V. R. Edman to the board of trustees, Wheaton College, October 28, 1957, Russell L. Mixter Papers, Special Collections, Buswell Library, Wheaton College. On the controversies over evolution at Wheaton College, see Numbers, *The Creationists*, pp. 181–83.

15. Bernard Ramm, *The Christian View of Science and Scripture* (Grand Rapids, Mich.: Wm. B. Eerdmans, 1954), pp. 180, 228, 293. The phrase "narrow bibliolatry" appears on p. 9 of the paperback edition, also published by Eerdmans. On "progressive creation," see also Edwin K. Gedney, "Geology and the Bible," in *Modern Science and Christian Faith: A Symposium on the Relationship of the Bible to Modern Science*, by Members of the American Scientific Affiliation (Wheaton, Ill.: Van Kampen Press, 1948), pp. 49–55.

16. Henry M. Morris, *The Troubled Waters of Evolution* (San Diego: Creation-Life Publishers, 1974), p. 16. On the renaissance of flood geology and its christening as "creation science," see Numbers, *The Creationists*, pp. 184–257.

17. J. R. Howitt to A. C. Custance, October 22, 1962, December 24, 1965, and August 25, 1973, A. C. Custance Papers, Special Collections, Redeemer College; J. R. Howitt to W. E. Lammerts, [late 1963], Walter E. Lammerts Papers, Bancroft Library, University of California, Berkeley. On creationism in Great Britain, see Numbers, *The Creationists*, pp. 323–30.

18. *Science and Creationism: A View from the National Academy of Sciences* (Washington, D.C.: National Academy Press, 1984), p. 7; Davis A. Young, *Christianity and the Age of the Earth* (Grand Rapids, Mich.: Zondervan, 1982), p. 10; Howard J. Van Till, Davis A. Young, and Clarence Menninga, *Science Held Hostage: What's Wrong with Creation Science and Evolutionism* (Downers Grove, Ill.: InterVarsity Press, 1988), pp. 45, 125. In Howard J. Van Till et al., *Portraits of Creation: Biblical and Scientific Perspectives on the World's Formation* (Grand Rapids, Mich.: William B. Eerdmans, 1990), written under the auspices of the Calvin Center for Christian Scholarship, Robert E. Snow defines a *"creationist"* as "someone who advocates the development of a science consistent with the view that creation was completed in six twenty-four-hour days, that the Earth and the universe are young (approximately 10,000 years in age), and that most of the Earth's geological features are attributable to the action of a worldwide flood" (p. 167). Two of the best recent studies of creationism in America are Edward J. Larson, *Trial and Error: The American Controversy over Creation and Evolution*, updated ed. (New York: Oxford University Press, 1989); and Christopher P. Toumey, *God's Own Scientists: Creationists in a Secular World* (New Brunswick, N.J.: Rutgers University Press, 1994).

11

A Sign for an Unbelieving Age

Evangelicals and the
Search for Noah's Ark

LARRY ESKRIDGE

During the summer of 1972, John D. Morris, a 26-year-old engineer and son of creationist Henry Morris, headed a five-man party representing the newly formed Institute for Creation Research in an attempt to find Noah's Ark on Mount Ararat in northeastern Turkey. Drawn by more than a century of alleged sightings of the ark, Morris's group was one of several on the mountain that summer. On the night of August 2, as Morris and two of his fellow climbers camped at about 11,000 feet, he became "overwhelmed by the feeling that at the top of the finger glacier we would see Noah's Ark. I just knew tomorrow would be a special day and related this to the others."[1]

He had no idea. Just after breakfast, the group avoided an early morning rock shower, dodging pebbles and careening boulders the size of Volkswagens. By early afternoon they found themselves in the midst of a howling blizzard. Suddenly, they were enveloped by thunder as lightning began to strike all the large rocks around them. Morris recalled a strong feeling of involvement in spiritual warfare. Pausing to rest for a moment, he remembered "thanking the Lord for protecting us, feeling that we would not be harmed, when the bolt struck." Morris lost the use of his legs; one of the other climbers was also immobilized and was sure his oddly twisted leg was broken; the third climber, his head covered with blood, had no idea who he was or where he was. Following a prayer for healing, Morris claimed he eventually regained use of his legs and his fellow climbers recovered sufficiently so that the trio was able to drag themselves to safety as the weather cleared. Near sundown, "strengthened by the fact that Satan" had been so determined to stop the group and failed, Morris wandered toward the edge of Ahora Gorge "positive that the Ark was in full view." Binoculars in hand, he searched in all directions but reported, "much to my disappointment, I did not see the Ark." Morris remembered that the group "had to settle for a comfortable place to sleep, hot food, and our lives that night.

. . . I'm sure that no one else [on Ararat] has had such a wonderful time of prayer and singing as we did that evening."[2]

In many ways, John Morris's harrowing adventure speaks volumes about an interesting phenomenon that has arisen within twentieth-century conservative American evangelicalism—the widespread conviction that the ancient Ark of Noah is embedded in ice high atop Mount Ararat, waiting to be found. It is a story that has combined earnest faith with the lure of adventure, questionable evidence with startling claims. The hunt for the ark, like evangelicalism itself, is a complex blend of the rational and the supernatural, the modern and the premodern. While it acknowledges a debt to pure faith in a literal reading of the Scriptures and centuries of legend, the conviction that the ark literally lies on Ararat is a recent one, backed by a largely twentieth-century canon of evidence that includes stories of shadowy eyewitnesses, tales of mysterious missing photographs, rumors of atheistic conspiracy, and pieces of questionable "ark wood" from the mountain. Fortified by grassroots creationist networks and the publicity of a string of articles, books, movies, and television specials, the quest for the ark has spawned a network of committed "arkeologists," thousands of dedicated supporters, and legions of the just plain convinced.

Charting the history and development of American evangelicals' hunt for the ark is in and of itself an interesting exercise. In many ways, it demonstrates the highly rationalist nature of the fundamentalist/evangelical worldview and its inherent tendency to "nail down" the theological and the supernatural in the here and now. It also parallels the story that Ronald Numbers tells so convincingly in his book *The Creationists*, of the spread of flood geology and creationism from Adventist circles to the larger realms of evangelicalism.[3] Moreover, it skirts the domain of pop pseudoscience and the paranormal, making the attempt to find the ark the evangelical equivalent of the search for Bigfoot and the Loch Ness Monster. In all these ways, it reveals much about evangelicals' distrust of mainstream science and the motivations and modus operandi of the scientific elite.

Beyond this, however, the attempt to find the ark peculiarly sheds light upon evangelicals' perception of their society and the times in which they live. For the search for the ark is, in a number of ways, as much an exercise in millennialism as in creation science, especially suited to the cosmic drama prevalent in the dispensationalism that pervades many sectors of evangelicalism.[4] The ark's enthusiastic hunters have continually seen in their quest the possibility of an end-times sign for all humanity. Hearkening back to Christ's Olivet Discourse in Matthew 24: 37–39—"As the days of Noah were, so also shall the coming of the Son of Man be"—the ark hunters have envisioned their search as potentially playing a key role in God's prophetic timetable. In their view, the uncovering of Noah's Ark would provide one last chance for the world to reject the presumptions of the modernist antichrist and his scientific prophets and embrace the truth of Christ and the Bible before God unleashes his final judgment upon mankind. The search for Noah's Ark then is part apologetics, part mystery, and part adventure with a purpose—all of which promise the ultimate end run around Darwinism and the structures of modern unbelief.

Background for the Search

Genesis 8: 4 says that the "ark rested in the seventh month, on the seventeenth day of the month, upon the mountains of Ararat." The mountain known to Western culture as Mount Ararat is known to the Turks as "Agri Dagh—the mountain of pain," to the Armenians as "Massis," and is actually but one contender among several sites associated with the "mountains of Ararat" in the story of Noah. The modern ark hunters' belief that this particular mountain is the site where Noah's Ark came to rest is based largely upon the accumulating traditions of Christian Armenia, tracing back at least to the eleventh and twelfth centuries, A.D.[5] These traditions filtered back to the Christian West through Renaissance travelers such as Marco Polo and the thirteenth-century French Franciscan William of Rubruck, and were later reinforced by post-Reformation notice of Armenian traditions about Ararat and the ark that came from travelers like the seventeenth-century Huguenot Sir Jean Chardin (1643–1713).[6]

That the first verifiable ascent of Ararat did not occur until 1829 is proof of both the native Armenians' and the Kurds' long-held tradition that it was not meant to be climbed,[7] as well as the imposing nature of Mount Ararat itself. Standing nearly 17,000 feet tall and covering an area of nearly 500 square miles, it may well be the most massive mountain in the world. Sudden storms, high winds, and lightning only add to the obstacles presented by poisonous snakes, bears, great sloping fields of loose stones, and crevasse-filled glaciers.[8]

For today's modern ark hunters, however, the proof of the Ark's existence on Ararat lies in a series of reported nineteenth-century and early twentieth-century "sightings," the vast majority of which have come to light since World War II. These stories, despite troublesome discrepancies and checkered histories, have served as the catalyst for the outpouring of interest, literature, and expeditions in the last 50 years. The first of these stories appeared in the Los Angeles–based magazine New Eden, in 1940. The story was a first-person account of an alleged sighting of Noah's Ark by an aviator in the czarist Russian Air Force during 1916–17. The pilot—a "Vladimir Roskovitsky"—went on to say that after he reported his sighting a ground expedition of czarist troops made their way to the exposed craft. Venturing inside, they found hundreds of rooms of varying sizes, some with very high ceilings as if meant to hold elephants and even larger animals, and others with cages seemingly designed to hold birds and small animals. The story claimed that complete measurements and plans were made of the ark and dozens of photographs taken. A few days after the expedition returned, however, the story claimed "the government was overthrown and Godless Bolshevism took over, so that the records were never made public."[9] Understandably, the fantastic story spread beyond the pages of the New Eden. Not all reaction was positive—the Assemblies of God monthly The Pentecostal Evangel after hearing the story in 1944 speculated that the flyers "must have been drinking too much vodka."[10] But the bulk of coverage seems to have been enthusiastic. Adventist broadcaster H. M. S. Richards read the story over the air,[11] the Pilgrim Tract Society of Randleman, North Carolina, put the story in tract form, and the tale was reprinted in the pages of The King's Herald

(November 1941), *Prophecy* (March 1942), and *Defender of the Faith* (October 1942).[12]

Floyd B. Gurley, the editor who first published the story in *New Eden*, was inundated by requests for further information but passed on all inquiries to the man he claimed as the source of his story—Benjamin Franklin Allen, a retired Adventist lawyer, amateur geologist, and head of the Society for the Study of Creation, the Deluge, and Related Science. Allen was outraged because the story was poles apart from the sources he had mentioned to Gurley—the families of two deceased men who had claimed that they had been part of Russian expeditions to the ark.[13] In a 1945 letter to the young up-and-coming Southern Baptist creationist Henry Morris, Allen relayed his frustration about the tale, characterizing it as "about 95% fiction, the one real part being some vague reports by two Russian soldiers in the World War I, which reports are being circulated by some of their relatives." Allen described Gurley as his "neighbor" and as "an off-center man . . . I know very well." He claimed that he had told Gurley about the stories and that he had "later abused my confidence and 'stole' the data, and worked it all up into a perfect deception."[14] Later that year, Gurley apologized to Allen, admitting that the "article was written up in story form with the intent of making it more interesting to read."[15]

Despite the discredited nature of the Roskovitsky story, the ark-hunting community has retained its belief in the story's basic essence while long knowing the details of its bogus origins. The key link in this strange development is Eryl Cummings, who came across a similar, related story in the American-based White Russian periodical *Rosseya* in October of 1945. Cummings, an Adventist real-estate agent who would become the dean of American ark hunters, pursued the *Rosseya* story and found its ghostwriter, Colonel Alexander A. Koor, a former White Russian officer who swore that an officer acquaintance told him in 1921 that his brother had actually been in the expedition to Ararat and that an aviator named Zabolotsky "may have" played a role similar to that of the fictional Roskovitsky.[16] Cummings was impressed with Koor's "integrity and sincere good will" as was later ark enthusiast John Warwick Montgomery, who had "no doubt of the Colonel's integrity and scholarly precision."[17] Thus, the Roskovitsky story of the aviator's sighting has been given life though long discredited by the ark hunters themselves, through Koor's alleged secondhand knowledge of the czar's expeditions to Ararat.[18]

In addition to the Roskovitsky-related tales, a flurry of mysterious evidence from the World War II era and the early 1950s has been a key factor influencing those who are convinced that the ark is on Ararat. As of today, none of this exists in anything beyond anecdotal form—"so much evidence and so little proof," as one ark hunter has described it.[19] However, the sheer number of seemingly credible people who have come forth over the years and claimed to have seen newspaper stories, photographs, and film of the ark dating back to this period has been enough to make those in the quest sit up and take notice.

In many ways, these stories seem to be an evangelical parallel to the phenomenon of modern urban legends and—like stories about Darwin's deathbed conversion and Madalyn Murray O'Hair's petition to ban religious broadcasting—have a life all their own.[20] One of the most frequently told stories purporting to support the existence of the ark is of an article and photographs that appeared in a ca. 1943 issue of the Armed Forces paper *Stars and Stripes*. According to those who claimed to have seen it, it told of the U.S. Air Force having found the ark and showed pictures of U.S. servicemen standing and pointing at the remains. Efforts to find the story in various "theaters' " editions of the paper—which apparently are incomplete—have to date failed to yield evidence of any such article or photos.[21]

A similar story that has emerged from people all across the country is a claim to have seen a "March of the Ages" newsreel during mid–World War II that featured film roughly paralleling the mysterious *Stars and Stripes* story. As with the story, no trace of this film has ever been found.[22] Other stories of World War II–era vintage photographs in the hands of, variously, American, Australian, and Soviet airmen have likewise turned up no physical evidence of any kind.[23]

Despite, as one exasperated chronicler lamented, the "amazing fact that none of these photographs can be relocated,"[24] these stories are still looked upon as evidence by devotees of the hunt. In 1976, one ark hunter made a plea to the armchair ark hunter to lend a hand in an attempt to uncover the missing clues: "Personally instigate a search for this material and other missing information. Leaf through the family Bible. Hunt through the albums and storage chests in the attic. Carefully investigate the old trunk containing your grandmother's most prized possessions, conveniently stashed away ever since she went to be with the Lord. It's there. It must be."[25]

The Modern Search for the Ark Begins

World awareness of claims that Noah's Ark rested on Ararat were awakened in late November 1948 when Associated Press correspondent Edwin Greenwald reported from Istanbul that the ark had been sighted. According to Greenwald, Shukru Asena, a 69-year-old landlord in the Ararat district, told of a Kurdish farmer named Reshit, who in an early September trip up the mountain came across an object he had never noticed in other trips up Ararat.[26] He circled around it and climbed higher to get a better look. There, the story related "was the prow of a ship protruding into a canyon."[27] Reshit supposedly spread the word about his find and peasants from all of the small villages near the base of the mountain excitedly clambered up the heights to see the relic.[28] The tale also sparked more than a little excitement in conservative religious circles in America. Aaron J. Smith, the dean of a holiness Bible college in Greensboro, North Carolina, was particularly interested. The 60-year-old Smith, a former missionary to China who had been "saved" and "sanctified" while on the mission field, determined to mount a search for the ark, forming the Oriental Archaeological Research Expedition.[29] In explaining his rationale and an appeal for funds, Smith noted that he was concerned with "the multitudes whose minds [had] been poisoned by the modernistic teachings of evolution" and had lost faith in God and the Bible. "We pray that those who have lost their faith in God and His Word, will regain it," Smith wrote, "before the impending judgment falls on this wicked generation."[30] Finding the remains of the ark on Ararat was one obvious way in which unbelievers could be won back.

Largely through the help of a Canadian physician, Smith was able to put together his expedition and landed in Turkey with three younger companions at the beginning of July 1949. Things went wrong from the start in a scenario of bureaucratic indecision and confusion and suspicion that would become a familiar part of the routine that has plagued nearly every ark-hunting expedition. Weeks were wasted in Istanbul and Ankara attempting to navigate the maze of Turkish bureaucracy.[31] The fact that one of the group hailed from Oak Ridge, Tennessee, spurred press speculation that the group was really there attempting to find deposits of uranium and accusations from the Soviet Embassy personnel that they were American spies.[32]

Finally, in late August the group, along with Greenwald, the AP reporter who had passed on the Reshit story, made it to the vicinity of Mount Ararat.[33] There, Smith's party made some scouting trips up the mountain while they attempted to contact Shukru Asena—and through him his client—Reshit. Asena replied that he would come and bring Reshit—for a sum equal to about $250 American dollars. The group divided over whether paying the fee would not bring a larger demand once the pair arrived.[34] Smith attempted to find Reshit on his own, but his search yielded no one who had heard either of the sighting of the ark or of Reshit.[35] By mid-September their funds were running low and the window for even minimally favorable weather on the mountain had passed. With a reluctant heart, Smith left for the United States.[36] A more elaborate expedition was put together in 1951 but neither Reshit nor the ark was found and Smith's dream was left unfulfilled before his death in 1960.[37]

One of the most publicized ark-connected finds was made a few years later by someone outside of the normal ranks of America's conservative Protestant ark hunters. Fernand Navarra, a wealthy French industrialist, claimed to have been bitten by the ark bug back in the late 1930s while serving in the French Army in Syria. Interested, Navarra collected information—including the Roskovitsky story—until he and four companions finally attempted to climb the mountain in 1952.[38]

During this trip Navarra and one of his party, Jean de Riquer, while out on a separate sortie up the mountain, claimed that they stumbled upon "an astonishing patch of blackness within the ice, its outlines sharply defined." Its shape was "unmistakably [like] that of a ship's hull: on either side the edges of the patch curved like the gunwales of a great boat. As for the central part, it merged into a black mass the details of which were not discernible. Conviction burned in our eyes: . . . *We had just found the Ark* . . . We would indeed have given ten years of our lives to have had radar equipment that day!"[39] However, conditions soon required that the group leave the mountain. Navarra returned alone in 1953 to confirm his find but was forced to end his search after a severe case of altitude sickness.[40]

Navarra's third, and most famous, expedition occurred in the summer of 1955. With his 11-year-old son, Raphael, as his sole companion, Navarra climbed the mountain without official government permission. One afternoon, at a height of nearly 14,000 feet, they reached a spot that Navarra believed was the one where he had spotted the outline of the ark under ice.[41] Climbing down a crevasse in the glacier toward what appeared to be a darker area under the ice, Navarra dug with his pickaxe until he saw a black piece of wood, "five feet long . . . and perhaps still attached to other parts of the ship's framework."[42] Upon his return to France, Navarra submitted his wooden finds for analysis at several laboratories. One agency—the Forestry Institute of Madrid—estimated the sample it examined to be at least 5,000 years old.[43] Navarra described his experiences and the results of the tests for his fellow Frenchmen in a briskly selling 1956 book, *J'ai trouvé l'arche de Noé* (I Have Found the Ark of Noah).[44]

The final major stimulus to the search surfaced in the 1950s and 1960s, when two reported eyewitness sightings of the ark came to the attention of Eryl Cummings. Both involved two elderly Armenian converts to Adventism who, some 60 years apart, claimed to have seen the ark during their childhood in the Ararat region. The first story came from a Pastor Harold H. Williams, who reported that while in school in California in 1915 he had taken care of an elderly invalid by the name of Haji Yearam who related a story from 1856 about "three vile men who did not believe the Bible . . . scientists and evolutionists" that enlisted his father and himself to guide them up Ararat.[45] After a hard climb, the party came upon the ark protruding from the ice. After exploring the ark, the dumbfounded scientists threatened to kill Haji and his father if they ever revealed their find to anyone. According to Williams, the old man had wanted to clear his conscience and tell the story before he died. Shortly after Yearam died in 1918, Williams was teaching school in Brockton, Massachusetts, when he claimed to have seen an item in a Boston paper about the deathbed confession of an old English scientist who sounded identical to the man in Yearam's story. Williams hung onto the newspaper, but unluckily it, along with the handwritten notes he had taken of Yearam's confession, were destroyed in a 1940 fire.[46] When Cummings heard the story, he was sure that God, in His mercy, had revealed the ark to the three scientists "trying to turn the so-called scientific world away from the alluring 'primrose path' on which it had set its feet." Had the scientists not "like Pharaoh of old—hardened their hearts in stubborn rebellion," Cummings believed that "the religious history of the entire civilized world would have been altered," and that "even Darwin himself . . . might have altered his opinions and cast his considerable influence on the side of truth."[47]

In the late 1960s another story came to Cummings's attention that, while lacking the melodrama of Haji Yearam's tale, provided more alluring evidence of the ark's existence. George Hagopian claimed that as a boy in the years between 1908 and 1910 his uncle twice took him up Ararat specifically to see the ark. He stated that the ark was long and rectangular, with a nearly flat roof, save for a "catwalk" containing fifty or more large windows. Although the vessel was largely covered with a green moss, the dark brown wood underneath was petrified—so hard that a blast from his uncle's musket barely made a dent in the ship. Cummings was utterly convinced by his story and put him in contact with ark hunter and artist, Elfred Lee. Hagopian spent hours with Lee, going over the details of the ark as he remembered it.[48] Lee's pictorial representation of Hagopian's description and comments is the most commonly seen depiction of the ark in ark-hunter literature.

The Search for the Ark Gains Momentum

Meanwhile, organized American attempts to search for the ark gained momentum in the 1950s and 1960s. Because of his timber and his book, Fernand Navarra was the reigning guru of ark hunters during this time, constantly courted by his American peers. However, for what he claimed were business-related reasons, Navarra did not return to Turkey until the late 1960s.[49] While Navarra stayed on the sidelines, other attempts were made to explore the mountain. Throughout this period, a predominantly Adventist group, the Archaeological Research Foundation (ARF), led by Cummings, flood geologists Clifford Burdick and Lawrence Hewitt, and television evangelist George Vandeman, plugged away stateside attempting to chase down evidence and funds for expeditions. Several ARF expeditions went to Ararat between 1960 and 1966. While useful in photographing and charting a great deal of the mountain, none claimed to find a trace of the ark.[50]

Parallel to the growth of influence of flood geology from Adventist to broader constituencies in quarters of evangelicalism, the search for the ark had by the early 1970s begun to attract the attention of more highly visible evangelicals. Their interest and subsequent involvement in attempts to discover the ark led to a spate of books and films that extended the curiosity and conviction about Noah's boat to not only the wider evangelical community but the general public. Tim LaHaye, a Southern Californian pastor and author of such popular volumes as *The Spirit-Controlled Temperament* (1967), had come into contact with Cummings while attempting to found his own Christian college and scientific research institute in San Diego.[51] LaHaye, who personally claimed to have seen while in the Air Force the *Stars and Stripes* story about the finding of the ark,[52] was enthusiastic about the possibilities:

> [H]umanistic ideas would have to change if Noah's Ark were ever discovered. . . . [A] successful search would ring the death knell to the already fragile theory of evolution. . . . [W]e would be reminded of God's past method of purging the world of sinful people and our attention would be focused on God's promise of another judgement in the very near future.[53]

Buoyed by these hopes, LaHaye volunteered for Cummings's 1970 expedition as "scribe and chaplain."[54]

Another important contact was John Warwick Montgomery, flamboyant professor of church history at Trinity Evangelical Divinity School and contributing editor to *Christianity Today*. Montgomery had likewise come to his interest in the ark via Eryl Cummings, having seen a notice about his plans in the newsletter of the American Scientific Affiliation. Cummings gave Montgomery access to his quarter-century collection of files on the ark while his wife, Violet, allowed the young professor to preview a manuscript she was putting together. "Its contents sent my pulse racing," Montgomery recalled, "Ark fever had most certainly set in."[55] Primarily interested in apologetics, Montgomery was excited about the possibility of finding the ark as a "most concrete indicator" of the end-times. He speculated: "Might the God of all grace—who as in the case of doubting Thomas, so often goes the second mile in offering His truth to the undeserving—not present one final confirmation of His Word to those who 'hearing can still hear'? before He brings down the curtain on human history?"[56] Montgomery was sure that such a strategy was entirely consistent with Scripture and reasoned that "in this light, Ark fever becomes not so much the product of an overheated brain as the consequence of dangerously close contact with a burning bush and tongues of fire."[57] He, too, volunteered for the 1970 expedition.

Unfortunately, "International Expedition '70" went wrong from the start. Several participants bowed out, including LaHaye, who was preoccupied with his new college. For a variety of reasons, Montgomery was late for the rendezvous. The expedition, reduced to Cummings, a Turkish guide, and Mark Albrecht, a Jesus freak from Berkeley's World Christian Liberation Front, began their climb but had to leave the mountain when a grounded expedition that had been denied permission to go near the mountain complained to Turkish authorities about unfair treatment. The government responded by forcing Cummings's group to leave the mountain for good measure. By the time Montgomery, accompanied by his 11-year-old son, finally arrived, there was no one to meet. Undaunted, Montgomery received permission to climb to the top of Ararat with a certified guide on the approved tourist route, dining on crevettes, Alsatian pâté de foie gras, and a bottle of Kronenbourg the night before their assault on the summit.[58]

Another expedition was planned for 1971, featuring Cummings, Clarence Burdick, and Montgomery. A new evangelical representation came in the person of John Morris, who, along with a high school biology teacher from Houston, represented his father's newly created Institute for Creation Research (ICR). Turkish officials, however, still would allow no one on the mountain during the 1971 season.[59]

Part of the difficulties the Cummings-Montgomery-ICR group faced with Turkish officials reflected back to a growing division that had begun to appear within the ARF group during the late 1960s. One faction, principally Adventist/ Evangelical in its makeup and led by Cummings, believed the ark was most likely in the Ahora Gorge area of the mountain associated with various eye-witness sightings. The other group, more diverse in its religious affiliation and secular in its public stance, assumed that Navarra's 1955 finds indicated that the real problem was how to uncover and move the ice-encased ark. As a result, a second organization was formed in early 1969, the Scientific Exploration and Archaeological Research Foundation, or SEARCH. Led by Adventist Ralph Crawford and largely bankrolled by oilman Jack Grim and Texan financier Bunker Nelson Hunt, the board included a number of Turkish officials and scholars, several Mormons, and Demos Shakarian, head of the Full Gospel Business Men's Association.[60]

In the summer of 1969 SEARCH sponsored a new Navarra-led expedition. Utilizing a hand-operated drilling device at likely spots on the glacier that Navarra's muddled directions led them to, the group came up with nothing but ice. Near the end of the group's allotted time on the mountain, however, Navarra disappeared for a day. Returning to camp the next morning, he announced that he had found a new site that might prove interesting. The new site, a small gathering pond for melting glacial ice, proved to be quite fruitful as the group dredged up five small pieces of apparently hand-hewn wood, one piece being nearly 17 inches in length.[61]

The new find resulted in publicity for SEARCH, Navarra, and the effort to locate the ark. Samples from the newly found pieces of wood were submitted for radiocarbon testing at various labs including the National Physical Laboratory in Teddington, England, and the University of Pennsylvania. However, the results that appeared a few years later were not as propitious as the less rigorous tests for his earlier find, coming up with estimated ages of anywhere from 600 to 1,700 years old.[62] This added ammunition to speculation from a small, but growing, contingent in the ark-hunting community that Navarra was a fraud who had brought aged wood from France or had purchased it from local Kurds and hauled it up the mountain.[63]

Undaunted, and convinced as the SEARCH committee was that the question was no longer finding the ark but uncovering it, a larger plan began to emerge for the excavation of the site and the future of the long-hidden craft. Various plans were bandied about, including hauling bulldozers and drilling rigs up the icy heights; painting the glacier black to use the sun's rays to melt the ice; and a strategy that employed chemical burning rods that would sear holes in the ice for the easy breaking and removal of huge blocks of glacier.[64] But probably the most ambitious plan SEARCH advanced was a proposed plastic bubble that would cover a portion of the mountain producing a mini-greenhouse effect. This, it was believed, would provide the happy benefits both of melting the glacier hiding the ark and protecting the work area from bad weather. Having thus solved the uncovering of the ark, it was only natural that plans for development were also being hatched. Among the possibilities envisioned by SEARCH were a modern airport and a 4,000-room luxury hotel at the base of the mountain that would connect with a 17-mile hoist and gondolas that would take tourists to the ark site.[65]

Unfortunately, Turkish authorities, always highly sensitive to problems along the Soviet border and the never-ending job of policing Kurdish tribesmen in the area, began to balk at all of the talk of bulldozers and plastic canopies. As a result, they began to take a much harder line toward ark hunting during the early 1970s.[66] Unfortunately for SEARCH, its future (and that of Turkish tourism?) was sealed in June 1972 with the appearance of an article in the *National Tattler* under the headline "Noah's Ark Found!!!" Besides repeating the normal canon of sightings of the ark, the story prominently featured information from someone within SEARCH. Among the allegations was the charge that the Russians were the real source behind the problems they had been experiencing. To make matters worse, the article contained a detailed list of bribes—complete with dates, names, and amounts—paid to Turkish officials over the previous few years.[67] SEARCH's attempts to find the ark effectively ended that summer.

The Search for the Ark Goes "Public"

While the various organizations' and expeditions' efforts to find the ark faltered, a new spate of books on the topic spread word of the endeavor to an increasingly wider public. Morris's previously cited trials and tribulations during the summer of 1972 served as the springboard for his 1973 book, *Adventures on Ararat*, published by the ICR.[68] Morris's volume was the third in a new round of books publicizing the hunt for the ark, joining Violet Cummings's 1972 book, *Noah's Ark: Fact or Fiction?* as well as John Warwick Montgomery's collection of documents and tale of his 1970 ascent of Ararat, *The Quest for Noah's Ark*.[69] The new tide of publicity was supplemented in 1974 when Dan Malanchuk, the entrepreneurial publisher of charismatic Logos Books, backed an updated English translation of Fernand Navarra's 1955 volume under the title *Noah's Ark: I Touched It*.[70]

The public's consciousness about reports of the existence of Noah's Ark took a real upswing during 1975 and 1976, however, with the release of two movies about the ark. Late 1975 saw the release of "The Ark of Noah," a secular effort by Los Angeles–based Bart LaRue's Janus Productions. This movie was largely built around film from Fernand Navarra's collection and the 1969 SEARCH expedition and film of LaRue's own illegal attempt to climb Ararat during the summer of 1974. The film was released regionally and had some popularity on the church circuit.[71]

By far the more noticeable was "In Search of Noah's Ark," a film by Utah's Sun Classic Pictures, makers of family films such as "The Life and Times of Grizzly Adams" (1973) and sensationalistic fare such as "The Lincoln Conspiracy" (1977). "In Search of Noah's Ark" was released nationwide during the spring of 1976 along with an accompanying mass-market paperback book of the same title that sold well over 500,000 copies. Structurally, the film featured long segments reenacting the story of Noah and his family with a great number of the best scenes devoted to Noah's chimpanzee helper. In terms of presenting the ark hunters' arguments, the film utilized the input of Cummings, Montgomery, Henry and John Morris, and a bevy of creationists and flood geologists.[72] The impact of "In Search of Noah's Ark" in terms of raising awareness about the claimed existence of the ark was intensified during 1977 when NBC purchased broadcast rights to the film. First shown on May 2, the film was shown again, with a heavier promotion campaign, on Christmas Eve 1977.[73]

After the flood tide of publication and publicity during the 1970s, the 1980s, by contrast, seemed comparatively quiet on the ark front. This was more a matter of appearances than anything else. In reality, the search for the ark continued apace, eased somewhat by better cooperation from Turkish officials.

One of the major players during the 1980s was Charles Willis, a medical doctor from Pinedale, California. Willis led four separate expeditions to the mountain in 1983, 1984, 1986, and 1988. Under colorful titles such as "The Apostle Thomas Expedition" and "The Snow Tiger Team," Willis's groups charted and surveyed several areas of the mountain, cut probe trenches into the ice, used radar equipment and a solar-powered drill, and eventually concluded that the eastern plateau of the mountain contained nothing but ice.[74]

A new evangelical notable in the hunt during the 1980s was former test pilot and astronaut James Irwin.[75] During the late 1970s, Irwin, a Southern Baptist, became interested in the ark story and used his reputation to lobby the Turkish government on behalf of the ark hunters.[76] Accompanying Eryl Cummings, Irwin made his first ascent of Ararat in 1982. The group took hundreds of photographs and "ruled out some sites as possible locations of the Ark."[77] The trip ended abruptly when Irwin took a 100-foot tumble on a glacier and suffered severe leg and face lacerations.[78] He returned to the Ararat region the next summer with special permission from the Turkish government to use a heli-copter to film the mountain but likewise found no trace of the ark.[79] In 1985 Irwin came back one more time, convinced that "finding Noah's Ark might signal the imminent return of the Messiah to Earth." Although his presence helped attract the coverage of ABC's "20/20," the expedition was forced off the mountain after two days due to Turkish skittishness about Soviet maneuvers just over the border.[80]

A flurry of excitement rocked Arkdom in September 1989 when Chuck Aaron, a devout Lutheran helicopter pilot from Orlando, Florida, and Robert Garbe, a member of the Church of Christ and president of the Creation Re-search Science Education Foundation of Winchester, Ohio, spotted and pho-tographed an "Ark-sized object" while circling Ararat. Both were sure that the object they saw fit drawings they had seen of George Hagopian's sighting but was "not nearly so tidy." A heavy snowfall obscured the object after two days' photography and videotaping and the group returned to the United States.[81]

In November, Aaron returned with John Morris and ICR geologist Grant Richards. Flying by the mountain they found the object to be relatively un-covered by snow. Richards concluded that the "ark" was probably a volcanic feature and Morris, while "still interested in it," admitted that he did not "really think [it was] the Ark."[82] These findings were echoed by a 1990 expedition headed by Carl Baugh of the Creation Evidences Museum in Glen Rose, Texas. Despite the letdown—and perhaps as always—"plans [were] underway to return to Mt. Ararat [in 1991] with technical instrumentation" for a ground expedition to investigate two other sites.[83]

Conclusion

And so it goes. After nearly 50 years of the hunt, the evangelical search for Noah's Ark continues despite the hardships and disappointments, and, perhaps more significantly—despite the criticism of skeptics both secular and religious.[84] However, there have been only a few attempts to tackle the ark hunters head-on, and at length, and their "success" at stemming the deluge can be assessed easily enough.[85] The notion that the ark is still there for the finding sticks in the throat of the secularist, scientific-oriented establishment. As the report of one survey of north Texas college students on paranormal and supernatural occurrences lamented, "when many college students believe in Noah's Ark . . . after completing courses that should teach them to know better, something is wrong with our system of science education."[86]

But the "problem" that an optimistic scientific community might perceive as simply a matter of inadequate pedagogy actually seems to engage deeper, more complex issues concerning evangelicalism—issues that have much to do with politics, social class, region, race and ethnicity, and—most crucially—sources of cultural authority. The same survey mentioned above showed that many students who scored high on a "creationist scale" had a pronounced tendency to reject pseudoscientific and paranormal claims for such things as UFOs, Bigfoot, and Atlantis.[87] This would seem to suggest that evangelicals are no more, and perhaps even less, credulous than the general public. Clearly, native intelligence and rationality is not the issue. What is intriguing is why many evangelicals would, in the case of the remains of Noah's Ark, be inclined to accept as evidence that which they would not find credible (secondhand anecdotes, "missing" photos, and unverifiable eyewitness claims) in other instances. Here, the questions of cultural authority, class, and interest-group conflict loom large. As evangelicals analyze the chaotic state of their society in recent decades, they blame the implementation of secularist political, economic, and cultural values and policies. Given this track record, there is little or no basis, in their opinion, to trust their opponents' analysis of scientific matters. For a variety of reasons, many conservative American evangelicals believe the world is going to Gehenna in a petri dish, and modern science and the cultural elites that support and revere it bear a great deal of the blame. In a line of argument that goes back to nineteenth-century attacks on Darwinism and World War I–era condemnations of "German Science," modern science has, in their opinion, fostered unbelief and the rampant relativism that threatens to choke belief in God and his Word, the Bible.[88] This in turn has led to a stunning explosion of immorality that threatens to destroy our culture. By all rights, unbelieving Science deserves nothing less than the judgment of an angry Creator.

But it is exactly here that evangelicals remember that the Scriptures teach that their God is "a gracious God, and merciful, slow to anger."[89] Perhaps even godless Science might yet be allowed a chance to repent of its sins of pride and unbelief. Such has been one of the main motivations for those who have been looking for the ark—the hope that God has spared that sacred vessel over the millennia for just this moment in time. Surely, the revelation that Noah's old ship yet rested upon the heights of Ararat would cause the skeptic to reexamine his doubt and unbelief. In one fell swoop modern science with all of the objections, all its so-called expertise, would be instantly discredited. And—not coincidentally—this great miracle would also serve to reveal to all the world who has been right all the while. There is much in the internal logic of this scenario to recommend it to devout evangelicals.

There is also the possibility, however, that the forces of doubt will win out over the intrepid hunters of the ark. Perhaps the continuing decades of few, if any, results will begin to winnow the ranks of those who believe that the ark remains buried in the high reaches of Ararat. As the mountain is combed by yet more expeditions armed with increasingly more sophisticated equipment, the element of expectancy and vindication may begin to fade and the hunt for Noah's Ark prove as ephemeral as the notion that Mussolini was the antichrist. The inherent logic of the quest and the rigors and vagaries of Mount Ararat, however, seem as if they may have enough power to sustain the phenomenon for yet awhile. Both of these possibilities seem to be working at one and the same time within now-veteran ark hunter, John Morris. In 1990 he acknowledged that his own inclinations told him that in an area of such heavy geologic and volcanic turmoil as Mount Ararat, "a wooden structure such as the Ark would not be likely to survive if it had landed there." The claims of eyewitnesses, he said, were "the only reason to be looking [there] at all." Yet Morris held out belief that God might yet find a way: "I am convinced that, if the Ark remains, it has been preserved all these years by God for a purpose. It will be found only when He is ready, when His eternal timetable calls for it, and in a way that will bring Him the glory. He will melt the glacier, move the rock, or do whatever it takes to reveal the Ark to a lost and dying world that needs it so."[90]

NOTES

1. John D. Morris, *Adventure on Ararat* (San Diego: Institute for Creation Research, 1973), pp. 54–59.

2. *Ibid.*, pp. 59–66.

3. Ronald Numbers, *The Creationists: The Evolution of Scientific Creationism* (Berkeley: University of California Press, 1992), see particularly pp. 184–240, 299–318.

4. For an example of the manner in which creation science and flood geology more broadly dovetail with the premillennialist ethos of much of evangelicalism, see Numbers, pp. 338–39.

5. Lloyd R. Bailey, *Noah: The Person and the Story in History and Tradition* (Columbia: University of South Carolina Press, 1989), p. 81.

6. John Warwick Montgomery, *The Quest for Noah's Ark* (Minneapolis: Bethany Fellowship, 1971), pp. 94–103. Chardin, being a good rational Calvinist, was rather skeptical of the stories the Armenian monks told him.

7. The Armenians based their view that Ararat could not be ascended particularly in the legend of a monk named Jacob, later bishop of Nisibis. According to the tale, Jacob was determined to climb the mountain but would climb half the way and awaken the next morning at the same spot from which he had begun. Finally, God sent an angel to Jacob with a piece of the ark and the message to rest himself for God had forbidden mankind access to the mountain (as told by Jean Chardin in Montgomery, pp. 102–3). The Kurds, on the other hand, tend to ascribe the ban to a less cooperative divine order. For example see Fernand Navarra, *The Forbidden Mountain*, translated by Michael Legat, (London: Macdonald, 1956), p. 145.

8. Howard M. Teeple, *The Noah's Ark Nonsense* (Evanston, Ill.: Religion and Ethics Institute, 1978), p. 91. A general survey of the literature dealing with the quest for Noah's Ark provides ample documentation of the problems involved climbing Ararat, from the

falling rocks and lightning that disrupted John Morris's expedition (see *Adventure on Ararat*, pp. 56–66), the poisonous snakes that killed a pack horse on John Warwick Montgomery's ascent (see *The Quest for Noah's Ark*, p. 266), the bears that attacked John Libi (see Tim LaHaye and John D. Morris, *The Ark on Ararat* [Nashville: Thomas Nelson, 1976], p. 140), and the Kurdish tribesmen who held several ark hunters hostage in the late 1980s (see Andrew Snelling, "Amazing 'Ark' Expose," *Creation Ex Nihilo* 14: 4 (Sept/Oct 1992): 37).

9. The text of the "Roskovitsky" story, and the best account of the whole affair is found in Tim LaHaye and John D. Morris, *The Ark on Ararat* (Nashville: Thomas Nelson, 1976), pp. 75–89.

10. *The Pentecostal Evangel* (April 22, 1944): 12.

11. Violet Cummings, *Has Anybody Really Seen Noah's Ark? An Affirmative Definitive Report* (San Diego: Creation Life Publishers, 1982), p. 24.

12. John Bright, "Has Archaeology Found Evidence of the Flood?" *The Biblical Archaeologist*, V:4 (December 1942): 59.

13. LaHaye and Morris, pp. 79–80.

14. Letter from Benjamin Franklin Allen to Henry C. Morris, June 1, 1945, printed in LaHaye and Morris, p. 80.

15. Letter from Floyd B. Gurley, "To Whom It May Concern," October 17, 1945 (postdated to August 1, 1940), printed in LaHaye and Morris, pp. 81–82.

16. Cummings, pp. 77–87.

17. Cummings, p. 83; Montgomery, p. 245.

18. The Roskovitsky story was cited verbatim as evidence for the ark's existence in several articles into the 1960s. For example, see Raymond Schuessler, "Hunting Noah's Ark," *Navy: The Magazine of Sea Power* (January 1961): 12–14; "Expeditions to Seek Remains of Noah's Ark," *Albuquerque Journal*, May 22, 1964, p. F-15. Moreover, the widely distributed 1976 Sun Classics film "In Search of Noah's Ark" presented the Roskovitsky story almost as fact, as did the accompanying paperback, Dave Balsiger and Charles E. Sellier, Jr., *In Search of Noah's Ark* (Los Angeles: Sun Classic Books, 1976), pp. 102–5.

19. LaHaye and Morris, pp. 5–6.

20. For examples of the persistence of folk rumors within the evangelical community see Tom B. McIver, "Ancient Tales and Space-Age Myths of Creationist Evangelism," *Skeptical Inquirer* 10 (1986): 258–76; Edward B. Davis, "A Whale of a Tale: Fundamentalist Fish Stories," *Perspectives on Science and Christian Faith* 43 (1991): 224–37; Daniel E. Wonderly, "Fanciful Bible-Science Stories' Harm: A Call to Action," *Perspectives on Science and Christian Faith* 44 (1992): 131–33, and James Moore, *The Darwin Legend* (Grand Rapids: Baker Books, 1994). The circulation of these stories resembles the wider cultural phenomenon dubbed "urban legends." The classic books on this subject are by Jan Harold Brunvand, *The Vanishing Hitchhiker: American Urban Legends and Their Meaning* (New York: W. W. Norton & Company, 1981), and *The Choking Doberman: And Other "New" Urban Legends* (New York: W. W. Norton & Company, 1984). A good example of a recent evangelical book that attempts to tackle various urban legends including evangelical legends is Kathryn Lindskoog, *Fakes, Frauds & Other Malarkey* (Grand Rapids: Zondervan, 1993).

21. LaHaye and Morris, pp. 103–4; Teeple, p. 107.

22. LaHaye and Morris, p. 107.

23. Cecil A. Roy, "Was It Hot or Not?" *Bible-Science Newsletter* 16 (July 1978): 1–2; A. J. Smith, *The Reported Discovery of Noah's Ark* (Orlando, Fla.: Christ for the World Publishers, 1949), p. 43; Balsiger and Sellier, Jr., pp. 157–58; LaHaye and Morris, p. 105.

Probably the most famous story of missing photographs of the ark is related by several friends and associates of John Jefferson Greene, an American mining engineer who is alleged to have taken photos of the ark while based in the Mideast in the early 1950s. Greene was murdered in British Guiana in 1962 and it is assumed that the missing pictures were removed from his briefcase as part of a robbery attempt (see Cummings, pp. 143–49).

24. LaHaye and Morris, p. 114.

25. *Ibid.*, p. 48.

26. Reprint of Edwin Greenwald Associated Press story, November 23, 1948, in A. J. Smith, *The Reported Discovery of Noah's Ark*, pp. 70–72.

27. *Ibid.*, pp. 71–72.

28. *Ibid.*

29. "Suspicion on the Mount," *Time* (April 25, 1949): 31; A. J. Smith, *The Reported Discovery of Noah's Ark*, pp. 7, 79–80.

30. Smith, *The Reported Discovery of Noah's Ark*, p. 74.

31. A. J. Smith, *On the Mountains of Ararat: In Quest for Noah's Ark* (Apollo, Penn.: West Publishing Company, 1950), pp. 11–92.

32. Smith, *On the Mountains of Ararat*, p. 71.

33. *Ibid.*, pp. 97–118.

34. *Ibid.*, pp. 120–21.

35. *Ibid.*, pp. 122–23.

36. *Ibid.*, pp. 127–28.

37. Werner Keller, *The Bible as History: A Confirmation of the Book of Books*, translated by William Neil (New York: William Morrow and Company, 1956; Bantam edition, 1974), pp. 42–43, mentions Smith's 1951 expedition briefly. Strangely, later ark hunters of the 1950s and 1960s, though eager to point to the Reshit story as evidence, never seem to have made much of an attempt to try and find the elusive Kurd.

38. Fernand Navarra with Dave Balsiger, *Noah's Ark: I Touched It* (Plainfield, N.J.: Logos International, 1974), pp. xiii–xiv; *The Forbidden Mountain*, pp. 11–27.

39. Navarra, *The Forbidden Mountain*, pp. 165–66; no doubt they also wish they had remembered the camera with which they took pictures of the rest of the expedition.

40. Navarra, *The Forbidden Mountain*, p. 170; *Noah's Ark: I Touched It*, pp. 38–39.

41. Navarra, *Noah's Ark: I Touched It*, pp. 40–51.

42. *Ibid.*, p. 62.

43. Navarra, *Noah's Ark: I Touched It*, pp. 123–36; Bailey, *Noah*, p. 94.

44. Fernand Navarra, *J'ai trouvé l'arche de Noé* (Paris: Editions France-Empire, 1956).

45. Letter from Pastor Harold L. Williams, "To Whom It May Concern," dated 1952, reprinted in LaHaye and Morris, pp. 43–45.

46. Cummings, pp. 119–29.

47. *Ibid.*, p. 129.

48. Cummings, pp. 223–27; LaHaye and Morris, pp. 68–72.

49. In his "tips" to expeditions during this period, Navarra had a tendency to point to various areas of a broad section of Ararat, as the place where he had found his famous piece of wood in 1955. Rene Noorbergen, *The Ark File* (Mountain View, Calif.: Pacific Press, 1974), pp. 161–63; Cummings, pp. 312–26; LaHaye and Morris, pp. 133–34.

50. "Hunt for Noah's Ark on Mt. Ararat Yields Wood Apparently From Boat," *Racine Journal-Times*, September 1, 1962, p. 14; Cummings, pp. 167–69; LaHaye and Morris, pp. 144–56.

51. LaHaye and Morris, pp. 168–69.

52. *Ibid.*, p. ix.

53. *Ibid.*, p. 4.

54. *Ibid.*, p. 168.

55. Montgomery, pp. 243–44.

56. *Ibid.*, pp. 27980.

57. *Ibid.*

58. John Warwick Montgomery, "Ark Fever," *Christianity Today* (July 7, 1971): 38–39; LaHaye and Morris, pp. 168–69; Montgomery, pp. 258–72; Noorbergen, pp. 171–73.

59. John Warwick Montgomery, "Arkeology 1971," *Christianity Today* (January 7, 1972): 50–51; Montgomery, pp. 293–95; Morris, pp. 1–2.

60. Noorbergen, p. 163; Cummings, pp. 328–29.

61. Bailey, p. 95; LaHaye and Morris, pp. 158–60; Navarra, *Noah's Ark: I Touched It*, pp. 70–93. Bart LaRue's film "The Ark of Noah" (Janus Productions, 1975) contains a great deal of film footage from the 1969 SEARCH expedition and Navarra's discovery.

62. "In the Wake of the Ark," *Science News* (June 13, 1970): 574; Bailey, *Where Is Noah's Ark?* (Nashville: Abingdon Festival, 1978), pp. 68–81; Noah, pp. 95–105; Teeple, pp. 119–20.

63. Cummings, pp. 331, 336–37; LaHaye and Morris, pp. 159–60.

64. LaHaye and Morris, pp. 163–64.

65. Cummings, pp. 352–53; LaHaye and Morris, p. 163.

66. LaHaye and Morris, pp. 168–71.

67. "Noah's Ark Found!!!" *The National Tattler* (June 4, 1972); LaHaye and Morris, p. 174.

68. John D. Morris, *Adventure on Ararat* (San Diego: Institute for Creation Research, 1973).

69. Violet Cummings, *Noah's Ark: Fact or Fiction?* (San Diego: Institute for Creation Research, 1972); John Warwick Montgomery, *The Quest for Noah's Ark* (Minneapolis: Bethany House Publishers, 1972).

70. Navarra, *Noah's Ark: I Touched It*.

71. "The Ark of Noah," Janus Productions, 1975. For some insight into LaRue and his project see "Clippings," *Bible-Science Newsletter* (July 1975): 6; (December 1977): 4; LaHaye and Morris, pp. 215–16, 219.

72. "In Search of Noah's Ark," Sun Classic Pictures, 1976; Dave Balsiger and Charles E. Sellier, Jr., *In Search of Noah's Ark* (Los Angeles: Sun International Books, 1976); Bailey, pp. 105–9; Teeple, pp. 3, 125–27. In test marketing in late 1976 the film actually finished second among all competing films in New Orleans and Seattle (Richard Dalrymple, "Demythologizing Noah's Ark," *Eternity* [January 1977]: 21, 66.) Besides advancing the view that Noah's Ark was still to be found on Mount Ararat, the film was credited with being the instrument of divine protection. A pastor from Estes Park, Colorado, claimed that during the summer of 1976 a flash flood killed 109 people in his community but harmed none of the members of his congregation. The reason? That night the entire church had gone to see "In Search of Noah's Ark" in a part of town untouched by the floodwaters ("Articles," *Bible-Science Newsletter* [December 1977]: 3).

73. Bailey, *Noah*, n. 199, p. 224; Teeple, pp. 2–3.

74. Charles D. Willis, "1983 Ararat Expedition," *Bible-Science Newsletter* 21:11 (November 1983): 1, 15; "1986 Mt. Ararat Expedition," *Bible-Science Newsletter* 24: 12 (December 1986): 12–13; "Mission to the Mountain of Pain," *Bible-Science Newsletter* 27:1 (January 1989): 1–2, 5; "1984 Mount Ararat Expedition Fund Appeal," *Bible-Science Newsletter* 22:5(May 1984): 10.

75. For insight into Irwin's life, his spiritual experiences on the moon, and his decision

to engage in parachurch ministry, see James B. Irwin, *To Rule the Night* (Nashville: A. J. Holman Company, 1973).

76. "The Search for Noah's Ark," *Five Minutes with the Bible & Science* 11:8 (September 1982): 4.

77. "Status Report: The Irwin-Cummings Trip to Ararat," *Bible-Science Newsletter* 20:10 (October 1982): 1.

78. James B. Irwin, obituary, *New York Times* (Saturday, August 10, 1991): 26-L.

79. "There's More to Explore: An Interview with James Irwin," *Eternity* (November 1983): 81–83; "New Evidence for Noah's Ark," *The Humanist* 44:6 (November/December 1984): 34.

80. "The Mystery of Noah's Ark," ABC News' "20/20," October 17, 1985; Bailey, *Noah*, pp. 204–5. A secularist pseudoscientific attempt to find the ark also received a fair amount of coverage during the 1980s and into the 1990s and was featured along with the Irwin-Cummings party in the 1985 "20/20" broadcast. The site was a mysterious boat-shaped impression about 12–15 miles south of Ararat that had first drawn attention in the late 1950s after publication of aerial photographs made by the Turkish Air Force. Examined by a 1960 ARF expedition, the site was judged to be nothing more than a "clay up-push in a lava flow" (LaHaye and Morris, pp. 145–146). In the mid-1980s the site was "rediscovered" by a team that included Dave Fasold, a self-proclaimed marine salvage expert, and Ron Wyatt, an anesthesiologist from Tennessee who also claims to have discovered Moses' stone tablets, the Ark of the Covenant, and chariot wheels from Pharoah's drowned army. The pair claimed that their survey of the site with metal detectors and a "molecular frequency generator" found a patttern of lines that corresponded to the remains of crossbeams of a boat's corroded iron nails or brackets. Evangelical ark hunters and creationists dubbed the claims ludicrous and criticized the unscientific methods used by the pair—particularly the molecular frequency generator, which they described as a pair of brass welding rods connected to a set of batteries in the operator's pocket. Although going their separate ways, Wyatt and Fasold and a small coterie of supporters have continued to tout their discovery—aided by the Turkish provincial governor who, despite contrary advice from Turkish scholars, had a visitors' center erected and the area declared a national park (Robert Sheaffer, "Levitated Linda, Ear Coning, and Arkeology," *Skeptical Inquirer* 17 [Spring 1993]: 268–69; John D. Morris, "Is It Noah's Ark?" *Creation Ex Nihilo* 12:4 [September/October 1990]: 16–18; Andrew A. Snelling, "Amazing 'Ark' Expose," *Creation Ex Nihilo* 14:4 [September/October 1992]: 26–38).

81. Paul A. Bartz, "Has Noah's Ark Been Found?" *Bible-Science Newsletter* 27:11 (November 1989): 1–2; Frank Vosler, "Noah's Ark May Be Found," *Bible-Science Newsletter* 27:12 (December 1989): 1–2, 5–6, 13.

82. "Noah's Ark May *Not* Be Found?" *Bible-Science Newsletter* 27:12 (December 1989): 5.

83. Don Schockey, "1990 Efforts to Find the Ark of Noah," *Bible-Science Newsletter* 29:2 (February 1991): 10.

84. Sometimes the critics have had the last laugh on the ark hunters, the media, and the public. Such was the case with the February 20, 1993, broadcast of "The Incredible Discovery of Noah's Ark." Veteran actor Darren McGavin interviewed George Jammal as part of the two-hour prime-time special broadcast nationwide on CBS. Jammal claimed that he had ascended Mount Ararat with a companion, "Vladimir," in 1984. He told of how they had found an intriguing crevasse during their climb. Deciding to investigate, they climbed into the fissure in the ice and suddenly found themselves inside a wooden structure. "We got very excited," Jammal remembered, "[W]e saw part of this room was made into pens, like places where you keep animals. We knew then that we had found

the Ark!" Vladimir snapped dozens of photographs and Jammal hacked off a piece of wood to document their find. Reemerging from the ice, Vladimir took more photos of Jammal, posing at the site. Suddenly, Jammal claimed, disaster struck. Backing up, Vladimir fell, the noise causing an avalanche that killed him and buried the precious film. As Jammal told the story, he was so upset by the turn of events that it took him over eight years to present his story, which, for the first time, he had told the producers of the special.

Unfortunately, Jammal did not tell the entire story. As it was revealed a few months later, Jammal turned out to be an actor and member of the Freedom From Religion Foundation who had never been near Mount Ararat. Intrigued at creationist claims about the ark, he contacted Duane Gish, vice president of the Institute for Creation Research, as early as 1985 with a story about having found the ark. Approached for the documentary in 1992, he was coached by his friend Gerald Larue, professor emeritus of biblical history and archaeology at the University of Southern California and senior editor of *Free Inquiry.* The wood from the ark that Jammal reverently described on camera as "so precious . . . a gift from God" was in reality a piece of pine found in Los Angeles that he had soaked in various juices and baked in the oven of his Long Beach home. Indeed, at the time of the filming, the "relic" literally reeked of teriyaki sauce, the last of its aging treatments. The production company that had been so easily taken in by Jammal was Sun International Pictures, Inc., of Utah, the same company that had produced the successful film "In Search of Noah's Ark," in the mid-1970s. Intimately involved with both projects was David W. Balsiger, whose other notable credits included being a coauthor of Mike Warnke's phenomenally best-selling—and later-proven fictional—autobiography *The Satan Seller,* and media director for evangelist Morris Cerullo's "Witchmobile." (Leon Jaroff, "Phony Arkaeology," *Time* [July 5, 1993]: 51; John D. Morris, "Noah's Ark Back in the News," *Acts & Facts* 22 (September 9, 1993): 3–4; James Lippard, "Sun Goes Down in Flames: The Jammal Ark Hoax," *Skeptic* 2:3 (1994): 22–33.)

85. While the 1970s' gush of literature and film undoubtedly raised awareness and convinced many people of existence of the ark, "In Search of Noah's Ark" was particularly responsible for a counteroffensive by skeptics. In 1978 two authors set out to debunk the notion that the ark had survived on Mount Ararat. Lloyd R. Bailey, an associate professor of Old Testament at Duke Divinity School, wrote *Where Is Noah's Ark?: Mystery on Mt. Ararat* (Abingdon/Festival, 1978), a pocket-sized paperback that calmly set forth objections to Ararat as the traditional site for the landing place of the ark, as well as pointing out contradictions and problems in more recent eyewitness claims. Howard Teeple, a "former believer in fundamentalism," retired librarian, and head of an Evanston, Illinois–based group called the Religion and Ethics Institute, rushed to print with *The Noah's Ark Nonsense* (Religion & Ethics Institute, 1978). Teeple's book attacked flood geology and fundamentalist hermeneutics as well as the ark hunters, the television industry, and the FCC for allowing such things as "In Search of Noah's Ark" on the airwaves. In 1989, Bailey published an expanded, updated volume, *Noah: The Person and the Story in History and Tradition* (Columbia: University of South Carolina Press) as part of the series Studies on Personalities of the Old Testament. This volume combined more in-depth biblical scholarship on Genesis and Noah with attempts to examine claims about the modern existence of the ark.

86. Francis B. Harrold and Raymond A. Eve, "Noah's Ark and Ancient Astronauts: Pseudoscientific Beliefs About the Past Among a Sample of College Students," *The Skeptical Inquirer* (Fall 1986): 61–75 (quote on p. 73).

87. *Ibid.,* p. 71.

88. For a good summary of the roots of this line of fundamentalist analysis, see George M. Marsden, *Fundamentalism and American Culture: The Shaping of Twentieth-Century Evangelicalism, 1870–1925* (New York: Oxford University Press, 1980): 212–21.

89. Jonah 4:2 (KJV).

90. John D. Morris, "Is It Noah's Ark?" *Creation Ex Nihilo* 12:4 (September/October 1990): 19.

PART V

WIDER DOMAINS

12

"The Science of Duty"

Moral Philosophy and the Epistemology of
Science in Nineteenth-Century America

ALLEN C. GUELZO

Begin by looking at everything from the moral point of view, and
you will end by believing in God.

— Thomas Arnold

There once lived, in the American nineteenth century, an intellectual child
called "moral philosophy." Knowing what we know today about morality and
philosophy in academe and how unlikely the two are to be seen together in
public, the suspicion is apt to arise that the parents of this child had been joined
together in something other than holy wedlock. And like the foundlings who
populate Dickens's novels, "moral philosophy" comes to us through the words
of historians dressed in all the tattered garments of intellectual poverty: *anemic,
wormy, naive* are only a few of the kinder cuts taken at it by Morton White,
Merle Curti, and Herbert Schneider. And like the foundlings again, the story
of the child's ignoble birth carries echoes of the Dickensian meeting of purity
and defilement, of highborn father and lowly mother. For "moral philosophy"
was, by most modern standards, the offspring of a misbegotten attempt to blend
Enlightenment science and Protestant theology, to turn the ever-quickening
pace of scientific experimentation and discovery as it emerged out of the eighteenth century, and blast its adolescence by extorting from it illusory proofs that
both physical nature and human nature were orderly and self-evident creations
of a benevolent God.

That, at least, was the assumption of hostile onlookers like Andrew Dickson
White and G. Stanley Hall, who were convinced that the proper trope for the
relationship of science and theology was warfare, not union. It is not merely
that nineteenth-century American moral philosophy comes to us full of overdrawn gestures and an elephantiasis of rhetoric; the Transcendentalists did the
same and yet we revere the baggy denizens of Concord, Massachusetts, as half-

divine sages. The real crime of moral philosophy (as Hall wrote in a savagely famous article in 1879) was that it attempted to pass off on an unsuspecting culture the old reactionary pre-Enlightenment Protestant theology, tricked out in what appeared to be the methods of scientific research and ostensibly claiming to discover by scientific means the truths and laws of human conduct, while "the great open questions of psychology and metaphysics are made to dwindle in number and importance as compared with matters of faith and conduct. . . . Hence all branches of mental science have come to be widely regarded as the special appanage of a theological curriculum" and mostly taught by instructors who "have no training in their department save such as has been obtained in theological seminaries."[1] What made the lineage of moral philosophy suspect to Hall was not any lack of benefit of clergy, but the abounding presence of too many of them.

It would be satisfying in Victorian terms to discover that these intellectual Fagins were wrong and that the much-despised child grew up Oliver Twist—like to bring forth sweetness, truth, and beauty. In fact, it did not: the career of moral philosophy as an academic discipline was fatefully short, lasting in real terms only from about 1789 (when the Alford Professorship of Natural Religion, Moral Philosophy, and Civil Polity was founded at Harvard College) until its last gasp with the publication of James McCosh's *Our Moral Nature* in 1892. Its great teachers—Francis Wayland, Francis Bowen, Joseph Haven, Archibald Alexander, Mark Hopkins, Laurens Perseus Hickok, Noah Porter, among other lesser lights—were almost always clergymen, who no matter what their aspirations to scientific reputations, remained such and therefore became increasingly suspect to a post–Civil War generation that had lost its faith in the moral authority of Protestant clergymen. Its customary position, as the capstone course of the senior year of collegiate instruction, was dethroned by the introduction of elective course systems and the preference of elite institutions to shift the burden of faculty work from instruction to research. And even today, modern evangelical historians are inclined, sometimes a little anxiously, to take the side of Fagin, suggesting not that science was being swindled by a liaison with religion but that the integrity of Protestant theism was being sacrificed to a rakish Enlightenment rationalism.[2]

Still, there is some doubt whether the actual shape of nineteenth-century American moral philosophy was either so enervating or so outrageous as that. "We painstakingly studied 'Mental' and 'Moral' Philosophy," recalled Jane Addams of her senior course at Rockford College in 1882, and "far from dry in the classroom," it "became the subject of more spirited discussion outside, and gave us a clue for animated rummaging in the little college library."[3] Andrew Preston Peabody recalled that the teaching of Harvard College president James Walker, who superintended (as most college presidents did before 1869) the senior instruction in moral philosophy, was "collectively and individually . . . intensely stimulating to industry, ambition, high moral resolve, and religious purpose."[4] Moral philosophy was, as Peabody and Addams heard it expounded, a compound of confidence and anxiety: *anxiety*, in that a case for corralling together science and religion had to be made in the American nineteenth century without either the cultural or legal scaffolding of established confessional churches around it; *confidence*, in the sense that the moral philosophers whom Hall hated so much believed that they had done more than merely harmonize science and religion. They had presided, or so they thought, over the birth of a third science, the science of human conduct. Moral philosophy was envisioned, not so much as containing proof of the reconciliation of science and theology, as in being itself that proof, both as method and substance. And it would occupy, for however brief a historical moment, a critical place in the chain of connections whereby American Protestants struggled to co-opt the Enlightenment, to fend off the threat of mechanism (as the wrong result of science) and romantic Transcendentalism (as the wrong result of philosophy), and to write a book of virtues for the first publicly non-Christian society in Western history.

I

"These are the days that must lay a new foundation of a more magnificent philosophy, never to be overthrown," wrote one of Robert Boyle's disciples in the 1690s, "that will empirically and sensibly canvass the phenomena of nature, deducing the causes of things from . . . the infallible demonstrations of mechanics."[5] This was precisely the attitude that disturbed pious believers and theologians across Western Europe for the following century, as more and more of the motion that animated the known universe fell under the rubrics of the "demonstrations of mechanics" rather than the will of a self-conscious and personal Creator, until at length science appeared, in the works of Hobbes, de la Mettrie, and the most radical of the *philosophes* to be ready to explain even human behavior by "mechanics." The canny Hobbes, for instance, began in the 1660s by describing the act of individual human willing as simply a response to the stimulation of the "*last* appetite"; little more than a century later, Thomas Jefferson was justifying a national political revolution as an act that "the course of human events" had made "necessary," and his fellow revolutionary James Madison would recast American politics in the tenth *Federalist Papers* as a closed system in which the self-cancelling rivalries of political factions would operate, of their own, to guarantee the greatest possible liberty to all.

The devout believer could, of course, "retire into his fortress," as Pierre Bayle had done in 1697, and respond only with "silence along with the shield of faith."[6] But it quickly became apparent that this option would prove viable only if European Christians were prepared, as Bayle was, to surrender all pretense to cultural hegemony, and the political form of that hegemony, the state-established church. Until the French Revolution, and for a lot longer outside France, that was a sacrifice beyond calm consideration. The Anglican Establishment, led by Samuel Clarke and Joseph Butler, championed a genteel and didactic accommodation with Newtonian physics, and in so doing preserved both the Established Church from a conflict it had little guarantee of winning and the normative position of Christian ethics for the Parson Woodfordes of the English countryside. In the new American republic, however, the competitive varieties of American Christianity and the surprising results of the American Revolution upset all such calculations. Except in those few places that clung temporarily to a severely attenuated form of religious establishment (and even that lasted only until 1833), all notion of a religious, much less Christian, hegemony evaporated, and Christian moralists were left to battle for a public voice with each other and with the "demonstrations of mechanics," a struggle that was not made the easier for them by the identification of most of the revolutionary elite—Jefferson, Franklin, Washington—with Enlightenment unbelief. It made little difference that precious few of that elite indulged anything more radical than deistic unorthodoxy, or indulged it very aggressively for that matter, or that the numbers of the orthodox provided an overwhelming numerical majority of adult Americans: no less than John Randolph of Roanoke believed that the early Republic was "the most ungodly country on the face of the earth," teeming with "a generation of free thinkers, disciples of Hume & Voltaire & Bolingbroke." And for the Princetonian Ashbel Green, it was not really the numbers of infidels at all but the legitimating of "open and avowed infidelity" by the Revolutionary leadership that convinced Green, who was a student at Princeton in the 1780s and later its president, that an "incalculable injury to religion and morals" was being done "throughout our whole country; and its effect on the minds of young men who valued themselves on their genius, and were fond of novel speculations, was the greatest of all."[7]

It is against this background that American moral philosophy emerged as a means for blunting, accommodating, and then turning the implications for politics and ethics of scientific "mechanics." Contemplating the unexpected consequences of religious disestablishment, John Witherspoon of Princeton laid down what became the fundamental raison d'etre of moral philosophy: that a republic is probably right in breaking thoroughly with the monarchical past by abolishing not only aristocracy but also compulsory religious establishments; but that republics (as everyone was supposed to know from reading Montesquieu) were fragile and depended, as monarchies did not, on the virtuous and disinterested public performance of all their privileged citizens; and that while science might teach us how the natural world operated, something was required to fill up the vacuum left by established religion in telling us how moral virtue operated.[8] The need to teach virtue could, of course, be supplied by Christianity, and Protestant revivalism offered one method for reinserting, by sheer numbers and energy, an undisguised Christian voice into the public sphere. But the problem with revivalism was that it went by fits and starts, and its voluntarism and its excesses offended both the Witherspoons (because it offered no stable platform for a public Christianity) and the Jeffersons (because revivalism made its demands for a public Christianity in too loud and too distinctively religious a voice). What was necessary, then, for Witherspoon (and his talented son-in-law Samuel Stanhope Smith) at Princeton, for Timothy Dwight at Yale, and elsewhere in the early republic's small colleges was to find a way of reshaping Christian moralism so as to put forward a Christian public voice, and yet to find a way of accommodating Christian theism to the secular voice of the Enlightenment. And it did so by discovering that Christian morality, and behind it Christian theism, could be reconceived as a science of virtue, whose methods and substance not even the most rabid republican secularist could question. By recognizing *science* as the dominant mode of Enlightenment discourse, Christian theists like Witherspoon, Smith, and Dwight sought, in effect, to co-opt science by insisting that human ethics was also a science, but a science that, in this case, led to Christian rather than mechanistic conclusions.

This co-optation began with the term *moral philosophy* itself: fundamentally what moral philosophy asked was that human conduct, or ethics, be understood to embody, or at least resemble, the methodology of science. Noah Porter defined moral philosophy as "moral science," and as "the science of duty"; Mark Hopkins called it "the science which teaches men their supreme end, and how to attain it," and Hopkins specifically stressed the structural parallel of moral philosophy to natural science by adding that, "As distinguished from Natural Science, which teaches what is, Moral Science teaches what ought to be."[9] In fact, for all practical purposes, "Philosophy and science, in the older usage of the term, are often almost identical," declared Amherst College president William A. Stearns.[10] This, of course, depended on defining *science* in strictly methodological terms, and apart from the cultural history it had acquired since the early seventeenth century; and so James Marsh innocently announced that making a science or philosophy of morals involved "simply to observe, to distinguish and arrange the facts of consciousness, as presented in our experience, aiming at nothing more . . . and thus to acquire a rational insight into the laws of our inward being."[11] Moral philosophy thus proposed to shift the scientific credibility of empirical observation and induction from the natural world to the world within, taking introspection beyond the boundaries of psychology to discover that morality had as objective and lawlike an existence within the human mind as any Lockean idea. That this scientific morality also turned out to be Christian was, of course, simply a convenient dividend. If everyone was playing by the proper rules of science, the authority that moral philosophy should command in the American public sphere was naturally augmented. "It is only in a modified sense that there can be such a thing as a Christian Moral Philosophy," Mark Hopkins cheerfully avowed in 1878, "a true moral science will, and must be, independent of revelation, and will be a test of anything claiming to be that, for nothing that can be shown to be really in opposition, either to the reason or to the moral nature of man, can be from God."[12]

In some respects, this bid to scientize and naturalize Christian ethics was only an extension of an ancient conversation on natural religion that, for Protestants at least, was as old as the Reformation and Protestant scholasticism, and that reflected a sincere confidence that diligent exploration of the natural world would exalt the Creator. Even in the seventeenth century, Protestant scholastics on a spectrum as broad as Henry More, the neo-Platonist, and Theophilus Gale, the Calvinist, all hoped to assimilate long-standing traditions of classical and natural ethics to Protestant Christianity; and in early America, the annual Dudleian Lectures at Harvard were reminding people from 1755 onward of the fundamental harmony of the religion one could deduce from nature with the religion revealed from on high.[13] The moral philosophers also owed a particular debt to the model of reconciling nature and religion offered by Anglican bishop Joseph Butler in 1736 in his celebrated *Analog of Religion Natural and Revealed, to the Constitution and Course of Nature*. It was Butler's great achievement to take the *nature* so beloved of the scientists and demonstrate, on the basis of reasonable probabilities, that Christian theism was wholly in accord with it; and in so doing, he paved the way for the moral philosophers to find that the inner world of human conduct was also governed by scientific principles that wholly accorded with Christianity. "No man" had stated the case for a "moral science" better or "more accurately than Bishop Butler," wrote Mark Hopkins, and Hopkins's own books on moral philosophy were, as he described them, little more than what "those facts, as stated by him, not only justify, but require."[14] Francis Wayland, who emerged as the most talented of the American moral philosophers, lauded Butler's *Analog* as "a work which has done more to promote the discovery and establish the truth of ethical philosophy, than any uninspired treatise in any age or language."[15] "All of his discourses," added George E. Emerson (Harvard College, 1817), upping the ante beyond the *Analogy*, "are of great practical value to the teacher who would teach a code of morals founded at once upon reason and the light of nature, and upon revelation."[16]

This long sweep of naturalized theology presented an already-worthy alternative to fideistic withdrawal; it required, however, the example set by the common-sense realism of the Scottish Enlightenment to effectively transfer the theologizing of external nature to the theologizing of human consciousness. The story of the influence of Scottish common-sense realism has become a thick one, too thick to bear much repeating here. But there is no question that American moral philosophy in the nineteenth century was given its most distinctive twist by the epistemology of the Scots. To the extent that the representationalist psychology marketed by Locke led ineluctably toward a skeptical uncertainty about whether our ideas had any sure connection to anything outside of our consciousness, the Scots argued that we not only have ideas but make intuitive judgments about the reality of the outward causes of those ideas, intuitive judgments that (precisely because they are intuitive) cannot be dismissed as unreliable. "It is self evident," announced Andrew Preston Peabody, "that all knowledge—every recognition of relation of thought to thought, every step of reasoning, every conclusion from premises—implies a belief in our own consciousness."[17] The Scots noted, in addition, that the same intuitive judgment is made in our consciousness, not only about the reality of external phenomena but about ethical judgments—about right and wrong—and hence our ethical responses are not mere culturally conditioned reactions. At the most forward edge of the Scots realists, they posited the existence of a "moral sense" within the consciousness that apprehended rightness and wrongness with the same reliability that the other senses apprehended hardness or extension. What had begun as an analysis of the *nature* of the understanding now opened up into a description of its *conduct*.

The canonical history of Scottish realism in America usually begins with Witherspoon and Samuel Stanhope Smith at Princeton; but it also sprouted almost simultaneously under Thomas Clap at Yale and David Tappan at Harvard, and it became the epistemological crossbeam on which moral philosophy rested its case.[18] For moral philosophy, in order to make its scientific methodology work, had to assume that there was a discoverable moral order within human beings upon which that methodology could operate—that there was what James Richards called "a constitutional propensity" to make judgments "and to do this as readily and with as much confidence in changes which take place in the physical as in the moral world."[19] And the insistence of the Scots that such a moral sense existed, and functioned so readily in the presence of moral data that its behavior seemed intuitive, gave the moral philosophers all the reason and all the credibility they needed for discovering a scientific moral order that would, incidentally, be in a position to prescribe Christian moral order without looking *too* Christian. "Mind is so constituted that it cannot but affirm obligation to will the good or the valuable as soon as the idea of the good or valuable is developed," wrote the revivalist-turned-college-president Charles Grandison Finney; grant that response, "and it only needs for us to take notice of what consciousness testifies, and we can settle the question as certainly as we can our own existence."[20] For Joseph Haven, "the mind is so constituted, that in view of such truth, it shall act as . . . recognizing the right and wrong of human conduct, measuring its actions and those of others by this standard, and approving or condemning accordingly."[21] By appealing in a "scientific" (or, as they preferred to call it, "Baconian," to further heighten the claims of moral philosophy as an empirical science) fashion to the judgments of commonly held human moral sense, the moral philosophers expected to discover an unambiguous ethical consciousness that would drive off mechanistic atheism and fend off the epistemological agnosticism of the Transcendentalists. "If I understand my own mode of philosophizing, it is the Baconian," declared Lyman Beecher in 1829.[22] Every occupant of the Alford Chair at Harvard before the Civil War was an enthusiastic disciple of the Scots; Clap, Dwight, Nathaniel William Taylor, and Noah Porter all preached it to the Yale undergraduates; Francis Alison established it at the University of Pennsylvania, Henry Philip Tappan at City College of New York (and later the infant University of Michigan); James McCosh, Archibald Alexander, and Charles Hodge in Princeton; Thomas C. Upham at Bowdoin, Francis Wayland at Brown; and Mark Hopkins at Williams.[23]

Articulating the content of the moral sense, however, required that the moral philosophers be seen scrupulously obeying the rules of scientific inquiry, and that was no small task since the single greatest methodological problem they encountered was their own indispensable assumption that the same inductive logic that ruled the scientific method when applied to physical nature could be transferred and applied to human nature. The moral sense would, they were confident, secure the epistemological ground for the morality they desired; but it required a hermeneutical principle before they could get the scientific method to work for them, and that was the principle of *analog.* "Analogy is the foundation of . . . moral reasoning," declared Levi Hedge in his Harvard logic textbook of 1827; as such, it allowed a critical transition to be made from thinking about the operations of nature, which Enlightenment science had already established to be regular, harmonious, and above all, observable, to thinking about moral nature, since analogy provided the means for saying that the empirical regularity that could be observed in physical nature should be assumed to govern moral nature as well. "He who understands one thing thoroughly, holds the threads of all knowledge in his hand," wrote Levi Hedge's son and successor at Harvard, Frederick Henry Hedge; and that allowed both Hedges to assume "that nature is consistent and uniform in her operations; so that from similar circumstances similar effects may be expected. . . ."[24] If regularity ruled physics, we must be allowed to assume it will rule ethics; hence the principle of analogy gives us the grounds for devising lawlike and scientized schemes of ethics as well. As Francis Wayland wrote, "Every law is found to be in perfect harmony with every other law . . . every thing teaches us that the universe, with all its changes, is nothing more than the realization of one single conception."[25] And since, as the natural religion tradition had all along been at pains to demonstrate, physical nature was analogous to Scripture in its revelation of a personal Creator, it would be perfectly scientific to discover that human conduct followed the same pattern. The construction of a public morality could then proceed, as Levi Hedge delightedly concluded, "similar in most respect to analytical induction."[26]

The logic of analogy worked itself out in the teaching of moral philosophy along four lines:

1. *The self-evidence of law*: Everyone, by the epistemological canons of common-sense realism, experiences inescapable intuitions about the existence of "facts," the most basic of which are, according to Francis Wayland, that "*certain things exist*, and that certain changes are taking place in them," and that those changes "do not take place at random, but in the order of a succession, at first, dimly, but, by close inspection, more clearly seen."[27] Finding these mental objects and their changes to be real, James McCosh wrote, it becomes "the object of the ordinary sciences, physical and mental, to discover their laws."[28] Mark Hopkins, in his 1867 Lowell Lectures, simply diagrammed the self-evidence of law as a progression from the intuition of "Being" to the discovery that "Being" exerts "Force," to the discovery that "Force" possesses "Uniformity" of operation towards "An End," and this process thus assumes the shape of "law."

2. *The universality of law*: All laws can, claimed Francis Wayland, be empirically demonstrated to have, more or less, a single pattern. If they did not, then we could scarcely talk about *law* at all, for every motion or every substance in the universe would be a law unto itself, and the result, as Wayland pointed out, would be "universal ruin." For instance, argued Henry Philip Tappan, "all researches in nature go upon the admission that every phenomenon has a cause, and that every cause has a rule of action." But if this intuition of *law* has any meaning at all, then we should expect that "the phenomena of mind must have causes and laws in like manner; for the axiom above named is a universal axiom, embracing all phenomena."[29] In fact, added James McCosh, such laws are "in the mind and deeply seated there, just as the power of gravitation is seated there."[30] There thus should be, as Mark Hopkins concluded, a "striking ground of analogy" between "the laws of things," which command the "putting forth of force uniformly," and the "laws of persons," which make certain ethical

choices "*obligatory*."[31] "Just as, from the acknowledged existence and reality of sensible impressions or perceptions, we may and do assume the existence and reality of the sensible world," said James Walker in 1834, "from the acknowledged existence, and reality of spiritual impressions or perceptions, we may and do assume *the existence and reality of the spiritual world*."[32]

3. *The lawlikeness of human conduct*: It did not take much to convince the moral philosophers that such lawlikeness was copied in human conduct. "The human mind is not a mere aggregation of states and exercises," argued Laurens Perseus Hickok, "but an organization held together by one law of unity."[33] And just as human minds naturally intuit the reality of physical laws and categories, the human mind should, on the expectation of universality, similarly intuit the' existence of moral law within. "No man was ever known to exist, who in any sense could be called a developed human being, who did not recognize certain ethical distinctions as real, and esteem them of supreme importance,)" wrote Noah Porter. "[W]e take them as we know them, whether civilized or savage."[34] Among those distinctions, said Joseph Haven, "must be included the notion of the *beautiful*, and also that of *right*."

> That these ideas are to be traced, ultimately, to the originative or intuitive faculty, there can be little doubt. They are simple and primary ideas. They have the characteristics of universality and necessity. They are My awakened intuitively and instantaneously in the mind, when the appropriate occasion is presented by sense. There are certain objects in nature and art, which, so soon as perceived, strike us as beautiful. There are certain traits of character and courses of conduct, which, so soon as observed, strike us a morally right and wrong.[35]

And among those "traits" and "courses," the moral philosophers easily found all the familiar constituents of Christian morality. "We know immediately and intuitively that love is good and malignity evil," Mark Hopkins declared; a man "knows he ought not to be selfish—ought to be benevolent," echoed Charles Grandison Finney. "He knows he is bound to love his neighbor as himself— bound to seek the higher at the sacrifice if need be of the lower good. . . . A child knows these things before he is taught, and cannot remember when he first had them."[36]

4. *The triumph of design*: Since law is a constant construct of both the natural and moral worlds, then, reflexively, the discovery of moral purpose and direction within returns us, by the logic of analogy, to the scientific study of the natural world with a renewed conviction that natural law will likewise reveal intelligent moral purpose, and through that, evidence of divine purpose and providence in ruling the universe. "The plan of God pervades the moral universe as really as the natural," announced James Harris Fairchild. "He accomplishes his plan, through the movement of his moral creatures, as really as through the natural forces in the material world."[37]

This discovery allowed the moral philosophers to continually shuttle analogically between the natural and moral realms in order to provide a scientific rhetoric for Christian ethics. Even the pious Harvard mathematician Benjamin Peirce excitedly insisted, "How can there be a more faithless species of infidelity, than to believe that the Deity has written his word upon the material universe and a contradiction of it in the Gospel?"[38] The analogy of nature forces us to see purpose in human ethics, an analogy that Mark Hopkins professed to see even in the ordinance of the Sabbath day. "From the opinion of many scientific physicians," reported Hopkins, it was clear that Sabbath keeping was not only an obvious moral obligation, but a natural requirement for good health; therefore, if such a divine *moral* imperative was written so clearly into the imperatives of *physical* nature, then not only was the joint nature of divine and moral law intuitively and scientifically unified, but both in turn pointed to the wisdom of the God who had ordained the Sabbath.[39] "When we contemplate the order which prevails in the natural world," wrote Mercer University president John Ledley Dagg, "we behold the exhibition of the wisdom which God's providence displays," for "the advantage resulting from its order meets us in every experience of life."[40] Once moral law had been established in human consciousness, it could then be read back into physical nature to demonstrate, by inductive analogy, that the physical order must also be guided by a grand Designer. "The analogy of the human soul," wrote Noah Porter, "furnishes a decisive argument in favor of the conclusion, that the creator and thinker is One Being."[41] There is, in fact, so much of what James McCosh called "harmonies pre-established between . . . the moral law and the physical laws" that the "harmonies" cannot be accounted for in any other way except to assume that "God has so ordered his physical government, that it is made in various ways to support his moral government."[42] As Harvard College president Cornelius Felton declared to the Concord Lyceum in 1829, "The existence of an Eternal God, as it is the grand truth on which all religion rests, is, I am convinced, no less the basis that supports the fabric of human knowledge."[43]

It is easy to say, in retrospect, that a good deal of this rested upon epistemological foundations that were by no means as secure as they seemed, and upon an act of hermeneutical daring that had something of the air of tautology to it. But in antebellum America, the epistemology of common sense and intuition had few challengers among either moralists or scientists. The Scots' intuitional judgments seemed unassailable: McCosh described realism with all sincerity as "what we spontaneously accept . . . everything falls in with it, confirms it." It was not simply the hegemony of clergymen in antebellum American colleges that led James Marsh (himself a Congregational clergyman) to complain to Samuel Taylor Coleridge in 1839 that pride of place in American college curriculums had "very generally given place to the Scotch writers; and Stewart, Campbell, and Brown are now almost universally read as the standard authors on the subjects of which they treat."[44]

Moreover, the discovery of harmonious realms of moral and natural law was regarded, and not just by the moral philosophers, as the starting point for reconstructing a genuinely moral order for the Anglo-American republicanism as it emerged from out of the shadow of traditional aristocratic and hierarchical orders that had, in their own heyday, claimed a similar identity between public policy and natural law. That such a moral law also stood as a sign for Christian ethics added the additional benefit of reintroducing Christian morality to the front of the public stage without awakening the hostility of the Enlightenment to explicit religious claims. Civil society, wrote the southern Methodist Albert Taylor Bledsoe in 1856, is not really "a thing of compacts, bound together by promises and paper," as Locke and Jefferson had supposed. It was "a decree of God"; and then, as if to cover a revelation too hard for a secular republic to stomach, Bledsoe immediately retreated to the tactical cover of moral philosophy, for this "decree of God" was also "the spontaneous and irresistible working of that nature, which, in all climates, through all ages, and under all circumstances, manifests itself in social organizations."[45]

It was through this carefully scientized methodology that the moral philosophers were able to leap from an analysis of the understanding to offering prescriptions for conduct that would rebuild the structure of Christian public ethics in the half-century after the American revolution. Through the intuitive response of a moral consciousness, Mark Hopkins rediscovered an intricate threefold class of duties for which human beings had been created, including an obligation to obtain "air, exercise, sleep, and clothing," but also in a more bourgeois vein, a "right to property" that "is graciously bestowed upon mankind for the purpose of rousing them from sloth and stimulating them to action."[46] Union College students in the 1850s found through Laurens Perseus Hickok that they had natural and self-evident moral obligations to "cleanliness of dress and person;" but they discovered by the same means that they also had obligations to privatize the post office, since "state interference" is "oppressive to the public freedom, and like all tyranny should at once be abated."[47] All of these intuited moral obligations climaxed, however, in what Francis Wayland called "the general obligation to supreme love to God," and this for Wayland led point by point to "the cultivation of a devotional spirit," to prayer, and even to Sabbath keeping. As Wayland happily concluded, "As everything which we can know teaches a lesson concerning God, if we connect that lesson with everything which we learn, everything will be resplendent with the attributes of Deity."[48]

II

Well, almost everything. The birth certificate of moral philosophy, which seemed from the witness of Wayland, Hickok, Hopkins, and the others to attest a legitimate offspring of the scientific and the religious, concealed several serious weak links of practice and reasoning, and under the pressure of postbellum social and intellectual change, the weaknesses became more and more apparent. The first of these weaknesses, curiously enough, concerned religion—not whether moral philosophy had too much of it, but whether it might have too little. "To make the validity of scientific inference the only possible basis of religion approaches very near to pure rationalism," wrote Charles Sanders Peirce, tweaking Noah Porter in a review of *The Human Intellect* in 1869, "a doctrine that is not in the interest of religion, because it subordinates religion to science." On those terms, the urge to scientize theism and ethics might end up turning both into mere science.

We are inclined to suspect that the metaphysician . . . must look upon his problems with the cold eye of science, and have no other feeling for the eternal interests of man than the curiosity with which he would examine a trilobite; and then, being in a state of mind essentially irreligious, he can arrive at no result that would really help religion, for at most he can only say to mortal man that it is most likely that there is a God, which is no assurance; or he must bring the feelings of a religious man into the inquiry, and then he is as incompetent to treat the problem as a physician is to judge of his own case.[49]

This has become a popular postmortem judgment on American moral philosophy, and there is a certain element of truth in it. Despite the official disclaimers about self-evident facts and Baconian methodology, the moral philosophers were, as almost all their readers knew, ordained clergymen whose scientific methodology never failed to reach explicitly religious conclusions before the last page of their textbooks; what was less clear was the specific shape of those religious conclusions. Although the moral philosophy textbooks strained to present a semblance of uniformity on moral basics that would give a sense of verisimilitude to the claim that they were only reflecting the common sense of every conscious mind, the clergymen who wrote these textbooks all had specific confessional loyalties to serve. It would prove highly inconvenient for a purely inductive moral science to stumble across facts of human behavior that might militate against their particular confessional identity; or worse still, to find themselves in entire agreement, morally speaking, with reverend gentlemen whom they were otherwise required to anathematize. This was a particular problem for Calvinists in the Presbyterian and Congregational churches and colleges, such as Hickok, Porter, and Alexander, who on the one hand found themselves allied in the cause of moral philosophy with Unitarians such as Francis Bowen or Levi Hedge, with Methodists such as Daniel Whedon, or with the Oberlin College band of Finney, Mahan, and Fairchild.

The free will question offers an instance of how easily the natural moral intuitions upon which moral philosophy rested its epistemological case could fail their promoters. For Calvinist moral philosophers, it was a central confessional dogma that God caused and ordered all events, whatsoever came to pass. And thus, to Calvinist moral philosophers such as John Ledley Dagg, it was entirely in order to find that the moral sense agreed, and that moral philosophy should teach, that "Analogy favors Necessity."[50] But not to Unitarians such as Andrew Preston Peabody, who found instead that "we are distinctly conscious, not only of doing as we choose, but of exercising our free choice among different objects of desire, between immediate and future enjoyment, between good and evil."[51] And to the Methodist Whedon, it was equally clear that "Edwardean Calvinism" and "d'Holbachian Atheism" were cut from the same cloth of "godless naturalism which threatens to overwhelm the thinking world with a base materialistic and lawless antichristianity."[52] It did not ease the pain of Calvinist moral philosophers that Peabody and Whedon actually had much of the Scottish Enlightenment's heroes, especially Reid and Hutcheson, on their side, or that the argument that free will was essential to genuine moral choice and responsibility clearly commanded increasing assent in an industrializing world where human technology more and more appeared to be the master of nature rather than its subject. And so the Calvinist moral philosophers agreed, in case after case, to put their Calvinism on the shelf whenever they spoke about moral philosophy.[53] The Amherst College Congregationalist Joseph Haven conceded that "it is a presumption in favor of freedom that there is among men, a very general, not to say universal conviction of freedom"; and not just a conviction, according to James Harris Fairchild, but "a self-evident principle that obligation is conditioned on ability."[54] No one less than the twin doyens of Princeton Calvinism, Archibald Alexander and James McCosh, decided that, for the purposes of moral philosophy, it was enough to believe in a self-evident, intuited freedom that, when they were speaking theologically, they did *not* believe in. "In answer to all arguments brought to prove that man is not a free moral agent," Alexander confidently informed his Princeton seminary students, "we appeal to the consciousness of every rational being. No arguments, however plausible, are of any force against intuitive first principles. Whether we can or cannot answer arguments against liberty, we know that we are free."[55]

Still, the embarrassment confessional Protestants must have felt about such concessions was not, at least for them, the same thing as Peirce's accusation that the whole enterprise was subverting the purity of true religion. In fact, Peirce's accusation tended to be the complaint, not of the anxious faithful who felt that something was being lost by the moral philosophers, but by Victorian post-Christians like G. Stanley Hall who hoped to use the most attentuated definitions of fideism as sticks to beat back the moral philosophers off their own scientific territory, or even to move dogmatic Christianity entirely out of the American collegiate system. "In its most developed forms," wrote Hall, in a voice that eerily (and one suspects, disingenuously) anticipated the complaints of fundamentalist Protestants half a century later, "Protestantism has more or less completely rationalised not only the dogmas of theology but their Scriptural data, and now inculcates mainly the practical lessons of personal morality and the duty of discriminative intellectual, political and aesthetical activity."[56] There is not much evidence that Hall was really motivated by his concern for the integrity of Protestant Christianity. But neither is there much evidence that moral philosophy seriously betrayed Christian principles or that the small evangelical colleges Hall criticized so ruthlessly in 1879 were mindless hotbeds of proselytization. To the contrary, there is ample evidence that, unlike twentieth-century Protestant fundamentalists, the moral philosophers and their pious colleagues resisted the temptation to demonize modern science—much less psychology and ethics—and instead engaged and even valorized an empirical "investigation" of consciousness and social policy.[57] It is just as arguable that, by appealing past all questions of science to the core value of evangelical fideism, which had ever since the seventeenth century been vulnerable to the suspicion that any form of natural theology might divert the mind from true piety, both Hall and Peirce were implicitly revealing how much they feared that engagement and how much they thought secularization had to gain from crying fire about the threat to piety. Even among the Harvard Unitarians, it became fear about piety, not fear of science, which fatally weakened the pace of moral philosophy, and Hall and Peirce were only too happy to throw such an apple of intellectual discord in the moral philosophers' path.[58]

If anything, the moral philosophers may have been almost too loyal to their confessions. The very fact that they were, most of them, ordained clergy and often the officers of denominationally backed institutions prevented them from setting up the kind of defensive professional organization that other budding academic disciplines in America were already using to promote their own disciplinary interests and the careers of their members. Finney, Hodge, Bowen, and Walker all had to swear to the existence of a natural, and therefore common, Christian morality; but their theological identities prevented any of them from joining arms in defense of either their discipline or that morality, and in the context of academic professionalization in the nineteenth century, that failure to organize any form of national professional association helped to delegitimate the whole endeavor. They thus found themselves confused by the urge to remain loyal to their own confessional traditions and the paralysis induced by the cynical suggestion that confessional tradition mandated that they withdraw from the enterprise entirely.

The second of these problems touched on moral philosophy's claims to a scientific parentage. Despite the spacious aspirations of the moral philosophers to be purely Baconian in their inductive methodology from the "facts" of consciousness, there was no real assurance that defining science in strictly methodological terms, or that using the principle of analogy as a bridge between the natural and moral worlds, would actually hold up under the scrutiny of scientists who did not also happen to be clergymen. The word *science*, as the moral philosophers used it, was (as Charles Peirce remembered), by the 1860s, coming to be considered "from the etymological point of view, already a misnomer." Contrary to Amherst's president Stearns, "what they meant, and still mean, by 'science' ought, etymologically, to be called *philosophy*."[59] Peirce did not mean this as a compliment to philosophy. It did not help, either, that the inductive Baconian methodology that the moral philosophers glorified as the essence of the scientific endeavor was under increasingly heavy fire for its inadequacies in the Anglo-American nineteenth century. Beginning with Macauley's critical survey of Bacon in the *Edinburgh Review* in 1827 and climaxing with John Stuart Mill's *System of Logic* in 1843, Baconian induction was increasingly subordinated to the logic of deduction, until in 1875 the *Encyclopedia Britannica* could authoritatively state the demise of Bacon as science: "The true scientific procedure is by hypothesis followed up and tested by verification: the most powerful instrument is the deductive method, which Bacon can hardly be said to have recognised."[60] If Bacon was no longer the father of science, then moral philosophy could not be science's offspring, and it was time for moral philosophy to fragment into the study of psychology, "a psychology," insisted James Mark Baldwin, "which is not a metaphysics, nor even a philosophy."[61] Lastly, the claims of moral philosophy to scientific status were resisted, not only as an epistemological intrusion, but as an act of professional aggression. Up until the 1840s, Anglo-American science had been intimately bound up with technology and the culture of what Roy MacLeod has called "the practical man"—the engineer, the mechanic, the inventor. But after mid-century, theoretical scientists struggled to place distance between "the creed of practice" and "the creed of science" (meaning *pure* rather than *applied* science, as articulated by T. H. Huxley, W. S. Jevons, and John Tyndall). The moral philosophers were nothing if not men of "practice," looking to discover a practical ethic; and postbellum scientists rejected their claims to scientific status with the same firm resentment with which they marginalized all other "men of practice."[62] And when in the 1870s, the elite institutions of American higher education came to conceive of themselves as research universities rather than teaching colleges, moral philosophy found itself even more methodologically handicapped, since, in a discipline where the first principles of study were intuited concepts, there was (and could be) nothing upon which to carry out experimentation and research.

Thus, the skeptical Utilitarian lawyer Richard Hildreth, whose *Theory of Morals* reads at many points like an acidic parody of the moral philosophy textbooks, could hope to throw the whole question of moral philosophy's scientific parentage into the shade simply by questioning whether either the epistemology of common sense or the hermeneutics of analogy had any reality:

> So long and so far as there is a perfect coincidence between what is called the reason, conscience, moral sense, or moral sentiment of all men, like that which exists in the perception of forms, colors, sounds, this theory answers sufficiently well. But it is precisely because there are great differences among men upon questions of morals, that the nature or law of moral distinctions becomes an object of such anxious inquiry. What we want is some text by which to distinguish, in cases of dispute, what is Right, and what is Wrong. But so long as each man appeals to his own particular Reason, his own particular conscience, his own particular moral sentiment, as the ultimate and infallible tribunal, just as he appeals to his eye in matters of color . . . no such test does, or can, exist. All consciences do not agree, like all ears and all eyes.[63]

Hildreth's sense that analogy might not work in quite the way the moral philosophers expected was already manifest in the 1840s in a series of quasi-scientific enthusiasms that boded nothing good for the integrity of moral philosophy. Phrenology, for instance, which tried to establish direct correlations between "character" and the physical outline of the cranium, offered a dramatic shortcut toward understanding human moral attributes simply by dropping out the need for analogies between physical and human nature and reading physical nature *as* human nature. A similar threat emerged from polygenetic racism, which did by means of racial distinctions what craniums had done for the phrenologists, that is, fuse the identity of human moral nature with simple differences in human physical nature, without the introspective need to consult a moral sense.[64] And this hardly begins to describe the difficulties posed to the serenity of academic moral philosophy by the general psychological traumas of the American Civil War, by the evidence of radical cultural (and ethical) diversity offered through the experience of colonialism, the appeal to liberal industrialism of Comte and Herbert Spencer (who were able to offer an alternative path to a "science" of social conduct), or the emergence of prehistoric anthropology arising from mid-nineteenth-century discoveries of archaic human remains in the Rhine valley and Belgium. The ultimate blow against analogy came, of course, in 1859, with Darwin's *Origin of Species*, not so much because it offered a radically new approach to understanding human origins, but because it so effectively catalyzed an already existing movement toward dispensing with the analogies of the natural theologians and moral philosophers, and gradually restricting them instead in utilitarian terms to the gradual development of species.[65] The evolutionism in Robert Chambers's notorious *Vestiges of the Natural History of Creation* (1844), for instance, was clearly aimed at critiquing the principle of analogy, and confining it entirely to the natural realm (as in "a very interesting analogy" Chambers found "between the mental characters of types in the quinary system of zoology and the characters of individual men").[66] Darwin's accomplishment was to break down the bridge of analogy completely. As Adam Sedgwick complained to Darwin after reading *The Origin of Species*:

> 'Tis the crown and glory of organic science that it *does*, through *final cause*, link material to moral. . . . You have ignored this link; and, if I do not mistake your meaning, you have done your best in one or two pregnant cases to break it. Were it possible (which, thank God, it is not) to break it, humanity, in my mind, would suffer a damage that might brutalize it, and sink the human race into a lower grade of degradation than any into which it has fallen since its written records tell us of its history.[67]

Sedgwick, of course, was wrong. Alexander Bain and James and John Stuart Mill, in the process of wrecking the reputation of Scottish realism, had already set out the beginnings of a purely associationalist psychology that easily outpaced the Scots in its reduction of all mental phenomena to empirically generated ideas, and all moral notions to simple association rather than the operation of an autonomous "moral sense." The influences of the Bain, Mill, and, Mill triangle in British philosophy, along with Darwin's evolutionism, were brought together in the early 1870s in America in the earliest version of pragmatism, and from that developed a dramatically new concept of the mind as an associative organ that, under the necessity to adapt itself to its changing environment, seeks out, not an abstract moral good, but whatever will relieve the "irritation" of doubt and inquiry.[68] Though Laurens Perseus Hickok might protest, impotently, that "these illustrations and analogical indications that life in its transformations comes in by evolution are illusive," it did no good.[69] The young Josiah Royce (the son of an itinerant Disciples of Christ preacher) remembered in the early 1870s how "with failing at heart" he rejected the arguments from analogy and moral sense that he heard from ministers around the infant University of California and bowed to "the modern theory of evolution as the real truth of nature." From 1873 until 1889, William James successfully campaigned to ease Francis Bowen out of the teaching of philosophy of Harvard; by 1908, when John Dewey collaborated with James Tufts in producing a textbook on ethics for the "American Science Series," all mention of analogy and moral philosophy had been effaced by pragmatism and social democracy.[70]

Still, moral philosophy's troubles were not merely a matter of certain intellectual challenges; what may have been its greatest flaw was its habit of making promises it could not keep. The easy access that the moral sense provided to what was right and what was wrong, and the triumphant assurance provided by analogy that these rights and wrongs were as immovable as the laws of nature, suggested a kind of radical moral absolutism that few of the moral philosophers, remote in their collegiate classrooms, showed much stomach for in practice. The unfettered operation of the moral sense, predicted Mark Hopkins, "can thus vindicate the supremacy of the moral nature, and, instead of a sweltering and chaotic mass of moral corruption, tending to a corruption still deeper, can cause society to present the order and beauty of the planetary spheres." But on the clearest question of moral contest in the American nineteenth century, slavery, the moral philosophers fell unaccountably silent, or betrayed a confusion that itself belied the unanimity of a moral sense. Joseph Haven confidently announced in 1859 that "Whatever enactment of human authority conflicts with this prior and supreme law" of moral sense "carries with it, at the bar of conscience, no power of obligation." And among those enactments thus lacking in obligation was slavery, for "slavery is a wrong, inasmuch as it not only deprives the slave of his natural right of self-disposal and control, but *subjects him to the lawless will of a master.*"[71] But Haven lifted no voice on behalf of abolition, nor did Mark Hopkins, Francis Bowen, or Noah Porter. Francis Wayland personally condemned slavery, but he weakly pleaded that "as citizens of the United States, we have no power whatever either to abolish slavery in the Southern States; or to do any thing, of which the *direct intention* is to abolish it . . . Whether slavery be bad or good, we wash our hands of it, inasmuch as it is a matter which the providence of God has never placed within our jurisdiction."[72] Moral philosophy claimed to have found an unambiguous stance for ethics in the moral sense that could transcend the factionalism and secularism of the republic; but when Wayland beheld the violent passions that the slavery debate unleashed, it was precisely the factionalism and secularism of the republic that he insisted forbade him from speaking.

Slavery was only the beginning of a series of public moral conflicts, extending into the goatish greed of the Gilded Age, for which the moral philosophers proposed only the most limited and personal solutions, despite their discipline's overweening claims to universally self-evident answers. And as those problems mutated, so did the self-perception of the purpose of moral philosophy. By the 1870s, moral philosophy, which had been fashioned as a means for outflanking the agnosticism of the republican ideology, now found itself, as Wayland did on slavery, justifying republicanism from the threat of radical change. The external pressure of that shift only added weight to the developing unsureness moral philosophy exuded concerning its scientific credentials. Unable to rationalize these contradictions and inconsistencies, and with analogy no longer able to bear significant scientific freight, and with social control rather than internalized virtue acquiring a higher premium among the managerial elites of industrial America, moral philosophy hemorrhaged legitimacy; by 1890, it had yielded all but the smallest corners of American academe to "the new psychology" of Wundt, Helmholtz, J. B. Watson, and William James, emptied of all significant religious or metaphysical content.[73]

And yet, if the claims of the moral philosophers to scientific universality fall somewhere short of legitimacy, theirs was still, like Icarus's, an important failure. The moral philosophers forced upon their hearers and readers an inescapable sense of their moral nature as human beings, and with it the need to order their lives on a plane considerably higher than the hedonism and indifference that their successors, pragmatism and psychology, ended up so dismally condoning.[74] "An education which looks only at the practical, may help to fill the purse, but it can never enrich the mind," warned Frederic Henry Hedge, in a puff of pedagogic idealism that seems almost admirably quaint beside the cynical accommodations of Social Darwinism or Deweyan pragmatism. "It can never impart that dignity of character, that respect for our intellectual nature, that veneration for the beautiful and the good, that zeal for improvement, that longing after the infinite, to impart which, is the true object of all education."[75] And yet these were exactly the qualities that Progressive critics of the Gilded Age, and the public philosophers of both the Left and the Right in the twentieth century, lamented losing to modernity and secularism. In that respect, Francis Wayland's moral blink in the face of slavery appears to us no less drastic than Dewey's shameless embrace of jingoism in 1917 and even more shameless neutralism in 1941.[76]

The moral philosophers also had, whatever their other inconsistencies, a clear conception of the universe as an integrated system of moral and natural law, and human society as an organism that had to conform to the intuitive dictates of moral duty. They dealt unashamedly in virtues, not mere "values," and the middle-class moralism that they seem (to us) to have championed was uttered, not as a means of controlling a resentful and rebellious working class, but of restraining a middle class becoming more relaxed and permissive as the nineteenth century wore on.[77] They were, no doubt, foundationalists, but it was a remarkably democratic foundationalism, rooted in the analogical interconnectedness of a universalized human nature with physical nature, rather than in aristocratic elitism or Burkean tradition. It was not Royce or Peirce or Dewey who first questioned the influence of atomistic individualism on American thought and society, but James Harris Fairchild, attacking the "extravagance of individualism, springing from our progressive democracy," and Laurens Perseus Hickok, urging that "that is the best government and those the best statutes which will best bind individuals and nations together as a brotherhood of fellowhelpers."[78] Royce's philosophy of "loyalty," and even Dewey's cooperative democracy were, in that light, not so much bold proposals for the future as a wistful effort to salvage a notion of moral community from the wreckage of a system they had done so much to demolish.

Above all, moral philosophy left open, for the last time in modern times, the avenue by which science could still join hands with doxology, in what Theodore Dwight Bozeman dared to call "an ennobling enterprise" that discovered living purpose and joy in the humblest of minds.[79] True, they feared and resented the mechanistic implications of Enlightenment science, but they did not fear the scientific endeavor itself; and even if their avowed dedication to scientific impartiality in the investigation of human action did not go unmixed with less objective desires for cultural hegemony, the practice (not to say the theory) of science in the twentieth century has permanently disabused us of the notion that evolutionary concepts of human conduct are any freer of those desires. It was, and has been, the lament of evolutionary humanism that it gave no joy, and less humanity, to America than it had at the hands of the moral philosophers.[80] Inscribed on the wall of the Harvard Memorial Church is a memorial to Andrew Preston Peabody: "he moved among the Teachers and Students of Harvard College and wist not that his face shone." No one that I know ever said the like of William James.

NOTES

1. Hall, "Philosophy in the United States," in *Mind* 4 (January 1879), pp. 90, 93. William James made a similar complaint in an 1876 article in *The Nation*, where he complained that "metaphysical thought" in American colleges "has always been haunted by the consciousness of the religious orthodoxy of the country, and either assiduously sought to harmonize itself therewith, or, if skeptical in character, it has been trammeled and paralyzed and made petty by the invidious presence of this polemic bias" ("The Teaching of Philosophy in our Colleges," in *Works of William James: Essays in Philosophy*, ed. F. H. Burkhardt et al. [Cambridge, MA: Harvard University Press, 1978], volume 5, p. 3). John Dewey, in an 1886 "Inventory of Philosophy Taught in American Colleges," had much the same judgment to make: "The philosophic discipline of the ordinary American college is a survival of that period of its existence when its especial deed was to furnish to the community well-fortified ministers of the gospel" (*John Dewey: The Early Works, 1882–1898*, ed. Jo Ann Boydston [Carbondale, Ill.: Southern Illinois University Press, 1969], p. 116).

2. Mark Noll, *The Scandal of the Evangelical Mind* (Grand Rapids, Mich.: Eerdmans, 1994), 95–99.

3. Addams, *Twenty Years at Hull-House, With Autobiographical Notes* (1910; New York: New American Library, 1981), p. 48.

4. Peabody, *Harvard Graduates Whom I Have Known* (Boston: Houghton, Mifflin, 1890), pp. 130–31.

5. Henry Power, in Richard Olson, *Science Deified and Science Defied: The Historical Significance of Science in Western Culture* (Berkeley, Calif.: University of California Press, 1990), volume 2, p. 31; J. R. Jacob, *Robert Boyle and the English Revolution* (New York: B. Franklin, 1977), pp. 159–76.

6. Bayle, "Paulicians," in *Historical and Critical Dictionary: Selections*, ed. Richard H. Popkin (Indianapolis, Ind.: Bobbs-Merrill, 1965), pp. 175, 193.

7. Henry F. May, *The Enlightenment in America* (New York: Oxford University Press, 1976), p. 330; "Letter XVIII from the Reverend Ashbel Green, D. D.," in William B. Sprague, *Lectures on Revivals of Religion* (1832; rept. Edinburgh: Banner of Truth Trust, 1978), p. 131.

8. Fred J. Hood, *Reformed America: The Middle and Southern States, 1783–1837* (University, Ala.: University of Alabama Press, 1980), pp. 5–26; Lawrence A. Cremin, *American Education: The National Experience, 1783–1876* (New York: Harper and Row, 1980), p. 2.

9. Porter, *Elements of Moral Science, Theoretical and Practical* (New York: Scribner, 1885), p. 2; Hopkins, *The Law of Love and Love as a Law; or, Moral Science, Theoretical and Practical* (New York: Scribner, 1869), p. 29. On the various uses of the term "moral philosophy"

and its special relationship to psychology, see K. E. Wetmore, "The Evolution of Psychology from Moral Philosophy in the Nineteenth Century American College Curriculum" (unpublished Ph.D. dissertation, University of Chicago, December 1991), p. 4ff.

10. Stearns, "Address," in *Opening of Walker Hall, Amherst College, Amherst, Mass., October 20, 1870* (Boston: Rand, Avery and Frye, 1871), p. 10.

11. Marsh, "Remarks on Psychology," in *The Remains of the Rev. James Marsh, D. D.* (1843; Port Washington, N.Y.: Kennikart Press, 1971), p. 242.

12. Hopkins, *An Outline Study of Man; or, the Body and Mind One System* (New York: Scribner, 1878), p. 280.

13. Benjamin Peirce, *A History of Harvard University, From its Foundation, in the Year 1636, to the Period of the American Revolution* (Cambridge, Mass.: Brown, Short-tuck 1833), pp. 201–02.

14. Hopkins, *The Law of Love*, p. 117.

15. Wayland, "The Philosophy of Analogy," in *American Philosophic Addresses, 1700–1900*, ed. Joseph L. Blau (New York: Columbia University Press, 1946), p. 357.

16. Emerson, *Moral Education: A Lecture Delivered at New Bedford, August 16, 1842, before the American Institute of Instruction* (Boston: Fowle and Copen, 1842), p. 4.

17. Peabody, *The Positive Philosophy: An Oration Delivered before the Phi Beta Kappa Society of Amherst College, July 9, 1867* (Boston: Gould and Lincoln, 1867), p. 8.

18. Elizabeth Flower and Murray Murphey, *A History of Philosophy in America* (New York: Putnam, 1977), volume 1, p. 236; G. Stanley Hall, "On the History of American College Textbooks and Teaching in Logic, Ethics, Psychology and Allied Subjects," in *Proceedings of the American Antiquarian Society* 9 (April 1894), pp. 145–46.

19. Richards, "On Creation," in *Lectures on Mental Philosophy and Theology* (New York: M. W. Dadd, 1844), p. 189.

20. Finney, *Lectures on Systematic Theology* (Oberlin: J. M. Fitch, 1846), volume 1, p. 27, and *Lectures to Professing Christians, Delivered in the City of New York in the Years 1837 and 1837* (New York: J. S. Taylor, 1837), p. 143.

21. Haven, *Moral Philosophy: Including Theoretical and Practical Ethics* (Boston: Gould and Lincoln, 1859), p. 70.

22. Beecher, in *Autobiography, Correspondence, etc. of Lyman Beecher, D. D.* (New York: Harper, 1865), volume 2, p. 175.

23. Daniel Walker Howe, *The Unitarian Conscience: Harvard Moral Philosophy, 1805–1861* (Cambridge, Mass.: Harvard University Press, 1970), p. 32; Herman Hovenkamp, *Science and Religion in America, 1800–1860* (Philadelphia: University of Pennsylvania Press, 1978), pp. 19–20; Ralph Henry Gabriel, *Religion and Learning at Yale: The Church of Christ in the College and the University, 1757–1957* (New Haven, Conn.: Yale University Press, 1958), pp. 65–77.

24. Levi Hedge, *Elements of Logick; or a Summary of the General Principles and Different Modes of Reasoning* (Buffalo, N.Y.: Phinney and Co., 1855), p. 83; F. H. Hedge, *An Introductory Lecture Delivered at the Opening of the Bangor Lyceum, November 15th, 1836* (Bangor, Maine: Nourse and Smith, 1836), p. 10.

25. Wayland, "Theoretical Atheism," in *Sermons Delivered in the Chapel of Brown University* (Boston: Gould, 1849), p. 10.

26. Hedge, *Elements of Logick*, p. 83.

27. Wayland, "Theoretical Atheism," p. 10; and "The Philosophy of Analogy," p. 348.

28. McCosh, *Realistic Philosophy Defended in a Philosophic Series* (New York: Macmillan, 1887), p. 6.

29. Tappan, *The Doctrine of the Will Determined by an Appeal to Consciousness* (New York: Wiley and Putnam, 1840), pp. 166–67.

30. McCosh, *Realistic Philosophy*, p. 39.

31. Hopkins, *The Law of Love*, pp. 34–35.

32. Walker, "The Philosophy of Man's Spiritual Nature," in *Reason, Faith and Duty: Sermons Preached Chiefly in the College Chapel* (Boston: Roberts Brothers, 1877), p. 54.

33. Hickok, "Course of Lectures Comprising a Body of Systematic Theology Delivered to the Middle Class of Auburn Theological Seminary, 1850–51," in L. P. Hickok Papers, Amherst College Archives, Amherst, Massachusetts.

34. Porter, *Elements of Moral Science*, pp. 113–14.

35. Haven, *Mental Philosophy: Including the Intellect, Sensibilities, and Will* (Boston: Gould and Lincoln, 1871), p. 262.

36. Hopkins, *Lectures on Moral Science Delivered before the Lowell Institute* (Boston, 1872), p. 228; Finney, "The Inner and the Outer Revelation," in *The Oberlin Evangelist* (February 15, 1854), p. 25.

37. Fairchild, *Elements of Theology, Natural and Revealed* (Oberlin: E. J. Goodrich, 1892), pp. 96–97.

38. Peirce, *Address of Professor Benjamin Peirce, President of the American Association* [for the Advancement of Science] *for the Year 1853, on Retiring from the Duties as President* (n.p., 1853), p. 11.

39. Hopkins, *The Law of Love*, p. 331.

40. Dagg, *Manual of Theology, In Two Parts* (Charleston, S.C.: Southern Baptist Publication Society, 1859), p. 119.

41. Porter, *The Elements of Intellectual Science* (New York: Scribner, 1871), p. 523.

42. McCosh, *The Method of the Divine Government, Physical and Moral* (New York: Robert Carter, 1851), p. 197.

43. Felton, *An Address Pronounced on the Anniversary of the Concord Lyceum, November 4, 1829* (Cambridge, Mass.: Hilliard and Brown, 1829), p. 28.

44. McCosh, *Realistic Philosophy*, p. 31; Marsh to Coleridge, March 23, 1839, in *Remains of the Rev. James Marsh*, p. 136; see also James Turner's comment that "seldom in Western Christianity had intuitionist claims loomed so large in belief," in *Without God, Without Creed: The Origins of Unbelief in America* (Baltimore: Johns Hopkins University Press, 1985), p. 105.

45. Bledsoe, *An Essay on Liberty and Slavery* (Philadelphia: Lippincott, 1856), p. 34.

46. Hopkins, *The Law of Love*, pp. 147, 183.

47. Hickok, *A System of Moral Science* (Schenectady, N.Y.: G. Y. Van Debogert, 1853), pp. 94, 266.

48. Wayland, *The Elements of Moral Science* (Boston: Gould and Lincoln, 1851), pp. 165–66.

49. Peirce, "Professor Porter's Human Intellect," in *Writings of Charles S. Peirce: A Chronological Edition*, ed. Edward C. Moore (Bloomington, Ind.: Indiana University Press, 1984), volume 2, pp. 280–81.

50. Dagg, *Manual of Theology*, p. 124.

51. Peabody, *A Manual of Moral Philosophy* (New York: A. S. Barnes, 1873), p. 3.

52. Whedon, *The Freedom of the Will* (New York: Eaton and Mains, 1892), pp. 108–109.

53. Edward H. Madden, "The Reidian Tradition: Growth of the Causal Concept," in *Nature and Scientific Method: Studies in Philosophy and the History of Philosophy, Volume 22*, ed. Daniel O. Dahlstrom (Washington, DC: Catholic University of America Press,

1991), pp. 291–301; Todd L. Adams, "The Commonsense Tradition in America," in *Transactions of the Charles S. Peirce Society* 24 (Winter 1988), pp. 11–13.

54. Haven, *Mental Philosophy*, pp. 539, 541; Fairchild, *Elements of Theology*, pp. 267–68.

55. Alexander, *Outlines of Moral Science* (New York: Scribner, 1860), p. 99; see McCosh, *Psychology: The Motive Powers* (New York: Scribner, 1887), pp. 258–60.

56. Hall, "Philosophy in the United States," p. 105.

57. Stanley M. Guralnick, "Sources of Misconceptions on the Role of Science in the Nineteenth Century American College," in *Science in America since 1820*, ed. Nathan Reingold (New York: Science History Publications, 1976), pp. 48–72.

58. Howe, *Unitarian Conscience*, p. 297; a half-century later, the same appeal to "piety" would be used by Protestant modernists to help weaken the demands of fundamentalists like J. Gresham Machen for intellectual consistency with traditional Protestant confessionalism (George M. Marsden, *Fundamentalism and American Culture: The Shaping of Twentieth-Century Evangelicalism, 1870–1925* [New York: Oxford University Press, 1980], pp. 184–95).

59. Peirce, "The Century's Great Men in Science," in *New York Evening Post* (January 12, 1901).

60. Richard Yeo, "An Idol in the Marketplace: Baconianism in Nineteenth-Century Britain," in *History of Science* 23 (June 1985), pp. 251–58; and Yeo, *Defining Science: William Whewell, Natural Knowledge and Public Debate in Early Victorian Britain* (Cambridge: Cambridge University Press, 1993), pp. 182–84, 250.

61. Baldwin, *Handbook of Psychology: Feeling and Will* (New York: H. Holt, 1891), p. iii.

62. MacLeod, "The Practical Man: Myth and Metaphor in Anglo-Australian Science," in *Australian Cultural History* 8 (1989), pp. 28–29, 30–34; see also Nicholaas A. Rupke, *Richard Owen: Victorian Naturalist* (New Haven, Conn.: Yale University Press, 1994), pp. 325–32.

63. Hildreth, *Theory of Morals: An Inquiry Concerning the Law of Moral Distinctions* (Boston: Little and Brown, 1844), p. 3.

64. Bozeman, *Protestants in an Age of Science: The Baconian Ideal and Ante-bellum American Religious Thought* (Chapel Hill: University of North Carolina Press, 1977), pp. 92–94; John M. O'Donnell, *Origins of Behaviorism: American Psychology, 1870–1920* (New York: New York University Press, 1985), p. 75.

65. Peter J. Bowler, *The Non-Darwinian Revolution: Reinterpreting a Historical Myth* (Baltimore: Johns Hopkins University Press, 1988), pp. 4–5.

66. Chambers, *Vestiges of the Natural History of Creation and Other Evolutionary Writings*, ed. James A. Secord (Chicago: University of Chicago Press, 1994), p. 351.

67. Sedgwick, in C. C. Gillespie, *Genesis and Geology: A Study in the Relations of Scientific Thought, Natural Theology, and Social Opinion in Great Britain, 1790–1850* (Cambridge, Mass.: Harvard University Press, 1951, 1969), p. 217.

68. Max Fisch, "Alexander Bain and the Genealogy of Pragmatism," in *Peirce, Semiotic, and Pragmatism*, ed. K. L. Ketner and C. J. W. Kloesel (Bloomington, Ind.: Indiana University Press, 1986), p. 100.

69. Hickok, "Comprehensive Evolution in Three Distinctive Grades," in L. P. Hickok Papers.

70. Howard M. Feinstein, *Becoming William James* (Ithaca, N.Y.: Cornell University Press, 1984), pp. 332–40; D. H. Meyer, *The Instructed Conscience: The Shaping of the American National Ethic* (Philadelphia: University of Pennsylvania Press, 1972), p. 131.

71. Haven, *Moral Philosophy*, pp. 122–23, 276.

72. Wayland, *The Limitations of Human Responsibility* (New York: D. Appleton, 1838), p. 173.

73. O'Donnell, *The Origins of Behaviorism*, pp. 119–21.

74. Daniel G. Wilson, *Science, Community, and the Transformation of American Philosophy, 1860–1930* (Chicago: University of Chicago Press, 1990), pp. 40–42.

75. Hedge, *Bangor Lyceum*, p. 23.

76. John Patrick, Diggins, *The Promise of Pragmatism: Modernism and the Crisis of Knowledge and Authority* (Chicago: University of Chicago Press, 1994), pp. 250–58, 272–75; Robert B. Westbrook, *John Dewey and American Democracy* (Ithaca, N.Y.: Cornell University Press, 1991), pp. 195–212, 510–17.

77. Gertrude Himmelfarb, *The De-Moralizing of Society: From Victorian Virtues to Modern Values* (New York: Knopf, 1995), pp. 28–31, 46.

78. Fairchild, *Moral Philosophy; or, the Science of Obligation* (New York: Sheldon and Co., 1869), p. 324; Hickok, *A System of Moral Science*, rev. Julius H. Seelye (Boston: Ginn. Heath and Co., 1882), p. 130.

79. Bozeman, *Protestants in an Age of Science*, p. 170.

80. Some modern sociologists, such as James Q. Wilson, have attempted to reassert the existence of innate moral sensitivities, such as sympathy, fairness, self-control, and duty, but this time as functions of evolutionary selection, since the possession of these qualities is part of a "particular psychological orientation" that the evolutionary process favors in the struggle for species survival. The difficulties with this reconstruction are, as Wilson acknowledges, that (a) he can specify no "sensory organ" that acts as the medium through which such an evolved "orientation" operates, and (b) this evolutionary "moral sense" describes only the existence of a general "shared moral nature" rather than "a set of moral absolutes" and is therefore "not always and in every aspect of life strong enough to withstand a pervasive and sustained attack." See Wilson, *The Moral Sense* (New York, 1993), pp. 23–24.

13

Toward a Christian Social Science
in Canada, 1890–1930

MICHAEL GAUVREAU
NANCY CHRISTIE

In the almost total absence of the development of the social sciences in Canadian universities before 1920, the Protestant churches served as the primary vehicles by which the social scientific disciplines entered Canadian culture. The enduring dominance of Canadian churches vis-à-vis the universities stood in marked contrast to the American "social gospel" movement which found itself overwhelmed and marginalized by the coincident rise of the social sciences in the universities during the 1890s. Because of the immense authority of Protestantism, the Canadian universities, unlike those in the United States, were extremely conservative in their defense of traditional humanities disciplines and remained astonishingly impervious to the scientism that so characterized American social science disciplines. Historians of Canadian higher education have wholly subscribed to the American pattern and chronology of the secularization of the academy as set forth most notably in the work of Laurence Veysey. Not only has this interpretation come under attack from American religious historians,[1] but as this chapter will demonstrate, such derivative conceptions of the preeminent role of the university in society have ignored the fact that in Canada there existed a close congruence between Christian thought and the social sciences. However, Protestant clergymen in Canada did far more than simply accommodate Christianity to modern social scientific thought. In Canada, Protestantism assumed the leading role in determining the character of the social sciences and maintained this position of strength well into the 1930s.

This uniquely close connection between mainline Protestantism and the social sciences in Canada gave the churches a preeminence in defining the scope and method of the social sciences and thus lent a peculiar cast to the importation of specialized knowledge of social problems from Britain and the United States. The churches' ultimate goal of creating the Kingdom of God on earth meant that they consistently eschewed the more objectivist forms of social science such as behaviorist psychology and value-free sociology in favor of social scientific investigation that, although empirical in its method, was firmly anchored to the pursuit of an ethical standard and the advocacy of a type of reform explicitly animated by the concerns of social Christianity. The power that the church continued to wield over the character and agenda of the social sciences extended not only to the training and employment of social scientists but more importantly to the identification of social problems and to the very definition of a legitimate scope of activity for the social sciences in modern Canada. Only in the later stages of the Depression, after "economic management" and "planning" had become the watchwords of both the political left and right in Canada[2] did university social scientists finally attain greater public authority vis-à-vis the churches.

The ambition of twentieth-century progressive church leaders to construct a reform coalition in which the church would function as the central clearinghouse for research, publicity, and the lobbying for reform legislation had a profound effect on both the intellectual training and social role of the rank-and-file minister. Where before 1900 biblical exegesis provided the intellectual foundation of a ministerial authority that remained largely confined to the institutional church, the new ideal of the minister stressed his wider cultural role as a community leader and thus necessitated the introduction of a new form of intellectual sustenance for Christian faith: modern social science. The historian Ramsay Cook has observed that the central flaw of social Christianity was that it lacked a "systematic intellectual underpinning" and thus failed to acquire the authority either of traditional biblical theology or the supposed rigorous social analysis brought to bear by radical and secular social thinkers.[3] In spite of this pejorative assessment, not only were ministers enjoined to read the works of contemporary Canadian social scientists at the urgent behest of vigilant field-secretaries such as Hugh Dobson in western Canada and Ernest Thomas in the East but they were exposed to a wide range of British and American social philosophy. This allowed Protestant clergymen to articulate a coherent and sophisticated Christian sociology that was instrumental in situating Canadian Protestantism on the cutting edge of the current transatlantic reevaluation of traditional liberalism. Moreover, church leaders believed that the introduction of modern social science was especially crucial in continuing to attract the best and the brightest of young men to the profession in an age when the ministry was experiencing competition from the rising prestige of business, law, and medicine. Through the introduction of the new social sciences, church progressives hoped to refashion the ministry into a more manly and activist profession whose arena was the public sphere of politics. For these church leaders, the creation of social welfare policies would be achieved through the scientific rigor of empirical investigation.

Prior to 1900 Canadian clergymen gracefully sidestepped many of the implications of Darwinism and social evolutionism by situating the wellsprings of Christian faith in a historical theology that saw the development of human civilization not as a natural process but as the fulfillment of divine revelation.[4] This relative lack of interest in the relationship between religion and the natural

sciences displayed by the Victorian clergy changed dramatically on the eve of
the twentieth century. By 1900, clergymen easily integrated social evolutionary
thought into the tenets of evangelicalism largely through their reading of history,
psychology, anthropology, and sociology, disciplines that after 1880 had incre-
mentally absorbed Spencerian and Darwinian notions of human development,
what James R. Moore has termed "Christian Darwinisticism."[5] The consequent
blending of idealist philosophy with evolutionary science led to the breakdown
of traditional compartments between science, morals, and religion. Once Spen-
cerianism shed its dubious associations with positivistic science, its central meta-
physic of society as an organism subject to the natural laws of development was
quickly incorporated into all forms of knowledge that treated the development
of the human mind and civilization.[6]

The popularization of evolutionary thought permeated the religious language
of the progressive age, when Darwinian thought was made accountable to religion largely through Lamarckian ideas of evolution, then in vogue among
scientists and social philsophers, because they were redolent of the older natural
theology and preserved the centrality of divine benevolence and design in both
natural and social evolution. Where Darwin had emphasized the randomness
and the morally blind mechanism of natural selection to explain biological
change, neo-Lamarckians such as Joseph LeConte and Henry Drinker Cope fell
back on the theory of use and disuse that implied that human agency was a
critical factor in determining the direction of evolutionary change. This revision
of Darwin made evolution palatable to an ethical vision of society because unlike
Darwin it was hopeful in suggesting that evolution was purposeful and progressive.[7]

In language resplendent with images borrowed from Victorian natural theology, Rev. W. A. Douglas described, in a pamphlet titled *The Church and Social
Relations*, how "in the testimony of the rocks, in the wondrous mechanism of
the heavens, in the sublimities and the harmonies of the universe, in the mar-
vellous adaptations of the physical forces, in the ineffable potencies of thought
and vitality" God's power was revealed to all classes, and from these fixed dictates of nature Douglas sought out the guiding tenets of twentieth-century social
democracy.[8] The Methodist preacher W. W. Andrews was no less confident
that in the merging of Darwinian science and Christianity, atheism would be
banished altogether from modern culture. Andrews deployed evolutionary
thought to buttress the new social evangelism. In his 1913 pamphlet *Nature and
Self-Sacrifice* he reworked Darwin's theory of the struggle for existence so that it
ultimately refuted Darwin's central idea of competition and conflict over scarce
resources as the mechanism of evolutionary change by contending that human
beings, like societies of plant life, do not "live for themselves" but are inter-
dependent upon "various classes . . . each performing different functions in the
life of the community." Through what he termed "conscious self-sacrifice"
human societies would evolve toward the highest form of life, classless interdependence characterized by social harmony.[9] Rev. Peter Bryce, a postwar
champion of national efficiency, was fascinated by Henri Bergson's theory of
creative evolution because it harkened back to the supreme role of both God

and humans in directing evolutionary social change. Bryce borrowed from Spencer's idea of the superorganic when he stated that "each member of society is a unit going to make up the whole of a complicated organism." For those evangelicals wishing to preserve individual piety within the new dictates of social Christianity, science provided compelling lessons that demonstrated the naturalness of the growth of individual responsibility that flowed in the wake of social development.[10]

Because the assumptions and methods of the social sciences had, by the beginning of the twentieth century, become increasingly informed either directly or indirectly by social evolutionary ideas, the acceptance of neo-Darwinian science by Canadian clergymen was an important intellectual hurdle to be jumped before the mainline Protestant churches could consistently advocate the teaching of the social sciences as the essential equipment of the modern minister. More generally, those Protestant clergymen committed to social Christianity were well apprised of the growing authority conferred on scientific investigation and the possession of specialized knowledge. The Presbyterian leadership, which was the first to advocate training in economics, sociology, and modern industrial problems, recognized that moral exhortation alone would not suffice in the modern world of rapid social change. To ensure their command over the direction of social reform movements, it was incumbent upon the churches to "be raising up a body of *trained and specialized workers*" for in the modern age "expert knowledge" was the only means by which they could garner public support. More importantly, Presbyterian progressives like J. G. Shearer and C. W. Gordon believed that the modern social sciences constituted the most crucial new departure that would revivify the prestige of the clerical profession among ambitious young men.[11]

Astutely aware of how scientific methodology—what he termed the "inductive method"—had come to permeate all areas of modern life, Samuel Dwight Chown, a leading Methodist advocate of social Christianity, impressed upon the Methodist church colleges the urgent necessity of shedding their obsolete commitment to Old Testament theology in favor of courses that would put the minister in "sympathetic touch with the intellectual world" of the modern day, for only through the acquisition of modern knowledge could young probationers be awakened to the wider social implications of their faith. In Chown's estimation, therefore, modern social science would preserve the church's autonomy because rather than replacing Christian faith, it served to amplify the minister's search for those truths that had been revealed in the Bible.[12]

In the estimation of church leaders like Chown, the addition of the social sciences to the intellectual preparation of the Canadian minister was indispensable in carving out a new role for the clergyman as a community leader. And by thus creating a strong civic leadership it was contended that the church's influence would naturally extend into all areas of public policy. Most importantly, these new disciplines conferred upon the Protestant churches an unchallengeable scientific authority that allowed them to capture the agenda and maintain the leadership of social reform movements. John A. Cormie, a persistent advocate of the study of rural sociology in theological colleges, warned church leaders that unless ministers exercised a "virile leadership" by keeping abreast of current scientific knowledge both in agriculture and community social problems, that the church, especially in rural areas, would surrender its function as the molder of public opinion: "A Church which has missed its opportunity of ministering to the social needs of the people cannot expect to retain its place of influence among them, still less to make a large place for itself in the life of the neighbourhood."[13]

Out of the fear for the decline in the church's influence in the community, Protestant progressives consciously recast both the role of the minister and the function of religion in terms which were broadly cultural and extrainstitutional. Under this new rubric, ministers were to become experts in the study of society and in community leadership. C. W. Gordon and J. G. Shearer believed that religion was the central unifying force that mediated between the demands of the state, economic groups and the individual, and thus viewed Rev. Dr. W. A. Riddell's rural survey of Swan River, Manitoba, as a contribution to the building of Christ's dominion on earth.[14] Likewise, Rev. A. E. Smith stated what many progressives contended, that the actual institution of the church was but a means to a larger religious end.[15] By thus making the Kingdom of God coterminous with every facet of human activity and by defining religion in terms of experience rather than ecclesiastical dogma, progressive clergymen sought to break down all distinctions between the sacred and the secular. This intellectual convergence was most cogently adumbrated by J. S. Woodsworth, himself a clergyman, social worker, and later politician, who wrote in 1902 to his cousin C. B. Sissons, later professor of classics at the University of Toronto, that

> the more I think about such matters the more the distinction between sacred and secular diminishes. Theoretically, for me, there is no such distinction. It is artificial, false—the product of a narrow view of life and the product of a withered ecclesiasticism and a more wretched secularism. Practically, the two are so interpenetrating each other, that I am gradually atuning my theoretical position in actual life. A man is called *to live*. Life itself is the greatest responsibility and one which no one can escape.... For if we have the one spirit the difference of gift is a minor consideration.[16]

This perspective on the unity of the sacred and the secular was also voiced in quarters well beyond the purview of the Protestant churches. The founder of the department of political economy at Queen's University, Adam Shortt, expressed the outlook of many Canadian university social scientists in the early twentieth century when he envisioned the principles of modern economics and sociology in terms of a wider elaboration of Christian service. Initially, Shortt believed that teaching Christ's doctrines had to be done exclusively within the formal church, but upon entering his professorial calling, he saw the university as one of the most powerful institutions for extending the Kingdom of God. He maintained that through the study of political economy, his students would learn of "[a] higher & purer nature . . . to which . . . they are primarily responsible. They are responsible to an internal principle . . . more truly divine in origin & nature than the external commands, which are but an imperfect expression of the dictates of this inner nature of man." It was Shortt's conviction that in modern society, personal salvation was contingent upon the individual working to elevate "the highest interests of all others".[17]

The view put forth by the Methodist and Presbyterian progressives that the broader social evangelism erased any distinction between the secular and the sacred was also advanced by the Baptist minister C. A. Dawson, who later taught sociology at McGill University. In taking up his position as director of the McGill School of Social Service, Dawson was implementing his ideal that Christian social endeavor must "organically unite" the church with industrial organizations, schools, and government agencies. In this way, this preacher-sociologist championed the creation of new extrainstitutional pathways that the mainline Protestant churches had established through the application of sociology to modern problems. "The church long ago realized," observed Dawson, "that the field of service and goodwill is more extensive than church organization, and that in social work as a separate instutition it could discover a new ally in achieving the goals of a more abundant life."[18] Dawson's biographer has interpreted his decision to become a professor rather than a clergyman as signaling his loss of Christian belief and of a growing commitment on the part of Canadian universities to the currents of secular thought.[19] However, rather than disrupting the marriage between evangelicalism and social reform, the development of modern social work in Canada was the creation of the expanding authority of the Protestant churches that were the promoters of scientific social work both at the University of Toronto and McGill University.[20] That the professionalization of social work was not inimical to Christian belief was best illustrated by Carl Dawson, one of the prime movers behind organizing the new profession of social work. Dawson castigated those who believed that social science was the adversary of the true functioning of the church. In his view, social scientific investigation could not be sundered from religious faith: "One of the foundations of the Christian faith—one of its fundamentals—is service . . . Social Science is one part of that service." Eschewing traditional theology, Dawson contended that the scientific rigor of sociology and social psychology, with their special knowledge of vice, crime, and the human frailties, provided the most powerful means by which the social service ideal could become part of modern Christian culture. Only by applying social Christianity through social work could the church become, once again, coterminous with the people and "be the relationship between man and his Maker and the foundation of Social Order."[21]

By 1908, as part of a wider program to promote the discussion of social questions within all church-sponsored agencies, the progressive wings of both the Methodist and Presbyterian churches had strongly endorsed the teaching of Christian sociology in the church colleges. This campaign to establish chairs of sociology in these institutions continued well into the 1920s and in contrast to the American example, where sociology emerged as a discipline out of the urban crucible of the 1890s, Canadian sociology grew directly out of explicitly Christian concerns.[22] The first chair of Christian sociology was established at Victoria

College in 1919 and was occupied by Rev. John Walker Macmillan, a Presbyterian minister who had studied political economy at the University of Toronto with W. J. Ashley, an English economist identified with the Christian
reformism of Arnold Toynbee and his social settlement ideal.[23] In 1891, after
attending Knox College, Macmillan was ordained and served 25 years as a minister when he became professor of social ethics and practical theology at the
University of Manitoba. There he forged close links with the well-known champions of labor, Salem Bland and J. S. Woodsworth, and became one of the chief
lecturers in Woodsworth's training class in social work at the University of
Manitoba, a group dominated by Protestant ministers.[24] This Winnipeg model
of teaching the principles of applying New Testament Christianity to child welfare, relief work, the investigation of industrial accidents, and the development
of modern social theories formed the basis for his later sociology courses at
Victoria College in Toronto.[25]

Although best known for introducing Mothers' Allowances in Manitoba and
Ontario and for his later chairmanship of the Ontario Minimum Wage Commission,[26] Macmillan retained the impress of Christian thought in his sociological
views. While undertaking postgraduate work in social ethics at the Union Theological Seminary in New York, Macmillan had his social outlook amplified by
the writings of Washington Gladden and Walter Rauschenbusch, prominent
leaders of the American social gospel whose own thinking was in turn shaped
by current sociological debates.[27] Despite the influence both of Herbert Spencer
and American social Darwinists upon him, Macmillan never doubted the tenets
of Christianity nor veered toward the secular ethics of modern philosophy.
While he advocated the importance of modern social psychology with its stress
upon the interdependence of the individual and the social order, Macmillan
grounded his conception of social progress upon the individual mind as the
primary mechanism of evolution. From Macmillan's perspective, the developmental process was wholly Christian in character because it culminated in the
highest form of the human species, Jesus Christ. Throughout his career Macmillan saw as his principal task the encouragement of sociology in the modern
pulpit. In 1921 he spoke to the Methodist Ministerial Association on "Sociology
and Its Relationship to the Pulpit" and later introduced the "Basic Principles
of Sociology" to the students at the Canadian School of Missions. Even as late
as 1930, Macmillan's growing espousal of government intervention in the sphere
of social welfare remained tempered by his belief that a cooperative society was
anchored upon the primary institutions of the family and the state, wherein the
church remained the critical linchpin between the public and private spheres.[28]
As the careers of Canada's two founding sociologists demonstrate, the essence
of Christian thought was not fundamentally altered by the social sciences.
Rather, because clergymen were the chief promoters of the social sciences, and
occupied the founding chairs in the universities, they, and not secular thinkers,
largely determined the direction and methodology of these new disciplines that
in Canada became tributary to and complimentary of the imperatives of social
Christianity.

There has grown up among Canadian historians such as Ramsay Cook and Richard Allen the notion that Protestant clergymen were cloistered from wider currents of thought, and they have thus concluded that Protestant analyses of contemporary social problems were by extension hopelessly jejune and naive. Such assessments have arisen as a result of an overweening focus upon the thought of American social gospelers Walter Rauschenbusch and Shailer Mathews as the sole intellectual influences. William McGuire King has recently argued that the boundaries between religion and social science were extremely porous well into the 1920s, and that social gospel writers should be viewed as synthesizers of contemporary social science and as critical social thinkers who themselves influenced the shape of academic social science.[29] This interpenetration of religion and social science was no less prominent in Canada, where clergymen were very well informed as to the latest currents in sociology, psychology, and political economy. One of the first decisions taken by both Methodist and Presbyterian departments of evangelism and social service was to invite social scientists such as Robert Magill, professor of political economy at Dalhousie, the Queen's political economists Adam Shortt and O. D. Skelton, and J. W. Macmillan and Robert MacIver of the University of Toronto to recommend a reading list of the latest literature on economics, the history of trade unionism, socialism, and practical sociology.[30] This impressive reading course, which contained the most outstanding works of British and American social science, was intended to form the basis of a curriculum in sociology that progressive leaders hoped to introduce to the church colleges across Canada. Not only did prominent church leaders lobby strenuously for the introduction of chairs of sociology into theological seminaries, but the Presbyterians established a scheme of scholarships that would enable students of the ministry to proceed to New York and Chicago to attend lectures on social questions. In addition Shearer sent copies of the reading course to every Presbyterian minister in the field.[31] The Methodist Church was even more vigilant in ensuring that local ministers applied the insights of modern social science to practical Christianity by having the district field-secretaries, such as Hugh Dobson in Saskatchewan, establish informal reading courses. Dobson was one of the foremost promoters of introducing sociology into the church colleges and accordingly his reading course of 1918 reflected his own interests in the labor problem, public health reform, and rural development. Dobson, in fact, became one of the chief purveyors of the work of the American sociologist E. A. Ross, professor of sociology at the University of Wisconsin, whose own concerns for the closing of the American frontier and the diminution of Anglo-Saxon values under the impact of European immigration struck a responsive chord among Protestant leaders on the Canadian Prairies.[32]

Prior to 1920, progressive clergymen who were preoccupied with the social problems of poverty, industrial unrest, unemployment, and public health turned to the works of English social thinkers and economists who were themselves attempting to reorient traditional laissez-faire liberalism toward the provision of general principles that could be applied to the solution of current social ills.

British sociologists, new liberals, and Fabians shared a commitment to a belief in the empirical investigation of social problems that had as its goal the definition of social values. This was precisely what Canadian church progressives meant when they stated that ministers should follow the example of Arnold Toynbee, the British reform economist and the progenitor of the social settlement ideal, by investigating "the facts of life" in a manner which was "clear, accurate, unbiased, scientific."[33]

Although not explicitly Christian, the new liberal notion that the goals of the individual and society would evolve toward harmonious social cooperation based on self-sacrifice and altruism bespoke a moral fervor and a strongly ethical perspective. The organic view of society espoused by new liberals—what Hobson termed the "moral rational organism"[34]—and its emphasis upon the mutual dependence of individual and society, converged with the social evangelism of Canadian clergymen. In the aftermath of the World War I, the influence of British new liberalism reached its apogee and found its clearest expression in Canada in the reform program of the Protestant churches as outlined in their statements on reconstruction in 1918, which pressed for child welfare laws, minimum wage legislation, social and health insurance, mothers' pensions, schemes of labor democracy such as the Whitley Councils, and the regulation of public utilities. British collectivist thought found immense favor among Canadian clergymen largely because its redefinition of democracy and its notion of positive liberty laid the groundwork for a broad interpretation of the human condition that was inclusive of all social groups,[35] a vision that accorded with the Canadian Protestant mission to found a classless Kingdom of God in Canada.

The counterpart of new liberalism in the United States was progressivism, and shared with it an ameliorative outlook and a focus upon poverty, delinquency, labor relations, and urban ills. Prior to 1920 these social problems acted as the central catalyst for the rise of sociology and the new economics, both of which were preoccupied with the search for order and sought through scientific knowledge the means to redefine progress in light of the social changes wrought by industrialization and immigration. This search for a harmonious liberal society imparted a particularly reformist and activist cast to the temper of American social science.[36] It was a sensibility that converged with the pragmatism of Canadian social Christianity. As late as 1900, the reading of prospective ministers had been dominated by theological and philosophical concerns, but after 1910, the book lists of Canadian clergymen featured the works of Albion Small, Charles Henderson, E. A. Ross, Charles Ellwood, and Richard Ely, the very figures who established the modern discipline of sociology in the United States and who were also responsible for deepening the already close alignment between American Protestantism and the social sciences and for directing the endeavor of sociology toward establishing the Kingdom of God on earth.[37]

One of the first American social scientists to translate the social inequalities of the Gilded Age into a new vision of statist reform was Richard T. Ely. Ely effectively drew upon both the millennial optimism of Christianity and the Protestant emphasis upon the priority of the rights of the organic community over unrestrained individualism to articulate a rigorous critique of capitalism that, more than that of any other social critic of his age, made him sympathetic to socialism. Ely dissented from classical political economy and sought to reorient the guiding principles of the discipline in the direction of the achievement of material abundance, which he viewed as the precursor to a truly harmonious social order.[38] In fact, Ely founded the American Economic Association with the central purpose of using historical economics as a salve for the conflict between capital and labor, and as the scientific basis for Christian reform.

Ely's student, Albion Small, a Baptist minister and founder of the department of sociology at the University of Chicago, brought his Christian outlook to bear upon sociology, which he viewed as the study of the process by which the conflict of social groups was resolved into a higher stage of accommodation and harmony. Small's conception both of social conflict and cooperation emanated directly from his evangelical belief in evil, the recognition of sin, and redemption. The consciousness of social sin was to be attained through the direct scientific observation of social groups in the urban laboratory of Chicago. However, the practical implementation of his sociological tenets was left to his colleague and fellow minister Charles R. Henderson, who to an even greater degree influenced Canadian clergymen. Through his courses in practical sociology given at the divinity school of the University of Chicago, Henderson developed the subdisciplines of criminology, the sociology of deviance, and rural sociology, and was responsible for establishing the investigation of social groups in their natural setting, a later preoccupation of the more celebrated sociologists of the "Chicago School," Robert Park and Ernest Burgess.[39]

However, the American sociologist whose views most directly mirrored the concerns of Canadian Protestant progressives was E. A. Ross, professor of sociology at the University of Wisconsin, whose theory of social control was an important counterweight to the dominance of the Smallian tradition at the University of Chicago.[40] His greatest contribution to Canadian Protestantism, however, lay in his skepticism concerning the naturalness of man's social state. Ross applied loosely Darwinian ideas of evolution to human society, but to an even greater degree than either Ely or Small, he was anxious to preserve the independence of individual behavior within the overwhelming presence of social or group interests in modern society, what he called "social ascendancy."[41] Guided less by a faith in Christian idealism, which tended to see a harmonious confluence between individual and society, Ross saw in the modern social state an artificial compulsion toward conformity. Having been raised a Presbyterian in the rural precincts of Iowa, Ross reacted against modern legalistic controls and sought the more natural and traditional bonds of opinion and custom, whereby those subtle psychological wellsprings of community life drew individuals together harmoniously. While like Small and Ely, Ross used his sociology to critique the acquisitive individualism of modern capitalism, the guiding principle of his thought was the recapturing of the liberal millennium that preserved the sanctity of individual free will, which Ross feared was being extinguished with the closing of the American frontier. Ross's overweening desire to preserve individualism in the face of modern social pressures was an issue with which Canadian clergymen also wrestled. Despite Ross's intellectual shedding of his evangelical origins, his notion that the chaotic drift of modern society could be arrested only through the inner psychological control located in the individual moral being had obvious affinities with the pietistic underpinnings of Protestantism. More importantly Ross's idea that social control was ultimately founded upon public opinion led him to a definition of "social religion," which he saw as the preeminent sanction for any communal order because it was based upon both the unity of man and the fatherhood of God. Like Canadian progressive clergymen who read his works, Ross rejected theological disputation, but retained a commitment to the beneficial agency of social Christianity in preserving liberal values amidst the complexities of modern society.[42]

By the end of World War I the injunction to make the social sciences the centerpiece of the education of modern clergymen was heeded by an ever-growing number of young Methodist and Presbyterian men who sought the ministerial profession as a means to express their commitment to social reconstruction. The ideal of a scientifically trained Christian leadership within the burgeoning social welfare organizations was realized when the Social Service Council of Canada was created in 1908. This research body was the offspring of the Protestant churches and until the late 1930s, when it foundered due to internal conflicts and financial constraints, it fulfilled a role comparable to that of the American Social Science Research Council, the National Bureau of Economic Research, and the large philanthropic foundations such as Rockefeller and Carnegie. What is distinctive about Canadian social research in this period was that it was not formulated primarily by university social scientists, but by clergymen who, like Claris Silcox, J. R. Mutchmor, and T. R. Robinson, had all studied in the United States. While American and Canadian "social gospel" clergymen articulated similar views regarding social reform, American clergymen never succeeded in usurping leadership of social reform largely because of the power of universities, independent secular reform organizations, and government institutions, all of which funded social research. By contrast, in Canada, where university departments of social science remained marginal until the World War II and there was a dearth of large philanthropic organizations with independent means and a government bureaucracy devoted to collection of social data, Protestant clergymen assumed a preponderant role in the arena of social policy creation. Significantly, even when university academics became involved in the creation of government social policy during the 1930s, they did so only under the auspices of the church-dominated Social Service Council.

It has become commonplace for historians to view the development of modern social policy in Canada as the product of the intersection of an elite cadre of university academics within the federal bureaucracy.[43] By focusing their attention upon the spate of welfare legislation introduced in the late 1930s and 1940s, these historians have too narrowly conceived the arena of policy making in terms of the legislative process alone, and have thereby ignored the important contribution of private bodies such as the Social Service Council of Canada, which were crucial catalysts both in creating a climate of opinion conducive to an increasingly interventionist state and in providing the social data indispensable to the creation of that policy. Between 1908 and 1935, the Social Service Council served as the research arm of both federal and provincial government by conducting social investigation of rural problems, immigration, child welfare, and unemployment. It consistently pressured both levels of government to implement legislation protecting the welfare of women and children, and general measures of comprehensive unemployment and health insurance appropriate for a modern society.[44] In truth, the Social Service Council lived up to its motto of being a clearinghouse for the modern state.

Far from being swept aside by the secular tendencies of modern thought, as many have argued, the Protestant churches in Canada were the chief exponents of the social sciences and the prime movers behind such "secular" institutions as the Canadian Council on Economic and Social Research. And far from being weak and marginal institutions who abjured modernism, the Protestant churches in Canada remained at the forefront of social science research between 1900 and 1930 and were essential to the transformation of government policy making by being among the first bodies to argue for the systematic collection and interpretation of social data. In their role as patrons, rather than as clients of the social sciences, Canada's Protestant churches demonstrated that, far from being hidebound and archaic bastions of traditionalism, they were the major conduits for embedding modern values into the wider culture.

NOTES

1. See George M. Marsden and Bradley J. Longfield, eds., *The Secularization of the Academy* (New York: Oxford University Press, 1992). For the traditional interpretation, see Laurence Veysey, *The Emergence of the American University* (Chicago: University of Chicago Press, 1965); and A. B. McKillop, *Matters of Mind: The University in Ontario, 1791–1951* (Toronto: University of Toronto Press, 1994).

2. The impact of the idea of "planning" on both social scientists and federal politics in Canada has been described by Doug Owram, *The Government Generation: Canadian Intellectuals and the State, 1900–1945* (Toronto: University of Toronto Press, 1986), chaps. 7 and 8; and Michiel Horn, *The League for Social Reconstruction: Intellectual Origins of the Democratic Left in Canada, 1930–42* (Toronto: University of Toronto Press, 1980).

3. See Ramsay Cook, "Francis Marion Beynon and the Crisis of Christian Reformism," in Carl Berger and Ramsay Cook, eds., *The West and the Nation: Essays in Honour of W. L. Morton* (Toronto: McLelland and Stewart, 1976), 203–4.

4. See Michael Gauvreau, *The Evangelical Century: College and Creed in English Canada from the Great Revival to the Great Depression* (Montreal and Kingston: McGill-Queen's University Press, 1991), 284–91.

5. Nancy J. Christie, " 'Prophecy and the Principles of Social Life': Historical Writing and the Making of New Societies in Canada and Australia, 1880–1920," Ph.D. thesis, University of Sydney, 1987; Christie, "Psychology, Sociology and the Secular Moment: The Ontario Educational Association's Quest for Authority, 1880–1900," *Journal of Canadian Studies*, 25:2 (summer 1990), 119–43; James R. Moore, *The Post-Darwinian Controversies: A Study of the Protestant Struggle to Come to Terms with Darwin in Great Britain and America, 1870–1900* (Cambridge: Cambridge University Press, 1979), 218–51.

6. James T. Kloppenberg, *Uncertain Victory: Social Democracy and Progressivism in European and American Thought, 1870–1920* (New York: Oxford University Press, 1986), 26,

140; Robert B. Westbrook, *John Dewey and American Democracy* (Ithaca: Cornell University Press, 1991), 11–21. For the importance of Spencer in American social scientific thought, see Robert C. Bannister, *Social Darwinism: Science and Myth in Anglo-American Social Thought* (Philadelphia: Temple University Press, 1979); Dorothy Ross, *The Origins of American Social Science* (Cambridge: Cambridge University Press, 1991).

7. For the popularity of neo-Larmarckism in the early twentieth century, see Peter J. Bowler, *Evolution: The History of an Idea* (Berkeley: University of California Press, 1984), 243–53; Bannister, *Social Darwinism*, 137–42; James R. Moore, *The Post-Darwinian Controversies: A Study of the Protestant Struggle to Come to Terms with Darwin in Great Britain and America, 1870–1900*, 217–51; David N. Livingstone, *Darwin's Forgotten Defenders: The Encounter Between Evangelical Theology and Evolutionary Thought* (Grand Rapids, Michigan: William B. Eerdmans, 1987); Robert J. Richards, *Darwin and the Emergence of Evolutionary Theories of Mind and Behavior* (Chicago: Chicago University Press, 1987). For the blending of Lamarckian and Darwinian ideas in anthropology and geography, see Nancy J. Christie, "Environment and Race: Geography's Search for a Darwinian Synthesis," in Roy MacLeod and P. F. Rehbock, eds., *Darwin and the Pacific* (Honolulu: University of Hawaii Press, 1994).

8. W. A. Douglas, *The Church and Social Relations* (pamphlet, DESS, #36, n.d.), n.p. United Church Archives (UCA) University of Toronto, Dobson Papers, Box A2, file G.

9. W. W. Andrews, *Nature and Self-Sacrifice: A Study* (pamphlet, June 1913), 3–9. UCA, Dobson Papers, Box A2, file G.

10. "National Social Efficiency," Presidential Address, Canadian Conference on Public Welfare, 25 Sept. 1917, Ottawa, 4–9. UCA, Dobson Papers, Box A6, file C.

11. "Minutes of the Meeting of the Executive." UCA, Presbyterian Church, Board of Moral and Social Reform, 16 Nov. 1910; Ibid., 9 Sept. 1908.

12. "Address to the Ecumenical Conference, Toronto, The Adaptation of the Church to the Needs of Modern Life," 10 Oct. 1911. UCA, Chown Papers, Box 11, file 294; "Extract from the Annual Report of the Department of Temperance and Moral Reform of the Methodist Church, 1908," UCA, Chown Papers, Box 1, file 1. According to David Hollinger, the "social gospel" of Christian social reform and the "intellectual gospel" of applying modern science to industrial and social problems, although rivals for cultural authority, in fact dovetailed in the early twentieth century: the former provided religious sanction for reform and the latter considered the production of the new knowledge as a "religious mission." See Hollinger, "Justification by Verification: The Scientific Challenge to the Moral Authority of Christianity in Modern America," in Michael J. Lacey, ed., *Religion and Twentieth Century American Intellectual Life* (Cambridge: Cambridge University Press, 1989), 116–35.

13. "Some Problems of Rural Life in Canada," n.d., 18, 26–27. UCA, University of Winnipeg, John A. Cormie Papers, PP6, folder F.

14. J. G. Shearer to C. W. Gordon, 17 Oct. 1914. University of Manitoba Archives, C. W. Gordon Papers, Box 17, folder 5; "The Inner Side of Christian Life and Service," sermon, n.d. University of Manitoba Archives, C. W. Gordon Papers, Box 29, folder 2.

15. "Autobiography," UCA, A. E. Smith Papers, 222.

16. J. S. Woodsworth to C. B. Sissons, 14 Feb. 1902. National Archives of Canada (NAC), MG 27 III F3, C. B. Sissons Papers, Vol. 5.

17. Adam Shortt to Elizabeth Smith, 14 Aug. 1883. University of Waterloo, Department of Special Collections, Elizabeth Smith Shortt Papers, Box 20, file 310.

18. C. A. Dawson, "Social Work as a National Institution," Presidential Address at the Canadian Conference on Social Work, Montreal, April 24–27, *Social Welfare*, 10:10, July 1928, 225–26. For a similar view, see "The Sociological Man," n.d., UCA, Samuel Dwight Chown Papers, Box 13, file 377.

19. See Marlene Shore, *The Science of Social Redemption: McGill, the Chicago School, and the Origins of Social Research in Canada* (Toronto: University of Toronto Press, 1987).

20. For Allen's belief that the professionalization of social work marked the displacement of the Protestant churches, see *The Social Passion: Religion and Social Reform in Canada, 1914–28* (Toronto: University of Toronto Press, 1971), 240–41, 284, 294–95. For a larger discussion of the primary role of the Protestant churches in the founding of schools of social work in Canada, see Nancy Christie and Michael Gauvreau, *"A Full-Orbed Christianity": The Protestant Churches and Social Welfare in Canada, 1900–1940* (Montreal and Kingston: McGill-Queen's University Press, 1996), chap. 4.

21. "Science Spoiled Christian Faith," *Montreal Star* , 25 Oct. 1922; C. A. Dawson, "Why a Canadian National Conference of Social Work?" Memorandum, n.d. NAC, MG 28 I10, Canadian Council on Social Development, Vol. 30, file 150, "Canadian Association of Social Workers, 1927."

22. "Extract from the Annual Report of the Department of Temperance and Moral Reform of the Methodist Church, 1908." UCA, Chown Papers, Box 1, file 1; Rev. Trevor Davies to William Creighton Graham, 16 Feb. 1927. UCA, United Church Commission on Courses of Study Records, 1926–28, 82.008, Box 1, file 3; A. E. Hewell, Department of Extension, University of Alberta to Graham, 8 Mar. 1927. UCA, Chown Papers, Box 1, file 3.

23. Ashley was a strong advocate of the application of economics to public policy. See Alfred Marshall to Cannan, 22 Sept. 1902. Edwin Cannan Papers, London School of Economics. Ashley was one of the early British promoters of economics as a tool for the solution of social problems and at Oxford was closely associated with collectivist social philosophers such as L. T. Hobhouse, D. G. Ritchie, M. E. Sadler and W. A. S. Hewins, later director of the LSE. See Edwin Cannan Minutebook. Oxford University, Bodleian Library, Oxford University Economic Papers, 1886–91. The society was founded in Ashley's college rooms 20 Oct. 1886. For Ashley's links with Arnold Toynbee, see Alon Kadish, *The Oxford Economists in the Late Nineteenth Century* (Oxford: Clarendon Press, 1982), 42–50.

24. "Report of the Hon. Secretary-Treasurer to the Board of Management of the Winnipeg Training Class in Social Work," 28 Sept. 1914. NAC, Woodsworth Papers, Vol. 2. This alliance between Christianity and social investigation became the matrix of Woodsworth's later work for the Bureau of Social Research. See "Bureau of Social Research, Governments of Manitoba, Saskatchewan and Alberta, Report of First Year's Work," 6 Dec. 1916. NAC, Woodsworth Papers, Vol. 15, file 7. Following Cook, Allen Mills has portrayed this period in Woodsworth's life as his transition to secular social philosophy. See *Fool for Christ: The Political Thought of J. S. Woodsworth* (Toronto: University of Toronto Press, 1989), 38–43.

25. John Walker Macmillan. University of Toronto Archives (UTA), Department of Graduate Records, A73/0026/292(51), Biographical Files; "Heard in College Halls," *Toronto Telegram* , 13 May 1919; "Death of Professor J. W. Macmillan," *Social Welfare* , 14:7, April–May, 1932, 123. Born 26 Sept. 1868, Macmillan later served as chaplain to the 66th Halifax Rifles at Fort Halifax. Macmillan died 18 Mar. 1932.

26. J. W. Macmillan, "Standards of Wages," *Social Welfare*, 3:5, Feb. 1921, 138; "Profit, Competition and Service," *Social Welfare* , 2:11, Aug. 1920, 311–12.

27. O. G. S, "Rev. John Walker Macmillan," *New Outlook* , 21 Dec. 1932.

28. Prof. J. W. Macmillan, "Unemployment and Its Causes," *New Outlook*, 12 Nov. 1930; *Happiness and Goodwill and Other Essays on Christian Living* (Toronto: McClelland and Stewart, 1922), 99.

29. William McGuire King, "The Reform Establishment and the Ambiguities of

Influence," in William R. Hutchison, ed., *The Travail of the Protestant Establishment in America, 1900–1960* (Cambridge: Cambridge University Press, 1989), 122–23.

30. "Minutes of Board of Moral and Social Reform," 9 Sept. 1908. UCA, Presbyterian Church. Ibid., 6 Sept. 1910; "Minutes of Moral and Social Reform Council of Canada," 26 Sept. 1911. NAC, Canadian Council of Churches. Although less well known than the other social scientists, Robert Magill had a distinguished career in university and government. Born in Ireland, he was educated at Queen's College, Belfast, the Royal University of Ireland, and the University of Jena, Germany. In 1903, he came to Canada as a professor at Pine Hill Theological College and was principal of that institution in 1907–08, before accepting an appointment as professor of political economy at Dalhousie, which he held from 1908 to 1912, when he was appointed chairman of the Board of Grain Commissioners. See "An Observer," "Robert Magill, M. A., Ph.D.," *Grain Growers' Guide (GGG)* 2 Jan. 1918, 24. Titles recommended were Stephen Leacock, *Elements of Political Science*; Woodrow Wilson, *The State*; Richard Ely, *Outlines of Economics*; Alfred Marshall; *Principles of Economics*; William Cunningham, *Growth of English Industry and Commerce*; E. R. A. Seligman, *The Economic Interpretation of History*; Sidney and Beatrice Webb, *Industrial Democracy*; John R. Commons, *Trade Unionism and Labor Problems*; Richard Ely, *Socialism and Social Reform*; Robert Flint, *Socialism*; O. D. Skelton, *Socialism*; John Spargo, *Socialism*; Francis Peabody, *Jesus Christ and the Social Question*; Walter Rauschenbusch, *Christianity and the Social Crisis*; Jane Addams, *Democracy and Social Ethics*; Charles Ellwood, *Sociology*; Helen Bosanquet, *The Family*; J. A. Hobson, *Evolution of Capitalism*; C. R. Henderson, *Social Settlements*; Charles Zeublin, *Municipal Progress*; E. A. Ross, *Social Control* and *Social Psychology*; Albion Small and George Vincent, *An Introduction to the Science of Society*; and Franklin Giddings, *The Principles of Sociology*.

31. "Minutes of the Board of Moral and Social Reform and Evangelism," 5–7 Sept. 1911. University of Manitoba Archives (UMA), Gordon Papers, Box 16, folder 1; Gordon to Shearer, 2 May 1914. UMA, Gordon Papers, Box 17, folder 7; "Minutes of Board of Moral and Social Reform, 6 Sept. 1910." UCA, Presbyterian Church.

32. For Dobson's reading course, see "A Recommended List of Books for Yorkton District Reading Course," n.d.. UCA, Dobson Papers, Box A4, file T; Dobson to J. M. Baird, Alma College, 8 Nov. 1918. UCA, Dobson Papers, Box 4A, file B; Dobson to H. A. Goodwin, 4 Jan. 1920. UCA Dobson Papers, Box A5, file G; Dobson to John Fitzpatrick, Tompkin, Sask. UCA, Dobson Papers, Box A5, file F; 21 Oct. 1920. Dobson to Rev. J. W. A. Henderson, Carnduff, Sask., 13 July 1920. UCA, Dobson Papers, Box A5, file H.

33. "Board of Moral and Social Reform," 16 Nov. 1910. University of Manitoba Archives, Gordon Papers, Box 16, folder 1.

34. Quoted in Michael Freeden, *The New Liberalism* (Oxford: Oxford University Press, 1978), 104.

35. T. Albert Moore, "Democracy and Law Observance," n.d. UCA, Methodist Church, Department of Evangelism and Social Service, Box 7, file 132.

36. For the ongoing affinity between American social science and American liberal exceptionalism, see Ross, *The Origins of American Social Science*, xiii–xv.

37. Cecil E. Greek, *The Religious Roots of American Sociology* (New York: Garland Publishing, 1992), vii–viii.

38. Ross, *The Origins of American Social Science*, 103, 187–88, 192.

39. Greek, *Religious Roots of American Sociology*, 122–39; Ross, *The Origins of American Social Science*, 125–31, 222–26. See also Jean B. Quandt, "Religion and Social Thought: The Secularization of Postmillennialism," *American Quarterly*, 25: 4 (Oct. 1973), 402.

40. For this alternate tradition, see Steven R. Cohen, "From Industrial Democracy

to Professional Adjustment: The Development of Industrial Sociology in the United States, 1900–1955," *Theory and Society*, 2:1 (Jan. 1983), 55–56.

41. See E. A. Ross to Lester Ward, 2 Feb. 1896, "The Ward-Ross Correspondence, 1891–1896," Bernhard J. Stern, ed., *American Sociological Review*, 3:3, June 1938, 391. Like Canadian clergymen, Ross was also a follower of the Lamarckian naturalist Joseph LeConte.

42. For Ross's rejection of theological disputation, see Ross to Ward, 13 Dec. 1891, in "The Ross-Ward Correspondence," 364.

43. See Doug Owram, *The Government Generation: Canadian Intellectuals and the State, 1900–1945* (Toronto: University of Toronto Press, 1986); Michiel Horn, *The League for Social Reconstruction* (Toronto: University of Toronto Press, 1980); J. L. Granatstein, *The Ottawa Men* (Toronto: University of Toronto Press, 1982).

44. For a longer discussion of the activities of the Social Service Council of Canada, see Nancy Christie and Michael Gauvreau, *"A Full-Orbed Christianity"*: *The Protestant Churches, the Social Sciences, and the Welfare State in Canada, 1900–1940* (Montreal and Kingston: McGill–Queen's University Press, forthcoming), chap. 6.

14

Evangelicals, Biblical Scholarship, and the Politics of the Modern American Academy

D. G. HART

In 1976, the famed year of the evangelical, Harold Lindsell dropped a bomb on a religious community relishing its notoriety. His book *The Battle for the Bible* addressed the increasingly disputed and disreputable doctrine of biblical inerrancy. While Lindsell, as well as Harold John Ockenga, who wrote the preface, thought the book was irenic, the second word of the title indicated that there were limits to how congenial discussions about the authority and meaning of Scripture would be. Indeed, the author wrote with a clear sense of alarm. "Those who call themselves evangelicals," Lindsell lamented, had departed markedly from a "viewpoint held by them for so long." More and more organizations and individuals in the evangelical world embraced and defended a view "that the Bible has errors in it."[1] This perspective contained the seeds of evangelical destruction. Without an inerrant Bible, evangelicals would soon abandon the fundamental doctrines of the faith just as Unitarians, Bishop Pike, the Church of England, American Lutherans, mainline Presbyterians, and the United Church of Christ had.[2] Lindsell, employing an argument well suited to the Cold War era, thus established the domino theory of theological infidelity, with inerrancy standing as the first line of defense.

A year later James Barr, the learned biblical scholar at the University of Oxford, came out with the book *Fundamentalism*. His perspective was markedly different from Lindsell's. To Barr the doctrine of inerrancy "seen from the outside" distorted and deranged "all sorts of relations which to the student of the Bible seem[ed] quite obvious." To add insult to injury he wrote that fundamentalism was a "pathological condition of Christianity." But despite obvious disdain for fundamentalism and its doctrine of Scripture, Barr evinced remarkable agreement with Lindsell about the centrality of inerrancy for conservative Protestantism. "The inerrancy of the Bible, the entire Bible, including its details," he wrote, "is indeed the constant principle of rationality with fundamen-

talism." Even more extraordinary was Barr's apparent second of Lindsell's proposition that inerrancy was *the* doctrine that defined not just fundamentalism but
also evangelicalism. While he conceded that the word "fundamentalist" was
synonymous with "narrowness, bigotry, obscurantism and sectarianism," Barr
still believed that the ideas and practices of most evangelicals differed little from
those of fundamentalists. Thus, Barr and Lindsell, though for different purposes,
agreed that the doctrine of inerrancy was the proverbial line in the sand that
separated conservatives from other Protestants.³

Call it harmonic convergence or great minds thinking alike, the Lindsell and
Barr books set off a lively debate—to put it euphemistically—and an avalanche
of books and articles on the doctrine of Scripture that has to count as the greatest
scholarly output per capita on biblical authority in the history of the Christian
church. To be accurate, rumblings over inerrancy were audible before the Lindsell and Barr books. Indeed, a variety of books published in the early and mid-
seventies revealed an internal debate within evangelicalism over what exactly it
meant to belong and the doctrine to emerge most prominently was inerrancy.⁴
Thus, in the decade after the appearance of Lindsell's book a spate of literature
on the authority and infallibility of the Bible appeared that was backbreaking if
not breathtaking.

Even if the warfare model of the history of science and religion has been
dismantled, the lively debate about biblical authority instigated by the Lindsell
and Barr books demonstrated that at least one battle between theology and
science was indeed being fought—this time over the Bible—with important
implications for assessing American evanglicalism's engagement with modern
science. From one angle the controversy over inerrancy exposed a significant
conflict over professional authority within the evangelical community. By making inerrancy central to evangelical identity, an older generation of evangelical
leaders tried to reign in both a movement that had become unwieldy and a
younger generation of biblical scholars who seemed to be uncomfortable with
the subculture. In effect, the contested doctrine of inerrancy raised the question
of whether in interpreting Scripture the doctrine of the word of God was more
authoritative than the scientific study of Bible. Thus, many of the defenders of
inerrancy were theologians and ministers, while those who balked at the doctrine tended to be freshly minted Ph.D.'s in biblical studies. In other words, the
battle pitted learned amateurs against scientific experts.

Yet most of the literature produced during the debate ignored the institutional dimension of the conflict, focusing instead on the intellectual merits of
inerrancy. Proponents appealed to traditional Protestant understandings of special
revelation and to the teaching of Scripture itself, while detractors pointed to the
philosophical and historical circumstances that occasioned inerrancy. Though
the former made a good case, the scholarly consensus after a decade's worth of
writing was that behind evangelicalism's defense of the infallibility and authority
of the Bible was a decidedly scientific hermeneutic.⁵ For instance, Jack B. Rogers and Donald K. McKim argued in *The Authority and Interpretation of the Bible*
that inerrancy was not the historic teaching of the Christian church but rather
the creation of late nineteenth-century Princeton theologians who combined

Protestant scholasticism with the epistemology of common-sense realism to for-mulate a "peculiar" view of Scripture.[6] Mark Noll came to similar conclusions in his 1986 book, *Between Faith and Criticism*, a masterful survey of evangelical biblical scholarship since the rise of the modern university.[7] As he noted in the afterword to the second edition of the book, evangelical biblical scholarship, despite increasing sophistication, continued to be discounted in the academy in part because among evangelicals "the influence of early modern science . . . remains strong, while in the university world modern and post-modern science . . . prevail."[8]

Looking at the controversy over inerrancy as a conflict over professional authority allows for a different conclusion, one that discounts the influence of certain conceptions of science and a realist epistemology on evangelical beliefs, and highlights the theology that has informed conservative Protestant attitudes toward and handling of Scripture. What follows, then, is an attempt to put the debate among evangelicals over inerrancy specifically and twentieth-century evangelical biblical scholarship more generally in a different light by situating conservative Protestant study of Scripture within the larger history of religious studies at American universities. From this perspective what emerges as partic-ularly unique about evangelical biblical studies has less to do with the philo-sophical or scientific baggage conservatives carry than their expectation that the Bible is the *very* word of God.[9] Indeed, it is not much of a stretch to say that what separates evangelical scholars from their liberal Protestant colleagues in the Society of Biblical Literature, for instance, or their secular peers at university departments of Ancient Near Eastern Studies is the belief that the Bible, though in the words of men, is a divine and direct revelation from the triune God of the universe. Unlike mainstream Protestants who justify the study of Scripture on grounds that the Bible is a special book but then falter at specifying what makes it special, or professors of Near Eastern studies who explore the Bible as part of the larger project of understanding ancient cultures and languages, evan-gelicals have little difficulty explaining the importance of what they do when they teach or study the Bible in colleges or seminaries.[10] To them the Bible is a book that gives life and, though riddled with various interpretive difficulties, is authoritative for all matters of Christian faith and practice.

The theological underpinnings of evangelical biblical scholarship are generally assumed but rarely examined, particularly in the context of the politics of Amer-ican higher education. If, as Mark Noll has observed, the history of mainstream American Bible scholarship has not been informed by the realization that biblical scholarship, "like other enterprises of the modern academia, is intensely politi-cal," involving questions of "ownership and control, of pecking order and pres-tige," then how much more is this the case with evangelicals where their theo-logical convictions have kept them on the margins of professional biblical scholarship?[11] In other words, the focus on science and epistemology, as im-portant as they are, has obscured the importance of theology for understanding the status of evangelical biblical studies within the modern academy. Yet the evangelical doctrine of Scripture has not been merely a conduit for maintaining a particular philosophical commitment or scientific practice. It has also been a conviction with significant political implications in the sense that the evangelical beliefs about the Bible have been a self-conscious means for conservative Protestants to oppose the defections of mainline Protestantism and the excesses of the modern university. By contributing to the oppositional posture of evangelicals, their doctrine of Scripture both prevented their assimilation into the mainstream academy and provided a mechanism for maintaining the boundaries of their religious community. As such, the doctrine of inerrancy needs to be understood as the means, whether wise or not, by which the evangelical community has attempted to retain its identity and preserve a Christian voice in the professional study of Scripture.[12]

Religious Studies in American Higher Education

The history of religious studies in the United States since the rise of the modern research university can be divided into three main periods. From 1870 to 1925, the first period, mainstream Protestants accommodated the institutions and methods of new learning signaled by research universities and adapted beliefs and practices to adjust to the new social arrangements that sustained the revolution in higher education. These adjustments culminated in the modernist-fundamentalist controversy, a struggle in which liberals and conservatives fought over modern approaches to the study of Scripture, and which saw conservatives roundly defeated and forced to the margins of American scholarship. The victors in this contest, the modernists, entered the second period, from 1925 to 1965, with the support of the academic establishment. Protestant scholars championed the argument that the academic calling was essential to the establishment of a righteous and just society and also positioned the study of the Bible and theology as an essential component in the heritage of Western civilization and, hence, vital to liberty and democracy. Even though mainstream biblical scholarship moved to the right, evangelical convictions still looked fundamentalist from the perspective of neo-orthodoxy. In the third and most recent period, Protestant divinity and biblical studies became objectionable to the degree that they had been so closely identified with the American way of life. Older rationales for studying religion unraveled and attempts to justify the study of Scripture on scientific grounds surfaced only to be overwhelmed by the postmodernist turn that assailed the Enlightenment methods of the academy as just another form of white, patriarchal oppression. During this time evangelicals made great strides to move from the sidelines of the academy to the center, but ironically this was the same time when the study of anything Christian smacked of Western imperialism, Victorian sexual ethics, and economic exploitation.[13]

The Fundamentalist Era

Turning then to the first period, it is important to remember that at the time of the emergence of the research university in the United States, either in the form of brand new institutions such as Johns Hopkins and Cornell or the transformation of older colleges such as Harvard and Yale into universities, the study of the Bible by Protestants was segregated in freestanding seminaries or divinity schools on the margins of the university. Only in rare cases did the Bible and related theological disciplines come under the purview of the new institution in higher education.[14] The scholars who comprised the Society of Biblical Literature and the American Society of Church History, for instance, labored primarily at schools whose primary purpose was the training of Protestant ministers. In other words, the formal study of the Bible and theology at the founding of the modern university was oriented primarily to the church rather than the academy.

Nevertheless, the isolation of the study of the Bible and theology from mainstream learning in the United States was not a function of overt secularization. In fact, a number of university presidents hoped that the new model of learning promoted at their institutions would prompt seminaries to reform their curricula and methods. Daniel Coit Gilman, for example, who presided at Johns Hopkins for its first 25 years, said that "American universities should be more than theistic; they may and should be avowedly Christian—not in a narrow or sectarian sense—but in the broad, open and inspiring sense of the Gospels." Other university presidents echoed such sentiments, contending that the new institutions actively promoted the Christian religion. Almost everywhere one looks in the late nineteenth century, the new university was justified, as President James Burrill Angell at the University of Michigan put it, on the university's "fair, liberal and honorable Christian character." Leaving aside the question of sincerity, these sentiments were of a piece with the religious and moral idealism that propelled the social gospel and progressivism.[15]

From one perspective, the modernist-fundamentalist controversy was a referendum on whether the Protestant churches would countenance the university's conception of Christianity. Did the study of Scripture and Protestant divinity fit with or was it antithetical to, or at least in a different category from, the progressive and Kingdom-of-God building aims of the university? The competing models for studying the Bible that lay beneath the battles over creation and eschatology related directly to different conceptions of the purpose of advanced study. Fundamentalist attitudes toward the Bible as the divine revelation of God's saving purpose and plan for human history were ill suited for the university because they pointed toward a transcendent and, more important, sectarian standard to which academic life should conform. Liberal Protestant convictions, however, which stressed God's immanence and revelation in the unfolding of Western civilization, were much more congenial to university leaders who believed that advanced learning would actually disclose and realize the will of the creator of the universe.

Even though the doctrine of inerrancy took a back seat to creationism and dispensationalism, the conservative Protestant defense of Scripture's authority conflicted directly with the prevailing academic understanding of the Bible's significance and the direction of human history. Since the late nineteenth century in the wake of the controversy over Darwinism, American Protestants had established a fairly reliable means for adjudicating the competing claims of science and Christianity. Religion, many said, concerned piety and morality while science explored what was observable, rational, and physical.[16] Fundamentalists, however, denied the separation between religion and science by arguing that the Bible was more than just a guidebook to morality and a source of religious experience, that it made claims that trespassed the boundaries of science. The increasing appeal of creation science is probably the most notable instance of the fundamentalist view that the Bible propounded truths that scientists needed to consider. But J. Gresham Machen's defense of Christianity, while avoiding the debate over evolution, also depended upon the idea that the Bible taught truths that impinged upon the findings of science. This was the point of his insistence that without certain historical facts Christianity ceased to be Christianity. As he wrote at the end of *The Virgin Birth of Christ*, to say that the authority of the Bible lies in the sphere of religion and ethics, not in the sphere of "external history" or science, was tantamount to saying that the very existence of Jesus Christ was irrelevant to the truth of Christianity.[17] So, too, the appeal of dispensationalism, which with its pessimistic reading of the direction of human civilization also challenged the progressive orthodoxy of the university by questioning whether the fruits of science were as beneficent as academics alleged.[18]

Even while fundamentalists made these plausible points, the Protestant establishment continued to propagate a view of the Bible that attempted to preserve the book's religious authority while dodging the scientific implications of biblical teaching. So, for instance, Harry Emerson Fosdick drew upon the older technique, first used with prominence by the transcendentalist Theodore Parker, of distinguishing between the permanent and the temporary in the Bible.[19] The various teachings of the Bible, Fosdick wrote, are "transient phrasings of permanent conviction and experiences. . . . What is permanent in Christianity is not mental frameworks but abiding experiences that phrase and rephrase themselves in successive generations' ways of thinking." With this distinction Fosdick thought it possible for modern, well-educated believers to continue to believe in the Bible without committing "intellectual suicide."[20] A similar distinction lay behind Shailer Mathews's affirmation that the Bible, "when interpreted historically, is the product and trustworthy record of the progressive revelation of God through a developing religious experience." By applying the insights of critical and historical methods, Mathews believed it possible to separate the "permanent attitudes and convictions of Christians" from the supernatural husk of the Bible.[21]

The irony of the fundamentalist-modernist controversy was that the fundamentalists were the party to emerge from the conflict thoroughly discredited within the academy. Even though conservatives were the ones who stressed the intellectual implications of biblical teaching and Christian convictions, because they did not accept all of the claims of the academic establishment they gained a reputation for constituting, as H. L. Mencken observed, "the most ignorant class of teachers ever set up to lead a civilized people . . . even more ignorant than the county superintendents of schools."[22] Meanwhile, liberal Protestants, who appealed to the college-educated and the findings of science in their efforts to refashion the Christian religion, came away from the controversy with the blessing of the academic establishment, much of which they still ran, even though, as Mencken also observed, what was left of Christianity after liberals were finished with it was little more than "a series of sweet attitudes, possible to anyone not actually in jail for felony."[23] Indeed, the "modern use of the Bible," as Fosdick called it, provided the religious ballast that university builders needed.

One of the reasons that the modernist approach to Scripture was useful to the university was that its rival, the fundamentalist notion, was not only intellectually suspect but also authoritarian and therefore hostile to the ideology of liberty and inquiry that fueled modern notions of learning. At the most basic level the fundamentalist understanding of the Bible was one to which moderns would not assent. As Fosdick claimed, "multitudes of people" were rebelling against the "older uses of the Bible." Miracles, demons, fiat creation, apocalyptic hopes, eternal hell, or Old Testament conceptions of Jehovah shocked "the modern conscience." In other words, modern men and women would not consent to the mental categories of premodern people. But the modern study of the Bible gave "intellectual liberation" from the old view by allowing the "imperishable Gospel freed from its entanglements" to be preached with "a liberty, a reasonableness, an immediate application to our own age."[24] Mathews was more explicit in drawing the connection between modern study of Scripture, academic freedom, and Protestant liberalism. It was not just that educated people needed a new understanding of an ancient book but also that the methods of liberal Christianity were in fundamental congruence with those of modern learning. "Modernists" reached their conclusions in the same way as chemists or historians. "They do not vote in conventions and do not enforce beliefs by discipline" the way fundamentalists threatened to do.[25] Indeed, what made fundamentalists most threatening was their intolerance, or willingness to exclude dissenters from churches and Christian organizations. By drawing the lines so clearly between authority and liberty, or intolerance and tolerance, liberal Protestants were further solidifying the connections in American culture between Protestantism and the Whig ideology of freedom of thought, intellectual progress, scientific discovery, and national assimilation.[26]

The Era of Neo-Orthodoxy

The repudiation of fundamentalist views in the academy, however, went beyond scientific methods or the spirit of inquiry upon which the university depended and to which liberal Protestants accommodated themselves. For at the very time that the fundamentalist doctrine of Scripture (and with it the notion of fixed authority in religious matters) lost in the intellectual arena, the study of the Bible and theology began to be included in the university with greater frequency and urgency. An important factor in the emergence of religious studies as an academic discipline concerned the Protestant establishment's unflinching support for liberty, democracy, and the American way of life. Thus, in the second period of this survey, roughly from 1925 to 1965, religion moved gradually from an extracurricular activity to a formal area of instruction at American colleges and universities. What was particularly crucial to the emergence of religious studies in mainstream learning was the cultural crisis produced by World War II, together with the questions about national identity that this crisis provoked. During the 1940s religious studies began to be recognized as one of the humanistic disciplines. With the war in mind, educators began to stress the humanities' relevance for living an ethically and socially responsible life, emphasizing the "spiritual," "moral," and "humanizing" character of liberal education. No longer associated with timeless truths or mental discipline, a liberal education became one that prepared students for life in a liberal democracy. The study of religion was a natural fit.[27]

In this environment the rationale for studying the Bible was predicated upon the idea that Scripture was special, even the word of God, but when Protestant educators were pressed to identify the Bible's uniqueness they resorted most often to older liberal pieties. For instance, the president of the National Association of Biblical Instructors in 1933 warned that the study of Scripture was becoming indistinguishable from the study of literature, sociology, and history. What college professors needed to do was teach the Bible as the "Word of God" because that is what the Bible is, "Religion, . . . full of wonder, power and regenerating energy," where students could learn to ask with the Rich Young Ruler, "What can I do to get the most satisfying thrill out of life?"[28] To be sure, some educators made the more plausible argument that the Bible should be studied because of its importance in the development of Western civilization, an especially attractive reason during and after World War II when American ideals were at odds with fascism and communism.[29] But during this time when the religious studies curriculum came into its own with its explicit Protestant stamp, most arguments for studying the Bible concerned not questions of historical or cultural significance but rather the students' and society's need for religious experience and moral guidance.

This is not to say that the biblical theology movement and the influence of neo-orthodoxy did not firm up the theology of mainstream religious studies. With the ecclesiastical right defeated in the 1930s, it was easier for the theological center in mainstream Protestantism to retreat from the excesses of liberal Protestantism. Here the lead of Barth, Brunner, and Bultmann injected some measure of self-conscious reflection about the nature of Scripture and, thus, a more substantial (i.e., theological) argument for studying the Bible.[30] Even though the biblical theology movement had its critics,[31] its influence at mainline Protestant institutions, such as Princeton, Union (New York), and Yale, the graduate schools that trained the most religious studies professors, insured that it would also trickle down and out to the broader academy.[32] Still, the biblical theology movement could not shake the legacy of liberalism. On the one hand, by avoiding any identification between God's word and the words of the Bible, the newer approach to Scripture often couched the significance of divine revelation in terms that were a throwback to the old liberal emphasis on religious experience.[33] On the other hand, while wanting to recover the religious significance of the Bible and move beyond the dry and dusty issues raised in higher criticism, the neo-orthodox could never countenance a position that smacked of fundamentalism.[34]

Thus, at the very same time when evangelicals were emerging from the dark days of fundamentalism, they were still peripheral to the academic mainstream. The reason for this had to do with the evangelical doctrine of Scripture. To say that the twentieth-century evangelical doctrine of Scripture is merely a footnote on Benjamin Breckinridge Warfield is perhaps an overstatement, though the reprinting of his original article on inspiration in the 1982 "reconstructed" edition of the *International Standard Bible Encyclopedia* (originally published in 1930) does suggest some truth to the caricature.[35] Between the years of 1920 and 1950 Warfield's views may not have always been studied but they undoubtedly informed evangelical convictions about the Bible, though this observation is difficult to prove because of the paucity of literature published about the nature of the Bible during the 1930s and 1940s. In fact, the only publication of note on the doctrine of Scripture was the symposium of the faculty of Westminster Seminary, *The Infallible Word* (1946). In the opening chapter of this book, John Murray articulated once again the characteristic features of the Old Princeton position on inscripturated revelation. "The Bible," he wrote, "is the Word of God, ... inspired by the Holy Spirit" and occupying "a unique place as the norm of Christian faith and life." But having affirmed the divine authorship of Scripture, Murray, like Warfield, did not flinch from taking fully into account the "human instrumentality" of Scripture. Unlike liberals and the neo-orthodox to the left, Murray, again like Warfield, argued that the human element in Scripture was fully compatible with the infallibility and inerrancy of the Bible. Murray would have nothing to do with those critics of inerrancy who erected "an utterly artificial and arbitrary" notion of historical and scientific precision and thus parodied the evangelical position. "In accord with accepted forms of speech and custom," Murray explained, "a statement can be perfectly authentic and yet not pedantically precise. Scripture does not make itself absurd by furnishing us with pedantry." Contrary to inerrancy's cultured despisers, *The Infallible Word* testified to the scholarly breadth and theological insight of the Old Princeton doctrine of Scripture.[36]

Soon other voices in the evangelical community also rallied to the defense of the Bible's divine authorship and, hence, its infallibility and inerrancy. E. J. Young, one of the contributors to *The Infallible Word*, devoted a whole book to the doctrine of Scripture, defending and nuancing the Old Princeton position against defections within the conservative Protestant camp as well as from the threats posed by neo-orthodoxy.[37] A year later, J. I. Packer demonstrated further the subtleties of Warfield's teaching on inerrancy.[38] In the same year Carl Henry marshaled the collective intelligence of conservative Protestant biblical scholars and theologians to avoid some of the "reactionary" statements of inerrancy and infallibility, show the willingness of conservatives to grapple with the phenomena of Scripture, and ultimately, underscore "the God-breathed character of the Bible."[39] To be sure, some within the loose coalition of post–World War II evangelicalism were unwilling to go as far as some of inerrancy's defenders, arguing that Scripture was still infallible without inerrancy,[40] but within the broader Protestant world, the evangelical position was unmistakable. As Mark Noll summarized, evangelical scholars believed 1) that the Scriptures are inspired and as such constitute divine revelation; 2) that the Bible is the church's primary source of revelation, that is, that Scripture contains and is the word of God; 3) that inspiration is plenary and verbal; and 4) that Scripture infallibly—and for many, inerrantly—accomplishes God's purpose in revealing himself.[41]

While mainline Protestants and critics of evangelicalism have faulted this view of Scripture for being rationalistic, overly propositional, and scientific, what has more often than not prevented evangelical views from being taken seriously in the academy is the confessional or dogmatic nature of their conception of the Bible as the word of God.[42] (Why evangelicalism's critics did not see that their own reasons for rejecting the biblical "facts" that conservatives defended also stemmed from a "scientific" view of truth that rejected the possibility of miracle is difficult to understand.) Despite the repetition of charges and countercharges from the fundamentalist-modernist controversy about the nature of religious truth and knowledge, rival theological convictions were also responsible for the differences between evangelicals and mainstream academics in the study of Scripture. A good bit of this rivalry concerned the divine character and authorship of the Bible. While evangelicals viewed the book ultimately as God's word (while also granting its human aspects), mainstream Protestants and students of Scripture in the academy stressed the Bible's human origin, and hence, its fallibility and limitations, if not backwardness. Indeed, book reviews of leading evangelical scholars faulted them for being overly defensive and apologetic, for starting with the assumption that the Bible is unique and authoritative because of its divine origin.

But as was the case with fundamentalists, the defensiveness of evangelicals about the Bible was understandable once the theological convictions that sustained the evangelical doctrine of Scripture had been taken into account. It was not merely the accuracy of the Bible and God's truthfulness that mattered to evangelicals. Rather, of overriding importance was what the Bible revealed. As Wilbur Smith wrote in a forum printed in the journal of mainstream Bible instructors, conservatives approached and defended Scripture on the grounds that it was "given by God to teach us those truths which we could not, otherwise, of our own ingenuity, attain to, but without which man does not have deliverance from sin, reconciliation with God, abiding joy, nor the sure hope of a life to come."[43] Indeed, what academics and mainstream Protestants, even those caught up in the theological renaissance of neo-orthodoxy, found unacceptable about evangelical biblical scholarship ultimately hinged, as Machen had argued in the 1920s, upon the doctrine of salvation. From the perspective of the academy and mainline churches, conservatives, like their fundamentalist ancestors, were guilty of a theology that was too otherworldly, too individualistic, too privatistic, and not sufficiently engaged with the sociopolitical realities of the Cold War world.[44]

The situation for evangelical biblical scholarship, then, during the period when religious studies became respectable in the university, also the heyday of neo-orthodoxy, was not unlike the situation of biblical studies in the nineteenth century. Evangelical scholars were on the margins of the academy, located predominantly at seminaries and evangelical colleges, separate from mainline Protestant institutions and the academic establishment. As Noll argues, the work done during this period by evangelical biblical scholars was good, clearly advancing the study of Scripture beyond either the excesses of pragmatic revivalism or apocalyptic dispensationalism. Conservatives made significant contributions in textual criticism and continued to produce solid commentaries.[45] Be that as it may, theological assumptions kept evangelical biblical scholarship on the sidelines even though some of the best and brightest, such as those who spearheaded the neo-evangelical movement, had hoped through academic achievements to gain a wider hearing in the academy and the wider public for conservative Protestant views.[46]

The Era of Multiculturalism

If evangelical biblical scholars had trouble engaging the academy in the post-fundamentalist era, their prospects darkened considerably in the post-1960s university. This assessment is ironic at least because this period witnessed a record number of evangelicals pursuing graduate training in biblical studies at non-evangelical institutions. Indeed, the neo-evangelical strategy of transforming the culture, especially through higher learning, seemed to pay huge dividends. As Noll well documents in his book on evangelical biblical scholarship, the younger generation of conservative Protestants obtained impeccable academic credentials. Whereas only 12 of the 50 contributors to the learned *New Bible Commentary*, published by Eerdmans in 1953, held research doctorates, in the ongoing series from Zondervan, *The Expositor's Bible Commentary*, only 5 of the 54 contributors do not have research doctorates, and of those 49 doctorates only 13 were earned at evangelical institutions. These and other figures demonstrate that in academic pedigree evangelical biblical scholars rivaled the faculty at mainline Protestant seminaries and university departments of religious studies.[47]

Yet the hospitality of the academy to evangelicals was predicated on more than neo-evangelical cunning or conservative chutzpa; it also depended on significant changes within the university regarding the study of religion, changes that would continue to make evangelical convictions unacceptable. When in 1982 Ernest W. Saunders noted in his centennial history of the Society of Biblical Literature that the rise of a "new scholastic conservatism in biblical studies" provided a fresh opportunity for a "productive dialogue" on theological, historical, and philological issues, he was almost as guilty of misreading the academic scene as Protestants had been a century earlier.[48] For at the same time that evangelicals were becoming more conspicuous in settings such as the Society of Biblical Literature, the study of the Bible within American higher education itself was moving to the margins. Indicative of the growing discomfort with biblical studies in mainstream American learning was the formation of the American Academy of Religion in 1964, previously called the National Association of Biblical Instructors, now reconstituted to undo the hegemony of mainline

Protestantism in the study of religion and to articulate a rationale for studying religion that was more academic and more sensitive to America's religious diversity.[49] As John F. Wilson, then a young professor in religious studies at Princeton, put it, the post–World War II rationale for studying religion in the university, a set of studies dominated by the Bible and Protestant divinity, had failed to acknowledge "the religiously pluralistic" character of American society. "Religion is socially divisive in a way that other subjects simply are *not*," Wilson warned, thus calling for a different justification for studying any religion in the academy, whether the sacred texts of Christians or those of Buddhists.[50]

Wilson's comments anticipated the changes that would transform religious studies in the next 25 years, the very era when evangelicals seemed to be prospering in academic circles. Shifts toward phenomenological approaches to religion as well as an increased reliance upon the social sciences made theology suspect.[51] But the shift in religious studies also stemmed from the wave of social protest that the 1960s unleashed, which severely jeopardized the older Protestant assumption that Christian values were essential to American ideals of liberty and equality. According to a recent AAR report, which testifies to the decentering of religious studies, the study of religion could no longer be content with "nineteenth century WASP theology" but had to "recover the repressed in American religious history: the unique religious vision of Blacks, of American Indians, of Chicanos, of American Orientals."[52] This commitment to give greater prominence to the religions of the oppressed did not make the university world a particularly comfortable one for biblical studies conducted by white, middle-class, conservative Protestants. If the old biblical theology now looked too narrow, how much more that of Protestants to the right of Barth and Niebuhr?

Of course, evangelicals could try to profit in some fashion from these trends by arguing that because they had been excluded in the past, evangelical studies should now be included in the university. This logic would appear to explain, at least in part, the boom of evangelical history in the last 15 years. While the new pattern of religious studies made room for the study of non-Christian religions, it also provided cover for scholarship about Protestants outside the Protestant establishment.[53] To the extent that evangelical biblical scholars perceived themselves as victims of intellectual discrimination they could side with postmodernists and deconstructionists who scored many points noting mainline Protestantism's record of excluding outsiders in religious studies. Thus, in the politically charged environment of the contemporary university emerged the unlikely possibility of conservative Protestants teaming up with the advocates of gay, African-American, and women's studies and alternative religious perspectives to argue for the inclusion of evangelical views in the academy.[54]

The problem, however, is that while evangelicals as a group may have been excluded from (or at least gave up on) the university during the fundamentalist controversy, to the extent that they still study the Bible as God's word and the only authority for faith and practice, their rationale for biblical study continues to be suspect. Even though older objectivist paradigms of knowledge may be discredited by some, as George Marsden has also argued, the naturalistic assumptions of most scholars—from feminist scholars to members of the National

Association of Scholars—will be a barrier to evangelical beliefs about the Bible.[55] What is more, the university's stress upon liberation from oppression, a refrain often trumpeted by postmodernists despite its obvious indebtedness to Enlightenment conceptions about the autonomous rational self, does not suggest an environment where evangelical views about biblical authority and submission to divine purpose will be well received.[56]

Another factor contributing to the dimmer prospects for evangelical biblical scholars in the contemporary university is that the "evangelical perspective" that the academy is supposed to include has become increasingly difficult to define. At the same time that evangelicals have become more comfortable in the university, the evangelical consensus on Scripture that made the movement a distinct and definable community unraveled. Part of the reason had to do with the better academic credentials that evangelical biblical scholars were now carrying. Whereas older generations of conservative Protestants began with the conviction that the Bible was God's word and then went on to explore the phenomena of Scripture from that perspective, while also discrediting the conclusions of critical scholarship, the rules of the academy demand that such confessional commitments be minimized in order for the text to be understood in its historical and cultural (i.e., original) context. To make their way in the academy, evangelical biblical scholars increasingly approach the text from its human side and bracket out, for the sake of academic etiquette, the divine character and canonical nature of Scripture. With fewer evangelical academics possessing ministerial credentials, the theological convictions that often harnessed academic specialization for the good of the community of faith are less in force. The irony is that at a time when it has become fashionable for scholars to admit how ideological biases inform academic work, evangelicals approach Scripture along the lines of the older scientific history, assuming it possible to arrive at an objective reading of the text without the prejudice of theological conviction or ecclesiastical membership.[57]

In fact, one way of reading the inerrancy debates of the 1970s and 1980s is as an episode in the history of a segregated religious community in the throes of assimilation. What appears to have occurred within the evangelical academy over the last three decades only confirms what historians have observed about the effects of academic professionalization on other Christian traditions. As believing academics become more comfortable in the world of mainstream learning, they invariably become less comfortable with the restraints imposed by the religious communities that reared them. Thus, the same process of academic assimilation that since World War II eroded the theological identity of American Roman Catholic scholars seems to be at work in the evangelical community.[58]

In the case of evangelicals what became increasingly evident in the 1970s was that while most scholars still affirmed that the Bible was God's word, hence infallible and authoritative if not inerrant, they did not agree on what the Bible meant. In other words, agreement about the Bible's divine origin did not settle questions of interpretation. The cultural upheaval of the 1960s and early 1970s, moreover, especially regarding the family and the role of women in both the home and the church, posed enough questions about seemingly settled interpretations of the Bible to prompt younger evangelical scholars who had been in graduate school during those years to regard the defense of inerrancy as a cover for opposing newer approaches to contested passages. As Donald Dayton wrote in 1976 for *Christian Century*, "The emergence of a socially activist 'young evangelical' consciousness has also given shape to new configurations. Young evangelicals have been overwhelmed to discover the extent of biblical material related to themes of social justice—material largely ignored in the theology and writings of their elders. The great defence of 'inerrancy' that was supposed to have assured a 'biblical faith' seems to have failed in this area."[59]

Moreover, the ethos of the academy has also made unattractive to the younger generation of evangelicals the theological combativeness that had characterized their theological forebears, whether fundamentalists or neo-evangelicals.[60] Aside from forced harmonizations, sloppy exegesis, and a conspiratorial mentality, what many readers of Lindsell's *Battle for the Bible* objected to was his authoritative and exclusive tone. According to one reviewer, Lindsell had written "a poorly researched, poorly reasoned, poorly targeted book" that would "bring dishonor" upon the Bible because of his dogmatism.[61] While this perspective might be expected from a professor at Union Theological Seminary (New York), evangelicals who did not agree with Lindsell also objected to the author's narrowness. According to Douglas Jacobsen, young evangelicals like himself "harbor a certain jealousy of the self-confident authoritative mood" of the older generation, a mood that in Jacobsen's estimate had "ceased to be an option for this new generation."[62] Even the judicious and usually winsome Mark Noll could not help but object to the "recriminations" that evangelicals expressed in debating Scripture, concluding that Lindsell, as well as some of his critics, were heir to "a long tradition of religious extremism that stretches back to eschatological conspiracy theories of the American revolution and also includes substantial evangelical participation in racist, exclusionary, anti-Catholic, and anticommunist hysteria."[63] Obviously, the debate over inerrancy touched a raw nerve.

The doctrine became even more objectionable when evangelical institutions appeared to take Lindsell's argument to heart and exclude from their ranks scholars who would not subscribe to inerrancy. For instance, in 1983 J. Ramsey Michaels was forced to resign from the faculty of Gordon-Conwell Divinity School after 25 years of service because an examining board deemed views in his book *Servant and Son* (1981) to be incompatible with the school's statement on inerrancy (though the deity of Christ was also at issue). In the same year, inerrantists won another battle when the Evangelical Theological Society forced Robert Gundry, professor of New Testament at Westmont College, to resign his membership because his commentary on the gospel of Matthew appeared to violate ETS's theological statement on inerrancy. These and other examples of evangelical bloodletting prompted Donald A. Hagner to conclude that "it was nothing less than shocking to see the extent to which the Lindsellian perspective seems to be winning the day."[64]

While a good deal of this disagreement concerned differing understandings of what inerrancy meant, the battle over the Bible also showed that a political dispute, similar to one a century earlier in Protestant higher education between learned clergy and academic specialists, was occurring over who would run the evangelical academy.[65] The older generation, the inerrantists, reflecting the mindset of clergy, wanted evangelical institutions of learning to reflect the theological boundaries of the religious community. A high view of Scripture, they argued, was in fact what had defined evangelicalism throughout much of the twentieth century. The younger generation, the critics of the inerrantists with better academic credentials, however, wanted the evangelical academy to reflect the rules and ethos of the modern university. Not only were they uncomfortable with older evangelical views on women, the family, and social justice but they also objected to the kind of line drawing, name calling, and fellowship breaking that inerrancy encouraged.

Why Study the Bible?

Whatever the problems with inerrancy and its usefulness for marking the boundaries of evangelical identity, it has nonetheless offered one of the few compelling rationales in American higher education for studying Scripture.[66] Despite evangelical Protestantism's apparent capitulation to a wooden rationalism or a benighted inductivism, the tradition has retained a view of the Bible that is unmatched in the academy. Rather than witnessing the corrosive effects of an unholy commitment to Enlightenment epistemology, evangelical study of the Bible, even though judged by the modern academy as unscientific and naive, has fostered a tradition of interpretation and scholarship that preserved not just a reverent approach to Scripture—what Mark Noll calls "believing criticism"— but also a forceful rationale for why students should even bother with a collection of ancient writings.[67] When compared to the arguments made by mainline Protestants or, more recently, Ancient Near Eastern Studies scholars, the idea that the Bible is the word of God which makes wise unto salvation has a peculiar force and urgency that is capable of withstanding shrinking departmental budgets or laments about the exclusion of various voices from the literary canon.

Obviously, the evangelical conviction about the Bible's divine origin is much easier to maintain at places like Wheaton College or Gordon-Conwell Seminary, which is another way of saying it is well suited for private religious institutions, not colleges or universities that strive to serve the public.[68] Nevertheless, the evangelical doctrine of Scripture provides an altogether different, and in many ways compelling, justification for requiring undergraduates and seminarians to take courses in the Bible and theology. As Robert W. Funk wrote almost two decades ago, long before the university capitulated to multiculturalism, "without the benefit of the scriptural ploy," American biblical scholars would be hardpressed "to justify their existence in the secular university."[69] So, too, more recently, Jon Levenson has argued that in an age of multiculturalism and shrinking departmental budgets the professional study of the Hebrew and Christian scriptures lacks force. "The very value-neutrality" of mainstream biblical scholarship, he writes, "puts its practitioners at a loss to defend the *value* of the enterprise itself."[70]

This point needs to be kept in mind as evangelical scholars reflect upon their intellectual resources and position themselves for greater engagement with the modern university. A number of evangelical academics have been especially vocal in summoning evangelicals from their academic and cultural ghettos and in calling for scholarship that is distinctively Christian and also academically acceptable.[71] To be sure, greater access to and prominence within the university is by no means without advantages. But the history of biblical scholarship also underscores the lesson that real perils confront Christian scholars in the modern academy. Within the university it is not possible to appeal to the theological grounds on which evangelical biblical scholarship has depended. Instead, the only acceptable (i.e., public) reasons for studying Scripture are appeals either to the historic importance of the Bible in Western civilization—an increasingly difficult case to make at multicultural U.—or to the need for understanding and preserving ancient Near Eastern cultures, an argument that flies in the face of evaporating budgets and the increasing demands for vocational training. The evangelical study of Scripture and the theology that has sustained it may not be sufficiently persuasive to be included by the mainstream academy, but evangelicals are one of the few remaining Protestant communities to believe they have a sacred book worth studying. Surely, in an age when the intellectual justification for higher education generally and religious studies specifically is increasingly uncertain, the evangelical rationale for studying the Bible is a healthy even if antiquated alternative.[72]

NOTES

1. (Grand Rapids: Zondervan, 1976), 20.

2. *Ibid.*, ch. 8.

3. (Philadelphia: Westminster Press, 1977), 53, 5, 3.

4. Gerald T. Shepard, "Biblical Hermeneutics: The Academic Language of Evangelical Identity," *Union Seminary Quarterly Review* 32 (Winter 1977), 81–94, gives a good overview of these debates. Throughout this chapter I am referring to evangelicalism in the way that George Marsden does when he defines it as a "transdenominational community with complicated infrastructures of institutions and persons who identify with 'evangelicalism.' " See "The Evangelical Denomination," in *Evangelicalism and Modern America*, ed. George Marsden (Grand Rapids: Eerdmans, 1984), ix.

5. For some of the literature on inerrancy, see *Inerrancy*, ed. Norman L. Geisler (Grand Rapids: Zondervan, 1979); *Biblical Errancy: Its Philosophical Roots*, ed., Norman L. Geisler, (Grand Rapids: Zondervan, 1981); *Challenges to Inerrancy*, ed. Gordon Lewis and Bruce Demarest (Chicago: Moody Press, 1984); *Inerrancy and the Church*, ed. John Hannah (Chicago: Moody Press, 1984); *Hermeneutics, Inerrancy, and the Bible*, ed. Earl Radmacher and Robert Preus (Grand Rapids: Academie Press, 1984); *The Foundation of Biblical Authority*, ed. James Montgomery Boice (Grand Rapids: Zondervan, 1978); Robert K. Johnston, *Evangelicals at an Impasse* (Atlanta: John Knox, 1979); William J. Abraham, *Divine Revelation and the Limits of Historical Criticism* (New York: Oxford University Press, 1982); Abraham, *The Coming Great Revival* (San Francisco: Harper & Row, 1984); John D. Woodbridge, *Biblical Authority: A Critique of the Rogers/McKim Proposal* (Grand Rapids: Zondervan, 1982); George M. Marsden, *Fundamentalism and American Culture: The Shaping*

of Twentieth-Century Evangelicalism, 1870–1925 (New York: Oxford University Press, 1980), especially chs. 12–14, and 24; Ernest R. Sandeen, *The Roots of Fundamentalism: British and American Millenarianism, 1800–1930* (Chicago: University of Chicago Press, 1970), especially ch. 5; and George M. Marsden, "Everyone One's Own Interpreter?: The Bible, Science, and Authority in Mid-Nineteenth-Century America," Timothy P. Weber, "The Two-Edged Sword: The Fundamentalist Use of the Bible," and Grant Wacker, "The Demise of Biblical Civilization," in *The Bible in America: Essays in Cultural History,* ed. Nathan O. Hatch and Mark A. Noll (New York: Oxford University Press, 1982), 79–100, 101–20, and 121–38 respectively.

6. (San Francisco: Harper & Row, 1979), 347. For their critique of Old Princeton see especially chs. 5 and 6.

7. *Between Faith and Criticism: Evangelicals, Scholarship, and the Bible in America* (San Francisco: Harper & Row, 1986).

8. 2nd ed. (Grand Rapids: Baker Book House, 1991), 202.

9. See, for instance, Paul L. Holmer, "Contemporary Evangelical Faith: An Assessment and Critique," in *The Evangelicals: What They Believe, Who They Are, Where They Are Changing,* ed. David F. Wells and John D. Woodbridge (Grand Rapids: Baker Book House, 1977), 91–95.

10. Jon D. Levenson, *The Hebrew Bible, The Old Testament, and Historical Criticism* (Louisville: Westminster/John Knox, 1993), discusses the tensions surrounding the study of religious texts in the public environment of the university, especially the inadequacy of older rationales for studying the Bible. See especially chs. 1, 4, and 5.

11. "Review Essay: The Bible in America," *Journal of Biblical Literature* (hereafter cited as *JBL*) 106 (1987), 506.

12. For nuanced defenses of inerrancy, ones that would take issue with Lindsell, see Moises Silva, "Old Princeton, Westminster and Inerrancy," in *Inerrancy and Hermeneutic: A Tradition, A Challenge, A Debate,* ed. Harvie M. Conn (Grand Rapids: Baker Book House, 1988), 67–80; and Dan McCartney and Charles Clayton, *Let the Reader Understand: A Guide to Interpreting and Applying the Bible* (Wheaton: Victor Books, 1994), 38–47.

13. Works that help to delineate these periods are D. G. Hart, "American Learning and the Problem of Religious Studies," in *The Secularization of the Academy,* ed. George M. Marsden and Bradley J. Longfield (New York: Oxford University Press, 1992), 195–233; George M. Marsden, *The Soul of the American University: From Protestant Establishment to Established Non-Belief* (New York: Oxford University Press, 1994); and Douglas Sloan, *Faith & Knowledge: Mainline Protestantism and American Higher Education* (Louisville: Westminster/John Knox, 1994).

14. See Hugh Hawkins, *Pioneer: A History of the Johns Hopkins University, 1874–1889* (Baltimore: Johns Hopkins University Press, 1960), 152–59 and 230–31; James P. Wind, *The Bible and the University* (Atlanta: Scholars Press, 1987); Robert S. Shepard, *God's People in the Ivory Tower: Religion in the Early American University* (Brooklyn: Carlson Publishing Co., 1991); and Robert W. Funk, "The Watershed of the American Biblical Tradition: The Chicago School, First Phase, 1892–1920," *JBL* 95 (1976), 4–22.

15. Gilman, *An Address Before the Phi Beta Kappa Society of Harvard University, July 1, 1886* (Baltimore, 1886), 33; Angell quoted in Marsden, *The Soul of the American University,* 170. For similar expressions, see Hart, "Faith and Learning in the Age of the University: The Academic Ministry of Daniel Coit Gilman," in *The Secularization of the Academy,* 131–33. On the connections between Progressivism and liberal Protestantism, see Robert M. Crunden, *Ministers of Reform: The Progressives' Achievement in American Civilization, 1889–1920* (New York: Basic Books, 1982); and David B. Danbom, *"The World of Hope":*

Progressives and the Struggle for an Ethical Public Life (Philadelphia: Temple University Press, 1987).

16. See D. G. Hart, *Defending the Faith: J. Gresham Machen and the Crisis of Conservative Protestantism in Modern America* (Baltimore: Johns Hopkins University Press, 1994), 85–88; and Sloan, *Faith & Knowledge*, ch. 4.

17. (New York: Harper & Row, 1930), 384.

18. D. G. Hart, "Fundamentalism and the Origins of the American Scientific Affiliation," *Perspectives on Science and Christian Faith* 43 (December 1991), 242–44.

19. On Parker, see William R. Hutchison, *The Transcendentalist Ministers: Church Reform in the New England Renaissance* (New Haven: Yale University Press, 1959), 105–10.

20. *The Modern Use of the Bible* (New York: Association Press, 1924), 103.

21. *The Faith of Modernism* (New York: Macmillan, 1924), 180, 36.

22. "Protestantism in the Republic," *Prejudices: Fifth Series* (New York: Alfred A. Knopf, 1926), 114.

23. "Doctor Fundamentalis," *Baltimore Evening Sun*, Jan. 18, 1937.

24. *Modern Use*, 5, 273.

25. *Faith of Modernism*, 22.

26. On Whig/Protestant ideology, see Marsden, *Soul of the American University*, ch. 4.

27. On these developments within the humanities, see Laurence Veysey, "The Plural Organized Worlds of the Humanities," in *The Organization of Knowledge in Modern America, 1860–1920*, ed. Alexandra Oleson and John Voss (Baltimore: Johns Hopkins University Press, 1979), 57; Bruce Kuklick, "The Emergence of the Humanities," *South Atlantic Quarterly* 89 (1990), 195–206; and John Higham, "The Schism in American Scholarship," in *Writing American History: Essays in Modern Scholarship* (Bloomington: Indiana University Press, 1970), 3–24.

28. Chester Warren Quimby, "The Word of God," *Journal of the National Association of Biblical Instructors* (hereafter cited as *JNABI*) 1 (1933), 4.

29. See, for instance, Dwight Marion Beck, "The Teacher of Religion in Higher Education," *Journal of Bible and Religion* (hereafter cited as *JBR*) 17 (1949), 91–99; and Russell J. Compton, "The Christian Heritage in Humanities Courses," *JBR* 20 (1952), 19–22.

30. See especially the work of scholars such as G. Ernest Wright, "Neo-Orthodoxy and the Bible," *JBR* (1946), 87–93, and the lead editorials in theological journals such as *Theology Today* and *Interpretation*, both of which were founded in the 1940s under the influence of neo-orthodoxy.

31. W. Norman Pittenger, "Biblical Religion and Biblical Theology," *JBR* 13 (1945), 179–183.

32. See W. Eugene March, " 'Biblical Theology' and the Presbyterians," *Journal of Presbyterian History* 59 (1981), 113–130.

33. "The House of the Interpreter," *Interpretation* 1 (1947), 49–51.

34. Gabriel Hebert, "The Bible and Modern Religions: VI. Fundamentalism," *Interpretation* 11 (1957), 186–203.

35. Vol. 2, (Grand Rapids: Eerdmans, 1955), 839–49.

36. "The Attestation of Scripture," in *The Infallible Word*, rev. ed. (Philadelphia: Presbyterian and Reformed Publishing Co., 1967), 1, 4 note 2.

37. *Thy Word is Truth: Some Thoughts on the Biblical Doctrine of Inspiration* (Grand Rapids: Eerdmans, 1957).

38. *"Fundamentalism" and the Word of God* (Grand Rapids: Eerdmans, 1958).

39. Henry, "Preface," *Revelation and the Bible: Contemporary Evangelical Thought*, ed. Carl F. H. Henry (Grand Rapids: Eerdmans, 1958), 9.

40. See Douglas Jacobsen, "From Truth to Authority to Responsibility: The Shifting Focus of Evangelical Hermeneutics, 1915–1986," *TSF Bulletin* 10 (March-April, 1987), 13–15.

41. *Between Faith and Criticism*, 1st ed., 149–50.

42. Gabriel Hebert, "The Bible and Modern Religions," 200, complained in 1957 that the fundamentalist doctrine of inerrancy was the product of a "materialistic notion of truth" and "our scientific-minded age," a complaint that would continue to haunt the evangelical doctrine of Scripture some three decades later. See, for instance, the review of the sixth volume of Carl Henry's *God, Revelation and Authority in the Journal of the American Academy of Religion*, 52 (1984), 785–86.

43. "A Conservative Speaks," *JBR* 14 (1946), 83.

44. See especially Hebert, "The Bible and Modern Religions"; "Editorial: The Peril of a Vacuum," *Theology Today* 2 (1945), 145–51; and Thomas S. Kepler, "The Liberal Viewpoint," *JBR* 14 (1946), 80–81.

45. *Between Faith and Criticism*, 116–19.

46. See George M. Marsden, *Reforming Fundamentalism: Fuller Seminary and the New Evangelicalism* (Grand Rapids: Eerdmans, 1987), especially ch. 3.

47. Aside from counting the lists of contributors to the Zondervan series, statistics come from *Between Faith and Criticism*, 122–31, quotation from 124.

48. Ernest W. Saunders, *Searching the Scriptures: A History of the Society of Biblical Literature, 1880–1980* (Chico, Calif.: Scholars Press, 1982), 84.

49. On the beginnings of the AAR, see Hart, "American Learning," 195–98, 212–13.

50. Wilson, "Mr. Holbrook and the Humanities, or Mr. Schlatter's Dilemma," *JBR* 32 (1964), 254.

51. On methodological changes within religious studies, see Hart, "American Learning," 214–20.

52. American Council of Learned Societies, *A Report to the Congress of the United States on "The State of the Humanities"* (New York: ACLS, 1985), 3–4.

53. D. G. Hart, "Introduction," *Reckoning with the Past: Historical Essays on American Evangelicalism from the Institute for the Study of American Evangelicals* (Grand Rapids: Baker Book House, 1995), 13–16.

54. Some scholars believe this is what George Marsden is proposing in *The Soul of the American University*. See, for instance, the letters to the editor, *Chronicle of Higher Education*, May 25, 1994, and June 1, 1994, for reactions to an article on religion in the university that featured Marsden.

55. See especially "The Soul of the American University," *First Things* no. 9 (January 1991), 35–47.

56. Even the talk in recent years about the politics of knowledge is predicated, it seems to me, on Enlightenment notions of autonomy and oppression. Advocates of the study of nonwestern religion rely unwittingly on Enlightenment premises by arguing that such studies help to liberate the autonomous rational self from the restrictions of Western society. Thus, despite appeals to communities of discourse, group identity, and cultural diversity, the rationale for the study of religion is still driven by a commitment to the rational detached individual as the final arbiter of truth and meaning.

57. This paragraph, admittedly, is based upon impressions rather than "hard evidence." Nevertheless, the point seems obvious. Perhaps the best way of testing this hypothesis is to compare the dissertations done by evangelicals at conservative Protestant institutions with those produced by evangelicals at places like Harvard, Yale, Brandeis, etc. Another would be to compare the scholarship produced by evangelicals for SBL,

IBR, and ETS meetings. Nonetheless, despite the obvious and necessary restraints upon evangelicals in the university world, it is unfortunate that no evangelical is making points that Brevard Childs and Jon Levenson are about the ways canonicity and communities of faith inform scholarship.

58. A very instructive essay on the academic assimilation of Roman Catholics is Philip Gleason, "Immigrant Assimilation and the Crisis of Americanization," in *Keeping the Faith: American Catholicism Past and Present* (Notre Dame: University of Notre Dame Press, 1987), ch. 3. For some of the work on post–World War II evangelical scholarship, see George Marsden, "Why No Major Evangelical University? The Loss and Recovery of Evangelical Advanced Scholarship," in *Making Higher Education Christian: The History and Mission of Evangelical Colleges in America*, ed. Joel A. Carpenter and Kenneth W. Shipps (Grand Rapids: Christian University Press, 1987), 294–304; Nathan O. Hatch, "Evangelicalism as a Democratic Movement," in *Evangelicalism in Modern America*, ch. 6; and Mark A. Noll, *The Scandal of the Evangelical Mind* (Grand Rapids: Eerdmans, 1994). But only Robert Wuthnow, *The Restructuring of American Religion: Society and Faith Since World War II* (Princeton: Princeton University Press, 1988), 155–70, and 185–91, appears to recognize the threat of academic assimilation to evangelical identity.

59. " 'The Battle for the Bible': Renewing the Inerrancy Debate," *Christian Century* 93 (Nov. 10, 1976), 978. See also Donald W. Dayton, "The Church in the World: 'The Battle for the Bible' Rages On," *Theology Today* 37 (1980), 79–84; Douglas Jacobsen, "The Rise of Evangelical Hermeneutical Pluralism," *Christian Scholar's Review* 16 (1986–1987), 325–35; and Noll, *Between Faith and Criticism*, 166–80.

60. On twentieth-century academic life, see, for example, David A. Hollinger, "Ethnic Diversity, Cosmopolitanism, and the Emergence of the American Liberal Intelligentsia," in *In the American Province: Studies in the History and Historiography of Ideas* (Bloomington: Indiana University Press, 1985), ch. 4; Philip Rieff, *The Feeling Intellect: Selected Writings*, ed. Jonathan B. Imber, (Chicago: University of Chicago Press, 1990), 247–64; and Wuthnow, *Restructuring of American Religion*, 155–71.

61. Donald W. Shriver, Jr., *Interpretation* 32 (1978), 216.

62. Jacobsen, "From Truth to Authority to Responsibility: The Shifting Focus of Evangelical Hermeneutics, 1915–1986 (Part II)," *TSF Bulletin* 10 (May–June 1987), 12.

63. Noll, "Evangelicals and the Study of the Bible," in *Evangelicalism and Modern America*, 109, 110.

64. Hagner, "The Battle for Inerrancy: An Errant Trend Among the Inerrancists," *Reformed Journal* 34 (April 1984), 19–22, quotation from 20. On these developments, see also Noll, *Between Faith and Criticism*, 167–74; and David L. Turner, "Evangelicals, Redaction Criticism, and Inerrancy: The Debate Continues," *Grace Theological Journal* 5 (1984), 37–45.

65. For some of the literature on this earlier dispute between clergy and scholars, see Laurence Veysey, *The Emergence of the American University* (Chicago: University of Chicago Press, 1965); Veysey, "Plural Organized Worlds of the Humanities"; and Kuklick, "Emergence of the Humanities."

66. This point is made implicitly in two reviews of Robert Alter's and Frank Kermode's *Literary Guide to the Bible*: Donald Davie, "Reading and Believing," *The New Republic*, Oct. 27, 1987, 28–33; and George Steiner, "The Good Book," *New Yorker*, Jan. 11, 1988, 94–98.

67. Noll, *Between Faith and Criticism*.

68. As Marsden shows in *The Soul of the American University*, the public rationale of many institutions was one of the chief factors undermining the theological identity of confessional colleges and universities.

69. Funk, "Watershed of the American Biblical Tradition," 21.

70. Levenson, *Hebrew Bible*, 109.

71. See, for instance, Noll, *Scandal of the Evangelical Mind*; George M. Marsden, "Why No Major Evangelical University? The Loss and Recovery of Evangelical Advanced Scholarship," in *Making Higher Education Christian*, 294–303; and Nathan O. Hatch, "Evangelicalism as a Democratic Movement," in *Evangelicalism and Modern America*, ch. 6.

72. Alisdair MacIntyre, *Three Rival Versions of Moral Inquiry: Encyclopedia, Genealogy and Tradition* (Notre Dame, Ind.: University of Notre Dame Press), shows the philosophically shaky grounds of the modern university and defends the academic rationales of closely bound moral and religious traditions.

AFTERWORD

15

The Meaning of Science
for Christians

A New Dialogue on Olympus

GEORGE MARSDEN

Introduction

Walter Lippmann provided some of the most astute reflections on the Scopes trial in his "Dialogue on Olympus," published in *American Inquisitors: A Commentary on Dayton and Chicago* (New York: Macmillan, 1928). In Lippmann's dialogue, Socrates challenges Thomas Jefferson and William Jennings Bryan to clarify their views on science, religion, and the state. A high point, for instance, is Socrates' response to Jefferson, after Jefferson has explained his views of religious freedom:

SOCRATES: I don't understand you. You say there were many people in your day who believed that God had revealed the truth about the universe. You then tell me that officially your citizens had to believe that human reason and not divine revelation was the source of truth and yet you say your state had no official beliefs. It seems to me it had a very definite belief, a belief which contradicts utterly the belief of my friend St. Augustine, for example. Let us be frank. Did you not overthrow a state religion based on revelation and establish in its place the religion of rationalism?[1]

In Lippmann's version Bryan's contribution to the dialogue is minimal since he is, on the whole, unable to follow the line of argument. For instance, Bryan's response to Socrates' observation just quoted is: "It's getting very warm in here. All this talk makes me very uncomfortable. I don't know what it is leading to." Then the dialogue proceeds essentially between Socrates and Jefferson alone.

Recently we have discovered an updated version, set on Mt. Olympus in the 1990s. In this version Bryan is taken somewhat more seriously—except, of course, by Jefferson. However, the updated version still does not do justice to

329

Bryan or to the other historical figures for that matter. In fact, the level of resemblance between these and the actual historical figures is somewhere between coincidental and irresponsible.

We pick up the discussion where the passage just quoted leaves off. (You will notice that Bryan has picked up the contemporary evangelical habit of excessive informality. Jefferson, too, is egalitarian but more reserved. Socrates, of course, calls everyone by one name, but retains some formality).

SOCRATES: But, Thomas, as I was saying, Did you not overthrow a state religion based on revelation and establish in its place the religion of rationalism?

WJB: (intervening): That's just the point, Tom. Soc's got it right. You have tried to establish a religion of reason in our public schools and your scientists are the high priests.

TJ: That's ridiculous. We don't impose beliefs on anyone. Everyone is free to make up his—that is, his *or her*—own mind. Freedom is what our country is about. That's also the essence of the scientific method—you start by freeing your mind of prejudices. Then you seek principles that are self-evident to all. That is the only way to discover universal laws of nature on which a just society may be built among diverse peoples.

SOCRATES: That is a noble ideal, Thomas. But suppose you had the misfortune to live among the benighted people of the late twentieth century whom we see down here before us. Suppose you lived when there was no consensus on self-evident first principles of morality, when people scoffed at the idea of natural law, and there was no hope that science could lead to such a consensus?

TJ: The world would be unbearable if they did not have some self-evident first principles from which we could derive a universal science of higher morality. In such a world the citizens would be victims of rule by unprincipled attorneys. I can't think of anything worse.

SOCRATES: Would that grim prospect make you rethink your faith in the scientific method as the best basis for building American society?

WJB: He's right, Tom. This old guy is *smart*.

TJ: (looking at Bryan): I just thought of something worse than rule by unprincipled attorneys. It would be rule by preachers—and by sectarian politicians who can't tell the difference between the American people and a Sunday-school class. Society would be just one shouting match until one sect took over. That's been proven by history.

No. The reason people need to trust the scientific method is that it's still the best thing we've got to adjudicate among conflicting sectarian opinions. You could not have a diverse republic without it. You'd just have sectarian enclaves at each other's throats. Look at Bosnia over there—they hated each other in my day and they're *still* fighting. They missed the Enlightenment.

The scientific ideal is still the best we have—it invites people to hold their conclusions in a tentative way.

SOCRATES: It seems to me, though, that the method of freeing one's mind of all prejudices would eventually teach people to doubt everything. Isn't that the inevitable outcome of the Enlightenment?

TJ: But, Socrates, didn't *you* teach us all to question everything?

SOCRATES: Questioning is different from doubting. I questioned because I trusted my reason (*and*, you might recall, I also trusted my voices from the divine).

TJ: But we *can't* just trust voices from the divine. There are too many of them. Each sect makes its conflicting claims. Only our reason can adjudicate among these claims. Reason is the only means by which we can gain wide consensus among men and women. That's why we have to trust it. Once religious establishments break down, there is no other way to construct a public order. So we have to trust reason and the scientific method. It doesn't work for everything, but it works better than anything else.

SOCRATES: But now you've made my point. You say you have to trust reason because it works. When you say "trust" you use the language of faith. You just put your faith in one method of settling arguments and religious people put their faith in another . . .

WJB: He's gotcha, Tom. He's gotcha. That's just what I was trying to say. It's your faith against mine. Maybe I'm not so dumb after all.

TJ: (sarcastically): Sure, Bill. That's why you ended up as the laughingstock of every educated person of your day.

SOCRATES: Gentlemen, gentlemen . . . break it up . . . what will our audience think? Let me raise one more question about what Thomas said. Thomas said that reason is the only thing that we have to adjudicate among the conflicting claims of the sects and so is our only way to establish consensus. That's why we have to trust it.

TJ: Right.

SOCRATES: So Thomas does have a "reason" for his faith in the scientific method. But it is not quite all that he and his friends thought. They thought that the ultimate reason was that the scientific method was the best guarantee of getting at the truth about the reality of things—the laws of nature—whether it be physics, first principles of morality, even the character of God. But the reason he gave was really that "it works" to settle some limited types of arguments.

So doesn't that mean that those who advocate the scientific worldview as a guide for all of life are just another sect or faith community, if you will? It's just that they are a sect who promote the goals of technological cooperation and keeping the peace in a diverse society.

WJB: Keeping the peace! They're a sect all right, but the only way they want to keep the peace is by winning the war. The real agenda of the sect of Jefferson and his crew is to impose a materialistic, atheistic philosophy on the whole nation. They make science the authority instead of the Bible. It's better to know the Rock of Ages than the ages of rocks. (I was always good at the turn of phrase.)

TJ: (aside): Oh, brother. And to think this guy ran for president three times— and as a Jeffersonian!

WJB: (continuing) . . . That's why the teaching of evolution of species in the public schools always leads to atheism.

SOCRATES: Whoa. Wait a minute. You just lost me there. I agree that an exclusive trust in science can foster an atheistic sect (or at least an agnostic one). But all of a sudden you lapsed into rhetoric. Why do you focus on biological evolution as a way of combating atheism?

WJB: Because it is materialistic. It assumes there is no God and that we must be products of natural forces alone. It promotes unbridled materialist capitalist competition. I opposed it because I believed in social reform based on moral principles.

Besides, evolution is just a bunch of guesses strung together. The only reason it is convincing to people is that they start out by eliminating God from the picture. That makes biological evolution seem a lot more probable, since without God there has to be *some* naturalistic explanation. So since natural selection is the best explanation going—it doesn't matter how many holes it has—it still comes to the top as the best explanation. The next thing, people are teaching kids that it's "fact."

SOCRATES: Your argument is more sophisticated than I had heard. But I still don't understand why you and your evangelical followers still talk about evolutionary biology so much. If it's a prior naturalistic or materialistic philosophy that is the problem, why not focus on that and attack materialistic philosophy?

Biological evolution as presently conceived may or may not be true. You can safely bet, though, that in three hundred years the best naturalistic explanations will look very different and people will look on the twentieth-century hypotheses about the way that twentieth-century people look on seventeenth-century views. In three centuries Darwinism will seem hopelessly quaint. But that doesn't mean that showing weaknesses in evolutionary theory today is going to change the minds of those who are committed to pure naturalism.

What do you think would happen if tomorrow's *New York Times* reported some fossil discoveries that blew current evolutionary theory to smithereens. Do you think that the Clarence Darrows or Stephen Jay Goulds of the world would become believers in the Bible?

WJB: Probably not. The human heart is perverse. They would just think up some other materialist explanation, equally absurd.

SOCRATES: And a lot of educated people would believe them. So they would just shift to another best materialistic explanation. Then they would use the prestige of natural science to promote their materialistic worldview, even though they're arguing in a circle.

WJB: That seems right.

SOCRATES: So when you evangelicals attack a particular scientific theory, aren't you attacking just the symptoms, but not the disease?

WJB: The disease is what we are after all right. What we need is a good way to really zero in on it—something the people can understand. Something that gets at the big picture, not just natural science.

Actually, I think the recent proposals for a school prayer amendment are a step in the right direction.

TJ: (aside): This guy *is* an idiot.

SOCRATES: (patiently): How would a school prayer amendment address the issue?

WJB: It would say to the world that there is more to education than just science. It would challenge the monopoly of atheists and materialists over the public domain.

TJ: It would also breach the wall of separation of church and state that James Madison and I so carefully designed. It's essential to modern life that religion and the state be seen as separate spheres.

SOCRATES: "Separate spheres." Is that the same concept I hear your feminist friends complaining about?

TJ: Er . . . no. They are very different issues.

SOCRATES: Really. I should have thought they were part of the same pattern. I don't want to put words in your mouths. So let me tell you why.

TJ: Words in my mouth! I've had the feeling that words have been being put in my mouth all evening.

WJB: Me, too. Except for a few of my deathless phrases that I managed to work in.

SOCRATES: We all get that feeling sometimes up here—it's the historians, you can't trust them. But let me make my point.

You moderns have built your civilization by making this sharp distinction between the public and private spheres. It seems to be related to your capitalist economy. In order to build efficient machinery—whether for the market—or government—or technology, you rationalize reality. You professionalize work—and so forth. I've learned a lot about this by dropping in on the dead white male sociologist club when it meets Tuesday nights. You should talk to Max or Emile, or maybe Jacques.

The problem though is that you have this image of walls of separation for these spheres and that idea keeps causing difficulties. It reminds me of the other walls you see this century with barbed wire or armed guards. Somebody or something is always getting arbitrarily excluded when you try to define separate spheres so strictly.

TJ: So where are we heading? These people that are listening to us came to hear about "the meaning of science for Christians" and I think they're getting restless.

Besides, I'm supposed to go out for drinks afterward with Newton and Einstein.

SOCRATES: Try the hemlock. It has a nice nutty flavor.

But if you can stay with us just a bit longer, I was just getting to the place of science. Natural science is an essential component of this artificially constructed public domain. So if you want to understand the meaning of science for Christians, don't we have to think about that question in the larger context of the meaning of the modern state for Christians—or for that matter, the meaning of capitalism for Christians?

TJ: I don't have any trouble with that. Science is essential to the public sphere. In fact, it is the purest prototype for that sphere since it makes it possible for people of diverse faiths to work together for common goals. That's why there should be a wall of separation between religion and the sciences. And there is where you really do need the wall—armed guards and all.

WJB: But you can't do that. Don't you see that if you define science so as to exclude religion and then define most of education as scientific, you end up excluding the Bible from public life and establishing nonbelief?

TJ: That's better than establishing idiocy and superstition. Look at your right-wing evangelicals today. They want to impose the Bible on public life and so are proposing to regulate everything from bedrooms to artists' studios. *They* are the great expanders of government and if they have their way there will be no room for privacy and individual choice. Even though they still call themselves Baptists, they act like Presbyterians, trying to take over and set up a Puritan commonwealth. Look at the influence of Theonomy.

WJB: That's an extreme.

TJ: I don't see how it's different from your view of science. They want to run the government on the basis of Old Testament law. You want to run natural science on the basis of Old Testament cosmology.

SOCRATES: But doesn't Thomas have a point there, William? You claim to put the Bible first, whether in government or science.

WJB: We *do* put the Bible first in all of life.

SOCRATES: So how is it, if you put loyalty to the bible first, you evangelicals are such American patriots? The fact is that you seem to have tremendous loyalty to democracy and to the whole liberal polity that Jefferson and his friends designed.

WJB: I resigned as secretary of state when I saw Woody's policies were leading to war.

SOCRATES: Admirable. But didn't you ultimately support the war effort?

WJB: Ultimately we have to play by the rules of the system.

SOCRATES: Why is that? If the system tends to favor Godless materialism—as clearly it does in some respects—why don't you try to get a new system? All you seem to be asking for is to be allowed to sit down at the table of liberalism—maybe to be allowed to pray or to win a few symbolic victories. If you Christians are really committed to your rhetoric of always putting God's will first, then why aren't you working to destroy your liberal political system and its phony neutrality, and trying to take over the government.

TJ: That's what they *are* trying to do. In my days you Presbyterians were always trying to take over.

WJB: That's a lie. We have always played by the rules in this country.

SOCRATES: By and large that seems to be true. But I wonder why, if I am to believe your own rhetoric. Why shouldn't you evangelicals adopt Theonomy and have a Puritan revolution? After all, shouldn't your goal be that there is not one square inch of creation that is not reclaimed in God's name? How can you compromise when you are talking about God's law?

WJB: The powers that be are ordained by God. We do not have to have a perfect system in order to have an obligation to play by its rules. Besides, the American system of democracy is the best thing that humans have come up with so far.

SOCRATES: So, if I understand you, you really end up defending the American political system because it works. It keeps the peace better than anything else. You end up sounding a lot like Thomas here. The justification is pragmatic.

WJB: Yes, I always claimed to be a Jeffersonian (of course, that was before I met Tom here). The difference was that I would not allow the system to become Godless. Our system of government is founded on principles from the Bible, too, not just on natural law or what works best.

SOCRATES: It sounds to me as though you want to have it both ways. You want to say both that you put the Bible first and that you are loyal to the pragmatic rule of American politics. Don't you have to choose one or the other? Or at least work out a good theory of how your two loyalties are related?

TJ: That's why we need walls of separation. The only alternative is for one religion or another to take over, whether they admit it or not. It doesn't matter that they do not do it consistently, they are still intruding *their* principles on everyone else.

SOCRATES: But now it seems that we have come around full circle from where we began. Thomas, you also enter the public domain with certain higher principles that you hold to, whether principles from natural law or whatever and these provide the context within which technical procedural activities take place. So you do not see a total separation of spheres between your higher principles and the public domain either. Even your feminists and postmodernists have nonnegotiable moral principles that they bring into the public domain.

TJ: That is hard to deny.

SOCRATES: So you would not say that there should be a *total* separation of spheres? Even in the public domain we need to work in the context of *some* higher principles, even if those principles cannot be derived from science. So I do not see how you could keep religious principles out of the public domain on the basis of a principle of total separation of spheres.

TJ: Religious views are relevant to the public domain, so long as religious people keep them to themselves. They are free to have any private beliefs they want.

SOCRATES: But suppose someone has a religious belief that is not strictly a private matter. Like William here thinks that the Bible teaches that we should be particularly concerned for the common person. He even championed the vote for women before that was popular. Should he be required to hide the biblical basis for his concerns for justice when he is acting in a public capacity, as a politician or as a teacher?

TJ: He could identify the source of his belief as a matter of self-identification—so people would understand his prejudices. In the public domain he is going to have to argue the case on some other grounds. It is just like natural science in that respect. If you are not dealing with evidence that is equally accessible to all, you are not doing natural science. So you cannot bring in your special revelations. It is just the way that part of the public sphere is defined.

SOCRATES: OK. So at least you would concede there is not a complete wall of separation between religious beliefs and the pragmatic public domain. People can argue for religiously based beliefs, so long as they argue according to the rules of the public domain, whatever they are.

TJ: That seems right.

SOCRATES: So might not the religious beliefs be relevant to the *scientific* enterprise in just about the same way that they would be relevant to politics—as background beliefs that control what you think is important or not important—like William's belief in the common person, and so forth?

TJ: Fair enough. But still they have to remain in the background. They have no relevance to the technical theorizing. There is no Christian version of 2 + 2 = 4. There is no distinct Christian view of photosynthesis. No Christian view of when we signed the Declaration. There is no Christian biology—not even a Christian history, if history is done as a science.

SOCRATES: But didn't you conflate two things when you said that background religious views had no relevance to technical theorizing. The examples you gave all had to do with *purely* technical processes. But what about the larger theoretical context within which even the technician works? What of the context that includes questions like: "Why am I doing this?" "What is the wider significance of this work?" "What questions are important to investigate in this field?" "What assumptions about the nature of reality are relevant to this work?" "Does this work tell us anything about the nature of reality, or only about the nature of our assumptions?" These and others are all big questions that bear even on technical work.

TJ: I suppose so. But this gets pretty subtle when you deal with everyday questions in natural science.

SOCRATES: But you forget, we have been assigned the topic of "the *significance* of science for Christians." When you get to significance, then you *are* dealing with the big questions. You are dealing with the larger issue of the significance of the public domain in modern life. That is why the analogy of politics is relevant to the question of a wall of separation between religion and science.

In politics its clear that you bring with you some major background commitments that—even if not made explicit—still determine even which technical questions you ask.

For instance, if you have a mathematician calculate whether a balanced budget amendment would help the poor, your moral and religious commitments have entered into the very asking of that question. If you had lived in a society—like mine—where politicians did not worry much about the poor—the calculation would never have been done. That's why the whole idea of a "wall of separation" seems too rigid. We need an image that is much more porous.

TJ: What image would work better?

SOCRATES: I'm glad you asked me that. It looks to me as though both of you do make a *distinction* between a public domain and other loyalties, but neither of you keeps them separate. Both of you are in fact loyal to the pragmatic American political system, but you also have religious and moral loyalties that you bring into it.

So how are these two realms actually related in the modern world? (And this question applies to science as well as politics.)

I think the best image would be that if we imagined that every city, town, county, and so forth had a separate territory within it that most everybody entered every day. This is the so-called public domain.

Now what is different about this territory is that as soon as you cross the border you have to speak a new language—the language of public discourse. Let's call this the "publican" language.

WJB: As in publicans and sinners?

SOCRATES: Actually that's not a bad allusion. The publican language is part of a larger set of pragmatic rules of the road that are necessary to get particular jobs done when not everyone believes the same things. These are the rules for tax collectors and the like. They are not derived directly from any one group's religion, so it may look as though this realm is just godless and pragmatic. But isn't it the case that you both agree that you need this realm so that even you, William, have learned its language and play by its rules?

TJ: All too well.

SOCRATES: But maybe there is nothing wrong with that even on William's own principles. Your Jesus dined with the publicans and sinners. And he did not tell them to cease being publicans—only to stop cheating people. William, you made more or less the same point when you said that your American system—which is the prototype of such a modern system—was ordained by God.

WJB: OK. I follow you.

TJ: *This* is a first.

SOCRATES: But, William, let me ask you a hard question. Isn't your problem that you identify this realm too much as your primary citizenship? Wouldn't it be better if you thought of the publican land just as an artificially constructed territory that you had to enter every day and a language you had to speak to be understood there? It seems to me that then you would not be likely to mistake it for your primary allegiance.

WJB: But politics was my life. My calling was to reform the system according to biblical principles.

SOCRATES: Ah. There's the rub. You Christians do have a duty to reform the publican realm—whether politics or science—by bringing your Christian principles to bear on it whenever appropriate. But that calling to reform seems to bring with it the temptation to take publican land too seriously. It tempts you to forget that it is an artificial construction that God has ordained for limited purposes—for keeping the peace and working together among diverse peoples. The temptation is for you Christians to think of this land as the primary location of the kingdom of God.

WJB: How did you become such an expert on Christianity?

SOCRATES: I've had lots of time. And Augustine and I talk a lot.

But to continue. If you saw the primary locus of the kingdom in the church—that is, in the hearts of communities of believers—then you would be clearer regarding modern pragmatic inventions like political systems or natural science. You would see that there is no way that believers with changed hearts are not going to bring their hearts—and hence the kingdom—with them into publican land; so that will influence everything they do—sometimes in direct ways, sometimes in indirect ways. It will influence the questions you ask. Sometimes it will control the theories you are willing to entertain. For instance, it rules out for you the theory that because natural scientific method works well for some questions, it is the highest test for all knowledge.

WJB: So I could work for reforms like keeping the state from mandating the teaching of Godless evolution in the publican schools?

SOCRATES: You could certainly insist that the "Godless" part does not follow. You could point out that that is the premise of the method, not the conclusion of any research. That gets back to our earlier discussion. That is a point of logic, not something drawn directly from the Bible.

The main thing to recognize is that publican land always has a tendency toward imperialism and that is what you should always be fighting in your reforms—but you can argue that in terms of justice and fairness that most people can understand.

WJB: But if I don't bring the Bible in directly—whether in politics or science—wouldn't I then be selling out? I'd be really making the publican rules the standard for my life half the day and Christianity the other half?

SOCRATES: Not necessarily. It's more like just observing the rules of the road for a particular cooperative purpose. When a Christian gets on a public road she enters publican land and agrees to the rule of driving on the right hand side of the street. That rule has a specific ad hoc purpose of keeping drivers from running into each other—and you can say it is God ordained that people should make up such rules. But accepting that rule for that ad hoc purpose is a secondary allegiance. If a person sees a child run out on her side of the road, she drives on the other side if she can—because she has higher loyalties than to the traffic rules. It should be the same for all these activities, Christians should just be clear about it.

TJ: What about non-Christians? They'll swerve to the other side also.

SOCRATES: True. That's the point I made earlier, that we all bring our higher principles into publican land. Though you have an additional problem as I see it, Thomas. It is not clear that you have any source of higher allegiance that is distinct from publican land. You ground your higher beliefs in science, in natural law, in universal principles accessible to all. In essence, you define all of life as publican land. So you need a revolution every generation if things are not going just as you like.

TJ: Seems to me, you had the same problem, Socrates. It's just that you resolved it in another way. Which is better, a revolution or to die a victim of unjust laws? You might have escaped Athens and then led an insurgency based on just principles.

SOCRATES: You're perfectly correct in seeing that we had the same problem. For me, like you, the state was all I had (even the gods I believed in were ultimately the gods of the state). So I had to die to uphold the law, even though I was its innocent victim.

TJ: So why aren't you recommending to others that they give their all to uphold the law of the city-state? Why this idea of a higher allegiance and limited ad hoc loyalty?

SOCRATES: Because you people profess to follow Jesus. Compare my death and that of Jesus.

TJ: I think of them as much the same. You both were innocent but were willing to die even when condemned unjustly.

SOCRATES: But my reason was very different. I died to uphold the law and the civil order, even when it acted unjustly. I thought the gods demanded such loyalty. Jesus accepted death by the unjust law. He rendered to Caesar what was Caesar's and he did not foster political revolution or destroy the regime with his legions of angels. He believed that the Roman law was ordained of God and he even told the publicans to reform their ways. But he would never have thought of dying to uphold the Roman law. His first allegiance was to a kingdom in which love would rule, and you are not going to get that from a state.

I'm just trying to get you Christians to think like Christians. I have since come to admire Jesus immensely, but I don't think most Christians follow him very closely.

TJ: I've always admired Jesus, too—enough to get rid of all the superstition about him.

SOCRATES: Ah, but here's the difference. You admired him only as an ethical teacher. You accepted Jesus only when you could fit him into the rules of science and of publican land—as though that were the only reality. You had no resort but to absolutize the principles of science and claim a universal natural law basis for your ideas. Science became your god and the god of your state. Now that science has failed to provide a basis for a universal morality, your followers are stuck. All they have is politics and resorts to power.

WJB: (wistfully): I wish Tom would repent. He would make a wonderful Presbyterian elder. But I'm afraid it's a lost cause.

TJ: I feel that I've been unfairly worked into a corner here. Next time we have a symposium, I want to ask the questions.

SOCRATES: Here on Mt. Olympus, I get to ask the questions.

TJ: This is Mt. Olympus? You mean with Zeus and Athena and that whole bunch. That's impossible!

SOCRATES: Believe it or not. Maybe you're the one hearing voices now?

WJB: (musing): Mt. Olympus? But that *is* impossible. This all must be a dream. Just my luck. All those good ideas from Socrates and as soon I and the audience wake up, they'll all be forgotten.

NOTES

I am grateful to the editors of this volume for permission to publish an abridged version of this as "A New Dialogue on Olympus: Science, Religion and the State," in *Books and Culture* I:1 (September/October 1995), 16–18.

1. From reprint in Gail Kennedy, ed., *Evolution and Religion: The Conflict Between Science and Theology in Modern America* (Boston: D.C. Heath, 1957), 54. As one might expect, there are a few points in the updated version at which a participant may make a remark similar to that which he made on the earlier occasion.

Index

158, 164–67; and moderate party, 146–
47, 149, 151–52, 158–59,161, 163. *See
also* Presbyterians
Church and state, separation of, 333
City College of New York, 273
Clap, Thomas, 272–73
Clapham Sect, 143, 146, 148, 161, 167
Clark, Harold W., 237–38
Clark, Ian, 147–48, 153, 161, 164
Clark, Robert E. D., 229
Clarke, Samuel, 163, 269
Clergy, evangelical, 154, 268; American,
300; authority of, 268, 291; Canadian,
293, 300; as community leader, 293–94;
Protestant, 297
Coal, 181, 184–85, 187
Cockburn, Dean, 18
Cohen, Floris, 76
Coleridge, Samuel Taylor, 276
College of New Jersey, 199, 208
Common Sense realism, 165, 201, 272,
274, 276, 308
Comte, Auguste, 281
Conbeare, William Daniel, 178
Conflict, 77; form of, 52–53; as model of
theology and science, 88. *See also*
harmonization; warfare
Congregationalism, 278
Conscience, argument from, 147; as
human, 168
Conversion, 144, 154; evangelical, 155
Cook, Ramsay, 291, 297
Cooper, Thomas, 179
Cope, Henry Drinker, 292
Copernicanism, 28, 71, 88
Cormie, John A., 293
Cornell University, 309
Corsi, Pietro, 158
Cotton, Elizabeth. *See* Hope, Lady
Cotton, John, 57
Courtenay, William, 78
Covenant theology, 70; of grace, 54, 59;
of works, 54–55, 60
Crawford, Ralph, 252
Creation, 30, 80–81, 84, 86–87 89, 177–
78, 211, 236–37; doctrine of, 78, 80; ex
nihilo, 211; literal understanding of,
184; Old-earth creation, 28
Creation Evidences Museum, 255

Creationism, 3, 5, 20, 234–35, 238, 240,
310; inclusive definition of, 239; and
neocreationism, 220, 229; as progres-
sive, 30, 239; Six-day, 178; Young-
Earth, 28, 240
Creation-Life Publishers, 228
Creation Research Science Education
Foundation, 255
Creation Research Society, 239
Creation science, 9, 239–40, 311
Creator, 235, 256, 269, 271, 274
Cummings, Eryl, 247, 250–52, 255
Cummings, Violet, 254
Cunningham, John William, 167
Curti, Merle, 267
Curtiss, Samuel I., 210
Cuvier, Georges, 156

Dabney, Robert L., 99
Dagg, John Ledley, 276, 278
Dana, James Dwight, 10, 186
Darwin, Charles, 5, 8, 20, 25, 27–28, 32,
35, 186, 188, 195–99, 201–02, 205, 222–
25, 227, 234–235, 250, 292; *Animals
and Plants under Domestication,* 209;
deathbed conversion of, 247; and
evolution, 299; *Origin of Species,* 235,
282; value of a chastened, 212
Darwinism, 28, 186, 197, 204, 210, 245,
256, 291–92, 310, 332; definition of,
234. *See also* evolution
Davis, Ted, 220
Dawson, Carl, 295
Dawson, John William, 186, 235–37
Day-age theory, 179, 236–38, 240; and
interpretation of Genesis, 186
Dayton, Donald, 319
De-conversion, and science, 32
Deism, 26, 150, 156, 158; and
unorthodoxy, 270
Descartes, René, 7, 80–87, 89, 155
Design, 26, 55, 166, 196, 199–200, 203,
275; argument from, 146–47, 149, 161
Desmond, Adrian, 33, 198
Dewey, John, 282
D'Holbach, Baron, 157
Dispensationalism, 245, 310–11, 316
Distinction between natural theology and
theology of nature, 144